THE ORIGINAL LISTS.

#

OF

PERSONS OF QUALITY;

EMIGRANTS; RELIGIOUS EXILES; POLITICAL REBELS;
SERVING MEN SOLD FOR A TERM OF YEARS; APPRENTICES;
—CHILDREN STOLEN; MAIDENS PRESSED; AND OTHERS
WHO WENT FROM GREAT BRITAIN TO THE
AMERICAN PLANTATIONS

1600-1700.

WITH THEIR AGES, THE
LOCALITIES WHERE THEY FORMERLY LIVED IN THE MOTHER COUNTRY,
THE NAMES OF THE SHIPS IN WHICH THEY EMBARKED,
AND OTHER INTERESTING PARTICULARS.

*FROM MSS. PRESERVED IN THE STATE PAPER DEPARTMENT OF HER
MAJESTY'S PUBLIC RECORD OFFICE, ENGLAND.*

EDITED BY

JOHN CAMDEN HOTTEN.

JANAWAY PUBLISHING, INC.
Santa Maria, California
2012

Notice

In many older books, foxing (or discoloration) occurs and, in some instances, print lightens with wear and age. Reprinted books, such as this, often duplicate these flaws, notwithstanding efforts to reduce or eliminate them. The pages of this reprint have been digitally enhanced and, where possible, the flaws eliminated in order to provide clarity of content and a pleasant reading experience.

Originally published
London, 1874

Reprinted by:

Janaway Publishing, Inc.
732 Kelsey Ct.
Santa Maria, California 93454
(805) 925-1038
www.janawaygenealogy.com

2012

ISBN: 978-1-59641-264-4

Made in the United States of America

To the Members of the

GENEALOGICAL AND HISTORICAL SOCIETIES

OF THE

UNITED STATES OF AMERICA,

THIS COLLECTION OF THE NAMES OF THE EMIGRANT
ANCESTORS OF MANY THOUSANDS OF AMERICAN FAMILIES,

IS RESPECTFULLY DEDICATED

BY THE EDITOR,

JOHN CAMDEN HOTTEN.

CONTENTS.

		PAGE
REGISTER OF THE NAMES OF ALL THE PASSENGERS FROM LONDON DURING ONE WHOLE YEAR, ENDING CHRISTMAS, 1635		33, 145

		Ship	Master	Pages
In the Ship		*Bonaventure*	J. Ricrofte, Master	35
"	"	"	J. Romsey, Master	38
"	"	*Hopewell*	I. Wood, Master	39
"	"	*Christian*	J. White, Master	42
"	"	*Planter*	N. Trarice, Master	43, 45, 47, 48, 50, 53, 55, 56
"	"	*Peter Bonaventure*	I. Harman, Master	43, 47, 51
"	"	*Hopewell*	W. Bundocke, Master	44, 46, 49
"	"	*Elizabeth*	W. Stagg, Master	48, 53, 53, 56, 57, 60, 61, 68
"	"	*Rebecca*	Hodges, Master	50, 54
"	"	*Paul*	Acklin, Master	50
"	"	*Eliza & Ann*	R. Cowper [or Cooper], Master	54, 57, 58, 61, 69, 72, 76, 77, 78
"	"	*Encrease*	R. Lea, Master	55, 57, 58, 60, 61, 64
"	"	*Susan & Ellen*	E. Payne, Master	59, 62, 76
"	"	*Falcon*	T. Irish, Master	63, 142
"	"	*Expectation*	C. Billinge, Master	67, 69
"	"	*Ann & Elizabeth*	J. Brookhaven, Master	70
"	"	*Abigail*	R. Hackwell, Master	73, 87, 88, 89, 90, 91, 92, 96, 97, 98, 99, 100
"	"	*Alexander*	Burche & G. Grimes, Masters	73
"	"	*Plain Joane*	R. Buckam, Master	78
"	"	*Matthew*	R. Goodladd, Master	80
"	"	*Speedwell*	J. Chappell, Master	82
"	"	*Thomas & John*	R. Lambard, Master	83
"	"	*Truelove*	R. Dennis, Master	85
"	"	*James*	J. May, Master	88, 107
"	"	*Defence*	—. Pearce, Master	89, 90

CONTENTS

				PAGE
In the Ship	*Defence*...	E. Bostocke, Master	89, 91, 98, 99, 100, 101,	
				105, 106
„	„ *Blessing* ..	... J. Lester, Master ...	...	93, 108
„	„ *Philip* ...	... R. Morgan, Master	...	... 94
„	„ *America* ...	... W. Barker, Master	...	... 95
„	„ *Transport*	... E. Walker, Master...	...	... 101
„	„ *Paul* ...	... L. Betts, Master ...	...	... 103
„	„ *Pied Cow*	... Ashley, Master ...	...	106, 110
„	„ *Love* ...	... J. Young, Master ..	...	... 109
„	„ *Alice* ...	... R. Orchard, Master	...	... 109
„	„ *Hopewell*	... T. Babb, Master ...	110, 123, 130, 144	
„	„ *Assurance*	... I. Bromwell & I. Pewsie, Masters	...	110
„	„ *Primrose*	... Douglass, Master ...	...	... 114
„	„ *Merchant's Hope* ..	H. Weston, Master	...	... 116
„	„ *Elizabeth*	... C. Browne, Master	...	... 117
„	„ *Bachelor* ...	... T. Webb, Master ...	...	... 118
„	„ *Globe* ...	... J. Blackman, Master	...	... 119
„	„ *Safety* ...	... J. Graunt, Master ...	...	... 121
„	„ *George* ...	.... J. Severne, Master ...	...	... 124
„	„ *Thomas* ...	... H. Taverner, Master	...	... 126
„	„ *William & John* ...	R. Langram, Master	...	... 127
„	„ *David* ...	... J. Hogg, Master ...	...	... 129
„	„ *Truelove*...	... J. Gibbs, Master ...	...	... 131
„	„ *Dorset* ...	... J. Flower, Master ...	...	... 132
„	„ *John* ...	... J. Waymoth, Master	...	... 134
„	„ *Amity* ...	... G. Downes, Master	...	... 134
„	„ *Constance*	... C. Campion, Master	...	... 136
„	„ *Abraham*	... J. Barker, Master ...	...	... 138
„	„ *Expedition*	... P. Blackley, Master	...	... 139
„	„ *Friendship*	... ———, Master ...	...	... 145

PASSENGERS BY THE COMMISSION AND SOLDIERS ACCORDING TO THE STATUTE, CHRISTMAS, 1631, TO CHRISTMAS, 1632 147-154

ENTRIES RELATING TO AMERICA, FROM THE PATENT ROLLS 155-168

LISTS OF THE LIVING AND DEAD IN VIRGINIA, 16 FEBY., 1623 169-196

WALLOONS AND FRENCH EMIGRANTS TO VIRGINIA ... 197-199

MUSTERS OF THE INHABITANTS OF VIRGINIA 201-265

	PAGE
PATENTS GRANTED TO SETTLERS IN VIRGINIA (CIRCA) 1626 266-274	
RETURNS OF THOSE WHO EMBARKED FROM IPSWICH AND WEYMOUTH FOR NEW ENGLAND, 1634 TO 1637 ... 275-286	

  From Ipswich, in the Ship *Francis* ... J. Cuttinge, Master ... 277, 279
   „ „ „ „ *Elizabeth* ... W. Andrewes, Master 277, 280, 281
   „ Weymouth, in the Ship ——— [1635] ... ———, Master ... 283-286

REGISTER OF PERSONS ABOUT TO PASS INTO FOREIGN
 PARTS, FROM MARCH TO SEPT., 1637 287-298

  From Ipswich, in the *John & Dorothy* ... W. Andrewes, Master ... 289
   „ Yarmouth, in the *Rose*   ... W. Andrewes, Junr. Master 289
   „ Southampton, in the *Virgin* [1639] ... J. Weare & J. Delahay, Masters 296
   „ „ „ *Bevis* [1638] ... ... R. Batten, Master ... 298

THE SUMMER ISLANDS, 1673 TO 1679 301-314

  Names of the Governor and Council of the Assembly, Aug., 1673 ... 301
  Account of the Lands belonging to the Summer Islands Company, taken
   out of Mr. Richard Norwood's Survey Book, made in 1662-3 ... 304

MONMOUTH REBELLION OF 1685 :—LISTS OF CONVICTED
 REBELS SENT TO THE BARBADOES AND OTHER PLANTA-
 TIONS IN AMERICA... 315

  Receipt for 100 Prisoners to be transported from TAUNTON, by John
   Rose, of London, Merchant 316
  Invoice of 68 Men-servants shipped on Board the *Jamaica Merchant*,
   Capt. Chas. Gardner, for Account of John Rose & Compy., they being
   to be sold for 10 Years 317
  Receipt for 100 Prisoners on Mr. Nepho's Account, to be sent to Barba-
   does. [Prisoners in DORCHESTER Gaol to be transported.] 317*
  Prisoners in EXETER Gaol to be transported 319
  Prisoners at WELLS to be transported 319
  List of the Convicted Rebels on Board the *Betty*, of London, at the Port
   of WEYMOUTH 320
  List of 72 Rebels Granted by his Majesty to Gerome Nepho, with the
   Names of their Masters in Barbadoes 322
  Sir Wm. Booth's Receipt for 100 Prisoners, on Account of James Kendall
   [Prisoners in DORCHESTER Gaol to be transported.] 326

CONTENTS.

PAGE

Certificate of the Disposal of Capt. Kendall's Rebels.—A List of 90 Rebels by the *Happy Return*, with the Names of their Masters to whom they were disposed 328

Sir Wm. Booth's List of Prisoners sent to Barbadoes, with the Names of the Towns in Somersetshire and Devonshire from whence they came ... 332

A List of 77 Convicted Rebels, imported from BRISTOL in the *John frigate* 336

Sir Wm. Booth's Receipt for 100 Prisoners—56 from the Bridewell at TAUNTON, 33 from BRIDGEWATER Prison at TAUNTON, and 11 from EXETER 341

The Sale of 67 Rebels, delivered by Capt. Charles Gardner, of the *Jamaica Merchant* 342

TICKETS GRANTED TO EMIGRANTS FROM BARBADOES TO NEW ENGLAND, CAROLINA, VIRGINIA, NEW YORK, ANTIGUA, JAMAICA, NEWFOUNDLAND, AND OTHER PLACES, 1678-9 345-418

BARBADOES :—PARISH REGISTERS—BIRTHS AND DEATHS — LISTS OF INHABITANTS — LANDED PROPRIETORS — SERVANTS, &C., 1678-9 418

Parish Registers of ST. MICHAEL'S—Baptisms 421
,,   ,,   ,,   ,,   Burials... 425
List of Inhabitants of ST. MICHAEL'S, with their Hired Servants, 'Prentices, Bought Servants, and Negroes 438
List of the Jews of ST. MICHAEL'S 449-50
Alphabetical List of Landowners in ST. MICHAEL'S, with the Number of their Acres, Hired Servants, Bought Servants, and Negroes ... 451-459
Owners of Land in the Parish of ST. GEORGE, Number of Acres, White Servants, and Negroes [1679] 460-464
Parish Registers of ST. GEORGE—Baptisms [1678-9] 465-6
,,   ,,   ,,   ,,   Burials 466-8
,,   ,,   ,, ST. ANDREWS—Owners of Lands, Number of Acres, Servants, Negroes, Christenings, Burials 469-472
Parish Registers of CHRISTCHURCH—Landowners, Acres, Servants, Negroes 473-488
Parish Registers of CHRISTCHURCH—Baptisms [1678-9] ... 489-93
,,   ,,   ,,   ,,   Burials [1678-9] ... 493-6
,,   ,,   ,, ST. JAMES'—Baptisms 496-7
,,   ,,   ,,   ,, Burials 497-9
,,   ,,   ,,   ,, Landowners, Servants, Negroes [1678-9] 500-507
Parish Registers of ST. JOHN'S—Baptisms [1678-9] 507-8

LIST OF SHIPS CONVEYING EMIGRANTS TO VIRGINIA BEFORE 1625-6, MENTIONED IN 201-265

Abigail	George	Phœnix
Ambrose	Gift	Prosperous
Ann	Great Hopewell	Return
Blessing	God's Gift	Sampson
Bona Nova	God Speed	Samuel
Bonaventure	Hercules	Sarah
Bonny Bessie	Hopewell	Seaflower
Charity	Jacob	Sea Venture
Charles	James	Southampton
Concord	Jonathan	Star
Delaware	John & Francis	Supply
Deliverance	London Merchant	Susan
Diana	Margaret	Swallow
Discovery	Margaret & John	Swan
Due Return	Marmaduke	Temperance
Duty	Mary Ann Margaret	Tiger
Edwin	Mary & James	Treasurer
Elianor	Mary Margaret	Trial
Elizabeth	Marygold	Truelove
Falcon	Mary Providence	Unity
Flying Hart	Neptune	Warwick
Francis Bonaventure	Noah	William & John
Furtherance	Patience	William & Thomas

INTRODUCTION.

LITTLE could even the most sanguine of the early emigrants to America have contemplated the subsequent effect which their action would work upon the world's history. Some of them, it is true, were men of position at home, with wealth and all its concomitant advantages at their disposal, but by far the greater number was composed of comparatively obscure men—men of little means, but possessed of hearts and consciences of too honest a nature to permit them quietly to submit to the intolerance which was forced upon them at home. But those whose names are recorded in the following pages, with many others of whom no such minute particulars have come down to us, were the seed-grains from which the mighty Republic has sprung—the rapid growth of which has no parallel in the world's history. Colonization was but imperfectly developed in those early days, and many attempted settlements proved abortive; but the first settlers in Virginia, and subsequently those in New England, carried with them the elements of success, resulting in permanent establishments.

Of the history of the Colonies, and the eventual establishment of Independence, I have nothing to say. My object is simply and briefly to point out some of the causes which contributed to the early emigration of English families to America; and then to estimate the practical value of the contents of the present volume as a means of assistance in making genealogical researches in the mother country.

One of the earliest acts of Charles the First,—an act which raised a storm of indignation throughout the country,—was the imposition of a forced loan without the grant of Parliament. The manner in which this unconstitutional measure was treated by those called upon to contribute towards the assessment, is well illustrated by the events which took place in Lincolnshire; and a relation of the part taken by the leading men of that locality, some of whom were related to, or intimately associated with, the principal agents in the subsequent emigration to Massachusetts, under JOHN WINTHROP, in 1630, will be of some interest to the descendants of the New England emigrants.

One of the richest men in the county of Lincoln, who strenuously opposed the forced loan, was ISAAC JOHNSON, who, as is well known, married the Lady ARABELLA FYNES, sister to THEOPHILUS, Earl of LINCOLN, who himself married a sister of the Lord SAY and SELE. These two noblemen took a very active part in denouncing the loan as dangerous and unconstitutional. Lord SAY and SELE, who, during the civil war, some years later, commanded a Parliamentarian regiment, openly asserted that he would rather lose half his estate than risk the impoverishment of his posterity by the establishment of so dangerous a precedent as a loan without the sanction of Parliament. But Lord LINCOLN'S opposition to the loan was more immediately productive of dissatisfaction. As soon as it was proposed he took upon himself to have an Abridgment of the Statutes prepared for distribution; and it is not unlikely that in the compilation of this document he was aided by his former steward, THOMAS DUDLEY, who subsequently went over to New England, and became Governor of Massachusetts. DUDLEY had received a legal education, under his relative, Sir AUGUSTINE NICHOL, one of the Justices of the Common Pleas, and was therefore peculiarly fitted for the work. The immediate result of this act on the part of Lord LINCOLN, was to bring down upon himself and his servants the resentment of the King and his party, and the Abridgment was rigorously suppressed. Not only was his lordship proceeded against in the Star Chamber, but more completely to crush out the attempts made to incense the people, a proclamation was issued for the apprehension of JOHN HOLLAND, Steward to the Earl, and ROBERT BLOW, the Clerk of his kitchen; and further, a Groom in the household of his lordship was condemned in the Star

Chamber to pay a fine of £3000 for his share in distributing the obnoxious work. The Earl was soon after committed a close prisoner to the Tower, where he remained in custody for some years. I have not found any evidence of what was the result of the attempts made to apprehend HOLLAND and BLOW, but there are reasons for supposing that both escaped detection. A ROBERT BLOW, in all probability the same person, was subsequently an ensign in the regiment of Lord SAY and SELE, the nobleman before mentioned. The only trace of HOLLAND we have met with brings out some information respecting the residence, at Boston, of THOMAS DUDLEY, and the estimated value of his yearly income.

Letter from Sir EDWARD HERON, addressed to Sir HUMPHREY MAY, Chancellor of the Duchy of Lancaster:—

"Cressye, 28 July, 1627.

"RIGHT HONORABLE,

"I had rather offende in too much officiousnes, then negligence, especially to the king's ma^{tie}. I have hearde that Mr. HOLLANDE who attended the earle of Lincolne, hath been in quest by the state; yf it be soe, I doe heare for certeine, that he was seene dyvers tymes, about a month or six weekes past vpon the terras-walkes at Sempringham; but since that tyme it is privately whispered that he is now removed to the house of one Mr. THOMAS DUDLYE, in Boston, whoe did allsoe of late tymes wayte vpon the sayde earle; and it is very p'bable, because Mr. HOLLANDS wyfe is observed to make often viages frome Sempringham vnto Boston, and there to abide sometyme 2 or 3 dayes, sometyme a weeke together. * * *   "EDWARD HERON.

"Yet maye you please further to vnderstande, that this Mr. DUDLYE beynge reported to have 300li p. an., some saye 400li, refused vpon our earnest request to beare 30s. towards the loane with a neyghbourgh that was deeply charged as we have informed in our certificatts vnto the lords of the councell, whereof I beseech your honor to direct the delyverye.

"Since the writinge hereof, I vnderstande that one ADDAM RESTON' brother in law vnto the s^d Mr. HOLLANDE, came ridinge through our streete on fridaye in the nyght, the 20th of this month, with a gentlewoman behinde him, supposed to be the wyfe of Mr. HOLLANDE goeynge towards Boston; and an other gent, seeminge vnwillinge to be knowne.

"You maye allsoe please to take into your consideration that one BENIAMINE DICKOSON of Boston adviseth, that the toune of Boston is able and ought to contribute to the charge and expence of theyre late mayor & EDW. TILLSON, or anye else, that suffer trouble in cause of the loane; and to helpe towards theyre losses. p JOHAN HOBSON, Collector.

"The same DYKCONSON was 3li lands, yet sett vnto 1li by the lords at Lincoln."*

A long list of Lincolnshire men who refused to contribute to the loan, has been preserved. Ten of the principal of them were immediately committed to prison :—Sir JOHN WRAY, Sir THOMAS GRANTHAM, and Sir EDWARD ASCOUGH, to the Gate House; Sir WILLIAM ARMYN, Sir THOMAS DARNELL, WILLIAM ANDERSON, Esq., the Mayor of Boston, and Alderman (EDWARD) TILSON of that town, to the Fleet; and WILLIAM TAROLD (THOROLD), Esq., and —. HORWOOD, Esq., to the Marshalsea. The Boston men who refused to lend, or to enter into bond for their appearance before his Majesty's Privy Council, beside the Mayor, and Alderman TILSON, were ATTERTON HOWGHE (ATHERTON HOUGH), EDMOND JACKSON, BENJAMIN DICONSON, THOMAS LEVERETT, THOMAS LOWE, THOMAS TOOLY, JOHN COPPYN, WILLIAM COTTINGTON (CODDINGTON), WILLIAM CONDY, and RICHARD WESTLAND. Of these, LEVERETT, CODDINGTON, and HOUGH subsequently went out to New England, and there attained positions of eminence. The London prisons were soon filled with the more important of the objectors, from various parts of the country, but chiefly from the city of London, Lincolnshire, Northamptonshire, Essex, and Gloucestershire. The

---

* State Papers, Chas. I., Domestic Series, Vol. 72, No. 36, Record Office.

gaols being filled to repletion, and moreover the expense of maintaining the prisoners proving a heavy charge upon the State—already impoverished—the great majority were liberated from confinement, but were not allowed, however, to return to their own homes for fear of their stirring up fresh disaffection among their neighbours. Thus a delinquent belonging to Essex would be sent, perhaps, to Wiltshire, or Yorkshire, and under pain of severe punishment, forbidden to leave the town in which he was located, where, by-the-way, under the semblance of being a free man, he was compelled to earn, or at least procure, his own living.

This was a very ill-advised proceeding on the part of the Government, for each man thus removed to a distant town soon formed a focus of discontent. One of the most energetic of these prisoners, in free custody, as it was termed, was RICHARD KNIGHTLEY, a gentleman belonging to Northamptonshire, an intimate friend of the leaders of the Massachusetts Colony, and connected by marriage with JOHN HAMPDEN, in conjunction with whom he was named as executor to the will of ISAAC JOHNSON.

Most of the proceedings against the remonstrants were taken in the Star Chamber, the decree-books of which are unfortunately lost, or we might readily have traced many, if not all the suits, citations, fines and censures instituted in, or imposed by, the Court. The Star Chamber was a tribunal taking cognizance of all kind of delinquencies, and there still remains in the Record Office an immense mass of documents appertaining to suits before the Court, in which, when they can be sorted, arranged, and made available to the public, we may hope to find some important information respecting the personal histories of some of the original settlers in New England.

The proceedings, which were taken chiefly against the Nonconformists, caused many English families to leave their homes. Unfortunately, the records of the High Court of Commission, which has been not inaptly called "The English Inquisition," are very imperfect, but enough remains to show that proceedings were taken in it against many of the ministers and public men who afterwards became eminent in the New England States. It was not until the Rev. JOHN COTTON, RICHARD BELLINGHAM, recorder, and WILLIAM CODDINGTON, a member of the corporation of the town of Boston (co. Lincoln), had been fined for nonconformity, that they gave up their English preferments and places to join their friends in Massachusetts. Other instances might be adduced of the same result attending prosecutions in that Court.

The imposition of Ship Money was the culminating measure that drove hundreds from England to find homes in America, and among other causes, was that which most of all contributed to bring about the war between the King and the Parliament. Though, after a long and tedious struggle, the levy of ship money was declared to be illegal, enough had been effected to make far-sighted men tremble for impending troubles, and no doubt the stand made by men of great influence and high position, such as HAMPDEN (who was intimately associated with the leaders of the Massachusetts settlement), had an immense weight with persons of an inferior standing in worldly wealth. By the Act of Parliament, which declared the illegality of the tax, it was ordered that all proceedings which had been taken should be cancelled, and in consequence a wholesale destruction of documents must have taken place, which, had they been preserved, would have been of great value to the topographer and genealogist, as the rolls of assessments were very minute. One volume of assessments only appears to have escaped the general fate, and this contains the names of all the persons assessed in the county of Essex (with the exception of four towns), numbering about 18,000, and, without doubt, includes many of the subsequent emigrants who went out from that county to New England, in the years 1637 and 1638. A copy of this very interesting document has been prepared for publication.

In 1860, Mr. SAMUEL GARDNER DRAKE, of Boston (Mass.), published his "*Result of some Researches among the British Archives, for information relative to the Founders of New England.*"

That work first suggested the desirability of making a systematic collection of authentic documents relating to the early settlers in America, not only to those who removed to the New England States but to those also who settled in Virginia, the Summer Islands, Barbadoes, Carolina, Jamaica, and other places. It is impossible to overestimate the value of these records, and it is a matter of the deepest regret that comparatively so few have survived to the present time. Those that we have, therefore, of undoubted authenticity, are all the more to be prized. It is a transcript of some of these documents which is here submitted. The aim of the transcriber has been to present an absolute copy of the originals. He has not even ventured to correct palpable mistakes in the spelling of names, or other clerical errors. Where such occur, and they are by no means infrequent, he has called attention to the fact, either by inserting the correct word in brackets, or by adding a foot-note, but the text is a faithful reproduction of the originals.

There are some papers included in Mr. DRAKE'S volume, which have not been deemed admissible in the body of this work, inasmuch as they are not in themselves official documents, but they may not inaptly be quoted here. The first to be noticed are the following lists, taken from the History of Sandwich, being transcripts of records belonging to the corporations of that port.

A LIST OR REGISTER

Of all such persons as embarked themselves in the good ship called the *Hercules*, of Sandwich, of the burthen of 200 tons, John Witherley, master, and therein transported from Sandwich to the plantation called New England in America; with the certificates from the ministers where they last dwelt of their conversation, and conformity to the orders and discipline of the church, and that they had taken the oath of allegiance and supremacy. (The certificates, all dated February and March, 1634, are here omitted.)

Masters of Families.	Children.	Servants.
NATHANL. TILDEN of Tenterden yeoman and LYDIA his wife	Seven by name	Seven by name
JONAS AUSTEN of Tenterden and CONSTANCE his wife	Four.	
ROB. BROOK of Maidstone mercer and ANNE his wife	Seven.	
THO. HEYWARD of Aylesford taylor and SUSANNAH his wife	Five.	
WILL. WITHERELL of Maidstone schoolmaster and MARY his wife	Three	One

	Children.	Servants
Masters of Families.		
FANNET ...... of Ashford hemp-dresser.		
THO BONEY and HEN. EWELL of Sandwich, shoemakers		
WILL. HATCH of Sandwich merchant and JANE his wife	Five	Six
SAM. HINKLEY of Tenterden and SARAH his wife	Four.	
ISAAC COLE of Sandwich carpenter and JOAN his wife	Two.	
		A Servant.
THO. CHAMPION of Ashford		
THO. BESBEECH of Sandwich	Six	three
JNO. LEWIS of Tenterden and SARAH his wife	One	
PARNEL HARRIS of Bow London		
JAMES SAYERS of Northbourn taylor		
COMFORT STARRE of Ashford chirurgion	Three	Three
JOS. ROOTES of Great Chart.		
EM. MASON of Eastwell wid.		
MARGT. wife of Will. Johnes late of Sandwich, now of New England, painter		
JNO. BEST of the said parish taylor.		
THO. BRIDGEN of Faversham husbandman and ...... his wife.		

History of Sandwich, by W. BOYS, 1792, pp. 750-1.

A TRUE ROLL OR LIST

Of the names, surnames, and qualities of all such persons who have taken passage from the town and port of Sandwich for the American plantations, since the last certificate of such passengers returned into the office of Dover Castle.

THOMAS STARR of Canterbury yeoman and SARAH his wife   1 child

EDWARD JOHNSON of Canterbury joiner and SUSAN his wife   7 children 3 servants

INTRODUCTION. xxi

NICHOLAS BUTLER of Eastwell yeoman and 3 children 5 serv.
JOICE his wife
SAMUEL HALL of Canterbury yeoman and JOAN 3 serv.
his wife.
HENRY BACHELOR of Dover brewer and 4 serv.
MARTHA his wife
JOSEPH BACHELOR of Canterbury taylor and 1 child 3 serv.
ELIZABETH his wife
HENRY RICHARDSON of Canterbury carpenter 5 children 1 serv.
and MARY his wife
JARVIS BOYKETT of Chanington carpenter
JOHN BACHELOR of Canterbury taylor
NATHANIEL OVELL of Dover cordwinder 1 serv.
THOMAS CALLE of Faversham husbandman and 3 children
BENNET his wife
WILLIAM EATON of Staple husbandman and 3 children 1 serv
MARTHA his wife
JOSEPH COLEMAN of Sandwich shoemaker and 4 children
SARA his wife
MATTHEW SMITH of Sandwich cordwinder and 4 children
JANE his wife
MARMADUKE PEERCE of Sandwich taylor and 1 serv.
MARY his wife

Certified under the seal of office of mayoralty 9th June, 1637.
History of Sandwich, by W. BOYS, 1792, p. 752.

We have next to notice the record compiled by Mr. DANIEL CUSHING, first printed in Mr. SOLOMAN LINCOLN'S Centennial Address, at Hingham, September 28, 1835. It contains the names of one hundred and seventy-five emigrants from the county of Norfolk, who emigrated between the years 1633 and 1638, almost wholly from Hingham, Windham, and other neighbouring parishes, and who consequently called their new settlement Hingham. But there is something to be said about this emigration, which it is believed has hitherto escaped notice—that is, that the movement was largely fostered by, if not directly traceable to, the influence of JOHN HAYNES, who was subsequently Governor of Connecticut.

The first name on the list referred to, is that of THEOPHILUS CUSHING, from Hingham, who lived several years upon the farm of Mr. HAINS, as he is described in the original. Hitherto, Governor HAYNES has always been regarded as an Essex man, and he is said to have married MARY, daughter of ROBERT THORNTON, of Nottingham. This is not in accordance with the facts of the case, for JOHN HAYNES was the son of another JOHN HAYNES, who lived at Great Hadham, and afterwards at Codicote, both in the county of Hertford, but inherited an estate in Essex, which had been purchased by his father. He married MARY, one of the three daughters and co-heirs of ROBERT THORNTON, who possessed a good estate in Hingham, Windham, and Wramplingham. Mr. THORNTON died when his daughter, who was afterwards Mrs. HAYNES, was very young, and there are reasons for the belief that after the marriage, JOHN HAYNES went to reside at Hingham, and that their first child, called JOHN (whose name is not recorded by any genealogist either in England or America), was born there. But, before he left England, Mr. HAYNES certainly took up his abode in Essex, on a newly-acquired property, called Copford. Taking then the residence at Hingham of a man of the character of HAYNES, it is easy to account for the emigration from that place, especially as the first portion of the company went out in the same year; indeed, there is every reason to suppose that they sailed in the same ship. There can be but little doubt that THEOPHILUS CUSHING was a trusted servant of JOHN HAYNES, and probably a family connection on his wife's side, her maternal grandmother being the heiress of EDMUND CUSHING, by which marriage the THORNTON family acquired the estates at Hingham, Windham, and Wramplingham, which they enjoyed at the time Mr. HAYNES married into that family.

This list of Mr. CUSHING'S is undoubtedly of great value, tending, as it does, to confirm other statements and unofficial lists, but as it is only a compilation made by a private individual, it is not inserted in this work.

INTRODUCTION. xxiii

There is another very interesting paper included in Mr. DRAKE'S work, which may be briefly noticed. It consists of extracts from the municipal records of Leyden, in Holland, made by the Hon. HENRY C. MURPHY. Many English families took refuge in Leyden, and the list referred to is a register of the births, marriages, and deaths which occurred there among the exiles. It was from Leyden that many of the first settlers in New England, popularly known as the Pilgrim Fathers, came, and embarking from English ports, sailed on board the ships *Mayflower, Fortune, Ann,* and *Little James.*

Among other notices contained in this list, are the following :—

WILLIAM BRADFORD, of Austerfield, Eng., m. Nov. 30, 1613, DOROTHY MAY, of Witzbuts, Eng.*

EDWARD WINSLOW, of London, m. 16 May, 1618, ELIZABETH BARKER, of Chetsum, Eng.*

JOHN JENNE, of Norwich, Eng., m. 1 Nov., 1614, SARAH CAREY, of Moncksoon.†

The three places here mentioned may be traced as Wisbeach, in Cambridgeshire; Chesham, in Buckinghamshire; and Monk Soham, in Suffolk. A family of the name of MAY certainly lived at Wisbeach at the time referred to, as did one of the name of BARKER at Chesham.

The foregoing extracts sufficiently demonstrate the nature of the Leyden records. Further notices are unnecessary, but the list of those who embarked in the before-mentioned ships is of sufficient value to entitle its insertion in this place, though it must be remembered that it is not absolutely official. It is taken from the interesting work of the Rev. Ashbel Steele, A.M., entitled "*Chief of the Pilgrims, or the Life and Times of William Brewster.*" Philadelphia, 1857, pp. 401—410.

---

* Both Bradford and Winslow sailed in the *Mayflower*.

† His wife probably died shortly afterwards, as the name of John Jenny is given alone in the following list as coming over in the *Ann,* or *Little James.*

LIST OF PASSENGERS IN THE *MAYFLOWER;*

Being the *names* of those who came over first, in the year 1620, and were the founders of New Plymouth, which led to the planting of the other New England Colonies. This list of their "names" and families, was preserved by Governor Bradford at the close of his History, and is here presented in the order in which he placed them. The value of such an accurate list cannot be too highly estimated.

Mr. JOHN CARVER; who was chosen their first Governor on their arrival at Cape Cod. He died the first spring. KATHERINE, his wife; she died a few weeks after her husband, in the beginning of summer.

DESIRE MINTER; afterwards returned to her friends, in poor health, and died in England.

JOHN HOWLAND; man servant, afterwards married the daughter of John Tillie, and had ten children.

ROGER WILDER; man servant, died in the first sickness.

WILLIAM LATHAM; a boy, after more than twenty years visited England, and died at the Bahama Islands.

A maid servant; who married, and died one or two years after.

JASPER MOORE; who died the first season.

Mr. WILLIAM BREWSTER; their Ruling Elder, lived some twenty-three or four years after his arrival. MARY, his wife; died between 1623 and 1627. LOVE BREWSTER; a son, married, lived to the year 1650, had four children. WRESTLING BREWSTER; youngest son.

RICHARD MORE and Brother; two boys placed with the Elder. Richard afterwards married, and had four or more children. His brother died the first winter.

Mr. EDWARD WINSLOW; Mr. W. afterwards chosen Governor, died in 1655, when on a commission to the West Indies. ELIZABETH, his wife; died the first winter. Mr. W. left two children by a second marriage.

GEORGE SOULE and ELIAS STORY; two men in Winslow's family. G. Soule married and had eight children. E. Story died in the first sickness.

ELLEN MORE; a little girl placed in Mr. Winslow's family, sister of Richard More, died soon after their arrival.

Mr. WILLIAM BRADFORD; their second Governor, author of the history of the Plymouth Colony, lived to the year 1657. DOROTHY, his wife; who died soon after their arrival. Governor Bradford left a son in England to come afterwards—had four children by a second marriage.

Mr. ISAAC ALLERTON; chosen first assistant to the Governor. MARY, his wife; who died in the first sickness. BARTHOLOMEW; son, married in England. REMEMBER and MARY, daughters. Remember married in Salem, had three or four children. Mary married in Plymouth, had four children.

JOHN HOOK; servant boy, died in the first sickness.

Mr. SAMUEL FULLER; their physician. His wife and child remained, and came over afterwards; they had two more children.

WILLIAM BUTTEN; servant, died on the passage.

JOHN CRACKSTON; who died in the first sickness. JOHN CRACKSTON, his son; who died some five or six years after.

Capt. MYLES STANDISH; who lived to the year 1656; chief in military affairs. ROSE, his wife; died in the first sickness. Capt. Standish had four sons living in 1650, by a second marriage.

Mr. CHRISTOPHER MARTIN and his wife; SOLOMON PROWER and JOHN LANGEMORE, servants; all died soon after their arrival.

Mr. WILLIAM MULLINS, his wife, JOSEPH, a son; these three died the first winter. PRISCILLA, a daughter; survived and married John Alden. ROBERT CARTER, servant; died the first winter.

Mr. WILLIAM WHITE; died soon after landing. SUSANNA, his wife; afterwards married to Mr. E. Winslow. RESOLVED, a son; married and had five children. PEREGRINE, a son; was born after their arrival at Cape Cod, he cannot therefore be numbered among the passengers proper; married, and had two children before 1650.

WILLIAM HOLBECK and EDWARD THOMSON, servants; both died soon after landing.

Mr. STEPHEN HOPKINS, and ELIZABETH, his wife; both lived over twenty years after their arrival, and had a son and four daughters born in this country. GILES, and CONSTANTIA, by a former marriage. Giles married; had four children. Constantia married; had twelve children. DAMARIS, a son, and OCEANUS, born at sea; children by the present marriage.

EDWARD DOTY, and EDWARD LITSTER, servants. E. Doty by a second marriage had seven children; after his term of service went to Virginia.

Mr. RICHARD WARREN; his wife and five daughters were left, and came over afterwards. They also had two sons; and the daughters married here.

JOHN BILLINGTON; he was not from Leyden, or of the Leyden Company, but from London. ELLEN, his wife. JOHN, his son; who died in a few years. FRANCIS, the second son; married and had eight children.

EDWARD TILLIE, and ANN, his wife; both died soon after their arrival. HENRY SAMSON and HUMILITY COOPER, two children, their cousins. Henry lived, married, had seven children. Humility returned to England.

JOHN TILLIE, and his wife; both died soon after they came on shore. ELIZABETH, their daughter; afterwards married John Howland.

FRANCIS COOKE; who lived until after 1650; his wife and other children came afterwards; they had six or more children. JOHN, his son; afterwards married; had four children.

THOMAS ROGERS; died in the first sickness. JOSEPH, his son; was living in 1650, married and had six children. Mr. Rogers' other children came afterwards, and had families.

THOMAS TINKER, wife and son; all died in the first sickness.

JOHN RIGDALE, ALICE, his wife; both died in the first sickness.

JAMES CHILTON, his wife; both died in the first sickness. MARY, their daughter; lived, married, and had nine children. Another married daughter came afterwards.

EDWARD FULLER, his wife; both died in the first sickness. SAMUEL, their son; married; had four children.

JOHN TURNER, two sons; names not given; all three died in the first sickness. A daughter came some years afterwards to Salem and there married.

FRANCIS EATON, SARAH, his wife; she died the first winter; by a third marriage he left three children. SAMUEL, a son; married and had one child.

MOSES FLETCHER, JOHN GOODMAN, THOMAS WILLIAMS, DIGERIE PRIEST, EDMOND MARGESON, RICHARD BRITTERIGE, RICHARD CLARKE; these seven died in the general sickness. The wife of D. Priest, and children, came afterwards, she being the sister of Mr. Allerton.

PETER BROWN; lived some fourteen years after, was twice married, and left four children.

RICHARD GARDINER; became a seaman, and died abroad.

GILBERT WINSLOW; after living here a number of years, returned to England.

JOHN ALDEN; "a hopeful young man," hired at Southampton, married Priscilla Mullens, as mentioned, and had eleven children.

JOHN ALLERTON.

THOMAS ENGLISH.

WILLIAM TREVORE, and — ELY; two seamen; are commonly, but incorrectly reckoned in the number of the first company of passengers for the Colony; Bradford himself says: "Two other seamen were hired to stay a year; * * when their time was out they both returned." Accordingly he says of the *Mayflower* company: "These being about a hundred souls, came over in the first ship." Afterwards he adds: "Of these one hundred persons who came over in this first ship together, the greatest half died in the general mortality, and most of them in two or three months' time." Omitting those two hired sailors who returned, and counting the person that died and the child that was born while on the passage as one passenger, we have the exact number—*one hundred* of the Pilgrim Company, "who came over in the first ship." And, as *fifty-one* died the first season, this enumeration makes good those other words of the historian, that, "the greater half died in the general mortality."

LIST OF PASSENGERS THAT ARRIVED, AFTER ONE YEAR, IN THE SECOND SMALL SHIP *FORTUNE;*

Being parts of families, with others, left in England or Holland the year before. They arrived at New Plymouth, on the 11th of Nov., 1621.

JOHN ADAMS.
WILLIAM BASSITE (Bassett, probably two in his family).
WILLIAM BEALE.
EDWARD BOMPASSE.
JONATHAN BREWSTER; the oldest son of Elder Brewster.
CLEMENT BRIGGES.
JOHN CANNON.
WILLIAM CONER.
ROBERT CUSHMAN; for several years the Leyden Company's agent in England. He returned in the *Fortune* to act still further as agent for the Company; was of great service in various ways; but died before coming again to settle in the Colony. THOMAS CUSHMAN, son of Robert, about twelve years old; came with his father in the *Fortune*, became an exemplary man in the Colony, and succeeded Elder Brewster in the eldership, in 1649.
STEPHEN DEAN.
PHILIP DE LA NOYE.
THOMAS FLAVELL and son.
WIDOW FORD and three children, WILLIAM, MARTHA, and JOHN.
ROBERT HICKES.
WILLIAM HILTON.
BENNET MORGAN.
THOMAS MORTON.
AUSTIN NICHOLAS.
WILLIAM PALMER (probably two in his family).
WILLIAM PITT.
THOMAS PRINCE, or PRENCE; married the Elder's daughter, Patience; was afterwards Governor.
MOSES SIMONSON.

HUGH STATIE.
JAMES STEWARD.
WILLIAM TENCH.
JOHN WINSLOW; brother of Mr. Edward Winslow.
WILLIAM WRIGHT.

LIST OF THOSE WHO CAME OVER IN THE *ANN* AND *LITTLE JAMES*.

The vessels parted company at sea; the *Ann* arrived the latter part of June, and the *Little James* some week or ten days later; part of the number were the wives and children of persons already in the Colony.

ANTHONY ANNABAL; afterwards settled in Scituate.
EDWARD BANGS; settled in Eastham.
ROBERT BARTLETT.
FEAR BREWSTER and PATIENCE BREWSTER; daughters of Elder Brewster.
MARY BUCKET.
EDWARD BURCHER.
THOMAS CLARKE. This Thomas Clarke's grave-stone is the oldest on the Plymouth Burial Hill.
CHRISTOPHER CONANT.
CUTHBERT CUTHBERTSON; was a Hollander.
ANTHONY DIX.
JOHN FAUNCE.
MANASSEH FAUNCE.
GOODWIFE FLAVELL; probaby the wife of Thomas Flavell, who came in the *Fortune*.
EDMUND FLOOD.
BRIDGET FULLER; apparently the wife of Samuel Fuller, the physician.
TIMOTHY HATHERLY.
WILLIAM HEARD.
MARGARET HICKES and her children; the wife of Robert Hickes, who came in the *Fortune*.

William Hilton's wife and two children. He had sent for them before his death.

EDWARD HOLMAN.

JOHN JENNY; had "liberty, in 1636, to erect a mill for grinding and beating of corn upon the brook of Plymouth."

ROBERT LONG.

EXPERIENCE MITCHELL.

GEORGE MORTON; he brought with him his son, Nathaniel, and four other children. NATHANIEL MORTON; son of George Morton, and afterwards Secretary of the Colony.

THOMAS MORTON, jr.; son of Thomas Morton, who came in the *Fortune*.

ELLEN NEWTON.

JOHN OLDHAM; a man of some note afterwards.

FRANCES PALMER; wife of William Palmer, who came in the *Fortune*.

CHRISTIAN PENN.

Mr. Perce's two servants.

JOSHUA PRATT.

JAMES RAND.

ROBERT RATTLIFFE.

NICHOLAS SNOW; settled in Eastham.

ALICE SOUTHWORTH; widow, afterwards the second wife of Governor Bradford.

FRANCIS SPRAGUE; settled in Duxbury..

BARBARA STANDISH; *i.e.*, second wife of Captain Standish, married after her arrival.

THOMAS TILDEN.

STEPHEN TRACY.

RALPH WALLEN.

It must not be imagined that the following pages furnish by any means a complete list of the early settlers in America. In 1637 Thomas

Mayhew was appointed, for a term of twenty-one years, to keep a record of all those persons who left England "to passe into forraigne partes," but of Mayhew's lists nothing is to be found but the fragment commencing at page 287, and that continues but for a few months. It cannot be doubted but that other lists were made, but they are either lost, or are among the mass of papers still uncatalogued at the Record Office. We learn incidentally that ships left England almost daily for America, but no records of them, or of their passengers, remain. Thus among the registers of deaths in the parish of Deal, co. Kent, we find that on the 4th of May, 1639, Margaret, wife of Thomas Waldigraue, bound for New England, was buried. Who was Thomas Waldigraue, and with what company did he sail?

We know that many ships sailed from Bristol, among others *The Angel Gabriel* and *The James*, conveying the Revd. Richard Mather and the Revd. Daniel Maude, but no records of departures from that port remain. Again, who were the companions who sailed in 1633 in the *The Griffin*, with John Haynes and the Revd. Thomas Hooker? Where are the lists of *The Arabella*, and other ships, in which John Winthrop and the founders of Massachusetts embarked? Who went out with the Revd. Ezekiel Rogers from Rowley, and with Fenwick, and the Revd. Henry Whitfield? These are but a few instances, to show how very imperfect are our records of the early settlers.

Further, it should be borne in mind that only the names of those were taken who legally left the shores of England. At page 142, for example, and elsewhere throughout the book, we find that the passengers were examined by the minister touching their conformity to the church discipline of England, and that they had taken the oaths of allegiance and supremacy; elsewhere (p. 106, &c.) we find it certified that they are no subsidy men, that is, men liable to the payment of a subsidy to the crown. Among the thousands who emigrated to New England, it cannot be doubted but that a very large number left to avoid payment of the hateful subsidy, and that they would not take the oaths of allegiance and supremacy. These, therefore, must have left secretly, and of such no record would exist.

It is perhaps hardly necessary to say, that where, in the following lists, it is stated that so many people were *transported* to New England, it does not mean that they were sent as felons, as the word, at the present time, usually implies. It simply means that they were conveyed. Those persons, however, who were convicted for upholding the cause of the Duke of Monmouth (pp. 315—342), were undoubtedly *transported*, as we now understand the word.

The Summer Islands, mentioned at pages 301—314, and elsewhere, are now called the Bermudas. In 1609, Sir GEORGE SOMERS, or SUMERS, was driven on the islands in the course of a voyage to Virginia, and from him the islands derived their name. The Virginia Company, who claimed the islands by the right of having discovered them, sold them to a company of a hundred and twenty persons, who, having obtained a charter for their settlement in 1612, sent out sixty settlers, with a governor. During and immediately after the civil war in England, many persons of eminence took refuge in the Bermudas, among others the poet WALLER, who celebrated their beauty in a poem, entitled "*The Battle of the Summer Islands*."

Enough has been said to show the great value of the lists here given, and I trust that others may be induced to make further search among the documents in the Record Office, to bring to light the treasures there hidden.

J. C. H.

May, 1873.

[Regi]ster of the names of all ẙ Passinger wch Passed from ẙ Port of London for on whole yeare Endinge at Xp^mas 1635.

Passinger wch Passed from y^e Port of London.

Post festum Natalis Christi 1634. vsq' ad festum Na: Christi 1635

Secundo Januarij 1634

THEIS vnder written are to be transported to Virginea imbarqued in ye Merch^t *bonaventure* JAMES RICROFTE M^r bound thither have taken ye oath of Allegeance.

	yeres		yeres
WIllM SAYER	58	ANDREW JEFFERIES	24
BAZILL BROOKE	20	W^M MUNDAY	22
ROBERT PERCY	40	ARTHUR HOWELL	20
CHARLES HILLIARD	22	JO: ABBY	22
EDWARD CLARK	30	JAMES MOYSER	28
JO: OGELL	18	MATHEW MARSHALL	30
RICHARD HARGRAVE	20	W^M SMITH	20
JO: ANDERSON	20	GARRETT RILEY	24
FRANCIS SPENCER	23	MILES RILEY	20
JOHN LEWES	23	WIllM BURCH	19
RICHARD HUGHES	19	PETER DOLE	20
JOHN CLARK	19	JAMES METCALF	22
W^M GUY	18	JO: VNDERWOOD	23
JOHN BURD	18	ROBERT LUCK	25
JAMES REDDING	19	JOHN WOOD	26
RICHARD COOPER	18	WALTER MORGAN	23

Henrie Irish	16	John Fountaine	18
George Greene	20	Henry Redding	22
Henry Quinton	20	Loughton Bostock	16
Jo: Bryan	25	John Russell	19
Robert Payton	25	Tho: Ridgley	23
Tho: Symond's	27	Robert Harris	19
Michell Browne	*35	Wiłłm Mason	19
Jo: Hodges	37	Victor Derrick	23
Jo: Edmond's	16	John Bamford	28
Garret Pownder	19	Geo: Session	40
Jo: Wise	†28	Jo: Cooke	47
Henry Dunnell	23	Tho: Townson	26
Symon Kenneday	20	Tho: Parson	30
Tho: Hyet	22	Michell Hopkinson	27
Tho: James	20	Wᴹ Surgisson	25
Jo Sotterfoyth	24	Edward Fisher	35
Emanuell Bomer	18	Robert Fisher	34
Leonard Wetherfield	17	Richard Ellis	29
James Lickburrowe	20	Jo: Atkinson	24
Tho: Singer	18	Jo. Hickcombottom	24
Jesper Withy	21	Joseph Washborn	22
Robert Kersley	22	Richard Pitt	19
Jo: Springall	18	Edward Maior	19
Tho: Jesopp	18	Jo: Favor	18
James Perkyns	42	Henry Anmer	16
Daniell Greene	24	Ellin Jones	18
Wᴺ Hutton	24	Wiłłm Ridgdell	24
Jo: Wilkinson	19	Christopher Carnoll	23
Hugh Garland	20	Jo: Feeldhouse	19
Richard Spicer	18	Tho: Taylor	19
Humfrey Topsall	24	Jo: Grimscroft	27
Tho: Stanton	20	Jesper Weston	27
Jo: Watson	28	John Lee	17
Tho: Murfie	20	John Skorie	16

* [This age is uncertain, the first figure having been altered; it, however, looks like a 3 followed by two 5's.]

† [It is doubtful whether this age is 18 or 28.]

Jo: Mosely	18	Henry Rogers	30
Jereemy Redding	18	Robert Smithson	23
Richard Ast	30	Nic^a: Harvy	30
John Rolinson	26	James Graston [or Grafton]	22
Richard Glaister	31	Daniell Daniell	18
Protherock Alis	24	Reginoll Hawes	25
John Towse	26	Geo: Burlingham*	20
Richard Cave	28	Jo: Hutchinson	22
Tho: Goodman	25	James Grame †	17
Phillipp Conner	21	Richard Harman	20
Launcelot Pryce	21	Sam: Ashley	19
Vxor Thomazin	18	Geo: Burlingham	20
Kat: Yates	19	Elizabeth Jackson	17
Averyn Cowper	20	Sara Turner	20
Jo: Dunn	26	Mary Ashley	24
Leonard Evans	22	Margerie Furbredd	20
Tho: Anderson	18	Margaret Huntley	20
Edward Cranfield	24	Richard Doll	25
vxor Ann Cranfield	18	Tho: Perry	34
Jo: Baggley	14	vxor Dorothy	26
Tho: Smith	14	Ben: Perry	4
Wiłm Weston	30	Mary Carlton	23
Tho: Townsend	14	Abram Silvester	40
Edward Davies	25	Tho: Bolton	18
Mary Saund^{rs}	26	Richard Champion	19
Jane Chambers	23	Richard Champion	18
Margaret Maddock's	21	Abram Silvester	14
Roger Sturdevant	21	Elizabeth Nuñick	20
John Wigg	24	Jo: Atkinson	30
John Greenwood	16	Ric^x Hore	24
Andrew Dunton	38	Ralph Nicholson	20
John Wise	30	Robert More	19
Wm Hudson	32	Joan Nubold	20
Tho: Edenburrow	37	Tho: Hebden	20
John Hill	50		

* [It will be observed that this name is repeated five lines below.]
† [It is possible that this name may be intended for GRAND; the last two letters are very badly written.]

vj° Januarij 1634.

THEIS vnder written names are to be transported to St Christophers ℞ the Barbadoes, JAMES ROMSEY M^r bound thither have taken ye oath of Allegeance.

	yeres		yeres
JOHN PHILLIPPS	21	JOHN BOWES	23
JOHN ALLIN	23	HENRY CUPPLEDIKE	20
DAVID JOHNES	24	ROB^T STRATFORD	16
W^M WHITE	30	ROBERT HOLLAND	19
HUMFREY DAVIES	22	THO: BORNE	22
W^M CANNION	21	EDWARD ROBERT'S	25
EDWARD LAMPEUGH	35	JOHN CARTER	26
GEORGE CLIFFE	26	GEORGE SUTTON	19
ABRAM J^N°SON	27	EDWARD JENNOR	24
HENRIE WELLS	23	JOSEPH GLADE	20
JOHN VSHER	26	PETER MONK	29
EDMOND KNIGHT	21	RICHARD COKE	38
THO: RASBOTTOM	23	ISACK PETER	20
W^M GRIGGSON	14	PHILLIPP SQUIER	20
RICHARD JONES	23	BARTHOLMEW FLUDE	24
MICHELL WHITE	18	RICHARD LAWRENCE	20
RICHARD BORNE	24	DANIELL SMITH	20
EDWARD FLETCHER	20	JOHN SYMES	17
FRANCIS SOWTH	19	ROBERT KETT	22
JOHN CONNY	20	SUZAN HUDSON	20
ROBERT SKARVILL	21	MARY SEA	16
EDWARD ROBINSON	18	JOHN SHETTLEWORTH	28
JOHN HOLLAND	15	RICHARD FRYME	26
EDWARD ASH	20	ROB^T HOLME	22
THO: SANDBY	17	JOHN MORE	28
THO: GREENE	24	RICHARD PERCE	45
MARK THEODY	18	EDWARD JONES	21
WILLM BURT	22	MARK ELLVYN	20

HENRY PURSTYNN	18	JOHN HIGGINS	20
RICHARD CHITTING	23	WiHm HODGSON	20
THO: MARFUTT	22	THO: JENKYNNS	23
RICHARD EDMOND'S	18	Jno GREENEWOOD	26
Wm PRICHARD	25	JOHN PLACE	22
THO: ARNOLD	18	Wm HAYMAN	36
RICHARD CHAMBLIS	19	EDWARD SAVAGE	20
EDWARD BRUNT	25	JO: CONNIERS	21
GEORGE STOKES	23	JOHN MORE	30
HENRY FOOKES	21	ROBT GROUND	22
ROBERT GRANGER	21	WILLIAM BRUTON	22
Wm WALTER	26	WILLIAM WALTON	22
JOHN RODS	20	WiHm SEWARD	26
EZECHELL CLEMENT'S	20	HENRY RYMES	40
THO: CARPENTER	20	HENRY ILES	17
THO: SMITH	17	BRYAN ERLE	21
JOHN WHITE	27	JOHN FOX	19
JOHN WATKINSON	22	ROBERT GILBY	18
JOSEPH PARDY	23	ROBERT BAKER	50
ROBERT LANGRIDGE	20	THO: PECK	20
Jno ETHERINGTON	17	WiHm HARRIS	35
GEORGE WHITE	27	JOHN TOWNE	27
THO: COCKEY	25	CHRISTIAN MYNNIKYN	19
Anto BLACKGROVE	24		

17 *Februarij* 1634.

THEIS vnder-written names are to be transported to thē Barbadoes imbarqued in yͤ *Hopewell* Capten THO: WOOD Mr bound thither. the passenges have taken the oath of Allegeance ℓ Supremacie.

	yeres		yeres
WiHm VSHER	22	JOHN HILL	19
RICn: HANBY	23	RICHARD CLYNTON	23
RICHARD JACKSON	17	Jno HARRISON	45

James Read	19	Jarvice Dodderidge	21
Dunston Kember	20	John Decborn	22
Wᴹ Owen	23	Wᴴᴍ Seriff	19
Jnᵒ Free	25	John Offword	24
Richard Gane	19	Tho: Lee	20
Thomas Richard's	19	Robert Richard's	18
John Nicks	23	George Hiter	18
Martin Perkynn	20	John Dreadd	17
Antᵒ Blades*	24	Arthur Wvnd	17
Robert Dymond	29	Richard Osborn	22
Tho: Dayes	20	John Phillipps	37
Wᴹ Walker	21	John Steevens	13
Ralph Harwood	23	John Reddhedd	28
Phillipp Philpott	30	Wᴹ Gibson	18
James Pallister	28	Tho: Waterman	27
Richard Clark	21	Tho: Jones	19
Daniell Baker	20	Jo: Nisom	23
John Tayler	23	Edward Layton	30
Thomas Prosser	20	Wᴴᴍ Benson	28
John Eaton	20	John Whitehedd	23
Tho: Smith	21	Richard Barnard	23
John Johnson	18	Henry Long	21
Richard Holmes	24	John Wilks	22
Ralph Terrett	24	Tho: Wellman	21
Henry Tatnum	20	Tho: Gaton	25
Alexander Smith	18	Wᴴᴍ Allin	25
John Crapp	37	Tho: Letteny	20
John Faux	36	Robert Porter	20
Joseph Bryan	20	John Hughes	20
Nevill Hutchins	20	Henry Atkyns	22
Wᴹ Walters	22	Robert Kember	21
Wᴴᴍ Puttex	20	Robert Mills	19
Archibald Weyer	18	John Davies	25
Nathaniell Cobham	17	Thomas Crowder	21

* [This name is very faintly written, but I do not think there can be any doubt about it.]

RICHARD PURNELL	21	THO: EVERIE	19
ROBERT LYNLEY	20	THO: MEDWELL	31
HENRY HOLMES	44	JO: BASHER	20
JOHN KEY	30	JAMES ELLERTON	18
JOHN WILLIAMS	21	RICHARD HANDS	19
JOHN FOWLER	24	MEDUSALA WATT'S	20
JOHN OWEN	20	THO: HAMES	19
OWEN WILLIAMS	21	PHILLIPP CARTWRITE	20
THO: DREW	26	JOHN LOFTIS	21
W^M BUMSTEDD	21	MICHELL ROCKS	21
EDWARD JN°SON	20	JO: LING	45
JOHN BOWND	20	THO: SHERMAN	26
JOHN HAIES	30	W^M JACKSON	30
JOHN LYON	18	JAMES GOLDINGHAM	32
Wiłłm CORSER	24	RIC^R: RAINOLDS	19
THOMAS TRIGG	21	JO: NOKES	20
ROBERT NISBETT	19	FRANC'S [FRANCIS] SYMOND'S	21
Wiłłm CADDY	21	THOMAS LURTING	21
JOHN CASSEDY	20	JAMES ANDERSON	19
ALEXANDER MORE	24	WALTER JAGO	20
RICHARD WELLYN	25	JOHN BEAD	22
RICHARD GRIFF'S [GRIFFITHS]	24	JOHN YOUNG	19
ARTHUR YEOMANS	24	THO: HUBBARD	20
NICHOLAS HOBSON	23	EDWARD BROWNE	24
W^M MARROW	25	W^M SEERE	22
FRANCIS DENE	21	W^M LEVYNS	22
JOHN PHILPOTT	16	JO: HAMOND	17
JOHN STRATTERGOOD	18	EDWARD PULLIN	27
W^M CANT	19	JAMES CULLIMOR	22
HENRIE SPECKMAN	27	JO: DE PARK	28
JOHN YAT'S	19	RICHARD WALTON	21
W^M RANSE	27	ROBERT COLLIE	20
GEORGE SELMAN	16	JOSEPH HEPWORTH	33
NICHOLAS BLADES	21	Wiłłm WALTERS	32
JOHN CLARK	24	DANIELL SMITH	33

RICHARD TRUEMAN	24	RANDALL OGDEN	19
Wᵐ MASTERS	21	THO: BROWNE	11
JO: CLERE	26		

xj° *Marcij* 1634

de pochia Sci Egiddij [*Giles*] Cripplegate. } **THEIS** vnder written names are to be transported to New England having brought Certificate from the Justices of the peace ℓ Minister of the pish the ptie hath taken the oaths of Allegeance ℓ Supremacie.

PETER HOWSON xxxj yeres ℓ his Wife ELLIN HOWSON 39 yeres old.

Turris Londoñ } **THEIS** vnder written names are are (*sic*) to be transported to New-England having brought attestacoñ ℓ Certific from the Justices of peace ℓ Minister of the pish according to the LLs [Lords] of the Councells order the ptie hath taken the oaths of Allegeance ℓ Supremacie.

	yetes
THOMAS STARES	31
SUZAN JOHNSON	12

16 *Marcij* 1634

Mildred Bredstret } **THEIS** vnder-written names are to be transported to New-England imbarqued in yᵉ *Christian* de Lo: JO: WHITE. Mʳ bound thither, the Men have taken yᵉ oath of Allegeance ℓ Supremacie.

	yeres		yeres
FRANCIS STILES	35	JO: HARRIS	28
THO: BASSETT	37	JAMES HORWOOD	30
THO: STILES	20	JO: REEVES	19
THO: BARBER	21	THO: FOULFOOT	22
JO: DYER	28	JAMES BUSKET	28

THO: COOP [COOPER]	18	THO: HAUKSEWORTH	23
EDWARD PRESTON	13	JO: STILES	35
JO: CRIBB	30	HENRIE STILES	40
GEORGE CHAPPELL	20	JANE WORDEN	30
ROBERT ROBINSON	45	JOAN STILES	35
EDWARD PATTESON	33	HENRY STILES	3
FRANCIS MARSHALL	30	JO: STILES	9. Mo:
RIC^R: HEYLEI	22	RACHELL STILES	28
THO: HALFORD	20		

22° *Marcij* 1634

THEIS vnder-written names are to be imbarqued in y^e *Planter* NIC^O: TRARICE M^r bound for New-England p Certificat from Stepney pish, and Attestacōn from S^r THO: JAY, & Mr SIMON MUSKETT 2 Justices of the Peace. the Men have taken the oaths of Supremacie & Allegeance.

	yeres		
NICHOLAS DAVIES	40	W^M LOCK	6
SARA DAVIES	48	A Sawyer JO: MADDOX	43
JOSEPH DAVIES	13	Glover JAMES LONNIN	26
ROBERT STEVENS	22	A Sawyer	
JOHN MORE	24	A Labourer	
JAMES HAIEWARD	22	4 servants	
JUDITH PHIPPIN	16		

26 *Marcij* 1635

THIS vnder written name is to be imbarqued in the *Peter Bonaventure*. THO: HARMAN M^r bound for ye Barbadoes & St Christophers p Certificate from St Androwes pish Holborne: And Attestacōn from Justice GRIMSTON & Justice SHEPPARD hath taken the oaths of Allegeance & Supremacie.

Wiħm BANKS.......................... 21 yeeres.

Primo Aprill 1635

IN the *Hopewell* of Lond m' Wm BUNDOCKE v^rs New Engld

JO^n COOPER..............	41 yers	of oney [Olney]* in Buckingham-sher	theis haue taken the othe of Alleg & supremcie
EDMOND FARRINGTON	47 yers		
Wm PARRYER	36		
GEO: GRIGG'S	42	of Landen [? Lavenden]*	in Bucking- hāsher
PHILLIP KYRTLAND ...	21	of Sherington	
NAth KYRTLAND	19	of Sherington	

THO. GRIGG'S	15 yers	Children of GEO: GRIGGS aforsaid
Wm GRIGG'S..............	14	
ELISA. GRIGG'S	10	
MARY GRIGG'S	6	
JAMES GRIGG'S	2	

  WIBROE .... 42 y^rs wife of JO^n COOPER
  ELIZA: .... 49 yers wife of EDMOND FARRINGTON
  ALYCE .... 37 yers wife of Wm PURRYER†
  ALYCE .... 42 ycrs wife of GEO. GRIGG'S

MARY COOPER	13	Children of JO^n COOPER aforsaid
JO^n COOPER..............	10	
THO. COOPER	7	
MARTHA COOPER	5	

  PHILLIP PHILLIPP .... 15 yers seru^t to JO^n COOPER

SARRA FARRINGTON...	14	Children of EDW.‡ FARRINGTON
MATHEW FARRINGTON	12	
JO^n FARRINGTON	11	
ELIZA. FARRINGTON...	8	

---

* [I have no doubt that Olney and Lavenden are meant; both which places, as well as Sherington, are in the Hundred of Newport.]

† [It is probable that this is intended for PARRYER, a name which appears above; it is however, clearly written PURRYER.]

‡ [So in the original; but doubtless intended for EDMOND, which name occurs above.]

MARY PURRYER*	7
SARRA PURRYER*	5
KATHREN PURRYER*	18 monthes

Children of Wᴹ PURRYER.*

27 psons

2° *Aprilis* 1635

THEIS vnder written names are to be transported to New-England imbarqued in the *Planter* NICᵒ: TRARICE Mʳ bound thither the pties have brought Certificate from the Minister of Sᵗ Sᵗ (*sic*) Albons in Hertfordshier ℗ Attestacon from the Justices of peace according to the Lords order.

	yeres		
A Mercer JO: TUTTELL	39	Husbandman GEO: GIDDINS	25
JOAN TUTTELL	42	JANE GIDDINS	20
JOHN LAWRENCE	17	THO: SAVAGE, a Tayler	27
Wᴹ LAWRENCE	12	A Taylʳ RICHARD HARVIE	22
MARIE LAWRENCE	9	Husb:man FRANC'S [FRANCIS] PEBODDY	21
ABIGALL TUTTELL	6		
SYMON TUTTELL	4	Lynnen wever Wᴹ WILCOCKSON	34
SARA TUTTELL	2		
JO: TUTTELL	1	MARGARET WILCOCKSON	24
JOAN ANTROBUSS	65	JO: WILLCOCKSON	2
MARIE WRAST	24	ANN HARVIE	22
THO: GREENE	15	A Mason Wᴹ BEARDSLEY	30
NATHAN HEFORD†	16	MARIE BEADSLEY	26
servant to JO: TUTTELL		MARIE BEADSLIE	4
MARIE CHITTWOOD	24	JOHN BEADSLIE	2
Shoemaker. THO: OLNEY	35	JOSEPH BEADSLIE	6. mo:
MARIE OLNEY	30	Husbandman ALLIN PERLEY	27
THO: OLNEY	3	Shoemaker Wiƚƚᴹ FELLOE	24
EPENETUS OLNEY	1	A Taylor FRANCIS BAKER	24

* [See note † on previous page.]
† [This name is very difficult to decipher.]

THO: CARTER 25
MICHELL WILLMSON [WIL-
   LIAMSON] .... 30 } servant's to GEO: GIDDINS prd
ELIZABETH MORRISON 12

3ᵈ Aprill 1635

       Statinor JAMES WEAUER......... 23 yers ℓ
Husbandman dwelge in } EDMOND WEAVER ... 28 yers ℓ his wife
Auckstrey in herefordsher   MARGRETT aged 30 yers.

THEIS vnder written names are to be transported to New-England imbarqued in yᵉ *Hopewell* Mʳ Wᵐ BUNDICK. the pties have brought Certificate from the Minister ℓ Justices of peace, that they are no Subsedy men. they have taken the oath of alleg: ℓ Supremacie.

Husbandman Jo: ASTWOOD ... 26
   Jo: RUGGELLS 10
   MARTHA CARTER 27
   MARIE ELLIOTT 13

Nazing in Essex.
Shoemaker Jo: RUGGELLS...... 44
   uxor BARBARIE RUGGELLS... 30
   Jo: RUGGELLS 2
   ELIZABETH ELLIOT 8
   GILES PAYSON 26
   ISACK MORRIS............... 9

Husbandman. Jo: PEAT 38
   of Duffill* pish
   in Derbieshier.

   EDWARD KEELE 14
   Jo: GOADBY 16
   Jo: BILL 13
   THO: GREENE 15

p Cert: from Stanstedd Abbey†
   in com Hert.
Husb:man LAWRENCE WHITTI-
   MOR 63
   ELIZABETH WHITTIMOR . 57
   ELIZABETH TURNER 20
   SARA ELLIOTT   6
   ROBERT DAY 30
   Wᵐ PEACOCK 12

Husbandman ISACK DISBROUGH 18
   of Ell-Tisley‡ in com
   Cambridge.
   ELIZ: ELLIOTT 30
   LYDDIA ELLIOT 4
   PHILLIP ELLIOT 2

Husbandman ROBERT TITUS
   of St. Katherins 35
   uxor HANNA TITUS 31
   Jo: TITUS 8
   EDMOND 5

---

* [Probably Duffield, in Appletree Hundred.]
† [Stansted Abbot is a Township in the Hundred of Braughin, Herts.]
‡ [Eltisley, a parish in the Hundred of Longstow.]

GEO: WOODWARD .... 35. ffishmonger.

p Certi from S^r GEO: WHITMOR ℓ S^r NIC^o RAYNTON two Justices of ye Peace in London. ℓ from JO: THORP Minister of ye pish of St Buttolphs Billings gate.

TO be Imbarqued In the *Peter Bonav^tr* de Lo. m' Capt HARMAN v^rs Barbades.

Theis pties here vnder expressed haue brought Certeficat from two Justices of peace that the toke the oathe of Allegā ℓ Sppremacie ℓ Also cer^t frō ye Ministr of the pishe this 3^d Aprill 1635

                            yers

THO: HATHORNE ....aged 22	ALCE MACE............ 22
Wm MORRISON..................... 23	MARGRETT ELLGATE 24
RALPH VAUGHAN .... 22 ℓ ½	MARGRETT HARTFORDE 22
JANE MADDOCKES 21	

4th *Aprill* 1635

IN the *Peter Bonav^tr* de Lo. m' Capt HARMAN for Barbades Theis two pties brought Cer^t from two Justices of peace ℓ the Ministr of their Conformity accord to order.

Wm CLERKE.................. 29 yers. | THO: SERGEANT............. 23 yers.

vj° *Aprilis* 1635

THEIS pties heerevnder menconed are to be transported to New-England: imbarqued in the *Planter* NIC^o: TRARICE M^r bound thither: they have brought Certificate from the Justices of Peace ℓ Ministers of ye pish that they are conformable to the orders of ye Church of England and are no Subsedy Men: they have taken the oath of Supremacie ℓ Allegeance die et An^o prd.

                                                  yeres

    A Carrier MARTIN SAUNDERS 40
        vxor RACHELL SAUNDERS............... 40

3 children {	Lea Saunders	10
	Judith Saundr's	8
	Martin Saunders	4
3 servant's {	Marie Fuller	17
	Richard Smith	14
	Ric^R: Ridley	16
Husb:	Francis Newcom	30
wife & 2 children {	Rachell Newcom	20
	Rachell Newcom...........	2½
	Jo: Newcom̄	9 moneths
A Glover	Ant^o Stannion..................	24
	Daniell Hanbury	29
	Francis Dexter	13
	Wiłm Dawes	15
	Marie Saunders	15

A Taylor	Clement Bates	40	⎫
	Ann Bates	40	⎬
5 children {	James Bates	14	Theis pties imbarqued in the *Eliz*. Mr Wm Stagg bound for New England p Cert: from the Justic's & Ministers of ye pish.
	Clement Bates	12
	Rachell Bates.........	8
	Joseph Bates...........	5
	Ben: Bates	2
servant's {	Jo: Wynchester	19
	Jarvice Gold*	30

More for the *Planter*

Husbandman	Richard Tuttell..............	42
	Ann Tuttell...................	41
	Anna Tuttell	12
	Jo: Tuttell	10
	Rabecca Tuttell.............	6
	Isbell Tuttell.................	70
	Marie Wolhouston...........	30

* ["The scribe made a brace against Jo: Wynchester, and began to write *servant* against the name, but stopped when he had written *se*, and wrote *servants* against Jervice (Jarvice) Gold."—*Drake.*]

Husbandman	WIḦM TUTTELL 26
	ELIZABETH TUTTELL 23
	JO: TUTTELL 3½
	ANN TUTTELL .... 2 a qʳ
	THO: TUTTELL .... 3. mo:
	SYCILLIE CLARK 16
	MARIE BILL 11

PHILLIPP ATWOOD 12	MARIE BUSHNELL 26
BARTHOL: FALDOE 16	MARTHA BUSHNELL 1
A Carpenter THO: PELL* 26	WIḦM LEA† 16
MARIE PELL 26	MARIE SMITH 18
MARIE PELL 1	ELIZABETH SWAYNE 20
Wᴹ LEA 16	MARGARET LEACH 15
A Carpenter FRANC'S BUSH-NELL 26	HANNA SMITH 18
	ANN WELLS 15

IN the *Hopewell* WIḦM BUNDOCK Mʳ bound for New-England &c.

	JAMES BURGIS 14
	ALEXANDER THWAIT'S 20
	JO: ABBOTT 16
	JO: BELLOWES 12
	JO: JOHNES 18
	CHRISTIOM ‡ LUDDINGTON 18
	MARIE ABBOTT 16
	MARIE COKE 14
	MARIE PEAKE 15
A Tayler THO: PELL	 22
A Glazier JO: BUSHNELL	 21

* [This and the three following names are crossed through in the original MS.]
† [It will be seen that this is a repetition of one of the crossed-out names in the first column.]
‡ [Probably intended for CHRISTIAN. The original, however, is distinctly written.]

7

IN the *Rabecca* of London, M^r   HODGES for New-England

  A Husbandman. PETER VNDERWOOD 22
      ISABELL CRADDOCK 30

---

vij° Aprilis 1635

THIS ptie vnder mencioned is to be imbarqued in the *Planter* bound for New-England, p Cert: from ALDERMAN FENN of his conformitie. he hath taken the oath of Allegeance & Supremacie.

  RICHARD FENN 27

---

3 *Aprilis* 1635 At Gravesend.

THEIS vnder written names are to be transported to St Christophers imbarqued in the *Paul* of London, JO: ACKLIN, M^r bound thither. there was Cert: brought from the Minister of St Katherins of their conformitie of their discipline & orders to ye Church of England the Men did take ye oath of Alleg: and Supremacie.

	yeres		yeres
RALPH REASON	23	THO: WATSON.....................	29
EDWARD MERRIFIELD	19	DAVID EVANS	22
ROBERT WADE	35	STEEVEN GARRET	19
WIllM HAIES	24	W^M BEDDLE	19
GEO: RISHFORD	24	RICHARD LOCK	20
MATHEW MOYSES	17	ABRAM WATSON..................	19
ROBERT RICHARDSON	20	JAMES CARTER	25
JO: MOUNTAIN	20	W^M SCARSBRICK	23
JO: WILLIS	29	W^M CHURCH.......................	21
JO: FRENCH	18	JOHN REINOLD'S..................	23

HENRY BAGIN	22	JO: WATT'S	21
Wᴹ Lamyn	21	EDWARD FISHER	27
HANNA ROPER	23	Rɪcʀ: CROWDER	28
HENRY LEE	30	Rɪcʀ: PRESTON	21
EDWARD SMALLMAN	21	Rɪcʀ: OLDER	24
ROBERT ATKINSON	23	Wᴹ KING	18
THO: FEARFAX	22	JO: HOLMES	22
MATHEW TURNER	46	Nɪcᵒ SEDEN	20
EDWARD GASS	20	FRA: STOTT	32
HENRY SENTENCE	20	PHILLIPP JEÑING'S	25
EDMOND DAVIES	21	ROBERT SPURR	24
EDWARD BARNES	16	THO: SPENDERGRASS	24
THO: NOTT	18	Nɪcᵒ: HOLLIS	20
JO: ADAMS	16	Rɪcʀ: DANES	20
EDWARD GRAY	32		
			49

IN the *Peter Bonaventure*, THO: HARMAN Mʳ bound for the Barbabodoes, theis vnder written names p order: they have taken yᵉ oaths of Supremacie and Allegeance.

	yeres		yeres
THO: BERKYNN	24	Rɪcʀ: LEECH	22
JO: WESTGARTH	28	Rɪcʀ: ABBOTT	20
JO: SWEETING	26	AMBROSE HUETT	27
JAMES TOWNSON	29	JO: WHITE	25
Rɪcʀ: DAWSON	28	JO: WESTON	26
THO: GREENWOOD	15	Wᴹ WESTON	16
THO: IVESON	36	Wᴹ HOWSEMAN	12
THO: HYWOOD	22	Rɪcʀ: CHAPMAN	40
Wᴹ BANK'S	23	THO: CUTLER	35
JO: GREENLY	20	JAMES JACKSON	33
DANIELL DAVIES	26	JO: SMITHEMAN	23
ROBERT BRABAN	29	ROBERT SAVAGE	21
JO: THOMAS	25	GEO: PENNY	24

Jo Pattman	23	Willm Beckkitt	26
Tho: Coke	30	Tho: Evans	20
Jo: Symonds	19	Jo: Hynd	24
Jo: Boone	12	Wm Mecham	20
Nico: Evans	16	Roger Wills	20
Jo: Wydhouse	15	Tho: Tedder	19
Ricʳ: Hollinby	20	Jo: Sessions	22
Wm Lodge	13	Daniell Dennis	22
Isack Pratt	22	Capten Jacob Lake	30
o: Evans	17	Luke Stokes	35
Ames Robard's	20	Richard Speed	35
Ricʳ: Clark	19	Phillipp Henson	21
Geo: Plunckett	19	Arthur Watkyns	25
Wm Maccowdin	19	Jo: Joyner	25
Jo: Alliday	20	Jo: Dent	30
Walter Gibson	25	Robert Jnoson	26
Jo: Wynkles	20	Jo: Sawcott	18
Jo: Vynn	17	Jo: Bunce	18
Robert Roe	19	Jo: Robinson	26
Maurice Willms [Williams]	18	Ricʳ: Pell	22
Dennis Mortagh	30	Jo: Disherd	22
Jo: Dukkarth	31	Tho: Lamberd	23
Ricʳ: Mansfield	22	Geo: Chapman	17
Gregorie Ogell	15	Wm Aston	17
Wm Whitlock	31	Adrian Coke	27
Jo: Long	20	Robert Philkynn	25
Jo: Thomson	31	Jno Sympson	29
Tho: Farmer	22	Steeven Greenly	16
Ricʳ: Brownley	19	Mary Loveley	35
Mathew Westwood	18	Ann Lovely	10
Jo: Mather	21	Margaret Lucock's	27
Robert Pendred	40	Annis Percy	24
David Robinson	20		

8 *Aprilis* 1635

THEIS pties herevnder mencioned are to be transported to New-England: imbarqued in the *Elizabeth* of London Wᴹ STAGG Mʳ bound thither: they have taken the oath of Allegeance ℓ Supremacie p Cert: from the pish of St Alphage Cropplegate [Cripplegate] the Minister there.

    Tanners Wᴹ HOLDRED 25
           ROGER PRESTON 21
           DANIELL BRODLEY 20
           ISACK STUDMAN*............ 30

That theis 3 pties prd̃ are no Subsedie men: wee whose names herevnto are written belonging to Blackwell Hall, do averr they are none.

                    ROBᵀᴱ FARRANDS.
                    THOMAS SMITH.

THEIS pties herevnder written are to be transported in the *Planter:* prd. p Cert: from the Minister of Kingston vpon Thames in the County of Surrey of their conformitie: ℓ yᵗ they are no Subsedy men.

    A Miller PALMER TINGLEY † 21
    An ostler Wᴹ BUTTERICK 20
    A Miller THO: JEWELL 27

---

ix° *Aprilis* 1635

IN the *Elizabeth* de London prd̃ Mʳ Wɪ̃ʟᴍ STAGG bound for New-England: Theis vnder-written names have brought Cert: from yᵉ Minister of Hauckust ‡ in Kent: ℓ Attestation from two Justices of

---

* [This fourth name is in a different handwriting from the preceding three, and was doubtless inserted after the succeeding paragraph (in which *three* only are referred to) had been written.]

† [The first letter of this name is very faintly marked; but, after close examination, I cannot doubt that it is a T.]

‡ [Hawkhurst, in the Lathe of Scray.]

Peace being conformable to the Church of England ℓ that they are no Subsedy Men.

		yeres
A Clothier	JAMES HOSMER	28
wife ℓ 2 children {	*Vxor* ANN HOSMER	27
	MARIE HOSMER	2
	ANN HOSSMER	3. mo:
maidserv^{ts} {	MARIE DONNARD	24
	MARIE MARTIN	19
	JO: STON	40
	EDWARD GOLD	28
	GEO: RUSSELL	19
	JO: MUSSELL	15

Nono die Aprilis 1635

IN the *Rabecca* M^r JO: HODGES bound for New-England.

Husbandman.	JACOB WELSH	32
	GEO: WOODWARD	35

THEIS vnder-written names are to be transported to New-England imbarqued in the *Rabecca* prd.

ELIZABETH WINCKOLL	52	W^M SWAYNE aged	16
JO: WINCKOLL	13	FRANCIS SWAYNE	14

17th *Aprill* 1635

IN the *Elisa* ℓ *Anne* m' RO. COWPER v^{rs} New England

THOMAS HEDSALL .... 47 yers.

IN the *Encrease* of Lond. m' ROBERT LEA v^rs New Engld

 a Mason GEO: BACON* .... 43 yers:
  SAMUELL .... 12 yers ⎫
  JO^N 8   ⎬ Children of the Said Mason*
  SUSAN 10   ⎭ [BACON].
 a Husbandman THO: JOSTLIN 43
  REBECCA his wife.................... 43
  ELIZA. WARD a maid seru^t............ 38
   REBECCA ...... 18 ⎫
   DOROTHY 11   ⎪
   NATHANIELL .. 08   ⎬ Children of the said
   ELIZA. 6   ⎪ THO: JOSTLIN
   MARY......... 1   ⎭

---

x° Aprilis 1635

THEIS vnder written names are to be transported in the *Planter* prd NIC°: TRARICE M^r bound for New Engl: p Cert: of the Minister of Sudburie in Suffolk ℓ from the Maior of the Towne of his conformitie to the orders ℓ discipline of the Church of England ℓ that he is no Subsedy man. he hath taken the oath of Alleg: ℓ Suprem:

             yeres
  Carrier RICHARD HASFELL† 54
   vxor MARTHA 42
    ⎧ MARIE HASFELL 17
    ⎪ SARA HASFELL 14
5 daughters. ⎨ MARTHA HASFELL 8
    ⎪ RACHELL HASFELL............ 6
    ⎩ RUTH HASFELL 3

---

* [This name was first written MASON, in mistake, and then altered to BACON; the correction, however, was not made for the children. I therefore suggest, in their case, what is doubtless the correct reading, within brackets.]

† [With some of the daughters, this name appears to be written HASFELL; it is, however, evidently intended for HASFELL: in the first name, that of RICHARD HASFELL, it is quite clear.]

| ALICE SMITH 40
| ELIZABETH COOP [COOPER] 24
| JO: SMITH 13
| JOB HAWKINS 15

IN the *Planter* prd: Theis vnder names are to be transported to New-England.

| EGLIN HANFORD 46
| 2 daughters { MARGARET HANFORD 16
| ELIZ: HANFORD 14
| RODOLPHUS ELMES 15
| THO: STANSLEY 16

IN the *Elizabeth* of London: Wm STAGG M^r bound for New-England.

| WIℏM WILD... 30
| PETER THORNE 20
| ALICE WILD 40

xj° die Aprilis 1635

IN the *Eliz:* prd Wm STAGG M^r bound for New-England: the pties vnder written have brought Certificate according to order

A Carpenter Wm WHITTEREDD 36	JO: CLUFFE 22
uxor ELIZABETH 30	JO: WILD 17
sonn THO: WHITTREDD .. 10	SAM͞VEL HAIEWARD 22
	JO: DUKE 20

IN the *Planter* prd: Theis vnder written names are to be transported to New-England p Certificate according to order

SARA PITTNEI 22	MARGARET PITNEY 22
2 children { SARA PITNEI .. 7	RACHELL DEANE 31
{ SAMVELL PITNEY 1:½	

xiij° Aprilis 1635

IN the *Elisabeth & Ann* Mr ROGER COOP [COOPER] bound for New-England p Cert: from the Maior of Evesham in com worc^r & from the Minister of ye pish. of their Conformitie.

MARGERIE WASHBORN	49
JO: WASHBORNE	14 } 2 sonns
PHILLIPP WASHBORNE	11

IN the *Elisabeth* de Lo: W^M STAGG M^r prd: theis vnder written names brought Certi. from the Minister of St Savio^rs Southwark: of their conformitie.

THO: MILLET	30	JOSUA WHEAT.............	17
vxor MARIE MILLET	29	JO: SMITH	12
VRSULA GREENOWAY.......	32	RALPH CHAPMAN	20
HENRIE BULL.............	19	THO: MILLET	2

THIS vnder written name is to be imbarqued in y^e *Increase* ROBERT LEA M^r bound for New-England.. p Cert. from Billerecay in Essex, from the Minister of ye pish that he is no Subsedy man.

Husbandmen W^M RUSCO	41
et vxor RABECCA	40
SARA RUSCO..........	9
MARIE RUSCO	7 } 4 children.
SAMVEL..............	5
W^M RUSCO	1

IN the *Increase* prd. Theis vnder written names are to be transported to New England: p Cert: from All Sts Stayning's Mark-lane of their Conformitie to the Church of England.

  A Taylor THO: PAGE 29
    ELIZABETH PAGE .... 28 ⎫
    THO: PAGE .... 2 ⎬ wife & 2 children.
    KATHERIN PAGE .... 1 ⎭
    EDWARD SPARK'S .... 22 ⎫ 2 serv^ts
    KAT: TAYLOR .... 24 ⎭

IN the *Elizabeth & Ann* ROGER COOP [COOPER] M^r: Theis pties herevnder expressed are to be imbarqued for New-England having taken the oaths of Allegeance & Supremacie & likewise brought Certificate both from the Ministers & Justices where their abiding's were latlie of their conformitie to the discipline & orders of the Church of England, & y^t they are no Subsedy Men.

Husb: ROBERT HAWKYNNS ..	25	THO: HUBBARD	10
JO: WHITNEY	35	THO: EATON	1
JO: PALMERLEY	20	MARIE HAWKYNNS	24
RICHARD MARTIN	12	ELLIN WHITNEY	30
JO: WHITNEY	11	ABIGALL EATON............	35
RICHARD WHITNEY	9	SARA CARTRACK	24
NATHANIELL WHITNEY	8	JANE DAMAND	9
THO: WHITNEY	6	MARY EATON	4
JONATHAN WHITNEY	1	MARIE BROOMER	10
NIC^o: SENSION..............	13	MILDRED CARTRACK........	2
HENRY JACKSON............	29	JOSEPH ALSOPP	14
Wm HUBBARD	35		

YE PORT OF LONDON. [1635

IN the *Suzan* & *Ellin* EDWARD PAYNE Mr for New-England Theis pties herevnder expressed have brought Certificate from the Minister & Justices of their Conformitie & that they are no Subsedy Men

Husbandman JOHN PROCTER	40	Husb: RICHARD SALTONSTALL	23
MARTHA PROCTER	28	MERRIALL SALTONSTALL	22
JOHN PROCTER	3	MERRIALL SALTONSTALL	9 Mo:
MARIE PROCTER	1	THO: WELLS	30
ALICE STREET	28	PETER COOP [COOPER]	28
Husb: WALTER THORNTON	36	Wᴹ LAMBART	26
JOANNA THORNTON	44	SAᴍVEL PODD	25
JOHN NORTH	20	JEREMY BELCHER	22
MARY PYNDER	53	MARIE CLIFFORD	25
FRANCIS PYNDER	20	JANE COE	30
MARIE PYNDER	17	MARIE RIDDLESDEN	17
JOANNA PINDER	14	JO: PELLAM	20
ANNA PYNDER	12	MATHEW HITCHCOCK	25
KATHERIN PINDER	10	ELIZABETH NICHOLLS	25
JO: PYNDER	8	TOMAZIN CARPENTER	35
RICHARD SKOFIELD	22	ANN FOWLE	25
EDWARD WEEDEN	22	EDMOND GORDEN	18
GEORGE WILBY	16	THO: SYDLIE	22
RICHARD HAWKINS	15	MARGARET LEACH	22
THO: PARKER	30	MARIE SMITH	21
SYMON BURD	20	ELIZABETH SWAYNE	16
JO: MANSFIELD	34	GRACE BEWLIE	30
CLEMENT COLE	30	ANN WELLS	20
JO: JONES	20	DYONIS TAYLER	48
Wᴹ BURROW	19	HANNA SMITH	30
PHILLIP ATWOOD	13	JO: BACKLEY	15
Wᴹ SNOWE	18	Wᴹ BATTRICK	18
EDWARD LUᴍUS*	24		

* It is very likely this name may be intended for Lam[m]as; the second letter is, however, plainly written *n*.

15 *May* 1635

PENELOPY PELLAM 16 yers to passe to her brother plantaoñ [plantation]

---

xiiij° Aprilis 1635

IN the *Increase* of London Mr ROBTE LEA bounde for New England

ROBERT CORDELL } SAMUELL ANDREWES aged 37 yrs } Theis haue taken the oathes of Allegance & Supremacye, and haue brought Certeficat of their conformety wch are this day filed
Gouldsmith in } ROBTE NANEY .... aged 22 yeres }
Limbert Stret* } ROBTE SANKEY .... aged 30 yeres }
sent them a Way } JAMES GIBBONS .... aged 21 yeres }

Also.

JANE the wife of thabouesaid SAM ANDREWES 30 yrs } All for newland [New England] in the *Increase* aforesaid
ELLYN LONGE her s'runte aged 20 yeares........ }
JANE ANDREWES her daughter aged 3 yeares .... }
ELIZABETH ANDROWES her daughter aged 2 yeares }

---

xvth·Aprill 1635

IN the *Eliza*. de Lond. m' WM STAGG vrs New Englād

RICH. WALKER .... 24 yers } theis ptis haue taken Oathe of Allegane & of Supremacy before Sr WM WHITIMOR & Sr NICHO: RANTON
JON BEAMOND .... 23 }
WM BEAMOND .... 27 }
THO: LETTYNE .... 23 }
JON JOHNSON .... 23 }

WiHM WALKER 15

---

* [Doubtless intended for Lombard Street.]

15th *Aprill* 1635

IN the *Eliza*.. ℓ *Anne* de Lon m' ROGER COOPER v^{rs} New England

PERCY KINGE 24 yers. a Maid seruant to m' RO: CROWLEY:

IN the *Eliza*.. de Lo. m' Wm STAGG vrs New England

JAMES WALKER 15 yers ℓ SARRA. WALKER 17 yers: Serut^{ts} to Joⁿ BROWNE a Baker ℓ to on Wm BRASEY linen drap in Cheapside Lond p Cert. of their Conformity.

---

xviij° *Aprilis* 1635

THEIS vnder written names are to be transported to New-England imbarqued in the *Increase* de Lo: ROBERT LEA M^r the ptie prd. having brought Certificat's from the Minister ℓ Justices of ye Peace of his conformitie to the Church of England

		yeres	
Glover	THO: BLOGGETT	30	
uxor	SUZAN BLOGGETT	37	
	DANIELL BLOGGET	4	} 2 children.
	SAMVELL BLOGGET	1½	

IN the *Increase* prd. The ptie vnder written hath brought Certificate from the Minister of Wapping ℓ from two Justices of peace, of his Conformitie to y^e Church of England: to passe in y^e said Ship for New-England

Lynnen wever	THO: CHITTINGDEN	51	
uxor	RABECCA CHITTINGDEN	40	
	ISACK CHITTINGDEN	10	} 2 children
	HEN: CHITTINGDEN	6	

THEIS vnder written names are to be transported to New-England imbarqued in the *Suzan* & *Ellin* EDWARD PAYNE M\$^r\$: the pties have brought Certificates from y\$^e\$ Ministers & Justices of the peace y\$^t\$ they are no Subsedy Men : & are conformable to y\$^e\$ orders & discipline of the Church of England

A Drap RALPH HUDSON	....	42
vxor MARIE HUDSON	....	42
3 children { HANNA HUDSON	....	14
ELIZ: HUDSON	....	5
JO: HUDSON	....	12
THO: BRIGGHAM	....	32
servant's { BEN: THWING	....	16
ANN GIBSON	....	34
JUDITH KIRK	....	18
JO: MORE	....	41
HENRY KNOWLES	....	25

GEO RICHARDSON	....	30
BEN: THOMLINS	....	18
EDWARD THOMLINS	....	30
BARBARA FORD	....	16
JOAN BROOMER	....	13
RICHARD BROOKE	....	24
THO: BROOKE	....	18
Husbandman SYMON CROSBY	....	26
vxor ANN CROSBY	....	25
THO: CROSBY ....8 week's } 1 Child		
Husbandman RIC\$^b\$: ROWTON	....	36
vxor ANN ROWTON	....	36
EDMOND ROWTON .... 6 } 1 child.		
A Husb:man PERCIVALL GREENE	....	32
vxor ELLIN GREENE	....	32

Jo: Trane	25 ⎫ 2 servant's
Margaret Dix	18 ⎭
Jo: Atherson	24
Ann Blason	27

Ben: Buckley	11
Daniell Buckley	9
Jo: Corrington	33
Mary Corrington	33

xiiij° Aprilis 1635

THEIS vnder-written names are to be transported to the Barbadoes imbarqued in the *Faulcon* de London, Tho: Irish Mr p Certificate from the Minister of the pish of their conformity to the orders of the Church of England, The Men have taken the oaths of Allegeance & Supremacie.

Gabriell Bolt	29	Henry Dye	20
Owen Bliss	30	Edward Bull	22
Geo: Say	26	Farford Goldsmith	22
Bassell Terry	22	Tho: Crispin	19
Marmaduke Turner	21	Francis Sheres	26
Jo: Bassett	19	John Bathe	23
Jo: Sheering	26	Smith Baker	28
Henrie Biddleston	17	James Hibbins	17
Tho: Lett	22	Jo: Belton	48
Samvel Stor*	17	Nicolas Flitcroft	16
James Burt	13	Wm Bingham	18
Charles Fall	19	Humfrey Morris	18
Wm Sennott	20	Jo: Dallinger	16
Jo: Browne	20	Jo: Rogers	34
Tho: Webb	18	Jo: Spyer	32
Jo: Hopwood	20	Francis Smith	20
Nico: Wade	19	Abraham Halloway	20
Robert Davers	14	Joseph Drap [Draper]	21

* [The last letter is very indistinctly written : the name *may* be read as Stor, Ston, or Stow.]

Tho: Bromby	59	Toby Hazell	20
Jo: Bromby	27	Geo: Clark	15
Jesper Giggon	18	Tho: Robert's	18
John Brumwell	22	Marmaduke Crosby	28
Ric^h: Dent	17	Geo: Harris	17
Thomas Gualmay	22	Roger Sawter	17
Richard Snathe	19	Marie Perry	18
Richard Cockman	20	Elizabeth Elson	18
Thomas Allin	22	Bridget Gerden	19
Valentine Love	18	Katherin Hill	20
Robert Haxley	21	Marie Newcom	17
Tho: Metcalf	20	Benedicter Sheriiack	20
Wm Knight	30	Marie Crew	19
Henrie Gilder	18	Elizabeth Long	21
George Lee	16	Winifred Hand	20
Ant^o: Boldsworth	18	Elizabeth Curtis	22
John Church	21	~~Wm Langley~~ *	14
John Scott	16	Wm Sturgis	18
Robert Jones	25	Tho: Knowles	16
Nathaniell Write	32	Peter Lostell	14
John Jones	24	Walter Holburd	24
Tho: Wallis	27		

xv° Aprilis 1635.

THEIS pties hereafter expressed are to be transported to New-England imbarqued in y^e *Increase* ROBERT LEA M^{r.} having taken the oathes of Allegeance & Supremacie : As also being conformable to the Governm^t & discipline of the Church of England whereof they brought testimony p Cert: from ye Justices & Ministers where there abodes have latlie been. (vizt.)

		yeres
Husbandman	SAMVELL MORSE	50
vxor	ELIZABETH MORSE	48

---

* [Crossed through in the original; the age is doubtful.]

Joseph Morse	20
Elizabeth Daniell	2
Alynnen wev' Philemon Dalton	45
vxor Hanna Dalton	35
Samvel Dalton	5½
Wᴹ White	14
Husbandman Marthaw Marvyn	35
vxor Elizabeth Marvynn	31
Elizabeth Marvinn	31
Mathew Marvynn	8
Marie Marvynn	6
Sara Marvynn	3
Hanna Marvynn	½
Jo: Warner	20
Isack More	13
Carpenter Samvell Ireland	32
vxor Marie Ireland	30
Martha Ireland	1½
Plowrite. Wiŀŀᴍ Buck	50
Roger Buck	18
A joyner. Jo: Davies	29
A Husbandman. Abram Flem̄ing	40
Husb: Jo: Fokar	21
Clothier. Tho: Parish	22
John Owdie	17
Butcher Wᴹ Houghton	22
Husb: Wiŀŀᴍ Payne	37
Anna Payne	40
Wᴹ Payne	10
Anna Payne	5
Jo: Payne	3
Daniell Payne	8. week's.

James Bitton	27	Jo: Kilborne	10
Wm Potter	25	James Roger	20
Elizabeth Wood	38	Richard Nunn	19
Elizabeth Beards	24	Tho: Barret	16
Suzan Payne	11	Jo: Hackwell	18
Aymes Gladwell	16		
Phebe Perce	18	Chirurgion Symon Ayres	48
Carpenter Henry Crosse	20	*vxor* Dorothy Ayres	38
Husb: Tho: Kilborne	55	Marie Ayres	15
vxor Francis Kilborne	50	Tho: Ayres	13
Margaret Kilborne	23	Symon Ayres	11
Lyddia Kilborne	22	Rabecca Ayres	9
Marie Kilborne	16	Jane Rawlin	30
Francis Kilborne	12		

      Husbandman Symon Stone 50
          vxor Joan Stone 38
             ⎧ Francis Stone 16
             ⎪ Ann Stone 11
    children ⎨ Symon Stone 4
             ⎪ Marie Stone 3
             ⎩ Jo: Stone .... 5 weekes

          Christian Ayres 7
          Anna Ayres 5
          Beniamin Ayres 3
          Sara Ayres .... 3. mo:

   A Sawy^r Steeven vpson 23
          Jo: Wyndell 16
            ⎧ Isack Worden 18
            ⎪ Nathaniell Wood 12
   seruants ⎨ Elizabeth Streaton 19
            ⎩ Marie Toller 16

16 *Aprilis* 1635

THEIS pties hereafter expressed are to be transported to the Island of Providence imbarqued in y^e *Expectacion* CORNELIUS BILLINGE M^r, having taken the Ooaths of Allegeance & Supremacie: As likewise being conformable to the Church of England; whereof they brought testimonie from the Ministers & Justices of Peace, of their Abodes

FRANCIS SMITH	36	MARY BAKER	42
THO: PALMER	18	ELISHA BRIDGES	16
LEONARD SMITH	22	WiłłM THORP	30
MATHEW HAMBLEN	38	ELIZABETH THORP	20
W^M LYNLIE	58	ELIZABETH THORP	2
CHRISTIAN WHETSTON	19	JOAN FELVER	50
W^M CAWDLE	19	MARGARET ROLLRIGHT	45
FLORENCE DICKENSON	19	ELLIN COOPER	24
JO: BAKER	42	ELIZABETH COKE	20
JO: MARTIN	30	MARIE CHADDOCK	20
W^M SMITH	20	ELIZABETH HAMOND	25
ANT^O DOWSELL	20	ALICE AWBREY	29
RICHARD SLIE	20	ELIZABETH LAWRENCE	26
FRANCIS DALES	20	ANN NOBLE	21
PETER AWBREY	32	MARIE HARROWIGG	21
THO: FELD	18	MILLICENT LEECH	28
EDWARD HASSARD	24	MARIE GOODWYNN	20
RICHARD BULL	17	KATHERIN WEBB	22
RICHARD REINOLD'S	16	ELIZABETH SCOTT	20
W^M EAKINS	15	MARIE HOWES	18
JO: TOTNELL	16	DOROTHY LAWRENCE	28
EDWARD HORSHAM	14	ELIZAB: HORSHAM	16
RICHARD TRENDALL	16	ALICE GOLDHAM	26
W^M READ	16	RICHARD PRICE	14
MATHEW PIPPIN	20	RICHARD LANE	38

ALICE LANE	30	ELIZABETH OWEN	30
SAMVEL LANE	7	MARIE MILWARD	21
JO: LANE	4	ISACK BARTON	27
OZIELL LANE	3	ABRAM RAY	20
JO: ATKINSON	36	DORCAS HORSHAM	40
LOVE ATKINSON	38	MARIE GRIFFINN	17

17 *Aprilis* 1635

THEIS pties herevnder expressed are to be transported to New-England imbarqued in y^e *Elizabeth* Wm STAGG M^r p Cert: from the Ministers & Justices of the Peace of their Conformitie to the Church of England: they have taken the oaths of Allegeance & Supremacie

	yeres		
Husb: JAMES BATE	53	*filia* MARY SMITH	15
ALICE BATE	52	PETER GARDNER	18
LYDDIA BATE	20	Wm HUBBARD	35
MARIE BATE	17	RACHELL BIGG	6
MARGARET BATE	12	PATIENCE FOSTER	40
JAMES BATES	9	HOPESTILL FOSTER	14
Husbandman EDWARD BULLOCK	32	FRANCIS WHITE	24
		JOAN SELLIN	50
ELIZABETH STEDMAN	26	ANN SELLIN	7
NATHANIELL STEDMAN	5	EDWARD LOOMES	27
ISACK STEDMAN	1	JO: HUBBARD	10
ROBERT THORNTON	11	JO: DAVIES	9
MARGARET DAVIES	32	MARIE DAVIES	4
ELIZABETH DAVIES	1	JO: BROWNE	40
DOROTHY SMITH	45		

THE ptie herevnder named with his wife & children is to be transported to New-England imbarqued in the *Elizabeth & Ann* W&M Cooper M^r bound thither the ptie hath brought testimony from the Minister of his conformitie to the orders & discipline of the Church of England & from the two Justices of peace y^t he hath taken the oaths of Allegeance & Supremacie.

ALEXANDER BAKER .... 28 ⎫
Vxor ELIZABETH .... 23 ⎬ yeres
ELIZABETH BAKER .... 3 ⎭
CHRISTIAN BAKER 1
CLEMENT CHAPLIN 48
Wm SWAYNE 50

24 *Aprilis* 1635

THEIS vnder written names are to be transported to the Island of Providence imbarqued in the *Expectacon* aforesaid, the pties have taken ye oath of Alleg:

	yeres		yeres
NICHOLAS RISKYMER	31	SAM: GOODENUFF	22
Wm RANDALL	26	EDWARD HASTING'S	23
ANDREW LEAY	24	THO: HOBBS	18
JO: LEAY	25	JO: SARACOLE	17
JO: BLOXSALL	28	THO: WILSON	18

27 *Aprilis* 1635

THEIS vnder written names are to be transported to New-England ROGER COOPER M^r bound thither, in the *Elizabeth & Ann.* the pties have brought Certificate from the Minister at Westminster: ℓ the Justices of the Peace of his Conformitie. the ptie hath taken the oaths of Alleg. ℓ Suprem:

 A Carpenter RICHARD BROCKE 31
    EDWARD SALL................ 24
    DANIELL PRESTON 13

THEIS vnder-written names are to be transported to the Barbadoes ℓ St Christophers, imbarqued in the *Ann* ℓ *Elizabeth* JO: BROOKEHAVEN Capten ℓ Mʳ having taken the oaths of Allegeance ℓ Supremacie. As also being Conformable to the orders ℓ discipline of the Church of England ℓ no Subsedy Men. whereof they brought test: from the Minister of St Katherins neere yᵉ Tower of London.

	yeres		yeres
JOHN CROFT'S	30	BARTHOLOMEW BENNET	18
NATHANIELL BEDFORD	19	THOMAS TYLER	21
JO: MASON	20	JOHN PRICHARD	20
JO: ORAM	21	GILES BARNES	19
CHRISTOPHER FISH	24	HUGH SADLER	20
OWEN ANDROWE	18	HARFORD YOUNG	20
ROBERT ANDERSON	22	JOHN WILLIAMS	16
JOHN GREENE	25	ANDREW EVANS	16
JOSEPH WALLINGTON	19	JOHN BARRET	16
JOHN HAIEWARD	22	JOSEPH WALKER	18
THOMAS MARTIN	16	JAMES TATE	17
EDMOND HOLLOWAY	17	JOHN SMITH	14
THOMAS PIERCE	19	NATHANIELL BOLTON	19
WILLIAM HAYWARD	18	Wᴹ LAYDON	17
EDWARD WILKINSON	17	THOMAS AVERY	18
RICHARD GALE	16	THO: LEAKE	18
ROBERT TRATT	21	DAVIE WILLIAMS	17
THOMAS REDDMAN	16	Wⁱⁱᵗᴹ HARRIS	23
Wⁱⁱᵗᴹ GRUBB	16	JOHN TURPIN	22
JOHN GOLDING	21	FRANCIS SAIEWELL	18
CLEMENT HUTCHINSON	20	MATHEW ROGERS	21

Bryan Bourk	19	Robert Laycock	18
Ant° Taylor	26	Michell Estplynn	18
Andrew Carr	23	James Bell	19
Owen Garret	20	Frend Picto	20
John Frazill	29	John Whithedd	22
John Porter	24	Jo: Mallion	21
Charles Pollington	26	Tho: Bedlam	24
Charles Jackson	18	Tho: Lone*	19
Edward Bacon	25	Thomas Wazell	21
Thomas Robinson	31	Edward Garrard	26
Patrick Conly [or Couly]	21	John Coke	22
George Goddin	31	Jeremy Hartley	30
Arthur Roker	20	Gilbert Holdsworth	30
Tho: Dale	28		
John Davies	19	*Women.*	
Tho: Burton	19	Katherin Lloyd	19
Hugh Wynstonly	20	Suzan Greene	20
Bartholmew Draper	20	Margerie Barran	19
Robert Brock	25	Elizabeth Benning	18
Hugh Tawyer	18	Elizabeth Bruster	18
Wm Greene	17	Joan Smith	27
Patrick Connyer	20	Suzan More	21
Richard King	23	Alice Dixon	21
Willm Barnes	17	Jane Stafford	24
Willm Taylor	23	Alice Hilton	18
Robert Sennodd	23	Katherin Russell	20
Thomas Perkynn	29	Mary Powell	23
Willm Longwith	26	Debora Winke	21
Tho Gullifer	28	Rabecca Bedding	18
John Davies	18	Mathew Page	20
Richard Cawood	25	Ann Spicer	26
Richard Dynley	19	Marie Jones	20
Dennis Peke	20	Margery Harding	20
Nicholas Greene	18	Marie Kinderslie	26

* [Perhaps intended for Loue, *i.e.* Love.]

29° *Aprilis* 1635

THEIS vnder written names are to betrans ported to New-England imbarqued in the *Elizabeth* ℓ *Ann* ROGER COOP [COOPER] M^r the pties have brought Certificate from the Minister of the pish ℓ Justices of Peace of their conformitie to the orders ℓ discipline of the Church of England ℓ y^t they are no Subsedy-men

RIC^R: GOARD	17	THO: POUNT*	21
A Smith THO: LORD	50	ROBERT LORD	9
vxor DOROTHY	46	AYMIE LORD	6
THOMAS LORD	16	DOROTHY LORD	4
ANN. LORD	14		
W^M LORD	12	JOSIAS COBBET	21
JOHN LORD	10	JO: HOLLOWAY	21
JAMES COBBETT	23	JANE BENNET	16
JOSEPH FABERR	26	W^M REEVE	22

eodem 29 *Aprilis* 1635

A Taylor CHRISTOPHER STANLEY 32
    vxor SUZANNA 31
    W^M SAMOND 19

4° *Maij* 1635.

THEIS vnder-written names are to be transported to New-England imbarqued in the *Eliz:* ℓ *Ann* prd. The pties have brought Certificate from the Minister ℓ Justic's of the Peace of their conformitie ℓ that they are no Subsedy Men.

A Tallow-Chandler HEN: WILKINSON 25
    ROBERT HAIES .... 19 A soapeboyler.

---

* [It is impossible to decide whether this name is PONNT or POUNT; it is so indistinctly written, that it may even be intended for POUND.]

THEIS vnder-written names are to be transported to New-England: imbarqued in the *Abigall* RICHARD HACKWELL M^r: The pties have brought Certificate from ye Minister & Justices of their conformitie to the orders & discipline of the Church of England

THO: BUTTOLPH	32	NATHANIELL TYLLY	32
vxor ANN BUTTOLPH	24	PETER KETTELL	10
Wm FULLER	25	THO: STEEVENS	12
JO: FULLER	15	ELIZ: HARDING	12

2° *Maij* 1635

THEIS vnder-written names are to be transported to ye Barbadoes imbarqued in the *Alexander* Capt: BURCHE and GILBERT GRIMES M^r p Certificate from the Minister where they late dwelt the Men tooke the oaths of Alleg. & Supremacie die et A° prd

	yeres		yeres
WiH'M RAPEN	29	Wm POWELL	19
LEONARD STAPLES	22	RALPH PROWD	26
JO: STANFORD	24	JO: BULLMAN	40
JAMES MANZER	27	JO: WATT'S	19
JO: WATTS	25	Wm DENCH	16
THO: CLARK	26	FRANCIS PECK	22
MICHELL KIMP	27	JO: BENSTEDD	24
HENRY BROUGHTON	20	SYMON PARLER	24
GEO: VENTIMER	20	RICHARD HOWSEMAN	19
ROBERT HARDY	18	WALTER JONES	20
THO: DABB	25	PHELIX LYNE	25
GEO: NORTON	22	ARTHUR WRITE	21
Wm HUCKLE	20	LEWES WiH'MS [WILLIAMS]	21
EDWARD KEMP	19	Wm POTT	18

	yeres		yeres
Thomas Gilson	21	Geo. Ridglie	17
Nico: Watson	26	Dennis McBrian [MacBrian]	18
Olliver Hookham	32	Jo: Bussell	36
Chri: Buckland	25	James Driver	27
Jo: Hill	23	Hugh Johnes	22
Anthony Skooler	20	Tho: Gildingwater	30
Jo: Anderson	21	John Ashurst	24
Wm Phillipps	17	James Parkinson	23
Jo: Besford	18	Wiłłm Young	21
Henry Yatman	21	Wm Smith	18
Robert Duce	18	Morgan Jones	31
Owen Williams	18	Jo: Richard	30
Jo: Write	24	Peter Flaming	16
William Clark	19	Miles Farring	24
Edward Halingworth	46	Robert Atkins	23
Richard Powell	32	Beniamin Mason	23
Henry Longsha	23	Tho: Rutter	22
Jo: Bush	22	Jo: Howse	41
Jonathan Franklin	17	Jo: Cole	20
Jo: Phillipps	20	James Watts	35
Richard Cribb	19	Wm Crowe†	17
Tho: Browne	18	Phillipp Lovell	34
Jo: Greenwich	21	uxor Elizabeth Lovell	33
Jo: Nedsom *	19	Rowland Mathew	27
Edward Church	18	Robert Sprite	30
Anto Threlcatt	19	Jo: Weston	41
Wm Willis	17	James Smith	19
Clement Hawkins	16	Jo: Smith	19
Lewes Hughes	19	Richard Lee	22
John Greene	22	Wm Seely	29
Richard Marshall	36	Edward Plunket	20
Mathew Calland	16	Tho: Plunkett	28
Lewes David	28	Rowland Plunkett	18
Geo: White	18	Teague Nacton	28

* [*Might* be read as Neesom.] † [Or, perhaps, Crome.]

Dermond ô Bryan	20	Richard Fane	15
Charles Galloway	19	Robert Robert's	18
James Montgomery	19	Wm Lake	14
J^{no} Mª Conry	28	Richard Iveson	16
Sam̄vell Priday	20	Humfrey Kerby	18
Samvell Farron	30	Edward Cokes	17
Edmond Montgomery	26	Henry Morton	20
Olliver Bassett	14	James Brett	17
Parry Wy	15	Tho: Dennis	18
Daniell Burch	14	Tho: More	33
Richard Stone	13	Jo: Lawrence	17
Thomas Tayler	27	Wm Martin	13
Edmond Nash	21	Richard Philpe	17
Jo: Herring	28		
Wm Beaton	24	*Women.*	
Tho: Roe	22	Barbarie Reason	20
Edward Bank's	35	Jane Marshall	21
Tho: Fludd	21	Diana Drake	19
David Collingworth	22	Mary Inglish	17
Wm Mathews	30	Annis Barrat	20
Tymothie Goodman	27	Marie Lambeth	17
Tho: Penson	20	Ann Mann	17
Willm Anderson	36	Elizabeth Warren	17
Geo: Merriman	41	Ann Skynggle	18
Jo: Dellahay	27	Alice Chump*	20
Robert Lee	33	Mathew May	21
Jo: Jackson	24	Elizabeth Chambers	20
Alexander de la Garde	27	Elizabeth Farmer	20
Francis Marshall	26	Margaret Conway	20
Walter Lutterell	20	Grace Walker	34
Jo: White	15	Edith Jones	21
Jo: Burton	17	Alice Guy	20
Symon Wood	14	Mary Spendley	17
Robert Mussell	14	Ann Gardner	36

* [It is possible this name may be intended for Champ.]

6 *Maij.* 1635

THEIS vnder-written names are to be transported to New-England imbarqued in the *Elizabeth & Ann* ROGER COOP [COOPER] M^r, the pties have brought Cert: from the Ministers where their abodes were: & from the Justices of peace of their conformitie to the orders & discipline of the Church of England, & y^t they are no Subsedy Men, they have taken the oaths of Alleg: & Suprem:

SAMVELL HALL	25	VYNCENT POTTER	21
W^M SWYNDEN	20	RIC^R: GOARD	17
†JO: HALSEY*	24	W^M ADAMS	15
		†HENRY CURTIS*	27

viij° *Maij* 1635.

IN the *Elizabeth & Ann* prd ROGER COOP [COOPER] M^r. Theis vnder written names are to be transported to New-England imbarqued in the said Shipp: They brought Cert. of their Conformite to the Church of England & y^t they are no Subsedy Men.

JOHN WYLIE	25	GEORGE ORRIS	21
JO: THOMSON	22	†JO: JACKSON*	27
EDMOND WESTON	30	ELIZABETH FABIN	16
GAMALIELL BEOMONT	12	GRACE BULKLEY	33
AWDRY WHITTON	45		

Nono die Maij 1635.

THEIS vnder-written names are to be transported to New-England, imbarqued in y^e *Susan & Ellin* EDWARD PAYNE M^r. The pties have brought Certificate from the Minister of the pish of their conformitie

---

* [The † is in the original.]

to the Church of England, & that they are no Subsedy Men. the pties have taken the oaths of Alleg & Suprem:

	yeres		yeres
PETER BULKLEY	50	RIC^d: BROOKE	24
THO: BROOKE	20	ELIZABETH TAYLOR	10
PRECILLA JARMAN	10	ANN LIEFORD	13

IN the *Elizabeth & Ann* prd ROGER COOP [COOPER] M^r bound for New-England.

		yeres	
	ROBERT JEOFFERIES	30	
	MARIE JEOFFERIES	27	
wife & 3 children	THO: JEFFERIES	7	
	ELIZABETH JEFFERIES	6	
	MARY JEFFERIES	3	
	HANNA DAY	20	} 2 maidserv^t's
	SUZAN BROWNE	21	
	ROBERT CARR	21	A Tayler
	CALEBB CARR	11	
	RIC^d: WHITE	30	
	THO: DANE	32	} Carpenters
	Wm HILLIARD	21	

xj° Maij 1635.

THEIS vnder-written names are to be transported to New-England imbarqued in the *Elizabeth & Ann* prd The pties have brought Certificate from the Minister & Justices of Peace of their conformitie to ye orders & discipline of the Church of England, & y^t they are no Subsedy Men.

A Shoemaker WIHM COURSER	26	
A Husbandman GEO: WYLDE	37	} yeres
A Carpenter GEO: PARKER	23	

xij° Maij 1635

IN the *Elizabeth & Ann* ROGER COOPER Mr bound to New-England : Theis vnder written names are to be transported p Certificate from ye Minister of *Benuandin* * in Kent of their Conformitie to ye orders & discipline of ye Church of England.

JOHN BORDEN	28	JEREMY WHITTON	8
vxor JOAN	23	MATHEW BORDEN	5
NICO: MORECOCK	14	ELIZ: BORDEN	3
BENNET MORECOCK	16	bro wever† THOMAS WHITTON	36
MARIE MORECOCK	10	SAMVELL BAKER	30

14 Maij 1635

THEIS vnder-written names are to be transported to New-England imbarqued in the *Elizabeth & Ann* ROGER COOPER Mr the pties have brought Certificatt from the Minister of the pish of his conformitie to the orders & discipline of the Church of England.

	yeres		
A Tayler RICHARD SANSOM	28	THO: OLDHAM	10
THO: ALSOPP	20	ROBT STANDY	22
JOHN OLDHAM	12		

xv° Maij 1635

THEIS vnder-written names are to Virginea : imbarqued in the *Plaine Joan* RICHARD BUCKAM Mr. the pties having brought Attestacōn of their conformitie to the orders & discipline of the Church of England.

---

* [Benendon is a parish in the Hundred of Rolvenden, in the Lathe of Scray.]
† [Meaning not clear.]

	yeres		yeres
Robert Briers	21	Richard Wolley	36
Jnº Johnson	20	Wiłłm Clark	27
Robert Coke	25	Wᴹ Baldwinn	24
Jo: Alsopp	50	Wᴹ Collins	20
Wᴹ Piggott	50	Tho: Pitcher	20
Wᴹ Topliss	30	Joseph Nelson	26
Tho: Arnold	30	Francis Gray	15
Wᴹ Paulson	23	Samvell Young	14
Jo: Northin	22	Robert Hutt	14
Tho: Turner	21	Jo: Raddish	23
Jo: Beddell	22	Tho: Bulkley	32
Jo: Barrowe	26	Robert Brooke	33
Jo: Trent	27	Richard Downes	34
Jo: Coker	21	Arthur Peach	20
Henrie Donoldson	25	Wᴹ James	26
Wᴹ Lavor	22	Tym: Blackett	40
Chri: Davies	22	Roger Koorbe	25
Chri: Taylor	22	Ann Perk's	27
Daniell Clark	33	Tho: Britton	26
Richard Day	32	Wᴹ Collins	34
Robert Lewes	23	Jo: Resburie	30
Luke Bland	20	Henry Jackson	24
Jo: Warren	27	Charles Mᵃ Cartie	27
James Ward	18	Owen Mˡ Cartie	18
Tho: Stump*	32	Charles Flane	18
Tobias Frier	18	Richard Lawrence	20
Willm Steddall	26	Tho: Godbitt	20
Chri: Thomas	26	Nicº: Kent	16
Richard Flem̄ing	24	Thomas Newman	15
Mathew Lem̄	20	Peter Sudburrowe	20
Henry Perpoynt	22	Tho: Lloyd	20
Tho: Hall	21	Wᴹ Hitchcock	27
Edward Wilson	22	Francis Barber	18
Jo: Palliday	23	Edward Wheeler	18

* [May, however, be read Stamp.]

JAMES MILLER	18	JO: HUGHES	30
JO: SHAWE	21	GEO: TALBOTT	18
JO: MARSHALL	21	ROBERT GILBERT	18
JO: ARIS	19	JO: BENNET	18
ROBERT WARD	22	JO: ROLLES	22
THO: VIPER	26	JAMES WYND	23
ROB^T SHINGLEWOOD	26	J^{NO} MARSH	26
GEO: SMITH	34	RALPH WRAY	64

21° Maij 1635

THEIS vnder-written names are to be transported to St Christophers, imbarqued in the *Mathew* of London, RICHARD GOODLADD M^r p warrant from ye Earle of Carlisle.

	yeres		yeres
THOMAS KNIGHT	21	ROBERT WENDEVER	25
JO: HILL	18	SAMVEL TRESE	20
JO: RAWLINS	18	EVAN JONES	19
FRANCIS PENN	22	GABRIELL DAVIES	38
GEORGE ALLERTON	23	EDWARD EELES	20
ROWLAND MILLINGTON	24	DAVIE THOMAS	40
RIC^h: THOMAS	40	RICHARD HORRIBYNN	31
ROGER THOMAS	22	CHRISTOPHER WATSON	21
RICHARD GRIGGSON	34	JAMES HUBBARD	27
JO: BRUÑING	20	W^M STOE	18
ROBERT COKE	32	MATHEW TOMLINSON	31
CLINTON CUTLER	20	THO: HALL	25
THO: TURNER	25	W^M MARSH	26
JO: WOOD	22	JO: HATTERTON	38
W^M ROBINSON	26	THO: TERRILL	18
EDWARD BICROFT	22	ROBERT FAUCE [*or* FANCE]	40
JO: STURDY	26	MILES COVENTRIE	18
ANT^O. NETBIE	20	JO: THOMAS	14

	yeres		yeres
THO: REEVE	24	PIERCE STAPLETON	22
LEWES AWBREY	30	GEO: EATON	27
JAMES WALKER	30	LEONARD HUNT	38
THO: VENN	27	JO: CAVE	34
GEO: BALL	51	W^M BARBER	22
THO: GOSLING	22	JO: HODDINS	50
JO: PALMER	19	ALEXANDER TADD	38
JAMES COTES	21	ROB^T WOODSTOCK	40
W^M HELAWE	21	JOHN OFFLENT	20
MATHEW HELY	21	NIC^O: WATTS	18
ORIGINALL LOWIS	28	RICHARD BROOKES	16
JO: THOMSON	34	THO: HADBIE	22
W^M BROOKES	25	THO: REINOLDS	18
JO: DOE	22	DARBY HURLIE	18
MATHEW WALKER	19	JO: HILLIARD	35
WALTER COLLINS	18	ROBERT LACIE	21
JO: CLINTON	19	THO: BELL	14
ADAM CHESTERMAN	19	ROWLAND MORTON	17
HUYN HALLOWELL	22	JAMES HIDE	22
W^M SALMON	25	RICHARD NELME	20
JO: LANGE	22	THO: HODGES	20
RICHARD LOVE	28	EDWARD THOMSON	18
JO: GREENE	29	THO: WILLIAMS	18
EDWARD WARREN	28	RIC^R: LEE	18
JO: PAPLE	21	WALTER ANTONY	23
ROBERT DENTON	26	CHARLES CAVERLIE	17
W^M ELVYN	23	THO: COXSON	21
GEO: TEMS [*or* TENIS]	20	THO: GOODWYNN	30
GEO: SWALES	19	NIC^O: WILCOCKS	21
MARMADUKE READ	25	GEO: EEKE	26
JO: KIBE	21	RIC^R: HUBBARD	18
THO: GARRETT	20	WiḦM RUSH	20
JO: GOSLINN	20	W^M DONN	22
THO: MILWARD	18	PAUL BOTTELL	32
MORGAN BRINT	19	JO: BOSWELL	17

PASSINGER W^{CH} *PASSED FROM* [1635

Jo: Woodgreene	16	Robt Sandley	20
Jo: Harlowe	16	Edward Mawfrey	15
Robert Warrington	20	Geo: Wade	16
Jo: Reinolds	20	Jo: Fulford	18
Ant^{o.} True	18	Geo: Smith	17
Wm Knight	13	Tho: Powell	24
Ant^{o.} Williams	14		
Jo: Barloe	22	*Women.*	
Wm Parker	17	Margaret Prichard	17
Jo: Wood	18	Jane Burrowe	17
Jo: Payne	18	Katherin Armstrong	20
Daniell Lee	25	Mary Barker	12
Tho: Powell	21	Eliz: Speere	20
Jo: Smith	22		
Geo: Dodd	17		

28 *Maij* 1635

THEIS vnder-written names are to be transported to Virginea imbarqued in the *Speedwell* of London Jo: Chappell M^r being examined by the Minister of Gravesend of their conformitie to the orders ℓ discipline of the Church of England ℓ have taken the oath of Allegeance.

Henry Beere	24	Willm Basford	19
Jo: West	30	Jo: Watson	22
Richard Morris	19	Jo: Gilgate	22
Nic^o: Tetloe	35	Robt Spynk	20
Wm Shipman	22	Richard Rowland	20
Nathaniell Faierbrother	21	Tho: Childs	30
Richard Baylie	22	Jo: Curden	22
Wm Spencer	17	Tho: Romney	19
James Lowder	20	Jo: Harris	20
Chri: Metcalf	19	Christopher Piddington	18
Jeremy Burr	20	Edmond Clark	16

	yeres		yeres
Jonas Smith	22	Tho: Willis	19
Wᴹ Hynton	25	Wᴹ Straughan	22
Jo: Mowser	22	Geo: Sympson	19
Samvell Tyres	21	Richard Phillips	20
Wᴹ Steevens	22	Arthur Saiewell	25
Tho: Busby	19	Melashus Mᵃ Kay	22
Richard Harvy	32	Richard Thomas	20
Tho: Robins	17		
Jo: Beeby	17	Katherin Richard's	19
Jo: Turner	19	Marie Sedgwick	20
Samvell Holmes	20	Elizabeth Biggs	10
Jo: Bever	24	Dorothie Wyncott	40
Jo: Talbott	27	Ann Wyncott	16
Edward Austin	26	Phillipp Biggs	6. mo:
Tho: Greene	24	Elizabeth Pew	20
Richard Browne	19	Francis Langworth	25
Wᴹ Appleby	32	Chri: Reinolds	24
Robert Parker	21	Abram Poore	20
Wᴹ Cunningham	21	Elizabeth Tuttell	25

vj° Junij 1635

THEIS vnder-written names are to be transported to Virginea imbarqued in the *Thomas & John* Richard Lambard Mʳ: being examined by the Minister de Gravesend concerning their conformitie to the orders & discipline of the Church of England: And tooke the oath of Allegeance.

	yeres		yeres
Richard Pew	23	Edward Dix	19
Richard Waynewrite	24	Wᴹ Chaplin	18
Chri: Houghton	19	Jo: Singleton	18
Richard Jones	24	Geo: Dickenson	19
Francis Garret	25	Geo: Hawkins	18
Richard Dally	18	Henry Rastell	30

FRA: SPIGHT 21	SYLUS FOSTER 22
Wᴹ AYMIE 26	EDWARD MOUNTFORT 20
Wᴹ HYNTON 20	HENRY NEWBY 24
JO: EDWARDSON 22	JO: EEDEN 19
THO: MANN 23	THO: SHERLY 23
ROBᵀ ALDRED 24	JO: THOMSON 24
ZACHARY TAYLOR 24	HENRY WARREN............ 15
HUMFREY GRUDGE 21	JO: WILKENSON 28
Wᴹ WHITE 22	RALPH HUDSON 17
JOSEPH MONNVS............. 21	THO: ALLIN................ 33
Wᴹ YARD 21	Wᴹ JONES.................. 17
CHRISTOPHER WHEATLY 28	THO: SHARPLES 20
ROBERT HEED.............. 27	Wᴹ CROOKE 23
EDWARD COLES 20	Wiłłm BEAD 15
MORRIS JONES.............. 28	LAWRENCE PLATT 15
WARDIN FOSSITT 22	ROBERT SPENCER 21
THO: CHAMBERLIN 20	SAMVELL WALDEN.......... 16
JO: SHORTER 26	HENRY MORLEY 25
ANTᵒ· TERRY 50	BEN: EASY 13
ROBERT Wiłłms [WILLIAMS].. 44	JO: MOSS 21
THO: ROSDELL 23	JANE WILKINSON 20
THOMAS TERRY 25	ANN BROOKES.............. 18
CHARLES WYNGATE 22	KATHERIN WISEMAN........ '19
JO: HAMPTON 30	JANE SCOTT 19
JO: EVANS 22	JANE CATESBY............. 20
ROBERT SEWAR 23	JAMES POWELL 12
RICHARD BERRY............ 23	Wᴹ MANN 25
OWEN HUGHES 27	THO: WARNER.............. 26
JO: SUTTON 24	THO: RAM 19
Wᴹ STONHOUSE 43	GRIFFIN JONES 21
Wᴹ CLARK 18	THO: TOLLIE 17
JO: DICKENSON 22	Wᴹ JONES 21
THO: BELL 17	MORRIS PARRY 30
Wᴹ BETT 20	MARMADUKE YOUNG........ 24
JAMES CROSS ·............. 27	Wiłłm WHITE 22

	yeres		yeres
JAMES SHERBONE	15	FRANCIS HUNTER	19
Wᵐ GARDENER	15	FRANCIS ASHBORN	20
JO: ROBINSON	19	Wᵐ DIXON	18
ROBERT TURNER	16	Wᵐ SMART	20
THO: CLARK	16	LAWRENCE PRESTON	21
GILES TERRY	33	Wᵐ WHEATLIE	17
EDWARD CRESSITT	20	Wᵐ LACY	18
THO: WAGGITT	17	JAMES BANK'S	30
MARY FORD	22	GEO: COBCRAFTE	22
KATHERIN WATERMAN	20	GEO: KENNYON	25
SUZAN SHERWOOD	22	JO: KENNYON	21
GRACE BYCROFT	20		

xᵒ *Junij* 1635

THEIS vnder-written names are to be transported to the Bormoodes or Somer-Islands, imbarqued in the *Truelove* de London, ROBERT DENNIS Mʳ, being examined by the Minister of Gravesend concerning their conformitie to the orders & discipline of the Church of England as it now stands established: And tooke the oath of Allegeance.

	yeres		yeres
HENRY MORE	19	DAVID HUSWITH	22
Wᵐ HOLT	19	HENRY HILL	24
JO: NORMAN	19	JO: WARREN	19
ANTᵒ GILLIARD	38	ZEVERIN VICCARS	18
ROBᵗ STOCK	26	GEO: NORMAN	25
THO: FOSTER	27	GABRIELL STOCKWELL	16
ROBERT HART	30	THO: TOOLIE	27
Wᵐ PENDLETON	27	EDWARD GODDIN	16
JAMES TAYLER	28	THO: DORRELL	22
CHRI: HART	20	RICHARD CAÑON	24
RICHARD ANDERSON	30	*vxor.* ELIZABETH CAÑON	23
THO: RICHARDS	24	BARNARD COLMAN	26
JO: NORRIS	18	CHRI: TUKE	16

	yeres		yeres
Wm Paul	20	Robt Poole	20
Wm Bates	17	Tho: Jones	17
Samvell Short	24	Tho: Ewynn	16
Wm Hooper	18	Symon Barcott	16
Richard Hurt	17	Geo: Calverlie	14
Willm Wells	17	Edward Parnell	16
Tho: Dene	17	Wm Lee	18
Jo: A Negroe	18	Wm Tayler	17
Jo: Richards	21	Edward Gibbs	17
Ant^o Bullock	19	James Reason	27
Thomas Bassit	18	Jacob Wilson	18
Edward Aleworth*	13	Ben: Strange	18
Edward Vyncent	18	Ralph Vennable	21
Jo: Trippatt	17	Tho: Bloes	10
Ant^o Cooper	17	Tho: Hedley	11
Jo: Lake	16	Tho: Thomson	17
Ric^r: Tayler	16	Hen: Stonword	13
Tho: Mordin	18	Samvell Hubbard	16
Edward Sell	18	Thomas Bull	13
Roger Willms [Williams]	16	Daniell Hamond	12
Jo: Baylie	18	Geo: Morgan	12
Francis Woodcott	16	Jo: Barnes	16
Jo: Bee	17	Abraham Claxson	17
Ric^r: Greene	17	James Aston	22
Geo: Palmer	18	Ric^r Daughton	13
Tho: Smith	14	Mathew Steevens	12
Nathaniel Willmson [Williamson]	17	Tho: Larkynn	15
Phillipp Wharton	14	David Jones	15
Wm Henry	18	George Hanmer	24
Geo: Saires	12	Roger Hodges	17
Nic^o: Gaughton	14	Wm Powell	15
Edward Hedley	13	Sampson Meverill	20
Wm Sares	17	Henry Carter	42
		Jo: Yates	48

* [May, however, be read as Aldworth.]

	yeres		
Jo: Browne.......................	16	Josias Forster	43
Francis Raynne [or Raymie]	10	Tho: Hall	24
Francis Hedges	13	Humfrey Smith	14
Davie Morris	18	Francis Watson	16
Tho: West	17	Katherin White........	18
Hugh Wentworth	44	Elizabeth Clark.......	18
Ann Taylor	24	Ellin Burrowes	30
Elizabeth Groves	35		
Jo: Groves	1 qr	Jo: Page	33
Blanch Robert's	20	Tho: Jennicom	21
		Sara Page	31
2 Ministers.		Sara Page	3
Jo: Oxenbridge...............	24	Mary Page	3. mo.
Henry Jenning's	24	Richard Harris	17
		Jeffery Wright	18
Beniamin Miller.............	30	Samvell Mayo	10
Henry Fletcher.............	35	Marie Goffe	18
Edward Staughton	50	Jo: Brookes	12

xv° Junij 1635

THEIS vnder written names are to be transported to New-England: imbarqued in the *Abigall* de Lo: Mr. H: HACKWELL: The ptie having brought Certificate from the Minister of Thisselworth* of his conformitie to the orders & discipline of the Church of England. He hath taken the oaths of Allegeance & Supremacie.

	yeres		
Dennis Geere	30	Anns Pancrust	16
wife & 2 children { Elizabeth Geere .	22	Eliz: Taselie..........	55
Elizabeth Geere .	3	Constunt Wood	12
Sara Geere	2		

* [Is it possible that this is intended for ISLEWORTH? I can find no THISSELWORTH.]

19 *Junij* 1635

THEIS vnder written names are to be transported to New-England imbarqued in y^e *Abigall:* HACKWELL M^r the pties having brought Certificate from the Minister of the pish of the litle Miniries of his conformitie & opinion of the discipline of the Church of England.

	yeres		
W^M TILLY	28	CHARLES JONES	21
ROBERT WHITEMAN	20	LIDDIA BROWNE	16

ABOARD the *James* Jo: MAY for N. England.

Tayler THO: EWER	40	SARA BEALE	28
SARA EWER	28	ELIZABETH NEWMAN	24
ELIZABETH EWER	4	JO: SKUDDER	16
THO: EWER	1½		

xx^th *June* 1635

THEIS vnder Written names are to be imbarqued in the *Abbigall* de Lnd [London] m' HACKWELL & bofid to New Engld haue taken oathe of Allegance & Supremacie & Conforable [conformable] to ye Ch as p Cert from Two Justices of Peace & minstr of St Lawrence in Essex

HENRY BULLOCKE	40 yers	husbandman
& SUSAN his wife	42	
iij Children { HENRY	8	
MARY	6	
THO:	2	

more xx*th* 1635

IN the *defence* de Lond m' PEARCE ℓ bōd for New Engḻd p Cert. frō ij Justices of Peace ℓ Ministr of All Saint's homan.* in Northapton.

    Wm HOEMAN............ 40 yers husbandman
    his wife WINIFRID ... 35
    ALCE ASHBEY .... 20 yers amaid Seruant.
5 Children { HANNA............ 8
      { JEREMY............ 6
    MARY.......... 4
    SARRA 2
    ABRAHAM......... 1 q^rtr

xx*th* *June* 1635

IN the *Abbigall* de Lo. m' HACKWELL bōd for New Engḻd p Cert from.† of his Conformity from Justices of Peace ℓ Ministr Eaton Bray‡ in Cō Bedford.

    JO^N HOUGHTON............ 4 [? 40] yers old.

7*th* *Jully* 1635

            BOSTOCKE‖
IN the *defence* de Lond. m' EDWARD§ ~~PEARCE~~ vrs New Engḻd p Cert frō ij Justices of peace ℓ ministr frō Dunstable in Com^t· Bedfordsher:

    ROBERT LONGE................... 45 yers Inholder
    ELIZA: his wife 30

---

* [There is no place bearing this name in Northampton. Query, is it a misspelling of the name HOEMAN in next line, wrongly written in here, and not afterwards erased?]

† [*Sic.* The word must be omitted, to make sense.]

‡ [Eaton Bray is a Township in the Hundred of Manshead.]

§ [*Or* EDMOND. The word is blotted in the original.]

‖ [So in the original. There would seem to have been more than one ship called the *Defence*, since we find the names of four different commanders to ships so named: EDWARD BOSTOCKE (as here); — PEARCE (June 20); EDWARD BOSWELL (June 22); THOMAS BOSTOCK (July 2).]

PASSINGER W^CH PASSED FROM [1635

	MICHELL	20	JOSHUA	3 qʳtrs old
	SARRA	18		
	ROBERT	16	LUCE MERCER	18. a seruant
	ELIZA	12		
x Children	ANNE	10		
	MARY	9		
	REBECCA	8		
	JOⁿ	6		
	ZACHERY	4		

xx^{th} June 1635

IN the *Defence* de Lond m'   PEARCE vrs New Engld p Cert frō two Justices of Peace ℓ Minstr of Towcester in Coᵗ· Northampton

    JOⁿ GOULD............. 25 yers   husbandman
    GRACE his wife .... 25 yers

xxij^{th} June 1635

IN the *Abbigall* de Lond. m'   HACKWELL vrs New Engld p Certᵗ frō Minstr of Cranebroke* in Kent.

    EDW. WHITE............. 42 yers   husbandman
    ℓ his wife MARTHA 39
    ij Children { MARTHA 10
               { MARY 08
    JOⁿ ALLEN..................... 30 yers   husbandman
    his wife ANNE 30
        p Cert hernehil* in Kent

* [Both Cranbrook and Herne-Hill are in the Lathe of Scray.]

IN the *Abbigall*.
p Cert· from Justice peace ℓ Ministr of Stepney.

   GEO: HADBORNE.......... 43 yers Glouer.
   his wife ANNE 46
2 Children { REBECCA 10
      { ANNA 4
JOSEPH BOREBANCKE .... 24 } Seruant's to GEO: HAD-
JOANE JORDEN .... 16 } BORNE.

22th

IN the *Defence* de Lo. m' EDW: BOSWELL vrs New England p Cert·
from Sr Henry Mildmay ℓ Ministr of Baddow* in Essex.

   JON BROWNE................. 27 yers. Taylor.
      { THO: HART 24
his 3 seruant's { MARY DENNY .. 24
      { ANNE LEAKE .. 19

26 *Jun ij* 1635

IN the *Abigall* ROBERT HACKWELL Mr to New-England p Cert:
from Northton Tho. Martin Maior ℓ 2 Justices

Shoemaker JO: HARBERT............... 23
Bricklayer RICHARD ADAMS 29
    SUZAN ADAMS 26

4th *Jully*

   HENRY SOMNER 15
   ELISA. SOMNER 18

---

* [There are two Baddows, Great and Little, in the Hundred of Chelmsford.]

17 *Junij* 1635

THEIS vnder written names are to be transported to New-England, imbarqued in the *Abigall* ROBERT HACKWELL M^r p Cert from the Minister & Justices of Peace of their Conformitie, being no Subsedy Men. they have taken ye oaths of Alleg: & Supremacy being all Husbandmen

	yeres		
RALPH WALLIS	40	MARY MONING'S	30
RALPH ROOTE	50	MARY MONNING'S	9
J^no FREEMAN	35	ANNA MONNING'S	6
WALTER GUTSALL	34	MICHELALIELL MOÑING'S	3
RICHARD GRAVES	23	ELIZABETH ELLIS	16
ROBERT MERE	43	ELLIN JONES	36
SAMVELL MERE	3	ISACK JONES	8
EDMOND MAÑING	40	HESTER JONES	6
THO: JONES	40	THO: JONES	3
GEO: DREWRIE	19	SARA JONES	3. mo:
Wm MARSHALL	40	CESARA COVELL	15
THOMAS KNORE	33	JOAN WALL	19
JOHN HALLJACK	38	Wm PAYNE	15
GEORGE WALLIS	15	NOLL KNORE	29
RABECCA PRICE	14	SARA KNORE	7
MARIE FREEMAN	50	ROB^T DRIVER	8
JO: FREEMAN	9	ELIZABETH MERE	30
SYCILLIE FREEMAN	4	JOHN MERE	3. mo:
JO: WEST	11		

IN the *Abigall* prd: p Cer^t: from the Minister of their conformitie & from the Justices, that they are no Subsedy men.

CHRISTOPHER FOSTER ...... 32 | *vxor* FRANCIS FOSTER 25

children { Rabecca Foster	5	Elizabeth Rookman	31
Nathaniell Foster	2	Jo: Rookeman	9
Jo: Foster	1	Hugh Burt	35
Edward Ireson	32	Ann Burt	32
Wm Almond	34	Wm Bassett	9
Mary Jones	30	Edward Burt	8
Awdry Almond	32	Tho: Freeman	24
Annis Almy	8	Wm Yates	14
Chri: Almie	3	Elizabeth Ireson	27
John Strowde	15	Jo: Fox	35
Edward Rainsford	26	Richard Fox	15
Robt Sharp	20	Jo: Payne	14
John Rookeman	45	Edmond Freeman	45

THEIS vnder-written names are to be transported to New-England imbarqued in the *Blessing* Jo: Lecester M^r the pties having brought Cert from the Minister ℓ Justices of their conformitie being no Subsedy Men, tooke ye oaths of Alleg: ℓ Supremacie.

Willm Cope	26	Robert Turner	24
Richard Cope	24	Eliza: Holly	30
Thomas King	21	Ann Vassall	6
Jo: Stockbridge	27	Margaret Vassall	2
Robert Saiewell	30	Mary Vassall	1
Wm Brooke	20	Elizabeth Robinson	32
Gilbert Brooke	14	Sara Robinson	1.½
Nathaniell Byham	14	Nic^o: Robertson	30
Jo: Wassell	10	Jo: Mory	19
Wm Vassall	42	Charles Stucbridge	1
Ric^k: More	20	James Saiewell	1½

Jo: Robinson	5	Sara Tynkler	15
Ann Stocbridge	21	Fra. Vassall	12
Suzan Saiewell	25	Thomazin Munson	14
Ann Vassall	42	Kat: Robinson	12
Suzan King	30	Mary Robinson	7
Judith Vassall	16	Robᵗ Onyon	26

20 *Junij* 1635

THEIS vnder-written names are to be transported to Virginea imbarqued in the *Phillip* RICHARD MORGAN Mʳ the Men have been examined by the Minister of the towne of Gravesend of their conformitie to the orders & discipline of the Church of England: And tooke the oath of Alleg. die et Aº prd.

John Hart	33	John Taylor	16
John Coachman	28	John Gorham	18
John Reddam	32	Richard Wilson	19
John Shawe	30	Robert Morgan	33
George Hill	23	Samvell Milner	18
George Bonham	31	Tymothie Featlie	23
Wᴹ Rogers	35	Wᴹ Arundell	32
Edward Halock	22	Alexander Leake	22
Ricʀ: Dawson	31	John Mason	16
Peter Johnson	36	Wiᵗᵗm Enson	33
Wiᵗᵗm Bransby	34	James Habroll	22
Nicholas Rippin	31	Thomas Trumball	22
James Quarrier	22	Richard Jnºson	19
Isack Owdell	22	John Lawters	17
Wᴹ Taylor	36	Thomas Edwards	20
James York	21	Robert Davies	28
Thomas Gorham	19	Richard Vppcott	26
Nathaniell Disnall	23	Thomas Poslett	23

		MARCIE LANGFORD	24
Women.		ELIZABETH WILLERTON	18
ELLIN BURGIS	45	SARA SHAWE	18
KATHERIN BOWES	20	MARIE BAKER	25
SUZAN TRASH [*or* TRASK]	25	ANN: BARNIE	23

23º *Junij* 1635

THEIS vnder-written names are to be transported to Virginea imbarqued in the *America* WiȞM BARKER Mʳ: p Cert: from the Minister of the Towne of Gravesend of their conformity to the orders ℓ discipline of the Church of England.

RICHARD SADD	23	RICHARD HERSEY	22
THOMAS WAKEFIELD	17	JOHN ROBINSON	32
THOMAS BENNETT	22	EDMOND CHIPPS	19
STEEVEN READ	24	THO: PRICHARD	32
WiȞM STANBRIDGE	27	JONATHAN BRONSFORD	21
HENRY BARKER	18	WiȞM COWLEY	20
JAMES FOSTER	21	JOHN SHAWE	16
THOMAS TALBOTT	20	RICHARD GUM̄Y	21
RICHARD YOUNG	31	BARTHOLMEW HOLTON	25
ROBERT THOMAS	20	JOHN WHITE	21
JOHN FAREPOYNT	20	THOMAS CHAPPELL	*33
ROBERT ASKYN	22	HUGH FOX	24
SAMVELL AWDE	24	DAVIE MORRIS	32
MILES FLETCHER	27	ROWLAND COTTON	22
WILLIAM EVANS	23	WILLIAM THOMAS	22
LAWRENCE FAREBERN	23	JOHN YATES	20
MATHEW ROBINSON	24	RICHARD WOOD	36
ISACK BULL	27	JAMES SOMERS	22
PHILLIPP REM̄INGTON	29	DAVIE BROMLEY	15
RADULPH SPRAGING	37	WALTER BROOKES	15
GEORGE CHAUNDLER	29	SYMON RICHARDSON	23

* [The original has been altered, and is not clear; it is possible the age should be 23.]

THOMAS JNºSON	19	THOMAS BOOMER	13
JO: AVERIE	20	GEORGE DULMARE	8
JOHN CROFTES	20	JOHN VNDERWOOD	19
THOMAS BROUGHTON	19	WIĦM BERNARD	27
BENIAMIN WRAGG	24	CHARLES WALLINGER	24
HENRY EMBRIE	20	THOMAS DYMETT	23
ROBERT SABYN	40	RYCE HOOE	36
GEORGE BROOKES	35	JOHN CARTER	54
THOMAS HOLLAND	34		
HUMFREY BELT	20	*Women.*	
JOHN MACE	20	ELIZABETH REMINGTON	20
WALTER JEWELL	19	KATHERIN HIBBOTT'S	20
WIĦM BUCLAND	19	ELIZABETH WILLIS	18
LAUNCELOT JACKSON	18	JOAN JOBE	18
JOHN WILLIAMSON	12	ANN NASH	22
PHILLIPP PARSONS	10	ELIZABETH PHILLIPS	22
HENRY PARSONS	14	DOROTHY STANDICH	22
ANDREW MORGAN	26	SUZAN DEATH	22
WIĦM BROOKES	17	ELIZABETH DEATH	3
RICHARD HARRISON	15	ALICE REMINGTON	26
THOMAS PRATT	17	DOROTHIE BAKER	18
JOHN EELES	16	ELIZABETH BAKER	18
RICHARD MILLER	12	SARA COLEBANK	20
ROBERT LAMB	16	MARY THURROGOOD	19

29 *Junij* 1635

BOARD the *Abigall*, ROBᵀ HACKWELL, Mʳ for New-England.

A Baker JOSEPH FLUDD	45	JOSEPH FLUDD	½
vxor JANE FLUDD	35	EDWARD MARTIN	19
ELIZABETH FLUDD	9	SUZAN HATHWAY	34
OBEDIAH FLUDD	4		

vltio Junij 1635

ABOARD the *Abigall* ROBERT HACKEWELL Mr p Cert from the Minister of Stepney pish of their conformitie : ῥ that they are no Subsedy men.

	yeres
Starchmaker HENRY COLLINS	29
vxor ANN COLLINS	30
3 children { HENRY COLLINS	5
JO: COLLINS	3
MARGERY COLLINS	2
JOSUA GRIFFITH	25 ⎫
HUGH ALLEY	27 ⎬ servant's
MARY ROOTE	15 ⎥
JO: COKE	27 ⎭
GEO: BURDIN	24

IN the *Abigall* prd p Cert from the Minister ῥ Justices according to order.

	yeres
EDWARD FOUNTAINE	28
	yeres
RALPH SHEPPARD	29
THANKES SHEPPARD	23 ⎫ Wife ῥ Daughter.
SARA SHEPPARD	2 ⎭

Primo die Julij 1635

IN the *Abigall* prd.

ANN GILLAM	28
sonn BEN: GILLAM	1
Husbandman THOMAS BRANE	40
THO: LAUNDER	22
Husb: WILLIAM POTTER	27
vxor FRANCIS POTTER	26

13

Joseph Potter	20 week's.	Phillip Drinker	39
Ric_R: Carr	29	uxor Elizabeth Drinker	32
Wm King	28	Edward Drinker	13
George Ram	25	Jo: Drinker	8
Jo: Stantley	34	Marg_t: Tucker	23
James Dodd	16	Ellner Hillman	33
Mathew Abdy	15	Jo Terry	32
Husb: Edward Freeman	34	Jo: Emerson	20
uxor Elizabeth Freeman	35	Ric^R: Woodman	9
Edmond Freeman	15	Elizab: Freeman	12
John Freeman	8	Alice Freeman	17
Jo: Jones	15	Hugh Burt	15
John Cooke	15* } servant	Annis Aldcock	18
Edward Belcher	18*	Tho: Thomson	18
Ann Williams	10		

Secundo die Julij

IN the *Abigall* prd. p Certificate from ye Minister of Shorditch pish ꝑ Stepney pish.

John Deyking 25
Jesper Arnold 40
Alice Deyking 30
Ann Arnold 39
} yeres. bound to New-England

Alice Steevens 22
Margaret Devocion.... 9
Ruth Bushell 23

THEIS vnder written names are to be transported to New-England imbarqued in the *Defence* Tho: Bostock, M^r the ptie hath brought testimony from the Justices of Peace ꝑ Minister in Cambridge

---

* [These figures are not clear in the original.]

of his conformitie to the orders ℓ discipline of the Church of England:
he hath taken ye oaths of Alleg: ℓ Suprem:

		yeres
A Taylor	ADAM MOTT	39
uxor	SARA MOTT	31
Mason.	HENRY STEEVENS	24
Husb:	JOHN SHEPPARD	36
	MARGARET SHEPPARD	31
	THO: SHEPPARD	3. mo.
	JO: MOTT	14 ⎫
	ADAM MOTT	12 ⎪
	JONATHAN MOTT	9 ⎬ children.
	ELIZABETH MOTT	6 ⎪
	MARY MOTT	4 ⎭

IN the *Defence* prd THO: BOSTOCK M^r for New England, p Cert:
from the Minister of Fenchurch of his conformitie ℓc.

THO: BOYLSON .... 20 yeres

4th *Jully* 1635

IN the *Abbigall* de Lo: p Cert from the Ministr ℓ Justice of peace
of St Oliues Southwarke:

	RALPH MASON	35 yers	Joyner
	his wife ANNE	35 yers	
3 Children {	RICHARD	5 yers	
	SAMUELL	3 yers	
	SUSAN	1 yere	

IN the *Defence* prd:

ELIZABETH FRENCH	30	FRANCIS FRENCH	10
ELIZABETH FRENCH	6	JO: FRENCH	5. mo.
MARIE FRENCH	2½		

13—2

iiijth *Jully* 1635

IN the *Defence* de Lond m' THOMAS BOSTOCKE vrs New Engld p Cer^t: from the Minstr ℘ Justice of Peace, of his Conformity to ye Gou'm^t [Government] of Churche of Engld ℘ No Subsidy man.

ROGER HARLAKENDEN aged 23 toke oathe of Allegance ℘ Supremacie
ELIZA his wife 18
MABLE his sister 21
ANNE WOOD his seru^t .... 23 ⎫
SAMUELL SHEPHERD ser^t .. 22 ⎪
JOSEPH COCKE .... 27 ⎪
GEO: COCKE............. 25 ⎬ Seruan^{ts} to ye afore said ROGER HARLAKENDEN.
Wm FRENCH .... 30 ⎪
ELISA. his wife........... 32 ⎪
ROBERT   a Man ser^t:.... — ⎪
SARRA SIMES .... 30 ⎭

6th *Jully*.

IN the *Defence* de Lond. m' THO: BOSTOCKE vrs New Engld

Jo^n JACKSON 30 yers whole Sale Man in Burchenlane p Cer^t from s^r GEO: WHITMORE ℘ Ministr of ye pish

x^o *Julij* 1635

IN the *Abigall* RICHARD HACKWELL M^r p Cer^t: from the Minister ℘ Justice of Peace of his conformitie to the Church of England ℘ that he is no Subsedy Man

	yeres		
JOHN WYNTHROPP..........	27	THO: GOAD	15
ELIZABETH WINTHROPP	19	ELIZABETH EPPS............	13
DEANE WINTHROPP	11	MARY LYNE.,..............	6

IN the *Defence* prd. p Cert from the Justic's ℓ Minister of his conformitie to the Church of England.

A Taylor JAMES FITCH...... 30 | *uxor* ABIGALL FITCH 24

4° Julij 1635.

THEIS vnder-written names are to be transported to Virginea imbarqued in the *Transport* of London EDWARD WALKER Mr p Certificate from the Minister of Gravesend of their conformitie to the orders ℓ discipline of the Church of England.

	yeres		
OLLIVER VAN HECK	35	JO: GODFREY	21
uxor KATHERIN VAN HECK ..	34	RICHARD CRITCH	27
PETER VAN HECK	7	ELLIS BAKER	21
RICHARD MATON	23	JONATHAN NEALE	12
Wᴹ PAGE	18	JO: BUSH	17
ROBERT KEVYNN	19	Wᴹ NESSE	23
PETER SMITH	25	JO: SPREATE	20
BRIAN Mᵃ GAWYN	3	THO: STEEVENS	25
DANIELL SYMPSON..........	17	JO: WATERS...............	29
PATRICK BREDDY	21	ROBᵀ FOSSITT.....	26
HENRY CASTELL	22	WALTER DOWNES	24
STEEVEN BLOCK............	18	SYMON JONES	40
GOWEN LANCASTER	28	ROBERT JENKINSON	18
ROBERT FARRAR	24	FRANC'S CLARK	28
BRYAN GLYNN	20	FRANCIS BICK.............	23
HUMFREY HADNET	22	THOMAS CRANFIELD	14
JO: WODDALL	18	THO: PAYNE	23
WIllM WALLINGTON	32	PHILLIP JONES	22
RICHARD SHARP...........	15	JOHN GOODSON	21
MARMADUKE KIDSON	18	STEEVEN BEANE............	20

GEO: BARBER 20	GEORGE JOHNSON 19
RICHARD WHEATLIE............ 32	JOHN VOSS 22
RICHARD LLOYD................. 28	ANDREW ADAMS 18
HENRIE BARNES.................. 22	JOHN WILSON.................... 32
THO: MORE 21	NATHAN ANLEY.................. 28
JOHN HARRISON.................. 30	ANTHONY GRIMSTON 20
W^M HUDSON 20	THO: HATCHET 19
W^M MASON 30	ROBERT HONNIBORN............ 21
MARK BRIGGOLL................... 21	JO: PARSON 18
HENRY PORTER 30	ALEXANDER BURLIE............ 18
PATRICK WODDALL 20	W^M HART.......................... 26
JOHN GEE 18	NATHANIELL PATIENT 16
RICHARD COOPER 28	HENRY ARMSTRONG 22
RICHARD EGGLESTON 24	*Women.*
W^M HARBERT 15	
JOHN WISE 18	KATHERIN LONG 34
THOMAS COLES 32	ELIZABETH SAMES 19
THO: WILLIAMS 18	JOAN HARDISS 18
GEORGE ASHON 22	ELIZABETH RILEY 18
PETER SEXSTON 20	ELLIN ROGERSON 20
THO: JOHNSON 23	ELIZABETH LINCOLN............. 23
THOMAS SAUNDERS 20	ELIZABETH CORKER 19
JOHN LEE 16	ANN WANDALL 18
ROBERT FAREST 20	SIBBELL LAKELAND 25
RICHARD BICK 18	ELLIN WHITE..................... 26
WIH^M HARDISSE.................. 22	W^M WHITE .... 7 weekes old
DANIELL ROSE 25	ELLENER ROGERS 19
RICHARD ANDERSON............ 17	DOROTHIE CHARLES 20
JAMES PHILLIPS 26	HESTER BROTHERTON 18
ROBERT TYNMAN 21	MARGARET WATSON 18
PETER WALLER 24	OLIFF SPRAWE 21
RICHARD PETLEY 22	ANN BRISCO 22
ROGER HOLLIDGE 19	ANN GUDDERIDGE............... 23
W^M REDDMAN..................... 18	RABECCA LANE 22
ROBERT GREENE 20	ELIZABETH YORE 23
HENRY MEDDOWES 20	

RALPH GOLTHORP	20	JO: SYARD	38
EDWARD THOMSON	24	GEO: MIDLAND	19
W^M WHITE	37	W^M WATSON	24
ROBERT LEWES	38	HARBERT JUDD	16
BARNABIE BARNES	35	JOHN FOX	33
EDWARD ISON	20	HENRY BURKET	34
JOHN SOMERTON	24	BENNET FREEMAN	20
JO: RUSSELL	14	EDWARD SALTER	19
ROBERT BATEMAN	20	ROBERT COVETT	25
W^M COOKE	20	THO: MORE	18
HENRY BANISTER	22	JO: RUSSELL	16
THO: RICHARDSON	26	EDWARD HUNT	19
JO: WALLER	19	ROBERT BECKWITH	21
RICHARD WEVER	27	JO: WITTON	16
JOHN TRUE	26	JOHN HARRIS	28
JO: HORNE	21	JO: BAYLIE	42
ROBERT MEDLEY	16	JO: HATHORN	20
RICHARD ATKINSON	21	EDWARD DRUE	18
JO: POWND	20	JO: ARP	19
EDWARD ROE	17	EDMOND PRYME	16
FRANCIS WEBSTER	27		

vj° Julij 1635

IN the *Paule* of London LEONARD BETTS M^r bound to Virginea p Certificate from the Minister of Gravesend of their Conformitie to the Church of England.

ADRIAN FORD	26	THO: GREENE	21
W^M EAST	23	JO: JONES	18
ROBERT CAPLIN	22	THO: BAREFOOTE	19
EDWARD WADE	24	ROBERT TAYLOR	18

Jo: Richardson	22	Francis Lattner	17
Richard Hughes	20	Wiłłm Berry	17
Robert Markcom	22	David Fludd	17
Peter Price	23	Jo: Hodges	17
John Davies	23	Samvell Burnet	17
Nicholas Parker	23	Francis Woddall	18
John Gill	19	Abram Bruster	16
Jo Aynis	21	Edward Hobson	22
Aron Everett	20	Henry Jacob	20
Launcelott Limrick	20	Richard Clayton	24
Wᴹ Strange	25	Thomas Webb	18
Wᴹ Palmer	18	Henry Worlidge	18
Phillip Bagley	19	Richard Davies	20
Ciprian Warner	21	Wᴹ Jackson	26
Henry Dudman	18	Tho: Draper	26
Tho: Hitchcock	22	Antº. Pott's	27
Giles Collins	20	Mark White	25
Jo: Machem	18	Wᴹ Hickey	22
Robert Wile [*or* Wild]	21	Francis Searle	28
John Thomkins	25	Wiłłm Riddell	16
Sylvester Thatcher	21	Jo: Potter	26
Nicholas Fox	20	William Capell	25
Jeremy Watts	21	Jo: Mynter	16
John Coop [Cooper]	24	Wᴹ Harefinch	30
Henry Bank's	19	Symon Simes	15
Nathaniel Deane	27	Anthony Day	22
Thomas Lister	22	Richard Eggleston	16
Edward Wygon	20	Jo: Courtney	32
Wᴹ Jackson	26	Robert Vnderwood	30
Tho: Simpson	17	Wᴹ Quyñie	40
Daniell Collier	30	Nicholas Clark	31
John Cooke	20	Samvell Symonds	30
Arthur Patient	22	Jo: Gill	34
Hugh Harrison	22	Mathew Bennet	18
Wᴹ Pack	27	Wiłłm Hind	35

MARGARET HINDE	30	SAMVELL DAVIES	24
AUGUSTIN HARWOOD	25	THO: WARNER	12
KATHERIN WILSON	28		
2 childr: { ROBERT WILSON	6	*Women.*	
RICHARD WILSON	5		
LEONARD WOOD	22	GRACE ALDERMAN	22
Wᴹ POSTELL	22	MARY HUSBAND	20
CHARLES FORD	33	ALICE FULLER	22
JOHN SCOTT	26	ELIZABETH RAYNTON	16
THOMAS FLEXNEY	23	ELIZABETH COLLINS	20
JOHN HERON	18	DOROTHIE BRADLIE	18
THO: BAKER	16	GRACE JONES	24
Wɪʟʟᴍ HUGHES	20	SYBBILL COURTNEY	33
JO: COXSHEDD	14	JOAN BOWDEN	24
PETER PRYER	26	ANNIS SEEDEN	22
BENIAMIN HOOKE	20	JOAN COLCHESTER	23
JO: GIBBS	35	ELIZABETH STACIE	20
GEO: DAWE	23	DOROTHY DAY	17
HUGH BEACON	25	ANN EMMERTON	20
JO: BISHOPP	23	MARTHA HOLLAND	24

xjᵒ die Julij 1635

THEIS vnder-written names are to be transported to New-England imbarqued in the *Defence* of Lndon [London], EDWARD BOSTOCK Mʳ p Certificate of his Conformitie in Religion ℓ that he is no Subsedy-man.

A Miller RICHARD PERK...... 33 ⎫
        MARGERY PERK ... 40 ⎪ yeres | HENRY DUHURST 35
        ISABELL PERK ...... 7 ⎬
        ELIZABETH PERK... 4 ⎭

14th *July* 1635

IN the *Defence* de Lond m' EDMOND BOSTOCKE v's New England p Cer' from the Minstr

ROBERT HILL, 20 yers seru' to m' CRADDOCKE.

---

xviij° *Julij* 1635

THEIS vnder written name is to be transported to New-England imbarqued in the *Pide-Cowe* p Cert: from the Minister of his conformitee & from S' EDWARD SPENCER resident neere Branford that he is no Subsedy man. hath taken the oathe of Alleg. & Suprem.

Wil+m Harrison	55 yeres old
Jo: Baldin	13
Wm Baldin	9

THEIS vnder-written names are to be transported to N. England imbarqued in the *defence* prd p Cert: from the Minist^{rs} & Justic's of their conformitie & y^t they are no Subsedy Men.

Sara Jones	34	Wm Sawkynn	25
Sara Jones	15	Husb: Wm Hubbard	40
Jo: Jones	11	Judith Hubbard	25
Ruth Jones	7	John Hubbard	15
Theophilus Jones	3	Wm Hubbard	13
Rabecca Jones	2	Wm Read	48
Eliz. Jones	½	Mabell Read	30
Tho: Donn	25	George Read	6
Suzanna Farebrother	25	Ralph Read	5
Eliz: Fennick	25	Justice Read	18 Mo:

Dorothie Knight	30	Martha Banes	20
Nathaniel Hubbard	6	Jasper Gonn	29
Richard Hubbard	4	Ann Gonn	25
Martha Hubbard	22	Febe Maulder	7
Mary Hubbard	20	Sym: Roger	20
Robert Colburne	28	Jo: Jenkynn	26
Edward Colborn	17	Robert Keyne	40
Dorothie Adams	24	Eliz Steerer	18
Francis Nutbrowne	16	Sara Knight	50
Wm Williamson	25	Ann Keyne	38
Marie Wiłłimson	23	Ben: Keyne	16
Luce Mercer	19	Jo: Burles	27
Jo: Fitch	14	Mary Bentley	20
Penelope Darno	29		

13 *July* 1635

THEIS vnder-written names are to be transported to N. England imbarqued in the *James* J^{no} May M^r for N. E. p Cert: from the Ministers of their conformitie in Religion ℘ that they are no Subsedy Men.

Husb: Wm Ballard	32	Wm Hooper	18
Elizabeth Ballard	26	Edmond Johnson	23
Hester Ballard	2	Samvel Bennet	24
Jo: Ballard	1	Ric^r: Palmer	29
Alice Jones	26	Ant^o Bessy	26
Eliza: Goffe	26	Edw: Gardner	25
Edmond Bridges	23	Wm Colbron	16
Michell Milner	23	Henry Bull	25
Tho: Terry	28	Salomon Martin	16
Robert Terry	25	wheelewrite. W^u Hill	70
Ric^r: Terry	17	Nic^o Buttry	33
Tho: Marshall	22	Martha Buttry	28

Grace Buttry	1	John Johnson	26
Shoemaker Jo: Hart	40	Suzan Johnson	24
Mary Hart	31	Eliza: Johnson	2
Shoemaker Henry Tybbot	39	Tho: Johnson	18 mo.
Elizabeth Tibott	39	Barber Ralph Farman	32
Jeremy Tybbott	4	Alice Farman	28
Samvell Tybbot	2	Mary Farman	7
Remembrance Tybbott	28	Tho: Farman	4
Cloth Worker Nico: Goodhue	60	Ralph Farman	2
Jane Goodhew	58		

THEIS vnder written names are to be transported to N. England imbarqued in the *Blessing* John Lester Mr the pties have brought Cert: from the Ministrs ꝑ Justices of their conformitie in Religion, ꝑ that they are no Subsedy Men.

fisherman Jo Jackson	40	Mary Spratt	20
Margaret Jackson	36	Ricᴿ: Hallingworth	40
John Jackson	2	Suzan Hallingworth	30
Jo: Manifold	17	Christian Hunter	20
John Burles	26	Eliz: Hunter	18
Jo: Fitch	14	Tho: Hunter	14
Nico: Long	19	Wᴹ Hunter	11
Christian Buck	26	Wᴹ Hollingworth	7
Barnabie Davies	36	Ricᴿ: Hallingworth	4
Suzan Danes [or Daues]	16	Suzan Hallingworth	2
Robert Lewes	28	Eliz: Hallingworth	3
Eliz: Lewes	22	Tho: Trentum	14
Edward Ingram	18	Tho: Bigg's	13
Henry Beck	18	Jo: Brigg's	20
Jo: Hathoway	18	Robᵀ Lewes*	28
Richard Sexton	14	Eliz: Lewes*	22
Mary Hubbard	24		

* [It will be observed that these names also appear in the first column.]

THEIS vnder-written names are to be transported to New-England imbarqued in the *Love* JOSEPH YOUNG Mr.

Baker WiȞM CHERRALL	26	SARA HARMAN	10
VRSULA CHERRALL	40	WALTER PARKER	18
JO: HARMAN	12	fisherman WiȞM BROWNE	26
FRANCIS HARMAN	43	MARY BROWNE	26

THEIS vnder-written names are to be transported to Virginea, imbarqued in the *Alice* RICHARD ORCHARD Mr the Men have taken the oaths of Allegeance ꝑ Suprem:

EDWARD HUGHES	21	CHRI: HUDSON	30
JAMES MORFY	21	JO: SMITH	20
ROBERT HAGGAR	33	JO: Coop [COOPER]	20
THO: ASKEW	21	EDWARD WAGGITT	20
RICᵈ: COOKE	21	JO: VICCARS	35
MILES ATKINSON	22	THO: ATKINSON	27
ROWLAND VAUGHAN	19	ROWLAND SUDGERNER	21
RICHARD NATT	18	Wᴹ MASSINGBURD	23
FRA: JENKINSON	28	JO: HUTTON	17
WiȞM KENDRIDD	20	ELIZABETH DEW	32
JO: WILSON	29	ANN DEW	9 mo.
ROBᵀ BAXTER	21	RACHELL ADAMS	16
JO: BENTLEY	34	AVIS DEACON	19
JO: HOLDSWORTH	20	HANNA GLIFFORD	20
JO: WRIGHT	21	ELIZ: BLANCH	20
CHARLES PEACOCK	28	SOPHIA ROTTRIE	16

23 July.

THIS vnder-written name is to be transported to New-England imbarqued in the *Tide-Cowe*, Mr ASHLEY: the ptie hath brought Certificate of his conformitie in Religion ℓ Attestacōn from the Justices that he is no Subsedy man.

Husb: ROBERT BILLS........ 32

28 July 1635

THEIS psons herevnder expressed are to be transported to New-England, imbarqued in the *Hopewell* of London, THO: BABB, M^r p Certificate, from the Minister of St Giles Cripplegate, that they are conformable to the Church of England. the Men have taken the oaths of Allegeance, ℓ Supremacie.

	yers		yeres
A Smith THOMAS TREDWELL	30	THO: BLACKLY	20
MARY TREDWELL	30	THO: TREDWELL	1

[24 July]*

THEIS vnder-written names are to be transported to Virginea imbarqued in the *Assurance* de Lo: ISACK BROMWELL ℓ GEO. PEWSIE M^r examined by the Minister of the Towne of Gravesend of their conformitie in o^r Religion. the men have taken the oaths of Allegeance ℓ Supremacie.

	yeres		
ROBERT BRIAN	27	RICHARD HAMEY [or HAMDY]	38
MAUDLIN JONES	60	W^M HOLLAND	35
ANN SHAWE	32	HENRY SNOWE	26
JO: DUNCOMB	46	MARIE SOUTHWOOD	22
SITH HAIEWARD	30	FRANCIS ROWLSON	29

* [There is no date to this list; but a *list of troops to be transported to Flanders*, which precedes it in the original MS., is thus dated.]

Name	Age	Name	Age
Jane Sowthern	19	Ricʳ: Rogers	48
Margerie Baker	39	Ricʳ: Lockley	51
Sara Rayne	18	Jo: Jakes	20
Andrew Vnderwood	22	Tho: More	19
Phillipp Johns	22	Jo: Baker	22
Henrie Marshall	35	Nehemiah Cason*	21
Henry Heiden	30	Robert Maves	28
Elizabeth Sherlocke	29	Richard Barnes	38
Tho: Hurlock	40	Jo: Buttler	50
Samvel Handy	25	Wᵐ Rebbell	19
Jo: Gater	36	Robert Wyon	22
Joan Gater	23	Mathew Dixon	18
Wᵐ Lee	36	John Wheeler	23
Josua Titloe	19	Jo: North	24
Jo: Middleton	23	Mountford Newman	27
Robert Haiward	22	Robert Steere	17
Samvel Powell	19	Wᵐ Lake	35
Richard Glover	24	Humfrey Wilkins	19
Tho: Pagitt	41	Antᵒ Stilgo	21
Mathew Holmes	21	Tho: Deacon	19
Elias Harrington	22	Robᵗ Rigglie	19
Richard Smith	35	Beniamin Pillard	18
Tho: Robinson	24	Robert Davies	28
Evan ap-Evan	19	Jo: Smith	20
Jo: Browne	21	Walter Merridith	33
Robert Frith	23	Tho: Phillips	24
Tho: Wilkinson	23	James Kingsmill	18
Dennis Hoggin	24	Jo. Bowton	20
Jo: Friccar	25	Walter Chapman	44
Richard Ridges	19	James Arnold	37
Edward Davies	27	Richard Leake	18
Theodorus Bakewell	21	Tho: Edwynn	13
Jo: Dermot	21	Handgate Baker	22
Jo: Morgan	27	Jo: Abrock	20
Tho: Baycock	46	Tho: Hall	15

[* Second letter not clearly written : the name *might* be read Coson.]

JAMES EDWIN 18	THO: LEONARD 18
EDWARD COm̄INS 28	THO: BESON............... 24
JO: GATER 15	CHRI: DIXON 24
NICº GIBSON 22	ISACK KEMP 23
JO: ROBERT'S 46	JEREMIE SLIE 19
GEO: MOSELY 20	JO: ô MULLIN 18
JAMES RAVISH.............. 20	ANTO PROCTER 16
JO: HALES 21	ROBERT HANDLEY 19
WARRAM TUCK 20	JO: AYMIES 18
JO: JONES 30	JO: TAYLER 21
Wᴹ COLTURE 19	Wᴹ ROFFIN 18
ROBERT SILBY.............. 19	RICᴿ: HALSEY 13
RICᴿ: BRUSTER 26	ANTº OTLAND 18
JO: SWANLEY 21	ROBERT OLDRICK 18
Wᴹ CHARLES 21	Wᴹ HALL 21
ANTHONY LEE 21	JO COPELAND 19
Wiłłm WILLIAMS............ 28	JOHN GOAD............... 18
HENRY GEORGE 19	JO: POOLY 17
JO: BILLINS 21	FRANCIS GAYER 18
Wᴹ WRITE 18	THO: CRAVEN 17
ROBERT LOVETT 20	RICᴿ: LUCAS............... 16
JOB JEFFERIE 19	GEO: CULLIDGE 18
HENRIE HALER 22	LAWRENCE BARKER 26
RICHARD SYMONDS 30	JO: BOWES 20
JAMES SPARK'S 57	JO: WOODBRIDGE 32
RICHARD KIRBIE 32	JO: JOHNSON 20
JAMES HINGLE 40	JO: CHAPPELL 38
THO: SAUNDERSON.......... 24	GEO: WHITTAKER 32
Wᴹ SPICER 20	RICHARD LIVERSIDGE 24
Wiłłm THOMAS 19	HENRIE WOOD 20
HENRY MADIN 30	ROBᵀ MAX 21
EDWARD EDNALL 21	JO: WARREN 18
THO: JEFFERIES 22	THO: TURNER 18
NICº: JACKSON............. 22	JO: GARLAND 19
THO: SPRATT 23	JO: HUMFREY 23

ISACK AMBROSE	18	ISABELL HAKESBY	23
W^M HUNCOTE	35	JOAN VALLINS	17
THO: WILLIAMS	19	MARIE CHAMBNEY	28
THO: FOXCROFTE	19	ELIZABETH ALLCOTT	20
THO: HOBBS	22	FRANCIS BAKEWELL	30
CHARLES COLLOHON	19	ELIZABETH PAYNE	21
HENRY DONN	23	ELIZABETH HUGHSON	22
ROGER QUINTIN	21	MARIE AVERIE	22
W^M SMALL	18	SARA ALPORT	25
W^M COLEMAN	16	MARIE LEE	22
ANT^O ANDROWE	21	ELIZABETH BATEMAN	23
JO: RICHARDSON	18	THOMAZIN MARKCOM	26
W^M CLADDIN	17	ANN GOLDWELL	17
THO: GUDDERIDGE	17	ANN GRIFFINN	26
ROGER BURLEY	17	JAMES BROOKES	28
THO: BARD	16	*vxor.* ALICE BROOKES	18
HENRY BUTLER	14	DORCAS MERCER	30
JO: BUDD	15	ELLIN DAVIES	23
J^{NO} MARSHALL	35	ALICE HARRIS	21
W^M READ	30	EEDIE HOLLOWAY	22
EDWARD MITCHELL	18	SARA COGGIN	20
ROBERT DREWRIE	16	ELIZABETH BAKER	20
RIC^R: WELLS	17	DOROTHIE DAVIES	17
JO: COTES	17	ELIZABETH RAYNARD	20
JO: STUBBER	17	MARIE OLLIVER	21
HENRY LEE	18	ALICE RIALL	18
RIC^R: BALL	17	RABECCA PARMETON	19
JO: COOKE	17	MARIE MIDDLETON	17
THO: SYER	14	KAT: FULDER	17
JO: PARTRIDGE	18	ELIZ: DICK'S	18
JO: JOHNSON	24	SARA GREENE	20
		MARGARET RICKORD	20
Women.		WINNIFREDD CONGRAVE	22
		MATHEW PLANT	23
ISBELL DAVIES	22	JO: MORE	28

Elizabeth Powell 17	Marie Lee.............. 14 weekes
Marie Shorter 26	Mathew Clatworthy 25

188

33*

27° *July* 1635

THEIS vnder-written names are to be transported to Virginea imbarqued in the *Primrose* Capten DOUGLASS, Mr p Certificate vnder ye Ministers hand of Gravesend, being examined by him touching their Conformitie to the Church Discipline of England   The Men have taken the oaths of Allegeance & Supremacie.

	William Sprawson 28	Wm Alderton 35
fetch off by Mr Secretary Windebanks Warrant.	Jo: Symond's 18	Tho: Clifton..................... 25
	Richard Webb 36	Wm Browne 19
	Luke Snoden 21	Alexander Masie 21
	Wm Starling..................... 18	Geo: Lee 16
	Lawrence Whithorse 17	Tho: Beane 21
	Robert Nuttall 18	Jo: Pew 16
	Jo: Hall 24	George Cottingham 20
	Mathew Burr 27	Jo: Swifte 23
	Tho: Daggett 21	Geo: Fowler 22
	Jo: Baldwynn 27	Tho: Farraby 20
	Tho: Bruxston................. 20	Robert Sharp 21
	Henry Banbridge 18	Wm Evans 25
	Nico: Petting 24	Wm Harris....................... 50
	Robert Williams.............. 21	Thomas Coke................... 24
	Wm Thorncome................ 19	Abram Swifte 2
	Tho: Wiggin 21	Oliver Fayrie 2
	Chri: Legg 19	Oliver Symon 30
	Henrie Robinson............... 26	Henry Maggitt 26
	Jo: Sherrick 19	Tho: Bales...................... 18
	Jo: Palmer 18	Wm Allinson.................... 2

* [There are 221 names in the list. It will be observed that adding these two numbers together, will yield 221.]

Walter Marshall	17	James Hall	18
Jo: Shipley	21	Robert Benton	18
Tho: Smith	18	Tho: Mason	19
Jo: Johnson	21	Tho: Saker	16
Jo: Wick's	26	Jo: Marsh	33
Ric$_R$: West	21	Francis Mursh*	28
Geo. Wade	19	Tho: Adams	21
W^M Perce	19	Philip Davies	25
Jo: Beetell	20	Edward Dannell	18
Francis Ratford	20	Henry Chapman	19
Jo: Morfin	20	Jo: North	22
Jo: Lee	25	Charles White	18
Jo: Balme	34	John Parry	27
Jo: Strowde	17	Godfrey Hundley	24
W^M Fox	21	Richard Watt's	24
Tho. Pynch	32	Clement Donn	22
Ric^R Gill	26	Ric^R Stanford	25
Henry Dikes	33	Ben: Gregorie	24
W^M Shawe	25	Edward Mills	30
Henry Smith	22	Robert Eelie	14
Ralph Hunt	22	Ric^R: Kellum	16
Jo: Lupton	25	Robert Page	17
James Rydie	45	Jo: Baldwyn	21
Garret Cooke	20	Ellis Harman	18
Jo: Merie	17	Jo: Bottomly	19
Olliver Clifford	18	W^M More	16
Wiłłm White	23	Samvell Boswell	23
Tho: Mortimer	20	W^M Swifte	21
Jo: Ridge	16	W^M Griffin	21
Tho: Vinson	18	Jo: Norman	20
Francis Dellicat	20	Richard Wardd	13
Tho: Ridge	23	Francis Jarvice	14
Richard Cary	17	Tho: Thomas	20
Tho: Manning's	16	Luke Richardson	17
W^M Parry	16	Jo: Fletcher	18

* [So in the original; but probably intended for Marsh.]

ROBᵀ HARRIS	20	SICILLIA WESTON	37
ROBERT FEAT'S	25	JANE PRYM̄	18
JO: SAKER	30	ANN VISHER	20
Wᴹ JOHNSON	26	KAT: YORK	19
JO: WEEKES	18	DOROTHY JAKES	29
EDMOND ARDINTON	20	AYMIE HUMFRIE	23
CHRISTO: BANBRIDGE	19	MARGARET JNºSON	20
ELIZ: MAYNARD	22	MARIE SAKER	24
ANN JACKSON	23	ELLIN SUTTON	20
JO: MOLIN	30	JO: SAKER	1
MARGARET CLARK	21	THO: POOLE	43
Wᴹ CLARK	1	JO: WHETSTON	20
ELLIN HALY	55	THOMAZIN MILLS	38
	100		
	38		

Vltimo Julij 1635

THEIS vnder-written names are to be transported to Virginea, imbarqued in yᵉ *Merchant's Hope* HUGH WESTON Mʳ: p examinacōn by the Minister of Gravesend touching their conformitie to the Church discipline of England ꝑ have taken the oaths of Alleg: ꝑ Suprem:

EDWARD TOWERS	26	CHARLES RILSDEN	27
HENRY WOODMAN	22	JO: EXSON	17
RICHARD SEEMES	26	Wᴹ LUCK	14
ALLIN KING	19	JO: THOMAS	19
ROWLAND SADLER	19	JO: ARCHER	21
JO: PHILLIPS	28	RICHARD WILLIAMS	25
VYNCENT WHURTER	17	FRANCIS HUTTON	20
JAMES WHITHEDD	14	SAVILL GASCOYNE	29
JOSIAS WATTS	21	RICᴿ: BULFELL	29
PETER LOE	22	RICᴿ: JONES	26
GEO: BROOKER	17	THO: WYNES	30
HENRY EELES	26	HUMFREY Wi̴lᵐs [WILLIAMS]	22
JO: DENNIS	22	EDWARD ROBERT'S	22
THO: SWAYNE	23	MARTIN ATKINSON	32

Edward Atkinson	28	Jo: Ballance	19
Wᵐ Edward's	30	Wᵐ Baldin	21
Nathan Braddock	31	Wᵐ Pen	26
Jeffery Gurrish	23	Jo: Geerie	24
Henry Carrell	16	Henry Baylie	18
Tho: Ryle	24	Ricʳ: Anderson	50
Gamaliel White	24	Robert Kelum	51
Richard Mark's	19	Richard Fanshaw	22
Tho: Clever	16	Tho: Bradford	40
Jo: Kitchin	16	Wᵐ Spencer	16
Edmond Edward's	20	Marmaduke Ella	22

Women.

Lewes Miles	19		
Jo: Kenneday	20	Ann Swayne	22
Saᵐ: Jackson	24	Eliz: Cote	22
Daniell Endick	16	Ann Ryce	23
Jo: Chalk	25	Kat: Wilson	23
Jo: Vynall	20	Maudlin Lloyd	24
Edward Smith	20	Mabell Busher	14
Jo: Rowlidge	19	Annis Hopkins	19
Wᵐ Westlie	40	Ann Mason	24
Jo: Smith	18	Bridget Crompe	18
Jo: Saunders	22	Mary Hawkes	19
Tho: Bartcherd	16	Ellin Hawkes	18
Tho: Dodderidge	19		
Richard Williams	18		

66
—
9

Primo die Augusti 1635

THEIS vnder-written names are to be transported to Virginea, imbarqued in the *Elizabeth* de Lo: Christopher Browne Mʳ examined by the Minister of Gravesend touching their conformitie to the ordⁿˢ ℘ discipline of the Church of England the Men have taken the oaths of Alleg: ℘ Supremacie.

Jo: Benford	20	Wᵐ Thurrowgood	13
Lodowick Fletcher	20	Samvell Mathew	14
Jo: Bagbie	17	Tho: Frith	17
Robᵗ Salter	14	Jo: Austin	24
Edward White	18	Paul Fearne	24
Steeven Pierce	30	Thomas Royston	25
Ricʳ: Beauford	18	Jo: Tayler	18
Ricʳ: Chapman	18		
Andrew Parkins	18	*Women.*	
Jo: Baker	16	Katherin Jones	28
Jo: Wakers	16	Eliz: Sankster	24
Jo: Vaughan	17	Ellin Shore	20
Yeoman Gibson	16	Alice Pyndon	19
Tho: Leed	16	Sara Everedge	22
Geo: Trevas	18	Margaret Smith	28
Wᵐ Shilborn	20	Elizab: Hoeman	20
Samvel Growce	38	Moules Naxston	19
Wᵐ Glasbrooke	21	Marie Burback	17
Edward Dick's	30	Eliz: Rudston	40
Jo: Bennett	18	Eliz: Rudston	5
Michell Saundby	25		
		26	
		13	

xjᵗʰ Augᵗⁱ 1635

IN the *Batcheler* de Lo: m' Tho. Webb vrs New Eng͞ld

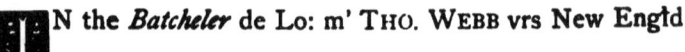

Lyon Gardner 36 yers ꝑ his wife Mary 34 yers, ꝑ Eliza. Coles 23 yers, their maid Seruanᵗ, ꝑ Wᵐ Jope 40 yers, who are to passe to new England, haue brought Cert. of their Conformity.

vij° Augusti 1635

THEIS vnder-writtcn names are to be transported to Virginea imbarqued in the *Globe* of London JEREMY BLACKMAN Mʳ, have been examined by the Minister of Gravesend of their Conformitie, & have taken the oaths of Alleg: & Supremacie.

Minister JOHN GOODBARNE	30	GEO: NETTELLFORD	19
EDWARD LEWES	21	THO: PARKER	22
JO: WHITWHAM	26	PHILIP MEREDITH	12
JO: BABINGTON	20	ROBERT COPPYN	11
Wᴹ SATCHILL	22	Wᴹ BROWNE	20
THO: GOWEN	18	ROBERT YATES	25
SYMON MOODY	20	Wᴹ GRIFFITH	18
THOMAS TUCKER	21	OLOUGH BERNE	19
JO: WATTON	20	JAMES COPLEY	22
JO: RAMSEY	30	THO: BLITHE	20
RICHARD BATES	16	Wᴹ HOWARD	16
Wiɫɫm BOWLER	14	JO: HALE	14
HENRY HOPES	23	NICHOLAS TAYLER	17
Wᴹ BARNES	22	BENEDICT ROLLS	16
HENRY SMITHICK	26	MARTIN PERKINS	18
THO: GRIGG	16	Wᴹ ENNIS	22
CHRISTOPHER LEGG	18	DAVIE VAUGHAN	18
RANDALL BURNE	20	JO: SEATON	19
HUMFREY BUCKLEY	18	THO: BOWYER	19
HENRY STON	27	ABRAM BENTLEY	20
PHILLIPP SHERRINGHAM	17	RICᴿ: ADAMS	22
THO: SHARP	17	JOHN RUSSELL	15
Wᴹ SAVORY	25	Wᴹ BURTON	20
EDWARD KING	21	MATHEW BATEMAN	20
NATHANIEL ROGERS	17	JO: BYNSTEDD	20
MICHELL VICTOR	18	MICHELL HAYNES	21
Wᴹ SHARP	21	THO: JNºSON	21
Wᴹ OSMOTHERLY	14	JOHN WHITFIELD	20

Henry Moston	23	John Peter	20
Allin Hamock	32	Richard Wollman	22
George Forth	27	Edward Cleiborn	20
Charles Smith	22	Nicholas Bate	24
Mathew Morton	19	Wm Bate	35
Wm Lewes	25	Richard Wells	26
Robert Arnold	30	Richard Guy	23
Jo: Thatcher	22	Jo: Swann	18
Wm Nash	22	Edward Lene	32
Peter Payton	22	Tho: Sawell	29
Robert Baldry	18	Tho: Whaplett	21
Edward Langstedd	18	Mabell Eaton	27
James Scott	21	Sara Cleyton	27
Wm Androwes	18	Ann Levynns	31
Jo: Bland	26	Mary Willis	22
Philip Westlake	20	Ann Creede	22
Jo: Marwood	17	Julian Merideth	38
Jo: Griffith	20	Lucie Buckle	18
Jo: Howgate	17	Joan Jernew	30
Luke Hanes [or Haues]	27	Eliz: Jernew	25
Jo: Stibbs	19	Robert Scriven	18
Jeffery Wynch	20	Robert Isham	14
Richard Abbott	25	Jo: Armsby	30
Ric^a: Steevenson	19	Wm Lennon*	19
Tho: Smith	30	Michell Whitley	23
Ant^o: Carter	22	Jo: Manning's	20
Geo: More	25	Wm Barloe	19
Robert Gannock	20	Edward Hollinbrigg	27
Ric^a: Cooke	46	Wm Manifold	20
Richard Townsend	28	Gregorie Allin	17
Nicholas Jernew	28	Wm Talbott	14
Tho: Wallis	32	Geo: Hawley	17
Willm Scarfield	22	Edward Hodgskynns	21
Samvel Stringer	17	Mark Gill	22
Nic^o: Reinold's	38	Tho: Harrwood	26

* [Or Lemon. The strokes of the letters are thick and clumsy.]

Abram Watson	17	Francis Townsend	21
Allin Rippin	28	Francis Townsend	2
John Hobson	25	Tho: Needham	13
Tho: Chapman	26	Tho: Axstell	35
Robert Vass	19	Jo: Reddman	46
Richard Ward	23	Robert Mascrie	32
Geo: Aldin	20	Robert Crouch	15
Wm Warner	25	Tho: Owen	23
Geo: Grace	25	Tho: Knibb	23
Christopher Hamond	32	Robert Waltum	26
Jacob Averie	33	Debora Barnie	23
Geo: Averie	23	Jo: Tyler	16
Francis Bullock	26	Tho: Gregorie	15
Richard Vpgate	21	Tho: Tate	22
Ann Willett	23	Tho: Hancock	15
Joyce Robinson	20	Fra: Pepper	16
Margaret Baylie	20	Wm Saund^r's	19
Mary Brackley	20		

x^o Aug^{ti} 1635

THEIS vnder-written names are to be transported to Virginea, imbarqued in the *Safety*, John Graunt M^r

	yeres		yeres
John Hardon	27	Mary Pitway	4
Richard Haieward	33	Jo: Jones	29
Barthol: Hoskyns	34	Mathew Gough	22
Ant^o Haies	24	Robert Boddy	19
Jo: Catts	23	Jo: Carter	22
Jo: Wazen	19	Thomas Heath	23
Henry Gadling	16	Jo: Hornwood	21
Richard Hopkins	25	Francis Barker	21
Robert Sutton	17	W Tighton	24
Robert Pitway	27	Christopher Wynn	20

Jo: Heming	25	James Bethell	27
Ralph Sympkynn	28	Jo: Browne	25
James Barnes	25	Jo: Gibson	30
Chri: Stope	24	Tho: Belk	37
Robert Lendall	20	Geo: Tucker	22
David Kiffin	24	Tho: Jennions	24
Wᵐ Symonds	32	Robert Perkins	25
Tymothy Trallopp	21	Jo: Martin	23
Henry Dugdell	20	Edmond Farrell	20
John Lownd	16	Wᵐ Hassell	24
James Atkinson	16	Edward Gifford	30
Nicᵒ: Watson	16	Roger Gilbert	16
Jo: Taylor	18	Richard Allin	22
Arthur Raymond	20	Jo: Wilkinson	14
Edward Spicer	21	Francis Vyons	25
Robert Harrwood	17	Wiłłm Davies	27
Richard Foster	16	Richard Alderley	26
Jo: Bell	30	Henry Dalleper	18
Gabriell Fisher	36	Rich: Hudson	30
Tho: Browne	18	Jo: Hill	22
Cornelius Maies	12	Edmond Mulleneux	20
Steven Gorton	35	Humfrey Blackman	16
Jo: Gloster	23	Richard Cotton	20
Jo: Pigeon	15	James Allin	19
Thomas Thorne	13	Martin Church	16
Jo: Write	15	Henry Gilbert	34
Richard Preston	17	Wᵐ Q'ny*	20
Andrew Stretcher	14	Brian Kelly	20
Alexander Harvie	15	Lewes Smith	22
Edmond Jenkins	15	Tho: Doe	33
Nicᵒ: Morton	17	Thomas Saunders	13
Jo: Bay	16	Edward Saunders	9
James Pattison	21	Thomas Carter	25
Wᵐ Lowther	24	Thomas ap Thomas	30
Edward Saunders	40	Richard Caunt	36

* [Clearly so in the original.]

RICHARD MOSS	20	HANNA WADDINGTON	16
JOHN PERRYN	21	ELIZABETH HOLLOWAY	26
HUGH LE ROY	19	ELIZ: GOLD	17
THOMAS REINOLDS	15	ELIZABETH FRISBY	24
JO: CURTIS	21	ELIZ: SMITH	50
ROBERT GLENESTER	25	MARGARET GARD	24
HENRY BUCKLE	30	MARGERIE SMITH	22
JO: NEWMAN	20	ELIZAB: PISCER	16
THOMAS GARDNER	22	ELIZABETH WARD	25
JO: NEWMAN	24	JOAN GRIFFIGE	35
ROBERT FRISTER	20	ELIZ: TURNER	44
RICHARD FIELD	20	JOAN ALLIN	20
GEO: HABBITTELL	26	MARIE BOOTH	19
WIḦM KARSEWELL	20	JANE CUTTING	17
WᴹGRASSON	20	Wᴹ HINDSLEY	23
RICHARD WRIGHT	23	KATHERIN SMITH	18
JO: BUTLER	21	THOMAZIN BROAD	24
JO: HENDRY	24	ANN WATERMAN	18
RICHARD BROOKES	20	JOAN TURNER	21
JO: MARTIN	17	JANE FOXSLEY	25
GEO: CASTELL	21	ROSE HILLS	22
JO: BILLINS	26	ANN CROFT'S	16
THO: WRENN	20	GRACE TUBLEY	20
ROBERT PISCER	44	MARGARET SNALES	22
		ANN HOLLAND	19
MARIE LERRIGO	19	ANN FOSSITT	34
MARGARET HOMES	23	DOROTHY MOYLE	24
ALICE ASHTON	20		

21th Aug^{ti} 1635

IN the *Hopewell* de Lo: m'   BABB, vʳˢ New Engld

HENRY MAUDSLEY 24 yers hath brought Cerᵗ· from the Ministr of his Conformity hath taken the oathe of Allegance.

21 *Aug^{ti}* 1635

THEIS vnder-written names are to be transported to Virginea, imbarqued in the *George* Jo: SEVERNE M^r bound thither p examination of the Minister of Gravesend p̃c.

	yeres		yeres
MICHELL MASTERS	21	MARY BURTWEZILL	18
THO: MORECOCK	26	ALICE WATSON	30
JO: GILLAM	21	JOAN LUDCOLE	18
THO: GILLAM	18	NATHAN: WILSON	23
HUMFREY HIGGINSON	28	THEODOR ROGERSON	20
MATHEW SILSBY	31	W^M THOMSON	22
THO: BULLARD	32	JO: JONES	17
THO: ROGERS	15	MICHELL HEDLY	24
NOWELL LLOYD	16	EDWARD ABBS	37
ANN HIGGINSON	25	W^M GOLDER	22
FRANCIS FOSTER	18	THO: HAND	20
ROBERT SCOTCHMORE	39	GEORGE FOX	14
JO: EVANS	19	JO: DAYNIE	20
RABECCA PALMER	19	W^M HAWKES	22
ARTH^R BODILIES	19	RALPH CLEYTON	20
PETER MANING	25	THO: BEST	33
DANIELL BOWYER	30	JO: HUNT	23
MICHELL WILLIAMS	18	JO: FELD	20
CHRI: KIRK	23	ELIZ: BRISTOWE	17
RICHARD GENNEY	20	MARY ROBINSON	18
CHRISTOPHER THOMAS	21	ELIZABETH WOODBRIDGE	22
WALTER WALKER	23	BRYAN HARE	27
JO: POPE	28	ROGER CUTTS	20
ANT^O HODGSKINS	22	W^M DICKENSON	21
JOHN BELL	21	W^M MITCHELL	15
ANN LAYFIELD	30	MARIE NEELE	13
JO: HUTCHINSON	47	ANN COOPER	20
ALICE LEVITT	16	GEO: TAYLER	20

Henry Kilby	27	Alexander Greene	40
Jo: Fynch	27	James Bankes	35
Geo: Quithor	25	Oliff Gibbins	13
Tho: Mothropp	21	Constance Fister	23
James Horner	24	Wm Scott	24
Jo: Ray	21	Ralph Browne	23
Ric^d: Dixon	20	Robt Morrison	21
Tho: Peacock	19	Edward Greene	6
Jo: Rogers	18	Tho: Bank's	4
Griffith Hughes	24	Eliz: Bank's	9 mo.
Ann White	19	Jo: Allin	21
Jo: Quyle	15	Lewes James	30
Tho: Allin	17	Tho: Wiggins	20
Jo: Butler	13	Sara Merriman	20
Tho: Purnell	16	Arthur Figiss	40
Valentine Bishopp	11	Wm Hinshawe	20
Wm Clowdlslie*	26	Roger Nevitt	20
Richard Verdin	24	Mathew Price	20
Jo: Baddam	40	Ric: James	33
Elias Wiggmore	24	Wm Neesam	21
Suzan Hare	24	Tho: Buck	17
Richard Hide	24	Geo: Smith	20
Robert Dunham	30	Joseph Mills	20
Jo: Goodridge	19	Tho: Rogers	16
Jo: Tiffing	19	Jo: Richards	17
Henry Cutling	40	Wm Saie	17
Leonard Richardson	43	Geo: Cranwell	23
Jesper Hodgskyns	24	Jo: Weston	20
Jo: Wynn	25	Francis Blake	18
Tho: Howell	20	Tho: Maynard	22
Lawrence Barwick	20	Jo: Price	34
Jo: Musgrave	37	Peter Starkie	22
Edward Lillie	19	James Hawkins	17
Jo: Goodson	25	Joseph Warrwell	17
Michell Prynn	25	Francis Young	21

* [So in the original: doubtless intended for Clowdeslie.]

Tho: Connier	22	Francis Havercamp	17
Tho: Perry	18	Edmond Jones	22
Jo: Staunton	27	Henry Hawley	34
Tho: White	16	Robert Burr	19
Ricʀ: Phillips	14	Wᴹ Miller	29
Jane Swifte	23	Wᴹ Curtis	19
Margery Carter	23	Tho: Beomont	29
Gressam Parkins	19	Jo: Covell	18
Wᴹ Block	23	Mary Lovett	18
Tho: Gadsby	19	Joan Vizard	18
Minister. Richard James	33	Wᴹ Steevens	22
Vrsula James	19	Tho: Horrock's	22
Arthur Figiss	33	Mary Soanes	26
			152

THEIS vnder-written names are to be transported to Virginea imbarqued in the *Thomas* HENRY TAVERNER Mr, have been examined by the Minister of Gravesend touching their conformitie in oʳ Religion, &c.

Jo: Lewes	16	Edward Erle	45
Wᴹ Greene	18	Richard Crane	32
Walter Smith	20	Adam Crowe	19
Wᴹ Burton	24	Jacob Denton	20
Jo: Hill	15	Hugh Stanley	16
Joseph Browning	20	Beniamin Symes	42
Tho: Fouch	16	Mary Jolly	21
Edward Sawnders	20	Eliz: Ayres	26
Wᴹ James	18	Humfrey Awdry	21
Jo: Tullie	20	Edward Johnson	28
Jane Gibbs	27	Jo: Collopp	22
Mary Chadd	17	Peter Ricard	19
Jane Colerack	22	Henry Gew	20
Alice Wright	21	Wᴹ Adams	24

Robᵗ James	18	Edward Robins	33
Jo: Browton	20	Geo: Dawe	23
Ricᴿ: Wheeler	24	Joseph Preston	20
Robert Wells	30	Ananiah Dyer	24
Jo: Gressam	22	Roger Wilkyns	33
Teague Quillin	20	Jo: Booth	19
Wᴹ Peas	19	Peter Harbynn	21
Bartholm: Furbank	20	Tho: Maltman [or Multman]	17
Robert Johnson	27	Nicᵒ: Folly	16
Mary Johnson	23	Hugh Fouche	17
Alice Jnᵒson	22	Michell Hutchinson	16
Eliz: Johnson	18	Wᴹ Pallmer	17
Mary Lucie	20	Wᴹ Chamberlin	16
Joan Looker	20	Nathan: Tooly	19
Suzan Jennoway	26	Henry Wilson	12
			58

Secundo die Septembris 1635

THEIS vnder-written names are to be transported to Sᵗ Christophers: imbarqued in the *William & John* Rowland Langram Mʳ. have been examined by the Minister of Gravesend & tooke the oaths of Alleg: & Supreīñ: die et Aᵒ pd

James Lampley	19	W Williams	21
Wᴹ Greene	18	Christopher Steevenson	19
Henry Daniell	20	Tho: Barnes	20
Rowland Davies	20	Robert Watler	20
Wᴹ Reddish	20	Andrew Young	40
Edward Broomish	20	Francis Hudson	36
Robert Fitt	18	Jo: Parr	19
Richard Lewes	26	Wᴹ Morley	24
Richard Corie	18	Ricᴿ: Gavyn	21
Richard Cristie	20	Tho: Phillipps	35
Jo: Brunt	24	Jo: Willard	16

Tho: Hanmer	14	Tho: Hames [or Haines]	16
Wᵐ Burnham	21	John Pinkley	30
Walter Wall	16	Robert Thomson	22
Wᵐ Bathoe	18	Wᵐ Davies	30
Tho: Tapper	21	Richard Beare	28
Wᵐ Baylie	23	Geo: Ford	19
Tho: Brookes	21	Tho: Lowynn	20
Nathaniell Bernard	22	Jo: Drake	18
Tho: Price	20	Robert Outmore	38
Geo: Frie	19	Hugh Hilton	23
Tho: Hart	25	Tho: King	27
Mathew Addison	17	Lawrence Adderford	26
Theobald Wall	18	James Dockkie	17
Robert Richardson	33	Ezechell Rennam	*13
Robert Leake	38	Tho: Haiden	15
Barnabie Brooke	20	Edward Brunt	26
Jo: Cock	18	Tho: Reinolds	16
Nicᵒ: Cobb	24	Wᵐ Benn	24
Jo: Hinson	21	Phillip Skorier	26
Tho: Ekkersoe	24	Wᵐ Worrall	23
Geo: Carter	28	Jo: Benson	27
Ricˢ: Harris	26	Henry Bugland	21
Henrie Nokes	27	Jo: Morton	24
Tho: Thomson	28	Jo: Ditchfield	22
Samvel Knipe	23	Nathaniell Simpkins	26
Jo: Watton	25	Wᵐ Procter	26
Jo: Byrall	29	Edward Gressam	17
Morris Parry	30	Wᵐ Steevens	21
Jo: Nayler	20	Tho: Whithedd	24
Edward Nayler	21	Tho: Clark	25
Geo: Noble	22	Wᵐ Stiffchynn	16
Wᵐ Cock's	20	Jo: Bonn	18
Martin Sowth	19	Wᵐ Dunbarr	15
Wᵐ Greenelefe	26	Jo: Morrish	18
Jo: Sawnders	17	Alexander Glover	37

* [Originally written 15, but afterwards altered.]

EDWARD KING	25	RICHARD MASON	29
JO: KENT	23	MANLEY RICHARDSON	21
ROBERT LYNT	21	ISACK BELT	23
EDWARD BELLIS	21	JOHN PICKERING	25
THO: GILL	30	THO: ARCHBOLD	19
Wᵐ GROVE	32	MATHEW WELLS	28
			*103

THEIS vnder written names are to be transported to Virginea imbarqued in the *David* JO: HOGG Mʳ· have been examined by the Minister of Gravesend, &c.

EDWARD BROWNE	25	JO: MORRIS	26
SAMVEL TROOPE	17	RICHARD BROOKES	30
Wᵐ HATTON	23	ROBERT BARRON	18
DANIELL BACON	30	JONATHAN BARNES	22
ROBERT ALSOPP	18	HENRY KENDALL	17
TEDDER JONES	30	THO: POULTER	31
THO: SIGGINS	18	JO: LAMB	22
ABELL DEXTER	25	THO: NUNN	22
RICᴿ: CATON	26	JO: STEEVENS	19
HENRY SPICER	28	EDWARD CRABBTREE	20
THO: GRANGER	19	Wᵐ BARBER	17
JO: BONFOLLY†	21	ANN BEEFORD [*or* BEDFORD]	25
ROGER MANNINGTON	14	MARTHA PORTER	20
JOSUA CHAMBERS	17	GURTRED LOVETT	18
HENRY MELTON	23	JANE JENNING'S	25
DAVID LLOYD	30	MARGARET BOLD	30
DONOUGH GORHIE	27	MARY ROGERS	20
GER: BUTLER	27	MARGARET WALKER	20
ADDAM NUNNICK	25	FREESE BROOMAN	20
JO: STANN	27	ELIZ: JONES	20
EDWARD SPICER	18		—
JO: FEELDING	19		41

* [It will be observed that these totals are not always correct; there are 104 names in this list. The next, too, is wrong.]

† [Possibly BONFILLY. The fifth letter is indistinctly written; it looks like an *o*, but has a *dot* above it.]

xj° Sept: 1635

THEIS vnder-written names are to be transported to New-England imbarqued in the *Hopewell* THO: BABB, m^r p Cert from the Ministers &c Justices of their conformitie in Religion to o^r Church of England: &c y^t they are no Subsedy Men. they have taken ye oaths of Alleg: &c Suprem.

	yeres		
Husb: Willm Wood	27	Robert Withie	20
Elizabeth Wood	24	Henrie Ticknall	15
Jo: Wood	26	Harnis maker Isack Heath	50
Robert Chambers	13	Elizabeth Heath	40
Tho: Jn°son	25	Elizabeth Heath	5
Marie Hubbard	24	Martha Heath	30
Jo: Kerbie	12	Wm Lyon	14
Jo: Thomas	14	Grace Stokes	20
Isack Robinson	15	Tho: Bull	25
Ann Williamson	18	Joseph Miller	15
Tanner. Jo: Weekes	26	Jo: Prier	15
Marie Weekes	28	Richard Hutley	15
Anna Weekes	1	Daniell Pryer	13
Suzan Withie	18	Katherin Hull	23
Robert Baylie	23	Mary Clark	16
Marie Withie	16	Jo: Marshall	14
Samvel Younglove	30	Joan Grave	30
Margaret Younglove	28	Mary Grave	26
Samvel Younglove	1	Joan Cleven	18
Andrew Hulls	29	Edmond Chippfield [Chipperfield]	20
Anthony Freeman	22		
Twiford West	19	Mary With	62
Roger Toothaker	23	Robert Edward's	22
Margaret Toothaker	28	Robert Edge	25
Roger Toothaker	1	Walter Lloyd	27

ELLIN LEAVES	17	JO: FORTEN	14
ALICE ALBON	25	GABRIELL RELD	18
BARBARY ROFE	20		
			54

xix Sept: 1635

THEIS vnder-written names are to be transported to New-England imbarqued in the *Truelove* JO: GIBBS M^r. the Men have taken the oaths of Alleg: ₽ Suprem.

	yeres		
Labouring man. THOMAS BURCHARD	40	RABECCA FENNER	25
		THO: TIBBALD'S	20
MARY BURCHARD	38	THOMAS STREME	15
ELIZABETH BURCHARD	13	JO: STREME	14
MARIE BURCHARD	12	Husb: RALPH TOMKINS	50
SARA BURCHARD	9	*vxor* KAT. TOMKINS	58
SUZAN BURCHARD	8	ELIZABETH TOMKINS	18
JO: BURCHARD	7	MARIE TOMKINS	14
ANN BURCHARD	18 mo.	SAMVEL TOMKINS	22
PETER PLACE	20	RICHARD HAWES	29
W^M BEERESTO	23	ANN HAWES	26
GEO: BEERESTO	21	ANNA HAWES	2½
Husbandmon EDWARD HOWE	60	OBEDIAH HAWES	6. mo
ELIZABETH HOWE	50	RALPH ELLWOOD	28
JEREMIE HOWE	21	GEO: TAYLER	31
SARA HOWE	12	ELIZABETH JENKINS	27
EPHRAIM HOWE	9	W^M PRESTON	44
ISACK HOWE	7	MARIE PRESTON	34
W^M HOWE	6	ELIZ: PRESTON	11
JO: SEDGWICK	24	SARA PRESTON	8
JEREMY BLACKWELL	18	MARIE PRESTON	6
LESTER GANTER [*or* GUNTER]	13	JO: PRESTON	3
ZACHARIA WHITMAN	40	W^M JOES*	28
SARA WHITMAN	25	WILLIAM BENTLEY	47
ZACHA: WHITMAN	2½	ALICE BENTLEY	15

* [This name *may* be read as IVES.]

Margaret Killinghall	20	John Done	16
Jo: Bentley	17	Roger Broome	17
Tho: Stockton	21	Dorothie Lowe	13
Geo: Morrey	23	Jo: Simpson	30
Richard Srayne	34	Tho: Brighton	31
Sarah Haile	11	Tho: Rumball	22
Samvel Grover	16	Edward Parrie	24
Robert Browne	24	Jane Walston	19
Tho: Blower	50		*66
Edward Jeofferies	24		

Tricessimo die Septembris 1635

BOARD the *Dors.* John Flower M^r bound for ye Bormodos.

John Redford [*or* Reeford]	16	Jo: Heth	21
Robert Ramsey	15	Nathaniell Bonnick	16
John Williams	16	Jo: Denman	14
Wiłł︤m Elliston	13	Tho: More	18
Lubas Wright	16	Wm Bruister	17
Humfrey Holt	18	George Hubbard	16
Tho: Joyner	16	Edw: Middleton	15
Ric^r: Tregagell	18	Francis Russell	23
Jo: Loe	18	James Rising	18
Josua Woodcock	11	Geo: Absolon	16
Robert Fisher	10	Jo: Mosdell	24
Tho: Sharp	17	Wm Stoker	19
Jo: Rowland	21	Edward Morris	18
Wm Wheeler	22	Wm Thomas	17
Wm Pennington	18	Ric^r: Bunting	17
Jo: Mathews	16	Tho: Stokes	30
Robert Vardell	20	Wm Rosden	16

* [So in the original. But there are 67 names in the list.]

Nathaniell West	15	Edward Grubthorn	14
Jo: Donn	14	Jonas Goldenham	16
Edward Edwynn	15	Judith Bagley	58
Jo: Sell	15	John Glassenden	14
Tho: Ireland	10	Wᴹ Harding	30
Edward Davies	17	uxor Sara Harding	30
Edward Simpson	13	Henry Rosse	31
Edward Aldin*	17	Tymothie Pynder	26
Tho: Atkins	16	Margaret Pynder	41
Tho: Riley	16	Jane Dart	17
Wᴹ Barnes	15	Minister Geo: Turk	40
Jo: Day	16	Ezia vyncent	30
Wᴹ Barrith	16	uxor Marthew	30
Jo: Tustin	16	Minister Daniell Wite	30
Jo: Nicklin	17	Sampson Lort	30
Jo: Harkwood	20	Jo: Miller	47
Humfrey Kemp	16	John Johnson	23
David Thomas	26	Richard Jenning's	35
Willm Alburie	15	uxor Sara Jenning's	18
Arthur Thorne	33	Richard Palmer	30
Wᴹ Cheeseman	20	uxor Ellis Palmer	21
John Mitchell	20	Tho: Griffin	32
John Casson	18	Ann Griffin	35
Alexander Brabant	30	Robert Ridley	23
Henry Fulcock	15	Elizabeth Ridley	30
Jo: Mansfield	19	Edward Chaplin	20
Willm East	15	Wᴹ Casse	19
Richard Haldin	14	Peternell Nowell	46
Geo: Palmer	27	Christian Wellman	43
Wᴹ Simpson	17	Eliz: Aldworth	15
Edward Simpson	13		95

* [Originally written Allin, afterwards altered to Aldin.]

2° die Octobris 1635

ABOARD the *John* of London JAMES WAYMOTH M^r bound to St Christophers

JOHN BATCHELLER...............	26	THO: WALKER.....................	19
SAM̃VEL PARKER	19	JO: MULLENEUX........	24
THO: JAMES........................	25	OSWELL METCALF	22
CHRI: THOMSON	21	EDWARD COOKE..................	22
ALEXANDER FLEETWOOD......	19	JO: SHERLOCK.....................	20
WALTER LEE	21	THO: FROST........................	28
EDWARD DODSON	21	LEWES EVANS.....................	25
GILBERT CLARK	19	JO THOMSON	19
GEO: HEELIS	19	RICHARD TOWNSEND............	19
RICHARD ELMES..................	21		
RICHARD SMITH...................	22	MARY GOODWINN	18
WILLM RICHARDSON	24	JANE GOODWYNN	20
EDWARD MEKINS	18	MARTHA LILLIOT	20
JO: CLYMER	30	ELIZABETH MURRIN	21
RICHARD EVANS..................	21	JOAN HILL	21
HENRIE FEELD	25	ELIZABETH FREEMAN	18
HENRIE RADFORD	20		
JO: HENMAN	19		33

13° die octobris 1635

ABOARD the *Amitie* GEORGE DOWNES M^r bound to St Christo͞phr^s

ISACK DRAKE	25	EDWARD FARR	28
RICHARD IVESON	24	W^M BURROWE	19
ROBERT BARNE	33	THO: BREWYNN	24
THO: HERNDEN	23	MARMADUKE BORNE...........	21

Wiłłm Creswell	22	Jo: Goddin	20
Henrie Hodgskynns	19	Richard Larkynn	32
Robert Payne	21	Richard Boeman	23
George Hatrell	32	Tho: Molton	20
Jo: Hippsley	19	David Owen	26
Wiłłm Stanley	22	Henrie Rowles	22
John Snape	22	Nico: Alford	28
Isack Buck	33	Samvell Sakell	23
Walter Ellitt	20	Robert Jones	30
Aymies Halfyard	19	Jo: Browne	33
Oliver Johnes	25	Peter Salmon	20
John Smith	23	Jo: Saunderson	23
Hamblet Sankey	22	Robert Rolfe	23
Edward Porter	21	John Jack	27
Tho: Galley	20	Tho: Yott	24
Tho: Pitt's	24	John Teirrer	24
Jo: Thomson	25	John Farmer	24
Richard Webster	24	Wm Daughton	20
Lewes Jones	20	Ric^e: Skynner	20
John Coombes	26	Wm Egerton	20
George Coop [Cooper]	20	James Makynn	20
Mathew Preston	22	Wm Harris	20
John Pynkston	27	Bastian Petite	23
Wm Geies	18	John Warren	20
Wiłłm Vbank	20	Ric^k: Phinnei	30
Charles Parker	18	James Brigg's	25
James Leachman	22	John Musick	19
Wm Cartwrite	18	Jo: Griddick	16
Richard West-Garrett	20	Wm Davies	40
Wm Harris	16	Robt Heath	30
Jer: Nicholls	16	Tho: Baggelay	24
Tho: Rodes	20	William Yateman	25
Jo: Boughei	21	Richard Grind	11
Edward Grindall	21	Wm Galler	20
Jo: Vaughan	23	Robert Downe	35

John Hye	36	Mary Wynd	18
Edward Webb	17	Margaret Coles	21
James Johnson	28	Marie Merriton	21
John Avery	22	Kat: Brewett	16
Daniell Cannelly	20	Ellin Chaunce [or Channce]	21
Rice Poke	30	Ann Palmer	29
Roger James	29	Alice Barker	30
James Curtis	18	Patient White	44
Clement Hames	22	Isack } Jacob... } Twynns	2
John Fynn	22		
Wiłhm Goff	30	Judith Lloyd	18
Andrew White	11	Marie Maxwell	21
John Billinghurst	24		
Morrice Davie	24		105
Wᵐ Rule	20		

24° Octobris 1635

ABOARD the *Constance*, Clement Campion Mʳ bound to Virginia.

	yeres		yeres
John Wade	21	Geo: Atkinson	16
Garret Nicholson	23	Robt Sexston	24
John Burrowes	18	Tho: Pursell	26
Wᵐ Bett	21	Davie Lupton	23
Thomas Simpson	24	Henrie More	20
Tho: Patrick	22	Michell Suckliff	18
John Till	20	George Atterborn	20
Joseph Prichard	17	Ricᴿ: Steere	24
Wᵐ Bennerman	18	Tho: Leer	18
Ricᴿ: Tayler	18	Wᵐ Prichard	34
John Griffin	26	James Cotes	22
Samvel Jackson	21	James Revell	20

	yeres		
Wᴹ Androwes	20	Jo: Palmer	12
Symon Garr	14	Griffin Maymor	21
Wᴹ Hunt	21	Francis Marsden	19
Tho: Jackson	23	Steephen Pack	22
Miles Coke	23	Geo: Davie	22
Chri: Chambers	24	Henrie Johnson	27
Davie Williams	24	Jo: Ashcrofte	33
Nicᵒ: Huggins	24	Mathew Gowgh*	28
Jo: Davies	20	Tho: Digglin	22
Wᵐ Jones	25	Robert Baskervile	22
Henrie Richardson	21	Nathaniell Young	20
Roger Williams	19	Tho: Hodson	20
Jo: Wythins	24	Sampson Alkynn	24
Tho: Jay	25	Jo: Coke	24
Elizabeth Brewer	17	John de Cane	20
Isack Bever	24	Jo: Elliott	36
Alice Brass	15	Wᴹ Gillam	27
Tho: More	26	Tho: Smith	24
Wᴹ King	21	Antᵒ Miles	11
Jo: Mitchell	22	Chri: Boyce	38
Tho: Hall	21	Tho: Saddock	17
Robert Ellis	22	Mary Parker	15
James Haies	28	Wᴹ Hulett	19
John Hancock	17	Walter Jenkyns	30
Ricᵉ: Gray	21	Edmond Porter	35
Wᴹ Tyse	20	Edward Herrott	35
Tho: Wathin	35	Hugh Douglas	22
Charles Hughes	50	Walter Colly	19
James Symonds	20	Joan Carraway	22
Joꜱ Clark	38	Tho: Hart	18
Geo: Dyos	38		—
			85

* [There is a *flourish* at the end of this name in the original; I do not think it is intended for a final *e*.]

ABOARD the *Abraham* of London JOHN BARKER M^r bound to Virginea.

TOBIE SYLBIE	20	HENRY DOBELL	20
ROBERT HARRISON	32	GEORGE BREWETT	18
Wiłłm LAWRENCE	22	FRANCIS STANLEY	23
JOHN JOHNSON	35	Wiłłm FREEMAN	46
Wm FISHER	25	EDWARD GRIFFITH	33
STEEVEN TAYLER	17	Wiłłm MANTON	30
THO: PENFORD	30	OWEN WILLIAMS	40
Wm SMITH	25	THO: FLOWER	32
THO: ARCHDIN	18	JO: BULLAR	32
RIC^s: MORRICE	17	JO: CLANTON	26
WALTER PIGGOTT	19	ALEXANDER SYMES	19
RICHARD WATKYNS	20	ANT^o. PARKHURST	42
JO: BRAUNCH	13	JO: HILL	36
JO: CLARK	20	ALEXANDER GREGORIE	24
GABRIELL THOMAS	30	MARTIN WESTERLINK	20
DAVIE JONES	21	PATRICK WOOD	24
ALEXANDER MADDOX	22	THO: KEDBY	25
FRANCIS TIPPSLEY	17	ROGER GREENE	24
EMANUELL DAVIES	19	Wiłłm DOWNES	24
Wm WILLIAMS	25	JO: BURNETT	24
ROGER MATHEWS	28	THO: ALLIN	31
JO: MASTERS	23	SIMON FARRELL	19
WILLM MATHEWS	18	THO: CLEMENT'S	30
JO: BRITTEN	18	Wm HUNT	20
GEORGE PRESTON	20	KATHERIN ALDWELL	33
ROBERT TOULBAN	23		51

20 *Novembris* 1635

THEIS vnder-written names are to be transported to the Barbadoes imbarqued in the *Expedition* PETER BLACKLER Mr· The Men have taken the oaths of Allegeance ℘ Supremacie: And have been examined by the Minister of the Towne of Gravesend touching their Conformitie to the ordrs ℘ discipline of the Church of England die et Ao prd

	yeres		yeres
Minister NICHOLAS BLOXĀ [BLOXAM] als INGLES	31	BRIAN ASTON	21
ABRAM HOLLAND	19	NICHOLAS COLLON	19
THOMAS HUDSON	16	HENRIE FIELD	24
BLACKWELL LAWRENCE	16	RICHARD SMITH	20
LEONARD BRIGGINS	17	JOHN KNOWLES	27
THOMAS CLARK	27	JOHN DICKENSON	24
MORGAN JENKINS	32	JOHN MANN	21
RICk: PRATT	18	THO: PEACOCK	17
THO: FREEMAN	19	EDWARD STEEVENS	53
Wiłłm GREEFESON	26	THOMAS WEEKES	23
RICHARD WARTUMBEE	21	HUGH CHESWOOD	21
HENRY BRYAN	21	JO: COERT	21
HUGH DAWSON	18	JOHN PIKE	30
MATHEW BEADS	19	GEORGE BLACKLOCK	32
CHARLES LAMBERT	23	JOHN COLEMAN	40
JO: LAKE	18	Wm WATTS	28
JO: SMITH	18	JOHN BONNER	18
ANTHONY HUTCHINS	32	Wiłłm SINGNELL	18
Wiłłm GIBSON	19	THO: HOBIN	20
JO: WILLIAMS	17	FRANCIS BARNIT	23
WILLIAM STEWARD	21	Wiłłm BUCKLEY	26
JOHN PIERCE	18	JOHN CLARK	16
HUGH EVANS	18	PHILLIPP MORLIN	21
		HENRY RAWLINS	25

Jo: Rudge	42	Willm Warr	19
Edward Evans	22	Mathew Wilkinson	18
John Hownsefield	20	Mathew Gibbons	20
Tho: Davie	20	Wm Awdley	19
Henry Gowde	19	James Kingston	22
Wm Mellison	25	Ricr: Smart	20
John York	26	Wm Walters	26
Wm Carpenter	19	Tho: Davies	23
John Wynter	23	Nathaniell Nordin	46
Jo: Waller	17	Wm Pitt	25
John Sumes	20	Jo: Chater	17
John Heron	20	Jo: Chapman	24
Willm Tayler	26	Geo: Sterry	24
John Parlin	21	Abram Cheynei	22
Wm Jackson	33	Jo: Sturton	18
John Medgley	21	Jo: Edens	19
Wm Wrench	21	Lawrence Brock	18
Robert Hurt	19	Ricr: Best	18
James Farebank	26	Robert Hobbs	26
Henrie Berrisford	32	Peter Jones	30
James Nettleton	22	Wm Topleife	18
Thomas Armetage	24	Jo: Robinson	19
Francis Mann	19	Morrice Jones	21
John Felkynn	20	Henry Stint	18
John Jones	20	Josias Weston	25
Richard Lightbound	22	Francis Birkenhedd	24
Christopher Hartlie	19	Edward Jones	29
Tho: Wood	23	Ellis Williams	18
Henrie Godfrie	36	Wm Tayler	40
Tho: Palmer	19	Tho: Burnham	18
Jo: Humfrey	20	Joseph Boyce	24
John Smith	22	Jo: Rainsecrofte	23
Ambrose Greene	23	Henrie Bostock	19
Jo: Hilliard	18	Jefferie Ship	24
Jo: Browne	26	Wm Brooke	26

Launcelott Lacon	32	Mary Lupton	30
Wᴹ Plomer	23	Ricʀ: Horne	22
Wᴹ Sheicrofte*	17	John Newton	29
Wᴹ Coke	18	Thomas Cowdell	17
Jo: Jenning's	18	Richard Gibson	25
Tho: Ossebrooke	27	Nicholas Nevell	19
Jo: Davenport	30	George Tayler	20
Geo: Burton	23	Wᴹ Goad	21
Wᴹ Morgan	20	Wᴹ Marritt	26
Davie Thomas	20	Roger Eritage	22
Ricʀ: Hannis	21	Davie Dodderidge	20
Peter Croningburk	20	George Fullwood	19
Jo: Hall	29	Ricʀ: Hamis	21
Jo: Compton	26	Ralph Webster	20
Clement Backford	30	Tho: Robinson	15
Robert Browne	18	Joseph Thomlinson	26
John Key	32	Baltazar Dederix	26
Howell Pryce	25	James Smith	24
Edward Aston	32	Nicᵒ: Flatter	27
Robᵗ Edwards	38	Nicᵒ: Whithedd	24
Richard Ash	24	Wᴹ Hinkynn	26
John Medley	26	Thomas Gilbert	26
Thomas King	24	Richard Seabright	21
Richard Snowe	28	Robert Greenewood	18
Robert Filborne	18	Anthony Ashmore	33
Pierce Morgan	23	Launcelott Bromley	44
Jo: Williams	17	Peter Spencer	15
Nicᵒ: Brogan	28	Thomas Phipps	15
Antᵒ: Smith	18	Davie Thomas	20
John Spenceley	24	Wiᴴᴹ Greene	23
Mathew Shore	46	Jo: Watts	20
Thomas SParlin†	19	Wᴹ Lock	21
Dorothy Symonds	40	George Leas	20

* [*Or* Shercrofte. The fourth letter is not clear.]

† [The first two letters are capitals in the original; possibly the name is intended for S[t] Parlin.]

John Spencer	19	John Chesting	21
Henry Antony	19	Roger Sanford	35
James Fassitt	34	Willm Cornwell	20
Henry Ellotts	23	Wm Gosselin	21
Henrie Coke	28	Jo: Coop [Cooper]	21
Richard Benes	25	Wm Price	22
Wm Cosson	20	Sam: Skynner	22
Wm Thomson	20	Robt Dunstarr	34
Thomas Vsherwood	28	Richard Buck	24
Wm Haning	30	Nico: Lynton	22
John Goad	22		
Richard Moncaster	32		205

19 Dec: 1635

THEIS vnder-written names are to be transported to the Barbadoes imbarqued in the *Falcon* Tho: Irish Mr the Men have been examined by the Minister of the Towne of Gravesend touching their conformitie to the Church Discipline of England: And also have taken the oaths of Alleg: & Suprem̃. Die et Ao prd

	yeres		yeres
Arnold Ownstedd	30	Jo: Barnet	20
Tho: Skyddell	28	James Spencer	25
Anto Cadwold	23	Jo Chubnell	21
Phillipp Miller	21	Wm Gunter	22
Maximillian Prichard	20	Jo: Thurrogood	20
Tho: Tiffin	28	Tho: Greene	16
Jo: Butler	21	Richard Richardson	36
Phines Trusedell	18	Rabecca Burgis	17
Bryan Cowly	30	Richard Panke	19
Jo: Mason	19	Leonard Robinson	20
Robert Harris	42	Francis Buck	20
Abram Shawe	20	John Hogg	21
Geo: Sabyn	21	Robert Symper	20
Wm Cartwrite	23	Tho: Page	20
Nathan: Murfitt	23	Dennis Brittin [*or* Britton]	20

Jo: Rogers	18	Jo: Scott	42
James Wolton	22	Tho: Evans	23
Jo: Burkitt	21	Wᴹ Phillips	28
Tho: Harrwell	29	James Cotesworth	21
Gregorie Booth	18	Ellinn Robb	27
Edward Howe	19	*filia* Elizabeth Robb	7
Robᵀ Clark	18	Tho: Clark	27
Francis Martin	18		—
Tho: Webb	22		46

25 *Decembris* 1635

THEIS vnder-written names passed in a Catch to the Downes: and were put aboard the aforesaid Shipp.

Wᴹ Rofe	20	Jane Hickles	25
Jo: Lawnder	16	Henry Van Luccom	24
Wᴹ Atwell	21	Jo: King	30
Hugh Perry	27	Wᴹ Flatter	18
Jo: Stotter	26	Jo: Weston	27
Ricʀ: Hughes	28	Tho: Clark	28
Tho: Davies	17	Wᴹ Conisby	31
Henry Benson	19	Robert Tissall	30
Jo: Welsh	35	Tho: Vnyon [*i.e.* Unyon]	19
Henry Southward	20	Tristram Ford	21
Ricʀ: Newbolt	28	Elias Carpenter	20
Lawrence Keysie	28	Richard Hames	18
James Robinson	15	Thomas Streter	21
Antᵒ Pope	28	James Lee	28
Jo: Lee	30		—
Griffinn Evans	40		32
James Terrill	20		—
Elizabeth Cossen	25	In all	78

21° July

JANE GIBBS of age. 25 yeeres resident in Virginea to passe to Flushing about certen her affares.

29 Augusti 1635

WILLIAM NORTON xxv yeres old is to transport himself to New-England ℓ to imbarque himself in the *Hopewell* p Cert: from the Minister of his conformitie to the Church discipline of England: he hath taken the oaths of Allegeance ℓ Suprem. die et A° prd

iiijth Sep^{tr} 1635

ROBERT EDWARD'S. 27 yers who is to passe to Virginia hath taken the oathe of Allegance

ROBERT EDWARDS:

v^{to} die Septembris

THOMAS TURNER of age xlij yeres to passe to New England imbarqued in the *Hopewell* hath brought Certificate of his Conformitie, ℓ tooke the oaths of Allegeance ℓ Supremacie.

THOMAS TURNER

viij° die Sept.

Turner ROBERT PENNAIRD of age 21 yeres ℓ THO: PENNAIRD x yeres old are to [be] imbarqued in* Mr BABB bound to New-England have brought Certificate from Doctor DENISON of his conformitie. he hath taken the oaths of Alleg ℓ Suprem̄

---

* [So in the original; name of ship omitted.]

THESE men Whose names are heere vnder written belonginge vnto the *Friendshipe* of London, nowe ridinge att An Ankere in the reuer of Themes bound for Vergenia: March 1636

LEONARD BETTS Master
JOHN GOODWENE Masters Mat
JOHN CHAMBERS ye other Mate
SAMVELL LAWSONE gunner
DAUEY SLAWCOME Carpenter
JOHN YONGES botsman
RICHARD DAUES Cooper
LARENCE WILLKISSON q': Master
JOHN HUCHENS Carpenters Mate
JOHN LEE
WILLIAM BLORKE
JOHN POLLEN
RICHARD BONNER
THOMAS REEUES
NICHOLAS PORTE
RICHARD FRYE
BENIAMONE WILLKISSON
JOHN BLAKE
THOMAS GRIBELL Cooke
HENERY JOYCE
and A boye

A Booke of Entrie for Passengers by yᵉ Comission, ᵉ Souldiers according to the Statute passing beyond the seas begun at Christmas 1631. and ending at Christmas 1632*

---

* [This is the title on the cover of the original. It really refers only to the book from which the matter in the next two pages has been extracted; but for convenience the lists, pp. 151—154, have been arranged under it. The "souldiers" were not for America, and their names are therefore not reprinted.]

A Booke of Entrie for Passengers, &c.

---

vij° Marcij 1631

THE names of such Men as are to be tr be [*sic*] transported New-England to be resident there vppon a plantacon ha tendred ſ taken the oath of allegeance according to the Statute
vizt:

THOMAS THOMAS
THOMAS WOODFORD.
JOHN SMALLIE.
JOHN WHETSTON.
Wm HILL.
WiĦm PERKINS
WALTER HARRIS
JOSEPH MANNERING

JOHN LEVINS
THOMAS OLLIVER.
JOHN OLLIVER.
THOMAS HAEWARD
EDMOND WYNSLOE
JOHN HART
WiĦm NORTON.
ROBERT GAMLIN

xij° Aprilis 1632

THE names of such Men women and children wch are to passe to New-England to be resident there vppon a Plantacōn have tendred ℰ taken the oath of allegeance according to ye Statute.

JOHN BARCROFTE.
JANE BARCROFTE.
HUGH MOIER.
HENRIE SHERBORN
JOHN GREENE
PERSEVERANCE GREENE.

JOHN GREENE.
JACOB GREENE.
ABIGALL GREENE.
SARA. JOHNES madserv^t.
JOSEPH GREENE.

xxij Junij 1632

THE names of such Men transported to New-England to the Plantacōn there p Cert: from Capten MASON have tendred and taken the oath of allegeance according to the Statute

WILLIAM WADSWORTH
JOHN TALLCOTT
JOSEPH ROBERT'S.
JOHN COXSALL
JOHN WATSON.
ROBERT SHELLEY.
WIllM HEATH.
RICHARD ALLIS
THOMAS VSFITT
ISACK MURRILL.
JOHN WITCHFIELD
JONATHAN WADE
ROBERT BARTLETT
JO: BROWNE.
JOHN CHURCHMAN.
TOBIE WILLET
WILLIAM CURTIS

NIC°: CLARK.
DANIELL BREWER
JO: BENIAMIN.
RICHARD BENIAMIN.
WILLIAM JAMES.
THOMAS CARRINGTON.
WILLIAM GOODWYNN.
JOHN WHITE.
JAMES OLMSTEDD.
WILLIAM LEWES
ZETH GRAUNT
NATHANIELL RICHARD'S.
EDWARD ELLMER.
EDWARD HOLMAR.
JO: TOTMAN.
CHARLES GLOWER.

THE Names of those psons that went from Dartmouth to the Barbadoes beinge sworne before me ALLEXANDER STAPLEHILL Maio^r of Dartmouth the 15th day of Aprill Año Dñi 1634

Impris DANIELL POWELL of Curmer.

A LIST of the names and surnames of those psons wch are bound for St Christoph^{rs} ℘ haue taken the oath of Allegeance before Mr WILLIAM GOURNEY Maio^r: of Dartmouth they beinge brought befor me the Twentyeth day of February in ye Yeare of o^r lord god 1634

Inprimis WILLIAM HAUKINS of Exōn A Glover Aged 25 years or there abouts
JAMES COURTNEY of Exōn A Blacksmith Aged 23 Years or thereabouts
RICHARD SKOSE of Newton Abbot A Seafaringe man 37 Years or thereabouts
FRANCIS BOYCE of London a Button hole maker aged 25 Yeares or thereabouts
WILLIAM CARKILLE of Plimouth A Saylemaker aged 21 Years or thereabouts
WILLIAM GURGE of Exōn a Shoemaker aged 20 Yeares or thereabouts
ALCE WHITMORE of Huniton in Devon Spinster Aged 25 Years or thereabouts
PHILIPP* STEPHENS of Ashberton in Devon Spinster Aged 28 Yeares or therabouts
SARA COOSE of Exon Spinster aged 18 Years or therabouts
JUDETH STEVENS of Exon Spinter [Spinster] aged 19 Years or therabouts
MARGARETT HARWOOD of Stoke-gabriell in Devon spinster Aged 22 Years or therabouts
EDWARD MORRIS of Exōn a Locker aged 21 years or therabouts
THOMAS BRYANT of Bampton in Devonshire a husbandman aged 23 Years or therabouts

---

* [Probably intended for PHILIPPA.]

WILLYAM MAY of Myniard in Somersett a sea man aged 32 Yeares or therabouts
HUTINNE OWETH of St Steevens in Cornwall a husbandman Aged 24
JOHN WILLS in Barnstable in Devon a Feltmaker Aged 35 Years or thereabouts
SYMON WEEKS of Exon̄ a Worsted weaver aged 16 years or thereabouts
THOMAS JERMAYNE of Exon̄ an Ostler aged 30 Years
JOHN FRENCH of Washford in Ireland a seaman 26 years
WILL^M HILL of great Torington in Devonshire a husbandman Aged 28 Years
JOHN HOCKSLEY of Stoke Cannon in Devon a Tayler aged 28 Years
JAMES ROSMAN of London a husbandman aged 21 years.
ELIZABETH REED of Exon a Spinster aged 19 Years or thereabouts
MARY HARTE of Lyme a Spinster aged 18 Years or there abouts
MARY HOPPINE of Exmister a spinster aged 20 Yeares
MARYES HARRIES of Stoke Pommeroy in Devon aged 23 Years or therabouts
ELIZABETH QUICKE of Barnstable in Devon aged 18 Years
ELIZABETH HILL of Brixam in Devon aged 24 Years
JOANE SHORTE of Exon Aged 20 Yeares
JOANE LANERS [*or* LAUERS] of Modbury in Devon aged 19 Years
JANE GOULDINGE of St Thom. the Apostle in Devon aged 16 years or therabouts

JAMES WORTHY
Deputy.

for M^r· THOROUGHGOOD

The Name of such as passed out of the Poart of Plimworth Ano Dnie 1634

*Plymouth
Febr:* 1633.

PASSENGERS.

IN the *Robert Bonaventure* for St Christophers.

GEORGE FORD of Exon aged 30 yeares.
STEPHEN WHITTINGTON of Lincolne 20 yeares.
JOHN THOMAS of St Tissey 26 yeares.

JOHN LIDDICOTT of Sᵗ Cullum 22 yeares.
Wᴹ CLARKE of Truro 20 yeares.
THO: FRETHY of Perintho 24 yeares.
MICHAELL BOWDEN of Helston 27 yeares.
JOHN BADLAND of Northill 22 yeares.
RICHARD SLAVELIE of Stonehowse 40 yeares.
RICHARD COCKE of Wincklye 33 yeares.
HENRY RENSBY [or REUSBY] of Sᵗ Stephens 28 yeares.
ANTHONY WEBB of Lanceston 20 yeares.
GREGORY SAM of Chidleigh 15 yeares.
CHRISTOPHER CARTER of Sᵗ Gilt 45 yeares.
MARTIN ROOBY of Guindiron 23 yeares.
Wᴹ CURKE of Monteratt 24 yeares.
HENRY THOMAS of Luxulian 15 yeares.
STEPHEN SYMON of Plimpton 18. yeares.
MATHEW ARTHUR of Plimpton 18. yeares.
JANE TREWIN of Plimpton 26 yeares.
Wᴹ JOHNSON of London 32 yeares.
REIGNOLD FROST of Tottnes 15 yeares.
JOHN FARREN of Peter Tany 2 yeares.
Wᴹ WADE of Bodmin 33 yeares.
NICHAS DABBIN of Sᵗ Stephens 40 yeares.
ANDREW PICKE of Great Dalby 34 yeares.
JOHN PENINGTON of Symon Ward 40 yeares.
THO: POLLARD of Paraneuth 23 yeares.
ELLIN NANCARRO of Penryn 20 yeares.
RAWLEIGH EDYE of Bodmyn 15 yeares.
Wᴹ DUN of Truro. 16 yeares.
ANTH: PEARSE of Sᵗ Breage 16 yeares.
EDWARD TREMINEERE of Helston 18. yeares.
ROBᵀ TRENEIGHAN of Helston 34 yeares.
TEGO LEANE [or LEAUE] of Corke in Ireland 30 yʳˢ

Rec. for these ———
All husbandmen bound to serve there some 3 and some 4 yeares.

1633.   1° m'cij [*March*].

IN the *Margarett* for St Christophers.

THOMAS ROSETER of Washford 20 yeares.
THO: MARTIN of Cardinham 24 yeares.
JOHN DUSTON of St Cullom 26 yeares.
RICHARD WILLIAMS of St Cullom 30 yeares.
JOHN NEWDON of St Tue 28. yeares.
JOHN HEWBRAYNE of Josias Newton 20 y^{rs}
ANTH: BURROWES of Jacobstow 20 yeares.
ROBERT OLIVER of Crediton 20 yeares.
BARTH: CORNEW, of Crediton 18. yeares.
CLEMENT BARRY of Exon 22 yeares.
FRANCIS PEDLER of St Breage 28 yeares.
ROB^T PEDLER of St Breage 22 yeares.
JOHN MERRY of Withiell 28. yeares.
WALTER BURLACY of Luggan 22 yeares.
SAMUELL FORGIUE of Wallen Lizard 26: y^{rs}
RICHARD EDWARD of St Vivian 28. yeares.
RICHARD SYMOND'S of Wantage 28 yeares.
ROB^T PAINE of Marrozion. 29 yeares.
W^M BADCOCKE of St Hillary. 20 yeares.
SIMON MARTIN of St Ives. 18 yeares.
JOHN MARTIN of St Ives. 18. yeares.
GEORGE GRIFFIN of Marozion 18 yeares.
THO: SLEMAN of St Hillary 18 yeares.
JOHN SANDERS of Marozion 18. yeares.
THOMAS BORINTHON of Helston 22 yeares.
W^M WIETT of Marozion. 17 yeares.
NICHAS. WATERMAN or [of] Marozion 15 y^{rs.}
SAMUELL PUREFOY of St Ives 13 yeares.
GEORGE MATHEW. of Ludswan 23 y^{rs}
TEAGE WILLIAMS Irishman 18. yeares

        li s d
  rec̄d. for them —— 0. 15 0
All husbandmen for the most p^t as the former.
       JOSEPH BOOLE
        is Debutie ther

[ENTRIES RELATING TO AMERICA, &c.,

TAKEN FROM THE

INDEXES TO THE PATENT ROLLS,

COMMENCING 4 JAMES I. (1606),

AND ENDING 14 WILLIAM III. (1702).]

[The following entries, (pp. 155—168*), relating to Proclamations, Commissions, and Grants of Offices, Land, &c., in different parts of America and elsewhere, are taken from the Indexes to the Patent Rolls in the Public Record Office, commencing in 1606 (4 James I.), and ending in 1702 (14 William III.). There are several entries of the appointment of Commissioners to administer oaths to persons desirous of passing beyond the seas, (officers being stationed for this purpose at the ports of London, Harwich, Weymouth, Kingston-upon-Hull, the Cinque Ports, &c.); and the student will find among them valuable hints upon which to base more detailed researches. These entries must embody very many memoranda throwing light upon questions of settlement in America. We may add, that licenses were necessary, on leaving England, not only for civilians, but also for soldiers, whether under command, or going singly to join their regiments. Reference to *Roll* and *Part* is given at the end of each paragraph.]

[ENTRIES RELATING TO AMERICA, &c.]

COMMISSION granted to Sir HENRY BILLINGSLEY and Sir WILLIAM ROMNEY, Knights, and others, to minister an oath to all women and persons under the age of One-and-twenty years, that shall desire to go over the seas, at our port of London, &c. (Pat. 4 Jac. I. part 12.)

Commissions granted to the Mayor of Kingston-upon-Hull; the Customer and Comptroller of the Haven of Harwich; the port or haven of Weymouth; to administer an oath to all persons under the age of One-and-twenty who are desirous to pass the Seas from the said ports; also to HENRY, EARL OF NORTHAMPTON, to appoint Deputies to administer an oath to all persons of convenient age who pass the seas at the Cinque Ports. (4 Jac. I. p. 12.)

Proclamation licensing all manner of persons under the age of One-and-twenty years upon due examination of them to pass beyond the Seas. (Pat. 4 Jac. I. p. 12.)

10 April. Grant to Sir THOMAS GATES, Sir GEORGE SOMERS, Knts. and others, special license to make habitation and plantation, and to deduce a Colony of people into that part of America called Virginia. (Pat. 4 Jac. I. p. 19.)

Commission granted to THOMAS, LORD ELLESMERE, Lord Chancellor of England, to award Commissions to divers men for examination of all such persons as go out of the kingdom at any of the Ports of London, Harwich, Weymouth, and Kingston-upon-Hull. (Pat. 4 Jac. I. p. 24.)

20 July. Grant to THOMAS, LORD ELLESMERE, Lord Chancellor of England, of a special Warrant for licensing such as go beyond the Seas. (5 Jac. I. p. 22.)

29 July. Grant to HENRY, EARL OF NORTHAMPTON, of a special license to appoint deputies for ministering the oath of Allegiance to such as pass beyond the Seas. (5 Jac. I. p. 22.)

21 May. Grant to HENRY, EARL OF NORTHAMPTON, Commission special, by his Deputies, to examine all such as shall pass from the Cinque Ports beyond the Seas, &c. (6 Jac. I. p. 20.) Another of the 10th Oct. (same year), p. 30.

7 October. Grant to THOMAS, LORD ELLESMERE, Commission special, to seal several Commissions directed to several persons for the Port of London, licensing persons going beyond the Seas. (6 Jac. I. p. 30.)

1 May. Grant to Sir THOMAS CROMPTON, Sir THOMAS SMYTH, Knts., and others, Commission special, to minister an oath to all passengers that desire to pass over the Seas at the Port of London, and to examine them. (6 Jac. I. p. 37.)

23 May. Grant to ROBERT, EARL OF SALISBURY, THOMAS, EARL OF SUFFOLK, HENRY, EARL OF SOUTHAMPTON, WILLIAM, EARL OF PEMBROKE, and divers others, to plant and inhabit in Virginia, and to incorporate by the name of Treasurer and Company of Adventurers and Planters of the City of London, for the first Colony in Virginia. (7 Jac. I. p. 8.)

2 May. Grant of Incorporation, by the name of the Treasurer and Company of Adventurers and Planters of the City of London and Bristol, for the Colony and Plantation in Newfoundland. (8 Jac. I. p. 8.)

12 March. Grant to the Treasurer and Company of Adventurers and Planters of the City of London, for the first Colony in Virginia, all the Islands in any part of the Ocean, bordering upon the Coast of the Colony in Virginia, &c., to their heirs and successors; with full power for keeping a Lottery. (9 Jac. I. p. 14.)

28 August. Grant to ROBERT HARECOURT, Esq., Sir THOMAS CHALLONER, Knt., and JOHN ROVENSON, Esq., and to the heirs of the said ROBERT, all that part of Guiana or continent of America lying between the River of Amazons and the River of Dessequebe, et alia. (11 Jac. I. p. 9.)

9 Aug. Commission to EDWARD LORD ZOUCH, Lord Warden of the Cinque Ports, concerning the examining and licensing of passengers, with Instructions touching the same. (13 Jac. I. p. 16.)

29 June. Incorporation of the Governor and Society of the City of London, for planting of the Summer Islands, &c. (13 Jac. I. p. 19.)

3 November. The King grants, ordains, establishes and confirms that LODOWICK, DUKE OF LENOX, GEORGE, MARQUIS OF BUCKINGHAM, and divers others, be the first modern and present Council established at Plymouth in the county of Devon, for the plant-

ing, ruling and governing of New England in America, and that they shall elect and choose others to the number of forty persons, and no more, to be of that Council, and that they shall be incorporated by the name of the Council established at Plymouth for the governing of New England in America. (18 Jac. I. p. 16.)

24 January. Grant to FRANCIS, LORD VERULAM, Warrant special, to make out divers Commissions to such Justices, Officers and Ministers, and to such ports of this Realm as he shall think convenient, for the taking of an oath of all such as shall pass beyond the Seas. (The form of oath is recited in this patent.) (18 Jac. I. p. 16.)

31 Dec. Grant to Sir GEORGE CALVERT, Knt., of Newfoundland. (20 Jac. I. p. 14.) Similar grant made to the said Sir GEORGE CALVERT, on the 7th April. (21 Jac. I. p. 19).

Proclamation against irregular and disobedient persons and disorderly trading into New England, in America. (20 Jac. I. p. 16.)

Commission directed to the Supervisor General of the Customs in the port of London, to examine such persons as pass beyond the Seas, and to minister unto them an Oath. A similar Warrant granted to JOHN, Bishop of Lincoln. (21 Jac. I. p. 19, *in dorso*.)

Commission directed to Sir WILLIAM JONES, Sir NICHOLAS FORTESCUE, Knts., and others, to view, peruse and consider all Charters, Letters Patent, Proclamations and Commissions concerning the Colonies or Plantations in Virginia. (21 Jac. I. p. 19.)

Commission directed to HENRY, VISCOUNT MANDEVILLE, WILLIAM, LORD PAGET, and divers others, giving them power and authority to take into their considerations the state of the Colony and Plantation in Virginia, and to consider of all matters concerning the people's safety, their strength and government. (22 Jac. I. p. 1.)

20 December. Grant to GEORGE, DUKE OF BUCKINGHAM, Lord Warden of the Cinque Ports, Commission special, for him, or his deputies, to examine upon oath all passengers going beyond the Seas from those Ports, and to grant them licences; with instructions. (22 Jac. I. p. 14.)

26 August. Grant to Sir FRANCIS WYATT, Knt., FRANCIS WEST, Sir GEORGE YARDLEY, Knt., and others, Commission special, for the better government of the people in Virginia. (22 Jac. I. p. 17.)

18 September. Commission, appointing Sir GEORGE YARDLEY, Knt., Governor in Virginia. (22 Jac. I. p. 17.)

9 November. The King constitutes EDWARD DICHFEILD and others to be his officers to search and see that no Tobacco be brought

into this Kingdom from foreign parts, except from Virginia and the Summer Islands. (22 Jac. I. p. 4.)

Proclamation for the settling the Plantation of Virginia. (1 Chas. I. p. 4.)

13 September. Grant to THOMAS WARNER, and others, the Custody of the Islands of St. Christophers, the Barbadoes and "Moncerat" [Mountserrat] in the Continent of America. (1 Chas. I. p. 6.)

19 May. Grant to GEORGE, DUKE OF BUCKINGHAM, WILLIAM, EARL OF PEMBROKE, PHILLIP, EARL OF MONTGOMERY, JAMES, EARL OF CARLISLE, and divers others, that they shall be one body politic and corporate of themselves, by the name of Governor and Company of Noblemen and Gentlemen of England, for the Plantation of Guiana; and that they shall have perpetual succession. (3 Chas. I. p. 5.)

26 March. Grant to JOHN HARVEY, FRANCIS WEST, and divers others, Commission special, to be the present Governor and Council for the Colony and Plantation in Virginia. (3 Chas. I. p. 3.)

4 March. Grant to SAMUEL ALDERSEY, THOMAS ADAMS, and others, all that part of New England, in America, lying and extending between the bounds and limits in an Indenture expressed, with divers liberties, jurisdictions and royalties, to them and their heirs for ever.—(4 Chas. I. p. 11.)

20 September. Grant to GEORGE ARCHBISHOP OF CANTERBURY, and others, Commission special, to reprieve and stay from execution such persons as stand convicted, or hereafter shall be convicted, for small offences, who for strength of body or other ability shall be thought fit to be employed in foreign discoveries, or other services beyond the Seas. (4 Chas. I. p. 23.)

4 Feb. Grant to Sir WILLIAM ALEXANDER, Knt., and others of a Commission special, to make a voyage into the Gulf and River of Canada and the parts adjacent for the sole trade of Beaver Wools, Beaver Skins, Furs, Hides and Skins of Wild Beasts. (4 Chas. I. p. 34.)

25 May. Grant to PATRICK CRAFORD and MATHEW BYRKENHEAD, the office of clerks for the writing and entering of licences and passes granted by any Commissioners to persons going beyond the seas from the ports of Bristol, Beaumaris, Chester and Liverpool. (6 Chas. I. p. 5.)

19 Nov. Commission special directed to all Mayors, Recorders, Customers and other Officers within all port towns, ports and havens to examine and minister an oath to all passengers beyond the seas, except merchants and their factors. (6 Chas. I. p. 6, *in dorso.*)

4 December. Grant to ROBERT, LORD BROOKE, and others, to incorporate by the name of the Governor and Company of Adventurers of the City of Westminster, for the plantation of the Island of Providence, Henrietta, and the adjacent Islands lying upon the Coast of America. (6. Chas. I. p. 1.)

Proclamation forbidding the disorderly trading with the "Salvages" in New England in America, especially the furnishing of the Navies in those and other ports of America, by the English, with weapons and habiliments of war. (6 Chas. I. p. 11.)

19 Nov. Grant to EDWARD THOROWGOOD, the office of Clerk for writing of licences and passes to be granted by Commissioners to any person going out of this Realm, for 21 years. (6 Chas. I. p. 6.)

22 June. Grant to ROBERT, EARL OF WARWICK, and others, Governor and Company of Adventurers of the City of Westminster, for the plantation of the Islands of Providence, Henrietta, and the adjacent Islands, lying upon the coasts of America; all other Islands not formerly granted unto them, beginning at 6 degrees from the Equinoctial line towards the North, and extending from thence to 24 in Latitude towards the Tropic of Cancer, and between the degrees of 290 and 310 of Longitude, and Meridian distance through all the said Latitude, as the said degrees are in common computation reckoned and accompted in this Kingdom, to their heirs and successors. (7 Chas. I. p. 14.)

27 June. Grant to EDWARD, EARL OF DORSET, HENRY, EARL OF DEN-BIGH, and others, Commission special, to consider how the Virginia Plantation now standeth, and to consider what commodity may be raised in those parts. (7 Chas. I. p. 20.)

11 May. Grant to SIR WILLIAM ALEXANDER, and others, to collect Beaver Skins, &c., similar to the Grant made 4 Feb., 4 Chas. I. p. 34, (which see). (9 Chas. I. p. 7.)

23 September. Grant to THOMAS YOUNGE, gent., Commission special, to discover, find out, and search what parts are not yet inhabited in Virginia and America, and other parts thereunto adjoining. (9 Chas. I. p. 1.)

3 April. Grant to ROBERT, EARL OF WARWICK, HENRY, EARL OF HOLLAND, WILLIAM, LORD SAY AND SELE, ROBERT, LORD BROOKE, and others, Merchants Adventurers of the City of London, trading into the parts of America. (11 Chas. I. p. 8.)

Commission Special, directed to the Recorder of the City of London, SIR PAUL PYNDER, Kn^t, and others, for the taking of oaths of such persons as shall desire to go beyond the seas, and for the doing of many other things, such as in discretion shall seem meet to them. (11 Chas. I. p. 9.)

2 April. Grant to Sir JOHN HARVYE, Knt., Commission special, to be the present Governor of the Colony and Plantation in Virginia, with several powers and authorities therein mentioned. (12 Chas. I. p. 21, *in dorso.*)

10 April. Grant to WILLIAM, ARCHBP. OF CANTERBURY, THOMAS, LORD COVENTRY, Keeper of the Great Seal, and others, Commission special, for the government of all persons within the Colonies and Plantations beyond the seas, according to the Laws and Constitutions there; and to constitute Courts as well Ecclesiastical as Civil for the determining of Causes there. (12 Chas. I. p. 21, *in dorso.*)

10 May. Grant to THOMAS MAHEWE, the office of clerk of the passes and licences in the Outports, and the writing and registering of the same, and of the names of all those that shall go out of this Kingdom beyond the Seas, for 21 years in reversion. (12 Chas. I. p. 14.)

13 November. Grant to JAMES, MARQUIS OF HAMILTON, HENRY, EARL OF HOLLAND, and others, all that whole Continent, Island or Region commonly called Newfoundland, bordering upon the Continent of America, to them and their heirs. (13 Chas. I. p. 32.)

Proclamation against the disorderly transporting his Majesty's subjects to the plantations within the parts of America. (13 Chas. I. p. 15.)

11 January. Grant to Sir FRANCIS WYATT, Knt., Commission special, to be Governor of the Colony and plantation in Virginia during pleasure. (14 Chas. I. p. 29.)

29 March. Grant to RICHARD MORISON, Esq., the office of Captain or Keeper of the Castle of "Poynte Comfort," within the Lordship of Virginia, during pleasure, in reversion. (14 Chas. I. p. 38.)

Proclamation to restrain the transporting of passengers and provisions to New England without licence. (14 Chas. I. p. 6, *in dorso.*)

16 December. Grant to HENRY ASHTON, Esq., PETER HAY, Esq., and others, Commission special, to declare in his Majesty's name, in all public assemblies and places of the Islands and province of Barbadoes, against HENRY HAWLEY, to be Governor or Lieutenant General of the said Island; and to charge and require him and his Deputy or Agents, under his and their Allegiance, forthwith to yield up the said office and place of government, and all the incidents thereunto, unto HENRY HUNCKES, or to such person or persons as the EARL OF CARLISLE shall appoint. (15 Chas. I. p. 23, *in dorso.*)

3 April. Grant to Sir FERDINAND GORGES, Knt., all that part, purpart and portion of the main land or country, now commonly called or known by the name of New England in America, to him and to his heirs. (15 Chas. I. p. 25.)

6 August. ROGER WINGATE, Esq., appointed King's Treasurer within the Lordship of Virginia for life. (15 Chas. I. p. 23.)

Commission to JAMES, DUKE OF LENNOX, and others, for the tendering of an Oath to all persons that go beyond the seas, except women, and children, and sailors. (16 Chas. I. p. 13.)

9 August. Grant to Sir WILLIAM BERKELEY, Knt., and divers others, Commission special, to be the present Council of and for the colony and plantation in Virginia, and to perform and execute the places, powers, and authorities incident to a Governor there. (17 Chas. I. p. 6.)

31 July. Grant to Sir WILLIAM BERKELEY, Knt., and others, Commission special, to be present Governor and Council of and for the colony and plantation in Virginia, and for the managing of affairs there, during pleasure. (12 Chas. II. p. 26, *in dorso*.)

22 December. Grant to all Mayors, Recorders, Customers, Comptrollers, Surveyors, and Searchers in all ports of England and Wales, a special Commission to minister an Oath to all and every person or persons that shall be licensed to go beyond the seas. (12 Chas. II. p. 31, *in dorso*.)

2 August. FRANCIS CRADDOCK, Esq., appointed Provost Marshal General of the Barbadoes for life. (12 Chas. II. p. 32.)

17 August. JOHN DAWES appointed Secretary of the Islands of Barbadoes, and to the Governor and Council there: also clerk of the several Courts there, during life. (12 Chas. II. p. 23.)

8 January. THOMAS LINCH appointed Provost Marshal of Jamaica for life. (12 Chas. II. p. 30.)

22 September. Grant to THOMAS MAYHEW, Esq., of the office of clerk and clerkship of all Licences or passes in the Outports made, and to be made, to any person or persons, to go unto any foreign parts or places beyond the sea; and also the office of Register [Registrar] of the names of all the said persons for the term of 21 years in reversion. (12 Chas. II. p. 24.)

26 January. Confirmation of several Laws, concerning the people in Newfoundland, and upon the sea adjoining, and the bays, creeks and fresh rivers there. (12 Chas. II. p. 17.)

10 January. RICHARD POVEY appointed Secretary of and for Jamaica for life. (12 Chas. II. p. 30.)

12 September. Major JAMES RUSSELL appointed Governor of Nevis, during pleasure. (12 Chas. II. p. 35.)

21 November. Grant to FRANCIS, LORD WILLOUGHBY, all and singular prize ships, vessels, ordnance, furniture, ammunition, tackle and apparel, goods, chattels, merchandize, and lading whatsoever in the late Wars between this nation and the Dutch taken and seized at sea, in harbour, and at land, in or near the Islands of Barbadoes, St. Christophers, and other Islands in the parts of America, not sold or disposed of, accompted for, and discharged by sufficient discharges or acquaintances, or not pardoned, and discharged by his Majesty, or authority of Parliament, without any accompt whatsoever to be rendered or made for the same. (12 Chas. II. p. 27.)

13 March. ELIE ASHMOLE, Esq., appointed Secretary of Suranam [Surinam] and clerk of the King's Courts there. (13 Chas. II. p. 44.)

27 Sept. THOMAS BREEDON appointed Governor of Laccady and Nova Scotia, during life. (13 Chas. II. p. 16.)

13 May. Grant to JOHN, EARL OF BATH, of 200 acres of land in the parish of St. George, Barbadoes, to him and his heirs. (13 Chas. II. p. 40.)

8 February. Commission appointing EDWARD DOYLEY to be Governor of Jamaica, with instructions. (13 Chas. II. p. 4.)

1 February. JOHN MANNE, gent., appointed Chief Surveyor of Jamaica during pleasure. (13 Chas. II. p. 8.)

Proclamation for the encouraging of Planters in Jamaica. (13 Chas. II. p. 17, *in dorso.*)

2 August. THOMAS, LORD WINDSOR, appointed Governor of Jamaica. (13 Chas. II. p. 46.)

10 June. Revocation of Letters Patent appointing THOMAS BREEDON Governor of Laccady and Nova Scotia. (14 Chas. II. p. 6.)

15 March. Grant to WILLIAM DAVIDSON and others, licence special to dig for all mines of gold and other metals in Jamaica, for two years. (14 Chas. II. p. 11.)

17 Feb. JAMES, DUKE OF YORK, appointed High Admiral of Dunkirk, New England, Virginia, &c. (14 Chas. II. p. 12.)

23 April. Grant to the Governor, &c., of the English Colony of Connecticut in New England, of an Incorporation with divers privileges. (14 Chas. II. p. 11.)

7 Feb. Grant to the Company for propagating of the Gospel in New England, an Incorporation with divers privileges. (14 Chas. II. p. 11.)

ENTRIES RELATING TO AMERICA, &c.

17 July. THOMAS TEMPLE, Esq., appointed Governor of Laccady, and other the territories in America, for life. (14 Chas. II. p. 5.)

18 November. Grant to FRANCIS, LORD WILLOUGHBY, all those Islands called the Caribee Islands, containing in them the Islands of St. Christopher's alias St. Aristooall, Granado alias Greinada, St. Vincent, St. Lucy alias St. Lucre, Barbidas alias Barbadoes, Mittalania alias Martenico, Domenico, and others, to hold the same for 7 years. (14 Chas. II. p. 20.)

24 March. Grant to GEORGE, DUKE OF ALBEMARLE, ANTHONY, LORD ASHLEY, and others, all that territory or track [tract] of land called Carolina. (15 Chas. II. p. 2.)

17 July. Commission to THOMAS TEMPLE, Esq., to be Governor of several places in America. (15 Chas. II. p. 18.)

Grant to JOHN CLARKE and others, Inhabitants of New England, of divers liberties, &c. (15 Chas. II. p. 15.)

9 April. Grant to THOMAS ROSSE and others, the office of Receiver General, of all sums of money due and payable from the several plantations in Africa and America, for life. (15 Chas. II. p. 11.)

Grant to the Governor and Company of Rhode Island of divers privileges. (15 Chas. II. p. 15.)

2 June. Grant to FRANCIS, LORD WILLOUGHBY, and others, of the main tract of land, being part of the continent of Guiana in America, called Surinam. (15 Chas. II. p. 10.)

13 August. Grant to JOHN COLLINS, of a moiety of the profits of the Isle of Barbada, alias Barbuda [Barbadoes], reserved to the King for 7 years, and after the expiration of the said 7 years, then grants it to the said JOHN for 31 years. (16 Chas. II. p. 11.)

26 April. JAMES DREBBLE appointed Escheator of the Isles of Barbadoes and Caribee, for life. (16 Chas. II. p. 3.)

12 March. Grant to JAMES, DUKE OF YORK, and his heirs, all that part of the main land of New England, and several Islands adjacent. (16 Chas. II. p. 8.)

17 Feb. Grant to THOMAS ELLIOTT, of certain Copper Mines and other metals in Nova Scotia, for 31 years. (16 Chas. II. p. 17.)

29 May. Grant to Sir GEORGE CARTERET, Knt., and JOHN TRETHEWY, one annuity of 500*l.* per annum, to be paid out of one moiety of the profits arising out of the Caribee Islands, and due or payable to the Crown during the lives of WILLIAM LEY and JAMES CARTERETT. (17 Chas. II. p. 5.)

3 April. Declaration that the commodities of Jamaica shall pay no customs for the space of five years. (17 Chas. II. p. 3.)

20 December. Grant to Sir JAMES MODYFORD, Knt., licence to distinguish the Island of Providence alias St. Katherine, into counties, towns, manors, lordships and other privileges. (18 Chas. II. p. 4.)

4 February. WILLIAM WILLOUGHBY, Esq., appointed Captain General of the Caribee Islands for three years. (18 Chas. II. p. 4.)

19 March. EDWARD SCARBURGH appointed Surveyor General of Virginia during life. (19 Chas. II. p. 8.)

8 May. Grant to HENRY, EARL OF ST. ALBANS, JOHN, LORD BERKELEY, Sir WILLIAM MORETON, and JOHN TRETHEWEY, all that entire tract, territory, or parcel of land in America, and bounded by and within the head of the rivers Tappahanocke, alias Rappahanocke, and Quiriough or Patawomack rivers, to them and their heirs. (21 Chas. II. p. 4.)

1 November. Grant to CHRISTOPHER, DUKE OF ALBEMARLE, WILLIAM, EARL OF CRAVEN, JOHN, LORD BERKELEY, ANTHONY, LORD ASHLEY, Sir GEORGE CARTERET, Sir PETER COLLITON, &c., all those Islands called the Bahama Islands or the Islands of Lucayos, lying in the degrees of 22 to 27, and all ports, havens, creeks, &c., to their heirs and assigns. (22 Chas. II. p. 9.)

11 January. Grant to EDWARD, EARL OF SANDWICH, RICHARD, LORD GORGES, WILLIAM, LORD ALLINGTON, THOMAS GREY, and HENRY BLOUNCKER, Esquires, Sir HUMPHRY WINCH, Sir JOHN FINCH, and EDMOND WALLER, several yearly salaries, vizt: to the EARL OF SANDWICH, 700*l.* per annum, and to the rest (to each) 500*l.* per annum, they being of the Council for Foreign Plantations. (22 Chas. II. p. 8.)

6 August. Grant to FRANCIS RAYNES, all the lands and estates of one HENRY EDLYN, lying and being in the Island of Barbados, escheated to the Crown by his being executed for the murder of his wife. (22 Chas. II. p. 1.)

8 July. EDWYN STEED appointed Provost Marshal General of the Barbadoes, for life. (22 Chas. II. p. 1.)

9 Sept. Grant to JOHN STRODE to farm the Imposts upon the growth of the Leeward Islands, for 7 years. (22 Chas. II. p. 5.)

23 March. Sir ERNEST BRYAN, Knt., appointed Escheator in the Barbadoes and the Caribee Islands, for life. (23 Chas. II. p. 3.)

4 April. Commission for JAMES, DUKE OF YORK, and others, to be of the Council for Foreign Plantations. (23 Chas. II. p. 2.)

7 March. CHARLES WHEELER appointed Captain General of the Caribee Islands. (23 Chas. II. p. 2.)

19 June.	Commission appointing Sir RICHARD TEMPLE, Knt., to be of the Council of Foreign Plantations. (23 Chas. II. p. 2, *in dorso.*) Another Commission (same part) dated 15 Aug.
17 November.	ALEXANDER CULPEPER appointed Surveyor in Virginia, during pleasure. (23 Chas. II. p. 8.)
16 September.	ROBERT CLOWES appointed Chief Clerk to attend the Supreme Council in the town of St. Iago, in Jamaica, during life. (24 Chas. II. p. 3.)
27 September.	Commission granting to ANTHONY, EARL OF SHAFTESBURY, and others, a standing Council for Trade and Traffic both at home and for the Foreign Plantations. (24 Chas. II. p. 4.)
19 July.	Grant to WILLIAM, EARL OF KINNOUL, in consideration of a surrender by him made of his interest in the Caribee Islands, one annuity of 600*l.* per annum for five years, to be paid out of the four and a half per cent. Customs from those Islands, and after the expiration of five years the like annuity of 1000*l.* per annum to be paid for ever. (24 Chas. II. p. 1.)
10 February.	Revocation of the Grant formerly made to Sir CHARLES WHEELER, of the Government of the Leeward Islands. (24 Chas. II. p. 2.)
10 February.	WILLIAM STAPLETON appointed Governor of the Leeward Islands during pleasure. (24 Chas. II. p. 2.)
6 July.	WILLIAM, LORD WILLOUGHBY, appointed Captain General, and Governor in Chief, of the Barbadoes and Caribee Islands, during pleasure. (24 Chas. II. p. 2.)
13 April.	Grant to LEONARD COMPEARE and THOMAS MARTYN, Esq., the office of Receiver of the Duties upon all Wines, Brandies, &c., imported into Jamaica, for life. (26 Chas. II. p. 2.)
29 June.	Grant to JAMES, DUKE OF YORK, of several Islands and main land, near New England, particularly bounded, to him and his heirs, &c. (26 Chas. II. p. 5.)
28 March.	RICHARD MORLEY, Esq., appointed Secretary of Barbadoes, and Clerk of the Courts there, during life. (26 Chas. II. p. 2.)
8 July.	THOMAS, LORD CULPEPER, appointed Lieutenant and Governor General of Virginia, during life. (27 Chas. II. p. 7.)
18 March.	Grant to GEORGE GOSSELYNG, of all the lands, tenements, goods, and chattels of his brother JAMES GOSSELYNG, in the Island of Jamaica, forfeited by his being an alien. (27 Chas. II. p. 2.)
27 January.	The King declares and confirms several Laws concerning his people in Newfoundland, and upon the sea adjoining, &c. (27 Chas. II. p. 11.)

Proclamation to prohibit commodities into Foreign Plantations, but from England only. (27 Chas. II. p. 10.)

11 March. JOHN RICHARDS appointed Secretary of the Barbadoes, for life. (27 Chas. II. p. 2.)

25 June. ROBERT THORNTON, gent., appointed Provost Marshal of Jamaica, for life. (27 Chas. II. p. 7.)

3 September. HARBOTTLE WINGFIELD, gent., appointed Clerk of the Court of Common Pleas at Port Royal, Jamaica. (27 Chas. II. p. 3.)

27 January. RALPH WYATT appointed Clerk of the Market in Barbadoes, during pleasure. (27 Chas. II. p. 11.)

10 October. Commission granted to Sir WILLIAM BERKELEY, to pardon the Rebels in Virginia upon their submission. (28 Chas. II. p. 1.)

10 October. HERBERT JEFFERY, and others, Commissioners appointed to enquire and report the grievances of the Inhabitants of Virginia. (28 Chas. II. p. 1.)

10 October. Captain ROBERT WALTER, Commissioner, appointed Governor of Virginia, in the absence of HERBERT JEFFERY. (28 Chas. II. p. 1.)

9 October. HERBERT JEFFERY appointed Governor of Virginia in the place of Sir WILLIAM BERKELEY. (28 Chas. II. p. 1.)

11 November. Commission granted for HERBERT JEFFERYES to be Lieutenant Governor of Virginia. (28 Chas. II. p. 3.)

9 March. GARRETT COTTER appointed Secretary and Marshal of the Islands of Nevis, Teago, and Mountserrat, for three lives. (28 Chas. II. p. 5.)

10 October. Grant to the Governor and Council of Virginia; a special pardon for passing Acts of State to the Rebels. (28 Chas. II. p. 1.)

Same date and part, the King confirms and grants to the Inhabitants of Virginia, privileges, &c.

Commission to JOHN WILLOUGHBY, and others, to administer an oath to Sir JONATHAN ATKINS, appointed Captain General of the Caribee Islands; another, to RANDOLPH RUSSELL, and others, to administer an oath to WILLIAM STAPLETON, appointed Captain General of the Caribee Islands, lying leeward of Guadaloup, and for WILLIAM STAPLETON to administer an oath to the Deputy Governors of the same. (29 Chas. II. p. 10.)

27 April. CHARLES HERBERT appointed Chief Clerk in the town of St. Iago de la Vaga, in Jamaica. (29 Chas. II. p. 4.)

1 March. CHARLES, EARL OF CARLISLE, appointed Governor and Captain General of Jamaica. (30 Chas. II. p. 6.)

13 April. The King confirms divers Laws made in Jamaica. (30 Chas. II. p. 7.) The heads of the Bills are forty in number.

26 September. Grant to EDWARD RANDOLPH, Esq., and others, Commission to administer an oath to JOSIAS WINSLOW, Governor of New Plymouth; also to BENEDICT ARNOLD, Esq., Governor of Rhode Island and Providence Plantation; to JOHN LEVERETT, Esq., Governor of Massachusetts Bay; and to WILLIAM LEET, Esq., Governor of the Corporation of Connecticut. (30 Chas. II. p. 1.)

20 April. Indenture between the King and ROBERT SPENCER, JOHN STRODE, CHARLES TUCKER, and HENRY DANIEL, Esquires, as to the Imposts and Customs due to the King, of four and a half per cent. in the Islands of Barbadoes, Nevis, Antegua, Mountserrat, and St. Christopher's for seven years. (30 Chas. II. p. 4.)

21 June. JOHN BINDLOSS and SIMON WINSLOW appointed Chief Clerk, Register [Registrar], and Sole Examiner in the Court of Chancery in Barbadoes for their lives. (31 Chas. II. p. 5.)

6 December. THOMAS, LORD CULPEPER, appointed Lieutenant and Governor General of Virginia, for life. (31 Chas. II. p. 2.)

2 August. GARRETT COTTER appointed Secretary and Marshal of the Islands of Nevis, St. Christopher's, Antegua, and Mountserrat, for three lives. (31 Chas. II. p. 6.)

Commission to JOHN CUTTS, and others, for governing the Colony of New Hampshire, in America. (31 Chas. II. p. 6.)

8 May. CHARLES JONES appointed Postmaster and Register of the Admiralty in Barbadoes. (31 Chas. II. p. 5.)

5 April. THOMAS ROBSON appointed Clerk of the Market in Bridgtown, in Barbadoes, during pleasure. (31 Chas. II. p. 5.)

20 March. NICHOLAS SPENCER appointed Secretary in Virginia, during pleasure. (31 Chas. II. p. 6.)

8 December. Concerning Laws to be made in Virginia: the confirmation of Tithes, &c. (31 Chas. II. p. 2.)

24 February. JOHN BINDLOSSE appointed Clerk of the Markets in Jamaica. (32 Chas. II. p. 2.)

6 March. JOSEPH CRISPE appointed Escheator in the Leeward Islands. (32 Chas. II. p. 2.)

19 May. WILLIAM BLATHWAITE, Esq., appointed Surveyor and Auditor General of all the Revenues in America. (32 Chas. II. p. 2.)

28 October. RICHARD SUTTON appointed Governor of Barbadoes, &c. (32 Chas. II. p. 3.)

28 February. Grant made to WILLIAM PENN, Esq., of a tract of land,

with the Islands belonging to it, in America, bounded on the east by Delaware, &c. (33 Chas. II. p. 2.)

2 September. Sir THOMAS LYNCH appointed Governor of Jamaica. (33 Chas. II. p. 2.)

21 April. OBEDIAH CLAYTON and SAMUEL TRAVEL appointed Clerks of the Passes, for 21 years. (33 Chas. II. p. 3.)

9 May. EDWARD CRANFEILD, Esq., appointed Governor of New Hampshire. (34 Chas. II. p. 1.)

14 Nov. CORNWALL SOMERS, gent., appointed Postmaster in Barbadoes, vice CHARLES JONES, deceased. (34 Chas. II. p. 8.)

14 December. TIMOTHY THORNHILL, of Barbadoes, created a Baronet. (34 Chas. II. p. 9.)

22 March. The King doth give and grant to JAMES, DUKE OF YORK, his heirs and assigns, the town of Newcastle, alias Delaware, and fort thereunto belonging, situate between Maryland and New Jersey; and all that tract of land within the circle of twelve miles about the said town situate upon the river Delaware; and all Islands in the said river; and the said river and soil thereof, lying north of the said circle; and all that tract of land upon Delaware river, beginning 12 miles south from the said town of Newcastle, alias Delaware, and extending south to Cape Lopin. To be holden of the manor of East Greenwich, co. Kent, in free and common socage, and not in capite or by knight's service, yielding and rendering therefore every year four beaver skins, when the same shall be demanded, or within ninety days after such demand made—with several powers and authorities, amongst others to exercise Martial Law. (35 Chas. II. p. 1.)

23 Nov. GEORGE HANNAH, Esq., appointed Provost Marshal General of Barbadoes. (35 Chas. II. p. 2.)

28 Sept. FRANCIS, LORD HOWARD of Effingham, appointed Lieutenant and Governor General of Virginia, during pleasure. (35 Chas. II. p. 2.)

1 January. RICHARD CONY, Esq., appointed Lieutenant Governor and Commander in Chief of the Bermuda or Summer Islands, during pleasure, with power of constituting officers; the places of Sheriff, Provost Marshal, and Secretary of the said Islands always excepted. (36 Chas. II. p. 7.)

11 December. JOHN MOUNTSTEVEN, Esq., appointed Provost Marshal General of Jamaica, during pleasure; to execute by deputy, first approved by the Governor, or some of the Council there, for the time being. (36 Chas. II. p. 8.)

17 December. JOHN TUCKER, gent., appointed Provost Marshal General, or Sheriff, and Secretary of Bermuda, alias the Summer Islands, to exercise by himself or deputy, during pleasure. (36 Chas. II. p. 8.)

2 July. THOMAS ROBSON, gent., appointed Clerk of the Markets of St Michael's, alias Bridge Town, Spikes Town, and all the Towns in the Barbadoes. (1 Jac. II. p. 1.)

11 April. JOHN MOUNTSTEVENS, Esq., appointed Provost Marshal General of Jamaica. (1 Jac. II. p. 4.)

17 October. GEORGE HANNAY, Esq., appointed Provost Marshal General of Barbadoes. (1 Jac. II. p. 8.)

15 October. EDWARD RANDOLPH, Esq., appointed Collector, Surveyor, and Searcher of the Customs, within the colonies of New England, which office was erected the 15 Oct., 33 Chas. II., with a salary of 100*l*. per ann. (1 Jac. II. p. 8.)

8 October. The King doth erect, constitute, and appoint a President and Council to take care of the territory and dominion of New England, commonly called Massachusetts Bay; and appoints JOSEPH DUDLEY, Esq., to be the first president. (1 Jac. II. p. 8.)

28 October. FRANCIS, LORD HOWARD, of Effingham, appointed Lieutenant and Governor General of Virginia. (1 Jac. II. p. 8.)

21 October. NICHOLAS SPENCER, Esq., appointed Secretary in Virginia. (1 Jac. II. p. 9.)

21 October. ALEXANDER CULPEPER, Esq., appointed Surveyor General in Virginia. (1 Jac. II. p. 9.)

17 October. REGINALD WILSON, of Jamaica, gent., appointed Clerk of the Naval or Navy Office in Jamaica. (1 Jac. II. p. 9.)

28 October. Sir PHILIP HOWARD, Knt., appointed Captain General and Governor in Chief, in and over Jamaica, and the other territories depending thereon. (1 Jac. II. p. 10.)

5 December. Grant to HUGH NODEN, Merchant Taylor of London, of five shares of land, with the edifices thereupon, situate in the Summer Islands alias Bermuda, to him and his heirs for ever. To be held in free and common socage, by fealty only. (1 Jac. II. p. 10.)

8 January. ARCHIBALD CARMICHAEL appointed Clerk of the Navy in Barbadoes. (2 Jac. II. p. 2.)

30 April. RICHARD CONY, Esq., is constituted Lieutenant Governor and Commander in Chief of Bermuda or Summer Island: a Quo Warranto being issued, and Judgment thereon entered against the Bermuda Company. (2 Jac. II. p. 6, *in dorso*.)

9 June. Grant to Colonel JOHN LEGG, CHRISTOPHER GUISE, and JOHN ROBINS, (upon the surrender of ROGER WHALEY,) the office of Master or Registrar, for the taking cognizance of the free consents of such persons as shall go into the plantations in America or elsewhere. (2 Jac. II. p. 7.)

29 June. JOHN TUCKER appointed Secretary and Provost Marshal General of the Bermuda or Summer Islands. (2 Jac. II. p. 9.)

3 June. Sir EDMUND ANDROS appointed Governor of New England. (2 Jac. II. p. 9.)

10 June. THOMAS DUNGAN, Esq., appointed Governor of New York. (2 Jac. II. p. 9.)

9 Sept. THOMAS MONTGOMERY appointed Attorney General of Barbadoes. (2 Jac. II. p. 10.)

9 Sept. Sir ROBERT ROBINSON appointed Governor of Bermuda. (2 Jac. II. p. 10, *in dorso*.)

28 Sept. Sir NATHANIEL JOHNSON to be Governor in and over the Islands of Nevis, &c., known by the name of the Caribee Islands. (2 Jac. II. p. 10, *in dorso*.)

25 Nov. Commission for the DUKE OF ALBEMARLE to be Governor of Jamaica. (2 Jac. II. p. 11.)

28 Dec. WILLIAM TYACK, gent., appointed Escheator of the Leeward Islands. (2 Jac. II. p. 12.)

4 March. Grant to CHRISTOPHER, DUKE OF ALBEMARLE, of all Wrecks of plate, gold, silver, &c., on the north side of Hispaniola, or about the Islands of Bahama and Florida. (3 Jac. II. p. 1.)

2 March. Grant to CHRISTOPHER, DUKE OF ALBEMARLE, of all Mines of Gold, &c., in the Colonies of America. (3 Jac. II. p. 2.)

12 August. Ratification of the Letters Patent made to the DUKE OF ALBEMARLE on the 4th March. (3 Jac. II. p. 7.)

23 August. Grant to the DUKE OF ALBEMARLE, the sole use of saw mills in the plantations of America, (New England excepted), for the term of 14 years. (3 Jac. II. p. 8.)

13 August. The King erects the office of Provost Marshal General of New England, and grants the same to Sir WILLIAM PHIPPS. (3 Jac. II. p. 8.)

12 November. HENRY HORDESNELL, Esq., appointed Justice, or Chief Judge of the Bermuda or Summer Islands. (3 Jac. II. p. 9.)

January 20. Proclamation for the more effectual reducing and suppressing pirates or privateers in America. (3 Jac. II. p. 9.)

4 November. MATHEW PLOWMAN appointed Collector and Receiver of New York, with a salary of 200*l.* per annum, vice LUCAS SANTEN. (3 Jac. II. p. 10.)

20 October. Grant to the EARL OF FEVERSHAM, of all Wrecks, &c., on the north side of the main land of America. (3 Jac. II. p. 10.)

28 February. Grant to ROBERT BRENT, all Wrecks, &c., in or upon any of the rocks, shelves, seas, or banks, on or near the coast of America, between the Bermudas and Porto Rico, or between Cartagena and the Havanna. (4 Jac. II. p. 3.)

5 May. The King authorises the DUKE OF ALBEMARLE, (during his being Governor of Jamaica), to confer knighthood upon any six deserving persons, according to his own discretion, in that Island. (4 Jac. II. p. 4.)

20 April. The King erects and establishes the office of Secretary and sole Register [Registrar] in New England, and grant the said office to EDWARD RANDOLPH, Esq. (4 Jac. II. p. 4.)

27 September. The King confirms to THOMAS, LORD CULPEPER, an entire tract of land in Virginia, bounded within the springs of the rivers of Tapphannock and Quiriough, to him, his heirs and assigns for ever—yielding and paying therefore, 6*l.* 13*s.* 4*d.* (4 Jac. II. p. 7.)

5 September. Grant to JOHN, EARL OF BATH, ANTHONY, LORD FALKLAND, and others, the use of the ship *Forsight*, to take up and recover Gold near Hispaniola. (4 Jac. II. p. 7.)

25 September. HENRY FIFIELD, gent., appointed Secretary and Provost Marshal General of the Summer Islands, alias the Bermudas. (4 Jac. II. p. 8.)

7 April. Sir EDMUND ANDROS appointed Captain General and Governor over the Massachusetts Bay, &c. (Pennsylvania and the county of Delaware only excepted, vide Pat. 3 June, 2 Jac. II.) (4 Jac. II. p. 8.)

6 April. Major HENRY CARRE appointed Provost Marshal General of Jamaica. (1 Will. & Mary, p. 1.)

19 July. HENDER MOLESWORTH, of Jamaica, Esq., created a Baronet. (1 Will. & Mary, p. 2.)

8 August. ARCHIBALD CARMICHAELL appointed Clerk of the Navy in the Barbadoes. (1 Will. & Mary, p. 4.)

25 July. Sir HENDER MOLESWORTH appointed Captain General of Jamaica. (1 Will. & Mary, p. 4.)

3 August. JAMES KENDALL, Esq., appointed Captain General of Barbadoes, St. Lucca, &c. (1 Will. & Mary, p. 4.)

14 September. CHIDLEY BROOKE appointed Collector and Receiver of New York. (1 Will. & Mary, p. 5.)

8 August. REGINALD WILSON appointed Clerk of the Navy in Jamaica. (1 Will. & Mary, p. 5.)

3 October. Grant to JAMES KENDALL, (who was made Governor of Barbadoes on the 3d of August last), a salary of 1200*l.* a year. (1 Will. & Mary, p. 6.)

3 October. Grant of a large Commission to JAMES KENDALL, lately made Governor of Barbadoes. (1 Will. & Mary, p. 6.)

26 October. CHRISTOPHER CODRINGTON, Esq., appointed Governor of the Islands of Nevis, &c. (1 Will. & Mary, p. 6.)

15 November. HENRY FIFEILD* appointed Secretary and Provost Marshal of Bermuda. (1 Will. & Mary, p. 7.)

8 November. ISAAC RICHIER appointed Governor of Bermuda, &c. (1 Will. & Mary, p. 7.)

23 December. WILLIAM, EARL OF INCHIQUIN, Lieutenant General of Jamaica, appointed Vice Admiral of the said Island. (1 Will. & Mary, p. 8.)

12 December. RICHARD LLOYD appointed Clerk of the Crown in Jamaica. (1 Will. & Mary, p. 8.)

6 November. The King erects an office to be called the Secretary of New York, and appoints MATHEW CLARKSON to the same. (1 Will. & Mary, p. 8.)

25 November. JOHN STEDE appointed Clerk of the Markets of St. Michael, alias Bridge-town, &c., in Barbadoes. (1 Will. & Mary, p. 8.)

4 January. HENRY SLATER appointed Governor of New York. (1 Will. & Mary, p. 8.)

7 October. WILLIAM, EARL OF INCHIQUIN, appointed Lieutenant or Governor General of Jamaica. (1 Will. & Mary, p. 8.)

13 December. THOMAS FERNELEY, Esq., appointed Secretary of the Islands of St. Christopher's, &c. (1 Will. & Mary, p. 9.)

12 December. EPAPHRODITUS HOUGHTON appointed Provost Marshal General of the Islands of St. Christopher's. (1 Will. & Mary, p. 9.)

17 January. Colonel WILLIAM COLE appointed Secretary in Virginia. (1 Will. & Mary, p. 9.)

31 December. CHRISTOPHER CODRINGTON, Captain General of Nevis, appointed Vice Admiral of the said Island. (1 Will. & Mary, p. 9.)

---

* [See 25 Sept., 4 Jac. II.]

25 February. GEORGE HANWAY appointed Provost Marshal General of Barbadoes. (2 Will. & Mary, p. 2.)

5 November. FRANCIS, LORD HOWARD of Effingham, appointed Governor General of Virginia. (2 Will. & Mary, p. 5.)

4 December. JOSEPH BATHURST and RICHARD DODINGTON, appointed Clerk of the Court of Common Pleas of Jamaica. (2 Will. & Mary, p. 6.)

25 November. Grant to THOMAS NEALE, Esq., of all Wrecks, &c., within twenty leagues of the Bermudas. (2 Will. & Mary, p. 6.)

27 June. LIONEL COPLEY, Esq., appointed Governor of Maryland. (3 Will. & Mary, p. 2.)

4 June. ROWLAND WILLIAMS, Esq., appointed Clerk of the Navy of the Leeward Caribee Islands. (3 Will. & Mary, p. 3.)

5 September. Sir THOMAS LAWRANCE appointed Secretary of Maryland. (3 Will. & Mary, p. 6.)

7 October. The King incorporates the inhabitants of Massachusetts Bay in New England, &c. (3 Will. & Mary, p. 7.)

1 October. THOMAS BELCHAMBER appointed Provost Marshal General of the Islands of St. Christophers, &c., vice EPAPHRODITUS HAUGHTON. (3 Will. & Mary, p. 7.)

30 November. JAMES VERNON, Esq., appointed Chief Clerk of St. Iago de la Vaga, Jamaica. (3 Will. & Mary, p. 8.)

11 January. JOHN PALMER, Esq., appointed Secretary of St. Christophers, &c. (3 Will. & Mary, p. 9.)

12 December. Sir WILLIAM PHIPPS appointed Captain of Massachusetts Bay. (3 Will. & Mary, p. 9.)

1 March. Sir EDMOND ANDROS appointed Lieutenant and Governor General of Virginia. (4 Will. & Mary, p. 1.)

18 March. BENJAMIN FLETCHER appointed Captain General and Governor of New York. (4 Will. & Mary, p. 2.)

1 March. SAMUEL ALLEN, Esq., appointed Governor of New Hampshire. (4 Will. & Mary, p. 2.)

5 July. Grant to THOMAS NEALE of all Wrecks, &c., on the Coast of Bermudas, or within 20 Leagues. (4 Will. & Mary, p. 5.)

16 July. Grant to THOMAS NEALE, of all Treasure Trove in the little Island called Ireland, near the Bermudas. (4 Will. & Mary, p. 5.)

20 September. WILLIAM BRODRICKE appointed Attorney General in Jamaica. (4 Will. & Mary, p. 6.)

20 September. WILLIAM BEESTON, Esq., appointed Governor of Jamaica. (4 Will. & Mary, p. 6.)

22 August. Grant to THOMAS NEALE of all mines of gold within their Majesties' plantations in America, for 51 years; yielding and paying a sixth part. (4 Will. & Mary, p. 6.)

19 August. The King and Queen, in consideration of 400*l.*, do give unto THOMAS NEALE, Esq., all Wrecks, &c., between Cartagena and Jamaica; and between either of those two places and the Havanna. (4 Will. & Mary, p. 6.)

16 January. CHRISTOPHER ROBINSON, Esq., appointed Secretary in Virginia. (4 Will. & Mary, p. 8.)

8 February. Licence granted to found a College in the West part of Virginia. (4 Will. & Mary, p. 9.)

21 October. BENJAMIN FLETCHER (lately made Governor of New York), appointed Governor of Pennsylvania. (6 Will. & Mary, p. 10.)

1 March. JOHN GODDARD, Esq., appointed Governor and Commander of the Bermuda or Summer Islands. (5 Will. & Mary, p. 1.)

20 February. The King pardons GEERRARD BEECKMAN, MYNDERT COARTEN, THOMAS WILLIAMS, JOHN VERNNILLIE, ABRAHAM BRASIER, and ABRAHAM GOVERNEUR, all of New York; all treasons and murders for the death of JOSIAH BROWN, of New York (is particularly mentioned). (5 Will. & Mary, p. 1.)

10 March. Grant to MAINHARDT, DUKE OF LEINSTER, of all Wrecks, &c., &c., between the Latitudes of 12 Degrees South and 40 Degrees North, by him to be recovered at any time within 20 years after the date hereof, (the Bermudas, Cartagena, and Jamaica excepted) for several terms of years, one full tenth of the premises reserved to the King and Queen. (5 Will. & Mary, p. 1.)

10 February. FRANCIS NICHOLSON, Esq., appointed Captain General and Governor of Maryland. (5 Will. & Mary, p. 2.)

27 January. WILLIAM BARNES, Esq., appointed Provost Marshal General of the Islands of St. Christopher's, Nevis, Mountserrat and Antegua, during pleasure. (5 Will. & Mary, p. 2.)

25 April. Grant to THOMAS NEALE, Esq., and JOHN TYZACKE, gent., all Wrecks, &c., &c., within 30 Leagues of the Isle of Stables, and betwixt 40 and 50 Degrees of North Latitude, to be gotten and recovered by them within seven years after the date hereof. (5 Will. & Mary, p. 3.)

15 April. Grant to the Widows and Children of JACOB LEISLER and JACOB MILBURNE, of New York, all the real and personal estates of the said LEISLER and MILBURNE, executed for

treason or supposed treason, in the Colony of New York. (5 Will. & Mary, p. 4.)

13 December. Grant to Sir JOHN HOSKYNS, of Harewood, co. Hereford, Knt. & Bart., all those Islands called Ascension, Trinidad, and Martin Vaz, to him, his heirs and assigns, for ever—yielding and paying the fourth part of the profits of all mines of gold and silver wrought in the said Islands on the 5th Nov. yearly. To be holden of the manor of East Greenwich, in socage, and not in capite, nor by knights service. (5 Will. & Mary, p. 5.)

26 December. FRANCIS RUSSELL, Esq., appointed Captain General and Governor in Chief of the Islands of Barbadoes, Sta. Lucia, Dominico, St. Vincent's, &c., commonly called the Caribee Islands, lying and being to windward from Guadaloupe. (5 Will. & Mary, p. 5.)

26 June. Colonel RALPH WORMLEY appointed Secretary of Virginia, (vice CHRISTOPHER ROBINSON, Esq., deceased,) to hold the same by himself or deputy, during pleasure. (5 Will. & Mary, p. 6.)

10 June. BENJAMIN FLETCHER, Esq., Governor of New York and Pennsylvania, to be Commander of the Militia of Connecticutt. (5 Will. & Mary, p. 7, *in dorso*.)

8 March. EDWARD CRANFEILD, Esq., appointed Clerk of the Navy in Barbadoes, vice ARCHIBALD CARMICHAEL, Esq., deceased, during pleasure. (6 Will. & Mary, p. 1.)

17 January. Revocation of the appointment of GEORGE HANNAH to the office of Provost Marshal of Barbadoes, and appoints JAMES HANNAH, Esq., to the said office. (7 Will. III. p. 4.)

16 April. JOHN PERRIE, Esq., appointed Provost Marshal General of the Islands of St. Christopher's, Nevis, Mountserrat, and Antegua, during pleasure, vice WILLIAM BARNES, Esq., deceased. (8 Will. III. p. 4.)

1 May. WILLIAM BRODERICK, Esq., appointed Attorney General of Jamaica. (8 Will. III. p. 6.)

26 June. WILLIAM PARTRIDGE, Esq., appointed Lieutenant Governor of New Hampshire, during pleasure. (8 Will. III. p. 8.)

4 January. SAMUEL DAY, Esq., appointed Lieutenant Governor and Commander in Chief of the Bermudas or Summer Islands. (9 Will. III. p. 3.)

22 February. EDWARD PARSONS, Esq., appointed Secretary of St. Christopher's, Nevis, Mountserrat, and Antegua, and other Leeward Caribee Islands, during pleasure. (9 Will. III. p. 4.)

18 June. RICHARD, EARL of BELLOMONT, appointed Captain General and Governor in Chief of Massachusetts Bay; also Governor and Commander in Chief of all that province of New Hampshire within New England, extending from three miles northward of Merrimac River unto the province of Main. (9 Will. III. p. 6, *in dorso.*)

18 June. RICHARD, EARL OF BELLOMONT, appointed Captain General and Governor in Chief of New York, (9 Will. III. p. 7.)

24 July. RALPH GREY, Esq., appointed Captain General and Governor in Chief of the Islands of Barbadoes, Sta. Lucia, Dominico, St. Vincent's, &c., and the rest of the Islands, &c., commonly called the Caribee Islands. (9 Will. III. p. 7.)

17 July. JOHN BABER, Esq., appointed Secretary of Jamaica, and Commissary of the Stores and Clerk of the Enrolment of Deeds, &c., during pleasure. (9 Will. III. p. 7.)

18 August. The King releaseth unto Sir WILLIAM BEESTON, Knt., Lieutenant Governor of Jamaica, all offences and neglects committed for his not taking the oaths, appointed to be taken by the Governors of Colonies in Asia, Africa, or America. (10 Will. III. p. 5.)

12 August. GEORGE GOLDING, Esq., appointed Provost Marshal General of Jamaica, during pleasure. (10 Will. III. p. 7.)

20 July. FRANCIS NICHOLSON, Esq., appointed Lieutenant and Governor General of Virginia. (He succeeded Sir EDWARD ANDROS, Knt., who obtained leave to return home for the recovery of his health.) (10 Will. III. p. 8.)

19 October. NATHANIEL BLAKESTON, Esq., appointed Captain General and Governor in Chief of Maryland. (10 Will. III. p. 9.)

20 September. THOMAS LAWRENCE, Esq., appointed Secretary of Maryland, during pleasure. (Letters Patent appointing Sir THOMAS LAWRENCE, Bart., of the 5th Sept., 3 Will. & Mary, are revoked.) (10 Will. III. p. 10.)

6 May. WILLIAM NEEDHAM, gent., appointed Clerk of the Crown and Clerk of the Peace of Jamaica, during pleasure. (11 Will. III. p. 1.)

25 March. WILLIAM WELBY, Esq., appointed Secretary of Barbadoes, during pleasure. (11 Will. III. p. 1.)

7 June. EDWARD JONES, gent., appointed Secretary and Provost Marshal General of the Bermudas, alias Summer Islands. (11 Will. III. p. 2.)

ENTRIES RELATING TO AMERICA, &c.

18 May. EDWARD CHILTON, of the Middle Temple, Barrister, appointed Attorney General of Barbadoes. (11 Will. III. p. 2.)

5 January. Sir WILLIAM BEESTON appointed Captain General and Governor in Chief of Jamaica, during pleasure. (11 Will. III. p. 4.)

17 March. ALLEN BRODERICK, Esq., appointed Attorney General of Jamaica, during pleasure. (11 Will. III. p. 5.)

29 August. ALEXANDER SKENE appointed Secretary of, and Clerk of the several Courts in Barbadoes, during pleasure. (11 Will. III. p. 6.)

13 May. CHRISTOPHER CODRINGTON, Esq., appointed Captain General and Governor in Chief over the Islands of Nevis, St. Christopher's, Mountserrat, Antegua, Barbadoes, Anquilla, &c. (11 Will. III. p. 6, *in dorso*.)

23 Nov. RALPH GREY, Esq., and others, appointed Commissioners at Barbadoes, Sta. Lucia, Dominico, St. Vincent's, &c., for examining of Piracies. Similar Commissions to STAFFORD FAIRBORE, and others, for Newfoundland; to BENJAMIN BENNET, Esq., and others, for the Bermudas or Summer Islands; to NATHAN BLACKSTON, Esq., for Maryland and Pennsylvania; to CHRISTOPHER CODRINGTON, Esq., for St. Christopher's, Mountserrat, Antigua, Barbouda, [Barbadoes] Anguilla, &c., commonly called the Caribee Islands; to FRANCIS NICHOLSON, Esq., for Virginia and Carolina; and to RICHARD, EARL OF BELLOMONT, for Massachusetts Bay, New Hampshire, and Rhode Island. (12 Will. III. p. 1.)

13 December. SAMUEL COX, Esq., appointed Clerk of the Navy Office in Barbadoes, during pleasure. (12 Will. III. p. 1.)

23 November. RICHARD, EARL OF BELLOMONT, and others, appointed Commissioners for examining of Piracies at New York, East and West, New Jersey, and Connecticut; also to Sir WILLIAM BEESTON, Knt., for Jamaica and the Bahama Islands. (12 Will. III. p. 1, *in dorso*.)

24 September. BENJAMIN BENNETT, Esq., appointed Lieutenant Governor and Commander in Chief of the Bermuda or Summer Islands, during pleasure. (12 Will. III. p. 2.)

4 March. THOMAS WEAVOR, Esq., appointed Collector and Receiver of New York (during pleasure), with a salary of 200*l.*, vice CHIDLEY BROOK, who was appointed 14 Dec., 1 Will. & Mary. (12 Will. III. p. 4.)

11 July. Sir THOMAS LAWRENCE, Bart., appointed Secretary of Maryland, during pleasure. (13 Will. III. p. 1.)

31 July. WILLIAM SELWYN, Esq., appointed Captain General and Commander in Chief of Jamaica, during pleasure. (13 Will. III. p. 1, *in dorso*.)

9 September. EDWARD HYDE, Esq., commonly called LORD CORNBURY, appointed Captain General and Governor in Chief of New York, during pleasure. (13 Will. III. p. 2.)

27 November. HENRY CARPENTER, Esq., appointed Secretary of the Islands of St. Christopher's, Nevis, Mountserrat, and Antegua, and other the Leeward and Caribee Islands, during pleasure, &c. (13 Will. III. p. 3.)

13 February. MITFORD CROWE, Esq., appointed Captain General and Governor in Chief over the Islands of Barbadoes, Sta. Lucia, Dominico, St. Vincent, &c. (14 Will. III. p. 1.)

13 February. JOSEPH DUDLEY, Esq., appointed Captain General and Governor in Chief of Massachusetts Bay, (14 Will. III. p. 1); also Governor and Commander in Chief of New Hampshire, during pleasure. (14 Will. III. p. 1, *in dorso*.)

Lists of the Livinge and Dead in Virginia Febr: 16th 1623.*

---

* [*i. e.* 162¾.]

A List of Names; of the Living in Virginia
february the 16 1623

Att yͤ Colledg Land.

THOMAS MARLETT
CHRISTOPHER BRANCH
FRANCIS BOOT.
WILLIAM BROWĪNG [BROWNING]
WALTER COOp [COOPER]
WILLIAM WELDER
LEONARD MORE
DANIELL SHURLEY
PEETER JORDEN
NICHOLAS PERSE
WILLIAM DALBIE
ESAIAS RAWTON
THEODER MOISES
ROBERT CHAMPER
THOMAS JONES
DAVID WILLIAMS
WILLIAM WALKER
EDWARD HOBSON
THOMAS HOBSON
JOHN DAY
WILLIAM COOKSEY
ROBERT FARNELL
NICHOLAS CHAPMAN
MATHEW EDLOW
WILLIAM PRICE
GABRIELL HOLLAND
JOHN WATTSON
EBEDMELECH GASTRELL
THOMAS OSBORNE

Att yͤ Neck of Land.

LUKE BOYS
Mͬˢ BOYS
ROBERT HALAM
JOSEPH ROYALL
JOHN DOD'S
Mͬˢ DOD'S
ELIZABETH PERKINSON
WILLIAM VINCENT
Mͬˢ VINCENT

THE LIVING IN VIRGINIA.

Living

ALLEXANDER BRADWAYE
his wife BRADWAYE
JOHN PRICE
his wife PRICE
ROBERT TURNER
NATHANIELL REEUE* [REEVE]
Seriant Wᴹ SHARP
Mʳˢ SHARP.
RICHARD RAWSE
THOMAS SHEPPY
WILLIAM CLEMENS
THOMAS HARRIS
his Wife HARRIS
ANN WOODLEY
MARGRETT BERMAN
THOMAS FARMER
HUGH HILTON
RICHARD TAYLOR
vx. TAYLOR
JOSUA CHARD
CHRISTOPHER BROWNE
THOMAS OAGE
Vx: OAGE
infans OAGE
HENRY COLTMAN
HUGH PRICE
Vx PRICE
infans PRICE
Mʳˢ COLTMAN
ROBERT GREENE
vx. GREENE
infans GREENE.

Living

Att West and Sherlow hundred
JOHN HARRIS
DORITHE HARRIS
infants { HARRIS
           { HARRIS
THOMAS FLOYD
ELLIAS LONGE
WILLIAM NICHOLLAS
ROGER RATCLIFE
ROBERT MILNER
ROBERT PARTTIN
MARGRETT PARTTIN
infantes { PARTTIN
           { PARTTIN
HENRY BENSON
NICHOLAS BLACKMAN
NATHANELL TATTAM
MATHEW GLOSTER
SYMON TURGIS
NICHOLAS BALEY
ANN BAYLEY
ELMER PHILLIPS
THOMAS PAULETT
THOMAS BAUGH.
THOMAS PACKER
JONAS RAYLEY
JOHN TRUSSELL
CHRISTOPHER BEANE
JOHN CARTTER
HENRY BAGWELL
THOMAS BAGWELL
EDWARD GARDINER
RICHARD BIGGS

---

* [Might possibly be read as REENE.]

THE LIVING IN VIRGINIA.

Living

Mrs BIGGS
WILLIAM BIGGS ⎫
THOMAS BIGGS. ⎬ fit
RICHARD BIGGS ⎭
WILLIAM ASKEW
HENRY CARMAN
ANDREW DUDLEY
JAMES GAY
ANTHONY BURROWS
REBECCA ROSSE
fil: { ROSSE
{ ROSSE
PETTERS, a maid.

At Jordans Jorney
SISLYE JORDAN
TEMPERANCE BAYLIFE
MARY JORDAN
MARGERY JORDAN
WILLIAM FARRAR
THOMAS WILLIAMS
ROGER PRESTON
THOMAS BROOKES
JOHN PEEDE
JOHN FREME
RICHARD JOHNSON
WILLIAM DAWSON
JOHN HELY
ROBERT MANUELL [*or* MANNELL]
ANN LINKON
WILLIAM BASSE
Mrs BASSE
CHRISTOPHER SAFORD
vx SAFORD
JOHN CAMINGE
THOMAS PALMER

Living

Mrs PALMER
filia PALMER
RICHARD ENGLISH
NATHANIEL CAUSEY
Mrs CAUSEY
LAWRANCE EVANS
EDWARD CLARKE
vx CLARKE
infans CLARKE
JOHN GIBBS
JOHN DAVIES
WILLIAM EMERSON
HENRY WILLIAMS
vx WILLIAMS
HENRY FISHER
vx FISHER
infans FISHER
THOMAS CHAPMAN
vx CHAPMAN
infans CHAPMAN
EDITH HOLLIS

At flourdien hundred
RICHARD GREGORY
EDWARD ALBORN
THOMAS DILLIMAGER
THOMAS HACH
ANTHONY JONES
ROBERT GUY
WILLIAM STRACHEY
JOHN BROWNE
ANNIS BOULT
WILLIAM BAKER
THEODER BERISTON
WALTER BLAKE
THOMAS WATTS

THE LIVING IN VIRGINIA.

Living

THOMAS DOUGHTY
GEORGE DEVERELL
RICHARD SPURLING
JOHN WOODSON
WILLIAM STRAUNGE*
THOMAS DUNE
JOHN LANDMAN
LEONARD YEATS
GEORGE LEVET
THOMAS HAWAY
THOMAS FILENST
ROBERT SMITH
THOMAS GRINDER
THOMAS GASKO
JOHN OLIUES [OLIVES]
CHRISTOPHER PUGETT
ROBERT PEAKE
EDWARD TRAMORDEN
HENRY LINGE
GIBERT PEPPET
THOMAS MIMES
JOHN LINGE
JOHN GALE
THOMAS BARNETT
ROGER TOMPSON
ANN TOMPSON
ANN DOUGHTY
SARA WOODSON
— ⎫
— ⎪
— ⎬ vj ⎧ Negors
— ⎪   Negors
— ⎭   Negors
              Negors
              Negors
              Negors

Living

GRIVELL POOLEY minster

SAMUELL SHARP
JOHN VPTON
JOHN WILSON
HENRY ROWNIGE [*or* ROWINGE]
NATHANIELL THOMAS
WILLIAM BARRETT
ROBERT OKLEY
RICHARD BRADSHAW
THOMAS SAWELL
JOHN BAMFORD
ANTHONY ⎫
WILLIAM ⎬ Negors men
JOHN   ⎪
ANTHONY ⎭
an Negors woman

the rest at West and Sherlow hundred Iland

CAP: ISACKE MADDESON
MARY MADDESON
THOMAS WATTSON
JAMES WATTSON
FRANCIS WEST
ROGER LEWIS
RICHARD DOMELOW
WILLIAN HATFEILD
THOMAS FOSSETT
ANN FOSSETT
JENKIN OSBORNE
WILLIAM SISMORE
MARTHA SISMORE
STEPHEN BRABY
ELIZABETH BRABY

* [I believe this is correct; but the third letter is blotted in the original; and there is, besides, a dot near the end of the word, which makes it possible to read it as STRAMIGE.]

Living
EDWARD TEMPLE
DANIELL VERGO
WILLIAM TATHILL boy
THOMAS HAILE boy
RICHARD MOREWOOD
EDWARD SPARSHOTT
BARNARD JACKSON
WILLIAM BROCKE
JAMES MAYRQ

At Chaplains choise
ISACKE CHAPLAINE
Mrs CHAPLAINE
JOHN CHAPLAINE
WALTER PRIEST
WILLIAM WESTON
JOHN DUFFY
ANN MICHAELL
THOMAS PHILLIPS
HENRY THORNE
ROBERT HUDSON
ISACKE BANGTON [or BAUGTON]
NICHOLAS SUTTON
WILLIAM WHITT
EDWARD BUTTLER
HENRY TURNER
THOMAS LEY
JOHN BROWNE
JOHN TRACHERN
HENRY WILLSON
THOMAS BALDWYNE
ALLEXANDER SANDERSON
DAVID ELLIS
SARA MORE
ANN a. Maid.

Living

At James Cittye and wth the Corporacon therof.
Sr FRANCES WYATT Goveno^r:
MARGRETT LADY WYATT
HANT WYATT Minister
KATHREN SPENCER
THOMAS HOOKER
JOHN GATHER
JOHN MATHEMAN
EDWARD COOKE
GEORGE NELSON
GEORGE HALL
JANE BURTT
ELIZABETH POMELL
MARY WOODWARD

Sr GEORGE YEARDLEY Knight
TEMPERANCE LADY YEARDLY
ARGALL YARDLEY
FRANCES YEARDLEY
ELIZABETH YEARDLEY
KILIBETT HICHCOCKE
AUSTEN COMBES
JOHN FOSTER
RICHARD ARRUNDELL
SUSAN HALL
ANN GRIMES
ELIZABETH LYON
— YOUNGE
— Negro ⎱
— Negro ⎰ women

ALICE DAVISON vid:
EDWARD SHARPLES

THE LIVING IN VIRGINIA.

Living

JONE DAVIES

GEORGE SANDS Trasu'
Cap: Wm PERCE
JONE PERCE
ROBERT HEDGES
HUGH W^m [WILLIAMS]
THOMAS MOULSTON
HENRY FARMOR
JOHN LIGHTFOOTE
THOMAS SMITH
ROGER RUESE
ALLEXANDER GILL
JOHN CARTWRIGHT
ROBERT AUSTINE
EDWARD BRICKE
WILLIAM RAVENETT
JOCOMB ANDREWS
vx ANDREWS
RICHARD ALDER
ESTER EVERE
ANGELO a Negar

Doc: JOHN POTT
ELIZABETH POTT
RICHARD TOWNSEND
THOMAS LEISTER
JOHN KULLAWAY
RANDALL HOWLETT
JANE DICKINSON
FORTUNE TAYLOR

Cap: ROGER SMITH
Mrs SMITH

Living

ELIZABETH SALTER
SARA MACOCKE
ELIZABETH ROLFE
CHRI: LAWSON
uxor eius LAWSON
FRANCES FOULLER
CHARLES WALLER
HENRY BOOTH

Cap: RAPH HAMOR
Mrs HAMOR
JEREME CLEMENT
ELIZABETH CLEMENT
SARA LANGLEY
SISLEY GREENE
ANN ADDAMS
ELKINTON RATCLIFE
FRANCIS GIBSON
JAMES YEMANSON

JOHN PONTES
CHRISTOPHER BEST.
THOMAS CLARKE
Mr REIGNOLD'S
Mr HICKMORE
vx HICKMORE
SARA RIDDALL

EDWARD BLANEY
EDWARD HUDSON
vx HUDSON
WILLIAM HARTLEY
JOHN SHELLEY
ROBERT BEW
WILLIAM WARD

THE LIVING IN VIRGINIA.

Living
THOMAS MENTIS [*or* MEUTIS]
ROBERT WHITMORE
ROBERT CHAUNTREE
ROBERT SHEPPARD
WILLIAM SAWIER
LANSLOTT DAMPORT
MATH: LOYD
THOMAS OTTWAY
THOMAS CROUCH
ELIZABETH STARKEY
ELINOR

Mrs PERRY
infans PERRY
FRANCES CHAPMAN
GEORGE GRAUES* [GRAVES]
vx GRAUES*
REBECCA SNOWE
SARA SNOWE
JOHN ISGRAUE [ISGRAVE]
MARY ASCOMBE vid
BENAMY BUCKE
GERCYON BUCKE
PELEG BUCKE
MARA BUCKE
ABRAM PORTER
BRIGETT CLARKE
ABIGALL ASCOMBE
JOHN JACKSON
vx JACKSON
EPHRAIM JACKSON

Mr JOHN BURROWS
Mrs BURROWS

Living
ANTHONY BURROWS
JOHN COOKE
NICHOLAS GOULDSMITH
ELIAS GAILE
ANDREW HOWELL
ANN ASHLEY

JOHN SOUTHERN
THOMAS PASMORE
ANDREW RALYE

NATH: JEFFERYS
vx JEFFERYS
THOMAS HEBBS

CLEM^T DILKE
Mrs DILKE
JOHN HINTON

RICHARD STEPHENS
WASSELL RAYNER
vx RAYNER
JOHN JACKSON
EDWARD PRICE
OSTEN SMITH
THOMAS SPILMAN
BRYAN CAWT

GEORGE MINIFY
MOYES STON

Capt: HOLMES
Mr CALCKER
Mrs CALCKER
infans CALCKER

---

* [Might be read as GRANES.]

THE LIVING IN VIRGINIA.

Living

PECEABLE SHERWOOD
ANTHONY WEST
HENRY BARKER
HENRY SCOTT
MARGERY DAWSE

Mr CANN
Cap: HARTT
EDWARD SPALDING
vx SPALDING
puer SPALDING
Puella SPALDING
JOHN HELIN
vx HELIN
puer HELIN
infans HELIN

THOMAS GRAYE *et vx*
JONE GRAYE
WILLIAM GRAYE
RICHARD YOUNGE
vx YOUNGE
JONE YOUNGE

RANDALL SMALWOOD
JOHN GREENE
WILLIAM MUDGE

Mrs SOTHEY
ANN SOTHEY
ELIN PAINTER

GOODMAN WEBB

Living

in the maine

RICHARD ATKINS
vx ATKINS
WILLIAM BAKER
EDWARD OLIVER
SAMWELL MORRIS
ROBERT DAVIS
ROBERT LUNTHORNE
JOHN VERNIE
THOMAS WOOD
THOMAS REES

MICHEALL BATT
vx BATT
vid's TINDALL
Mr STAFFERTON
vx STAFFERTON
JOHN FISHER
JOHN ROSE
THOMAS THORNEGOOD
JOHN BADSTON
SUSAN BLACKWOOD

THOMAS KINSTON
ROBERT SCOTTESMORE
ROGER KID
NICHOLAS BULLINGTON
NICHOLAS MARTTIN

JOHN CARTER
CHRISTOPHER HALL
DAVID ELLIS
vx ELLIS
JOHN FROGMORTON
ROBERT MARSHALL

THE LIVING IN VIRGINIA.

Living

THOMAS SWNOW*
JOHN SMITH
LAWRANCE SMALPAGE
THOMAS CROSSE
THOMAS PRICHARD
RICHARD CROUCH

CHRISTOPHER REDHEAD
HENRY BOOTH

RICHARD CARVEN
vx CARVEN
JOHN HOWELL
WILLIAM BURTT
WILLIAM STOCKER
NICHOLAS ROOTE

SARA KIDDALL
infans { KIDDALL
{ KIDDALL
EDWARD FISHER
RICHARD SMITH
JOHN WOLRICH
Mrs WOLRICH
JONATHIN GILES
CHRISTOPH: RIPEN
THOMAS BANKS
FRANCES BUCHER
HENRY DAWLEN
ARTHUR CHANDLER
RICHARD SANDERS
THOMAS HELCOTT
THOMAS HICHCOCKE

Living

GRIFFINE GUNIE†
THOMAS OSBOURN
RICHARD DOWNES
WILLIAM LAWRELL

THOMAS JORDAN
EDWARD BUSBEE
HENRY TURNER
JOSUA CREW
ROBERT HUTCHINSON
THOMAS JONES
vx JONES
REIGNOLD MORECOCKE *et* vx
RICHARD BRIDGWATTER *et* [vx]

Mr THO: BUN
Mrs BUN
THOMAS SMITH
ELIZABETH HODGES

WILLIAM KEMP
vx KEMP

HUGH BALDWINE
vx BALDWINE
JOHN WILMOSE

THOMAS DOE
vx DOE

GEORGE FRYER
vx FRYER
STEPHEN WEBB

* [Clearly so in the original.]
† [Apparently so; but it might also be read as GUME, or GUINE.]

Living
in Jams iland
JOHN OSBOURN
vx OSBOVRN [OSBOURN]
GEORGE POPE
ROBERT CUNSTABLE

WILLIAM JONES
vx JONES
JOHN JOHNSON
vx JOHNSON
infans { JOHNSON
{ JOHNSON
JOHN HALL
vx HALL
WILLIAM COOKSEY
vx COOKSEY
infans COOKSEY
ALICE KEAN

ROBERT FITTS
vx FITTS
JOHN REDDISH

JOHN GREVETT
vx GREVETT
JOHN WEST
THOMAS WEST
HENRY GLOVER

GOODMAN STOIKS*
vx STOIKS
infans STOIKS
Mr ADAMS
Mr LEET

Living
WILLIAM SPENCE
vx SPENCE
infans SPENCE
JAMES TOOKE
JAMES ROBERTS
ANTHONY HARLOW

SARA SPENCE
GEORGE SHURKE
JOHN BOOTH
ROBERT BENNETT

yͤ neck of land.
Mr KINGSMEALE
vx KINGSMEALE
infans { KINGSMEALE
{ KINGSMEALE
RAPH GRIPHIN
FRANCES COMPTON
JOHN SMITH
JOHN FILMER
EDWARD a Negro
THOMAS SULLEY
vx SULLEY
THOMAS HARWOOD
GEORGE FEDAM
PETER STABER
THOMAS POPKIN
THOMAS SIDES
RICHARD PERSE
vx PERSE
ALLEN his man
ISABELL PRATT

---

* [First written STOCKS, then altered.]

THE LIVING IN VIRGINIA.

Living

THOMAS ALNUTT
vx ALNUTT
JOHN PAINE
ROGER REDES
ELINOR SPRAD

Ouer the River

JOHN SMITH
vx SMITH
infans SMITH
JOHN VERGO
RICHARD FENN
WILLIAM RICHARDSON
ROBERT LINDSEY
RICHARD DOLFEMB
JOHN BOTTAM
JOHN ELLIOTT
SUSAN BARBER
THOMAS GATES
vx GATES
PERCIVALL WOOD
ANTHONY BURRIN
WILLIAM BEDFORD
WILLIAM SAND'S
JOHN PROCTOR
Mrs PROCTOR
PHETTIPLACE CLOSE
HENRY HORNE
RICHARD HORNN
THOMAS FLOWER
WILLIAM BULLOCKE
ELLIAS HINTON
JOHN FOXEN
EDWARD SMITH

Living

JOHN SKINNER
MARTINE DE MOONE
WILLIAM NAILE
THOMAS FITTS
ELIZABETH ABBITT
ALICE FITTS

At ye Plantacon ouer ag^t James Cittie

Capt: SAM: MATHEWS
BENIAMIN OWIN
RICE AP WILLIAMS
JIRO a Negro
WALTER PARNELL
WILLIAM PARNELL
MARGREAT ROADES
JOHN WEST
FRANCIS WEST *Vid*
THOMAS DAYHURST
ROBERT MATHEWS
ARTHUR GOULDSMITH
ROBERT WILLIAMS
MORICE LOYD
ARON CONWAY
WILLIAM SUTTON
RICHARD GREENE
MATHEW HAMAN
SAMWELL DAVIES
JOHN THOMAS
JOHN DOCKER
ABRAM WOOD
MICHEALL LUPWORTH
JOHN DAVIES
LEWIS BALY

Living
JAMES DARIES
ALICE HOLMES
HENRY BARLOW
THOMAS BUTTON
EDMOND WHITT
ZACHARIA CRISPE
JOHN BURLAND
THOMAS HAWKINS
THOMAS PHILLIPS
PAULE REINOLD'S
NICH: SMITH
ELIZABETH WILLIAMS
HUGH CRUDER
EDWARD HUDSON
ROBERT SHEPPARD
THOMAS OTTAWELL
THOMAS CROUCH
ROBERT BEW
JOHN RUSSELL
ROBERT CHANTRY
GEORGE RODGERS
LANSLOTT DAMPORTT
JOHN SHULE
NATH: LOYD
WILLIAM SAWYER
WILLIAM WARD
WILLIAM HARTLY
JERIME WHITT
Lieutenñt PURFREY
EDWARD GRINDALL
Mr SWIFT
WILLIAN HAMES*

Living
GEORGE GURR
HENRY WOOD
JOHN BALDWINE
JOHN NEEDOME
WILLIAM BINCKS
NICHOLAS TOMPSON
JOHN DENCY [*or* DEUCY]
ERASMUS CARTTER
JOHN EDWARD'S
GEORGE BAYLEY
GEORGE SPARKE
NICHOLAS COMIN
NICHOLAS ARRAS
MARTTIN TVRNER
JOHN STONE *infans*
DAVY MANSFIELD
JOHN DENMARKE
ELIZABETH RUTTEN
GOODWIFE BINCKS
a servant of mr MOREWOOD'S

the glase howse
VINCENCIO ———
BERNARDO ———
OULD SHEPPARD his sonn
RICHARD TARBORER
Mrs BARNARDO

At Archurs hoop.
Leftennat HARRIS
ROWLAND LOTTIS
ux LOTTIS

---

* [There is a *dot* above this word, but I fancy it is of later date than the original writing If it *be* part of the word, we must read the name as HAINES.]

Living

JOHN ELISON
vx ELISON
GEORGE SANDERS
THOMAS CORDER
JOSEPH JOHNSON
GEORG PRAN
JOHN BOTTOM
THOMAS FARLY
vx FARLY
a Child
NICHOLAS SHOTTON

At Hogg Iland

DAVID SAND⁹ mſister [minister]
JOHN VTIE [UTIE]
Mʳˢ VTIE
JOHN VTIE infuas [infans]
WILLIAM TYLER
ELIZABETH TYLER
RICHARD WHITBY
WILLIAM RAMSHAW
RICE WATKINS
THOMAS FOSKEW lost
HENER ELSWORD
THOMAS CAUSEY
GEORGE VNION* [UNION]
HENRY WOODWARD
ROGER WEBSTER
JOHN DOUSTON
JOSEPH JOHNSON
RICHARD CROCKER Child
WILLIAM HICHCOCKE, lost
GEORGE PROWSE
ROBERT PARRAMORE

Living

JOHN JARVICE, als, GLOVER
JOHN BROWNE
WILLIAM BURCHER
JOHN BURCHER
JOHN FULWOOD
THOMAS BRANSBY
THOMAS COLLY
THOMAS SIMPSON
THOMAS POWELL
NICHOLAS LONGE

At martins hundred

WILLIAM HARWOOD
SAMWELL MARCH
HUGH HUES
JOHN JACKSON
THOMAS WARD
JOHN STEVANS
HUMPHRY WALDEN
THOMAS DOUGHTIE
JOHN HASLEY
SAMWELL WEAVER
Vid's JACKSON
filia JACKSON
Mʳˢ TAYLOR |
ANN WINDOR
ELIZABETH BYGRAUE
Mʳ LAKE
Mʳ BURREN
JOHN STONE
SAMWELL CULLEY
JOHN HELLINE
vx HELLIN

---

* [I am not quite sure as to this name; it certainly *might* be read as VINON.]

Living

a french man *et vx*
THOMAS SIBERY

At Warwick Squeake

JOHN BATT
HENRY PINFFE
WASSELL WEBLIN
ANTHONY READ
FRANCES WOODSON
HENRY PHILLIPS
PETTER COLLINS
CHR: REINOLD'S
EDWARD MABIN
JOHN MALDMAN
THOMAS COLLINS
GEORGE RUSHMORE
THOMAS SPENCER
GEORGE CLARKE
RICH: BARTLETT
FRANCS BANKS
JOHN JENKINS
THOMAS JONES
WILLIAM DENHAM
PETER }
ANTHONY } negres
FRANC'S }
MARGRETT }
JOHN BENNETT
NICHOLAS SKINNER
JOHN ATKINS
JOHN POLLENTIN
RACHELL POLLENTIN
MARGRETT POLLENTIN
MARY a maid

Living

HENRY WOODWARD
THOMAS SAWYER
THOMAS a boye

At the Indian thickett

HENRY WOODALL
GREGORY DORY
JOHN FOSTER
JOHN GREENE
JOHN WARD
CHRISTÔ: WINDMILE
RICHARD RAPIER
CUTBERT PEIRSON
ADAM RUMELL
RICHARD ROBINSON
JAMES a french mā

At Elisabeth Cittye

Cap ISACKE WHITTAKERS
MARY WHITTAKERS
CHARLES ATKINSON
CHARLES CALTHROP
JOHN LANKFEILD
BRIDG'S FREEMAN
NICHOLAS WESELL
EDWARD LOYD
THOMAS NORTH
ANTHONY MIDDLETON
RICHARD POPELY
THOMAS HARDING
WILLIAM JOY
RAPH OSBORNE
EDWARD BARNES
THOMAS THORNGOOD

THE LIVING IN VIRGINIA. 183

Living
ANN ATTKINSON
    LANKFEILD
    MEDCLALFE*
GEORGE NUCE
ELIZABETH WHITTAKERS
GEORGE ROADS
EDWARD JOHNSON
WILLIAM FOULLER
REINOLD GOODWYN
JAMES LARMOUNT
JOHN JACKSON
vid's JOHNSON
vid's FOWLER
2 french men
GEORGE MEDCALFE
WALTER ELY
THOMAS LANE
BARTHELMEW HOPKINS
JOHN JEFFERSON
ROBERT THRESHER
JOHN ROWES
Mr YATES
ROBERT GOODMAN
vx ELY
infans ELY
Cap RAWLEIGH CRASHAW
ROBERT WRIGHT
JAMES SLEIGHT
JOHN WELCHMAN
JOHN MORE
HENRY POTTER
Mr ROSWELL
WILLIAM GAWNTLETT

Living
OSBORNE SMITH
vx MORE
vx WRIGHT
vx WRIGHT
filia WRIGHT
THOMAS DOWSE
SAMWELL BENNETT
WILLIAM BROWNE
WILLIAM ALLEN
LEWIS WELCHMAN
ROBERT MORE
Mrs DOWSE
vx BENNETT
pue { BENNETT
      { BENNETT

At Bucke Row
THOMAS FLINT
JOHN HAMPTON
RICHARD PEIRSBY
WILLIAM ROOKINS
ROWLAND WILLIAMS
STEVEN DIXON
THOMAS RISBY
HENRY WHEELER
JAMES BROOKS
SAMWELL KENNELL
JOHN CARNING
THOMAS NEARES
ROBERT SALVADGE
WILLIAM BARRY
JOSEPH HATFIELD
EDWARD MARSHALL
AMBROSE GRIFFITH

* [Query MEDCALFE. See twelve lines below.]

THE LIVING IN VIRGINIA.

Living

PETTER ARRUNDELL
ANTHONY BONALL } french men
LA GAURD
JAMES BONALL
JOHN ARRUNDELL
JOHN HANIE [*or* HAINE]
NICH: ROW
RICHARD ALTHROP
JOHN LOYD
vx HAME*
vx HAMPTON
ELIZABETH ARRUNDELL
MARGREAT ARRUNDELL

At Basse Choise

Cap: NETHANIEL BASSE
SAMWELL BASSE
BENIAMIN SIMES
THOMAS SHEWORD
BENIAMINE HANDCLEARE
WILLIAM BARNARD
JOHN SHELLEY
NATHANIELL MOPER
NATHA: GAUMON
MARGRETT GILES
RICHARD LONGE
vx LONGE
infans LONGE
RICHARD EVANS
WILLIAM NEWMAN
JOHN ARMY
PETER LANGDEN

Living

HENRY
ANDREW RAWLEY
PETTER

more at Elizabeth Cittie

Liuetennat SHEPPARD
JOHN POWELL
JOHN WOOLEY
CATHREN POWELL
JOHN BRADSTON
FRANC'S PITTS
GILBERTT WHITFEILD
PETER HEREFORD
THOMAS FAULKNER
ESAW DE LA WARE
WILLIAM CORNIE
THOMAS CURTISE
ROBERT BRITTAINE
ROGER WALKER
HENRY KERSLEY
EDWARD MORGAINE
ANTHONY EBSWORTH
AGNES EBSWORTH
ELINOR HARRIS
THOMAS ADDISON
WILLIAM LONGE
WILLIAM SMITH
WILLIAM PINSEN

Cap Wm TUCKER
Cap NICH: MARTEAW
Leftennt ED: BARKLY

---

* [It is possible that a *dot* may have been omitted from this word, and that the lady's name should be read HANIE or HAINE ; she may have been wife to the man mentioned four lines above.]

Living	*Living*
DANIELL TANNER	ANN LAYDON
JOHN MORRIS	VIRGINIA LAYDON
GEORG THOMSON	ALICE LAYDON
PAULE THOMSON	KATHERNE LAYDON
WILLIAM THOMSON	WILLIAM EVANS
PASTA CHAMPIN	WILLIAM JULIAN
STEPHEN SHERE	WILLIAM KEMP
JEFFERY HALL	RICHARD WITH'E [WITHERE]
RICH: JONES	JOHN JORNALL
WILLIAM HUTCHINSON	WALTER MASON
RICHARD APLETON	SARA JULIAN
THOMAS EVANS	SARA GOULDOCKE
WESTON BROWNE	JOHN SALTER
ROBERT MOUNDAY	WILLIAM COALE
STEVEN CVLLOE	JERENY DICKENSON
RAPH ADAMS	LAWRANCE PEELE
THOMAS PHILLIPS	JOHN EVANS
FRANCIS BARRETT	MARKE EVANS
MARY TUCKER	GEORGE EVANS
JANE BRAKLEY	JOHN DOWNEMAN
ELIZABETH HIGGINS	ELIZABETH DOWNEMAN
MARY MOUNDAY	WILLIAM BALDWIN
CHOUPOUKE an Indian	JOHN SIBSEY
ANTHONY } Negres	WILLIAM CLARKE
ISSABELLA }	RICE GRIFFINE
Leftenñt LUPO	JOSEPH MOSLEY
PHILLIP LUPO	ROBERT SMITH
BARTHOLMEW WETHERSBY*	JOHN CHEESMAN
HENRY DRAPER	THOMAS CHEESMAN
JOSEPH HAMAN	EDWARD CHEESMAN
ELIZABETH LUPO	PETTER DICKSON
ALBIANO WETHERSLY*	JOHN BAYNAN
JOHN LAYDON	ROBERT SWEET

* [Sic in orig.]

THE LIVING IN VIRGINIA.

Living	*Living*
John Parrett	Elizabeth Booth child
William Fouks	Cap: Tho: Davies
John Clackson	John Davies
John Hill	Thomas Huges
William Morten	William Kildridge
William Clarke	Alexandr Mountney
Edward Stockdell	Edward Bryan
Elizabeth Baynam	Persivall Ibotson
George Davies	John Penrice
Elizabeth Davies	Robert Locke
Ann Harrison	Elizabeth Ibotson
John Curtise	Ann Ibotson
John Walton	Edward Hill
Edward Aston	Thomas Best
Toby Hurt	Hanna Hill
Cornelius May	Elizabeth Hill
Elizabeth May	Robert Salford
Henry May. child	John Salford
Thomas Willowbey	Phillip Chapman
Oliuer Jenkinson	Thomas Parter
John Chandeler	Mary Salford
Nicholas Davies	Francis Chamberlin
Jone Jenkins	William Hill
Mary Jenkins	William Harris
Henry Gouldwell	William Worlidge
Henry Prichard	John Forth
Henry Barber	Thomas Spilman
Ann Barber	Rebecca Chamberlin
John Hutton	Alice Harris
Elizabeth Hutton	Pharow Phlinton
Thomas Baldwin	Arthur Smith
John Billiard	Hugh Hall
Reynold Booth	Robert Sabin
Mary	John Cooker

THE LIVING IN VIRGINIA.

Living

HUGH DICKEN
WILLIAM GAYNE
RICHARD MINTREN Junior
JOANE FLINTON
ELIZABETH FLINTON
REBECCA COUBBER
RICHARD MINTREN senior
JOHN FRYE
WILLIAM BROOKS
SIBILE BROOKS
WILLIAM BROOKS
THOMAS CRISPE
RICHARD PACKE
MILES PRICHETT
THOMAS GODBY
MARGERY PRICHETT
JONE GOODBY
JONE GRINDRY
JOHN JUIMAN
MARY GRINDRY
JOHN GRINDRY child
JOHN WAINE
ANN WAINE
MARY ACKLAND
GEORGE ACKLAND
JOHN HARLOW
WILLIAM CAPP'S
EDWARD WATTERS
PAULE HARWOOD
NICH: BROWNE
ADAM THROUGOOD
RICHARD EAST
STEPHEN READ
GRACE WATTERS

Living

WILLIAM WATTERS
WILLIAM GANEY
HENRY GANEY
JOHN ROBINSON
ROBERT BROWNE
THOMAS PARRISH
EDMOND SPALDEN
ROGER FARBRACKE
THEODER JONES
WILLIAM BALDWIN
LUKE ADEN
ANNA GANY
ANNA GANY *fillia*
ELIZABETH POPE
REBECCA HATCH
THOMASIN LOXMORE
THOMAS GARNETT
ELIZABETH GARNETT
SUSSAN GARNETT
FRANCES MICHELL
JONAS STOCKTON
THIMOTHEE STOCKTON
WILLIAM COOKE
RICHARD BOULTEN
FRANCES HILL
JOHN JACKSON
RICHARD DAVIES
ANN COOKE
DICTRAS CHRISMUS
THOMAS HILL
ARTHUR DAVIES
WILLIAM NEWCOME
ELIZABETH CHRISMUS
JOANE DAVIES

THE LIVING IN VIRGINIA.

Living

THOMAS HETHERSALL
WILLIAM DOUGLAS
THOMAS DOUTHORN
ELIZABETH DOUTHORN
SAMWELL DOUTHORN a bo[y]
THOMAS an Indian
JOHN HAZARD
JOANE HAZARD
HENRY
FRANCES MASON
MICHEALL WILCOCKS
WILLIAM QUERKE
MARY MASON
MAUDLIN WILCOCKS
Mr KETH mister
JOHN BUSH
JOHN COOP [COOPER]
JONADAB ILLETT
JOHN BARNABY
JOHN SEAWARD
ROBERT NEWMAN
WILLIAM PARKER
THOMAS SNAPP
CLEMENT EVANS
THOMAS SPILMAN
THOMAS PARRISH

At the Eastern Shore

Cap WILLIAM EPPS
Mrs EPPS
PETTER EPPS
WILLIAM —
EDMOND CLOAKE
WILLIAM BIBBY

Living

THOMAS CORNISH
JOHN FISHER
WILLIAM DRY
HENRY WILSON
PETTER PORTER
CHRISTO: CARTTER
JOHN SUMFILL
NICHOLAS GRAUNGER
JAMES vocat PIPER
EDWARD
JOHN
THOMAS
GEORGE
CHARLES FARMER
JAMES KNOTT
JOHN ASCOMB
ROBERT FENNELL
PHILLIP
DANIELL COULEY
WILLIAM ANDREWS
THOMAS GRAUES
JOHN WILCOCKS
THOMAS CRAMPE
WILLIAM COOMES
JOHN PARSONS
JOHN COOMES
JAMES CHAMBERS
ROBERTT BALL
GOODWIFE BALL
THOMAS HALL
ISMALE HILLS
JOHN TYERS
WALTER SCOTT
GOODWIFE SCOTT

THE LIVING IN VIRGINIA.

Living
ROBERT EDMOND'S
THOMAS HICHCOCKE
JOHN EVANS
HENRY WATTKINS
PEREGREE WATTKINS
DANIELL WATTKINS
JOHN BLOWER
GODY BLOWER
JOHN
a boy of Mr CANS [*or* CAUS]
JOHN HOW
JOHN BUTTERFEILD
WILLIAM DAVIES
PETTER LONGMAN
JOHN WILKINS
GOODWIFE WILKINS
THOMAS POWELL
GODY POWELL
THOMAS PARKE

Living
WILLIAM SMITH
EDWARD DREW
NICHOLAS HOSKINS
  and his Child
WILLIAM WILLIAMS
Mrs WILLIAMS
JOHN THROGMORTON
BENNANINE* KNIGHT
CHAD GUNSTON
ABRAM ANALIN [*or* AUALIN,
  i.e. AVALIN]
THOMAS BLACKLOCKE
JOHN BARNETT
THOMAS SAVADGE
WILLIAM BEANE
SALOMAN GREENE
JOHN WASBORNE
WILLIAM OUILLS.

* [Evidently a misspelling for BENJAMINE.]

A List of the names of the Dead in Virgn^a since Aprill last
february 16: 1623

Colledg

JOHN WOOD
WILLIAM MORE
THOMAS NAYLOR } kild
JOHN HUNTER
JAMES HOWELL
WILLIAM LAMBERTT

At the neck of land

MOSES CONYERS
GEORGE GRIMES
WILLIAM CLEMENTS
THOMAS FERNLEY kid [killed]
EDWARD —

At Jurdains Jorney

ROGER MUCH
MARY REEFE
ROBERT WINTER
ROBERT WOOD'S
RICHARD SHREIFE
THOMAS BULL
JOHN KINTON
DANIELL —

At west and Sherlow hundred

SAMWELL FOREMAN
ZOROBABELL

2 Indians
one Negar
THOMAS ROBERTS
JOHN EDMONDS
JOHN LASEY
DANIELL FRANCKE
Cap: NATH WEST
CHRISTOPHER HARDING kild

At flower de hundred

JOHN MAYOR
WILLIAM WAYCOME
THOMAS PRISE
ROBERT WALKIN
JOHN FETHERSTON
JOHN AP ROBERTS
RICHARD JONES
RICHARD GRIFFIN
RICHARD RANKE [*or* RAUKE]
WILLIAM EDGER
JOHN FRY
DIXI CARPENTER
WILLIAM SMITH
JAMES CINDUARE*
EDWARD TEMPLE
SARA SALFORD

* [Spelling not very clear ; *may* be read CINDNAME or CINDVARE.]

THE DEAD IN VIRGINIA.

Dead	*Dead*
John Stanson	Robert Raffe
Christo: Evans	Ambrose Fresey
	Henry Fry
At James Cittie	John Dinse
Mr Sothey	Thomas Tindall
John Dumpont	Richard Knight*
Thomas Browne	John Jeffereys*
Henry Sothey	John Hamun*
Thomas Sothey	John Meridien*
Mary Sothey	John Countwane*
Elizabeth Sothey	Thomas Guine [or Gunie]*
Thomas Clarke	Thomas Somersall
Margrett Shrawley	William Rowsley
Richard Walker	Elizabeth Rowsley
Vallentyn Gentler	a maid of thers
Petter Brishitt	Robert Bennett
Humphry Boyse	Thomas Roper
John Watton	Mr Fitziefferys
Arthur Edward's	Mrs Smith
Thomas Fisher	Petter Marttin
William Spence } lost	James Jakins
Mrs Spence	Mr Crapplace
George Sharks	John Lullett
John Buth	Ann Dixon
Mr Collins	William Howlett
vx	Mr Furlows child
Mr Pegden	Jacob Prophett.
Petter De maine	John Reding
Goodman Ascomb	Richard Atkins his child
Goodman Witts	John Bayly
William Kerton	William Jones his svant
Mr Atkins	John Mr Pearns servant
Thomas Hakes	Josias Hartt
Petter Gould	Judith Sharp

* [See next page, where these names are repeated.]

Dead

ANN OUAILE
  REIGNOLD'S
WILLIAM DIER
MARY DIER
THOMAS SEXTON
MARY BAWDRYE
EDWARD NORMANSELL
HENRY FELL
  ENIMS [*or* EUIMS]
ROGER TURNOR
THOMAS GUINE [*or* GUNIE]*
JOHN COUNTWAY*
JOHN MERIDAY*
BÉNIAMINE VSHER†
JOHN HAMAN*
JOHN JEFFERYES*
RICHARD KNIGHT*
JOHN WALKER
  HOSIER
WILLIAM JACKSON
WILLIAM APLEBY
JOHN MANBY
ARTHUR COOKE
STEPHEN —

At y͞e Plantacon ouer against James Cittie

HUMPHRY CLOUGH
MORRIS CHALONER
SAMWELL BETTON
JOHN GRUFFIN
WILLIAM EDWARDS
WILLIAM SALSBURY

Dead

MATHEW GRIFFINE
ROBERT ADWARD'S
JOHN JONES
THOMAS PRICHARD
THOMAS MORGAINE
THOMAS BIGGS
NICHOLAS BUSHELL
ROBERT WILLIAMS
ROBERT REYNOLD'S
EDWARD HUIES
THOMAS FOULKE
NATHEW JENINGS
RICHARD MORRIS
FRANCES BARKE
JOHN EWINS†
SAMWELL FISHER
JOHN EWIS
JAMES CARTTER
EDWARD FLETCHER
ADERTON GREENE
MORICE BAKER
ROBERT Mr EWINS man
ROBERT PIDGION
THOMAS TRIGGS
JAMES THURSBY
NICHOLAS THIMBLEBY
FRANCES MILLETT
JOHN HOOKS
THOMAS LAWSON
WILLIAM MILLER
NICHOLAS FATRICE
JOHN CHAMP
JOHN MANING

* [It will be noticed that these names, although in some cases with different spellings, are given above (see previous page).]   † [Repeated on next page.]

THE DEAD IN VIRGINIA.

Dead	*Dead*
Richard Edmonds	Nicholas Dorington
David Collins	Raph Rogers
Thomas Guine [or Gunie]*	Richard Frethram
John Vicars	John Brogden
John Meridie*	John Beanam
Beny Vsher*	Frances Atkinson
John Cantwell	Robert Atkinson
Richard Knight*	John Kerill
Robert Hellue	Edward Davies
Thomas Barrow	Percivall Man
John Euines*	Mathew Staueling
Edward Price	Thomas Nicholls
Robert Taylor	2 Childrens of yᵉ french men
Richard Butterey	John Pattison ⎫
Mary Lacon	vx Pattison ⎬ kild
Robert Baines	Edward Windor ⎭
	Thomas Horner
Joseph Archer	John Walker
Thomas Mason	Thomas Pope
John Beman	Richard Ston
Christo: Pittman	John Catesby
Thomas Willer	Richard Stephens
Samwell Fulshaw	William Harris
John Wamsley	Christopher Woodward
Abram Colman	Joseph Turner
John Hodges	
Naamy Boyle	*At Warwicke Squeak*
At Hog Iland	Josias Collins
William Brakley	Clement Wilson
Petter Dun	William Robinson
John Long	Chr: Rawson
	Thomas Winslow
At martins hundred	vx Winslow
Henry Bagford	*infans* Winslow
Nicholas Gleadston	

* [Again repetitions. See previous page.]

Dead

ALEXANDER SUSSAMES
THOMAS PRICKETT
THOMAS MADDOX
JOHN GREENE
NATHANEL STANBRIDG
JOHN LITTON
CHRISTO: ASH
vx ASH
infans ASH
NETHANIEL LAME [*or* LAINE] } kild
JANE FISHER
PHILLIP JONES
EDWARD BANKS
JOHN SYMONS
THOMAS SMITH
THOMAS GRIFFIN
GEORGE CANE
ROBERT WHITT
SYMON an Italian

At Elizabeth Cittie

CHARLE MARSHALL
WILLIAM HOPKICKE
DORITHIE PARKINSON
WILLIAM ROBERTTS
JOHN FARRAR
MARTIN CUFFE
THOMAS HALL
THOMAS SMITH
CHRISTOPH' ROBERTTS
THOMAS BROWNE
HENRY FEARNE
THOMAS PARKINS
Mr HUSSY

Dead

JAMES COLLIS
RAPH ROCKLY
WILLIAM GEALES
GEORGE JONES
ANDREW ALLINSON
WILLIAM DOWNES
RICHARD GILLETT
GOODWIFE NONN [*or* NOUN]
HUGO SMALE
THOMAS WINTERSALL
JOHN WRIGHT
JAMES FENTON
CISELY a Maid
JOHN GAVETT
JAMES } Irishmen
JOHN }

JOCKY ARMESTRONGE
WOLSTON PELSANT
SAMPSON PELSANT
CATHRIN CAPPS
WILLIAM ELBRIDG
JOHN SANDERSON
JOHN BENBRICKE
JOHN BAKER kild
WILLIAM LUPO
TIMOTHY BURLEY
MARGERY FRISLE
HENRY WEST
JASPER TAYLER
BRIGETT SEARLE
ANTHONY ANDREW
EDMOND CARTTER
THOMAS ———

Dead	Dead
William Gauntlett	Innocent Poore
Gilbert —— kild	Edward Dupper
Christo: Welchman	Elizabeth Davies
John Hilliard*	Thomas Buwen
Gregory Hilliard	Ann Barber
John Hilliard*	William Lucott
William Richards	Nicholas —— kild
Elizabeth a maid	Henry Bridges
Cap: Hitchcocke	Henry Payton
Thomas Keninston	Richard Griffin
Cap: Lincolne	Raphe Harrison
Chad: Gulstons	Samwell Harvie
ux Gulstons	John Box
infans Gulstons	Benianine Box
George Cooke	Thomas servant
Richard Goodchild	Frances Chamberline
Chrismus his child	Bridgett Dameron.
Elizabeth Mason	Isarell Knowles
Symon With	Edward Bendige
Whitney Guy	William Davies
Thomas Brodbanke	John Phillips
William Burnhouse	Daniell Sauewell
John Sparks	
Robert Morgaine]	William Jones
John Locke	Robert Balls wife
William Thompson	Robert Leauer
Thomas Fulham	Huch Nichcott
Cutberd Brooks	John Knight.

* [Sic in orig.]

UT of the Ship cald the *Furtherance*

JOHN WALKER	JOHN MANBY
HOSIER	ARTHUR COOKE
WILLIAM JACKSON	STEVEN
WILLIAM APLEBY	

UT of the *Gods gift*
          Mr CLARE master
          WILLIAM BENNETT

UT of the *Margrett and John*.

  Mr LANGLEY
  Mr WRIGHT
  the gunner of the *William and John*.

[1621? *Promise of certain "WALLOONS and FRENCH" to Emigrate to VIRGINIA.*]

[IN the centre of a large sheet of paper is written in French, "*We promise my Lord Ambassador of the Most Serene King of Great Britain to go and inhabit in Virginia, a land under His Majesty's obedience, as soon as conveniently may be, and this under the conditions to be carried out in the articles we have communicated to the said Ambassador, and not otherwise, on the faith of which we have unanimously signed this present with our sign manual.*"

[The signatures and the calling of each are appended in the form of a round robin, and in an outer circle the person signing states whether he is married, and the number of his children. *Endorsed by Sir Dudley Carleton*, "Signature of such Wallons and French as offer themselfs to goe into Verginia." The names with an * have only signed their marks. Total 227, including 55 men, 41 women, 129 children, and two servants. As stated above, the original document is in French. The version here given has the authority of Mr. Sainsbury, of Her Majesty's Public Record Office. *The signatures are very indistinctly written.*]*

MOUSNIER DE LA MONTAGNE, medical student; marrying man.
MOUSNIER DE LA MONTAGNE, apothecary and surgeon; marrying man.
JACQUE CONNE, tiller of the earth; wife and two children.

---

* [The Answer of the Virginia Company is dated Aug. 11, 1621, and a contemporary copy is preserved in the State Paper Department of Her Majesty's Public Record Office. It is signed by JOHN FERRAR, Deputy. The substance is to the effect that the Company do not conceive any inconvenience, provided the number does not exceed 300, and they take the oath of allegiance to the King and conform to the rules of government established in the Church of England. Cannot recommend the King to aid them with shipping; the exhausted stock of the Company prevents them from affording any help. Land will be granted to them in convenient numbers in the principal cities, boroughs, and corporations in Virginia.]

Henry Lambert, woollen draper ; wife.
*George Béava, porter ; wife and one child.
Michel Du Pon, hatter ; wife and two children.
Jan Bullt, labourer ; wife and four children.
Paul de Pasar, weaver ; wife and two children.
Antoine Grenier, gardener ; wife.
Jean Gourdeman, labourer ; wife and five children.
Jean Campion, wool carder ; wife and four children.
*Jan De la Met, labourer ; young man.
*Antoine Martin ; wife and one child.
François Fourdrin, leather dresser ; young man.
*Jan Leca, labourer ; wife and five children.
Theodore Dufour, draper ; wife and two children.
*Gillain Broque, labourer ; young man.
George Wautre, musician ; wife and four children.
*Jan Sage, serge maker ; wife and six children.
*Marie Flit, in the name of her husband, a miller ; wife and two children.
P. Gantois, student in theology ; young man.
Jacques de Lecheilles, brewer ; marrying man.
*Jan Le Rou, printer ; wife and six children.
*Jan de Croy, sawyer ; wife and five children.
*Charles Chancy, labourer ; wife and two children.
*François Clitdeu, labourer ; wife and five children.
*Philippe Campion, draper ; wife and one child.
*Robert Broque, labourer ; young man.
Philippe De le Mer, carpenter ; young man.
*Jeanne Martin ; young girl.
Pierre Cornille, vine dresser ; young man.
Jan de Carpentry, labourer ; wife and two children.
*Martin de Carpentier, brass founder ; young man.
Thomas Farnarcque, locksmith ; wife and seven children.
Pierre Gaspar.
*Gregoire Le Jeune, shoemaker ; wife and four children.
Martin Framerie, musician ; wife and one child.

Pierre Quesnée, brewer ; marrying man.
Pontus Le Gean, bolting-cloth weaver ; wife and three children.
*Barthelemy Digaud, sawyer ; wife and eight children.
Jesse de Forest, dyer ; wife and five children.
*Nicolas De Le Marlier, dyer ; wife and two children.
*Jan Damont, labourer ; wife.
*Jan Gille, labourer ; wife and three children.
*Jan de Trou, wool carder ; wife and five children.
Philippe Maton, dyer, and two servants ; wife and five children.
Anthoine de Lielate, vinedresser ; wife and four children.
Ernou Catoir, wool carder ; wife and five children.
Anthoin Desendre, labourer ; wife and one child.
Abel de Crepy, shuttle worker ; wife and four children.
*Adrian Barbe, dyer ; wife and four children.
*Michel Leusier, cloth weaver ; wife and one child.
*Jerome Le Roy, cloth weaver ; wife and four children.
*Claude Ghiselin, tailor ; young man.
*Jan de Crenne, glass maker ? [fritteur] ; wife and one child.
*Louis Broque, labourer ; wife and two children.

[MUSTERS

OF THE

INHABITANTS IN VIRGINIA.

1624.]

[MUSTERS

OF THE

INHABITANTS IN VIRGINIA.

1624.]

Colledg
Land
Henrico

THE MUSTER of the Inhabitant's of the Colledge: Land in Virginia taken the 23th of January 1624.

Liuetennt THOMAS OSBORNE arived in the *Bona Nova* November 1619

Servant's

DANIELL SHERLEY aged 30 yeres came in the *Bona Nova* 1619
PEETER JORDEN aged 22 in the *London Marchannt* 1620
RICHARD DAVIS aged 16 yeres in the *Jonathan* 1620*

ROBERT LAPWORTH came in the *Abigaile*

JOHN WATSON came in the *William & Thomas*

EDWARD HOBSON came in the *Bona Nova* 1619

CHRISTOPHER BRANCH came in the *London Marchannt*
MARY his wife in the same Shipp
THOMAS his sonne aged 9 Month's

WILLIAM BROWINGE came in the *Bona Nova*

MATHEW EDLOW came in the *Neptune* 1618

WILLIAM WELDON came in the *Bona Nova* 1619

---

* [The *short rules* here and hereafter in these "Musters," indicate the omission of lists of the stores brought by passengers, given in the original, but omitted here as of no general interest.]

Colledge Land.

FRANCIS WILTON came in the *Jonathan*

EZEKIAH RAUGHTON came in the *Bona Nova*.
MARGRETT his wife in the *Warwick*.

WILLIAM PRICE came in the *Starr*

ROBERT CAMPION came in the *Bona Nova*

LEONARD MOORE came in the *Bona Nova*

THOMAS BAUGH came in the *Supply*

THOMAS PARKER came in the *Neptune*

THEODER MOYSES came in the *London Marchannt*

Neck-of-Land. Corporation of Charles Citty.

The MUSTER of the Inhabitant's of the Neck-of-Land in the Corporation of Charles Cittie in Virginia taken the 24th of January 1624.

LUKE BOYSE aged 44 yeares arived in the *Edwine* in May 1619
ALLICE his wife arived in the *Bona-Noua* in Aprill 1622

Servant's

ROBERT HOLLAM aged 23 yeares in the *Bonaventure* August 1620
JOSEPH ROYALL aged 22 yeares in the *Charitie* July 1622

The MUSTER of JOSUAH CHARD

JOSUAH CHARD aged 36 yeares in the *Seaventure* May 1607
ANN his wife aged 33 yeares in the *Bony besse* August 1623

The MUSTER of JOHN DOD'S

JOHN DOD'S aged 36 yeares in the *Susan Constant* Aprill 1607
JANE his wife aged 40 yeares

The MUSTER of WILLIAM VINCENE

WILLIAM VINCENE aged 39 yeares in the *Mary & James*
JOANE his wife aged 42 yeares

Neck-of-Land
Charles Cittie   The MUSTER of THOMAS HARRIS

THOMAS HARRIS aged 38 yeares in the *Prosperous* in May
ADRIA his wife aged 23 yeares in the *Marmaduke* in November 1621
ANN WOODLASE theire kinswoman aged 7 yeares

       Servant's
ELIZABETH aged 15 yeares in the *Margrett & John* 1620

The MUSTER of JOHN PRICE

JOHN PRICE aged 40 yeares in the *Starr* in May
ANN his wife aged 21 yeares in the *Francis Bonaventure* August 1620
MARY a Child aged 3 Months

The MUSTER of HUGH HILTON.

HUGH HILTON aged 36 yeares in the *Edwine* in May 1619

The MUSTER of RICHARD TAYLO[R]

RICHARD TAYLOR aged 50 yeares in the *Mary Margrett* September 1608
DOROTHY his wife aged 21 yeares in the *London Marchaunt* May 1620
MARY theire Child aged 3 months.
      Servant's
CHRISTOPHER BROWNE aged 18 yeares in the *Dutie* in May 1620

The MUSTER of THOMAS OAGE

THOMAS OAGE aged 40 yeares in the *Starr* in May
ANN his wife in the *Neptune* in August 1618
EDWARD theire sonn aged 2 yeares.

26—2

**Neck-of-Land,
Charles Cittie**

The MUSTER of Robert Greenleafe

ROBERT GREENLEAFE aged 43 yeres in the *Tryall* August 1610
SUSAN his wife aged 23 yeres in the *Jonathan* May 1620
THOMAS theire sonn aged 3 yeres
ANN a daughter aged 22 week's

The MUSTER of Henery Coltman

HENERY COLTMAN aged 30 yeres in the *Noah* August 1610
ANN his wife aged 26 yeres in the *London Marchannt* May 1620

The MUSTER of Hugh Price

HUGH PRICE aged 35 years in the *William & John* January 1618
JUDITH his wife aged 24 yeres in the *Marygold* May 1619
JOHN his sonn aged 2 yeres.

The MUSTER of Thomas Farmer

THOMAS FARMER aged 30 yeres in the *Tryall* 1616

The MUSTER of Thomas Sheppey

THOMAS SHEPPEY aged 22 yeres in the *Supply* January 1620

The MUSTER of Allexander Bradway

ALLEXANDER BRADWAY aged 31 yeres in the *Supply* January 1620
SISLEY his wife aged 28 yeres in the *Jonathan* May 1620
ADRIA theire daughter aged 9 Months.

<small>Neck-of-Land.
Charles Cittie</small>   The MUSTER of WILLIAM SHARP

WILLIAM SHARP aged 40 yeres in the *Starr* in May
ELIZABETH his wife aged 25 yeres in the *Bonaventure* August 1620
ISACK his sonn aged 2 yeres
SAMUELL his sonn aged 2 Months
                Servant's
RICHARD VAUSE aged 20 yeres in the *Jonathan* May 1620

<small>West & Sherley
hundred.
Charles Cittie</small>   The MUSTER of the Inhabitant's of West and Sherley Hundred taken the 22th of January 1624.

RICHARD BIGG's his MUSTER

RICHARD BIGG'S aged 41 yeres arived in the *Swann* in August 1610
SARAH his wife aged 35 yeres in the *Marygold* May 1618
RICHARD theire Sonn aged 3 yeres
THOMAS TURNER his Cozen aged 11 yeres in y^e *Marygold* 1616
SUSAN OLD his Cozen aged 10 yeres in the *Marygold* 1616
                Servant's
JAMES GUY aged 20 yeares in the *Marygold* 1622
WILLIAM BROCK aged 26 yeres in the *Margrett* in May 1622
EDWARD TEMPLE age 20 yeres in the *Margrett* May 1622
MARY PEETERS aged 16 yeres in the *London Marchant* May 1620

WILLIAM BAYLEYS MUSTER

WILLIAM BALEY aged 41 yeares in the *Prosperous* in May 1610
MARY his wife aged 24 yeres in the *George* 1617
THOMAS his Sonn aged 4 yeares

West &
Sherley
hundred.

Robert Partins MUSTER

ROBERT PARTIN aged 36 yeares in the *Blessinge* in June 1609
MARGRETT his wife aged 36 in the *George* 1617
ROBERT } theire Children { aged 4 Months.
AVIS } { aged 5 yeares.
REBECCA } { aged 2 yeares.

Servant's

THOMAS HALE aged 20 yeares in the *George* 1623 in October
ELLIN COOKE aged 25 yeares in the *London Marchannt* June 1620

Christopher Woodward's MUSTER

CHRISTOPHER WOODWARD aged 30 yeares in the *Tryall* in June 1620
JOHN HIGGINS } his ptn's { aged 21 yeres in the *George* 1616
RICE HOWE } { aged 26 yeres in the *Gifte* 1618

Servant's

MATHEW GLOSTER aged 20 yeres in the *Warwick* 1621
WILLIAM TOTLE aged 18 yeres in the *George* 1623
JOHN CANON aged 20 yeres in the *Abigaile* 1622

The MUSTER of Amias Bolte]

AMIAS BOLTE aged 23 yeares in the *Neptune* in August 1618

The MUSTER of John Collins

JOHN COLLINS aged 30 yeares in the *Suply* 1620
SUSAN his wife aged 40 yeres in the *Treasuror* 1613
ANN VSHER aged 8 yeares born heare

<small>West & Sherley hundred.</small> The MUSTER of Henery Benson

Henery Benson aged 40 yeares in the *Francis Bonaventure* August 1620

Nicholas Blackman his ptner aged 40 in the same Shipp

<small>West & Sherley hundred. Charles Cittie</small> m' Thomas Pawlett's MUSTER

Thomas Pawlett aged 40 yeares in the *Neptune* in August 1618

Servant's

John Trussell aged 19 yeres in the *Southampton* 1622

The MUSTER of William Askew

William Askew aged 30 yeres in the *Prosperous* in May 1610

The MUSTER of Rebecca Rose Widdow

Rebecca Rose aged 50 yeares in the *Marygold* in May 1619

Marmaduke Hill } Children { aged 11 yeres } in the same Shipp
Jane Hill   { aged 14 yeres }

The MUSTER of m's Mary Maddison Widdow

Mary Maddison aged 30 yeares in the *Treasuror* 1618
Katherin Layden a Child. aged 7 yeares

Servant's

James Watson aged 20 yeares in the *George* 1623
Roger Lewes aged 19 yeares in the *Edwin* in May 1617

West & Sherley hundred.
Charles Cittie

The MUSTER of ROBERT* BAGWELL &c.

HENERY* BAGWELL aged 35 yeares in the *Deliuerance* 1608
SYMON TURGIS aged 30 yeares in the *William & Thomas* 1618

Servant's

RANDALL BAWDE aged 30 yeares in the *Due Returne* 1623
CHARLES   aged 19 yeares in the *Jacob* 1624

Sherley hundred.
Charles Cittie

The MUSTER of ROBERT MILNER &c

ROBERT MILNER aged 24 yeares in the *Francis Bonaventure* August 1620
JOHN PASSEMAN aged 29 yeres in the *Jonathan* May 1620
JENKIN OSBORN aged 24 yeres in the *George* 1617
WILLIAM WESTON aged 25 yeres in the *Jonathan* May 1620

The MUSTER of JOHN THROGMORTON &c.

JOHN THROGMORTON aged 24 yeares in ye *William & Thomas* 1618
CHYNA BOYSE aged 26 yeres in the *Georg* in May 1617

Servant's

EDWARD SPARSHOTT aged 31 yeares in the *Scafloure* 1621
FRANCIS DOWNING aged 24 yeres in the *Returne* March 1624
ELLIS RIPPING aged 23 yeares in the *Returne* 1624

The MUSTER of ROGER RATLIFE

ROGER RATLIFE aged 44 yeares in the *Georg* in May 1619
ANN his wife aged 40 in the *George* in May 1619
ISACK his Sonn aged 9 Months

---

* [So in the original. It will have been observed, that generally the name in the *heading* is the same as the first name in the list.]

Sherley hundred.
Charles Cittie

The MUSTER of NATHANIELL TATAM

NATHANIELL TATAM aged 20 yeares in the *George* May 1619

The MUSTER of m's KATHERINE BENETT Widdow

KATHERINE BENETT aged 24 yeres in the *Abigall* 1622
WILLIAM BENETT her sonn aged 3 week's

Servant's

RANDALL CREW aged 20 yeres in the *Charles* 1621

DEAD at WEST & SHERLEY, and at SHERLEY HUNDRED. 1624.

ANDREW DUDLEY, came in the *Trueloue* 1622
RAPH FREEMAN. in the *Margett and John* 1622
m' WILLIAM BENET Minister in the *Seafloure* 1621
Cap.t ISACK MADDESON
JAMES CROWDER in the *Returne* 1623
DANIELL VIERO in the *George* 1623
BARNARD JACKSON in the *Margrett & John* 1623
THOMAS WESTON in the *George* 1623
JAMES ROLFE Liuetennt GIBB'S Man ⎫
JOHN MICHAELL ⎬ slaine by the Indians.
FRANCIS   Cap.t MADISONS Man. ⎭

Jordans
Jorney.
Charles
Cittie

The MUSTER of the Inhabitant's of JORDANS JORNEY taken the 21th of January 1624

The MUSTER of m' WILLIAM FERRAR & m's JORDAN

WILLIAM FERRAR aged 31 yeares in the *Neptune* in August 1618
SISLEY JORDAN aged 24 yeres in the *Swan* in August 1610

27

Jordans Jorney.
  Charles Cittie

MARY JORDAN her daughter aged 3 yeares ⎫
MARGRETT JORDAN aged 1 yeare   ⎬ borne heare.
TEMPERANCE BALEY aged 7 yeares   ⎭

     Servant's

WILLIAM DAWSON aged 25 yeres in the *Discouery* March 1621
ROBERT TURNER aged 26 yeres in the *Tryall* June 1619
JOHN HELY aged 24 yeares in the *Charles* November 1621
ROGER PRESTON aged 21 yeares in the *Discouerie* March 1621
ROBERT MANUELL aged 25 yeres in the *Charles* November 1621
THOMAS WILLIAMS aged 24 yeares in the *Dutie* May 1618
RICHARD JOHNSON aged 22 yeares in the *Southampton* 1622
WILLIAM HATFEILD aged   in the *Southampton* 1622
JOHN PEAD 35 yeares old in the same Shipp
JOHN FREAME aged 16 yeares in the same Shipp

The MUSTER of THOMAS PALMER

THOMAS PALMER arived in the *Tyger* November 1621
JOANE his wife in the same Shipp
PRISILLA her daughter aged xj yeares

     Servant's

RICHARD ENGLISH aged xj yeares in the *James* 1622

The MUSTER of ROBERT FISHER

ROBERT FISHER arived in the *Elsabeth* May 1611
KATHERINE his wife in the *Marmaduk* October 1621
SISLY theire daughter aged 1 yeare

     Servant's

IDYE HALLIERS a Maid servant aged 30 yeares in ye *Jonathan* 1619

Jordans Jorney
Charles Cittie

The MUSTER of JOHN CLAYE

JOHN CLAYE arived in the *Treasuror* February 1613
ANN his wife in the *Ann* August 1623
    Servant's
WILLIAM NICHOLL'S aged 26 yeres in the *Dutie* in May 1619

The MUSTER of CHRISTOPHER SAFFORD

CHRISTOPHER SAFFORD arived in the *Treasuror* 1613
JOHN GIBB'S his ptner in the *Supply* 1619
    Servant's
HENERY LANE aged 20 yeres in the *Southampton* 1623

The MUSTER of HENERY WILLIAMS

HENERY WILLIAMS arived in the *Treasuror* 1613
SUSAN his wife in the *William & Thomas* 1618

The MUSTER of WILLIAM BRANLIN

WILLIAM BRANLIN arived in the *Margrett & John* 1620
ANN his wife in the *Trueloue* 1622

The MUSTER of JOHN FLUDD

JOHN FLUDD arived in the *Swan* 1610
MARGETT his wife in the *Supply* 1620
FRANCES FINCH her daughter in the *Suply* 1620
WILLIAM FLUDD his sonn aged 3 week's.

Jordans Jorney.
Charle, Cittie

The MUSTER of THOMAS CHAPMAN*

THOMAS CHAPMAN arived in the *Tryall* 1610
ANN his wife in the *George* 1617
THOMAS his sonn aged 2 yeare
ANN theire daughter aged 6 week's

The MUSTER of JOSEPH BULL

JOSEPH BULL arived in the *Abigaile* 1622

The MUSTER of JOHN DAVIES &c.

JOHN DAVIES arived in the *George* 1617
WILLIAM EMERSON his ptner in the *Sampson* 1618

Servant's
WILLIAM POPLETON aged   in the *James* 1622
EUSTICE DOWNES aged 25 yeares in the *Abigall* 1622

The MUSTER of THOMAS CAWSEY.

THOMAS CAWSEY arived in the *Francis Bonaventure* 1620

The MUSTER of THOMAS IRONMONGER

THOMAS IRONMONGER arived in the

The MUSTER of RICHARD MILTON

RICHARD MILTON arived in the *Suply* 1620

---

* [The fifth letter of this name is not clear; the word begins with an ascending letter, and *might* be read as CHAPLAIN; but it is certainly CHAPMAN in the next line.]

<small>Jordans Jorney.
Charles Cittie</small>   The MUSTER of NATHANIELL CAWSEY

NATHANIELL CAWSEY arived in the *Phœnix* 1607
THOMASINE his wife in the *Lyon* 1609

     Servant's
EDWARD DENISON aged 22 yeares ⎱ arived in the *Trueloue* 1623
JAMES BONNER aged 20 yeares ⎰
JAMES DORE age 19 yeares in the *Bona Nova* 1621
LAURANCE EVANS aged 15 yeares in the *James* 1622
JOANE WINSCOMB aged 20 yeares in the *George* 1618

DEAD at JORDANS JORNEY 1624

LIDIA SHERLEY came in the *George* 1623
SUSAN SHERLEY an Infant.

<small>Chaplains Choise.
Charles Cittie</small>   The MUSTER of the Inhabitant's of CHAPLAINS CHOYSE and the *Trueloues* Company taken the 21ᵗʰ January 1624

The MUSTER of Ensigne ISACK CHAPLAINE

ISACK CHAPLAINE arived in the *Starr* 1610
MARY his wife in the *James* 1622
JOHN CHAPLAINE his kinsman aged 15 yeares in the *James* 1622

     Servant's
ROBERT HUDSON aged 30 yeares ⎫
HENERY THORNE aged 18 yeares ⎬ arived in the *James* 1622
JOHN DUFFILL aged 14 yeares ⎪
IVIE BANTON a Maid servant ⎭
ANN MIGHILL a Maid servant arived in the *George* 1619

<small>Chaplains Choise.
Charles Cittie</small> ### The MUSTER of Walter Price &c.

WALTER PRICE arived in the *Wiłłm & Thomas* 1618
HENERY TURNER arived in the *John & Francis* 1615
     Servant's
EDWARD FALLOWES aged 30 yeares in the *Hopewell* 1623

The MUSTER of Thomas Keie

THOMAS KEIE aged 30 ariued in the *Prosperous* June 1619
SARAH his wife in the *Trueloue* 1622

The MUSTER of John Browne

JOHN BROWNE aged 28 yeares in the *Bona Nova* Aprill 1621

The MUSTER of John Trehearne

JOHN TREHEARNE aged 33 yeares in the *Trueloue* 1622

The MUSTER of David Jones

DAVID JONES aged 22 yeares in the *Trueloue* 1622

The MUSTER of John Box

JOHN BOX aged 23 yeares in the *Trueloue* 1622

Murderers for the forte............ 3

DEAD at Chaplins Choise 1624.

Henery Wilson came in the *Trueloue* 1622 slaine by ye Indians
Nicholas Sutton in the *James* 1622 slaine by the Indians
Nicholas Baldwin in the *Trueloue* 1622 slaine by the Indians
William Barnett in the *Trueloue* 1623.

<small>Pierseys hundred.</small> The MUSTER of the Inhabitant's of Peirseys Hundred taken the 20th of January 1624.

Samuell Sharpe arived in the *Seaventure* 1609
Elizabeth his wife in the *Margrett and John* 1621

Servant's
Henery Carman aged 23 yeares in the *Duty* 1620

The MUSTER of m' Grivell Pooley Minister

Grivell Pooley arived in the *James* 1622

Servant's
John Chambers aged 21 yeares in the *Bona Nova* 1622
Charles Magner aged 16 yeres in the *George* 1623

The MUSTER of Humfrey Kent

Humfrey Kent arived in the *George* 1619
Joane his wife in the *Tyger* 1621
Margrett Arrundell aged 9 yeares in the *Abigaile* 1621

Servant's
Christopher Beane aged 40 yeares in the *Neptune* 1618

Pierseys hundred.

The MUSTER of Thomas Doughtie

THOMAS DOUGHTIE arived in the *Marigold* 1619
ANN his wife in the *Marmaduke* 1621

The MUSTER of Edward Auborn

EDWARD AUBORN arived in the *Jonathan* 1620

The MUSTER of William Baker

WILLIAM BAKER arived in the *Jonathan* 1609

The MUSTER of John Woodson

JOHN WOODSON } in the *George* 1619
SARAH his wife

The MUSTER of Edward Threnorden

EDWARD THRENORDEN arived in the *Diana* 1619
ELIZABETH his wife in the *George* 1619

The MUSTER of Nicholas Baly

NICHOLAS BALY arived in the *Jonathan* 1620
ANN his wife in the *Marmaduk* 1621

The MUSTER of John Lipps

JOHN LIPPS arived in the *London Marchannt* 1621

Pierseys hundred.

The MUSTER of m' ABRAHAM PEIRSEYS Servant's.

yeres.

THOMAS LEA ....aged 50
ANTHONY PAGITT 35
SALOMAN JACKMAN 30
JOHN DAVIES aged 45
CLEMENT ROPER 25
JOHN BATES aged 24
THOMAS ABBE..................... 20
THOMAS BROOK'S 23
WILLIAM JONES 23
PEETER JONES..................... 24 } arived in the *Southampton* 1623
PIERCE WILLIAMS 23
ROBERT GRAUES.................. 30
EDWARD HUBBERSTEAD 26
JOHN LATHROP 25
THOMAS CHAMBERS 24
WALTER JACKSON 24
HENERY SANDERS 20
WILLIAM ALLEN 22
GEORG DAWSON 24

JOHN VPTON aged 26 in the *Bona nova* 1622
JOHN BAMFORD aged 23 yeares in the *James* 1622
WILLIAM GARRETT aged 22 in the *George* 1619
THOMAS SAWELL aged 26 in the *George* 1619
HENERY ROWINGE aged 25 yeares in the *Temperance* 1621
NATHANIELL THOMAS aged 23 yeres in the *Temperance* 1621
RICHARD BROADSHAW aged 20 yeares in the same Shipp
ROBERT OKLEY aged 19 yeares in the *William & Thomas* 1618
Negro
Negro
Negro } 4 Men
Negro

Pierseys hundred.
ALLICE THOROWDEN } maid servant's arived in the *Southampton* 1623
KATHERINE LEMAN
Negro Woman.
Negro Woman and a yong Child of hers.

S' SAMUELL ARGALL'S Cattell

DEAD at PEIRSEYS HUNDRED Anno Dñi 1624

JOHN LINICKER.	JOHN ENGLISH.
EDWARD CARLOWE.	CHRISTOPHER LEES Wife.
ROBERT HUSSYE.	ELIZABETH JONES.
JACOB LARBEE.	

Pasbehayghs Corporation of James Citty

The MUSTER of the Inhabitant's of PASBEHAYS & the MAINE taken the 30th of January 1624 belonging to the Corporation of James City

ADAM DIXON arived in the *Margrett & John*

JOSEPH RYALE arived in the *William & Thomas*

GEORGE FRIER arived in the *William & Thomas*
VRSULA his wife in the *London Marchant*

ALLEN KENISTON arived in the *Margrett & John*

ROBERT PARAMOUR arived in the *Swan*

WILLIAM KEMP arived in the *George*
MARGRETT his wife in the *George*
ANTHONY his Sonn aged 7 week's

RICHARD BRIDGWATER arived in the *London Marchaunt*
ISBELL his wife in the same Shipp

HUGH HAWARD arived in the *Starr*
SUSAN his wife in the *George*.

Pasbehaighs
James Citty

HENERY TURNER arived in the *London Marchannt*

JOSEPH CREW arived in the *London Marchannt*

THOMAS JONES arived in the *London Marchannt*
MARGRETT his wife in the same Shipp

EDWARD BOURBICTH in the *London Marchannt*

REVOLL MORCOCK arived in the *Jonathan*
ELIZABETH his wife
THOMAS his Sonne aged 1 yeare.

EDWARD FISHER arived in the *Jonathan*
SARAH his wife in the *Warwick*
EDWARD KILDALE her sonn aged 6 yeares
CLARE REN a girle aged 10 yeares.

JOHN MOONE arived in the *Returne* 1623

Servant's.
JULIAN HALLERS aged 19 yeares ⎫
GILES MARTIN aged 23 yeares ⎬ in the *Trueloue* 1623
CLINION RUSH aged 13 yeares ⎭

RICHARD SMITH arived in the *London Marchannt*

The MUSTER of the Governors Men at Pasbehaighs

THOMAS JORDEN aged 24 came in the *Diana*.
JOHN MILNHOUSE aged 36 in the *London Marchannt*
RICHARD SANDERS aged 25 in the *Francis Bonaventure*.
GRIFFIN WINNE aged 28 in the *Francis Bonaventure*.
ARTHURE CHANDLER aged 19 in the *Jonathan*.
WILLIAM DORRELL aged 18 in the *Trueloue*.
CHRISTOPHER RIPPING 22 in the *Francis Bonaventure*.
THOMAS OSBORN aged 18 in the *Francis Bonaventure*.
GEORGE NELSON aged 19 in the *Francis Bonaventure*.
FRANCIS BUTLER aged 18 in the *Francis Bonaventure*.

Pasbehaighs
James City
THOMAS BLANCK'S aged 17 in the *Francis Bonaventure*.
HENERY DOWTIE aged 19 in the *Jonathan*.

JOHN SWARBECK came in the
the Maine.

James Citty.
THOMAS MARLOE came in the *Bona Nova*.

THOMAS BUNN
BRIDGITT his wife
THOMAS his sonn aged 1 yeare
                    Servant's
JOHN SMITH aged 30 yeares } in the *Abigaile*
THOMAS SMITH aged 16 yeres }
THOMAS JONES aged 35 in the *Bona Nova*
JAMES ROBESONN aged 35 in the *Swan*.
ELIZABETH HODGES a Maid servant in the *Abigaile*

THOMAS SWINHOW came in the *Diana*.
                    Servant's
LAWRANCE SMALEPAGE aged 20 yeres in the *Abigaile*

JOHN CARTER came in the *Prosperous*.

DAVID ELLIS in the *Mary Margrett*
MARGRETT his wife in the *Margrett & John*

JAMES TOOKE arived in the

WILLIAM BINK'S came in the *George*
ANN his wife in the *George*

MICHAELL BATT came in the *Hercules*.
ELLIN his wife in the *Warwick*.

ROBERT LINCE came in the *Treasuror*.

HUGH BALDWINE came in the *Tryall*
SUSAN his wife in the

the Maine.
James Citty

ROBERT SCOTCHMORE came in the *George* 1623
THOMAS KNISTON cane [KENISTON came] in the *George* 1623

Servant's

ROGER KIDD aged 24 yeares in the *George* 1623

ROBERT CHOLMLE .... } came in the *Charitie*
JAMES STANDISH....................

The MUSTER of DOCTO' POTT's Men in the MAINE

THOMAS LEISTER aged 33 yeares
ROGER STANLEY aged 27
THOMAS PRITCHARD aged 28
HENERY CROCKER aged 34 } came in the *Abigaile* 1620
THOMAS CROSSE aged 22
JOHN TRYE aged 20
WALTER BEARE aged 28
RANDALL HOLT aged 18 yeares in the *George* 1620
  The rest of his servant's, Provisions, Amunition &ct. at JAMES CITTY.

DEAD at PASBEHAIGHS & in the MAINE 1624.

JOACHIM ANNDREWS.
HENERY SCOTT.
RICHARD } 2 Men of m' BUNNS.
RICHARD

James Citty The MUSTER of the Inhabitant's of JAMES CITTIE
taken the 24th of January 1624

The MUSTER of Sr FRANCIS WYATT K^t &ct.

Sr FRANCIS WYATT K^t Governo' &^{c.} came in the *George* 1621

Servant's

CHRISTOPHER COOKE aged 25 in the *George* 1621

James Citty.
GEORG HALL aged 13 in the *Suply* 1620
JONATHAN GILES 21 in the *Triall* 1619
JOHN MATHEMAN 19 in the *Jonathan* 1619
JANE DAVIS 24 in the *Abigaile* 1622

The MUSTER of Sʳ GEORGE YEARLEY Kᵗ &ct.

Sʳ GEORGE YEARLLEY Kᵗ &c. came in the *Deliuerance* 1609
TEMPERANCE LADY YEARLLEY came in the *Faulcon* 1608
m' ARGALL YEARLLEY aged 4 yeares
m' FRANCIS YEARLLEY aged 1 yeare } Children borne heare
m's ELIZABETH YEARLLEY aged 6 yeres

   Servant's at JAMES CITTY

RICHARD GREGORY aged 40
ANTHONY JONES 26
THOMAS DUNN 14 } came in the *Temperaunce* 1620
THOMAS PHILDUST 15
THOMAS HATCH 17 in the *Duty* 1619
ROBERT PEAKE 22 in the *Margrett & John* 1623
WILLIAM STRANGE 18 in the *George* 1619
ROGER THOMPSON 40 in *London Marchaunt* 1620
ANN his wife
RICHARD ARRUNDELL in the *Abigall* 1620
GEORG DEVERILL 18 in the *Temperaunce* 1620
THOMAS BARNETT 16 in the *Elsabeth* 1620
THEOPHILUS BERISTON 23 in the *Treasuror* 1614
Negro Men. 3
Negro Woemen. 5.
SUSAN HALL in the *William & Thomas* 1618
ANN WILLIS in the *Temperance* 1620
ELIZABETH ARRUNDELL in the *Abigall* 1620.
  The rest of his servant's at HOG ILAND.

James Citty.   ## The MUSTER of Docto' John Pott

Docto' JOHN POTT .... } arived in the *George* 1620
m's ELIZABETH POTT .... }

Servant's.
RICHARD TOWNSHEND aged 19 yeares in the *Abigaile* 1620
THOMAS WILSON aged 27 yeares in the *Abigaile* 1620
OSMOND SMITH aged 17 yeares in the *Bona Nova* 1620
SUSAN BLACKWOOD a Maid servant in the *Abigaile* 1622

The MUSTER of Capt Roger Smith

Capt ROGER SMITH came in the *Abigaile* 1620
m's JOANE SMITH came in the *Blessinge*
ELIZABETH SALTER aged 7 yeares came in the *Seafloure*
ELIZABETH ROLFE aged 4 yeares } borne in Virginia.
SARAH MACOCK aged 2 yeares.   }

Servant's
CHARLES WALLER aged 22 came in the *Abigaile* 1620
CHRISTOPHER BANKUS aged 19 yeares in the *Abigaile* 1622
HENERY BOOTH aged 20 in the *Dutie*
HENERY LACTON aged 18 yeares in the *Hopewell* 1623

The rest of his men theire Provisions Armes &ct. Over the Watter.

The MUSTER of Capt Raph Hamor

Capt RAPH HAMOR
m's ELIZABETH HAMOR
JEREMY CLEMENT   } her Children.
ELIZABETH CLEMENT }

Servant's
JOHN LIGHTFOOTE in the *Seaventure*
FRANCIS GIBB'S a boy in the *Seaflower*.
ANN ADDAMS a Maid servant.

The rest of his servant's, Provisions Armes &^{c}. at HOG-ILAND.

James Citty   The MUSTER of Capt WILLIAM PIERCE

Capt WILLIAM PIERCE came in the *Sea-venture*
m^s JONE PIERCE his wife in the *Blessinge*

                 Servant's

THOMAS SMITH aged 17 yeares in the *Abigaile*
HENERY BRADFORD aged 35 yeres in the *Abigaile*
ESTER EDERIFE a maid servant in the *Jonathan*
ANGELO a Negro Woman in the *Treasuror*.

    The rest of his servant's; Provisions, Armes, Munition &ct at
                MULBERY ILAND.

      The MUSTER of m^r ABRAHAM PEIRSEY Marchannt

m^r ABRAHAM PEIRSEY came in the *Susan* 1616
ELIZABETH his daughter aged 15 yeres } came in the *Southampton* 1623
MARY his daughter aged 11 yeres

                 Servant's.

CHRISTOPHER LEE aged 30 yceres
RICHARD SERIEANT aged 36 yeres } came in the *Southampton* 1623.
ALICE CHAMBERS } maid servant's.
ANNIS SHAW

       The rest at Peirseys Hundred.

       The MUSTER of m^r EDWARD BLANEY.

m^r EDWARD BLANEY came in the *Francis Bonaventure*

             Servant's

ROBERT BEW aged 20 came in the *Dutie*.
JOHN RUSSELL aged 19 in the *Bona Nova*.

   The rest of his Servant's Armes &ct at his Plantacon Over ye Watter.

ROBERT POOLE came in the ———

JAMES HICMOTT came in the *Bonaventure*
his wife in the ———.

James Cittie.
JOHN SOUTHERN came in the *George* 1620
Servant's.
THOMAS CRUST aged   came in the *George* 1620

RANDALL SMALEWOOD came in the

GEORGE GRAUE came in the *Seaventure*
ELNOR his wife in the *Susan*
JOHN GRAUE theire sonne aged 10 yeares
REBECCA SNOW ⎫
SARA SNOW   ⎭ her daughters.

EDWARD CADGE came in the *Marmaduke*
NATHANIELL JEFFREYS came in the *Gift*.

JOHN JACKSON came in the
JOHN JACKSON his sonn aged 9 yeares
GERCIAN BUCK aged 10 yeares

THOMAS ALNUTT came in the *Gifte*
his wife in the *Marygold*
Servant's.
ROGER ROED'S aged 20 yeares in the *Bony bess*.

PEETER LANGMAN came in the *William & Thomas*.
MARY his wife came in the
PEETER ASCAM her sonn aged 1 yeares
ABIGAILE ASCAM her daughter aged 4 yeres.
BENOMY BUCK aged 8 yeres
PELEG BUCK aged 4 yeres
Servant's
ABRAHAM PORTER aged 36 yeares in the
THOMAS SAWIER aged 23 yeares in the

---

m' JOHN BURROWES came in the
BRIDGETT his wife
MARA BUCK aged 13 yeares

James Citty.

Servant's
JOHN COOKE aged 27 yeares
NICHOLAS GOULDFINCH aged 19 yeres
JOHN BRADSTON ~~aged 18 yeres~~*
THOMAS THOROWGOOD aged 17 yeres
ELLIAS GAILE aged 14 yeares
ANDREW HOWELL aged 13 yeres
ANN ASHLEY aged 19 yeres

The Cattell belonging to m' BUCKS Children

ELIZABETH SOOTHEY came in the *Southampton*
ANN SOOTHEY her daughter

JOHN JEFFERSON came in the *Bona Nova*
WALGRAUE MARK'S in the *Margrett & John.*

WILLIAM MUTCH came in the *Jonathan*
MARGERY his wife in the *George* 1623

RICHARD STEEPHENS came in the *George* 1623

Servant's.
WASSELL RAYNER aged 28 yeres came in the
THOMAS SPILLMAN aged 28 yeres in the *George* 1623
EDWARD PRISE aged 29 yeres in the *George* 1623
JOANE RAYNER wife of WASSELL RAYNER

GEORGE MINIFIE arived in the *Samuell* July 1623

Servant's
JOHN GRIFFIN aged 26 yeares in the *William & John* 1624
EDWARD WILLIAMS aged 26 yeres came in the same Shipp.

JOHN BARNETT aged 26 yeres came in the *Jonathan* 1620

---

* [Thus erased in the original.]

James Ileand

JOHN STOAK'S
ANN his wife } came in the *Warwick.*

RICHARD TREE came in the *George*
JOHN his Sonne aged 12 yeres

Servant's
SILVESTER BULLEN aged 28 yeres came in the

Wiłłm LASEY
SUSAN his wife } came in the *Southampton* 1624

JOHN WEST came in the *Bony bess*
THOMAS CROMPE came in the

JOHN GREEVETT came in the
ELLIN his wife in the

THOMAS PASSMORE
JANE his wife } came in the *George.*

Servant's.
THOMAS KERFITT aged 24 yeares in the *Hopwell*
ROBERT JULIAN aged 20 yeares in the *Jacob.*
JOHN BUCKMUSTER aged 20 yeres in the *Hopwell.*

CHRISTOPHER HALL came in the

ROBERT FITT came in the *George.*
ANN his wife in the *Abigaile*

GEORGE ONION came in the *Francis bona venture.*
ELIZABETH his wife in the same Shipp.
FRANCIS PALL a boy aged 6 yeares
THOMAS PALL a boy aged 4 yeres

JOHN HALL came in the *John & Francis.*
SUSAN his wife in the *London Marchant*

James Iland.

Robert Marshall came in the *George*
Ann his wife in the same Shipp

Thomas Grubb came in the *George*

John Osborn came in the
Mary his wife in the

William Spencer came in the *Sarah*.
Allice his wife in the
Allice theire daughter aged 4 yeres.

Thomas Graye came in the
Margrett his wife in the
William theire Sonn aged 3 yeres
Jone theire daughter aged 6 yeres.

Gabriell Holland came in the *John & Francis*.
Rebecca his wife in the same Shipp

Josias Tanner aged 24 yeres came in the
Andrew Railey came in the
William Cooksey
Thomas Baglen
William Carter

John Johnson
Ann his wife
John his sonn aged 1 yeare
Ann his daughter aged 4 yeres
Alice Kean a Maid servant.

John Hitchy
Thomas de la Maior.

DEAD at JAMES CITTIE & in the ILAND 1624

RICHARD MUMFORD
GEORGE CLARKE
BARTLOMEW BLAKE
WILLIAM WAÑERTON
SIBILL ROYALL
GOODWIFE JEFFEREYS
THOMAS POPKIN
THOMAS SIDES
THOMAS WEST
Wᴹ SPENCER a Child
 a servant of mʳ KETHS
mˢ PEIRSE
JOHN GEE
 a servant of PEETER LANGMAN
 PHINLOE
mˢ SUSAN KETH.

Neck of Land nere James Citty. The MUSTER of the Inhabitant's of the Neck-of-Land neare JAMES CITTY taken Febr the 4ᵗʰ 1624.

RICHARD KINGSMELL came in the *Delaware*
JANE his wife in the *Susan*
NATHANIELL his sonne aged 5 yeares.
SUSAN his Daughter aged 1 yeare.
   Servant's
HORTEN WRIGHT aged 20 yeres came in the *Susan*
JOHN JACKSON aged came in the *Abigall.*
EDWARD a Negro
ISBELL PRATT came in the *Jonathan*

JOHN SMITH came in the *Bonaventure.*

THOMAS BAGWELL came in the

Neck of Land neare
  James Citty

THOMAS BENETT came in the *Bona Nova*
MARGERY his wife in the *Guift*
SARAH BROMEDG a Child of 2 yeares old.

JOHN REDDISH came in the ―――

m^r ALNUTT and his servant here Planted reconed before in the Muster of JAMES CITTIE.

DEAD in this Plantacon 1624

a Man servant of m^r KINGSMELL'S.

LIUING

RICHARD PIERCE } came in the *Neptune*.
ELIZABETH his wife }

Archers Hope
  James Citty

THOMAS BRANSBY came in the *Charitie*

Servant's
NICHOLAS GREENHILL aged 24 yeres }
CHADWALLADER JONES aged 22 yeres } came in the *Marmaduk* 1623
ROBERT CREW aged 23 yeares }

JOHN ELLISON came in the *Prosperous*
ELLIN his wife in the *Charitie*

Servant's
JOHN BADELEY aged 24 yeres came in the *Hopwell* 1623

THOMAS FARLEY came in the *Ann* 1623
JANE his wife in the same Shipp.
ANN a Child

Servant's
NICHOLAS SHOTTEN aged 40 yeres in the *Ann* 1623

Archers Hope.
James Citty
JOSEPH JOHNSON came in the *William & Thomas*
MARGRETT his wife in the *Abigaile*
GEORGE PROUSE came in the *Diana*

DEAD at ARCHERS HOPE 1624
GEORGE ELLISON a Child
        a Maid servant of m' BRANSBYES.
WILLIAM BROWNE.

Burrows Hill
James Citty
m' BURROWES and six of his men wch are planted heare are recoñed,
   wth theire Armes Provisions &c, at JAMES CITTIE
JOHN SMITH came in the *Elizabeth* 1611
SUSANNA his wife in the *Bona Nova* 1619
FRANCIS SMITH his sonne aged 1 yeare
                Servant's
JOHN ELLATT aged 15 yeres in the *Margrett & John* 1621

GEORGE PELTON came in the *Furtherance* 1622

RICHARD RICHARD'S came in the *London Marchant* 1620
RICHARD DOLPHINBE came in the *Guift* 1618

Paces Paines
James Citty
JOHN PROCTOR came in the *Seaventure* 1607
ALLIS his wife in the *George* 1621
                Servant's
RICHARD GROUE aged 30 yeres in the *George* 1623
EDWARD SMITH aged 20 in the *George* 1621
WILLIAM NAYLE aged 15 in the *Ann* 1623

PHETTIPLACE CLOSE came in the *Starr* 1608
DANIELL WATTKINS in the *Charles* 1621
                Servant's
MARTIN DEMON aged 15 yeres in the *George* 1617
JOHN SKINNER in the *Marmaduk* 1621

Paces Paines
  James Citty

THOMAS GATES came in the *Swan* 1609
ELIZABETH his wife in the *Warwick*. 1620
WILLIAM BEDFORD in the *James* 1621

FRANCIS CHAPMAN came in the *Starr* 1608

[C]ap¹ Smiths Plant.   The MUSTER of CAP^T ROGER SMITHS men
  James Citty   Over ye Watter

FRANCIS FOWLER aged 23 yeres

CHRISTOPHER LAWSON
ALCE his wife

CHRISTOPHER REDHEAD aged 24

STEPHEN WEBB aged 25 yeres

JOHN BUTTERFEILD aged 23 yeres

WILLIAM BAKER aged 24 yeres

RICHARD ALFORD aged 26 yeres

THOMAS HARVIE aged 24 yeres

THOMAS MOLTON aged 25 yeres

m^r Blaneys Plant.   The MUSTER of m' EDWARD BLANEYS Men
  James Citty   Ouer ye Watter.

RICE WATKINS aged 30 yeres came in the *Francis bonaventure*.
NATHANIELL FLOID aged 24 in the *Bona Nova*.
GEORG ROGERS 23 ....⎫
JOHN SHELLEY 23 .... ⎬ in the *Bona Nova*.
THOMAS OTTOWELL 40 ....⎪
THOMAS CROUCH 40 ....⎭
ROBERT SHEPPEARD 20 in the *Hopwell*.
WILLIAM SAWIER 18 in the *Hopwell*.
ROBERT CHAUNTRIE 19 in the *George*

m^r Blaneys Plant.
  James Citty

WILLIAM HARTLEY 23 in the *Charles*
LAWLEY DAMPORT 29 in the *Duty*
WILLIAM WARD 20 in the *Jonathan*
JEREMY WHITE 20 in the *Tyger*
JOHN HACKER 17 in the *Hopwell*
ROBERT WHITMORE 22 in the *Duty*

Capt Mathews Plant
  James Citty

Capt SAMUELL MATHEWS came in the *Southampton* 1622
m' DAVID SAND's Minister came in the *Bonaventure* 1620

Servant's.

ROBERT MATHEWS aged 24 ⎫ cam
ROGER WILLIAMS......... 20
SAMUELL DAVIES......... 18
HENERY JONES............ 25 ⎬ came in the *Southampto* 1622
AARON CONAWAY 20
JOHN THOMAS 18
MICHAELL LAPWORTH... 16 ⎭

WILLIAM LUSAM .... 27 ⎫
WILLIAM FEILD .... 23 ⎬ in the *Charles* 1621
PEETER MONTECUE...... 21 ⎭

ROBERT FERNALL 31 in the *London Marchant* 1619
WALTER COOP [COOPER] 33 in the *Jonathan* 1619
WILLIAM WALTERS 27 in the *Bona Nova* 1618
NICHOLAS CHAPMAN 31 in the *Jonathan* 1619
GREGORY SPICER 22 in the *Triall* 1618
NICHOLAS PEIRSE 23 in the *Falcon* 1619
ROBERT PENN 22 in the *Abigaile* 1620
WILLIAM DALBY 28 in the *Furtherance* 1622
THOMAS HOPSON 12 in the *Bona Nova* 1618
ABRAHAM WOOD 10 in the *Margrett ℰ John* 1620

Cap¹ Mathews Plant
   James Citty
WILLIAM KINGSLEY 24 ...... ⎫ in the *Marmaduk* 1623
THOMAS BRIDGES 12 .... ⎭
ARTHURE GOLDSMITH 26 came in the *Diana* 1618

Crowders Plant.
   James Citty
m' HUGH CROWDER came in the *Bona Nova* 1619

Servant's

RICHARD BALL in the *George* 1617
THOMAS HAWKINS in the *James* 1622
PAULE RENALLES in the *Tryall* 1619
NICHOLAS SMITH a boy of 18 yeres in the *Bona Nova* 1621
JOHN VERIN a boy of 14 yeares in the *George* 1623

---

mr Treasurors Plant.

The MUSTER of m' GEORG SAND'S Esquire

m' GEORG SANDIS Esquire Treasuro' &c came in the *George* 1621

Servant's

MARTIN TURNER   ⎫
GEORGE BAILIFE   ⎪
JOHN SPARK'S   ⎪
JOHN DANCY   ⎪
JOHN EDWARD'S   ⎬ came in the *George* 1621
NICHOLAS TOMPSON   ⎪
ROSAMUS CARTER   ⎪
JOHN STONE a boy   ⎭
NICHOLAS COMON   ⎫ in the *Guifte* 1622
NICHOLAS EYRES a boy ⎭
DAVID MANSFEILD   ⎫ in the *Bona Nova* 1619 hired servant's
JOHN CLAXON   ⎭
THOMAS SWIFTE   ⎫ in the *Tyger* freemen. 1622
JOHN BALDWINE   ⎭

m' Treasurors Plant.

hired.   DANIELL POOLE a french man
his wife
a yong Child of theires

m' Treasurors Plant.
    James Citty

The MUSTER of those that Liue in ye TREASURORS Plant.

ROBERT SHEAPERD came in the *George* 1621
JAMES CHAMBERS in the *Dutie* 1620
JOHN PARSONS ⎫
WILLIAM BENGE ⎪
JOHN EVENS ⎬ in the *Marygold* 1619
ROBERT EDMUND'S ⎪
JOHN COMES ⎭
JOHN TYOS ⎫
WILLIAM PILKINTON ⎪
ELIAS LONGE ⎬ in the *Bona Nova* 1620
THOMAS HALL ⎭
MARGRETT PILKINTON ⎱ weomen
JANE LONG ⎰
m' VINCENCIO the Italian
m' BERNARDO
his wife
a Child

ZACHARY CRIPP'S came in the *Margrett & John* 1621
EDWARD WHITE in the *Bona Nova* 1620
MATHEW HAMON in the *Southampton* 1622
PHILLIP KITHLY in the *Furtherance* 1622
ANTHONY WEST in the *James* 1622

m^r Treasurors Plant.
James Citty

DEAD at all these PLANTATIONS Over the Watter 1624

JOHN PHILMOTT
WILLIAM PLANT
THOMAS ROWLSON
EDWARD JONES
JOHN DIMSDALE
JOHN DOCKER
ROBERT ALDRIDGE
RICHARD GREENE
JAMES DAVIS
DAVID WILLIAMS
JOHN FOXEN

ELIAS HENTON
THO: FITCH
ENECHA FITCH
JOHN SERE
WILLIAM SAND'S
GEORG GURR ⎫ slaine by the
WILLIAM COMES ⎭ Indians
ROBERT EVARS.
PEACEABLE SHEREWOOD.
WILLIAM HALL

Hog Iland

The MUSTER of CAP^T RAPH HAMORS servant's

JEFFEREY HULL came in the *George*
MORDECAY KNIGHT in the *William & John*
THOMAS DOLEMAN in the *Returne*
ELKINTON RATLIFFE in the *Seafloure*
THOMAS POWELL in the *Seafloure.*
THOMAS COOPER in the *Returne*
JOHN DAVIES in the *Guifte.*

The MUSTER of LIUETENNT BARKLEY.

Liuetennt EDWARD BARKLEY in the *Vnitie.*
m^s JANE BARKLEY in the *Seafloure.*
JANE BARKLEY his daughter.

Servant's

THOMAS PHILLIP'S ⎫
FRANCIS BARRETT ⎭ in the *Bona Nova*

Hog Iland

ROBERT MARTIN in the *George*.
KATHERIN DAVIES in the *Southampton*.

JOHN VTY came in the *Francis Bonaventure*
ANN his wife in the *Seafloure*.
JOHN his Sonn in the *Seafloure*.
Servant's
WILLIAM BURT } in the *Bony besse*
WILLIAM STOCKER }
RICHARD BICKLEY in the *Returne*.

JOHN CHEW came in the *Charitie*.
SARAH his wife in the *Seafloure*.
Servant's.
ROGER DELK in the *Southampton*.
SAMUELL PARSON in the *Hopewell*.
WALTER HASLEWOOD in the *Due Returne*.

HENERY ELWOOD } in the *Francis Bonaventure*.
WILLIAM RAMSHAW }
JOHN STONE in the *Swann*
SISLY his wife in the *Seafloure*.
HENERY CROCKER in the *Marygold*
JONE his wife in the *Swan*.
HENERY WOODWARD in the *Diana*.
JANE his wife
THOMAS HITCKOCK in the *Marygold*
ALICE his wife
ROGER WEBSTER
JOANE his wife
JOANE DAVIS.

Hog Iland.

The MUSTER of Sʳ Georg Yearlleys Men

Maximillian Stone aged 36 came in the *Temperance* 1620
Elizabeth his wife in the same Shipp.
Maximillian his sonn aged 9 months.
Robert Guy 22 in the *Swann* 1619
Edward Yates 18 in the *Duty* 1619
Cesar Puggett 20 in the *Diana* 1619
Allexander Sanders 24 in the *Trueloue* 1623
William Strachey 17 in the *Temperance* 1620
George Whitehand 24 in the *Temperance* 1620
Henery King 22 in the *Jonathan* 1620
John Day 24 in the *London Marchannt* 1620
The wife of John Day in the same Shipp

John Root in the *Guift* .... ⎫
Walter Blake in the *Swan* ...... ⎬ Dwellers.
Thomas Watt's in the *Treasuror*. ⎭

    David Dutton...... ⎫
    Rich: Baker......... ⎬ Dead

The rest of his servant's. Provisions
Armes &ct reconed at James Citty

Martins Hundred.

The MUSTER of the Inhabitant's of Martins Hundred taken the 4ᵗʰ of February 1624.

mʳ William Harwood came in the *Francis Bonaventure*

                  Servant's

Hugh Hughs came in the *Guifte*.
Ann his wife........................ ⎫
Thomas Doughtie aged 26...... ⎬ came in the *Abigall*.
John Hasley aged 22 yeres...... ⎭
Samuell Weaver 20 in the *Bony bess*
Elizabeth Bygraue 12 came in the *Warwick*.

Martins Hundred
ELLIS EMERSON ....
ANN his wife......................... } came in the *George* 1623.
THOMAS his sonn aged 11 ....

      Servant's.
THOMAS GOULDING aged 26 yeres came in the *George* 1623
MARTIN SLATIER aged 20 cam frō Canada in the *Swan* 1624

ROBERT ADDAMS..................... } came in the *Bona Nova*.
AUGUSTINE LEAK ....
WINIFRED LEAK his wife came in the *George* 1623

      Servant's
RICHARD SMITH aged 24 yeres came in the *George* 1623.

STEEPHEN BARKER came in the *James*
HUMPHREY WALDEN in the *Warwick*

JOHN JACKSON .... } came in the *Warwick*.
ANN his Wife...............
A Child aged 20 week's

      Servant's.
THOMAS WARD aged 47 yeres ... } came in the *Warwick*
JOHN STEEPHENS 35 yeres ......

SAMUELL MARCH came in the *William & Thomas*.
COLLICE his wife in the *Ann* 1623
SAMUELL CULLEY came in the *London Marchamt*

ROBERT SCOTCHMORE and his Company now planted heare are reconned
 before in the MAINE

DEAD at MARTINS HUNDRED this yeare
ALLICE EMERSON a girle
ROBERT   a boy of m' EMARSONS
      a girle of JOHN JACKSONS
      a Child of SAMUELL MARCH.

Mulburie Iland.

The MUSTER of the Inhabitant's att MULBURY ILAND taken the 25th of January 1624.

The MUSTER of Capt WILLIAM PIERCES servant's

RICHARD ATTKINS aged 24 came in the *London Marchaunt*
ABIGALL his wife .... ⎫
WILLIAM BAKER aged 20 . ⎭ came in the *Abigall*
ROBERT ASTON 29 in the *Treasuror*
HUGH WING 30 ⎫
ROBERT LATHOM 20 ⎬ came in the *George* 1620
RICHARD ALDON 19 ⎪
THOMAS WOOD 35 ⎭
ROGER RUCE came in the *Charles*
ALLEXANDER GILL 20 in the *Bony bess*
SAMUELL MORRIS 20 in the *Abigall*
THOMAS ROSE 35 in the *Jonathan*
ROBERT HEDGES aged 40 yeres in the

JOHN VIRGO came in the *Treasuror*
SUSAN his wife in the same Shipp

JOHN GATTER came in the *George* 1620

WILLIAM RICHARDSON came in the *Edwine*

RICHARD FINE came in the *Neptune*

JOHN NOWELL came in the *Margrett & John*

RICHARD DOWNES came in the *Jonathan*

JOHN CRANICH came in the *Marygold*

PERCEVALL WOOD came in the *George*
ANN his wife in the *George*.

WILLIAM RAYMONT came in the *Neptune*

WILLIAM BULLOCK came in the *Jonathan*

Mulbury Iland
ANTHONY BARAM came in the *Abigall*
ELLIZABETH his wife in the *William & Thomas*

THOMAS HARWOOD came in the *Margrett & John* 1622
GRACE his wife in the *George*

Servant's.
THOMAS READ aged 65 yeres

Wariscoyack.

The MUSTER of the Inhabitant's at WARISCOYACK taken the 7th of Febr 1624.

The MUSTER of m' EDWARD BENNETT's servant's

HENERY PINKE came in the *London Marchannt* 1619
JOHN BATE in the *Addam* 1621
PEETER COLLINS in the *Addam* 1621
WASSELL WEBLING ⎫
ANTONIO a Negro ⎭ in the *James* 1621
CHRISTOPHER REYNOLD'S ⎫
LUKE CHAPPMAN ⎬ in the *John & Francis* 1622
EDWARD MAYBANK ⎭
JOHN ATTKINS ⎫
WILLIAM DENUM ⎬ in the *Guifte* 1623
FRANCIS BANK'S ⎭
MARY a Nergro Woman in the *Margrett & John* 1622

[Basses Choyse]

A MUSTER of the Inhabitance of BASSES CHOYSE

CAPT NATHANIELL BASSE his MUSTER

NATHANIELL BASSE aged 35 in the *furtherance* 1622
WILLIAM BARNARD aged 21 in the *furtherance* 1622
EDWARD WIGGE aged 22 in the *Abigall* 1621

Basses Choyse

The MUSTER of Thomas Phillipes

THOMAS PHILLIPES aged 26 in the *William and Thomas* 1618
ELZABETH PHILLIPES aged 23 in the *sea Flower* 1621

The MUSTER of Thomas Bennett

THOMAS BENNETT aged 38 in the *Neptune* 1618
MARY BENNETT aged 18 in the *Southampton* 1622
ROGER HEFORD aged 22 in the *Returne* 1623
BENIAMINE SIMES aged 33 in the

RICHARD LONGE his MUSTER

RICHARD LONGE aged 33 in the
ALICE LONGE aged 23 in the *London Marchant* 1620
ROBART LONGE a Child borne in Virginia

Wariscoyack

RICHARD EVAND'S his MUSTER

RICHARD EVAND'S aged 35 in the *Neptune* 1618

WILLIAM NEWMAN his MUSTER

WILLIAM NEWMAN aged 35 in the *Furtherance* 1622
JOHN ARMY aged 35 in the *Furtherance* 1622

HENRIE WOODWARD his MUSTER

HENRIE WOODWARD aged 30 in the
JOHN BROWNINGE aged 22 in the *Abigall* 1621

Servant's
AMBROSE aged 25 in the *Marmiducke* 1621
PEETER aged 19 in the *Margett and John* 1620

MUSTERS OF THE INHABITANTS IN VIRGINIA.

Wariscoyack

A list of the DEAD in WARISCOYACKE 1624.

JOHN SELLEY
NATHANIELL HAUKWORTH [or HANKWORTH]
THOMAS SHEWOUD
BENIAMIN HANDCLEARE

MARGRETT SYMES
NATHANIELL ⎫
THOMAS   ⎭ Servant's
of Mr BENNET'S men
slayne by the Indianes ⎬ 5

Newportes newes

Mr DANNIELL GOOKINES MUSTER

Servantes

WILLIAM WADSWORTH aged: 26
WILLIAM FOOCKES aged: 24
THOMAS CURTIS aged: 24
PEETER SHERWOOD aged: 21
GILBERT WHITFILD aged: 23
RISE GRIFFIN aged: 24
WILLIAM SMITH aged: 23
ANTHONIE EBSWORTH aged: 26
} All wch Came in the *Flyinge Harte.* 1621:

ISAYE DELYWARR aged 22
HENRIE CARSLEY aged: 23
ROGER WALKER aged: 22
EDMOND MORGON aged: 22
WILLIAM CLARKE aged: 25
JOSEPH MOSLEY aged: 21
JOHN PARRATT aged: 36
ROBART SMITH aged: 22
WILLIAM CRONEY aged: 24
WILLIAM LONGE aged: 19
ANNE EBSWORTH aged: 44
ELLNOR HARRIS aged: 21
in the *Prouidence* 1623*

DEAD in this Plantatō

one ARMESTRONGE

---

* [I suppose this refers to the whole of the names from DELYWARR to HARRIS; but there is no "brace" in the original.]

Elizabeth Cittie

CAPT WILLIAM TUCKER his MUSTER

Capt WILLIAM TUCKER: aged: 36: in the *Mary and James:* 1610
Mʳˢ MARY TUCKER aged: 26: in the *George:* 1623.
ELZABETH TUCKER borne in Virginia in August:
GEORGE TOMSON aged: 17 ....⎫
PAULE TOMSON aged: 14............ ⎬ in the *George* 1623:
WILLIAM THOMSON — 11 ....⎭
PASCOE CHAMPION aged 23......... ⎱ in the *Ellonor* 1621:
STRENGHT SHEERE aged: 23 ...... ⎰
THOMAS EVAND'S aged: 23 ....⎫
STEPHEN COLLOWE aged: 23 ...... ⎬ in the *George:* 1623.
ROBART MUNDAY aged: 18 ....⎭
MATHEWE ROBINSONN aged: 24 in the *greate hopewell* 1623:
RICHARD APPLETON aged: 19: in the *James* 1622.
JOHN MORRIS aged 24: in the *Bona Noua:* 1619.
MARY MORRIS aged 22: in the *George* 1623
WILLIAM HUTCHINSON aged 21: in the *Diana* 1618
PEETER PORTER aged 20 in the *Tyger* 1621.
WILLIAM CRAWSHAW an Indean Baptised.
ANTONEY Negro: ISABELL Negro: and WILLIAM theire Child Baptised

JOHN DOWNEMAN his MUSTER

JOHN DOWNEMAN aged: 33: in the *John and Francis:* 1611:
ELZABETH DOWNEMAN aged: 22: in the *Warwicke* 1621.
MOYSES STONES aged: 16: in the *Bone Bes* 1623

JOHN LAYDON his MUSTER

JOHN LAYDON aged 44: in the *Susan* 1606
ANNE LAYDON aged 30: in the *Mary Margett* 1608

Elzabeth Cittie
VIRGINIA LAYDON ....
ALCE LAYDON .... } borne in Virginia.
KATHERIN LAYDON...... ....
MARGERETT LAYDON ....

WILLIAM COLE his MUSTER

WILLIAM COLE aged 26 in the *Neptune* 1618
FRANCIS COLE aged 27 in the *Susan* 1616
ROGER FARBRASE aged 26 in the *Elzabeth* 1621

MILES PRICKETT and FRANCIS MITCHELL their MUSTERS.

MILES PRICKETT aged 36 in the *Starr:* 1610
FRANCIS MITCHELL aged 38 in the *Neptune* 1618
MAUDLIN MITCHELL aged 21 in the *Bona Noua* 1620
JOHN MITCHELL borne in Virginia 1624

RICHARD YONGE his MUSTER

RICHARD YONGE aged 31 in the *George* 1616
JOANE YONGE aged 26 in the *Guifte* 1618
JOANE YONGE aged 2 borne in Virginia
SUSAN   aged 12 in the *Swan* 1624

LEIUETEN: ALBIANO LUPO his MUSTER

ALBIANO LUPO aged 40 in the *Swan* 1610
ELIZABETH LUPO aged 28 in the *George* 1616
TEMPERANCE LUPO aged 4 borne in Virginia
Servant's
HENRIE DRAPER aged 14 in the *George* 1621
JOSEPH HAM aged 16 in the *Warwicke* 1621

Elzabeth Cittie

JOHN POWELL his MUSTER

JOHN POWELL aged 29 in the *Swallowe* 1609
KATHREN POWELL aged 22 in the *flyinge Hart* 1622
JOHN POWELL borne in virginia

Servant's

THOMAS PRATER aged 20 in the *Marie Prouidence* 1622

LARENCE PEALE his MUSTER

LARENCE PEALE aged 23 in the *Margett and John* 1620
WILLIAM SMITH aged 30 in the *Jacob* 1624

ROBART BRITTIN his MUSTER

ROBART BRITTIN aged 30: in the *Edwin* 1618

MIHELL WILCOCKES and JOHN SLATER their MUSTER

MIHELL WILCOCKES aged 31 in the *Prosporouse* 1610
ELZABETH WILLCOCKES aged 23 in the *Concord* 1621
JOHN SLATER aged 22 in the *George* 1617
ANNE SLATER aged 17 in the *Guyft* 1622

Servant's

JAMES FEILD aged 20 in the *Swan* 1624
JOHN JORNALL aged 20 in the *Ann* 1623
THEODORE JOONES aged 16 in the *Margett and John* 1620

JOSEPH COBB his MUSTER

JOSEPH COBB aged 25 in the *Treasoror* 1613
ELZABETH COBB aged 25 in the *Bone Bes* 1623
JOHN SNOWOOD aged 25 in the

Elzabeth Cittie

CORNELIUS MAY his MUSTER
CORNELIUS MAYE aged 25 in the *Prouidence* 1616

WILLIAM MORGAN ats BROOCKES his MUSTER
WILLIAM MORGAN aged 30 in the *Starr* 1610
WILLIAM MORGAN aged 2 borne in Virginia

Mr WILLIAM JULIAN his MUSTER.
WILLIAM JULIAN aged: 43: in the *Hercules* 1609
SARA JULIAN aged 25 in the *Neptune* 1618
WILLIAM KEMP aged 33 in the *William and Thomas* 1618
THOMAS SULLY aged 36 in the *Sara* 1611
MAUDLYN SULLY aged 30 in the *London Marchant* 1620

Servant's

THOMAS FLOWER aged 22 in the *George* 1623
WYATT MASONN aged 16 in the *Ann* 1623

LEIUETEN THOMAS PURFRAY his MUSTER
THOMAS PURFRY aged 43 in the *George* 1621
CHRISTOPHER COLETHORPE aged 18: in the *Furtherance* 1622
DANNIELL TANNER aged 40 in the *Sampson* 1618

Servant's

HENRIE FEELDES aged 26 in the *Jacob* 1624
WILLIAM BAULDWIN

JOHN BARNABE his MUSTER
JOHN BARNABIE aged 21: in the *London Marchant* 1620

Elzabeth Cittie

JOHN HAZARD his MUSTER

JOHN HAZARD aged 40 in the *William and Thomas* 1618

Servant's

ABRAHAM PELTEARE aged 14 in the *Swan* 1624.

JERIMIAH DICKINSON his MUSTER.

JERIMIAH DICKINSON aged 26 in the *Margett and John* 1620
ELZABETH DICKINSON aged 38 in the *Margett and John* 1623

PHILLIP LUPO his MUSTER

PHILLIP LUPO aged 42 in the *George* 1621

ENSIGNE THOMAS WILLOBY his MUSTER

THOMAS WILLOBY aged 23 in the *Prosporouse* 1610

Servant's

JOHN CHAUNDLER aged 24 in the *Hercules* 1609
THOMAS aged 20 in the *greate hopewell* 1623
ROBERT BENNETT aged 24 In the *Jacob* 1624
NICCOLAS DAVIS aged 13 in the *Mariegould* 1618

JOHN HATTON his MUSTER

JOHN HATTON aged 26 in the *Tresorer* 1613
OLIUE HATTON aged 32 in the *Abigall* 1620

Mr CISSE Minister his MUSTER

Mr GEORGE KETH aged 40 ....⎫
JAMES WHITINGE aged 16 .... ⎬ in the *George* 1617
JOHN KETH aged 11 .... ⎭

Elzabeth Cittie

Susan Bush her MUSTER

SUSAN BUSH aged 20 in the *George* 1617
SARA SPENCE aged 4 borne in virginia

Servant's

CLEMENT EVAND'S aged 30 in the *Edwin* 1616
WILLIAM PARKER aged 20 in the *Charles* 1616
JOHN SEWARD aged 30 in the *Geife* 1622
GILBERT MARBURIE aged 32 in the *Southampton* 1622
THOMAS KILLSON aged 21 in the *Trueloue* 1623

Capt Niccolas Martue his MUSTER

NICCOLAS MARTUE aged 33 in the *Francis Bonaventure*
PETER ECCALLOWE aged 30 in the *Southampton*
WILLIAM STAFFORD aged 17 in the *furtherance*

Mr John Banum and Robart Sweete theire MUSTER

JOHN BANUM aged 54 in the *Susan* 1616
ELZABETH BANUM aged 43 in the *Bona Noua*, 1620
ROBART SWEETE aged 42 in the *Neptune* 1618

Servant's

NICCOLAS THREDDER aged 30 in the *Katherin* 1623
RICHARD ROBISONN aged 22 in the *Bona noua* 1620
JOHN HILL aged 26 in the *Bona Noua* 1620
WILLIAM MORTON aged 20 in the *Margett and John* 1620
JAMES PASCOLL aged 20 in the *Warwicke* 1621
ROBART DRAPER aged 16 in the *Jacob* 1624
SARA GOULDINGE aged 20 in the *Ann* 1623

Elzabeth Cittie

RICHARD MINTRENE his MUSTER

RICHARD MINTRENE aged 40 in the *Margett and John* 1620
WILLIAM BEANE aged 25 in the *Diana* 1618
EDWARD MINTRENE aged 12 in the *Margett and John* 1620
JOHN INMAN aged 26 in the *falcon* 1619
WILLIAM BROWNE aged 14 in the *Southamton* 1622

ANTHONEY BURROES his MUSTER

ANTHONEY BURROES aged 44 in the *George* 1617

JOHN WAINE his MUSTER

JOHN WAINE aged 30 in the *Neptune* 1618
AMYTE WAINE aged 30 in the *Swan* 1610
GEORGE ACKLAND aged 7 } borne in Virginia
MARY ACKLAND aged 4 }
JOHN HARLOW aged 28 in the *Sampson* 1619
ROBART SABYN aged 30 in the *marget and John* 1622
PHILLIP CHAPMAN aged 23 in the *flyinge Hart* 1621

M' ROBART SALFORD his MUSTER and JOHN SALFORD.

M' ROBART SALFORD aged 56 in the *John and Francis* 1611
JOHN SALFORD aged 24 in the *George* 1616
MARY SALFORD aged 24 in the *Bona Nova* 1620

Servant's

WILLIAM ELLISON aged 44 in the *Swan* 1624
THOMAS FAULKNER aged 28 in the *Mary Prouidense* 1622

Elzabeth Cittie

BARTHOLEMEW WETHERSBIE and RICHARD BOULTON their
MUSTERS

BARTHOLEMEW WETHERSBIE aged 30 in the *Providence* 1616
DORYTHIE WETHERSBIE aged 30 in the *London Marchant* 1620
RICHARD BOULTON aged 28 in the *Mary and James* 1610
RICHARD aged 15 in the *Swan* 1624

JOHN GUNDRIE his MUSTER

JOHN GUNDRIE aged 33 in the *Starr* 1610
MARIE GUNDRIE aged 20 in the *George* 1618
JOHN GUNDRIE aged 2 borne in Virginia

FRANCIS MASON his MUSTER

FRANCIS MASON aged 40 in the *John and Francis* 1613
ALICE MASON aged 26 in the *Margett and John* 1622
FRANCIS MASON borne in Virginia

Servant's
WILLIAM QUERKE aged 30 in the *Marmaducke* 1621
THOMAS WORTHALL aged 14 in the *Marmaducke* 1621
WILLIAM STAFFORD aged 16 in the *furtherance* 1622
HENRIE GANY aged 21 in the *Dutie* 1619
JOHN ROBINSON aged 21 in the *Margett and John* 1622

FARRAR FLINTON his MUSTER

FARRAR FLINTON aged 36 in the *Elzabeth* 1612
JOANE FLINTON aged 38 in the *Elzabeth* 1612
WILLIAM BENTLIE aged 36 In the *Jacob* 1624

Elzabeth Cittie

Servant's
ARTHUR SMYTH aged 25 } in the *Marget and John* 1622
HUGH HALL aged 13
MATHEW HARDCASTELL aged 20 in the *Jacob* 1624
HENRIE NASFEILD aged 19 in the *Swan* 1624

JAMES SLEIGHT and FRANCIS HUFF theire MUSTER

FRANCIS HUFF aged 20 in the *Swan* 1624
JAMES SLEIGHT aged 42 in the *Tryall* 1610

LEIUETEN JOHN CHISMAN his MUSTER

JOHN CHISMAN aged 27 in the *flyinge hart* 1621
EDWARD CHISMAN aged 22 in the *Providence* 1623

M' THOMAS SPILMAN his MUSTER

THOMAS SPILMAN aged 24 in the *George* 1616
HANNA SPILMAN aged 23 in the *Bona Noua* 1620
ELIZABETH HILL borne in Virginia

Servant's
ROBART BROWNE aged 25 in the *Mary gould* 1618
REBECCA BROWNE aged 24 in the *Southampton* 1623
THOMAS PARRISH aged 26 in the *Charity* 1622
JOHN HARRIS aged 21 in the *Jacob* 1624.

OLIVER JINKINES his MUSTER

OLIVER JINKINES aged 30, in the *mary James* 1610
JOANE JINKINES aged 26 in the *George* 1617
ALLEXAND' JINKINES borne in Virginia

Elzabeth Cittie

WILLIAME GAYNE and ROBART NEWMAN theire MUSTER

ROBART NEWMAN aged 25 in the *Neptune* 1618
WILLIAM GAYNE aged 36 in the *Bona Noua* 1620
JOHN TAYLOR aged 34 in the *Swan* 1610
REBECCA TAYLOR aged 22 in the *Margett and John* 1623
JOHN COKER aged 20
RICHARD PACKE aged 23 in the *Warwicke* 1621
ABRAHAM AVELIN aged 23 } in the *Elzabeth* 1620
ARTHUR AVELIN aged 26 }

THOMAS GODBY his MUSTER

THOMAS GODBY aged 38 in the *Deliu'ance* 1608
JOANE GODBY aged 42 in the *Flyinge Hart* 1621
JOHN CURTIS aged 22 in the *Flyinge Harte* 1621
CHRISTOPHER SMITH aged 23 in the *Returne* 1624

M' EDWARD WATERS his MUSTER

EDWARD WATERS aged 40 in the *Patience* 1608
GRACE WATERS aged 21 in the *Diana* 1618
WILLIAM WATERS } borne in Virginia
MARGERETT WATERS }
WILLIAM HAMPTON aged 40 in the *Bona Noua* 1620
JOANE HAMPTON aged 25 in the *Abigall* 1621
THOMAS LANE aged 30 in the *Treasorer* 1613
ALICE LANE aged 24 in the *Bona Noua* 1620
THOMAS THORNEBURY aged 20 in the *George* 1616
Servant's
ADAM THOROGOOD aged 18 } in the *Charles* 1621
NICCOLAS BROWNE aged 18 }
PAULE HARWOOD aged 20 in the *Bona Noua* 1622
STEPHEN REEDE aged 17 in the *George* 1618

Elzabeth Cittie
MATHIAS FRANCISCO aged 18 in the *Jacob* 1624
ROBART PENRISE aged 12 in the *Bona noua* 1620

Capt THOMAS DAVIS his MUSTER

Capt THOMAS DAVIS aged 40 in the *John and Francis* 1623
THOMAS HEWES aged 40 in the *John and Francis* 1623

Mr FRANCIS CHAMBERLIN his MUSTER

FRANCIS CHAMBERLIN aged 45 in the *Marmaducke* 1621
REBECCA CHAMBERLIN aged 37 in the *Bona Noua* 1622
FRANCIS CHAMBERLIN aged 3 borne in Virginia.

Servant's
JOHN FORTH aged 16 } in the *Bona Noua* 1622
WILLIAM WORLIDGE aged 18
SIONELL* ROWLSTON aged 30 in the *God's Guifte* 1623
RICHARD BURTON aged 28 in the *Swan* 1624

PERCIVALL IBOTTSON his MUSTER

PERCIVALL IBOTTSON aged 24 in the *Neptune* 1618
ELZABETH IBOTTSON aged 23 in the *Flyinge Hart* 1621
JOHN DAVIS aged 24 in the *John and Francis* 1623

Servant's
WILLIAM GREENE aged 28 in the *Hopewell* 1623
ROBART LOCKE aged 18 in the *Warwicke* 1621

Mr DANNIELL COOKINS his MUSTER

| WILLIAM WADSWORTH aged 26 | THOMAS CURTIS aged 24 |
| WILLIAM FOULKE aged 24 | PEETER SHEREWOOD aged 21 |

* [So in the original: probably intended for LIONEL

Elzabeth Cittie   THOMAS BOULDINGE his MUSTER

THOMAS BOULDINGE aged 40 in the *Swan* 1610
WILLIAM BOULDINGE borne in Virginia.
WILLIAM COXE aged 26 in the *Godspeede* 1610
RICHARD EDWARD'S aged 23 } in the *Jacob* 1624.
NICCOLAS DALE aged 20

REYNOLD BOOTH his MUSTER

REYNOLD BOOTH aged 32 in the *Hercules* 1609
ELIZABETH BOOTH aged 24 in the *Ann* 1623

Servant's
GEORGE LEVETT aged 29 in the *Bona Noua* 1619
THOMAS SEYWELL aged 20 in the *Tyger* 1623

THOMAS GARNETT his MUSTER

THOMAS GARNETT aged 40 in the *Swan* 1610
ELZABETH GARNETT aged 26 in the *Neptune* 1618
SUSAN GARNETT aged 3 borne in Virginia
AMBROSE GYFFITH aged 33 in the *Bona Noua* 1619
JOYSE GYFFITH aged 20 in the *Jacob* 1624

THOMAS DUNTHORNE his MUSTER

THOMAS DUNTHORNE aged 27 in the *Margett and John* 1620
ELZABETH DUNTHORNE aged 38 in the *Tryall* 1610

Servant's
WILLIAM TOMSON aged 22
GEORGE TURNOR aged 27 } in the *Swan* 1624
GEORGE BANCKES aged 15
THOMAS an Indian Boaye
ELZABETH JOONES aged 30 in the *Patience* 1609
SARA JOONES aged 5 borne in Virginia

Elzabeth Cittie

Thomas Stepney his MUSTER

Thomas Stepney aged 35 in the *Swan* 1610

Mr Stockton his MUSTER

Jonas Stockton aged 40 in the *bona Noua* 1620
Richard Popeley aged 26
Richard Davis aged 22
Walter Barrett aged 26
Timothey Stockton aged 14
} in the *Bona Noua* 1620

Servant's
William Duglas aged 16 in the *Margett and John* 1621
John Watson aged 24 in the *Swan* 1624

Tobias Hurst his MUSTER

Tobias Hurst aged 22 in the *Treasurer* 1618

Mr William Gany his MUSTER

William Gany aged 33 in the *George* 1616
Anna Gany aged 24 in the *Bona Noua* 1620

Servant's
Anna Gany borne in Virginia
Thomasin Eester aged 26 in the *Falcon* 1617
Elizabeth Pope aged 8 in the *Abbigall* 1621
John Wright aged 20
William Clarke aged 20
Hather Tomson aged 18
Thomas Savadge aged 18
} in the *Ambrose* 1623

Elzabeth Cittie

ALLEXANDER MOUNTNEY his MUSTER

ALLEXAND' MOUNTNEY aged 33 in the *Mary James* 1610.
LENORD MOUNTNEY aged 21 in the *Bona Nona* 1620
JOHN WALTON aged 28 in the *Elzabeth* 1621
BRYAN ROGERS aged 18 in the *Elzabeth* 1621
JOHN WASHBORNE aged 25 in the *Jonathan* 1619

A list of the BURIALLES in ELZABETH CITTY 1624.

WESTON BROWNE Aprill. 20.
RICHARD WIFFE Aprell 26
JOHN MILEMAN Aprell 28
JOHN JACKSON Maye 12
EDWARD HILL Maye 15
PEETER   Maye 16
JAMES MORE June 24
M' TOMSON
PHILLIP COOCKE July 8
THOMAS EBES July 12
M' CHAMBERLINS Man July 17
SIBILL MORGON July 18
           WETHERSBY August 8
JAMES CHAMBERLIN August 11

M' FENTON Minister Septemb' 5.
WILLIAM WHITE Septemb' 12.
JAMES CHAMBERLIN Septemb' 22
MARY DOWNEMAN a Child Nonemb' 23.
JOHN STAMFORD Septemb' 30
THOMAS DAVIS
PEETER DICKENSON
RICHARD EASTE
THOMAS HUNTER
JOHN SIMNELL.*
HENRIE MIDDELLTON
SAMMUELL LAMBERT
JOHN BUSH.

A MUSTER of the Inhabitente of ELIZABETH CITTIE beyond Hampton River. Beinge the Companyes land.

CAP^T FRANCIS WEST his MUSTER

Capt FRANCIS WEST Counseler aged 36 in the *Mary Ann Margett* 1610
Mrs FRANCIS WEST Widdowe in the *Supply* 1620
NATHANIELL WEST borne in Virginia

---

* [This name has been altered from some previous spelling: but it is doubtless correct as printed.]

Elzabeth Cittie   Servant's
JOANE FAIRECHILD aged 20 in the *George* 1618
BENIAMIN OWIN aged 18 in the *Swan* 1623
WILLIAM PARNELL aged 18 in the *Southampton* 1622
WALTER COUPER aged 22 in the *Neptune* 1618
REINOULD GODWIN aged 30 in the *Abigall* 1620
JOHN PEDRO a Neger aged 30 in the *Swan* 1623

Capt JOHN MARTIN his MUSTER

Capt JOHN MARTIN
SACKFORD WETHERELL aged 21
JOHN SMITH aged 31   } in the *Swan* 1624
JOHN HOWARD aged 24
JOHN ANTHONIE aged 23

GEORGE MEDCALFE his MUSTER

GEORGE MEDCALFE aged 46
SARA MEDCALFE aged 30 in the *Hopewell* 1624
JOANE A Child.

EDWARD JOHNSON his MUSTER

EDWARD JOHNSON aged 26 in the *Abigall* 1621
                         in the *Bona Noua* 1621
A Child borne in Virginia

JOHN LAUCKFILD his MUSTER

JOHN LAUCKFILD aged 24 in the *Bona Noua* 1621
ALICE LAUCKFILD aged 24 in the *Abbigall* 1621
SAMMUELL KENNELL aged 30 in the *Abigall* 1621

Elzabeth Cittie

WILLIAM FOWLER his MUSTER

WILLIAM FOWLER aged 30 in the *Abigall* 1621
MARGRETT FOWLER aged 30 in the *Abigall* 1621

WALTER ELY his MUSTER

WALTER ELY
ELZABETH ELY aged 30 in the *Warwicke* 1622
ANN ELY borne in Virginia

WILLIAM TILER his MUSTER

WILLIAM TILER in the *Francis Bonaventure* 1620
ELIZABETH TILER in the *Francis Bonaventure* 1620

Servant's

ROBART MORE aged 50 in the *Prouidence* 1622
WILLIAM BROWNE aged 26 in the *Prouidence* 1622
ROBART TODD aged 20 in the *Hopewell* 1622
ANTHONIE BURT aged 18 in the *Hopwell* 1622
SAMIELL BENNETT aged 40 in the *Prouidence* 1622
JOANE BENNETT in the *prouidence* 1622

THOMAS FLYNT his MUSTER

THOMAS FLYNT in the *Diana* 1618
THOMAS MERRES aged 21 in the *Francis Bona Venture* 1620
HENRIE WHEELER aged 20 in the *Tryall* 1620.
JOHN BROCKE aged 19 in the *Bona Noua* 1619
JAMES BROOKES aged 19 in the *Jonathan* 1619
ROBART SAVADGE aged 18 in the *Elzabeth* 1621

Elzabeth Cittie

John Ward his MUSTER

JOHN WARD in the *Elzabeth* 1621
ADAM RIMWELL aged 24 in the *Bona noua* 1619
CHRISTOPHER WYNWILL aged 26 in the *Bona Noua* 1619
OLIUER JENKIN aged 40
JOANE JENKIN ℰ a littell Child
HENRIE POTTER aged 50
ANN POTTER in the *London Marchant*
ROBART GOODMAN aged 24 in the *Bona Noua* 1619

Gregorie Dorie his MUSTER

GREGORIE DORIE aged 36 in the *Bona Noua* 1620.
his wiffe ℰ a littell Child borne in Virginia

John More his MUSTER

JOHN MORE adge 36 in the *Bona Noua* 1620
ELZABETH MORE in the *Abigall* 1622.

Sargent William Barry his MUSTER

WILLIAM BARRY in the *Bona Noua* 1619

Servant's

RICHARD FRISBIE aged 34 in the *Jonathan* 1619
WILLIAM ROOKINES aged 26 in the *Bona Noua* 1619
JOSEPH HATTFILD aged 24 in the *Bona Noua* 1619
CUTBERT SEIRSON aged 22 in the *Bona Noua* 1619
JOHN GIBBES aged 24 in the *Abigall* 1621
FRANCIS HILL aged 22 in the *Bona Noua* 1619
JOHN VAGHAN aged 23 in the *Bona Noua* 1619
EDWARD MARSHALL aged 26 in the *Abigall* 1621

Elzabeth Cittie
WILLIAM JOYCE aged 26 in the *Abigall* 1621
WILLIAM EVAND'S aged 23 in the *Bona Noua* 1619
RALPH OSBORNE aged 22 in the *Bona Noua* 1619
MORRIS STANLEY aged 26 in the *hopewell* 1624
NICCOLAS WEASELL aged 28 in the *Abigall* 1621
STEPHEN DICKSON aged 25 in the *Bona Noua* 1619
THOMAS CALDER aged 24 in the *Bona Noua* 1619

WILLIAM HAMPTON his MUSTER

WILLIAM HAMPTON age 34 in the *Bona Noua* 1621.
JOANE HAMPTON
JOHN ARNDELL age 22 in the *Abigall* 1621

ANTHONIE BONALL his MUSTER

ANTHONIE BONALL age 42 } in the *Abigall* 1621
ELIAS LEGARDO age 38 }
ROBART WRIGHT age 45 in the *Swan* 1608
JOANE WRIGHT and two Children borne in virginia
WILLIAM BINSLEY age 18 in the *Jacob* 1624
ROBART GODWIN age 19 in the *Swan* 1624

VIRBRITT } two frenchmen in the *Abigall* 1622
OBLE HERO }

ROBART THRASHER his MUSTER

ROBART THRASHER age 22 in the *Bona Noua* 1620
ROLAND WILLIAMES age 20 in the *Jonathan* 1623.
Servant
JOHN SACKER age 20 in the *Marget and John* 1623

JOHN HANEY age 27 in the *Margett and John* 1621

Elezabeth Cittie
ELZABETH HANIE in the *Abigall* 1622
NICHOLAS ROWE in the *Elzabeth* 1621
MARY ROWE in the *London Marchant* 1620

Servant's

THOMAS MORELAND } age 19 in the *Abigall* 1621
RALPH HOOLE ......

A list of the DEAD beyond Hampton River

of M' BONALES Servant......... 1
M' DOWSE his men............... 2
M' PEETER ARNDELL

The Easterne Shore. A MUSTER of the Inhabitance of the Easterne Shore ouer the Baye.

CAP^T WILLIAM EPES his MUSTER. (in the *William and Thomas*

MARGRETT EPES in the *George* 1621

Servant's

NICCHOLAS RAYNBERD age 22 in the *Swan* 1624
WILLIAM BURDITT age 25 in the *Susan* 1615
THOMAS CORNISH age 25 in the *Dutie* 1620
PEETER PORTER age 19 in the *Tiger* 1621
JOHN BAKER age 20 in the *Ann* 1623
EDWARD ROGERS age 26 in the *Ann* 1623
THOMAS WARDEN age 24 in the *Ann* 1623
BENIAMINE KNIGHT age 28 in the *Bona Noua* 1620
NICCOLAS GRANGER age 15 in the *George* 1618
WILLIAM MUNNES age 25 in the *Sampson* 1619
HENRIE WILSON age 24 in the *Sampson* 1619
JAMES BLACKBORNE age 20 in the *Sampson* 1619
NICHOLAS SUMERFILD age 15 in the *Sampson* 1619

The Easterne Shore.   CAP^T JOHN WILLCOCKES his MUSTER

Capt JOHN WILLCOCKES in the *Bona Noua* 1620
HENRIE CHARLTON age 19 in the *George* 1623

Ancient THOMAS SAUAGE his MUSTER

THOMAS SAVAGE in the *John and Francis* 1607
ANN SAVAGE in the *Sea Flower* 1621
Servant's
JOHN WASHBORNE age 30 in the *Jonathan* 1620
THOMAS BELSON age 12

CAP^T THŌ: GRAUES his MUSTER

Capt THOMAS GRAUES in the *Mary and Margrett* 1607

WALTER SCOTT his MUSTER

WALTER SCOTT in the *Hercules* 1618
APPHIA SCOTT in the *Gift* 1618
PERCIS SCOTT borne in Virginia

THOMAS POWELL his MUSTER

THOMAS POWELL in the *Sampson* 1618

WILLIAM SMITH his MUSTER

WILLIAM SMITH age 26 in the *Sampson* 1618

EDWARD DREWE his MUSTER

EDWARD DREWE age 22 in the *Sampson* 1618

Easterne shore   CHARLES HARMAN his MUSTER

CHARLES HARMAN age 24 in the *Furtherance* 1622
JOHN ASKUME age 22 in the } *Charles* 1624
ROBERT FENNELL age 20 in the
JAMES KNOTT age 23 in the *George* 1617

NICHOLAS HODGSKINS his MUSTER

NICHOLAS HODGSKINES age 27 in the *Edwin* 1616
TEMPORANCE HODGSKINES in the *Jonathan* 1620
MARGRETT HODGSKINS borne in virginia

SOLLOMAN GREENE his MUSTER

SOLLOMAN GREENE age 27 in the *Diana* 1618

THOMAS GASKOYNE his MUSTER

THOMAS GASKOYNE age 34 in the *Bona Noua* 1619

WILLIAM ANDROS at the age 25 in the *Treasuror* 1617
DANNIELL CUGLEY age 28 in the *London Marchant* 1620

JOHN BLORE his MUSTER

JOHN BLORE age 27 in the *Star* 1610
FRANCIS BLORE age 25 in the *London Marchant* 1620
Servant's
JOHN PARRAMORE age 17 in the *Bona Venture* 1622
JOHN WILKINES

Easterne shore

ROBART BALL his MUSTER
ROBART BALL age 27 in the *London Marchant* 1619

WILLIAM BIBBIE his MUSTER
WILLIAM BIBBIE age 22 in the *Swan* 1621*
THOMAS SPARKES age 24 in the *Susan* 1616

JOHN HOME his MUSTER
JOHN HOME age 25 in the *Margerett and John* 1621

JOHN WILKINES his MUSTER
JOHN WILKINES age 26 in the *Mary gould* 1618
BRIGGETT WILKINES age 20 in the *Warwicke* 1621

PERREGRIM WATKINES his MUSTER
PERREGRIN WATKINES age 24 in the *George* 1621

WILLIAM DAVIS his MUSTER
WILLIAM DAVIS age 33 in the *William and Thomas* 1618

DEAD in this Plantation 1624
THOMAS HELCOTT.
JOHN WILKINES.

---

* [Not quite clear: may be 1620, blotted.]

[PATENTS GRANTED, &c.]

THE CORPORACŌN OF HENERICO*
[1626.]

ON the Northerly side of James River, from the Falles downe to Henerico. Contayning about x Miles in length, are yᵉ publique Land's, reserved & laid out, wherof 10,000: Acres, for the Vniuersitie Lands, 3000 Acres for the Companys Lands, wᵗʰ other Land belonging to the Colledge; the Comōn Land for the Corporacōn 1500 Acres.

On the Southerley side begining from the Falles, their are these PATTENTS graunted (vizt.

JOHN PETERSON	100: Acres	
ANTHONY EDWARD'S	100:	
NATHANELL WORTON	100:	
JOHN PROCTER	100:	
THOMAS TRACY..................	100:	
JOHN BILLIARD..................	100:	
FRANCIS WESTON...............	300:	
PHETTIPLACE CLOSSE	100:	By Pattent.
JOHN PRICE	150:	
PETTER NEVMART†	120:‡	
WILLIAM PERRY	100:	
JOHN BLOWER	100: Surrendred	
for the vse of the Iron Workes.		
EDWARD HUDSON	100:	
THOMAS MORGAN................	150:	
THOMAS SHEFFIELD............	150:	

* [There is a duplicate of this list, but it agrees in the main: we have indicated in notes all differences of any importance in the spelling of names.]

† [NEWMART in the duplicate list.]

‡ [Apparently 120, though blotted; but in the duplicate list it is 100.]

In COXENDALE, w^{th}in the same Corporacon of HENERICO.

EDWARD BARKLEY............	12 Acres	
RICHARD-BOLTON	100	
ROBERT AUKLAND*	200	
JOHN GRIFFIN	50	By Pattent.
PETTER NEINNEART†	40	
THOMAS TINDALL	100	
THOMAS READE	100	
JOHN LAYDEN	200	

THE CORPORACON OF CHARLES CITTIE

GEORGE GRINES‡	30 Acres	planted	
WILLIAM VINCENT	100	planted	
RICHARD TAYLOR	100	planted	
ROBERT PARTTEN	50		
THOMAS DOUSE	400		
GEORGE CAWCOTT	100		
ISACKE CHAPLINE	50		
THOMAS ROSSE	100		By Pattent.
JOHN OWLYE	50		
JOSUAH CHARDE	100		
JOHN DODD'S	50		
WILLIAM SHARPES	40		
JAMES VSHUR................	100		
WILLIAM CRADOUKE	100		
JOHN OWLY	150		
THEOPHILUS BERISTON	100		

* [ACKLAND in the duplicate list.]   † [NEIMART in the duplicate list.]
‡ [GRIMES in the duplicate list.]

JOHN HARRIS.....................	200 Acres	planted
ROBERT PARTTIN	100	planted
NATHANIELL CAUSEY	200	
JOHN CARTTER	40	
Captaine MADDISON	250	planted
RICHARD BIGGS	150	planted
FRANCIS MASON	50	
HENRY BAGWELL	50	
SAMUELL JARRATT*	100	
JOHN DADE.......................	100	} By Pattent.
THOMAS SWINHOW	300	
THOMAS HOBSON	150	
SYMON FORTESCUE	100	
THOMAS OAGUE..................	100	
WILLIAM BALY	100	
JOHN WRITTERS	100	
Leift: RICH: CRUDGE............	250	
JOHN CARR.......................	100	
RICHARD TAYLOR	100	
ROBERT BOURNE	250	planted

Laid out for the Company Land belowe SHERLEY HUNDRED Iland 3000 Acres

Claimed by CAPTAINE FRANCIS WEST, att WESTOUER 500 Acres

Vppon APMATUCKE RIVER

WILLIAM FARRAR	100 Acres	
HENRY MILWARD	250	
CHARLES MAGNOR	650	} By Pattent.
SAMUELL SHARPE	100	
HUMPHERY KENT...............	50	

* [JERRATT in the duplicate list.]

Mr ABRA: PERSEY	1150 Acres	
RICHARD SYMONS	100	
ARTHUR ANTONYE	150 Acres	} By Pattent
WILLIAM SIZEMORE	100 Acres	
WILLIAM DOWGLAS	250 Acres	

Here is Land laid out for CHARLES CITTIE, and the Comon Land.

The Territory of GREATE WEYONOKE.

CHRISTOPHER HARDING	100 Acres		
WILLIAM BAILY	50		
RICHARD PRATT	150		
WILLIAM JARRET*	200		
Capt Jo: WOODLIFFE............	550		
TEMPERANCE BAILY	200		} By Pattent
SAMUELL JORDAN	450	planted	
TEMPERANCE BAILY	200	planted	
ISACKE CHAPLIN	200	planted	
Capt: NATHANIELL POWLE ...	600 Acres		

Mr SAMUELL MAICOCKES Diuident.

PERSEYS hundred .... 1000 Acres planted

TANKS WAYONOKE ouer against } 2200 Acres.
   PERSEYS hundred

Captaine SPILLMANS Diuident.

MARTTIN BRANDON belonging to Captaine JOHN MARTTIN by Pattent out of England (planted).

Vppon the easterly Side of Chapokes Creeke, is appointed 500 Acres, belonging to ye place of Treasure by order of Courtt

JOHN MARTTIN	100 Acres	
GEORGE HARRISON	200	} By Pattent
SAMUELL EACH	500	

* [JERRATT in the duplicate list.]

On the Northerly Side, is the land belonging to Southampton hundred Containeing 100000: Acres, extending from Tanks Wayonoke downe to the mouth of Chicahomny River.

THE CORPORACON OF JAMES CITTIE

Adioyneing to the mouth of Chicohominy River ther are 3000 Acres of Land, laid out for ye Company 3000 Acres, laid out for the place of the Gouerner (planted) in wch are Some smale parcells, graunted by Sir THOMAS DALE and Sir SAMUELL ARGALL (planted)

Mr RICHARD BUCKE	750 Acres planted	} By Pattent
The GEABE [GLEABE] LAND	100	

In the Iland of James Cittie, are many parcells of land, graunted to the inhabitant's by Pattent, and order of Courtt

The Territory of TAPPAHANNA ouer against JAMES CITTIE.

JOHN DODD'S......................	150 Acres		
JOHN BURROWS	150	planted	
RICHARD PACE	200	planted	
FRANCIS CHAPMAN	100		} By Pattent
THOMAS GATES	100		
Mr JOHN ROLFE	400	planted	
Capt Wm POWELL*	200	planted	
Capt SAMUELL MATHEWS Diuident planted			
Captaine JOHN HURLESTONS Diuident planted			
JOHN BAINHAM..................	200 Acres planted		
Mr GEORGE SANDYS	300	planted	
EDWARD GRINDON	150	planted	
WILLIAM EWENS	1000	planted	} By Pattent
Capt Wm POWELL*	550	planted	
Ensigne JO: VTIE	100		
ROBERT EUERS	100 Acres		

* [POWLE, in each case, in the duplicate list.]

In Hog Iland MARY BAILY 500 Acres planted (by pattent
Southāpton hundred in Hog Iland planted
Captaine RAPHE HAMAR* by Clame in Hog Iland. 250 Acres
   planted

ARCHERS HOPE

Capt ROGER SMITH............	100 Acres planted	⎫
RICHARD KINGSMELL	200	⎬ by order of Courtt.
Mr Wᴍ CLAYBOURNE...........	250	⎭
Ensigne Wᴍ SPENCE .... ⎫	300 Acres planted	⎫
ℓ JOHN FOWLER .... ⎭		
JOHN JOHNSON	100	
RICHARD KINGSMELL	300	
WILLIAM FAIRFAX	200	
JOAKIN ANDREWES	100	⎬ By Pattent.
JOHN GRUBB	100	
JOHN JEFFERSON	250	
GEORGE PERRY	100	
RICHARD STAPLES..............	150	
RICHARD BREWSTER...........	100	⎭

MARTTINS HUNDRED Containeing as is Alledged 80000 Acres part
   planted

Nere MULBERY ILAND

NATHANILL HUATT†	200 Acres	⎫
Capt Wᴍ PEERCE .... ⎫		⎬ By Pattent
Mr JOHN ROLFE with some ⎬	1700: Acres planted	
others .... ⎭		⎭

---

* [HAMOR in the duplicate list.]

† [Apparently so, though the second and third letters are blotted; but it is clearly HUTT in the duplicate list.]

WAROSQUOIACKE Plantacōn Contayneing downe ward's, from Hog Iland xiiij^ten miles by the River side, in wch are these pattents following (vizt):

JOHN CARTER....................	100 Acres	
CHRISTOPHER DANIELL	100	
ADAM DIXSON	100	
JOHN BERRY	100	
THOMAS WINTER	100	
JOHN POLLINGTON	600	} By Pattent
THOMAS POOLE	100	
ANTHONY BARHAM	100	
Capt NETHA: BASSE	300	planted
GILES JONES	150	planted

BLUNT POINTE

Mr Wm CLAYBOURNE	500 Acres	by orde' of Court
JOHN BAINHAM	300 Acres	by pattent
Capt RAPHE HAMER*	500 Acres	by order of Court
GILBERT PEPPETT	50 Acres planted	} By pattent
FRANCIS GIFFORD	50 Acres planted	

Captaine SAMUELL MATHEWS his Diuedent by order of Court. planted.

THOMAS HETHERSALL	200 Acres	
CORNELIUS MAY	100	
RICHARD CRAUEN...............	150	
RICHARD TREE	50	} By Pattent.
RICHARD DOMELAWE	150	
PERSIUALL IBBISON	50	
EDWARD WATTERS	100 Acres	

* [HAMOR in the duplicate list.]

Belowe BLUNT POINT

Capt JOHN HURLESTONE	100 Acres	} by pattent
ROBERT HUTCHINS	100 Acres	
JOHN SOUTHERNE	40 Acres	} by Order of Courtt
Sr FRANCIS WYATT	500 Acers	
MORRIS THOMSON	150 Acres	
JOHN SALFORD	100	
PHARAOH FLINTON	150	} by pattent
LEIFT GILES ALINGTON	100	
WILLIAM BENTLEY	50	
THOMAS GODBY................	100 Acres	

THE CORPORACON OF ELIZABETH CITTIE

NEWPORTS NEWES	1300 Acres	plantd	
The GLEAB LAND	100	planted	
Mr KEYTH*	100	planted	} by pattent
THOMAS TAYLOR	50	planted	
JOHN POWELL	150	planted	
Capt Wm TUCKER	150	......	
RICHARD BOULTON	50 Acres	Claimed & planted	
JOHN SALFORD	50 Acres	planted	
ROBERT SALFORD†	100	planted	
ROBERT SALFORD†	100		
MILES PRICKETT	150	planted	
JOHN BUSH	300	planted	
WILLIAM JULIAN	150	planted	
LEIFT: LUPO	350	planted	} by pattent
ELIZABETH LUPO	50		
THOMAS SPILMAN................	50	planted	
EDWARD HILL	100	planted	
ALEXANDER MOUNTNEY......	100	planted	
WILLIAM COLE	50	planted	
WILLIAM BROOKS................	100	planted	
The GLEAB LAND	100	planted	
ELIZA: DONTHORNE‡	100	planted	} by pattent
WILLIAM GANY................	200	planted	

* [KETH in the duplicate list.]   † [Thus repeated in the original.
‡ [DUNTHORNE in the duplicate list.]

WILLIAM CAPPS divident planted

WILLIAM LANDSDELL	100 Acres	plantd
Mr Wm CLAYBOURNE	150	planted
JOHN GUNNERY	150	planted
MARY BOULDIN................	100	planted
THOMAS BOULDIN	200	planted
Mr PETTER ARUNDELL	200	
BARTHOLMEW HOSKINS	100	
Capt RAUGHLY CROSHAW betweene Fox hill & Pemonkey River...............	500	

} by Pattent.

THO: WILLOWSABY about 2 miles wthin the mouth of Pemonkey River } 200 Acres, by order of Court

On the Easterly Side of Southampton River, their are 3000 Acres, belonging to the Company at Elizabeth Cittie, planted, And 1500* Acres Comon Land,

---

On ye South Side of the maine River against ELIZABETH CITTIE

THOMAS WILLOUGHBYE......	100 Acres
THOMAS CHAPMAN	100
THOMAS BREWOOD	200
JOHN DOWNMAN†	100
Capt Wm TUCKER	650
JOHN SIPSEY....................	250
LEIFT: JO: CHEESMAN‡	200

} by pattent

The Easterne shore Ouer the Bay

JOHN BLOWER .... 140 Acres
Ensigne SALVADGE his Diuident
Sir GEORGE YARDLY at Hangers 3700 Acres by Order of Court

 Certaine others have planted their, but no Pattents haue bene graunted them, the Companyes and the Secretaryes Tennants, were alsoe their Seated but no land ordered, to bee laid out for them, as in the other 4 Corporacōns.

---

* [150 in the duplicate list.]   † [DOWNEMAN in the duplicate list.]
    ‡ [CHESMAN in the duplicate list.]

[PORTS OF IPSWICH AND WEYMOUTH.

RETURNS OF THOSE WHO EMBARKED FOR NEW ENGLAND.

1634—1635.]

[RETURNS OF THOSE WHO EMBARKED FOR NEW ENGLAND.
1634 —1635.]

To the right honno^{ble} the Lords & others of his Ma^{ts} moste honno^{ble} privie Councell.

The humble peticon & Certificates of JOHN CUTTINGE Ma^r of the Shipp called the *Francis*, and WILLIAM ANDREWES Ma^r of the *Elizabeth*, both of Ipsw^{ch}

Right honno^{ble} accordinge to yo' Lopps order, wee doe heerewth presente vnto yo' Lopps, the names of all the Passengers that wente for Newe-England in the said Shipps the Tenth daye of Aprill laste paste.

Humblie intreatinge yo' Lo^{pps} (they havinge pforemed yo' honno's order) that the bond's in that behalfe given may bee delivered back to yo' peticon's.

And they as in dutie bound will daylie praye for yo' honno's healthes & happynes

---

IPSWICH   A Note of all the names and ages of all those which did not take the Oath of Allegiance or Supremacy being vnder age shipped in our Port In the *Francis* of Ipswich Mr JOHN CUTTING: bound for New England the last of Aprill 1634

WILL: WESTWOOD:* { JOHN LEA ………aged 13 yeres
{ GRACE NEWELL …aged 13 yeres

---

* [The " braces " are not in the original, but have been inserted for the sake of clearness.]

Robᵗ: Rose:	John Rose ....aged 15 [yeeres] Robert Rose ....aged 15 Eliz: Rose ....aged 13 Mary Rose ....aged 11 Samuell Rose ......aged 9 Sarah Rose...........aged 7 Danyell Rose ......aged 3 Darcas Rose ....aged 2
Will: Freebourn:...	Mary Freebourne . aged 7 Sarah Freebourne aged 2
Jnᵒ: Bernard:	John Aldburgh......aged 14 Fayth Newell ......aged 14 Henry Haward..... aged 7
Abrahā: Newell...	Abraham Newell...aged 8 John Newell ....aged 5 Isaacke Newell ...aged 2
Edward: Bugby......	Sarah Bugbye ......aged 4
John: Pease:	Fayth Clearke......aged 15 Robert Pease.........aged 3 Darcas Greene......aged 15
Rowland: Stebing:	Thomas Stebing ...aged 14 Sarah Stebing ......aged 11 Eliz: Stebing ....aged 6 John Stebing.........aged 8 Mary Winche.........aged 15
Mary: Blosse:	Richard Blosse......aged 11
Tho: Sherwood: ...	Anna Sherwood ...aged 14 Rose Sherwood......aged 11 Thomas Sherwood. aged 10 Rebecca Sherwood aged 9
Robᵗ: Cooe:	John Cooe ....aged 8 Robert Cooe ....aged 7 Beniamin Cooe ......aged 5
Rich: Pepper:.........	Mary Pepp [Pepper] aged 3 and halfe Stephen Beckett...aged 11

EMBARKED FOR NEW ENGLAND. 279

ELIZ: HAMOND: .. ... { ELIZ: HAMOND ....aged 15 [yeeres]
SARAH HAMOND ....aged 10
JOHN HAMOND ....aged 7

Ipswich Customehouse this xijth of Nouember 1634

PHIL: BROWNE   EDW: MANN Compt
p Custr.

IPSWICH   A Note of the names and ages of all the Passengers which tooke shipping In the *Francis* of Ipswich M' JOHN CUTTING bound for new England the last of Aprill 1634

	yeeres		[yeeres]
JOHN BEETES............aged	40	ROBERT PEASE ....aged	27
WILLIAM HAULTON......aged	23	HUGH MASON ....} aged }	28
NICHOLAS JENNING'S ...aged	22	HESTER his wife ......} aged }	22
WILLIAM WESTWOODE } aged }	28	ROWLAND STEBING ...} aged }	40
BRIDGETT his wife......} aged }	32	SARAH his wife ....} aged }	43
CLEARE DRAP [DRAPER] aged	30	THOMAS SHERWOOD...} aged	48
ROBERT ROSE ....} aged}	40	ALICE his wife ....} aged	47
MARGERY his wife......} aged}	40	THOMAS KING ....aged	19
JOHN BERNARD.........} aged }	36	JOHN MAPES ....aged	21
MARY his wife ....} aged }	38	MARY BLOSSE ....aged	40
WILLIAM FREBOURNE { aged}	40	ROBERT COOE ....} aged }	38
MARY his wife ....} aged }	33	ANNA his wife ....} aged }	43
ANTHONY WHITE........aged	27	MARY ONGE ....aged	27
EDWARD BUGBYE ......} aged}	40	THOMAS BOYDEN ....aged	21
REBECCA his wife ......} aged }	32	RICHARD WATTLIN ......aged	28
ABRAHAM NEWELL ...} aged }	50	JOHN LYUERMORE ......aged	28
FRANCIS his wife ......} aged }	40	RICHARD PEPp [PEPPER] } aged 27
JUST HOULDING ....aged	23	MARY his wife ....} aged 30
JOHN PEASE ....aged	27	RICHARD HOULDING ...aged	25
ROBERT WINGE... ....aged	60	JUDETH GARNETT ......aged	26
JUDITH his wife...........aged	43	ELIZ: HAMOND ....aged	47
JOHN GREENE ....aged	27	THURSTON CLEARKE ...aged	44

These psons aboue named tooke the Oath of Allegeance and Supremacy at his Maties Custome house in Ips^wch^ before vs his Maties Officers according to the order of the Lords & others of his Maties most hono^ble^ Priuy Councell: This xij^th^ of Nouember 1634

    Ipswich Customehouse   THO CLERI scr
                           EDW: MANN Compt
         PHIL BROWNE
           p Custr.

IPSWICH   A Note of the names and ages of all the Passengers which tooke shipping In the *Elizabeth* of Ipswich Mr WILLIĀ ANDREWS bound for new EngLand the last of Aprill 1634

Name	aged	yeeres	Name	aged	[yeeres]
JOHN SHERMAN	aged	20	JOHN BERNARD	aged	30
JOSEPH MOSSE	aged	24	PHEBE his wife	aged	27
RICHARD WOODWARD	aged	45	THOMAS KILBORNE	aged	24
ROSE his wife	aged	50	ELIZABETH his wife	aged	20
EDMOND LEWIS	aged	33	JOHN CROSSE	aged	50
MARY his wife	aged	32	ANNE his wife	aged	38
JOHN SPRING	aged	45	ROBERT SHERIN	aged	32
ELINOR his wife	aged	46	HUMPHRY BRADSTREET	aged	40
THURSTON RAYNOR	aged	40	BRIDGETT his wife	aged	30
ELIZABETH his wife	aged	36	HENERY GLOUER	aged	24
THOMAS SKOTT	aged	40	WILLIAM BLOMFIELD	aged	30
ELIZABETH his wife	aged	40	SARAH his wife	aged	25
HENERY KEMBALL	aged	44	ROBERT DAY	aged	30
SUSAN his wife	aged	35	MARY his wife	aged	28
RICHARD KEMBALL	aged	39	SARAH REYNOLD'S	aged	20
VRSULA his wife	aged		ROBERT GOODALL	aged	30
ISAACKE MIXER	aged	31	KATHERIN his wife	aged	28
SARAH his wife	aged	33	SAMUELL SMITHE	aged	32
MARTHA SCOTT	aged	60	ELIZABETH his wife	aged	32
GEORGE MUNNING'S	aged	37	THOMAS HASTING'S	aged	29
ELIZABETH his wife	aged	41	SUSAN his wife	aged	34

EMBARKED FOR NEW ENGLAND. 281

	[yeeres]		[yeeres]
SUSAN MUNSON ....aged	25	JOHN PALMER ....aged	24
MARTIN VNDERWOOD } aged	38	DANYELL PIERCE ....aged	23
MARTHA his wife ...... } aged	31	JOHN CLEARKE..........aged	22
HENERY GOULDSON... } aged	43	JOHN FIRMIN...............aged	46
ANNE his wife .... } aged	45	REBECCA ISAACKE ......aged	36
ANNE GOULDSTON ......aged	18	ANNE DORIFALL ....aged	24
WILLIAM CUTTING ......aged	26		

These psons aboue named tooke the Oath of Allegeance and Supremacy, at his Mat's Custome house in Ipswich before vs his Maties Officers according to the order of the Lords & others of his Mat's most Hono^ble Priuy Councell : This xij^th of Nouember, 1634.

THO CLERI Scr

Ipswich Custome House
    PHIL. BROWNE   EDW: MAN
       p Custr   Compt

IPSWICH A Note of all the names and ages of all those which did not take the oath of Allegiance or Supremacy being vnder age shipped in o' Port In the *Elizabeth* of Ipswich Mr WILLIĀ ANDREWES, bound for New England the last of Aprill 1634

ED: LEWIS:	{ JOHN LEWIS: aged 3 yeeres { THOMAS LEWIS: aged 3 quarters
RICH: WOODWARD:......	{ GEORGE WOODWARD: aged 13 { JOHN WOODWARD: aged 13
JOHN: SPRING:	{ MARY SPRING: aged 11. { HENRY SPRING aged 6 { JOHN SPRING aged 4 { WILLIAM SPRING aged 3 quarters
THURSTON: RAYNOR:...	{ THURSTON RAYNER aged 13 { JOSEPH RAYNOR aged 11 { ELIZABETH RAYNOR aged 9 { SARAH RAYNOR aged 7 { LIDIA RAYNOR, aged 1 { EDWARD RAYNOR aged 10 { ELIZABETH KEMBALL aged 13

Tho: Scott:	Elizabeth Scott aged 9 [yeeres]
	Abigail Scott aged 7
	Thomas Scott aged 6
	Isaack Mixer aged 4
Hen: Kemball:...........	Elizabeth Kemball aged 4
	Susan Kemball aged 1 and halfe
	Richard Cutting aged 11
Rich: Kemball	Henry Kemball aged 15 yeeres
	Richard Kemball aged 11
	Mary Kemball aged 9
	Martha Kemball aged 5
	John Kemball aged 3
	Thomas Kemball aged 1
George: Munnings:...	John Lauericke aged 15
	Eliz: Munning's aged 12
	Abigail Munning's aged 7
Jno: Bernard:	John Bernard aged 2
	Samuell Bernard aged 1
	Tho: King aged 15
Hump: Bradstreet:...	Anna Bradstreet aged 9
	John Bradstreet aged 3
	Martha Bradstreet aged 2
	Mary Bradstreet aged 1
Willi: Blomfield: ...	Sarah Blomfield aged 1
Sam: Smith:	Samuell Smith aged 9
	Mary Smith aged 4
	Eliz: Smith aged 7
	Phillip Smith aged 1
Robt: Goodale:	Mary Goodale aged 4
	Abraham Goodale aged 2
	Isaacke Goodale aged halfe a yeere
Hen: Gouldson:	Mary Gouldson aged 15

Ipswich Custome house this xijth of Nouember 1634
    PHIL: BROWNE.   THO CLERI scr
       p Custr.   EDW: MAN
                   Compt

BOUND FOR NEW ENGLAND

WAYMOUTH
  yᵉ 20ᵗʰ of
  March 1635*

1 JOSEPH HALL of Somersᵗ a Ministr aged 40 year
2 AGNIS HALL his Wife aged .... 25 yʳ
3 JOANE HALL his daughtʳ aged 15 Yeare
4 JOSEPH HALL his sonne aged 13 Yeare.
5 TRISTRAM his son aged......... 11 Yeare
6 ELIZABETH HALL his daughtʳ aged 7 Yeare
7 TEMPERANCE his daughtʳ aged 9 Yeare
8 GRISSELL HALL† his daughtʳ aged 5 Yeare
9 DOROTHY HALL† his daughtʳ aged 3 Yeare
10 JUDETH FRENCH his s'vamt aged 20 Yeare
11 JOHN WOOD his s'vaunt aged 20 yeare
12 ROBᵀ DABYN his s'vamt aged 28 Yeare
13 MUSACHIELL BERNARD of batcombe Clothier
   in the County of Somersett 24 Yeare
14 MARY BERNARD his wife aged 28 yeare
15 JOHN BERNARD his sonne aged 3 Yeare
16 NATHANIELL his sonne aged 1 Yeare
17 RICH: PERSONS salter (? his s'vant: 30: yeare
18 FRANCIS BABER Chandler aged 36 yeare
19 JESOPE Joyner aged 22 Yeare
20 WALTER JESOP Weaver aged 21 Yeare
21 TIMOTHY TABOR of Som'sᵗ of Batcombe
   in taylor aged 35 Yeare ———
22 JANE TABOR his Wife aged 35 Yeare
23 JANE TABOR his daughtʳ aged 10 Yeare
24 ANNE TABOR his daughtʳ: aged 8 yeare
25 SARAH TABOR his daughtʳ aged 5 Yeare

---

* [Really 163⅔.]   † [So in the original.]

EMBARKED FOR NEW ENGLAND.

  26 Wiɫɫm Fever his s'vaunt aged 20 Yeare
  27 Jnᵒ: Whitmarck   aged 39 yeare
  28 Alce Whitmarke his Wife aged 35 yeare
  29 Jmᵒ* Whitmarcke his sonne aged 11 yeare
Portus
Waymouth 30 Jane his daughtʳ aged   7 Yeare
  31 Ouseph [*or* Onseph] Whitmarke his sonne
    aged 5 yeare
  32 Ricħ: Whytemark his sonne aged 2 Yeare
  33 Wiɫɫm Read of Batcombe Taylor in
  34† Som'sᵗᵗ aged 28 Yeare ——————
  35 Susan Read his Wife aged 29 Yeare
  36 Hanna Read his daughᵗʳ aged 3 yeare
  37 Lusan‡ Read his daughtʳ aged 1 yeare
  38 Ricħ: Adams his s'vante 29 Yeare
  39 Mary his Wife   aged 26 yeare
  40 Mary Cheame his daughtʳ aged 1 yeare
  41 Zachary Bickewell   aged 45 Yeare
  42 Agnis Bickwell his Wife aged 27 yeare
  43 Jnᵒ Bickwell his sonne aged 11 Yeare
  44 Jnᵒ Kitchin his servaunt 23 yeare
  46§ George Allin   aged 24 Yeare
  47 Katherin Allyn his Wife aged
    30 yeare ——————
  48 George Allyn his sonne aged 16 yeare
  49 Wiɫɫm Allyn his sonne aged 8 year
  50: Mathew Allyn his sonne aged 6 yeare
  51 Edward Poole his s'vaunt aged 26 yeare
  52 Henry Kingman   aged 40 Yeares
  53 Joane his wife beinge aged 39
  54 Edward Kingman his son aged 16 year
  55 Joane his daughtʳ aged 11: yeeare

---

 * [Sic. But doubtless intended for John.]
 † [It will be noticed that No. 34 is placed against the name of a place instead of that of a person.]
 ‡ [Probably intended for Susan.]   § [There is no No. 45.]

56 ANNE his daught^r aged ...... 9 Yeare
57 THOMAS KINGMAN his sonne aged 7 Yeare
58 JOHN KINGHMAN his sonne aged 2 yeare
59 Jⁿ FORD his servaunt aged 30 Yeare
60 WILLIAM KINGE   aged 40* Yeare
61 DOROTHY his Wife   aged 34 yeare
62 MARY KINGE his daught^r aged 12 year
63 KATHERYN his daught^r aged 10 Yeare
64 Wiłłm KINGE his sonne aged 8 year
65 HANNA KINGE his daught^r: aged 6 year
66† Somm'. [Somerset.]
     THOMAS HOLBROOKE of Broudway aged 34: yeare
67 JANE HOLBROOKE his wife aged 34 Yeare
68 JOHN HOLBROOKE his sonne aged 11 yeare
69 THOMAS HOLBROOKE his sonne aged 10 yeare
70 ANNE HOLBROOKE his daught^r aged 5 yea[re]
71 ELIZABETH his daught^r aged 1 yeare
72 THOMAS DIBLE husbandm̄ aged 22 yeare
73 FRANCIS DIBLE soror aged   24 Yeare
74 ROBERT LOVELL husbandman aged 40 Year
75 ELIZABETH LOVELL his Wife aged 35 year
76 ZACHEUS LOVELL his sonne 15 yeares
78‡ ANNE LOVELL his daught^r: aged 16 yeare
79 JOHN LOVELL his sonne aged 8 yeare
     ELLYN his daught^r aged ... 1 yeare
80 JAMES his sonne aged......... 1 yeare
81 JOSEPH CHICKIN his servant 16 year
82 ALICE KINHAM aged......... 22 yeare
83 ANGELL HOLLARD aged ... 21 yeare
84 KATHERYN his Wife 22 yeare
85 GEORGE LAND his servaunt   22 yeare
86 SARAH LAND§ his kinswoman 18 yeare

---

* [*Or* 30. One figure is written over the other, and I cannot tell which is the later.]
† [Thus in the original. This number should evidently come against the next line.]
‡ [There is no No. 77; but it will be observed that two lines below there is a name without number.]   § [Originally written LANG.]

	87	RICHARD JOANES of Dinder.........	
	88	ROBᵀ MARTYN of Badcombe husbandm̄	44
	89	HUMFREY SHEPHEARD husbandm̄...	32
	90	JOHN VPHAM husbandman	35 ......
	91	JOANE MARTYN	44 ......
	92	ELIZABETH VPHAM	32 ......
	93	JOHN VPHAM Juñ	07 ......
	94	WILLIAM GRAUE [GRAVE]	12 ......
	95	SARAH VPHAM	26 ......
	96	NATHANIELL VPHAM	05 ......
	97	ELIZABETH VPHAM	03.
Dorsᵗ		RICHARD WADE of Simstuly	
	98*	Cop [Cooper] aged	60 ......
	99	ELIZABETH WADE his Wife	6† ......
	100:	DINAH his daughʳ...................	22 ......
	101	HENRY LUSH his s'vant aged	17 ......
	102	ANDREWE HALLETT his s'vaunt	28 ......
	103	JOHN HOBLE husbandm̄	13 ......
	104	ROBᵀ HUSTE husbandm̄	40 ......
	105	JOHN WOODCOOKE	2 ......
	106	RICH PORTER husband	3 ......

JOHN PORTER Deputy
Cleark to EDW:
THOROUGHGOOD

---

* [This number should be in the line above.]   † [Sic in orig.]

A Register of the . . . .
of such persons a
and vpwards and haue t
to passe into forraigne partes from . .
march 1637 to the 29th* day of [S]ept.
by vertu of a commission granted to
m^r thomas mayhew gentleman.

---

* [The list does not go beyond the 19th of September 1637; the above date must therefore be an error. It should be mentioned that many passages to Holland are included in the original document: these we omit, as not pertinent to our object. The last passage for *America* is dated May 15. The dots indicate parts of the indorsement eaten away by age.]

[A REGISTER OF PERSONS ABOUT TO PASS
INTO FOREIGN PARTS.
1637.]

THESE people went to New England: with WILLIAM:* ANDREWES: of Ipswich M^r of the: *John: and Dorethey:* of Ipswich and With WILLIAM ANDREWES his Sone. M^r of the *Rose:* of Yarmouth.

Aprill the / 8th / 1637. The examinaction of JOHN: BAKER: borne in No^rwch in No^rffolck Grocar / ageed / 39 yeres and ELIZABETH: his Wife / ageed / 31 yeares with 3 Children ELIZABETH: JOHN: and THOMAS—and 4 Saruants. MAREY: ALXARSON: aged / 24 yeares ANNE: ALXARSON: aged / 20 yeares / BRIDGETT BOULLE: aged / 32 ycares / and SAMUELL: ARRES: aged 14 yeares ar all desiroues to goe for / Charles Towne in New England ther to inhabitt and Remaine ///

Aprill the / 8th / 1637. The examinaction of NICHO: BUSBIE: of No^rwch in No^rff / Weauer / aged / 50 yeares and / BRIDGETT: his Wife / aged / 53 yeares with / 4 / Children. NICHO: JOHN: ABRAHAM: and SARATH: ar desirous to goe to boston in New England to in habitt ///

Aprill the / 8th / 1637 The examinaction of MICHILL: METCALFE: of No^rwch Do^rnix Weauear / aged. 45 yeares and / SARRAH: his Wif / aged / 39 yeares with. / 8 Children / MICHILL: THOMAS: MAREY: SARRAH: ELIZABETH: MARTHA: JOANE: and REBECA:

---

* [We follow the very peculiar punctuation of this list throughout.]

and his Saruant THOMAS COMBERBACH: aged / 16 / yeares ar desirous to passe to boston in New England to inhabitt /¹/

Aprill. the / 8ᵗʰ / 1637   The examinaction of JOHN: PERS: of Noʳwch in Noʳff Weauear aged 49 yeares / and ELIZABETH: his Wife aged / 36 yeares / with 4 Children. JOHN: BARBRE: ELIZABETH: and JUDETH and one Saruant / JOHN: GEDNEY aged / 19 yeares. are desirous to passe to boston in New England to inhabitt ///

Aprill. the / 8ᵗʰ / 1637. The examinaction of WILLIAM: LUDKEN: of Noʳwch in Noʳff / Locksmith ther boʳne / aeged 33 yeares / and ELIZABETH: his Wife / ageed. / 34 yeares. With one Child and one Saruant / THOMAS: HOMES: are desirous to goe to Bostone in Newe England there to inhabitt / and Remaine ///

. . . . *ES: of Noʳwch in Noʳff / Cordwynar aged / 28 yeares and. / . . . . with / 4 / Children SAMUELL: JOHN: ELIZABETH: and DEBRA: . . . . NS: aged / 18 yeares and ANNE: WILLIAMES: aged / 15 yeares / . . . . England to Inhabitt ///

. . . . RANCIS: LAWES: boʳne in Noʳwch in Noʳff and their liuing Weauear / aged . . . . nd LIDDEA: his Wife / ageed / 49 yeares / With one Child MAREY: and 2 saruants. SAMUELL: LINCORNE: aged 18 yeares / and ANNE: SMITH: aged. 19 yeares ar desirous to passe foʳ New-England to inhabitt ///

. . . . 8 1637. The examinaction of WILLIAM: NICKERSON: of Noʳwch in Noʳff / Weauear / ageed 33 yeares. and. ANNE: his Wife / aged / 28 yeares with / 4 Children / NICHO: ROBARTT: ELIZABETH: and ANNE: ar desirous to goe to Bostone in New England ther to Inhabitt ///

Aprill the / 8ᵗʰ / 1637. The examinaction of SAMUELL: DIX: of Noʳwch in Noʳff Joynar ageed 43 yeares / and JOANE: his / Wife / aged 38 yeares with 2 Children PRESELLA: and ABEGELL: and 2 Saruantes WILLIAM: / STOREY: and DANIELL: LINSEY: the one aged / 23 the other / 18 yeares / ar all desirous to pass to Boston in New England there to Inhabitt ///

---

* [The dots here and after indicate parts of the original MS. eaten away by age or damp.]

ABOUT TO PASS INTO FOREIGN PARTS.

Aprill. the / 11th / 1637 The examinaction. of HENRY: SKERRY: of great yarmouth in the County of No^rff / Cordwynar. / ageed / 31 yeares and ELIZABETH : his Wife / ageed / 25 yeares / with one Child HENRY: and / one Aprenties / EDMUND: TOWNE: aged / 18 yeares. / ar desirous to passe fo^r New England to inhabitt ///

Aprill. the / 11th / 1637 The examinaction of JOHN: MOULTON: of Ormsby in No^rff husbandman. aged. 38 yeares., and. ANNE: his Wife / ageed / 38 yeares with 5 Children. HENRY: MAREY: ANNE: JANE: and / BRIDGETT: and / 2 Saruants. ADAM: GOODDENS: aged. 20 yeares and ALLES: EDEN: aged 18 yers / ar all desirous to passe to New England there to inhabitt ;// and abide ////

Aprill. the / 11th / 1637 The examinaction of MAREY: MOULTON: of Ormsby in No^rff / Wydow, ageed / 30 yeares and 2 / Saruants. JOHN : MASTON: aged / 20 yeares and MERREAN: MOULTON: ageed / 23 yeares / are desirous to goe to New England to inhabitt and dwell /;/

Aprill. the / 11th / 1637 The examinaction of RICHARD: CARUEAR: of Skratby.* in the County of No^rff / husbandman / ageed / 60, yeares, and GRACE: his Wife. ageed, 40 yeares. with / 2 Children. ELIZABETH: /// ageed / 18 yeares and, SUSANNA: aged 18, yeares. being twynes. / mo^r 3 Saruants ISACKE: HARTT: ageed, 22 yeares and THOMAS: FLEGE: aged / 21 yeares. and one MARABLE: VNDERWOOD: a mayd. Saruant / ageed, 20 yeares. goes all for New England to Inhabit / and Remaine /;;/

Aprill. the / 11th / 1637 The examinaction of RUTH: MOULTON: of Ormsby in No^rff. Singlewoman. ageed / 20 yeares. is desirous to passe for New England there to Inhabit and dwell /;/

Aprill . the / 11th / 1637 The examinaction of ROBERTT: PAGE: of Ormsby in No^rff. husbandman, ageed 33 yeares and / LUCEA: his Wife. aged 30 yeares with / 3 Children / FRANCES: MARGRETT: and SUSANNA: // and 2 Saruants / WILLIAM: MOULTON: and ANNE: WADD: the one aged 20 yeres the other / 15 yeares. and are all desirous to passe fo^r New England to inhabitt and Remaine. /;/

* [Perhaps Scratley, a part of Ormsby.]

Aprill. the / 11ᵗʰ / 1637   The examinaction of HENREY: DOWE: of Ormsby in Noʳff husbandman, ageed, 29 yeares. / and JOANE: his Wife / ageed 30 yeares with 4 Children, and one Saruant / ANNE: MANING, ageed / 17 yeares. are desirous to passe into New England to inhabitt ///

Aprill. the / 11ᵗʰ / 1637   The examinaction of ROBERTT:.............. Singleman. is desirous to passe ....

Aprill. the / 11ᵗʰ / 1637   The examinaction of ELLEN: ROBENSONE: of g............. desirous to passe into New England ther to in............

Aprill. the / 11ᵗʰ / 1637. The examinaction of WILLIAM: WILLIAMES: of great yarm .... 40 yeares. and ALLES: his Wife / ageed. 38 yeares with / 2 Children .... ar desirous to goe foʳ New England to inhabitt ///

Aprill. the / 11ᵗʰ / 1637   The examinaction of ELIZABETH: WILLIAMES: of Yaʳmouth. in Noʳff / Singlewoman ageed 31 yeares / is desirous to passe into New England ther to inhabitt and Remaine ///

Aprill. the / 12ᵗʰ / 1637   The examinaction of KATHREN: RABEY: of Yarmouth / a Wattermanes. Wydow. / ageed. 68 yeares. is desirous to passe into New England there to Remaine With her Sone /

Aprill. the / 12ᵗʰ / 1637   The examinaction of RICHARD: LEEDS: of great ya'mouth. Marrinar. ageed 32 yeares. and JOANE: his Wife / ageed. 23 yeares / with one Child / are desirous to passe foʳ New England and there to inhabitt / and dwell ///

Aprill. the / 12ᵗʰ / 1637   The examinaction of HENRY: SMITH: of Newbucknam husbandman / ageed 30 yeares. / and ELIZABETH: his Wife ageed. 34 / yeares. with 2 / Children JOHN: and SITHE: ar desirous to passe into New England /// to inhabitt ///

Aprill. the / 13ᵗʰ / 1637   The examinaction of JOHN: ROPEAR: of New Bucknam Carpentar. / ageed. 26 yeares. and ALLES: his Wife / ageed, 23 yeares / with / 2 Children. ALLES: and ELIZABETH: are desirous to goe for New England there to Remaine* ///

---

* [Here come a number of entries of passages for Holland.]

.. ese people went to New England with WILLIAM: / GOOSE: m^r of the *Marey: Anne:* of Yarmouth: ///

............1637 The examinaction of THOMAS: PAINE: of Wrentom in Suffolcke / Weauear / ageed / 50 yeares / and ELIZABETH: his Wife / ageed / 53 yeares with / 6 / Children / THOMAS: JOHN: MAREY: / ELIZABETH: DORETHEY: and SARAH: are desirous to goe for Salame in New England to inhabitt

May: the / 10th / 1637 The examinaction of MARGRETT: NEAUE: of great yarmouth in No^{rff} / Wydow. / ageed / 58 yeres / and RACHELL: DIXSON: her grand Child is desirous to passe into New England to inhabitt /

May: the / 10th / 1637 The examinaction of BENIEMEN: COOPER: of Bramton in Suffolck / husbandman / ageed / 50 / Yeares / and. ELIZABETH: his Wife / ageed / 48 yeares With / 5 Children LARWANCE: MAREY: REBECA: BENIEMEN: and FRANCIES: FILLINGHAM: his Sone / in Lawe / ageed / 32 yeares allso his Sister aged / 48 yeares / and 2 Saruants / JOHN: KILIN: and FELEAMAN: DICKERSON: ar all desirous to goe for Salam in New England and there. to inhabitt ///

May: the / 10th / 1637. The examinaction of ABRAHAM: TOPPAN: of yarmouth Cooper / ageed / 31 yeares and SUSANNA: his Wife / ageed. 30 yeares With / 2 Children PETTER: and ELIZABETH: and one Mayd / Saruant / ANNE: GOODIN: ageed / 18 yeares are desirous to passe to New England to / inhabitt ///

May: the / 10th / 1637 The examinaction of WILLIAM: THOMAS: of great Comberton in Wo^rstershire husbandman / Singleman / ageed / 26 yeares. is desirous to passe to Exerden / in New England to inhabitt

May: the / 10th / 1637 The examinaction of JOHN: THURSTON: of Wrentom in Suff / Carpentar / ageed, 30 yeares. and MARGRETT: his Wife / ageed. 32 yeares. With / 2 Children THOMAS. and JOHN: ar / desirous to passe to New England /// to inhabitt ///

May: the / 10th / 1637 The examinaction of LUCE: POYETT: of No^rwch Spinster / ageed. 23 yeares is desirous to pass into New England and there to Remaine ///

May: the / 10th / 1637 The examinaction of JOHN: BOROWE of yarmouth Cooper / aged 28 yeares. and ANNE: his / Wife / ageed / 40 / yeares is desirous to passe to Salam in New England and ther to inhabitt

May: the / 11th / 1637 The examinaction of WILLIAM: GAULT: of yarmouth Cordwynar / Singleman / ageed 29 / yeares is desirous to passe to New England and there to Remaine ///

May: the / 11th / 1637 The examinaction of JOANE: AMES: of yarmouth. Wydow / ageed / 50 yeares with / 3 Children RUTH: ageed / 18 yeares WILLIAM: and JOHN: are desirous to passe for. New England and there to inhabitt and Remaine ///

May: the / 11th / 1637 The examinaction of AUGSTEN: CALL........ .... ALLES: his Wife / ageed / 40 / yeares............ desirous to goe to Salam in New Eng..............

May: the / 11th / 1637 The examinaction of JOHN: DARRELL: of...... ....passe into Salam in New England and there............

May: the / 11th / 1637 The examinaction of JOHN: GEDNEY: of No^{r}wch in No^{r}ff Weauear.... to passe fo^r New England / with his Wife SARAH: aged 25 yeares. .... LEDIA: HANAH: and JOHN: mo^r / 2 Saruantes / WILLIAM: WALKER: aged .... BURGES: ageed / 26 yeares / ar desirous to passe fo^r Salam ///

May: the / 11th / 1637 The examinaction of SAMUELL: AIRES: of No^{r}wch an apintes / aged / 15 yeares is desirous [to] passe into New England to his Mr JOHN: BAKER: as he had apointed him ///

This man was for byden passage. by. the Commission^n and went. not. from. yramouth

{ The examinaction of JOHN: YONGES: of St Margretts: Suff / Minister / aged 35 yeares. and. / JOAN: his Wife / ageed / 34 / yeares with / 6 / Children / JOHN: THO: ANNE: RACHELL: MAREY: and / JOSUEPH: ar desirous to passe fo^r Salam: in New England to inhabitt ///

May: the / 12 / 1637 The examinaction of SAMUELL: GRENSILD: of No^{r}wch Weauear / ageed, 27 yeares, and BARBREY: his Wife / ageed / 35 yeares. With two Children MAREY: and BARBREY: and JOHN: TEED: his Saruant / ageed, 19 yeares ar all desirous to passe into New England to inhabitt ///

May: the / 12th / 1637 The examinaction of THOMAS: JOANES: of Elzing in No^rff, Buchar / Singleman / ageed. 25 yeres is desirous to passe into New England: and there to Remaine ///

May: the / 13th / 1637 The examinaction of THOMAS: OLLIUER: of No^rwch Calinder / ageed / 36 yeares. and MAREY: his Wife / ageed. 34 yeares, with 2 Children. THO: and JOHN: and 2 Saruants / THOMAS: DOGED: aged, 30 yeares and MAREY: SAPE: ageed / 12 yeares ar desirous to passe fo^r New England. to inhabit

May: the / 15th / 1637 The examinaction of WILLIAM: COCKRAM: of Southould in Suff / Marinrar / ageed 28 yeares. / and CHRISTEN: his Wife ageed. 26 yeares with 2 Children and / 2 Saruantes desirous to passe fo^r new england to inhabitt ///

[*Then follow more passages for Holland; and the whole is signed:*]

HENRY: HILL Deputy for m' THOMAS MAYHEW Gentleman.//

SOUTHAMPTON.

PORTUS SOUTHTON. A List of the Names of such Passengers as were shipped in the *Virgin* of Hampton of 60 tonnes JOHN WEARE M^r for the Barbathoes, & JOHN DE LA HAY merchant who haue taken the oathes of Allegiance & Supremacy the 30th of Marche. 1639 [1640]. Viz^t.

Aged.	
*57. yeares.	MICHAELL EDMOND'S of Crawley Com Southt husband.
28.	JEREMY ROBINSON of Singleton Com Suss hoopmaker.
29.	JOHN VENNELL de eod Cordwayner.
25.	Wm FRANCIS of Catterington Com Southt sergweau'. [serge-weaver]
20.	JAMES WILSON of Glascowe husbandm.
20.	Wm BARNES of Wimborne Com Southt shoemak^r
22.	NICHAS BARDIN of Southton Smith
22.	ANDREWE DRUDG of Southton p'd husbandm
27.	ABRAHAM SAD of Southton p'd sergeweau'
24.	JAMES BARREY of Dorchester husbandm
16.	JOHN STEVENS of Ringwood Com Southt husbandm
15.	GYLES WEEKEHAM of Bansteed Com Surr husbandm.
18.	PETER WOODLAND of Southton Ropemaker.
16.	RICHARD SHINGLE of Bevis hill nere Southton.
17.	JAMES HACKER of Andiver Com Southt.
15.	WIIIM TUCKE of Husborne nere Andiver p'd.
30.	JOHN HUDLICE of Newport in ye Isle of wight taylo^r.
16.	JAMES BLANCHE of the Isle of Wight p'd.
31.	RICHARD TRODD of Southstoneham husbandm.

* [The first figure is almost effaced.]

Aged.
14.	Robᵀ Clitson of Andiver p'd.
12.	Henry Harris of Southton p'd.
12.	Wiħm Decke of Wimborne p'd.
14.	Walter Smalle of the Isle of Wight p'd.
12.	John Bassett of Christchurch.
11.	Robᵀ Bruton of Andiver p'd.

These sixe vnder yeares, & not sworne.

THE names of such as were sworne the 8th of Aprill, & passed in the same Shipp.

Aged.
29. yeares.	Andrewe Bullaker of Southton barboʳ.
24.	Michaell Oxford of Bevis hill husbandm̄.
24.	Robᵀ Maijor of Southton, Chaundler.
19. 14.	Thomas Gretrick ℞ Rich. Warren servᵗˢ
14.	Thomas Turner vnder age ℞ not sworne.
22.	Daniell de la Hay seaman.
45.	John Newman of Brading in the Isle of wight.
30.	Thomas Holmes of Southton Currier.
24.	Wiħm Cockerell. Com̄ Staff Tayloʳ.
24.	Henry Dainty of Bymestʳ Com̄ Dorsᵗ shoemakʳ.
25	Henry Pressey of Hamsteed Com̄ Berk glou' [Glover]
26.	Gerrart Sister a form' Inh'itant there.
29.	Charles Darvall. of Southton clothworker.
14.	Francis Desart of Southton.
14.	Wiħm Gilbert of Southton p'd.
	eight servᵗ maydes, Not sworne.

These & the former which passe in this
Shipp were noe Subsidy men, but
people & servants of meane condiĉon.

PORTUS SOUTHTON;

28. June 1639. REGNALD ALLEN* of Kent of 30. yeares gent, GERRARD HAUGHTON of 30. yeares Com̄ Oxōn geñ ℘ DAVID BIXE of 35. yeares Com̄ Kanc̄ geñ free planters of the Barbathoes.
JOHN EVENSON of the County of Chest^r ℘ THO: EVENSON his broth^r, ANDREW WALLER of 18. yeares Com̄ Hert̄f, HUMPHRY BURGIS of 19. yeares of Cornewall, JOHN WETHERED of 22—yeares in the County of Yeorke serv^{t's} to the Planters aboue named, they passe in the *Boldadventure* of Hampton for the Isle of Guarnzey, ℘ from thence they take shipping for the Barbathoes, who haue taken the oathes vt sup^a [ut supra]

[*May* 1638.]

SOUTHTON   The list of the names of Passeng^{rs} Intended to shipe themselues, In the *Beuis* of Hampton of Cl Tonnes, ROBERT BATTEN M^r for Newengland; And thus by vertue of the Lord Tresurers Warrant of the second of May. wch was after the restrayne[t] & they some Dayes gone to sea Before the Kings Mat^{es}.. Proclamacōn Came vnto Southton.

Ages.
JOHN FREY of Basing wlelwrite. [wheelwright] his wife.
05—& three Children.
40—RICHARD AUSTIN tayler of Bishopstocke. his wife
05—& two Children.
ROBERT KNIGHT his seruant Carpenter.

---

* [Three entries of passengers for Jersey and Guernsey precede this in the original.]

[Ages]
37—CHRISTOPHER BATT of Sarum Tanner. }
32—ANNE his wife. }
20—DOROTHIE BATT there sister. & fiue
10 & vnder. Children vnder tenne yeares.
24.—THOMAS GOOD .... }
22.—ELIZA: BLACKSTON .... } serv{ts}
18.—REBECCA POND............... }

62.—WILLIAM CARPENTER...... } of Horwell Carpent{rs}
33.—WILLIAM CARPENT jun ... }
32.—ABIGAEL CARPENTER.
10 & vnder & fower Children.
14—THO: BANSHOTT Servt

38—ANNIS LITTLEFEILD & six Children
   JOHN KNIGHT Carpenter... } seru{ts}
   HEUGH DURDAL .... }

26—HENERY BYLEY of Sarū tanner.
22—MARY BYLEY ....
   THO: REEUES Serv{ts}
20—JOHN BYLEY............

40	RICHARD DUM' [DUMMER] of Newengland.
35	ALCE DUM'
19	THO: DUM'
19	JOANE DUM'
10	JANE DUM'
*09	STEEPHEN DUM' husbandman.
06	DORATHIE DUM'.
04	RICHARD DUM'.
02	THO: DUM'.

---

* [Evidently either the age or the occupation must be wrong here.]

[Ages]		
30	JOHN HUCHINSON Carpent'	
26	FRAUNCIS ALCOCKE Virg.	
19	ADAM MOTT tayler...........................	
22	Wīll WACKEFEILD.	
20	NATHANUEL PARKER of London Backer	Serv^{ts}
18	SAMUEL POORE	
14	DĀYELL POORE	
20	ALCE POORE.....................................	
15	RICHARD BAYLEY	
20	ANNE WACKEFEILD	

The numb' of the passeng'^{s} aboue mentioned are Sixtie & one Soules,

HEN: CHAMPANTE Cust^r THO: WULFRIS Coll & Fa$_r$

   N. DINGLEY Compt^r

[THE SOMMER ISLANDS.

1673—1679.]

[THE SOMMER ISLANDS.]

August the 23d 1673

THE Names of y^e Govern' & Councill of y^e Assembly

J HEYDON: D. G. [Deputy Governor.]

HENRY TUCKER seni'.	S^t* GEORG TUCKER
RICHARD WOLRICH	THOMAS KERSEY
HENRY MOORE	EDWARD CHAPLAIN
JOHN HUBBARD	GEORG BASCOMB
JOHN WAINWRIGHT seni'.	WILLIAM BASDEN
THOMAS WOOD	PHILLIP LEA
JONATHAN TURNER seni^r.	JOHN RAWLINS sen'.
THOMAS LECRAIFT	NICHOLAS THORNTON
CORNELIUS WHITE secretary	JOHN ARTHUR
	JOHN STOW
CHARLES WHETENHALL Speaker	JOHN SQIRE
JOHN BRISTOW Juni'.	JOHN HUTCHINS
SAMUELL BRANGMAN	RICHARD HANGER
BOAZ SHARP	GEORG HUBBARD
THOMAS SHAW	WILLIAM MILBORN
JAMES FARMER	LAWRENCE DILL
JOHN WELCH	JOHN COX
THOMAS STOW	JOHN SOMERSALL Sen'.
EDWARD SHERLOCK Sen'.	RICHARD JENNINS
ROBERT DICKONSON	RICHARD PENISTON

* [But possibly S_r, *i.e.* Sir.]

SEVERN VICARS
WILLIAM RIGHTON Seni'
THOMAS HALL
GEORG BALL
JOHN MORRICE Seni'.
Will. BURCH

THOMAS FORSTER
RICHARD MATHELIN
NATHANIELL BUTTERFIELD
HAMOND JOHNSON Clerk
of ye Assembly

N Accompt of the Generall Lands belonging to the Somer Islands Comp^a taken out Mr RICHARD NORWOODS Survey booke by him made in the yeares 1662: 1663:

GENERALL LANDS*

N^o   acr': roo: Perch

   Begining with St Georges Island

1 The Governo' holds of the Hono^{ble} Comp^a as belonging to his place Twelve Shares of Land at the East End of St Georges Island Containeing p Estimacon 300 00 00

                  Namely in the Occupacon of

DAVID STOKES p Estimation .... 1: share
JOSEPH GOODFAITH p Estimat............... 1: sha:
JOHN MILLS p Estimat .... ½ sha:
JOHN BEDWELL p Estimat 1½
JOHN MILLS p Estimat .... 1 sha:
ROBERT POWELL p Estimat .... 1 sha.
CORNELIUS EVANS MATTHEW NORMAN and ROGER BROWNE p Estimat ...... } 1 sha
ALEXANDER SMITH p Estimacon............ 1 sha:
JOHN WELSH JOHN BRISTOWE MARSHALL, ROGER BAYLEY HANNAH HOLLOWAY, EDWARD MIDDLETON, THO: SHAW JOHN HURT, these seaven hold p Estimacon 2 sha:

The residue of these twelve Shares are in the Occupacon of the Governo' himselfe.

---

* [There are two copies of this list, one going down to No. 26 only (see p. 307), the other to the end, as here. We have printed from the longer and more complete one. There are, however, no important variations in them, so far as they both extend.]

THE SOMMER ISLANDS.

Nº		acr:	roo:	Perch
2	Gleabe in the Tenure of mʳ: SAMᵘˡ· SMITH the psent Minister there Two shares Containeing p stimat. [estimation]	50	00	00
3	The Sheriffe Mʳ JOHN NICHOLLS as belonging to his Office Fower Shares of Land containeing p Estimat.	100	00	00
4	The Secrary Mʳ HENRY TUCKER as belonging to his Office holds of the Honoᵇˡᵉ Compᵃ 2 shares Containeing p Estimat	050	—	—
5	Mʳ JOHN VAUGHAN holdeth by Lease from mʳ CASEWELL of the Compᵃˢ Land 1 sha: containeing p Estimat	025	00	00
6	Leut: EDWARD BRACKLEY holdeth of the Honᵇˡᵉ Compᵃ at Will 2 sha: containeing p Estimat	050	00	00
7	Mʳ JOHN BRISTOWE Marshall holdeth of the Honᵒᵇˡᵉ Compᵃ as belonging to his Office 2 sha: Containing p estimat	050	00	00
8	Mˢ STALVERS holdeth of the Honoᵇˡᵉ Compᵃ as belonging to the Ferry 2 sha: Containeing Estimat	50	00	00

Sume 27: shares

But the whole Island (as formerly measured) conteynes 706: acres that is 28: sha: and Six acres.

The Small Islands neare Sᵗ Georges.

9	Two Islands against the East End of Sᵗ Georges Lyeing in Comon containeing	05	00	06
10	Pagetts Fort whereof Captaine FRANCIS TUCKER is Comander wᵗʰ the Island whereon it stands sometimes called Penestons Island and a Tenemᵗ or Dwelling house there in the Occupacon of Leivt: JONATHAN STOKES as belonging to the Fort cont	31	01	18

Nº	Generall	acr	roo:	perch.
11	Smiths Fort whereof Captaine GODHEARD ASER is Comander the Island Containeing	00	02	30
12	Smiths Island in the tenure of Captaine GODHEARD ASER from the Hono^{ble} Comp^a as Comander of Smiths Fort cont	61	02	10
13	An Island Called Hen-Island neare the West End of Smiths Island Lyeing in Comon and Containeing	03	01	04
*13	A small Island Lyeing betweene Hen-Island aforesaid and Smiths Island Lyeing in Comon ℓ Containeing	00	01	20
*14	Long Bird Island in the Tenure and Occupacon of JAMES STIRRUP and RALPH WRIGHT Weavers wch they hold of the Hono^{ble} Comp^a containeing	46	02	06
*15	Conny Island Lyeing at Burnt Point in the Occupacon of Mr HENRY STALVERS containeing	14	03	02
*16	Certaine small Islands in ye towne harbor Mullett bay ℓ towards burnt point about Tenn in number cont p estim..................	02 : 00 : 00		
	Sum of all these Islands lyeing neare S Georges	165 : 2 : 16		

Davids Island and first the Easterne part thereof which is Called ye Companyes land there

17	Capt FRANCIS TUCKER Comand' of Pagetts Fort			
18	holdeth of ye hono^{ble} Comp^a A parcell of Land neare Davids head in ye occupacon of his Leivetennt JONATHAN STOKES			
	Item another pcell there in ye occupacon of JOHN HURT, both pcells lyeing together ℓ cont p estim	60:	00:	00
19	MILES HIGGES holdeth of ye hono^{ble} Compa 1 sha: cont p est..................	25:	00:	00

---

* [This and the succeeding numbers, in the other list, read—14, 15, 16, 16.]

N°:	Landes	Acr:	roo:	per
20	HUGH HARDING holdeth of ye hono^ble Compa 1 Share cont p estimat..	25:	00:	00
21	WILLIAM ALLEN holds as aforesaid 1 share cont p est	25:	00:	00
22	Capt RICHARD JENNYNGS of Smiths tribe comand^r of Southampton fort holds of ye hono^ble Compā as belonging to ye Fort ℓ in ye occupaçon of JOHN GRAZBURY ℓ RANDALL DAVIS p estim 2 sha: of Land cont	50:	00:	00
23	Lievt THO: HILTON holds of ye hono^ble Compā p est 2 sh: con:	50:	00:	00
24	ROBT. BURCHER holds as afores^d p est 1 sh: cont......	25:	00:	00
25	Lievt EDWARD BRANGMAN and his sonne SAMUEL BRANGMAN holds as aforesaid p est 1 sha: cont ...	25:	00:	00
26	WILLIAM BELL holds of the Hono^ble Compā two pcells of Land namely one pcell on the South side cont p est 13 acres and another pcell on ye North side next ye Bay cont p est 12 acres both pcells cont p est one Share or	25:	00:	00

	acr:		
The sume of these Lands in S Davids called ye Companyes	310:	00:	00

	acr:	roo:	Per

The Lands in S Davids Island given by ye hono^ble Company to Harrington a̅l̅s Hamilton tribe

27	THO: SPARKE of Davids Island holdeth freely a pcell of land wch formerly belonged to two shares in Hamilton tribe that sometimes were Capt JOHN BERNARDS and are there marked (No: 19) cont p estimat	10:	00:	00
28	THO: SPARKE afores^d holdeth of m^r JOHN MILNER as belonging to ye two shares in Hamilton tribe where he dwells and another share In ye occupaçon of M's COX widdow In all three Shares being ye Lands of Mr PERIENT TROTT ℓ numbred there: 9 ℓ 20 he holdeth I say as belonging to these 3 sh p est	15:	00:	00

	Generall	acr:	roo:	Per
29	WILLIAM ADAMS holdeth of JACOB AXTON as belonging to ye Share of Mr MATTHEW WICKS in Hamilton tribe (No there 11th) p est	05:	00:	00
30:	M^s MARY MOUNTAINE (formerly MARY STOW) holdeth a pcell of Tenn acres belonging to two Shares in Hamilton tribe now Mr SOUTHERNES (No: 21) Item another pcell of Five acres belonging to a share in Hamilton tribe in ye free tenure of JOHN PLACE (No 30: both pcells lyeing together ℓ cont p estimat	15:	00:	00
31	MARY MOUNTAINE afores^d holdeth as belonging to two shares in Hamilton tribe being the Shares of Capt GEORGE HUBBART of Devonsheire tribe (No 12) a pcell cont p est	10:	00:	00
32	Leivt JOHN FOX holdeth of Capt GODHEARD ASSER as apperteyneing to ye 3 shares in Hamilton tribe whereon he the said Capt ASSER dwells wch were Late Mr DELBRIDGE A pcell cont p estimat	15:	00:	00
33 34	HENRY SHARPE holdeth freely a pcell of thirty acres of wch 15 acres did formerly belong to ye three shares of Capt COVELLS in Hamilton tribe (No 27: 28) the whole lyeing together ℓ Cont p est	30:	00:	00
35	JOHN LYDDALE holdeth of M^r SAM^{ll} WHITNEY of Sandys tribe as apteyneing to ye Land formerly m^r DYKES in Hamilton tribe a pcell Cont p estimacon	30:	00:	00
36:	Mr JOHN MOORE holdeth freely a pcell wch was heretofore JOHN DAY and apperteyneing to a share in Hamilton tribe now Mr WEBBS (No 16) cont p estimat	05:	00:	00
37	JOHN MOORE afores^d holdeth of Mr MIHIL BURROUGHES a parcell of Land apperteyneing to Two shares in Hamilton tribe in ye occupacon of ye said MIHIL BURROWES (No 22) cont p est	10:	00:	00

Nº	Landes	acr: roo: per
38	ELIZABETH NAILER holdeth of M' WATERMAN (wch was heretofore M' RICH: CASWELLS a pcell of Land belonging to Five shares in Hamilton tribe wch are thought to be the shares in the tenure of Mr STAFFORD M' STRINGER ℓ M' WRIGHTON cont p est (No: 13: 14: 15)	25: 00: 00
39	THO: STOW of Davids Island holdeth freely A pcell of Island belonging to a share now or Late in ye tenure of Capt CANTER (No. 29) cont p est	05: 00: 00
40	THO STOW afores^d holdeth of M' JOHN STOWE ℓ he of M' PERIENT TROTT a pcell of Land lyeing at ye Stocks pointe belonging to Five shares in Hamilton tribe whereof Fower were ye Earle of WARWICKS (Nom': 23 24 25 26: ℓ one y^t Lyes at ye Flatts No: 36. the whole pcell here Lyeing together ℓ Cont p estimat...	25: 00: 00
	The sume of these lands in Davids Island belonging to: 40: sh: in Hamilt tribe is p estim	200: 00: 00

Soc ye whole Islands of S Davids divided as aforesaid cont p estimat 510: acres

But as it was formerly measured it cont 527: acres

The Islands in Southampton halbo' als Castle Harbor

		acr: roo: per
41	Certaine small Islands to ye Number of Tenn lyeing in Comon neare to Davids Islands, and on the South side thereof (for the most pt) cont p estimat	08: 00: 00
42	The Island called Coopers Island in the tenure and occupacon of DAVID MING wch he holds of ye hono^{ble} Comp^a conteyneing	77: 2: 20
43	Foure small Islands lyeing in Comon betweene Davids Island ℓ Coopers Island cont p estimat	03: 2: 20
44:	Five other small Islands lyeing in Comon neare ye South end of Coopers Island cont p estimat.........	02: 2: 00

	Generall	acr:	roo:	per
45:	The Island called None-such lyeing in Comon cont	15:	2:	13
46.	Three Small Islands about Nonesuch lyeing in Comon cont	01:	00:	00
47	South-hampton Fort vnder ye Comand of Capt RICH JENYNGS wth ye Island whereon it stands cont p estimat	01:	2:	24
48	The Fellow of it lyeing next toward y^c Northeast in Comon	00:	3:	30
49	Kings Castle vnder ye Comand of our hono^{ble} Governo' Capt FLORENTIO SEYMOR, wth ye Island whereon it stands cont.	03:	2:	00
50	Charles Fort now decayed (onely there remaine two peeces of ordinance dismounted, y^c Island cont p estimat	03:	3:	00
51	Three Islands lyeing neare Charles Fort Island cont p estimat	01:	00:	00
52	Some other Small Islands lyeing in Comon in Southampton harbor als Castle Harbor cont p estimat	01:	3:	00
	Sume of these Islands in Southampton harbor	120:	3:	27

		acr:	roo:	per
N^o	The Generall Land at Tuckers Towne.			
53	Gleab Land in the tenure of m^r Abo=Cromby wth the Gleabe house cont p estimat 2 sha:	50:	00:	00
54	Mr W^M MOORE $\rlap{\rlap{(}\rlap{)}}$ Mr JOSEPH MOORE his sonne holdeth of y^e hono^{ble} Compā two Tenem^{ts} $\rlap{\rlap{(}\rlap{)}}$ two shares of Land cont p estimat	50:	00:	00
55	SAM^{LL} ATKINSON holdeth of the Hono^{ble} Compā a Tenem^t $\rlap{\rlap{(}\rlap{)}}$ 1 share of Land cont p estimat	25,	00:	00
56:	DANIEL MARROW holdeth as aforesaid a Tenem^t and One share of Land cont p est	25:	00:	00
57	NATHANAEL NORTH holdeth of y^e Hono^{ble} Compā a Tenem^t $\rlap{\rlap{(}\rlap{)}}$ one share of Land cont p estimat	25:	00:	00
58	PARNEL WILKINSON Widd holdeth of y^e hono^{ble} Compā a tenem^t $\rlap{\rlap{(}\rlap{)}}$ one share of Land cont p estimat some thinke she hath more.	25:	00:	00

THE SOMMER ISLANDS. 311

No.	Landes:	acr:	roo:	per
59	Leivetennt Wm JONES, Leift at y^e Castle holds as belonging to his place A tenem^t in his owne occupacon, Item another tenem^t in the occupacon of JAMES GRAZEBURY Item another tenem^t in ye occupacon of his Mother MARY JONES wth two Shares of Land in ye occupacon of himselfe and his said assignes cont p estimat..................	50:	00:	00
60	THO CLINCH Wm NEWMAN JOHN BROWNE each of them a Tenem^t & some pcells of Land wch together wth ye wast & Comon Land extending from Tuckers towne bay allmost to ye Castle cont p estimat	95:	00:	00
	Sume of these Generall Lands at Tuckers towne and extending thence to ye point neare ye Castle is	345:	00:	00

Touching some of ye Lands at Tuckers towne as alsoe in Davids Island I could not bee throughly Informed though I made seu'all Journyes & Inquiries, but have sett them downe according to ye best Informacon I could Gather.

	acr:	roo:	per
The Island called s Georges conteyneing by estimat 27 shares but by measure	706:	2:	00
The other Lands in ye towne Harbor & soe to Burnt pointe cont	165:	2:	16
Davids Island cont by estimacon 510 acres but by measure	527:	3:	00
Coopers Island Nonesuch and the other small Islands there cont..	120:	3:	27
The Generall Land at Tuckers Towne and extending to ye pointe neare ye Castle conteynes by estimacon 345 acr but there seemes to be neare one share more by measure namely...	370:	00:	00

	acr:	ro	pe
Sume totall of ye Generall Lands	1890:	03:	3:

Islands ~~in~~ Comon

No:

		acr:	ro.	per.
	The Islands in ye Great & Little Sound lyeing in Comon to all the Tribes............			
No: 1	The Bigger Island at ye bottome of ye Little Sound against ye Lands of m' JOHN HUBBART cont p estimat............	01:	02:	20
2	The Two Lesser conteyneing p estimat............	00:	00:	20
3	Another Small Island in ye Little Sound neare to Diggs his Dale in Smiths tribe Cont p estimat	00:	02:	00
4	An Island Att Bailyes Bay on ye North side of Hamilton tribe cont p estimat............	00:	02:	30.
5	Another there more Westerly cont p estimat............	00:	01:	00
6	The Greater of ye Islands in ye Little Sound called Trunck Islands in ye occupacon of JOHN ROBERTS cont	03:	00:	00
7	The next there to ye Northwards in ye occupacon of ye said JOHN ROBERTS cont p estimat	01:	00:	10
8	Two other small Islands there conteyneing p estimat	00:	01:	26

In the Greate Sound

9	An Island in Crow Lane (lyeing against ye Share of Schoole Land given by Mr COPELAND) in ye occupacon of EVAN OWEN for yearely rent wch he payes to ye Governo' or Sheriffe for public vses as doe ye rest of these Islands y^t are Lett out this Island cont p estimat	03:	00:	00
10	Another Island in Crow lane over ag^t M' STOWES house to ye Southward lyeing in Comon & and cont estimat............	03:	00:	00
11	Six small Islands at ye Entring of Crow Lane lyeing over from Mr STOWES pointe to Salt Kettle pointe lyeing in Comon & Cont p estimation	03:	01:	00

No.	To all the Tribes:	acr	ro:	per
12	Another Island there in ye occupacon of THO: ACKLAND wth the Tenem^t thereon cont p estimat	28:	2:	20
13	Two small Islands lyeing betweene y^t last before entred and warwicke tribe cont. p estimat	00:	3:	00
14	An Island in Bosses hole lyeing as aforesaid in Comon and Cont p estimat	00:	21:	00
15	Another Island there at ye Mill or Mouth of Mangrow bay &c cont p estimat	00:	1:	00
16	Another more Southerly Lyeing in Comon & cont p estimat	00:	2:	30
17	Another there more Southerly lyeing &c & cont p estimat	01:	00:	00
18	Another there more Southerly lyeing &c & cont p estimat	00:	2:	00
19	A Long Island at ye Entrance of Daniels bay wth a smaller further into ye bay, both lyeing in Comon & Cont p estimat	01:	1:	00
20	A Bigger Island lyeing agt Mr STOWES pointe shares to ye westward lyeing in Comon & Cont p estimat	03:	01:	00
21	Foure Smaller Islands to ye Westwards lyeing &c cont	01:	01:	00
22	An Island wth a bay on ye South side of it wth another Lesser Island toward's ye Northeast both in ye occupacon of LAZARUS OWEN wth the Tenem^t there Cont p estimat	28:	1:	30
23	Another Small Island next ye Two former lyeing in Comon & cont p estimat	00:	3:	10
24	Three small Islands to ye Westwards of LAZARUS OWEN lyeing in Comon & Cont p estimat	01:	2:	00
25	A Bigger Island Northwest from LAZARUS OWEN in ye occupacon of NATHANAEL VEAZEY or his assignes cont p est	13:	3:	00
26	Another Island neare adioyneing to ye West end in ye occupation of ye said NAT VEAZEY or his assignes cont p estimat	09:	2:	00

No	Islands in Comōn	acr:	ro:	per
27	Elizabeth Island wth a tenem^t there in the occupacon of JOHN BURT cont p estimat	21:	00:	10
28	An Island at ye North head of Elizabeth Island lyeing in Comon ℓ cont p estimat...............	00:	03:	20
29	Another Island at ye Northwest end of Elizabeth Island lyeing in Comon ℓ Cont p estimat	01:	02:	00
30	The Island called pearle Island wth another small Island at Spanish pointe ℓ another neare Ireland all lyeing in Comon ℓ cont p estimat	02:	01:	00
31	An Island to ye Southwestward of ye West end of Elizab^th Island lyeing in Comon ℓ Cont p estimat	01:	02:	00
32:	Another Island there more Southerly lyeing in comon cont p estimat	02:	01:	30
33	Three small Islands more Southerly comon cont p estimat.................................	03:	00:	00
34	An Island called Roundhill Island in ye occupacōn of HENRY WARD cont p estimat..................	16:	01:	20
35	A smaller Island to ye Southward of y^t last entred in ye occupacōn of ye said HENRY WARD cont p estimat.................................	02:	00:	00
36	An Island called Tuckers Island wth a Tenem^t there in ye occupacōn of NATHANIEL CONYARD cont p estimat.................................	21:	00:	00
37	The next on ye Northside called ye Lesser Tuckers Isłd in ye occupat of THO WARD cont p estimat ...	07:	03:	00
38	Two Small Islands to ye Westward of ye Two Last lyeing in Comon ℓ Cont p estimat	00:	02:	00
39	An Island betweene Tuckers Island ℓ Brother Islands sometimes called Graves Island lyeing in comon ℓ cont	06:	02:	00
40	The Westermost of ye Brother Islands lyeing next to Georges pointe wth a Tenem^t there in ye occupat of JOHN RIVERS cont p estimat	20:	01:	20
41	The easternmost of ye Brother Islands lyeing in comōn ℓ Cont p estimat............................	13:	3:	30

No	To all the Tribes:	acr:	roo:	per
42	An Island neare ye Shore at ye Partition line betweene the Lands formerly ye Earle of Southamptons & M' Scotts lyeing in Comon & Cont p estimat..........	02:	01:	20
43	Two small Islands neare Jews bay lyeing in Comon cont p estimat..	03:	00:	00
44 45	Two Islands before ye Entrance of Hearne bay one in ye occupacon of JOHN HELYN ye other in ye occupacon of his mother wth a tenem^t both Cont p estimat	17:	01:	00
46	Two other small Islands w^thin White hearne bay lyeing in Comon & Cont p estimation	01:	00:	10

The sume of these Islands lyeing in Comon to
all ye tribes is 253: acr: 2 roo: 36 per:

The totall of all ye shares of land sett apart for publique use
as p this booke are eighty six shares

    vera Copia Ex p   HENRY DANDG
                                      RI: BANNER.

[Indorsed:]
"Rec^d from Mr BANNER Secry to y^e Company 25 Sept: 1684."

[MONMOUTH'S REBELLION OF 1685.

LISTS OF THE "CONVICTED REBELS" SENT TO THE BARBADOES AND OTHER PLANTATIONS IN AMERICA.]

[MONMOUTH'S REBELLION OF 1685.]

Som's.
[Somerset.] ECEIPT for one hundred Prisoners to be transported from Taunton by JOHN ROSE of London Merchant.

DANIELL RUTTER	PERCIVALL NOWIS
JEREMIAH POOLE	WILLIAM SAUNDERS
JOHN BAKER	WILLIAM VEIYARD
ROBERT PEARCE	HENRY CHAMBERS
LEONARD STAPLE	THOMAS ROWSEWELL
EDWARD KENT	MATHEW COOKE
CHARLES BENNETT	JOHN CRANE
JOHN PARSONS	CHARLES BURRAGE
JOHN GIBBS	WILLIAM LEY
JOHN BRYER	JOHN ROBINS
THOMAS GOOLD	LUKE PORTER
JOHN HARTEY	THOMAS PREIST
WILLIAM PITTS	CORNELIUS RADFORD.
JAMES WEBB	PHILLIP CHEEKE
NICHOLAS COLLINS jun^r	ROBERT EARLE
RICHARD KING	JOHN MOGRIDGE
EMANUELL MARCHANT	HENRY RANDALL
WILLIAM MARCHANT	JAMES MAYNARD
JOHN SLADE	JOHN CULVERWELL
SAMUELL BOND	GEORGE TRUBBS
JOHN ROGERS	SYLVESTER LYDE
BERNARD LOVERIDGE	WILLIAM PHELPES

Elias Lockbeare	Robert Richards
Sylvester Poole	Christopher Row
Thomas Moore	Mathew Craft jun[r]
Lawrence Preist	Richard Peircy
William Gould	John Miller
Henry Preist	George Snow
Enock Gould	Samuell Collins
John Bennett	John Cockram
John Baker	James Cockram
Samuell Mountstephen	Christopher Hoblyn
Thomas Buglar	John Marwood
Stephen Jeffreyes	John Timothy
John Morse	Thomas Austin
William Scurrier	Moses Osborne
John England	Walter Hucker
Jacob Powell	Randall Babington
John Godsall	John Knight
John Andrewes	Job Hunt
Samuell Sweeting	William Woodcocke
George Rowsell	John Adams
Edward Bellamy	Thomas Pomfrett
William Crosse	James Patten
Jonas Browne	Thomas Bambury
John Crosse	James Clift
Christopher Knight	Thomas Chamberlyne
Thomas Meade	Humfrey Justine
John Needes	Isack Dyer
Thomas Pitts	Richard Symons

Receiued according to his Ma[ties] order the warrant from the Lord Cheife Justice wth a Sohedule therevnto annexed of one hundred persons attainted of High Treason w[ch] are by John Rose Merch[t] to be transported into his Maties Island of Barbadoes or other his Maties plantacōas [plantations] in America according to a Condicōn of a Recognizance entred into by me for that purpose In Wittnesse whereof I haue herevnto put my hand this 12th day of October in the first yeare of his Maties Raigne. Annoq, Dñi 1685º

JOHN ROSE

Wittnesse herevnto
ROBᵣ HYDE
GILES CLARKE.

Mᴿ Rose's LIST*

INUOICE of Sixty Eight Men Seruants Shipped on board Capⁿ Charles Gardner in yᵉ *Jamaica Merchant* for accoᵗ of Mᵣ John Rose & Compⁿ, they being to be Sold for ten Yeares theire Names as followeth Viz:

	Age		Trades
Isaack Dyer	25 year		Comber
James Webb	18 „		Hosbanman
William Woodcoke	19 „		Comber
Humphry Justin	17 „		Ditto.
Richard Pearcey	20 „		Ditto.
James Cockram	21 „		Ditto.
Daniel Rutter	20 „		Sarge Weauer
James Clift	20 „		Weauer
Xopher Holbin	40 „		Ditto
Thomas Pitt	18 „		Comber
John Timothy	29 „		Riben Veauer
Enoch Gould	15 „		Wauer
Jerimiah Poole	30 „		Clothier
William Scurrier	22 „		Weauer
Emanuel Merchant	20 „		Plowman
Edward Bellamy	27 „		Carpenter
John Godsall	27 „		Boucher
George Rousell	30 „		Woolle Comber

* [It will be noticed that so far as names are concerned, this list is in large part a repetition of that previously given.]

	Age		Trades
THOMAS GOULD	35 years		Tayler
LUKE PORTER	20	„	Showmaker
JOHN MAGERIDGE	23	„	Weauer
JOHN CROSS	18	„	Plowman
JOHN ROGERS	38	„	Clothier
ROBERT RICHARDS	28	„	Tayler
JAMES MAYNARD	22	„	Plowman
ROBERT PEARCE	25	„	Clothier
NICHOLAS COLLINGS	20	„	Weauer
JOHN GIBBS	19	„	Plowman
THOMAS MEADE	22	„	Glouer
RICHARD SIMONS	33	„	Weauer
JOHN COCKRAM	18	„	Comber
BERNARD LOUERIDGE	22	„	Sope boyler
ROBERT EARLE	24	„	Plowman
SAMUEL BOND	20	„	Serge Weauer
PERCIFULL NOWES	23	„	Hatter
WILLIAM LEE	20	„	Plowman
WILLIAM PHILLIP	26	„	Plowman
SILUESTER POOLE	24	„	Boucher
EDWARD KENT	19	„	
WILLIAM SANDERS	19	„	Clothier
CORNELIUS RADFORD	20	„	Weaer
CHARLES BURRAGE	27	„	Comber
JOBE HUNT	26	„	Carrier
LEONARD STAPLES	20	„	Plowman
JOHN SLADE	25	„	Sergeweauer
JONAS BROWNE	20	„	Plowman
JOHN BAKER	35	„	Sergeweauer
PHILLIP CHEEKE	16	„	Plowman
THOMAS PREIST	20	„	Sergeweauer
WILLIAM VERRYARD	17	„	Carpenter
MATHEW COOKE	21	„	Plowman
MATHEW CRAFT	19	„	Weauer
JOHN BAKER	27	„	Mason

LISTS OF CONVICTED REBELS.

	Age		Trades
JOHN CHAMBERLIN	20 years		Shoomaker
SILUESTER LYDE	27 „		Boucher
JOHN BRUER	25 „		Mason
GEORGE tRUBBS	28 „		Plowman
WILLIAM PITTS	28 „		Woollecomer
RICHARD KING	18 „		Plowman
JOHN ANDREWS	27 „		Woollecomer
JOHN MILLER	35 „		Plowman
HENRY PREIST	22 „		Ditto
GEORGE SNOW	19 „		Commer
ELIAS LOCKEBEAR	18 „		Tanner
XTOPHER ROW	34 „		Weauer
HENRY CHAMBER	25 „		Woollcomer
THOMAS AAUSTIN	27 „		Mercer

(*in dorso*) 9 *Dec*: 1685

The men whose names are conteined in the within written list are Shipt upon the acc^t of JOHN ROSE & company on board the *Jam^e Merch^t* to be landed & disposed of in Barbados or in Jamaica :

JOHN ROSE

 RECEIPT for one hundred Prisoners on Mr NEPHO'S Acc^o to be sent to Barbudos*

Prisoners in Dorchester Goale to bee Transported

JOHN MEGGERIDGE	JOHN FACY
THOMAS QUICK	W^M GREENWAY
NICHOLAS SALTER	RICHARD DANIEL
FRANCIS SMITH	PETER KENT
RICHARD GREEN	CHRISTOPHER JEWELL
W^M MATHEWES	ABRAHAM THOMAS

* [There are three copies of this list, as well as the certificate given in p. 320, each differing in some points from the other. Important variations are mentioned in the footnotes; the differences in spelling, common at that time, I have not indicated. I have chosen as "copy" that which appears, from the signatures, to have been the original document.]

LISTS OF CONVICTED REBELS.

John Baker	Wm Deale
Samuel Pinson	Wm Haynes
Robert Clarke	Thomas Franklyn‖
George Ebdon	Wm Guppy
Samuel Dolebeer	~~Malachi Mallocke~~ ⎫ being
Benjamin Whicker*	Azarias Pinney ⎭ wittnesse¶
John Whicker	John Bovett
John Hitchcott	Robert Sandy
Thomas Forcey	Thomas Dolling
Wm Gyles	Edward Marsh
Joseph Gage	John Easemond
Robert Mullens	John Vincent
Roger Bryant	Allen England
Charles Broughton	Robert Vater
Richard Parker	John Prew
John Hayne	Oliver Hobbs
John Connett	Philip Cox
Barnard† Lowman	Peter Tickin**
John Heathfeild	Wm Clarke
Edward Venn	Walter Osborne
Richard Pine	Richard Hoare
Thomas Pester‡ [not found there and so not deliuered to me]	Robert Foane
	Daniell Parker
John Sam	Pr†† Bagwell
Henry Simes§	

* [Thus in two lists; WHITKER in one.]   † [BERNARD in the other two lists.]

‡ [In two copies of this list he is called LESTER: in *this* list it was first so written, and then altered to a P. The bracketed words are found only in *one* of the copies.

§ [In one copy clearly written SUNES.]

‖ FRANCLYON in one of the copies; FRANCKLYN in the other.

¶ In both the copies MALACHI MALLOCKE'S name is left unerased: one differs from the original only in using the word "evidences" instead of "witnesses." The other reads thus:—

MALACHI MALLOCKE taken out of my custody for a wittnes

AZARIAS PINNEY sent away to Bristoll.

This explains why MALLOCKE's name is erased; for PINNEY, see the letter in note *, p. 320.]

** [Written thus in two lists; TINKIN in one.]

†† [PETER in two lists.]

LISTS OF CONVICTED REBELS.

Prisoners in Exeter Goale to bee transported

- ABRAHAM HUNT
- CHRISTOPHER COOPER
- EDMUND* BOVETT
- JOHN FOLLETT
- PETER BIRD
- JOHN KEMPLYN†
- WALTER TEAPE

Prisoners att Wells to bee Transported

- JOHN JOLIFFE
- ROBERT PEIRCE
- JOHN DODDS
- HENRY PITTMAN
- NATHANIEL BEATON
- PETER‡ CORDYLION
- Wᴹ BIGGS §
- Wᴹ PUTTMAN
- JOHN COOKE
- JOHN HARCOMBE
- JOHN COLLINS
- NATHANIEL STANDERWICK ‖
- RICHARD DYKE
- JOHN DENHAM
- ABRAHAM GOODEN
- JOHN MEAD
- JOHN BRICE ¶
- ANDREW HOLCOMBE
- JOHN HOOPER**
- THOMAS VENNER
- LAWRENCE CASWELL
- THOMAS CHYN
- SAMUEL WEAVER
- ROBERT BATT
- JOHN HOOPER**
- JOHN GOALD
- JOHN COOKE
- JOHN JOHNSON
- JOHN WILLIS
- RICHARD NASH als LYLLANT
- JOHN FOOT
- JOHN REEVES
- JOHN GILL juñ

Recd according to his Maties direccons ye Warrt from ye LORD CHEIFE JUSTICE wth a Schedule thereunto annexed of one hundred psons attainted of High Treason wch are by JEROM NEPHO to bee transported into some of His Majesties Plantacons in America according to a Condicon of a Recognizance entred into by me for that purpose In witnes

---

* [Thus in two lists; EDMOND in one.] † [SCAMPLYN in the two other lists.]
‡ [PETARD in one list.] § [Thus in two lists; BRIGGS in one.]
‖ [SANDERWICK in one of the two copies; SANDERWICKE in the other.]
¶ [Thus in two lists. PRICE in the other.]
** [Thus repeated in the original and other lists.]

whereof I have hereunto putt my hand this six ℓ Twentieth day of September In the first yeare of his now Majesties reigne Añoq̄, D͞ñi 1685

              GEORGE PENNE
  Witness   CHARLES WHITE
    ROB^r HYDE
    SAM^L GEE *

CERTIFICATE of Mr NEPHO's Prisoners Landed at Barbados.†

A LIST of the Convicted Rebells put on Board the *Betty* of London at the Port of Waymouth in the County of Dorsett, JAMES MAY Comander, and is according to Bill of Ladeing by him signed bound for the Island of Barbados, Uiz^t.

JOHN WHICKER	PETER BAGWELL
BENJAMIN WHICKER	ABRAHAM THOMAS
ROGER BRYANT	JOHN BAKER

---

* [At the end of one of the copies the following is written :

        These men are to bee transported to Barbados.
                GEO: PENNE.

That same list is preceded by the following letter :

      Mr NEPHO'S Acc^t of Prisoners.

S^r

Where as you haue signified to me that you are ordered to giue me an exact Acc^tt of ye hundred Rebells which his Ma^{tes} was pleased to grant you, in whome you haue transported your Right unto me to be transported according to his Ma^{tes} order to some of his Plantacions In America pursuant to ye Recognizance which I have entered Into, I doe assure you that there are in Goale sixty fiue of them at Dorchester one wounded man by name EDMUND BOUETT now Remaining In Exeter Goale, and three and thirty at Ilchester besides AZARIAS PINNEY who was sent in Custody to Bristoll to be transported who it will be made appeare upon ye Return of my Express sent for that purpose hath been shipd for some one of his Ma^{tes} Plantacions according to his Ma^{tes} order, of ye Rest I haue here annexed an exact List and expect with in feue daies by my afore-mentioned messenger the Cirtificat there of I am

21st Oct. —85. | ye humble Seruant
                   GEORGE PENNE

  The men that are to bee transported as in the list annexed, are to bee Sentt in the Ship *Rebecca*, the Commander is Capt JAMES MAY; wittness my hand GEORGE PENNE.

It will be observed that the ship in which the men sailed is called the *Betty*, in the certificate given above.

† [There is another copy of this list—an "Invoyce" of the prisoners made out before they started for the Barbadoes. The following are all the important differences in spelling of names &c., as given by it and in the above-printed list. See list for the corresponding numbers.

WILLIAM BIGGS
JOHN FOOT
JOHN DODDS
RICHARD PARKER
THOMAS QUICKE
NICHOLAS SALTER
EDWARD VENN
JOSEPH GAICH
SAMUELL PINSON
PETER KENT
CHRISTOPHER JEWELL
FRANCIS SMITH
JOHN UINCENT
JOHN EASTMOND
PHILLIP COX
JOHN REEUES
ROBERT MULLENS
JOHN CONNET (1)
JOHN FACEY
JOHN HAYNE
THOMAS FRANCKLYN
DANIELL PARKER
JOHN HEATCHFEILD (2)
JOHN MOGERIDGE
ABRAHAM HUNT
WILLIAM CLARKE
JOHN SAM
ROBERT VAWTER.
WILLIAM MADDER.
JOHN FOLLETT
JOHN COLLINS
JOHN COOKE (3)

WILLIAM GREENWAY
WILLIAM GUPPY
ALLEN ENGLAND
EDWARD HOARE (4)
RICHARD DANIELL
LAWRENCE CASWELL
RICHARD PINE
SAMUELL DOLBEARE
ROBERT CLARKE
ROBERT PEARE (5)
OLIVER HOBES (6)
RICHARD GREEN
JOHN WILLIS
ROBERT SANDY
THOMAS PESTOR
THOMAS VENNER
WILLIAM HAYNE
JOHN HITCHCOCK
WILLIAM GYLES
CHARLS BRAGHTON (7)
JOHN KEMPLIN (8)
PETER BIRD
RICHARD NASH
ANDREW HAULKON (9)
THOMAS FORCY
CHRISTOPHER COOPER
JOHN HILL (10)
JOHN HARCOMB
PETER CORDELON (11)
JOHN BOVETT
HENRY SIMS
WILLIAM DALE (12)

(1) CUNNET.
(2) HEATHFEILD.
(3) COCKE.
(4) RICHARD HOARE.
(5) PEARCE.
(6) HOBBS.
(7) BROUGHTON.
(8) KAMPLINN.
(9) HAWLKOM.
(10) GILL.
(11) PETARD CORDELION.
(12) DEALE.

NATHANIELL STANDERWICK (13)	ROBERT FAWN (15)
THOMAS DOLLEN	SAMUELL WEAVER
ABRAHAM GODEN	HENRY PITMAN
EDWARD BOVETT (14)	WILLIAM PITMAN
EDWARD MARSH	and one Servant woman by name
JOHN PREW	SUSANNAH TOLEMAN (16)

The Bill of mortallity of the said Rebells that dyed Since they were reced on Board and were thrown over board out of the said Ship are these uiz. December the sixteenth THOMAS VENNER, Seaventeenth Wᵐ GUPPY, Eighteenth JOHN WILLIS, Nineteenth EDWARD VENN, the same day PHILLIP COX one and Twentieth ROBERT VAWTER, Five and Twentieth Wᴹ GREENWAY Jannuary the First PETER BIRD, Witnessed by the Comander, Marchᵗ and officers of the said Ship this Eighth day of Janu'y 1685*

         JOHN MAY
         JOHN PENNE
         JOHN MADDISON
         GABRIEL WHITHORN
         MALCUM FRASER

Barbados.

    By the Rᵗ Honᵇˡᵉ the Leiuᵗ Gouernor

  CAPTAINE JAMES MAY Comander of the ship *Betty*, JOHN PENNE Marchᵗ Jnº MADDISON Mate, GABRIELL WHITHORN Boatswain & MALCUM FRASER Dcor of sᶜʰ Shipp, personally appeared before mee and made oath on the Holly Evangelists of Allmighty God, that the within servants or Convicted Rebells by the said MAY taken in at the Port of Waymouth in the County of Dorsett, are the very same Convicted Rebells that were delivered to, and by the said MAY brought in the said Ship to this Island, and that they were all of them here

---

(¹³) STANDERICK.   (¹⁴) EDMUND.   (¹⁵) FOWNE.   (¹⁶) SUSAN DOLEMAN.
           * [1685-6.]

landed and delivered to m' CHARLS THOMAS and Company Factors to JEROM NEPHO or his assignes Except Eight of them wch dyed on board the said ship in the voyage, and buried in the sea, whose names are mentioned in the within Bill of Mortallity. Giuen vnder my hand the 8th day of Jannuary 1685*

A true Coppy attested this
Nineth day of Janu'y 1685*   EDWYN STEDE
J N^o WHETSTONE Dep^ty Secr^ty

Warr for Delivery of Rebells convict to M^r· NEPHO.

AUG^T S^s

Whereas the severall persons whose names are conteyned in a Schedule hereunto annexed remaine now in yo' custody being attainted of high Treason for leavying Warr against his Sacred Matie vnder the late Duke of Monmouth, before mee and other his Maties Justices of Oyer and Terminer for this Westerne Circuit ; And whereas his Matie has been pleased to signifie to mee, his Royall pleasure of his gratious intentions to extend his mercy to the s^d persons, and to pardon them their lives vpon Cond;cōn of Transportation into some of his Maties Plantacons beyond the Seas And for that purpose the said persons should bee delivered to JEROME NEPHO or Order, he haveing allready pursuant to his Maties Comānds entred into a Recognizance for their safe and speedy transportacōn into his s^d Maties

Jeffreys   Plantations beyond the Seas according to his Royall directions, and is alsoe obliedged to discharge you and all yo' Officers & Ministers from further trouble and the Country from further charge, relateing to the said persons within tenn dayes after the date of these p'sents, and upon such other Conditions as his Matie has required.

These are therefore in his Maties name to will and require you forthw^th vpon sight hereof to deliver unto the said JEROME NEPHO or his

* [1685-6.]

Order the said severall persons in the s^d Schedule named, in order to their Transportacōn as aforesaid, and you are hereby directed to take a receipt from the person or persons to whome you shall deliver the said Prisoners Pursuant to this Order of the Receipt of them, and for soe doeing this shall bee yo' Warrant Giuen vnder my hand and seale this p'sent 25th day of September, in the first yeare of the Reigne of our Soveraigne Lord King James &c Annoq, Dñi 1685.

To the High Sherriffs of the Counties of Dorsett
Devon and Somersett, & to his ℓ their
Deputies & all other Officers whome these
may concerne.

A true Coppy attested this
9th day of Jannuary 1685
JNo WHETSTONE Dep^{ty} Secr^{ty}

[BARBADOES.]

LIST* of Seaventy two Rebells by his Ma^{tyes} Mercy granted to GEROME NEPHO to bee transported to this Island by the *Betty* JAMES MAY Master received by CHARLS THOMAS and JOHN PENNE, by order of GEORGE PENNE Esq' being the order of JEROM NEPHO

Masters.	Rebells
RICHARD WALTERS	WILLIAM BIGGS
	WILLIAM HAYNE
	WILLIAM DEALE
	EDMOND BOVETT
MICHAELL CHILD......................	SAMUELL WEAVER
	ROBERT MULLINS
	WILLIAM GILES
	DANIELL PARKER
	JOHN FACEY

* [The names of the "Rebels" in this List have been given in "*A Receipt for* 100 *Prisoners on Mr. Nepho's Account,*" on page 317*; but it was deemed advisable to print the following second list, made on their arrival in the Barbadoes, because of its including the names of the Masters to whom they were sold. The variations in the orthography of names have been already referred to.]

Masters.	Rebells
Thomas Gibbs	John Easman
Richard Cheesman	Henry Sims
Cap^{tn} John Sutton	John Collins
Cap^{tn} Robert Harison	Joseph Gaich
	John Follett
William Chester Esq'	Thomas Dollen
	Lawrence Casewell
Cap^{tn} John Gibbs................	John Foot
	Richard Pine
Nicholas Maynard	Peter Bagwell
	John Heathfeild
	John Hercombe
John Smart	John Reeves
	John Dodds
John Chace	Richard Parker
	Edward Marsh
Thomas Berresford	John Sams
	Nathaniell Standericke
Thomas Pearce	Thomas Franklyn
	John Cooke
	Robert Clarke
Peter Flewilling	Andrew Haukom
	John Prew
	Samuell Pinson
	John Gill
Rebecca Beal	Christopher Jewell
	Richard Nash
	Thomas Pestor

LISTS OF CONVICTED REBELS.

Masters	Rebells
BARNABAS CHATER	BENJAMINE WHICKER
Lt Coll^{oll} RICHARD VINTER	JOHN HAYNES THOMAS FAUCEY
THOMAS HOLEMAN	ROBERT PEIRCE
WILLIAM MARCHANT	SAMUELL DOLBEARE JOHN CONNETT
JOHN SHAHANY	OLIVER HOBBS
RALPH LANE	ROBERT FOANE NICHOLAS SALTER ABRAHAM THOMAS THOMAS QUICKE JOHN BAKER WILLIAM CLARKE
Coll^{oll} JOHN WATERMAN	ALLEN ENGLAND
CHRISTOPHER WILLIAMS	RICHARD GREEN
MATHEW CHAPMAN	RICHARD HOARE
THOMAS PROTHERS	PETER KENT
THOMAS AUSTIN	JOHN HITCHCOCKE
ELIZABETH FOSTER	JOHN MOGERIDGE
THOMAS LINTON	ROGER BRYANT
JOHN GOLDINGHAM	ROBERT SANDY
Cap^{tn} JOHN KING	JOHN VINCENT
DANIELL DEUSBURY	CHARLS BRAUGHTON
Maj^r GEORGE BUSHELL	FRANCIS SMITH
EDWARD HENLEY	ABRAHAM HUNT

LISTS OF CONVICTED REBELS.

Masters	Rebells
RICHARD SCOTT	ABRAHAM GODDING
JOHN JACKMAN..................	PETTARD CORDELION
CHARLS THOMAS and Company ..	JOHN WHICKER
	CHRISTOPHER COOPER
	JOHN BOVETT
	RICHARD DANIELL
ROBERT BISHOPP	HENRY PITMAN
	WILLIAM PITTMAN
HESTER FOSTER	JOHN KEMPLIN
	Wm MADER dead

CERTIFICATE of the Disposall of the Rebells sent by Mr NEPHO.

Barbados' By the R^t Hon'^{ble} the Leiu^t Gouernor.

M' CHARLS THOMAS and m' JOHN PENNY Factors for JEROME NEPHO Esqr to whom the within Convicted Rebells menconed in this List were consigned, personally appeared before mee and made oath on the Holy Evangelists of Almighty God, that the said Rebells were delivered them out of the ship *Betty* of London, whereof JAMES MAY is Comander, and were all of them by the said THOMAS and PENNY, Sold and disposed of here to the Seuerall persons menconed in the Said List, Except one of the said Rebells by name WILLIAM MADDER that dyed on Shoar Since the Arriveall of the said Ship Giuen vnder my hand the First day of February 1685*

EDWYN STEDE

A true Coppy attested this }
Second day of February 1685* }

JN^o WHETSTONE Dep^{ty} Secr^{ty}

* [1685-6.]

S͟I͟R WILLIAM BOOTH'S Receipt for the Prisoners within mencon'd on the Account of JAMES KENDALL Esqr· to be sent to Barbados*

Prisoners in Dorchester Gaole to bee Transported

EDWARD LUTHER(1)	THOMAS HOARE
JOHN DOWNE	PETER ROW
BENJ: CROWE	JOHN LOVERIDGE
THOMAS BENNETT	ELIAS STEPHENS(10)
JOHN FISHER	JOHN BRIDLE
JOHN MANNING	THOMAS PARSONS(11)
ROBERT LUMBARD(2)	NICHOLAS PALMER
Wm WADFORD(3)	THOMAS WILLIAMS
RICHARD KEECH(4)	MATHEW HUTCHINS(12)
GEORGE PLUMLEY	NICHOLAS SMITH
THOMAS ALLEN	EMANUELL COLLINS
JOHN REASON	ROGER HOBBS(13)
JOHN SPEERING	JOHN GAY(14)
MATHEW PORTER	JOSEPH HALLETT(15)
ROBERT SPURWAY(5)	NATHANIEL WEBBER(16)
JOHN EDWARDS	EDWARD MORETON(17)
JOHN HARDIMAN	JAMES SALTER
BARNARD BRYANT	WILLIAM LOVERIDGE(18)
JOHN MINIFIE(6)	AMBROSE ASHFORD
JOHN WHITE(7)	ROGER FRENCH(19)
JAMES POMEROY(8)	NICHOLAS WARREN(20)
ROBERT SHALE(9)	WILLIAM WILLS(21)

* [There is an "attested copy" of this Receipt, in which the following (see references after the names in list) are the more important alterations in spelling, &c. :—

(1) LUTTER.	(8) POMREY.	(15) *Left out.*
(2) LUMBERD.	(9) *Left out.*	(16) WHEELER.
(3) MADFORD.	(10) STEVENS.	(17) MORTEN.
(4) KEATCH.	(11) PASSENS.	(18) *Left out.*
(5) SPURNAY.	(12) HUGHENS.	(19) *Left out.*
(6) *Left out.*	(13) HOBES.	(20) *Left out.*
(7) WITTE.	(14) GUY.	(21) WILLIAMS.

LISTS OF CONVICTED REBELS.

JOHN PRYOR
Wm TUCKER
Wm BROWNE
SAMUEL LAWRENCE
JOHN HUTCHINS (22)
Wm CLARKE
JOHN BROWNE
ROBERT BURRIDGE
HENRY TUCKER
THOMAS BURRIDGE
JOHN ALLAMBRIDGE (23)
THOMAS CORNELIUS
HUMPHRY MOLETON
EDWARD WILLMOTT (24)
Wm WILLIAMS (25)
THOMAS MARSHALL
RICHARD PAUL
JOSEPH PAUL
HUGH WILLMOTT (26)
JOHN JOHNSON
RICHARD ALLENS
JOHN PITTS
STEPHEN GAMMAGE (27)
ANDREW RAPSON
Wm COZENS (28)
THOMAS TOWNESEND
JASPER DYAMOND (29)
THOMAS GREGORY

JOHN ALLEN (30)
ROBERT HELLYER (31)
THOMAS ALLEN (32)
THOMAS BEST
THOMAS HELLYER (31)
JOHN LONG
Wm BENNETT (32)
JOHN MARKES (32)
JOHN MITCHELL
JOHN MADDERS
THOMAS HALLETT
JOHN ALSTON
GEORGE MACY
JOHN PINNEY (33)
CHARLES STRONG
Wm FOODE (34)
Wm SAUNDERS
JAMES SPENCE (35)
JOHN WILSON
EDWARD ADAMS
JOHN ADAMS
ARTHUR LUSH (36)
JOHN HUTCHINS (37)
THOMAS BOVETT
JOHN TRUREN (38)
JAMES FOWLER
JOHN WHITE (39)
FRANCIS LANGBRIDGE

(22) HUGENS.
(23) ALIMBRIDGE.
(24) WILLMATT.
(25) WILLS.
(26) WILLMATT.
(27) GAMIDGE.
(28) COUSSENS.
(29) DIMAND.
(30) ALLENS.
(31) HILLIER, and THOMAS's name is twice given
(32) *Left out.*
(33) PENNY.
(34) *Left out.*
(35) JOHN SPENCE.
(36) LUCH.
(37) HUGENS.
(38) *Left out.*
(39) WITTES.]

Recd according to his Majesties direccons the Warr^t from the LORD CHEIFE JUSTICE wth a Schedule thereunto annexed of One hundred persons attainted of High Treason wch are by JAMES KENDALL Esqr to bee transported into his Majesties Island of Barbadoes or other his Majesties Plantacons in America according to a Condicon of a Recognizance entred into by me for that purpose In witnes whereof I have hereunto putt my hand this Five and twentieth day of September In the first yeare of his now Majesties reigne Ano q_h Dñi 1685

            WILL: BOOTH

 Wittness herevnto
  SAM: GEE
  ROBT: HYDE*

CERTIFICAT of the Disposall of CAPTAIN KENDALLS Rebells.

BARBADOS. A List of Ninety Rebells by the *Happy Returne* of Pool Cap^{tn} ROGER WADHAM Comander, with the Names of their Masters to whom they were disposed to, by the Hon'^{ble} Colloll JOHN HALLETT and Company for acco^t of Sr WILLIAM BOOTH and Cap^{tn} JAMES KENDALL, December 1685†

Servants Names	Masters Names
BENJAMIN CROW	⎫
JOHN GUY	⎬ Coll^{oll} JOHN HALLETT
JOHN ALSTONE........................	⎪
WILLIAM BROWN:	⎭
EDWARD WILLMOTT..................	PETER FLEWELLIN
RICHARD ALLEN	WILLIAM LEWGAR Esqr.
JOHN BROWN	BENJAMIN BIRD

* [The attested copy (dated Jan. 9, 1685 [1685-6]) states that the prisoners were put on board the *Happy Returne*, at Weymouth, in Portland Road, ROGER WADHAM Commander, &c. They were delivered to Mr. JOHN BROWNE and Company, Factors for Sir WILLIAM BOOTH, Knt., at the Barbadoes.]

† [It will be noticed that the same names are in some cases very differently spelt in this and the preceding list.]

Servants Names	Masters Names
ELIAS STEVENS	Cap{tn} JOHN STEWART
WILLIAM CLARKE	⎫
WILLIAM WILLS	⎬ Cap{tn} Wm MARSHALL
JAMES POMREY	⎬
EDWARD MORTON	⎭
JAMES SALTER	AGNIS FENTON
JOHN EDWARDS	Cap{;n} MATHEW HAVILAND
JAMES FOWLER	⎫
THOMAS CORNELIUS	⎬ Collo{ll} JOHN FARMER
ROBERT SPURWEY	⎭
THOMAS TOUNSEND	⎱
JOHN HUGENS	⎰ Cap{tn} TOBIAS FRERE
NATHANIELL WEBBER	⎱
JOHN LOVERIDGE	⎰ WILLIAM WEAVER
JOHN SPEERING	Majr GEORGE LILLINGTON
THOMAS HALLETT	Collo{ll} SAM{ll} TITCOMB
JASPER DIAMOND	RICHARD HARWOOD Esqr.
WILLIAM WILLIAMS	⎱
ROBERT BURRIDGE	⎰ Majr JOHN JOHNSON
PETER ROW	⎱
FRANCIS LAUGHBRIDGE	⎰ HESTER FOSTER
JOHN WILSON	STEPHEN GIBBS
NICHOLAS SMITH	HUGH WILLIAMS
Wm COSSENS	RALPH FRETWELL
JOHN ADAMS	⎱ JAMES THORPE
EDWARD ADAMS	⎰
THOMAS BOVETT	PHILLIP FOUSIIER
THOMAS ALLEN	⎫
ROBERT HELLIER	⎬
SAMUELL LAWRENCE	⎬
JOHN PITTS	⎬
THOMAS HELLIER	⎬ Collo{ll} RICHARD WILLIAMS
JOHN FISHER	⎬
JOHN ALAMBRIDGE	⎭

42

Servants Names	Masters Names
THOMAS HOAR	
ARTHUR LUSH	
JOHN PRIOR	
JOHN LONG	
WILLIAM MADFORD	
THOMAS ALLEN	
RICHARD KEATCH	
WILLIAM TUCKER	
STEPHEN GAMADGE	RICHARD LINTOTT
JOHN WHITE	
JOHN MADDERS	
EMANUELL COLLINS	
MATHER PORTER	
GEORGE PLUMLEY	
THOMAS WILLIAMS	NICHOLAS PRIDEAUX
JOHN MANNING	
JOHN JOHNSON	
ANDREW RAPSON	
THOMAS BURRIDGE	JOHN HETHERSELL Esq'
THOMAS BENNETT	
HENRY TUCKER	
BARNARD BRYANT*	
THOMAS BEST	
THOMAS MARSHALL	JOHN BURSTON
HUGH WILLMATT	
JOHN BRIDLE	
JOHN HARDEMAN	JOHN HOW
NICHOLAS PALMER	
JOHN PENNY	Cap{tn} GEO: TERWIGHT
CHARLS STRONG	
EDWARD LUTHER	
WILLIAM SANDERS	Colloll J{no}: SAMPSON.
THOMAS REASON	

* [The "brace" against this and the four following names is not in the original.]

Servants Names	Masters
JOHN MITTCHELL	⎫
THOMAS PARSONS	⎪
JAMES SPENCE	⎪
JOHN ALLIN	⎬ Cap^{tn} J^{no} PARNELL
JOSEPH PAUL	⎪
THOMAS GREGORY	⎪
RICHARD PAUL	⎭
JOHN HUTCHINS	JOHN HAYWOOD
MATHEW HUTCHINS	THOMAS HAYSE
HUMPHRY MOULTON	⎫
AMBROSE ASHFORD	⎬ Cap^{tn} WALTER SCOT
GEORGE MASEY	⎭
ROGER HOBES	Cap^{tn} ROBERT HARRISSON
JOHN DOWNE	STEPHEN DEVORAX
JOHN WITTE	⎱ RICHARD ADAMSON
ROBERT LAMBERT	⎰

Barbados,

By the R^t Hon'^{ble} the Lt Gouernor.

Mr JOHN BROWNE one of the Factors for s^r Wm BOOTH K^t to whom the aboue and within Convicted Rebells men͞coned in this List were consigned personaly appeared before mee and made oath on the Holy Evangelists of Allmighty God that they were delivered him and Company, out of the ship *Happy Returne* of Pool, ROGER WADHAM Comander, and were all of them by him and Company sold and disposed of here to the severall persons men͞coned in the said List, Giuen vnder my hand the 8th day of Janu'y 1685*

             EDWYN STEDE

 A true Coppy Attested this ⎫
 Nineth day of Janu'y, 1685.* ⎭
  J^{no}: WHETSTONE Dep^{ty} Secr^{ty}

* [1685-6.]

R WILL: BOOTH'S LIST of Prisoners sent to Barbados.*

Summersett. Shire.

WIll: DREW of Bridgwater
JOHN SEAMER of Chilton
WILLIAM SMITH of Road
WILLIAM HALL of Cheard
JUSTINEAN GUPPY of Tanton (1)
GEORGE CARROW of Bridgwater
THOMAS DENNIS of Bridgwater
AMBROSS WINTER of West Buckland
THOMAS GALHAMTON(2) of West Zoyland
WILLIAM DAW of Tanton
HENRY GIBBONS of Tanton
ROB: EASTON of Tanton
GEORGE MICELL of Bridgwater
DANIEL PUMREY(3) of Tanton.
EDWARD COUNSELL of Allerton
JOHN. WALL of Bridgwater
JOHN LEAKER(4) of Hunspill [Huntspill]
EDWARD VILDY of Tanton
ROBERT TEAPE of Bridgwater
JOSEPH WICKHAM of Burnam
JEREMIAH ATKINS of Tanton
SAMUEL BOONE of Tanton
JOHN BUSTON of Milverton
JOHN WALTERS of Tanton
ROB: SEASE of Tanton (5)
GEORGE MULLINS of Tanton
THOMAS BROCKE of Tanton

---

* [In an "attested copy" the under-named differences of spelling of names occur (see the reference numbers) :—
  (¹) JUZTIPHER GUPPY.   (³) JUMREY.   (⁵) SEARS.
  (²) GILHAMTON.   (⁴) LEAKE.

LISTS OF CONVICTED REBELS.

Rob: Seaman of Tanton
Laurance Hussey of Wellington
Will. Tiverton of Bridgwater
George Warren of Milverton
Rob: Coward of Road
John Chappell of Petherton
Will: Burrow's of Corfe (6)
Will: Haynes of Beckington
George Keele of Chilton (6)
Stephen Rodeway (7) of Frome
Henry Quant of Tanton
Will: Mead of Bridgwater
Thomas Gamage of Tanton
James Baker of Milverton
Humphery Pope of Tanton
John Warrin of Milverton
Joseph Vinicott(8) of Bridg Water
Henry Mire of Bridgwater
John Harris of Hunspill
Francis Came of Hunspill
Richard Stephens(9) of North Carre
George Nowell of Tanton
Morris Fusse of Milverton
James Hillman of Milverton
John Stoodly of Trent
Will: Barnard of Hust
Bartholomew Randall (10) of West Coter
John Rodgers (11) of Mackington
Rob: Mitchell of Illton
Jonas Crosse of Cullington
Richard Allin of Creech
Thomas Midleton of Tanton

(⁶) *Left out.* (⁹) Stevens.
(⁷) Rodway. (¹⁰) Rendell.
(⁸) Vincott. (¹¹) Rogers.

RICHARD BICKHAM (12) of Dosin
JOHN BUDGE of Cheard
ROBART PAUL of Illton
OSMOND READ (13) of Tanton
JOHN BURGES of Tanton
WILLIAM PARKER of Tanton
JOHN FARMER of Tanton
ABRAHAM POLLARD of Cheard

Devon—Shire

TIMOTHY HAWKER of Thorn Combe
JOHN MITCHILL of Thorn Come
JOHN BAGG of Thorncome
WILLIAM SMITH jun: of Vpportre [Uppottery]
MICELL POWELL of Neath Glomorging
WILLIAM WALTER'S of Membery
HUMPHERY TRUMP of West Sanford
JOHN BARTLETT of Pitmisser
JOHN CHILCOT (14) of Tiverton.
WILLIAM HARVEY of Memre
WILLIAM HUTCHINGS (15) of Vpportre
JOHN SMITH of Hunington
JOHN CLODE of Vppertre
JOHN CANTLEBURY of Sanford Pefrin
RICHARD WADHAM of Froome
WILLIAM WOOLRIDGE of Tiverton
SIMON POOLE of Bemister
WILLIAM COMBE of Broad Winser
RICHARD EDGAR of Mosterton.
Wiłł: PHIPPIN (16) of High Church
JOHN GALE (17) of Coscam

(12) BRICKHAM.
(13) SYMOND REID.
(14) CHILLICOTT.
(15) HUTCHINS.
(16) SHIPPIN.
(17) JOSEPH GALL.

THOMAS MATTHEWS of Chiddicke
JOHN KEELE of Chilton

Put on board the *John frigget* cap WILL: STOKES comand' ninty Prisonners consined for the burbadous dated at Dorchester oc^br the 24 1685

WILL: BOOTH

Shipt at Bristoll

Barbados *

By the Right Honble the Leiv^t Governo':

JOHN ROGERS Cheife Mate, and WILLIAM ALEXANDER Second Mate of the Ship *John Friggott* of Bristoll, whereof WILLIAM STOAKES deceased was lately Master, personally appeared before mee, and made Oath on the holy Evangelist of Almighty God, that the above convicted Rebells by the s^d STOAKES taken in att the Port of Bristoll, are the very same Rebells, that were delivered to, and by the said STOAKES brought in the said Shipp to this Island, and that they were all of them here landed, and delivered to M' JOHN BROWNE and Company Factors for S' WILLIAM BOOTH Kn^t except JOSEPH WICKHAM who dyed on board the said Shipp in Kingroad, and was from thence carryed on Shoare in the Port of Bristoll and there buryed, as alsoe twelve more of them which dyed on board the said Shipp on the voyage and were buryed in the Sea, whose names are as followeth vizt JUSTIPHER GUPPY, THOMAS GILHAMPTON, GEORGE MICELL, EDWARD COUNCELL, GEORGE KEALE, WILLIAM SMITH jun'. WILLIAM HUTCHINS, SYMON POOLE, W^M MEAD FRANCIS CAME JONAS CROSS and ROBERT PAUL Given under my hand this 28th day of January 1685.†

EDWYN STEDE

A true Coppy Attested this }
First day of February 1685† }
JN° WHETSTONE Dep^ty Secr^ty

---

* [This certificate, as will be seen from its ending, is taken from the attested copy.
† [1685-6.]

A list of seaventy seaven Convicted Rebells by the *John Friggat* of Bristoll Cap^tn Wm STOAKS Comander Imported this Island are all the very same Rebells that was taken on board the said ship at the Port of Bristoll, Except thirteen of them that dyed before the Arriveall, and one since the arriveall of the said ship to this Island:

Masters	Rebells
Cap^tn WALTER SCOTT	JOHN LEAKE EDWARD VILDY ROBERT EASTON JOHN STOODLY RICHARD BICKHAM THOMAS DENNIS GEORGE CARROW WILLIAM SMITH jun' JOHN BARTLETT ROBERT MITCHELL MICHAELL POWELL HENRY QUANT JOHN FARMER RICHARD ALLEN
J^no & Wm HOLDER	JOHN WALL AMBROSE WINTER JOHN CANTLEBURY RICHARD EDGAR RICHARD STEVENS Wm TIVERTON.
	THOMAS GAMADGE ROBERT COWARD GEORGE WARREN

Masters	Rebells
Ann Gallop..........................	John Walters Stephen Rodway George Nowell John Warrin John Burgis William Parker John Chilcott George Seaman
Coll^{oll} John Farmer	John Seamar
Henry Quintyne Esqr	William Haynes Robert Sease John Bagg
Samuell Smart	William Phiffin
John Buston	William Burrowes William Drew Humphry Pope John Clood John Gale Osman Read William Coomb John Budge
Coll^{oll} John Hallett...............	Humphry Trumpe Thomas Brocke
Wm Hectrop......... .	George Mullins
Richard Harwood Esqr	Thomas Middleton James Hilman John Smith

Masters	Rebels
Colloll JOHN SAMPSON	TIMOTHY HAWKER JOHN MITCHELL RICHARD WADHAM Wm BARNARD
Captn STOAKS	JAMES BAKER BARTHOLOMEW RANDALL
Dcor BATTYN	HENRY MYRE MORRIS FUSS
Dcor JOHN SPRINGHAM	HENRY GIBBONS
JOHN ALCHORNE	THOMAS MATHEWS
OTHNIELL HAGGAT	JOHN BUSTON
JOHN SUMERS	JOSEPH VINICOTT
SILUS MARCHANT	WILLIAM HALL
Major JOHNSON	JOHN RODGERS
JOHN HETHERSELL Esqr	JOHN HARRIS
HUGH WILLIAMS	ROBERT TEAP
WILLIAM ALLAMBY	JOHN CHAPPELL
JOHN DENNER	DANIELL POMRE
THOMAS BURKE	WILLIAM HARVEY
WILLIAM SLOGRAVE	LAWRENCE HUSSE
SAMUELL WARNER	WILLIAM WALTERS
ANTHONY PALMER	WILLIAM DAW
WILLIAM MARCHT	ABRAHAM POLLARD

LISTS OF CONVICTED REBELS.

Masters	Rebells
JOHN BROWNE	{ JEREMIA ATKINS SAMUELL BOON WILLIAM WOOLRIDGE

JOHN KEAL Dead

Barbados

By the R^t Hon'^{ble} the Leiu^t Gowernor.

Mr JOHN BROWNE one of the Factors for Sr WILLIAM BOOTH K^t to whom the within convicted Rebells menconed in this List were consigned; and m' DANIELL RICHARDSON personally appeared before mee and made oath on the Holy Evangelists of Allmighty God, that the said Rebells were delivered him the said JOHN BROWNE and Company out of the ship *John Friggat* of Bristoll, whereof WILLIAM STOAKS deceased was lately Master, and were all of them by him the said BROWNE and Company sold and disposed of here to the seuerall persons menconed in the said List, Except one of the said Rebells by name JOHN KEALE that dyed on shoar Since the arriveall of the said Ship Giuen vnder my hand the 29th Jann'y: 1685

EDWYN STEDE

A true Coppy Attested this }
First day of February 1685 }

    J^{no} WHETSTONE Dep^{ty} Secr^{ty}

R WILLIAM BOOTH'S Receipt for the Prisoners within mencon'd

Att the Bridewell at Taunton

RICHARD STEVENS	CHARLES LUCAS
*RICHARD EDGAR	GEORGE GRAY

* [The names marked with an asterisk are mentioned in previous Lists.]

John Bartlett
*John Stoodley
*Robt Paul
*Robt Mitchell
*John Gale
*Bartho: Randall
*John Rogers
*Wᵐ Haynes
*Willm Barnard
*Thomas Mathewes
*Henry Meyer
John Bressett
*Richard Allen
John Poole
*John Burges
*John Farmer
*Richard Bickham
*Henry Gibbons
John Bason
*George Nowell
*Morris Furse als Voss
*Humphrey Trump
*John Warren
*George Warren
*Humphrey Pope
*Osmond Read
*Henry Quant
*Willm Burroughs
*Wᵐ Daw
*Wᵐ Parker
*Robt Sease
*Thomas Midleton
*James Hillman
John Bray
*Ambrose Winter

*Laurence Hussey
*Robt Seaman
Edward Lyde
*John Chappell
*Robt Easton
*John Walter
*Thomas Brocke
George Mollins
*Daniell Pumroy
*Jeremy Atkins
*Samˡˡ Boone
John Edwards

Out of Bridgwater Prisonˢ that came from Taunton

*George Michill
*Wᵐ Drew
*Thomas Dennis
John Avoake
*Wᵐ Tiverton
*Joseph Vinicott
John Seymer
*John Leaker
*Symon Poole
*John Wale
*Richard Wadham
*Stephen Rodway
*Francis Came
*Michell Powell
*John Kerle
*Thomas Galhampton
*George Carrow
*Abraham Pollard
*John Budge

*W︎ᴹ Harvey
*Wᴹ Hall
*Wᴹ Phippen
*John Chilcott
*Robt Coward
*John Cantlebury
*Wᴹ Woolridge
*Wᴹ Smyth
John Smyth
*Wᴹ Mead
*George Keel
*Edward Councell
*Joseph Wickham
John Harris

Out of the Prison'ˢ that came from Exeter to Taunton.

*Robt Teap
*Tymothy Hawker
*Wᴹ Smyth
Joseph Newberry
*John Smyth
John Clode
*Jonas Cross
*John Bragg
*Wiłłm Hutchins
*John Mitchell
*Edward Vildy
*Justinian Guppy
Wᴹ Combe
*James Baker
*Thomas Gamage
*Wᴹ Walter

Received According to his Maᵗⁱᵉˢ direccons the Warrᵗ from the Ld Cheif Justice wᵗʰ a Schedule therevnto annexed of One hundred persons attainted of high Treason wᶜʰ are by me to be transported in to his Maᵗⁱᵉˢ Island of Barbadoes according to a Condicon of a Recognizance entred into by me for that purpose in Wittness whereof I have herevnto put my hand this present 25ᵗʰ of September in the 1ˢᵗ year of his now Maᵗⁱᵉˢ reigne Annoqᵤ Dom 1685.

            WILL: BOOTH

Witness
 Robᵗ: HYDE
 Samˡ GEE

    (in-dorso) Prison'ˢ 100

Bridwell at Taunton ..	56
Bridgewater Prison'ˢ at Taunton	33
Exeter Prison'ˢ att Taunton	11
	100

LISTS OF CONVICTED REBELS.

THE sale of Sixty Seaven Rebells delivered by Cap^{tn} CHARLS GARDNER Comander of the *Jamaica Marchant* to CHARLS THOMAS and THOMAS SADLER for acco^t of Messrs JOHN PALMER JOHN RICHARDSON SAMUELL YOUNG and WILLIAM ROSE the 12th day March 1685. Viz^t

Masters	Rebells
WILLIAM CHESTER Esqr	THOMAS PITT
FRANCIS BOND esq^r	JOHN BRUER
	WILLIAM CROSS
	ROBERT RICHARDS
	JOHN MILLER
	JOHN CROSS
BENJAMIN MIDDLETON	LUKE PORTER
EDWARD JOURDEN	JOHN SLATE
	DANIELL RUTTER
DANIELL PARSONS	ISACK DOYER
	SAMUELL BOND
MATHEW GRAY	JOHN MAGRIDGE
NICHOLAS GIBBS	JAMES COCKRAM
THOMAS ESTWICKE	WILLIAM SANDERS
RICHARD FORSTALL	JOHN ADAMS
JOHN GRAY	CHRISTOPHER HOLBIN
Maj^r RICHARD SALTER	HENRY CHAMBERS
FRANCIS YOUNG	SILVESTER LOYD
JOSEPH JONES	PERCYFULL NOWIS
WILLIAM BARON	JOHN CHAMBERLIN
ARCHIBALD JOHNSON	GEORGE RUSSELL
	HUMPHRY JUSTIN
	LEONARD STAPLE
	THOMAS GOOLD
	GEORGE SCRUBS
	WILLIAM VARIER
	ROBERT PEARCE

Masters	Rebells
Maj^r ABELL ALLEN	RICHARD SIMMONS
	ENOCK GOOLD
	JEREMIAH POOL
	JAMES CLIFT
	EMANUELL MARCH^T
GEORGE HANNAY esq^r	GEORG SNOW
	WILLIAM CURRIER
	JOHN COCKRAM
JOHN BAWDEN Esqr	JAMES WEBB
	RICHARD KING
JOHN HETHERSALL Esqr...	RICHARD PEARCE
	EDWARD BELLEMIE
GEORGE HARPER	CORNELIUS RADFORD
	JOB HUNT
Maj^r GEORGE BUSHELL	JOHN BAKER
Coll^{oll} THOMAS COLLETON	THOMAS BUGLER
	NICHOLAS COLLINS
	MATHEW COOKE
	CHRISTOPHER ROE
	THOMAS MEADE
	JOHN BAKER
	THOMAS PREIST
NICHOLAS PRIDEAUX	WILLIAM PHILLIPS
	JAMES MAYNARD
ROBERT KELLY.......................	HENRY PREIST
WILLIAM ALEMBY	EDWARD KENT
MICHAELL CHILD.....................	JOHN GIBBS
Cap^{tn} JOHN SUTTON................	ROBERT EARLE
	WILLIAM PITTS
MUSE WALFORD	JOHN GODSAL
Maj^r GEORGE LILLINGTON	SILVESTER POOL
	JONAS BROWNE
JOHN SUMMERS.......................	JOHN ROGGERS
ANN WALTERS	JOHN TIMOTHY

Masters	Rebells
Cap^{tn} THOMAS MORRIS	MATHEW CRAFTS
	BARNARD LOVERIDGE
CHARLS THOMAS & THOMAS SADLER	WILLIAM WOODCOCKE
	THOMAS AUSTIN
EDWARD HURLSTONE	PHILLIP CHEEK
	CHARLS BURRAGE
	WILLIAM LEE dead before the ship arrived in Barbados

Barbados

By the R Honble the Lt Gouernor.

Mr THOMAS SADLER one of the Factors to whom the within convicted Rebells menconed in this List were consigned to, personally appeared before mee and made oath on the Holy Evangelists of Allmighty God that they are the very same Rebells that were delivered him and m' CHARLS THOMAS the other Factor for Messrs JOHN PALMER, JOHN RICHARDSON, SAMUELL YOUNG & W^M ROSE out of the Ship *Jamaica March^t*, whereof CHARLS GARDNER is Comand^r and where all of them by the said SADLER disposed of there to the Severall persons menconed in the said List, Except one of the said Rebells that dyed at Sea by name WILLIAM LEE, and was thrown over board, as appeared by the oaths of the Said Comander, and JOHN LLOYD Mate of the Said Shipp, Giuen vnder my hand this 24th day of March (1685)

EDWYN STEDE

A true Coppy attested this
25th day of March 1686

J^{no} WHETSTONE Dep^{ty} Secr^{ty}*

---

* [There is "An Account of one Hundred and three Convict Rebells taken on board the *Jamaica March^t* CHARLS GARDNER Comander, at the Port of Waymouth in old England, vizt. thirty ffive p bill of loading, for acco^t of s^r CHRISTOPHER MUSGRAVE, and to bee delivered to Cap^{tn} SYMON MUSGRAVE in Jamaica, and sixty Eight for acco^t of Messrs JOHN PALMER, JOHN RICHARDSON, SAMUELL YOUNG and W^M ROSE, delivered on the Island of Barbados to m' CHARLS THOMAS and THOMAS SADLER, the 12th March 1685." But all the names contained in this account have been mentioned in other Lists printed in this book.]

[TICKETS GRANTED

TO EMIGRANTS FROM BARBADOES, TO NEW ENGLAND, CAROLINA, VIRGINIA, NEW YORK, ANTIGUA, JAMAICA, NEWFOUNDLAND, AND OTHER PLACES.
1678—1679.]

[BARBADOS.—TICKETS.]

LIST of what TICQ^tts. have been granted out of the Secr^tys Office of the Island aforesaid for the departure off this Island of the several psones hereafter menconed begining in January 1678 & ending in December following. (Viz^t.)—

February y^f 26th 1678:
ALBERCHT HENNIGO in the Ship *Judith*, for London ROBERT KINGS-
LAND Command^r·   time out

March y^f 11th 1678
ARMITAGE HENRY in the ship *Society*, for Boston, WILLIAM GUARD
Comander.   Security

March y^f 20th 1678:
ARIS JOHN in the ship *Indeavour* for London, JAMES GILBERT Coman-
der   time out

Aprill the 26th: 1679
ADAMSON GEORGE in the Ketch *Vnity* for Virginia JAMES RAINY,
Comander   time out

Aprill ye 26th 1679:
ADAMS THOMAS in the Ship *Defeyance* for London Wm CREED Comander.
                                                                                                  time out

TICKETS GRANTED.

Aprill the 28th 1679.
ALBERT ANN in the ship *Mary* for Carolina NICHº LOCKWOOD Comander   time out

Aprill yᵉ 28th 1679
ANDERSON MARGRET in the Ketch *Unity* for Virginia JAMES RAINY Comander.   time out

Aprill yᵉ 29th 1679
ARMSTRONG ANN in the Ship *Francis* for Antegoa PETER JEFFERYS Comander.   time out

May the first 1679
ABRAHAM AGNUS in the Ketch *Francis & Susan* for Boston PHILLIP KNELL Comandʳ.   time out

May 2ᵈ 1679
ARTHUR KATHERINE in the Ketch *Prosperous* for Virginia DAVID FOGG Comander   time out

May the 2ᵈ 1679
ADAMS GEORGE in the Ship *Adventure* for Londº Wᵐ JOHNSON Comandʳ.   security

May yᵉ 22 1679
AUST HENRY in the Ship *Industry* for Bristoll JAMES PORTER Comandʳ   time out

May the 27th 1679
ALLIN ELIAZER in the ship *Prudence and Mary* for Boston JACOB GREEN Comandʳ   time out

June the 14th 1679
ALLISON THOMAS in the ship *Johns Adventure* for Jamaica EDWARD WINSLOW Comandʳ   time out

TICKETS GRANTED.

July the 8th 1679
ALDERSON THOMAS in the ship *Friendship* for London JOHN WILLIAMS Comander   time out

August the 18th 1679
AVERY MARY in the Ship *Golden Fleece* for London HENRY PASCALL Comand^r   time out

October the 4 1679
ATHERTON W^m in the Ship *Nathaniell* for Boston Wm CLARKE Comand^r   time out

November the 25th: 1679
ABUDIENT ABRAHAM in the Ketch *Phœnix* for Antegoa ROBERT FLEXNY, Comand   security

November the 25. 1679
ARE SARAH in the Sloop *Katherine* for Antegoa ANDREW GALL, Comand^r   security

Novemb^r 27th 1679
ALSOP KATHERINE in the Sloop *Katherine* for Antegoa ANDREW GALL Comand^r   security

*Februray 13 1678**
BOWDLER ANDREW in the ship *James* for New Yorke WILLIAM SWEETLAND Comander   time out

February the 17th 1678
BROWN RACHAELL, in the Barq. *Adventure* for Antegoa CHRISTOPHER BERROW Comander   security

February 18th 1678
BLAKE JOHN in the sloop *Resolution* for Montseratt JOHN INGLEBY Comander   time out

* [1678-9.]

March first 1678

BARWELL JOHN in the *Constant Warwick* friggott for Londo Capt RALPH DELAVALL Comandr   time out

March the 5th 1678

BILFORD JAMES in the Pink *Seaventure* for Antegoa GEORGE BATTERSBY Comandr   time out

March the 12th 1678

BARTON JAMES in the Ketch *Wm and Susan* for New England RALPH PARKER Comandr   time out

March the 22 1678

BANCKS JOSEPH in the Ketch *Wm & Susan* for New England RALPH PARKER Comander   time out

March the 27th 1679

BARNARD HUMPHRY Senior and Junr in the Ketch *Mary and Sarah* for Carolina GEO: CONWAY Comandr   time out

Aprill the first 1679

BATES RICHARD in the ship *Expedition* for London JOHN HARDING Comander   time out

Aprill the third 1679

BROWNING ANN in the Ship *Martin* for Newfoundland CHRISTOPHER MARTIN Comander.   time out

Aprill 4th 1679

BAGNALL JOHN in the Sloop *Rutter* for Jamaica EDWARD DUFFEILD Comander   time out

Aprill the 7th 1679

BICKLE THOMAS in the Sloop *May Flower*, for Bermudes EDWARD HUBBERT Comandr   security

Aprill the 11ᵗʰ 1679
BURGOSS ABRAHAM in the Ketch W^m ℓ *John* for New England JOHN
SANDERS Comander time out

Aprill the 15ᵗʰ 1679
BRETT JOHN in the Ship *Honor* for London THOMAS WARREN
Comander time out

Aprill the 17ᵗʰ 1679
BARNES NICHOLAS in the Barqᵦ *Blessing* for Prouidence FRANCIS WAT-
LINGTON Comandʳ. time out

Aprill the 17ᵗʰ 1679
BUSHELL Wᴹ in the Ship *Pearle* for Antegoa, RICHᴰ WILLIAMS
Comandʳ time out

Aprill the 19ᵗʰ 1679
BALL JAMES in the ship *Pelican*, for London JOHN COCKE, Comander
security

Aprill the 22ᵈ 1679
BALRICK THOMAS in the Ship *Hope* for London JOSEPH BALL Comander. security

Aprill yͤ 29ᵗʰ 1679
BAGWELL FRANCIS in the Keatch *Calicta* for Topsham SAMUELL PAUL
Comandʳ time out

May yͤ 5ᵗʰ 1679
BINCKS CHARLES Esqʳ in the Ship *Expcrim*ᵗᵗ for London ALLAN COCK
Comandʳ time out

May the 5ᵗʰ 1679
BREARLY MARTIN in the Ship *White Fox* London JOHN LEE Comandʳ
time out

May the Sixth 1679

BOX ANN in the Ketch *Prosperous* for Virginia DAUID FOGG, Comander   time out

May the 6th 1679

BURNE DENNIS A servant belonging to Mr. HENRY APLEWHITE in the Ketch *Prosperous* for Virginia DAVID FOGG Comander

May the 7th 1679

BROWN Wm in the Ship *Merchants Adventure* for Leverpool JOHN GREIGS Comandr   time out

May ye 8th 1679

BLACKLEECH JOHN Senior and Junr for Boston in ye Ketch *May Flower* ROBERT KITCHIN Comandr   time out

May the 10th 1679

BISHOP ROBERT in the ship *experiment* for London ALLAN COCK Comandr.   security

May the 16th 1679.

BROME JOHN in the Ketch *Prouidence* for Boston MARKE HUNKING Comandr   time out

May the 17th 1679.

BOLTON AMBROSS in the ship *New Concord*, for Londo JAMES STRUTT Comandr   time out

May ye 29th 1679

BOND THOMAS in the Ketch *Eliz*. for Boston JOHN FLETCHER Comander   time out

May the 21st 1679

BERROW CHRISTOPHER in the ship *Society*, of Bristoll EDMOND DITTY Comandr   time out

June the 2ᵈ 1679

BOWHANE TEAG in the ship *Society*, for Bristoll EDMOND DITTY Comand.ʳ time out

June yᵉ 22ᵈ 1679

BREAD THOMAS, in the Ship *Providence* for Boston TIMOTHY PROUT Comandʳ time out

July the first 1679

BIRD HENRY in the Ship *Amity* for London BENJᴬ GROVE Comandʳ
time out

July the 2ᵈ 1679

BRADLEY MICHAELL in the ship *Amity* for London BENJᴬ GROVE Comandʳ time out

July yᵉ 4ᵗʰ 1679

BUTLER JOHN in the Ketch *New London* for ditto ADAM PICKETT Comander time out

July the 7ᵗʰ 1679

BOLTON SAMUELL in the Ship *Bare* for London Wᵐ DICKINS Comandʳ
security

July yᵉ 12ᵗʰ 1679

BROWNE HUGH in the ship *Bachelor* for London Wᵐ KNOTT Comandʳ
time out

July the 21 1679

BROGRAVE HENRY in the Ship *Malligoe Merchᵗˢ* for London ROGER HOMER Comandʳ time out

August the first 1679

BODKIN MARTIN in the ship *Young Wᵐ* for Virginia THO. CORNISH Comander time out

August the third 1679

BODKIN NICH⁰ in the ship *Young William* for Virginia THO CORNISH Comander   time out

August the 9th 1679

BARKER JOHN Laborer in the ship *friendship* for London JOHN W^{ms} Comander   time out

August the 11th 1679

BEVENISTER ELIAM* in the Ship *friendship* for London JOHN WILLIAMS Comander   time out

August. ye 12th 1679

BEARD JOHN in the ship *friendship* for Lond⁰ JOHN WILLIAMS Comand^r time out

August the 15th 1679

BODINGHAM JOHN in the Ship *friendship* for New Engt^d Wm MURPHY Comander   security

August y^e 19th 1679

BUTLER ELINOR A Seru^{tt} belonging to Mr Wm BULKLEY in the Ketch *Neptune* for Virginia JO: KNOTT Comand

September y^e 16: 1679

BROWNE FRANCIS in the Barq$_e$ *blessing* for Burmudos FRANCIS WATLINGTON Comander   time out

September the 30th 1679

BRANDBY ELIZ^a a Servant belonging to DAVID WATKINS in the sloop *Rutter* for Jamaica ED: DUFFEILD, Comd

---

* [There is a doubt as to this name; it has been written over another which is only partially erased.]

October yᵈ 2ᵈ 1679
BLUNT GEORGE in the Ship *Lixboa Merchᵗ* for New Yorke ROGER WHITFEILD Comander   time out

---

October the third 1679
BARTON CHRISTOPHER in the Ship *Barbados Merchant* for Virginia JAMES COCK Comandʳ   security

---

October the 4ᵗʰ 1679
BELFOUR JAMES in the Sloop *true friendship* for Antegua CHARLES KALLAHANE Comandʳ˙   time out

---

October yᶠ 4ᵗʰ 1679
BISHOP THOMAS in the Ship *Virgin* for Leward Islands THOMAS ALUMBY Comander   security

---

October yᶠ 4ᵗʰ 1679
BANISTER RICHᴰ in the sloop *true Freindship* for Antegoa CHARLES KALLAHANE Comander   time out

---

October yᶠ 6ᵗʰ 1679
BUTCHER JOHN in the Sloop *true friendship* for Antegua CHARLES KALLAHANE Comandʳ   security

---

October yᶠ 9ᵗʰ 1679
BENSON MARY in the Sloop *Endeavor* for Carolina THOMAS SHAW Comandʳ   security

---

October yᶠ 13ᵗʰ 1679
BATTISON JULIAN in the Barqᵗ *Endeavor* for Carolina THOMAS SHAW Comandʳ   time out

---

October the 20ᵗʰ 1679
BUTTLER WALTER in the Keatch *John & Sarah* for New Yorke JAMES SHOARE Comander   security

TICKETS GRANTED.

November yᵉ 7ᵗʰ 1679
BABBINGTON THOMAS a Servant belonging to THO: GLADDIN in the Barq Adventure for Jamaica EDWARD DUFFEILD Comandʳ

November yᵉ 20ᵗʰ 1679
BENTLY MARTIN in the Ketch Mary & Sarah for providence GEORGE CONWAY Comander   security

November 25ᵗʰ 1679
BREAD THOMAS in the Ketch Phœnix for Leward Islands ROBERT FLEXNY Comander   security

November yᵉ 25 1679
BREAD ARTHUR in the Ketch Phœnix for the Lewᵈ· Islands ROBERT FLEXNY Comander   security

December the 18ᵗʰ 1679
BARROW, REBECCA in the ship Ann and Jane for London RICHᴰ RADFORD Comander   time out

December the 24ᵗʰ 1679
BROOK THOMAS in the ship Recouery for Jamaica JAMES BROWN Comander   time out

December 24ᵗʰ 1679
BULKLY Wᴹ in the ship Ann & Jane for London RICHARD RATFORD Comander   security

December the 29ᵗʰ 1679
BARNEWELL ROBERT in the Ship Recouery for Jamaica JAMES BROWN Comander   time out

December the 30ᵗʰ 1679
BURKE JEOFFERY in the Sloop true friendship for Antegoa CHARLES KALLAHANE Comandʳ   time out

January the 4*th* 1678*

CRILLICK JANE a Servant belonging to JOHN FOLLITT in the ship *Old head* of Kingsale ROBERT BARKER Comand^r for Lew^d.

January the 7*th* 1678

CARTER ELINOR in the ship *Joseph and Ann* for Carolina SAMUELL EVANS Comander   security

January the 15*th* 1678

CHAPLIN JEREMIAH in the Ship *Joseph & Ann* for Carolina SAMUELL EVANS, Comand^r security

January the 31*st* 1678

CRAGG JOHN in the Ketch *Freindship* for New England JOSEPH HARDY Comand^r time out

February ye 22*d* 1678

CLAYPOOLE NORTON in the Ship *Bachelors Delight* for NYorke ROBERT GREENWAY Comander   time out

March the first 1678

CLARKE ANN in the ship *Samuell* for London JOHN CLARKE Comander   time out

March the 5*th* 1678

CLAYPOOL JOHN in the Ship *Patience* for Lond^o THOMAS HUDSON, Comander   time out

March the 6*th* 1678

COOPER THOMAS in the Pinke *Blessing* for New Yorke JOHN THWING Comand^r time out

March the 10*th* 1678

CARY RICHARD in the Pink *Seaventure* for Antegua GEORGE BATTERSBY Comander   security

* [1678-9.]

March the 10th 1678

CANTING DENNIS in the Ship *Mary* for Carolina NICHº LOCKWOOD, Comand^r   time out

March the 11th 1678

COLLYER AMBROSS in the Ship *Society* for Boston Wm GUARD Comander
                                                time out

March the 21 1678

COLWELL SAMUELL in the Ketch *W^m ℓ Susan* for New England RALPH PARKER Comand^r   time out

March the 21st 1678

CORNELIUS FRANCIS in the Barq *Joseph* for Saltertudos STEPHEN CLAY Comander   time out

March ye 24th 1678

CLARKE PORCAS in the ship *Supply* for London JOSEPH FREEMAN Comand^r   time out

Aprill the first 1679

CHAMBERLAINE MARMADUKE in the Ship *Endeavor* for London JAMES GILBERT Comander   time out

Aprill the first 1679

CAMPANELL MORDICAY in the Ketch *Swallow* for Newengland JOSEPH HARDY Comand^r   time out

Aprill the first 1679

CROSSING W^M in the Ship *Blessing* for Boston SAM^ll RICKARD Comand^r
                                                security

Aprill the third 1679

COOPER MARY in the Ship *Mary* for Carolina NICHOLAS LOCKWOOD Comand^r the said COOPER a seru^tt of ROB^T DANIELL.

Aprill the 22^d 1679

CAREW THOMAS in the Ship *Benj^a* of Topsham ROBERT LYDE Comander   time out

April ye 25th 1679

COLTHROUGH PETER in the Ship *Samuell and Eliz^a* for London THOMAS ORCHARD Comander   time out

May the 3^d 1679

CURSTIS JOHN in the Ship *Concord* for London JAMES STRUTT, Comander   time out

May the 10th 1679

CLARKE MARY in the Ship *Experiment* for Lond^o ALLAN COCK Comander   security

May the 22: 1679

COULBURNE JOHN in the Ship *Conclusion* for London W^м BEEDING Comand^r

May the 28th 1679

CORNISH EDWARD A Serv^{tt} belonging to JOHN HARRIS in the ship *W^m & John* for Boston, SAM^{ll} LEGG Comand^r

May the 31st 1679

CLOVAN THO.* in the Sloop *true friendship* for Neuis CHARLES KALLAHANE Comand^r security

July the first 1679

COLE THOMAS Junr in the Ship *Prevention* for Surranam BARNARD BOOGHERT Comander   time out

---

* [See the entry of Oct. 2nd, where this man is re-entered as for Antegua.]

July the 2ᵈ 1679

COLLINS JOHN in the Ketch *Neptune* for Carolina JOSEPH KNOTT Comander — time out

July the 28ᵗʰ 1679

CAWFEILD RICHᴅ in the Ship *Young William* for Virginia THOMAS CORNISH Comandʳ — security

August the 2ᵈ 1679

COTTINGHAM KATHERINE in the Ship *Elizᵃ·* for Jamaica SILVANUS PAINE Comander — time out

August the 9ᵗʰ 1679

COLLINS JOHN in the Barqᵗ *Platacon* for Carolina ASER SHARPE Comander

August the thirteenth 1679

CALLAY THOMAS in the Keatch *Neptune* for Virginia JOSEPH KNOTT Comander — time out

August yᵉ 25ᵗʰ 1679

COX FRANCIS in the ship *John and James* for New England GILES HAMLIN Comandʳ — time out

September 2ᵈ 1679

COLE JAMES in the Sloop *John and Francis* for Antequa JOHN HOWARD Comander — security

September the 18ᵗʰ 1679

COLLIS ALEXANDER in the Ship *Hope* for New England JOHN PRICE Comander — time out

September yᵉ 20ᵗʰ 1679

CHESTER SAMPSON in the Ship *Malligo Merchant* ROGER HOMER Comander for Londᵒ — time out

TICKETS GRANTED.

September 22ᵈ 1679

CHAPLIN THOMAS in the Ship *Malligo Merch^t* for London ROGER HOMER Comander   time out

October the 2ᵈ 1679

CLOVAN* THOMAS in the Sloop *true friendship* for Antegua CHARLES KALLAHANE Comander   time out

October the 6ᵗʰ 1679

CHARLES EUAN in the Sloop *true friendship* for Antegua CHARLES KALLAHANE Comander   time out

November the 3ᵈ 1679

COTINHO MOSES HENRIQUES in the Barq. *Adventure* for Jamaica EDWARD DUFFEILD Comander   time out

November yᵉ 6ᵗʰ 1679

COURTNEY Wᴹ in the Sloop *Hopewell* for Antegua Wᴹ MURPHY Comander   time out

November the: 27ᵗʰ 1679

CORBETT WILLIAM in the Sloop *Katherine* for Antegua ANDREW GALL Comander   time out

December the 15ᵗʰ 1679

CRISP ROGER in the Ship *Ann and Jane* for Londᵒ RICHᴰ RADFORD, Comandʳ   time out

February 14ᵗʰ 1678

DANG MARGARETT in the Sloop *Resolution* for Nevis JOHN INGLEBY Comander   time out

---

* [In the entry of May 31st he is bound for Nevis.]

February 21st 1678

DENTON JOHN in the Ship *Endeavour* for Virginia ABRAHAM NEWMAN Comander   time out

March the first 1678

DOLDRON GRACE in the Ship *Samuell* for London JOHN CLARKE Comander   time out

March the 10th 1678

DOLEBERRY ANDREW in the Ship *Society* for Boston Wm GUARD Comander   time out

March the 20th 1678

DEVENISH JOHN in the Ship *Endeavor* for London JAMES GILBERT Comander   time out

Aprill the first 1679

DICKINSON FRANCIS in the ship *Blessing* for Boston SAMUELL RICKARD Comander   security

Aprill the fourth 1679

DANIELL ROBERT in the Ship *Mary* for Carolina NICHOLAS LOCKWOOD Comander   time out

Aprill the 7th 1679

DUKES W^m in the Barq. *Adventure* for Carolina DANIELL RIDLEY Comand^r time out

Aprill the 9th 1679

DANIELL JOHN in the Barq. *Johns Adventure* for Antegua JOHN WELCH Comand^r time out

Aprill 22: 1679

DAVIES ELIZ^a. A serv^{tt} belonging to HILLIARD HOLDIP in the ship *Lond^o Merch^{tt}* for Lond^o EDW: DESWORTH, Comd

TICKETS GRANTED.

Abrill the 22ᵈ 1679
DRAX HENRY Esqʳ in the Ship *Honor* for Londᵒ THOMAS WARREN Comander   time out

Aprill the 22 1679
DENSY JANE in the Ship *Hope* for London JOSEPH BALL Comander   security

Aprill the 25ᵗʰ 1679
DRAYTON THOMAS junʳ in the ship *Mary* for Carolina NICHOLAS LOCKWOOD Comandʳ   time out

Aprill the 28ᵗʰ 1679
DAVIES JANE A Servant to RICHᴰ TOWNSEND in yᵉ Ship *Nathaniell* for Boston Wᴹ CLARKE Comandʳ

May the 2ᵈ 1679
DAVIES SAMUELL in the Ketch *Prosperous* for Virginia DAVID FOGG Comander   time out

May the 13: 1679
DAVIES JOHN junʳ in the Ship *Roe Buck* for London Wᴹ SHAFTO Comandʳ   security

May 13ᵗʰ 1679
DOWELL DENNIS in the Ship *Industry* for Bristoll JAMES PORTER Comander   time out

May the 14ᵗʰ 1679
DANGERFEILD WALCUP in the ship *Bachelor* for Bristoll ROGER BAGG Comander   time out

May the 23ᵈ 1679
DUNNOHOE TEAG in the ship *Margaret* for Bew Morris* ALEXANDER WOOD Comandʳ   time out

* [*i.e.*, Beaumaris.]

May the 24 1679

DUBOYES JOHN in the Ship *Supply* for Boston JOHN MELLOWES Comander — time out

June the 11th 1679

DUNNOHOE CORNELIUS and JEFFORY in the ship *Margrett* for Bew Morris ALEXANDER WOOD Comand^r — time out

June the 11th 1679

DAVIES, JOHN in the ship *Coast Friggott* for Londo PHILLIP VARLOE Comander — time out

June the 11th 1679

DAVIES JOHN of Christ Church in the Ketch *Joseph* for New Yorke ABRAHAM KNOTT Comander — security

July the 21 1679

DAVIES PETER in the Pinke *Neptune* for Carolina JOSEPH KNOTT Comander — time out

July the 29th 1679

DRAN MAREN A servant belonging to JACOB LEROUX in the Ketch *Dove* for Antegoa JOHN GRAFTON Comand^r

August the first 1679

DUNDAS W^m in the ship *Young William* for Virginia THO: CORNISH Comander — time out

August the 2d 1679

DAWSON TREMMIT in the ship *Eliz^a* for Jamaica SILVANUS PAYNE Comander — time out

August the 2d 1679

DAVIES KATHERINE a servant belonging to JOHN AUSTIN in the ship *Young William* for Virginia THOMAS CORNISH

TICKETS GRANTED.

Septemb' the 27th 1679

DANIELL WILBERT in the Ship *Supply* for Virginia JOHN ADY Comander   time out

November y' 15th 1679

DEWER STEPHEN in the Barq, *Resolution* for Antegoa THO GILBERT Comander   time out

Decemb' the 15th 1679

DEXTER W^M in the Ship *Ann and Jane* for Lond^o RICHARD RATFORD Comander   time out

December the 22^d 1679

DOUSE BRIDGETT in the Ship *Ann & Jane* for Lond^o RICHARD RATTFORD Comander   time out

December the 22: 1679

DOWNING JOHN in the Ship *Lawrell* for Nevis ROBERT OX Comander
                                                                                               time out

December the 24th 1679

DAVY ROBERT in the Ship *Ann and Jane* for London RICH^D RATFORD Comander   time out

December y' 24th 1679

DE WEVER LEWIN in the ship *Blossom* for Surranam RICH^D MARTIN Comander   security

March the 13th 1678

ENDERBEE OLIUER in the Ship *Ann and Mary* for Antegua JOHN JOHNSON Comander   security

March the 20th 1678

ELSON W^M in the Ketch *Begining* for New Yorke W^M PLAY Comander
                                                                                               time out

Aprill the 25 1679
EVANS LEWIS in the Ketch *Unity* for Virginia JAMES RAINY Comander
time out

Aprill the 26th 1679
EARLE JOHN in the ship *Defyance* for London, Wm CREED Comandr
security

Aprill the 26th 1679
ELLISTON GEORGE in the ship *Nathaniell* for Boston Wm CLARKE Comander
time out

Aprill the 28th 1679
EDWARDS JOHN in the ship *Society* for Bristoll EDMOND DITTY Comander
time out

May the 24 1679
ELLICOTT VINES in the ship *Supply* for Boston JOHN MELLOWES Comander
security

June the 20th 1679
EUANS Wm in the ship *Wm and Robert* for London GILES BOND Comander
time out

July ye 21: 1679
EVANS EDWARD in the Pink *Neptune* for Carolina JOSEPH KNOTT Comander
time out

July the 26th 1679
EASTCHURCH WILLIAM in the Ship *Joseph* for Lond.

July the 31 1679
EMERY JOHN a Servant belonging to Lievt. Collo. HALLETT in the Ship *Young William* for Virginia THO CORNISH Comandr

September the 12*th* 1679
ELLINSWORTH W^m in the Pink *Portsmouth* for Road Island JOSEPH BRIAR Comand^r   time out

October the 2*d* 1679
ELLIOTT HENRY in the Sloop *true friendship* for Antegoa CHARLES CALLAHANE Comand^r   time out

Feb^r the 6*th* 1678
FANNING ANDREW a servant belonging to DANIELL STANTON in the Ship *Diligence* for New England JER: JACKSON

February the 13*th* 1678
FORBUSH JAMES in the Ship *two Brothers* for Jamaica RICE JEFFERYES Comander   time out

March the 4*th* 1678
FITZRANDOLPH PHILLIP in the ship *Vnity* for Saltertudos ABRAHAM WISE Comand^r   security

March the 19*th* 1678
FYERS JONE in the ship *Katherine* for Bristoll ROBERT DAPWELL Comander   time out

March the 24*th* 1678
FITZ JAMES EDWARD in the Ship *Merch^{tt} Bonadventure* for London Wm BULKLEY Comander   time out

March the 26*th* 1679
FRANKLIN THOMAS in the Ship *Supply* for Lond^o JOSEPH FREEMAN Comander   time out

March the 29th 1679
Fox Stephen in the ship *Mary* for Carolina Nich⁰ Lockwood Comander   time out

March the 29th 1679
Fox Phillis in the ship *Mary* for Carolina Nich⁰ Lockwood Comander   time out

March the 31: 1679
Fransum Joseph in the Barq̃ *Blessing* for Prouidence Francis Watlington Comander   time out

April the 29th 1679
Fitz Nichols Mary a Serv$^{tt.}$ belonging to Rich^{D} Michell sen^r in the ship *Nathaniell* for Boston Wm Clarke Comander

May the Sixth 1679
Feaghery Thomas in the Ship *John & Tho:* for Prouidence Tho. Jenour Comander   time out

May the 8th 1679
Finn Teage in the Ship *Industry* for Bristoll James Porter Comander   time out

May the 14th 1679
Foster Hester in the ship *Ann and Eliz*$^{a.}$ for Leverpoole Hugh Reynolds Comander   time out

May the 21 1679
Fitz Jarrell John in the ship *Swallow* for Leverpoole Tho Withington Comander   time out

May the 23 1679

FONTLEROY JAMES in the ship *Prudence and Mary* for Boston JACOB GREEN Comander   time out

May the 26*th* 1679

FARRER JAMES in the ship *Conclusion* for Londo· Wᴹ BEEDING Comander   time out

May the 28*th* 1679

FRENCH SAMUELL in the Ketch *Joseph and Mary* for New Yorke ABRAHAM KNOTT Comandʳ   time out

May the thirtieth 1679.

FOWLER JOSHUA in the ship *John and Mary* for London JOHN UREE Comandʳ ·   security

June the fourth 1679

FLEMG [? FLEMING] EDMOND in the ship *Society* for Bristoll EDMOND DITTY Comandʳ   time out

June the 11*th* 1679

FELL LIDIA in the Ketch *John and Sarah* for New Yorke PETER CAROW Comander   time out

July the 21: 1679

FRITH SAMUELL in the Pinke *Rebecca* for Virginia THOMAS WILLIAMS Comander   time out

July the 26*th* 1679

FORD FRANCIS in the ship *Mallego Merch^{tt.}* for London ROGER HOMER Comandʳ   time out

47

October the first 1679
FEAR FRANCIS in the ship *Barbados Merchant* for Virginia JAMES COCK Comander   time out

October ye 29th 1679
FARRELL HUGH in the Barq{h} *Dove* for Nevis ANTHONY JENOUR Comander   time out

November the 26th 1679
FARRELL ROGER in the Sloop *Katherine* for Antegua ANDREW GALL Comander   security

December the 22 1679
FAVELL CHRISTOPHER in the ship *Ann and Jane* for London RICH{D} RATTFORD Comand{r}   time out

December 24th 1679
FARROR EDMOND in the ship *Ann & Jane* for London RICH{D} RATTFORD Comand{r}   time out

March the 10th 1678
GRIGG ROBERT & ALCE GRIGG in the ship *Mary* for Carolin[a] NICHOLAS LOCKWOOD Comander   time out

March the 11th 1678
GARDNER GEORGE in the Ship *Samaritan* for Leverpo[ol] VALENTINE TRIM Comand{r}   time out

March the 18th 1678
GRESTNINH JACOBUS in the Pink *Desire* for Pool THO WADHAM Comander   security

TICKETS GRANTED.

March the 20*th* 1678

GOLDING PERSIVALL in the ship *White Fox* for London JOHN LEE Comander time out

---

March the 22*d* 1678

GERISH BENJAMIN in the Ketch *Mary* for Boston JOHN GARDNER Comander time out

---

Aprill the 7*th* 1679

GODFRY MARY in the Ship *Mary* for Carolina NICH⁰· LOCKWOOD Comand^r time out

---

Aprill the 12*th* 1679

GOODING JOSEPH in the Barq$_h$ *Boneta* RICH^D RIPLY Comand^r for Jamaica time out

---

Aprill the 25*th* 1679

GITTES HENRY in the Ship *Mary* for Carolina NICHOLAS LOCKWOOD Comander time out

---

May the 6*th* 1679

GOLDING PERCIVALL in the Ship *Concord* for London JAMES STRUTT Comand^r

---

May the 6*th* 1679

GIBBS RICH^D in the ship *Bachelor* for Bristoll ROGER BAGG Comand^r time out

---

May the 14*th* 1679

GIBBS EDWARD in the ship *Roe Buck* for Lond⁰ W^M SHAFTO Comander time out

May the 23 1679

GOGIN WILLIAM in the ship *Bachelor* for Bristoll ROGER BAGG Comander time out

July the 22ᵈ 1679

GRAY ROBERT in the Keatch *Endeavor* for New England LAWRENCE CUTT Comander time out

August the 9ᵗʰ 1679

GORDEN GEORGE in the ship *Plantacon* for Carolina ASER SHARPE Comander time out

August the 16ᵗʰ 1679

GORTON JOHN A servant belonging to JOHN BROWNE in the Ketch *Neptune* for Virginia JOSEPH KNOTT Comandʳ

August the 19ᵗʰ 1679

GODFFREE GILBERT a seruᵗᵗ belonging to Mʳ Wᵐ BULKLY in the Ketch *Neptune* for Virginia JOSEPH KNOTT Comand

September yᵉ 2ᵈ 1679

GRIFFIN DENNIS in the sloop *John and Francis* for Antegua JOHN HOWARD Comandʳ

October the first 1679

GOTHER HENRY in the Sloop *Rutter* for Jamaica EDWARD DUFFEILD Comander time out

October the 2ᵈ 1679

GORTON RICHᴰ in the Sloop *Rutter* for Jamaica EDWARD DUFFEILD Comander time out

TICKETS GRANTED. 373

October the 7th 1679

GREENSLATT THOMAS in the Sloop *true friendship* for Antegua CHARLES KALLAHANE Comand^r   security

Novemb^r the 25th 1679

GIDION ROWLAND in the Ketch *Phœnix* for Antegua ROBERT FLEXNY Comand^r   security

February 11th 1678

HAYEM ABRAHAM in the ship *James* for New Yorke Wm SWEETLAND Comander   time out

March the 3^d 1678

HATTON ROBERT in the Sloop *Hunter* for Surranam WALTE[R] ASSUEROS Comander   time out

March the 3^d 1678

HOLLARD THOMAS in the *Constant Warwick* Frigott for London Capt RALPH DELAVALL Comand^r   security

March the 11th 1678

HOLLOWAY RICH^D in the ship *Samaritan* for Leverpool VALENTINE TRIM Comander   time out

March the 12th 1678

HERRICK ISAAC in the Ketch *W^m & Susan*, for New Engla[nd] RALPH PARKER Comander   time out

March the 20th 1678

HARVEY, GRIFFITH, in the ship *Merch^{tt} Bonadventure*, fo[r] London Wm BULKLY Comander   time out

March the 21 1678
HAMILTON ADAM in the Ketch *W^m & Susan* for New England RALPH PARKER Comand^r. time out

---

March the 24th 1678
HEYWOOD JOHN in the Pinke *Submission* for London CHRISTOPHER NEWHAM Comander time out

---

March the 24th 1678
HIGLEY JOHN in the Ketch *Mary* for Boston JOHN GARDNER Comander time out

---

March the 28th 1678 [? *should be* 1679].
HASELL WILLIAM in the Ship *Olliue Tree* for Bristoll THOMAS SHELLAM Comander time out

---

Aprill the first 1679
HAWTON GERARD in the ship *Expedition* for London JOHN HARDING Comander time out

---

Aprill the first 1679
HAVILAND MILES in the Ketch *Swallow* for Rhoad Island JOSEPH HARDY Comander time out

---

Aprill the 2^d 1679
HENDLY DANIELL and ELIZ^A in the ship *Olive Tree* for Bristoll THOMAS SHELLAM Comand^r time out

---

Aprill the 9th 1679
HETHERINGTON KATHERINE in the Pink *Greyhound* for London JOSEPH WASEY Comander time out

Aprill the 10ᵗʰ 1679

HOWELL SARAH in the Barq, *Prouidence* for Burmudos FRANCIS WAT-
LINGTON Comander   time out

Aprill the 10ᵗʰ 1679

HURLES, ELIZᴬ in the ship *Martin* for Newfoundland CHRISTOPHER
MARTIN Comandʳ   time out

Aprill the 19ᵗʰ 1679

HIGGISON HENRY in the ship *freinds Adventure* for Londᵒ JOHN
BLADES Comander   time out

Aprill the 19ᵗʰ 1679

HOLLIDAY MARY in the ship *Recouery* for New Yorke THOMAS CHIN-
NERY Comander   time out

Aprill the 22ᵈ 1679

HOLDIP HILLIARD in the Ship *Londᵒ Merchtt* for London EDWARD
DESWORTH Comander   security

Aprill the 22 1679

HOLT ROWLAND in the Ship *Honor* for London THOMAS WARREN
Comander   time out

Aprill the 30ᵗʰ 1679

HACKER FERDINANDO in the ship *Faireffax* for London NICHᵒ FAIRE-
FAX Comander   time out

May the 2ᵈ 1679

HEALY Wᴹ in the ship *Society* for Bristoll EDMᴰ DITTY Comander
    time out

May the third 1679

Hurst W^m in the Ship *Adventure* for Lond° Wm Johnson Comand^r
                    time out

May the third 1679

Holsey Richard in the Sloop *Batchelor* for Leward Peter Swaine Comand^r
                    time out

May the 23th 1679

Hackett Robert in the ship *Society* for Bristoll Edmond Ditty Comand^r
                    time out

May the 23^d 1679

Haley Dennis in the ship *Society* for Bristoll Edmond Ditty Comander
                    time out

May the 31 1679

Helmes John in the Ketch *Nicl^e & Rebecca* for New Yorke Nicholas Blake Comand^r
                    time out

June the 2^d 1679

Hook W^m in the Barq_h *Hopewell* for Boston Nicholas Morrell Comander
                    security

June the 13 1679

Hunt Dennis in the ship *Coast Friggott* for London Phillip Varloe Comander
                    time out

June the 14 1679

How Eliz^a in the Ship *Johns Adventure* for Jamaica Edward Winslow Comander
                    time out

June the 17th 1679
HOOPER DANIELL in the Ketch *Joseph* for New Yorke ABRAHAM KNOTT, Comand^r   time out

June the 21 1679
HARRIS EDWARD in the Ship *Experiment* for Lond^o. HENRY SUTTON Comand^r   time out

June the 21 1679
HILL JOHN in the ship *Charles* for Lond^o THOMAS NASH Comander   security

June the 21 1679
HOUGH W^m in the Ship *W^m & Robert* for London GILES BOND Comander   time out

June the 28 1679
HUNT JOHN in the ship *Providence* for Boston TIMOTHY PROUT Comander   time out

July the third 1679
HORNE GUSTAVUS ADOLPHUS in the ship *W^m & Ann* for London PHILLIP HANGER Comander   time out

July the 10th 1679
HUGHS ANDREW in the ship *Amity* for Lond^o BENJ^A GROVE Comand^r   time out

July the 31 1679
HALL GILES ju^r in the Ketch *John & Mary* for Boston JOHN PARRECK Comand^r   security

August the 14 1679
HERBERT HENRY in the Ship *John & Henry* for Bristo[l] THOMAS CADES Comander   time out

August the 20*th* 1679
HOBBS ELIZ*a* in the ship *Robert* for Lond*o* RICHARD COCK Comander
                                                                            time out

September the 17*th* 1679
HARKER JOHN in the ship *Hope* for New Engl*d* JOHN PRICE Comander
                                                                            time out

September the 18*th* 1679
HOLDSWORTH ARTHER in the Ship *Thomas & Sarah* for Lon[don] JAMES DAY Comander   time out

October the 7*th* 1679
HOTEN MARGERY in the Sloop *Affrica* for Leward Islands ANTHONY BURGESS Comander   security

October the 7*th* 1679
HILK JOHN in the Sloop *true friendship* for Antegua CHARLES KALLAHANE Comander   security

October the 7*th* 1679
HANCOCK ALEXANDER in the Sloop *true freindship* for Antequa CHARLES KALLAHANE Comander   security

October the 20*th* 1679
HASELL PETER in the Ship *Happy returne* for London ISAAC RAGG Comand*r*   time out

October the 29*th* 1679
HALE BARNABIE and THO HOW Seru*tts* belonging to Coll*o* CHRISTOPHER CODRINGTON in the Barq, *Doue* for Nevis ANTHONY JENOUX Comander

October the 29*th* 1679
HOLT JOSEPH in the Sloop *Hopewell* for Antegoa JOHN AYRES Comand*r* time out

November y° 6*th* 1679
HUNT LUKE in the Barq, *Adventure* for Jamaica EDWARD DUFFEILD Comander time out

November the 27*th* 1679
HANNAH, ANDREW a Serv*tt* belonging to W*m* STICKLAND in the Sloop *Katherine* for Antegua ANDREW GALL Comander

December the 24*th* 1679
HOLEMAN ROGER in the Sloop *true freindship* for Antegua CHARLES KALLAHANE Comand*r* time out

March the 11*th* 1678
JARMIN SYMON in the Ship *Society* for Boston W*m* GUARD Comander
time out

March the 14*th* 1678
JACCSON W*m* in the ship *Ann and Mary* for Antegoa JOHN JOHNSON Comander time out

March the 20*th* 1678
JACCSON GEORGE in the Ship *Merch*tt *Bonadventure* for London W*m* BULKLEY Comand*r* time out

48—2

March the 29*th* 1679

JIPSON SARAH in the ship *Mary* for Carolina NICH⁰ LOCKWOOD Comand^r   time out

---

Aprill the 9*th* 1679

JACOB JOHN in the Ketch *Providence* for New England MARKE HUNKING Comander   time out

---

Aprill the 19*th* 1679

JOHNSON NATHANIELL in the *friends Adventure* for Antegua, JOHN LONG Comander   time out

---

May the 9*th* [? 19] 1679

JONES JOHN jun^r in the ship *Ann and Eliz*^a for Leverpool HUGH REYNOLDS Comander   time out

---

May the 20*th* 1679

JONES ROBERT in the Ship *Rose and Crown* for London THOMAS CROFTS Comander   security

---

May the 22*d* 1679

JORDAN W^m, in the Ship *Prudence and Mary* for Boston JACOB GREEN Comander

---

May the 22*d* 1679

JOHNSON JOHN in the Ketch *Joseph* for New Yorke ABRAHAM KNOTT Comander   time out

---

May the 22*d* 1679

JONES RICH^D in the Ship *Battchelor* for Bristoll ROGER BAGG Comander   time out

TICKETS GRANTED. 381

May the 23ᵈ 1679

JAMES WILLIAM in the Ship *Society* for Bristoll EDMOND DITTY
Comander   time out

June the 11ᵗʰ 1679

JELSON JOELL in the Ship *Bachelor* for Bristoll ROGER BAGG Comander
    time out

June the 11ᵗʰ 1679

IRISH GEORGE in the ship *Bachelor* for Bristoll ROGER BAGG Comander
    time out

June the 17ᵗʰ 1679

JENKINS OWEN in the Ketch *Johns Adventure* for Jamaica EDWARD
WINSLOE Comandʳ   time out

June the 18ᵗʰ 1679

JONES SAMUELL in the Ketch *Johns Adventure* for Jamaica EDWARD
WINSLOE Comandʳ   security

June the 27ᵗʰ 1679

INGLEBY NICHOLAS in the ship *Providence* for Boston TIMOTHY PROUT
Comandʳ   security

August the 13ᵗʰ 1679

JACCSON JAMES in the Barq, *Hopewell* for Virginia THO CURLE
Comander   time out

August the 14ᵗʰ 1679

JONES ELIZᴀ· in the Barq, *Plantacon* for Carolina ASER SHARPE
Comander   security

TICKETS GRANTED.

September the fourth 1679
JAMES RICH[D] A serv[tt] belonging to Coll[o] SAM[ll.] NEWTON in the ship *Joseph* for New Yorke STEPHEN CLAY Comand[r]

September the 13th 1679
JOHNSON NATHANIELL in the Sloop *true freindship* for Antegua CHARLES KALLAHANE Comander   time out

September the 13 1679
JORDAN JAMES in the ship *Mallego Merch[tt]* for London ROGER HOMER Comander   time out

September the 19th 1679
JENKINS JANE in the Ship *Lixboa Merch[tt]* for New Yor[k] ROGER WHITFEILD Comander   security

September the 26th 1679
JENNINGS MICHAELL in the Sloop *Rutter* for Jamaica EDWARD DUFFEILD Comand[r]   time out

October the 7th 1679
JENNINGS WILLIAM, in the Sloop *True friendship* for Antegu[a] CHARLES KALLAHANE Comand[r]   security

October the 29th 1679
JOHN MORGAN in the Barq[h] *Dove* for Neuis ANTHONY JENNOR, Comander.   time out.

Nouember the 7 1679
JONES WILLIAM in the Sloop *Hopewell* for Antegua W[m] MURPHY Comand[r]   time out

Nouember the 7th 1679
JONES HECTOR in the Sloop *Hopewell* for Antegua Wm MURPHY Comander — time out

Aprill the 24th 1679
KING WILLIAM in the ship *friends Adventure* for Lond^o EDWARD BLADES Comander — security

May the 2d 1679
KENNEDY JOHN and ELLINOR his wife in the Ship *Society* for Bristoll EDMOND DITTY Comander — time out

May the 28th 1679
KYTE JOHN in the Ship *Prudence and Mary* for Boston JACOB GREEN Comand^r — time out

August the 2d 1679
KEITH HENRY in the Ship *Young William* for Virginia THO: CORNISH Comand^r — time out

November the 29th 1679
KEW NICHOLAS in the Barq *Resolution* for Antegua THO GILBERT Comander — security

Feb^{ry} 17th 1678
LYNCH NICHOLAS and ALICE his Wife in the Barq *Adventure* for Antegua CHRISTOPHER BERROW Comand^r — time out

March the 18th 1679 [167¾]
LOCK ANN in the Ketch, *W^m & Susan* for New England RALPH PARKER Comand^r — time out

March the 20th 1679 [167¾]

LYTTCOT LEONARD in the Ship *Supply* for Londo JOSEPH FREEMAN Comander   security

---

Aprill the first 1679

LEE HENRY in the Ketch *Unity* for Virginia JAMES RAINY Comander   time out

---

Aprill the third 1679

LEE HENRY in the Ship *Martin* for Newfoundland CHRISTOPHER MARTIN Comandr   time out

---

Aprill the 16th 1679

LANGLEY Wm in the Ship *Brothers Adventure* for New Yorke JOHN SELLOCK Comandr   time out

---

Aprill the 21st 1679

LOPES ABRAHAM in the ship *Hope* for Londo JOSEPH BALL Comandr   time out

---

Aprill the 22d 1679

LOWTHER CHRISTOPHER a servant belonging to Collo HENRY DRAX in the Ship *Honor* for Londo THO WARREN Comandr

---

May the 12th 1679

LANGTON THOMAS in the Ketch *Prosperous* for Virginia DAUID FOGG Comandr   time out

---

May the 28th 1679

LYDIATT TIMOTHY in the Ship *Wm & John* for Boston SAMUELL LEGG Comander   time out

June the 17*th* 1679

LONGSON WILLIAM in the Ketch *John's Aduenture* for Jamaica EDWARD WINSLOW Comand^r   security

July the 17*th* 1679

LEE RICH^D in the Pinke *Rebecca* for Virginia THOMAS W^ms Comander   time out

July the 29*th* 1679

LEROUX JACOB in the Ketch *Dove* for Antegua JOHN GRAFTON Comand^r   security

August the 8*th* 1679

LEWGAR JOHN in the ship *freindship* for London JOHN WILLIAMS Comand^r   time out

August the 13*th* 1679

LADSON JOHN in the Barq, *Plantacon* for Carolina ASER SHARPE Comander   time out

August the 28*th* 1679

LLOYD JOHN in the ship *Barbados Mercht* for Leward Islands   time out

September the 2*d* 1679

LANGFORD HARRY in the Ship *Joseph* for New Yorke STEPHEN CLAY Comander   time out

September the 15*th* 1679

LYNN ROBERT in the Ship *Mallego Mercht* for Londo ROGER HOMER Comand^r   time out

September the 16th 1679

LYNCH RICHARD in the Sloop *true friendship* for Nevis CHARLES KALLAHANE Comand^r   time out

October the 25th 1679

LEE HENRY in the Ship *Happy returne* for Londo ISAAC RAND Comand^r   security

Nouember the 24th 1679

LILBURNE RICH^D in the Ketch *Mary & Sarah* for Prouidence GEORGE CONOWAY Comand^r   security

November the 29th 1679

LYNCH MORGAN in the Barq, *resolution* for Antegua THOMAS GILBERT Comand^r the said LYNCH being a Seru^{tt} belonging to JOHN CODRINGTON Esqr.

December the 22: 1679

LYNE CHRISTOPHER Esqr in the Ship *Recouery* for Jamaica JAMES BROWNE Comand^r

December the 31. 1679

LOPEZ TELLES ABRAHAM in the ship *Recouery* for Jamaica JAMES BROWN Comand^r   time out

January the 4th 1678

MAYNARD JAMES A Seru^{tt} belonging to MATHEW W^{ms} in the ship *Old head* of Kingsale for Lew^d ROBERT BARKER Comand

January the 28th 1678

MARSHALL JARVIS in the Ship *James* for New Yorke JAMES SWEETLAND Comander   time out

TICKETS GRANTED.

Feby 11*^{th}* 1678

MASTUS JOSEPH and MARTHA MASTUS in the Ship *Patience* for London THOMAS HUDSON Comand^r   time out

March the 10*^{th}* 1679 [1678]

MORRIS W^m in the Ship *Society* for Boston Wm GUARD Comand^r   time out

March the 14*^{th}* 1678

MELONY TIMOTHY in the Ship *Ann and Mary* for Antegua JOHN JOHNSON Comand^r   security

March the 18*^{th}* 1678

MORRIS ISAAC in the Ketch *Begining* for New Yorke Wm PLAY Comand^r   time out

March the 19*^{th}* 1678

MADDOX JONE in the Ketch *Begining* for New Yorke Wm PLAY Comand^r   time out

Aprill the 7*^{th}* 1679

MATTSON BENJ^a in the Ship *John and Mary* for Lond^o EDWARD CALCOTT Comand^r   time out

Aprill the 8*^{th}* 1679

MANNEN ANDREW in the Ship *Mary* for Carolina NICHOLAS LOCKWOOD Comand^r   time out

Aprill the 10*^{th}* 1679

MAUL THOMAS in the Ketch *W^m & John* for New England JOHN SAUNDERS Comand^r   time out

Aprill the 17th 1679

Major W^m in the Barq. *Blessing* for Prouidence Francis Watlington Comander — time out

Aprill the 28th 1679

Mahony Daniell in the ship *freinds Adventure* for Antegua John Long Comand^r — time out

Aprill the 25th 1679

Michell Rich^d in the Ship *Nathan^{ll}* for Boston Wm Clarke Comander — security

Aprill the 25 1679

Michell John in the Ship *Nathan^{ll}* for Boston Wm Clarke Comander — time out

May the 8th 1679

Morgan John in the Ship *Society* for Bristoll Edmond Ditty Comander — time out

May the 8th 1679

Maccmash Charles in the Ship *Roe Buck* for Lond^o Wm Shafto Comander — security

May the 13th 1679

Murphy Daniell in the Ship *Industry* for Bristoll James Porter Comander — time out

May the 14th 1679

Morgan Thomas in the Ship *Bachelor* for Bristoll Roger Bagg Comand^r — time out

May the 14*th* 1679
MAGWAINE OWEN in the ship *Industry* for Bristoll JAMES PORTER Comand^r   time out

May the 17*th* 1679
MATHER GEORGE in the Ship *Hannah and Eliz* for Londo RICH^D PIX Comand^r   security

May the 19*th* 1679
MASON SYLAM in the Ship *W^m & John* for Boston SAMUELL LEGG Comander   time out

May the 23*d* 1679
MARROW CORNELIUS & KATHERINE in the Ship *Society* for Bristoll EDMOND DITTY Comander   time out

May the 24*th* 1679
MOSELY RICHARD in the Ship *W^m & John* for Boston SAMUELL LEGG Comander   time out

May the 24*th* 1679
MORGAN EDWARD in the Ship *Society* for Bristoll EDMOND DITTY Comander   time out

May the 24*th* 1679
MAHANE JOHN in the ship *Industry* for Bristoll JAMES PORTER Comand^r   time out

May the 28*th* 1679
MORRELL NICHOLAS in the Ship *Prudence and Mary* for Boston JACOB GREEN Comander   time out

May the 30*th* 1679
MACCLAHEN OWEN in the Ship *Society* for Bristoll EDMOND DITTY Comander   time out

June the 18*th* 1679
MATTSON MATHEW in the Ship *Concord* for Londo Wm FOSTER Comander   time out

June the 14*th* 1679
MAROH THOMAS, MARY & SARAH in the Ship *Society* for Bristoll EDMOND DITTY Comandr   time out

July the 7*th* 1679
MACCENREE JOHN in the Pink *Revecca* for Virginia THOMAS Wms Comandr   time out

July the 16*th* 1679
MATTHEWS GEORGE in the Pink *Eliz^a* for Boston JOHN BONNER Comander   time out

July the 21*st* 1679
MANSELL ROBERT in the Ship *Rich^d and Mary* for New England SAMUELL FITCH Comandr   security

August the 12*th* 1679
MAHONE JAMES A Seruant belonging to HENRY QUINTYNE Esqr in the Barq, *Plantacon* for Carolina ASER SHARPE Comandr

August the 13*th* 1679
MACCDANIELL PATRICK in the Ketch *Neptune* for Virginia JOSEPH KNOTT Comandr   time out

August the 14th 1679.
MIDLETON ARTHUR in the Barq̄ *Plantacon* for Carolina ASER SHARPE Comand^r
 time out

September the 16th 1679
MOUNTACK ANDREW in the Ship *Eliz*ᵃ for Holland ALLEXANDER MATTISON Comand^r
 security

October the first 1679
MADEN PATRICK in the Sloop *true friendship* for Antegua CHARLES KALLAHANE Comand^r
 time out

October the 2d 1679
MUSKETT W^M in the Sloop *Rutter* for Jamaica EDWARD DUFFEILD Comander
 time out

October the fourth 1679
MELLOLY JAMES in the Ship *Virgin* for Virginia THO: ALLUMBY Comander
 security

October the 7th 1679
MOUNTAINE JOHN in the Sloop *true freindship* for Antegua CHARLES KALLAHANE Comand^r
 security

October the 25th 1679
MORECOCK THOMAS in the Ship *Happy returne* for London ISAAC RAND Comand^r
 security

November the 21 1679
MANERICK NATHANIELL in the Ketch *Phœnix* for Antegua ROBERT FLEXNY Com̄ander
 security

December the 23ᵈ 1679
MARRIOTT ROBERT in the Ship *Recouery* for Jamaica JAMES BROWNE Comandʳ   time out

March the 7ᵗʰ 1678
NEUILL JOHN in the ship *Society* for Boston Wᴹ GUARD Comander   time out

July the 15ᵗʰ 1679
NEWTON ABIGALL in the Ship *Elisʳ* for Boston JOHN BONNER Comandʳ   time out

July the 22ᵈ 1679
NEEDLER JOHN in the Pink *Rebecca* for Virginia THOMAS WILLIAMS Comandʳ   time out

August the 4ᵗʰ 1679
NEAGLE MARTIN in the Ship *Young William* for Virginia THOMAS CORNISH Comandʳ   time out

September the 4ᵗʰ 1679
NEUILL JOHN in the Ship *Pearle* for Leward Islands EDWARD PEIRSON Comander   security

September yᵉ 18ᵗʰ 1679
NASY DANIELL in the ship *Hope* for New England JOHN PRICE Comander   time out

October the 14ᵗʰ 1679
NUTTALL THOMAS in the ship *Happy returne* for Londᵒ ISAAC RAND Comandʳ   time out

TICKETS GRANTED.

October ye 2^d 1679

ONEAL ANN in the Sloop *Rutter* for Jamaica EDWARD DUFFEILD Comand^r   time out

Nouemb^r the 10th 1679

OLDRIDGE ABELL in the Sloop *Hopewell* for Antegua Wm MURPHY Comand^r   time out

Nouember ye 20th 1679

OGLE JOHN in the Ketch *Mary and Sarah* for Prouiden [Providence] GEORGE CONOWAY Comand^r   security

Nouember ye 24th 1679

OSBURNE ROBERT a Seru^{tt} belonging to RICH^D LILBURNE in ye Ketch *Mary and Sarah* for Prouidence GEORGE CONWAY Comand^r

January the 13th 1678

PATY ELIZ^A in the Ship *Joseph and Ann* for Carolina SAMUELL EVANS Comand^r   time out

February the 21: 1678

PEIRCE JOHN in the Ship *Judith* for Lond^o ROBERT KINGSLAND Comander   time out

February 28th 1678

PEARSON JOHN in the Ship *Samuell* for London JOHN CLARKE Comander

March the third 1678

PIPER W^m in the Ship *begining* for Virginia THO: BOSSINGER Comand^r   time out

TICKETS GRANTED.

March the third 1678
PERRIN MARGARETT in the ship *Arthur* for Londo HENRY COSKER Comand[r] security

March the fifth 1678
PERWIDGE JOB in the ship *Expedition* for Virginia JOHN HARDING Comander time out

March the 13 1678
PILE W[m] in the Barq. *Susanna* for Carolina HUGH BABELL Comander time out

March the 21 1678
PARRIS OWEN in the Barq. *Joseph* for Saltertudos STEPHEN CLAY Comand[r] security

March the 28th 1679
PERWIDG JOB in the Ship *Endeavor* for London JAMES GILBERT Comander renewed

Aprill the first 1679
PEAD THOMAS in the Keatch *Swallow* for Road Island JOSEPH HARDY Comand[r] time out

Aprill the fifth 1679
PLUMER JOHN in the Barq. *May fflower* for Prouidence EDWARD HUBBERT Comander time out

Aprill the 5th 1679
PENISTON SAMUELL in the Barq. *May fflower* for Providence EDWARD HUBBART Comand[r] time out

Aprill the 16*th* 1679

PRIMATT HUMPHRY in the *Honor* for London THO: WARREN Comand^r security

Aprill the 16*th* 1679

POLEGREEN JOHN in the Ship *Honor* for London THOMAS WARREN Comander security

Aprill the 22*d* 1679

POPE CHARLES in the Ship *Honor* for Lond^o THOMAS WARREN Comander time out

Aprill the 22*d* 1679

PENNIMAN JANE in the Ship *Honnor* for London THOMAS WARREN Comand^r time out

Aprill the 25*th* 1679

PIDDOCK W^m in the Ship *Freinds Adventure* for London EDW^D BLADES Comand^r time out

Aprill the 28*th* 1679

POSLETT RICH^D in the Ship *Conclusion* for Lond^o Wm BEEDING Comander time out

May the 2*d* 1679

PINKE JOHN in the Ketch *Prosperous* for Virginia DAVID FOGG Comander time out

May the 8*th* 1679

PARSONES FRANCIS in the Ship *Concord* for Lond^o JAMES STRUTT Comand^r time out

May the 13th 1679

POTTLE CHRISTOPHER in the Pink *Dymond* for Topsham EZEKIAH VASS Comander   time out

May the 14th 1679

PRICE JOHN in the Ship *Bachelor* for Bristoll ROGER BAGG Comand^r time out

May the 19th 1679

PRICE JOHN in the Ship *Bachelor* for Bristoll ROGER BAGG Comand^r time out

May the 19th 1679

PEMMELL THOMAS in the Ship *Rose and Crown* for Lond^o THOMAS CROFTS Comand^r time out

**June the* 16th 1679

PLATT JOHN in the Ketch *Joseph* for New Yorke ABRAHAM KNOTT Comand^r time out

June the 17th 1679

PECHEY LAMBERT in the ship *Ruth* for Lond^o Wm TAYLOR Comand^r time out

June the 28th 1679

PHILLIPS ELIAZER in the Ship *Providence* for Boston TIMOTHY PROUT Comand^r time out

†*July the* 22^d 1679

PEARSHOUSE CHESTER in the Pink *Rebecca* for Virginia THO W^{ms} Comand^r time out

---

* [In the original the name of RICORD precedes this; but in order to keep to the alphabetical arrangement I have transposed it among the R's, and to its proper date (see p. 400).]

† [A similar remark applies to the name RICHARD, which stands here in the original (see p. 401).]

July the 29th 1679
POOR MILES in the KETCH *Doue* for Antegua JOHN GRAFTON Comand[r]
                     time out

August the 9th 1679
POWELL ARTHUR in the Ship *Friendship* for Lond[o] JOHN WILLIAMS Comand[r]

August the 18th 1679
POOR MARY A seru[tt] belonging to M[r] W[m] BULKLEY in the Ketch *Neptune* for Virginia JOSEPH KNOTT Comander

August the 19th 1679
PICKFORD ROBERT in the Ketch *Neptune* for Virginia JOSEPH KNOTT Comand[r]   time out

September the 1st 1679
POLLARD JOSEPH in the Pinke *Trent* for Boston GEORGE MUNJOY Comand[r]   time out

September the 4th 1679
PICKFORD ROBERT in the Ship *Pearle* EDW[D] PEIRSON Comand[r] for Lew[d] Islands   renewed

September the 8th 1679
PENDLETON MARY in the Ship *Trent* for Boston GEORGE MUNJOY Comand[r]   time out

September the 15th 1679
PILSON EDWARD in the Ship *Hope* for New England JOHN PRICE Comander   time out

October the 11th 1679
PORTMAN CHRISTOPHER in the Sloop *Endeavor* for Carolina THOMAS SHAW Comand^r   time out

October the 11th 1679
POPPLE MAGNUS in the Sloop *Endeauor* for Carolina THOMAS SHAW Comand^r   time out

October the 29th 1679
PARKER JOHN a Seruant belonging to Coll^o CHRISTOPHER CODRINGTON in the Barq. *Doue* for Neuis ANTHONY JENNOR Comand^r

October the 29 1679
PAGE JOHN a Seruant belonging to Coll^o CHR: CODRINGTON in the Barq. *Doue* for Neuis ANTHONY JENOUR Comand

Nouember the 27th 1679
PARRIS OWEN in the Barq. *Resolution* for Antegua THOMAS GILBERT Comand^r   time out

December the 23^d 1679
PERSIVALL ANDREW in the Ship *Ann & Jane* for Lond^o RICH^D RATTFORD Comand^r   security

March the 13th 1678
QUERK JOHN a Seryant belonging to THOMAS ALLEN in the Ketch *W^m & Susan* for New England RALPH PARKER Comand^r

August the 12th 1679
QUINTYNE RICH^D in the Barq. *Plantaĉon* for Carolina ASER SHARPE Comand^r   time out

TICKETS GRANTED.

February the 25th 1678

ROSE CHRISTOPHER in the Ship *Patience* for Londo THOMAS HUDSON Comand^r — security

February the 27th 1679 [1678]

ROYDON W^m in the *Constant Warwick* Friggott for London Capt RALPH DELAUALL Comand^r — time out

March the 3^d 1678

RYDER SYMON A seruant belonging to GEORGE MOOR in the Ship *Vineyard* for Virginia HENRY PERRIN Comand^r

March the third 1678

ROANE BANCKS in the Sloop *Hunter* for Surranam WALTER ASSUEROS Comand^r — time out

March the 12th 1678

ROBINSON ALLEXANDER in the Ship *Ann & Mary* for Antegua JOHN JOHNSON Comand^r — security

March the 21 1678

ROSS WILLIAM in the Ketch *W^m & Susan* for New England RALPH PARKER Comand^r — time out

March the 26: 1679

ROBERTS W^m in the Pinke *Endeauor* for Londo JAMES GILBERTS Comand^r — time out

Aprill the 2^d 1679

RIDLEY GEORGE in the Sloop *Rutter* for Jamaica EDW^d DUFFEILD Comand^r — time out

Aprill the 12th 1679

ROW LAWRENCE in the ship *Robert* for Boston NATHAN HAYMAN Comander   time out

---

Aprill the 19th 1679

ROTH RICH^D in the Ship *Recovery* for New Yorke THOMAS CHINERY Comander   time out

---

Aprill the 30th 1679

REMNANT JAMES and JONE his Wife in the Ship *Industry* for Bristoll JAMES PORTER Comand^r time out

---

May the 6th 1679

RAINY LUKE A servant belonging to Mr HENRY APLEWHITE in the Ketch *Prosperous* for Virginia DAUID FOGG Comand^r

---

May the 13th 1679

RICHBELL RICHARD in the Ship *Experim^{tt}* for London ALLEN COCK Comander   security

---

May the 19th 1679

RAVENSCROFT BENJ^A in the Ship *Rose and Crowne* for Lond^o THOMAS CROFTS Comand^r time out

---

May the 20th 1679

REMNANT JAMES & JONE in the Ship *New Concord* for Lond^o JAMES STRUTT Comand^r renewed

---

[May the 24th 1679

RICORD CHARLES in the Ship *Society* for Bristoll EDMOND DITTY Comander   time out]

---

* [This name is entered among the P's in the original, as is the case with RICHARD, JAMES, at bottom of next page.]

May the 28*th* 1679

RAINSFORD EDWARD in the Ship *W^m & John* for Boston SAMUELL LEGG Comand^r   time out

May the 28*th* 1679

RUSSELL EDWARD in the Ship *W^m & John* for Boston SAMUELL LEGG Comand^r   time out

May the 28*th* 1679

RICHBELL ROBERT in the Ship *W^m & John* for Boston SAMUELL LEGG Comander   time out

June the 28*th* 1679

RICH ROBERT Senior in the Ship *Amity* for London BENJ^A GROVES Comander   time out

July the first 1679

RICHBELL JOHN in the ship *Prouidence* for Boston TIMOTHY PROUT Comander   security

July the 10*th* 1679

RULE THOMAS in the Pinke *Rebecca* for Virginia THO: WILLIAMS Comander   time out

July the 17*th* 1679

RUDGE THOMAS in the Briganteen *Brother's Aduenture* for New Yorke ROBERT DARKIN Comand^r   security

[*July the* 21 1679

RICHARD JAMES in the Pinke *Rebecca* for Virginia THOMAS WILLIAMS Comand^r   time out]

August the third 1679

RICE JAMES and JOHN in the Ship *Young W^m* for Virginia THOMAS CORNISH Comand^r   time out

August ye 15th 1679

RICH ROBERT in the ship *Postilion* for New England JOHN PRAUL Comand^r   security

August ye 15th 1679

RUDLE ROBERT in the Ship *John and Henry* for Bristoll THOMAS CADES Comander   time out

September the 4th 1679

ROBOTHAM WILLIAM in the Ship *Joseph* for New Yorke STEPHEN CLAY Comand^r a serv^{tt} belonging to Coll^o SAM^{ll} NEWTON

Nouember the third 1679

REDDIN KATHERINE a Serv^{tt} belonging to MARTIN HAYES for Jamaica in the Barq *Aduenture* EDW^D DUFFEILD Comander

January the fourteenth 1678

SLAUGHTER WILLIAM a Serv^{tt} belonging to JOHN JENNINGS in the ship *Joseph & Ann* for Carolina SAM^{ll} EUANS Comand^r

January the 14th 168 [1678]

SERJEANT RICH^D in the Ship *Joseph and Ann* for Carolina SAMUELL EVANS Comander   security

January the 28th 1678

SMITH PHILLIP in the Ship *James* for New Yorke Wm SWEETLAND Comand^r   time out

February the 11*th* 1678
SYMONS SAMUELL in the Ship *James* for New Yorke Wm SWEETLAND Comand^r   time out

---

February the 13: 1678
STOCKLEY JOHN and MARY in the ship *two Brothers* for Jamaica RICE JEFFERYS Comander   time out

---

February the 13*th* 1678
SHERWOOD SAMUELL in the ship *Two Brothers* for Jamaica RICE JEFFERYS Comand^r   time out

---

February the 17*th* 1678
STEEL MARY in the ship *Merch^{tt} Bounduenture* for London Wm BUCKLEY Comand^r   time out

---

February the 25*th* 1678
SMITH HESTER in the Barq, *Plantacon* for Carolina ASER SHARPE Comand^r   time out

---

March the 8*th* 1678
STOAKES MICHAELL in the Ship *Society* for Boston WILLIAM GUARD Comander   time out

---

March the 11*th* 1678
STACY W in the Ship *Society* for Boston Wm GUARD Comand^r   time out

---

March the 12*th* 1678
SMITH EDWARD in the Barq, *Susannah* for Carolina HUGH BABELL Comander   security

51—2

TICKETS GRANTED.

March the 18th 1678

SANDERS BENJ^a in the Ketch *begining* for New Yorke Wm PLAY Comand^r   time out

---

March the 26th 1679

STEEL MARY* in the Ship *Supply* for London JOSEPH FREEMAN Comand^r   renewed

---

March the 29th 1679

SAILES RICH^d in the Ketch *Swallow* for New England JOSEPH HARDY Comander   time out

---

March the 31st 1679

SEWER JOHN in the ship *John and Thomas* for Prouidence THOMAS JENOUR Comander   time out

---

March the 31st 1679

SCOTT BENJ^a in the Ship *Expedition* for Lond^o JOHN HARDING Comand^r   time out

---

Aprill the first 1679

SMITH W^m in the Ketch *Unity* for Virginia JAMES RAINY Comand^r   time out

---

Aprill the 3d 1679

SALT SAMUELL in the Ship *Change* for London Wm KING Comander   time out

---

Aprill the 12th 1679

SANDIFORD HENRY in the ship *Robert* for Boston NATHAN HAYMAN Comander   time out

---

* [See under date Feb. 17, in previous page.]

Aprill the 15th 1679
SFRANE ALMONS in the Ship *Eliz* for Neuis PETER MAJOR Comand^r time out

---

Aprill the 19th 1679
STEPHENS NATHANIELL in the Ship *Recouery* for New Yorke THOMAS CHINERY Comander time out

---

Aprill the 19th 1679
SEDGWICK RALPH in the Ketch *Unity* for Virginia JAMES RAINY Comander time out

---

Aprill the 22d 1679
SPICER SAMUELL in the Ship *Hope* for London JOSEPH BALL Comander time out

---

Aprill the 26th 1679
SMITH MARGERETT a Seru^tt belonging to THOMAS DOXEY in the Ship *Brother's Aduenture* for New Yorke J^no SELLECK Com^r

---

Aprill the 28th 1679
SNACKNELL RICH^D in the Ship *Nathan^ll* for Boston W^M CLARKE Comand^r time out

---

May the 2d 1679
SOUTHWORTH FRANCIS in the Ketch *Prosperous* for Virginia DAUID FOGG Comander time out

---

May the fifth 1679
STAPLETON WALTER in the Ship *Society* for Bristoll EDMOND DITTY Comander time out

May the 10th 1679
STANTON PEARCE in the Barq. *Resolution* for Antegua JOHN INGLE-
BEE Comand^r   time out

May the 12th 1679
SHORT WALTER in the Ship *Bachelor* for Bristoll ROGER BAGG
Comand^r   time out

May the 14th 1679
SKAHANE TEIGE in the Ship *Industry* for Bristoll JAMES PORTER
Comand^r   time out

May the 14th 1679
SMITH ISAAC in the Ship *Supply* for Boston JOHN MELLOWES
Comand^r   time out

May the 19th 1679
SANDOME RICH^D in the Ship *Swallow* for Leuerpoole THO WITH-
INGTUN Comander   time out

May the 20th 1679
SMITH WILLIAM in the Ship *New Concord* for Lond^o JAMES STRUTT
Comand^r   time out

May the 20th 1679
STEPHENS SYLVESTER in the Ketch *Nich^o & Rebecca* for New Yorke
NICHOLAS BLAKE Comand^r   time out

May the 22^d 1679
SHERLAND JOHN jun^r in the Ship *Prudence and Mary* for Boston
JACOB GREEN Comand^r   time out

TICKETS GRANTED.

May the 28th 1679

SERFATTY JOSHUA in the Ship *Morneing Starr* for Surranam JOHN UANDERSPIKE Comand^r   security

May the 29th 1679

SPARKES SAMUELL in the Ship *W^m & John* for Boston SAM^LL LEGG Comand^r   time out

May the 29th 1679

SALTER RICH in the Ketch *W^m & John* for Boston SAM^LL LEGG Comander   time out

June the 25th 1679

SUTTON JOHN in the ship *Prosperous* for Londo THOMAS WOODCOCK Comand^r   time out

July the 9th 1679

SMITH THOMAS in the Ship *Bachelor* for London W^N KNOTT Comander   time out

July the 15th 1679

SCOTT THOMAS in the Pink *Rebecca* for Virginia THOMAS WILLIAMS Comander   time out

July the 22d 1679

STANNADGE THOMAS in the Pinke *Rebecca* for Virginia THOMAS WILLIAMS Comand^r   time out

July the 22d 1679

STRAUSE ELIAS in the Ship *Experim^tt* for London THOMAS AUBONY Comand^r   time out

August the 2ᵈ 1679

STONE JOHN in the ship *Bachelors Delight* for Londo ROBERT GREENWAY Comander   time out

August the 16ᵗʰ 1679

SEALY HENRY in the Ketch *Neptune* for Virginia JOSEPH KNOTT Comandʳ   time out

August the 16ᵗʰ 1679

SMITH THURLO a Servᵗ belonging to HENRY SEALY in the Keatch *Neptune* for Virginia JOSEPH KNOTT Comandʳ

September the 16ᵗʰ 1679

SONE GEORGE in the Barqᵏ *Blessing* for Burmudos FRANCIS WATLINGTON Comander   security

September the 20ᵗʰ 1679

STANLEY ROBERT in the Ship *Malligo Merchᵗᵗ* for London ROGER HOMER Comander   time out

September the 22ᵈ 1679

SEAMAN THOMAS in the Ship *Thomas & Sarah* for London JAMES DAY Comander   time out

October the first 1679

SHORT MARTHA in the Ship *Barbados Merchᵗᵗ* for Virginia JAMES COCK Comand.   time out

October the first 1679

SANDFORD JOHN in the Ship *Barbados Merchᵗᵗ* for Virginia JAMES COCK Comandʳ   time out

October the 2ᵈ 1679

SEARLE RICHᴰ A Servᵗᵗ belonging to JAMES COATES in the Sloop *Rutter* for Jamaica EDWᴰ DUFFEILD Comandʳ

October the 7ᵗʰ 1679

SWINNY THOMAS in the Sloop *true friendship* for Antego CHARLES KALLAHANE Comander security

---

October the 29ᵗʰ 1679

SENIOR JACOB in the Barq̧ *Doue* for Neuis ANTHONY JENOUR Comandʳ security

---

October the 29ᵗʰ 1679

SMITH JOHN a Servᵗᵗ belonging to Collᵒ CHRISTOPHER CODRINGTON in the Barq̧ *Doue* for Nevis ANTHᵒ JENOR

Nouember the 3ᵈ 1679

SWEETING RICHᴰ in the Barq̧ *Aduenture* for Jamaica EDWARD DUFFEILD Comander time out

---

Nouember the 6ᵗʰ 1679

SIDDY HENRY in the Barq̧ *Aduenture* for Jamaica EDWARD DUFFEILD Comandʳ security

---

Nouember the 7ᵗʰ 1679

SALTER GEORGE in the Sloop *Hopewell* for Antegua Wᴹ MURPHY Comandʳ time out

---

Nouember the 29ᵗʰ 1679

SPITTLE ROBERT in the Sloop *Katherine* for Antegua ANDREW GALL Comandʳ time out

December the 15th 1679
SIDNEY JOHN in the Ship *Lawrell* for Lew^d ROBERT OXE Comand^r
security

December the 22^d 1679
SMITH JOHN in the Ship *Ann and Jane* for Lond^o RICH^D RATTFORD Comander
time out

December the 24th 1679
SMART JOHN in the ship *Ann & Jane* for Lond^o RICH^D RATTFORD Comander
security

December 24th 1679
SHERWIN JOHN in the Ship *Ann & Jane* for Lond^o RICH^D RATTFORD Comander
security

December the 24th 1679
SINDRY JOHN in the ship *Recouery* for Jamaica JAMES BROWNE Comander
time out

December the 30th 1679
SWANLEY ROBERT in the Ship *Ann and Jane* for London RICH^D RATTFORD Comander
time out

December the 31st 1679
SHARPE MARY in the Ship *Recouery* for Jamaica JAMES BROWNE Comand^r
time out

February the 21st 1678
TRAVIS RICHARD in the Ship *Fellowship* for Antegua THOMAS PIM Comand^r
time out

March the first 1678:

TIPPIN JOHN in the *Constant Warwick* Friggott for London Capt RALPH DELAVALL Comander   time out

Aprill the 11th 1679

TINICO JACOB in the Ketch *W^m and John* for New England JOHN SANDERS Comander   time out

Aprill the 19th 1679

TOOLES MORGAN in the Ship *Freinds Aduenture* for London EDWARD BLADES Comander   time out

Aprill the 25th 1679

THORNTON W^m in the ship *Freinds Adventure* for Lond^o EDWARD BLADES Comander   time out

Aprill the 28th 1679

TOWNSEND RICHARD in the Ship *Nathan^{ll}* for Boston Wm CLARKE Comander   time out

Aprill the 29: 1679

TURNER JOHN in the ship *Nathaniell* for Boston Wm CLARKE Comander   time out

May the 10th 1679

TERRY CHRISTOPHER jun^r in the Ship *Experiment* for London ALLAN COCK Comander   time out

May the 24th 1679

THOMAS GEORGE in the Ship *Prudence and Mary* for Boston JACOB GREEN Comander   time out

June the 26 : 1679

TEAGE JOHN in the ship *Freindship* for London JOHN WILLIAMS Comander   time out

July the 12th 1679

TOLLO DEMEUEREZ LEWIS in the ship *Bachelor* for Lond^o Wm KNOTT Comander   time out

July the 17th 1679

THAYER NATHANIELL in the ship *Society* for Boston Wm GUARD Comander   time out

August the 16th 1679

TURDALL JOHN in the Ketch *Neptune* for Virginia JOSEPH KNOTT Comand^r a Serv^{tt} belonging to HENRY SEALY

September ye 18th 1679

TAPPER THOMAS in the ship *Malligo Merch^{tt}* ROGER HOMER Comander for London   time out

Nouember the 7th 1679

TREMILLS W^m in the Sloop *Hopewell* for Antegua Wm MURPHY Comander   time out

December the 11th 1679

THORPE JOHN in the ship *Ann and Jane* for London RICH^D RATTFORD Comander   time out

---

March the 10th 1678

VINER ANTHONY in the Ship *James* for Antegua PAUL CREAN Comander   time out

TICKETS GRANTED. 413

May the 2ᵈ 1679

VAUX JOHN in the Ship *Roe Buck* for London Wᴍ SHAFTO Co-
mander   time out

July the 16ᵗʰ 1679

VERIN NATHANIELL in the Pink *Rebecca* for Virginia THOMAS
WILLIAMS Comander   time out

Nouember yᵉ 8ᵗʰ 1679

URQUHART ALLEXANDER in the Sloop *Hopewell* for Antegua Wᴍ
MURPHY Comander   time out

December yᵉ 24ᵗ 1679

VERNON PETER in the ship *Ann and Jane* for Londᵒ RICHᴰ RATT-
FORD Comander   security

January the 4ᵗʰ 1678

WILLIAMS MATTHEW in the Ship *Old head* of Kingsale for Leward
ROBERT BARKER Comander   time out

February 11ᵗʰ 1678

WILLIS HENRY in the Ship *Dilligence* for Boston JEREMIAH JACSON
Comander   time out

February the 17ᵗʰ 1678

WILLS JOHN in the ship *Endeauour* for Virginia ABRAHAM NEWMAN
Comandʳ   time out

March the 10ᵗʰ 1678

WELTDEN ANTHONY in the Ship *Society* for Boston Wᴍ GUARD
Comander   security

TICKETS GRANTED.

March the 12th 1678
WHITELIFF GEORGE in the Ship *Samaritan* for Leverpool VALENTINE TRIm [? TRIMMER] Comand[r]   security

March the 19th 1678
WHITTEE MARY in the Ketch *begining* for New Yorke W[m] PLAY Comand[r]   time out

March the 19th 1679 [1678]
WRIGHT ROBERT and MARY in the Ketch *begining* for New Yorke W[m] PLAY Comand[r]   time out

March the 21st 1678
WILKS NATHANIELL in the ship Merch[tt] *Bonadventure* for London W[m] BUCKLEY Comander   security

March the 27th 1679
WRIGHT RICH[d] in the Ketch *Mary and Sarah* for Carolina GEORGE CONOWAY Comand[r]   time out

March the 31st 1679
WHITEFOOT AMOS in the ship *Robert* for Boston NATHAN HAYMAN Comand[r]   time out

Aprill the 10th 1679
WILKINSON DANIELL in the Barq[,] *Resolution* for Prouidence DANIELL ACKLIN Comand[r] y[e] said WILKINSON a Seru[tt] belonging to ROBERT HALL

Aprill the 15th 1679
WEBSTER HENRY in the ship *Robert* for Boston NATHAN HAYMAN Comand[r]   time out

Aprill the 19*th* 1679

WILSE FRANCIS in the ship *Hope* for Lond⁰ JOSEPH BALL Comand^r   time out

Aprill the 26*th* 1679

WEBSTER EDWARD in the Ship *Nathan*^n for Boston Wm CLARKE Comand^r   time out

Aprill the 26*th* 1679

WILKINS JOHN in the ship *Nathan*^n for Boston Wm CLARKE Comander   time out

Aprill the 26*th* 1679

WILLIAMS SYMON in the ship *Francis* for Leward PETER JEFFERYS Comander   security

May the 2*d* 1679

WHITFEILD MATHEW in the Ketch *Prosperous* for Virginia DAVID FOGG Comand^r   time out

May the 5*th* 1679

WHEELER W^m in the Sloop *Bachelor* for Leward PETER SWAINE Comander   time out

May the 8*th* 1679

WINGATT JOHN in the Ketch *Prosperous* for Virginia DAVID FOGG Comand^r   time out

May the 20*th* 1679

WICKHAM BENJ^a in the Barq *Resolution* for Antegoa JOHN INGLEBE Comand^r   security

May the 26th 1679

WHITEING W^m in the ship *Francis and Susan* for Boston PHILLIP KNELL Comander   time out

---

May the 26th 1679

WATTKINS PHILLIP in the ship *Prudence and Mary* for Boston JACOB GREEN Comander   time out

---

June the 18th 1679

WOLFE EMANUELL in the Ship *Thomas and Susan* for Boston DAVID EDWARDS Comand^r   security

---

June the 18th 1679

WOOD JAMES in the ship *Thomas and Susan* for Boston DAUID EDW^ds Comand^r   time out

---

July the 15th 1679

WILLSON W^m in the Barq *Rebecca* for Virginia THO WILLIAMS Comand^r   time out

---

July the 18th 1679

WELCH EDMOND a Seru^tt belonging to JOHN HOPCROFT in the Pink *Rebecca* for Virginia THO: W^ms Comander

---

August the first 1679

WHEELER JOHN jun^r in the Ship *Returne* for New Engl^d THOMAS HARVEY Comand^r   security

---

August the 19th 1679

WOLFINDEN JEREMIAH in the Sloop *true freindship* for Nevis CHARLES KALLAHANE Comand^r   time out

August y⁶ 28ᵗʰ 1679

WHELER CHRISTOPHER in the Ship *Robert* for London RICHᴅ COCK Comander   security

---

September the first 1679

WICKHAM ELIZᴬ in the Sloop *John & Francis* for Antegua JOHN HOWARD Comander   time out

---

September the first 1679

WESTBURY THOMAS in the Ship *Barbados Merchᵗᵗ* for Lewᵈ Islands EDWARD GRIFFIN Comandʳ   time out

---

September the 3ᵈ 1679

WATLINGTON MARY in the Sloop *John & Frances* for Antegua JOHN HOWARD Comandʳ   time out

---

September the 16ᵗʰ 1679

WEAVER THOMAS in the Ship *Mallego Merchᵗᵗ* for London ROGER HOMER Comander   time out

---

September y⁶ 22 1679

WOODCOCK THO: in the ship *Thomas & Sarah* for Londᵒ JAMES DAY Comandʳ   time out

---

October the 6ᵗʰ 1679

WICKHAM THOMAS in the Sloop *True freindship* for Antegoa CHARLES KALLAHANE Comandʳ   security

---

October y⁶ 7ᵗʰ 1679

WALL SAMUELL in the Sloop *true freindship* for Antegua CHARLES KALLAHANE Comandʳ   security

---

October y⁶ 8ᵗʰ 1679

WILLOUGHBY OLIVER in the Sloop *Affrica* for Antegoa ANTHONY BURGESS Comandʳ   security

TICKETS GRANTED.

October y⁰ 17ᵗʰ 1679
WILDE Wᴹ in the Ship *Happy Returne* for Londᵒ ISAAC RAND Comandʳ time out

October y⁰ 24ᵗʰ 1679
WAINWRIGHT JAMES in the ship *Happy Returne* for London ISAAC RAND Comandʳ time out

Nouember y⁰ first 1679
WHITEHEAD JOSEPH in the Ship *Three Brothers* for New Yorke PETER BOSS Comandʳ security

Nouembʳ y⁰ 7ᵗʰ 1679
WILLIAMS ARTHUR in the Sloop *Hopewell* for Antegua Wᴹ MURPHY Comandʳ time out

Decembʳ y⁰ 6ᵗʰ 1679
WARNER NATHANIELL in the Sloop *Unity* for Jamaica LAWRENCE SLUCE Comander time out

May the 2ᵈ 1679
YATES THOMAS A Seruᵗ belonging to FRAN: SOUTHWORTH in the Keatch *Prosperous* for Virginia DAUID FOGG Comd.

July y⁰ 18ᵗʰ 1679
YOUNG MATHEW in the Pink *Rebecca* for Virginia THOMAS WILLIAMS Comandʳ time out

Nouembʳ y⁰ 4ᵗʰ 1679
YARWOOD THOMAS in the Barq̄ *Endeavor* for Carolina THOMAS SHAW Comandʳ time out

Total of Men 523
Total of Women 60

In all 583

BARBADOES.

PARISH REGISTERS :—BIRTHS AND DEATHS, LISTS OF INHABITANTS, LANDED PROPRIETORS, SERVANTS, &c.

1678—1679.]

[PARISH REGISTERS.]

BARBADOS *The Parish of St Michaels.*

BAPTISMS.

1678

March 31.	JOICE y^e daughter of CHARLS & MARGARET YATES.
	THOMAS y^e Son of HENRY & ANNE SMITH.
April. 2.	ESTHER ye daughter of FRANCIS & ELISABETH HALL.
16.	MARY ye daughter of CALEB & ELISABETH POWEL.
25.	MARY ye daughter of JANE SCOT.
	LOVEL ye Son of JOHN & ELINOR HOBCRAFT.
	JANE ye daughter of JONE DAVIS.
May. 5.	MARY ye daughter of WILLIAM & MARY STANDON.
7.	SUSANNA ye daughter of JOHN & ANNE HALL.
15.	WILLIAM ye Son of STEVEN & MARGARET LANSDALE.
19.	MARY ye daughter of FRANCIS & KATHARINE HARDING
	DAVID ye Son of JOHN & ELISABETH MURRAL.
19.	JOHN ye Son of RICHARD & ELISABETH PERKIN.
	EDWARD ye Son of THOMAS & KATHARINE PROUT.
20.	EDWARD ye Son of EDWARD & HANNAH MATTHEWS.
28.	RICHARD ye Son of Maj^r THOMAS JELLY & MARY his Wife.
June. 3.	MARGARET ye daughter of Mr JOHN CRISP & SARAH his wife.

1678.

June. 9. WILLIAM yᵉ Son of WILLIAM & MARGARET STICKLAND.
ELISABETH yᵉ daughter of JOHN & ELISABETH GOSNEL.
KATHARIN yᵉ daughter of SIMON & ANN WILLIAMS, Christian Negroes.

16. ELISABETH yᵉ daughter of URSULA PEASE.
MARY yᵉ daughter of JOHN & JUDITH SMITH.

20. ANDREW yᵉ Son of ANDREW & SARAH GODFREY.

24. ARTHUR yᵉ Son of RICHARD & SARAH MENDAM.

25. PETRONILIA yᵉ daughter of GEORG & ELISABETH PARR.

28. ANN yᵉ daughter of THOMAS & ELISABETH CLARK.

July. 25. HANNAH yᵉ daughter of Dʳ JOHN SPRINGHAM, & SARAH his wife.

26. JANE yᵉ daughter of Mʳ SAMUEL SHENTON & GRACE his wife.

August. 9. WILLIAM yᵉ Son of STEPHEN & MARGARET LANDSDALE.

19. MARY yᵉ daughter of NICHOLAS & ELISABETH MAYNARD.
LAKE yᵉ Son of Capt WILL. MARSHAL.

21. CLEMENT yᵉ Son of ROBERT & REBECCA LANIERE.

25. ELISABETH yᵉ daughter of JOHN & SUSANNA NEWPORT.

September. 7. FRANCES yᵉ daughter of Mʳ ROBERT CODRINGTON & ELISABETH his Wife.

8. WILLIAM yᵉ Son of ROBERT & MARY ELLIS.

22. HANNAH yᵉ daughter of JOHN & MARY LISWEL.

26. THOMAS yᵉ Son of RICHARD & ELEN WHITE.

28. DAVID yᵉ Son of HUGH & JANE DAVIS.

October. 7. CHRISTOPHER yᵉ Son of Major JOHN HALLET & MARY his Wife.

13. JOHN yᵉ Son of JOHN & MARGARET AWMAN.
EDWARD yᵉ Son of BRASIL & REBECCAH BENFIELD.

14. ELISABETH yᵉ daughter of Mʳ THOMAS PIERCE & ELISABETH his Wife.

20. MARY yᵉ daughter of Mʳ JOHN SMITH & PHILIPPA his Wife.
SARAH yᵉ daughter of SAMUEL & SARAH ~~his Wife~~ *PERROT.

November. 3. MARY yᵉ daughter of THOMAS & ANN KANNIDAY.

---

* [Thus crossed through in the original.]

1678.

November. 10. PETER, alias THOMAS yᵉ Son of ROBERT & JANE PORTER.
11. JONATHAN yᵉ Son of JONATHAN & SARAH PEACH.
14. EDWARD yᵉ Son of Mʳ NATHANIEL BRANCKER & MARY his Wife.
17 ELISABETH yᵉ daughter of JACOB & PRISCILLA ALLEN.

December. 8. RICHARD yᵉ Son of JOHN & MARY BUTCHER.
12. FRANCIS yᵉ Son of Mʳ FRANCIS BOND & ELISABETH his Wife.
13. WILLIAM yᵉ Son of WILLIAM & ANN PARIS.
15. THOMAS yᵉ Son of DANIEL & ELISABETH FRISEL.
17. ELISABETH yᵉ daughter of Mʳ WILLIAM BARNS & SARAH his Wife.
22. ANN yᵉ daughter of NICHOLAS & DORCAS WILLOUGHBY.
27. JOHN yᵉ Son of STEPHEN & ELISABETH CORNISH.
ANN yᵉ daughter of JOHN & MARY HARWOOD.

January. 1. WILLIAM yᵉ Son of WILLIAM & MARGARET ROPER.
JOHN yᵉ Son of LAWRENCE & MARY ENGLAND.
8. THOMAS yᵉ Son of Mʳ THOMAS FERGUSSON & ELISABETH his Wife.
9. THOMAS yᵉ Son of JOHN & ELISABETH WILLIS.
12. KATHARIN yᵉ daughter of Mʳ JOHN SUTTON & MARY his Wife.
14. CHARLS yᵉ Son of CHARLS CAVENAUGH.
20. NICHOLAS yᵉ Son of ARCHIBALD & FRANCES MACQUIN.
22. JOHN yᵉ Son of HILLIARD HOLDIP & FRANCES his Wife.

February. 6. DOROTHY & THOMASIN yᵉ daughters of Capt. THOMAS MORRIS & SARAH his Wife.
ROGER yᵉ Son of Mʳ ROGERS & MARY his Wife.
9. ELISABETH yᵉ daughter of Mʳ GEORG CHENEY & MARY his Wife.
23. SAMUEL yᵉ Son of FRANCIS & MARY THATCHER.
27. ELISABETH yᵉ daughter of ROGER COWLEY Esqʳ, & SUSANNA his Wife.

March. 6. FRANCIS yᵉ Son of Capt. FRANCIS BURTON & JUDITH his Wife.

1678.

March. 13. SARAH ye daughter of CHARLS & MARTHA LEIGH.
   19. REBECCA ye daughter of NICHOLAS PRIDEAUX & REBECCA his Wife.
   22. FRANCES ye daughter of Mr JOHN OGILBY & ELISABETH his Wife.
—— 23. ANN ye daughter of DANIEL & BARBARA LAWRENCE.
1679 30. JAMES ye Son of JOHN & ELENOR FITZGERARD.
    JOHN ye Son of JOHN & SUSANNA CRAG.
April. 13. CORNELIUS ye Son of JOHN & SUSANNA MACKENNY.
   14. ABRAHAM ye Son of THOMAS & MARY HAWKINS.
   19. ALICE ye daughter of THOMAS & BRIDGET JOHNSON.
   25. JOSEPH ye Son of GEORG & HANNAH OATS.
May. 13. GILES ye Son of GILES & MARY ELDRIDG.
June. 3. JOHN ye Son of Mr JOHN STEWARD & MARGARET his Wife.
    4. THOMAS ye Son of MARY KING.
    8. JOHN ye Son of ANTHONY & ELISABETH SUILLIVANT.
   16. MATTHEW ye Son of FRANCIS & THOMASIN CHRISTIAN.
   22. THOMAS ye Son of JOHN & JANE JANES.
    JOHN ye Son of THOMAS & JANE WEST.
July. 15. WILLIAM ye Son of WILLIAM & ELISABETH HERBERT.
   24. ELISABETH ERPEY.
   25. THOMAS ye Son of DANIEL & SARAH GUN.
    MARY ye daughter of MARTHA TURNER.
   27. EDWARD ye Son of JEFFRY & PRISCILLA BATLEY.
   29. HENRY ye Son of ANN SMITH, Wid.
August. 5. ELISABETH ye daughter of Mr RICHARD BUNNY and HANNAH his Wife.
   10. TIMOTHY ye Son of TIMOTHY & MARGARET ENNYS
    NICHOLAS ye Son of NICHOLAS & MARGARET MORREL.
    DARBY ye Son of LANTHIL & MARY HALLOWAY.
   17. SUSANNA ye daughter of ROBERT & ELISABETH PAIN.
    ELISABETH ye daughter of JOHN & MARGARET TINE.
   22. EDWYN ye Son of EDWYN STEED Esqr & CALIA his Wife.
   26. MUNDUSIA ye daughter of JOHN & ELISABETH SMITH.
   28. ELISABETH ye daughter of Mr ROBERT & SUSANNA BECKLES.

1679.

September. 2. MARY yᵉ daughter of ANDREW & MARY MAIN.
    5. WILLIAM yᵉ Son of LEONARD & ANN ROBINSON.
  10. ESTHER yᵉ daughter of EDMUND & ELISABETH MORGAN.
  12. GEORG yᵉ Son of Capt. FRANCIS BURTON & JUDITH his Wife.
  21. ELISABETH & MARGARET yᵉ daughters of Mʳ BENJAMIN & MARGARET MATSON.
  25. MARGARET yᵉ daughter of Mʳ THOMAS & MARGARET DOD·

107.

BARBADOS   *The Parish of Sᵗ Michaels.*

URIALS.

1678

March 26ᵗʰ JOHN SWAN Master of yᵉ *Hope* of Amsterdam.
  28. Mʳ WILLIAM FLETCHER.
  30. FRANCIS BOYS'S child.
  31. FRANCIS VARNAM.
April. 1. WILLIAM FELLOW.
  2. VRSULA GREY.
    ROSE FORD.
  3. ALICE yᵉ daughter of HENRY & MARY LELAM.
    ROGER JONES from yᵉ Almshous.
  4. MARTHA CLAY.
  8. EDWARD ROBERTS.
    Mʳ ROBERT RAMSEY.
  14. JOHN HUGHS.
  15. JONE ALLEN a Widdow.
  16. WILLIAM TRUSDAL.
    HENRY JENNISON.
  17. Mʳ THOMAS PARIS, Merchᵗ
    WILLIAM MILLER.

1678.

April. 18. MARY ye daughter of CALEB & ELISABETH POWEL.
19. AGNES ye daughter of Mr THOMAS FORRESTER & JANE his Wife.
MARGARET ye daughter of RICHARD & ELISABETH RICHARDSON.
22. ELISABETH ye daughter of JOHN & JANE CARN.*
HANNAH ye wife of JOHN WADE.
MARGARET, a distracted Woman.
24. RALPH WARNER.
WILLIAM FERRIMAN.
27. KATHARINE MILLER.
Mr HECTOR STEVENS.
28. PATRIC KILHAMMY.
29. SUSANNA WITHERS.
May. 4. EDMUND JOY.
5. Mr JOHN JONES chief Mate of y^e *Arany Marchant*, Mr JOHN HALL, M^r
SUSANNA STEDMAN.
THOMAS ye Son of HENRY & ANN SMITH.
6. SUSANNA ROSE.
7. GEORG HILL.
9. THOMAS STEVENS Gunner of y^e *Thomas & Susan* of London, GEORG PYE Commander.
11. JANE ye Wife of Capt. HENRY HAWLEY.
13. THOMAS WALKER.
15. JOHN ROBINSON.
16. HUMILITY HOBS, from ye Almshous.
18. JONE WILEY.
20. ANDREW WOOD.
JOHN WASHBURN.
DANIEL SUILLIVANT.
THOMAS ENGLISH, from ye Almshous.
21. SARAH BUNTING.
EDWARD RUSSEL, from ye Almshous.

---

* [Seems to have been originally written CORN, and then altered to CARN.]

1678.

- May. 22. EDWARD MATTHEWS.
  - 27. THOMAS JAMES.
  - 28. JOHN HOLLIN.
  - 29. JOHN WILLIAMS, from yᵉ prison.
  - 31. KATHARINE yᵉ daughter of DENIS & ALICE DAYLEY.
- June. 4. WILLIAM RAYNER.
  - 5. MARY COPELAND.
  - 15. HUMPHREY ROSSER.
  - 17. ELISABETH yᵉ daughter of URSULA PEASE.
  - 19. THOMAS BAL.
  - 20. ROBERT HORTON Mate to WILLIAM SHACKERLY. HENRY GRIFFIN.
  - 21. JOHN yᵉ Son of Mʳ THOMAS WARNER & ANN his Wife. THOMAS ⁎ a Servᵗ to L.Col. JOHN CODRINGTON. MARY yᵉ daughter of JOHN & JUDITH SMITH.
  - 23. MARY JACKSON.
  - 25. ARTHUR yᵉ Son of RICHARD & SARAH MENDAM.
  - 28. JOHN yᵉ Son of ANN AUSTIN, Widdow.
  - 29. ANN yᵉ daughter of THOMAS & ELISABETH CLARK. PHILLIP LE VOH. ROGER yᵉ Son of THOMAS & LÆTITIA CLARK. GEORG yᵉ Son of GEORG & ELISABETH DODSON.
- July 3. JOHN FILKS, a Servᵗ to RICHARD WHITING. KATHARIN MORRIS.
  - 5. NOAH FLETCHER.
  - 7. JOHN WILSON.
  - 8. JAMES REYNOLDS. SAMUEL PEACOCK, mate of yᵉ *Africa* C JOHN HURLOCK Comᵈᵉʳ·
  - 9. DAVID ROGERS.
  - 10. JOHN DAN.
  - 12. FRANCES yᵉ daughter of Mʳ JOHN OGILSBY & ELISABETH his Wife.

⁎ [Blank in original.]

1678.

- July 13. Two daughters of JOHN PEARSON, infants.
  - 15. GUALTER GRIFFIN.
  - 15. MARGARET SUILLIVANT.
  - 16. ALICE y daughter of Mr ROBERT CODRINGTON.
  - KATHARIN HOSKINS.
  - 17. MARGARET ADAUDLY.
  - HENRY OVERBURY.
  - 20. RICHARD HUGHS.
  - BENJAMIN MIDDLETON, an Infant.
  - 21. ISABELLA LEVANT.
  - 22. ANN SMAL.
  - EDMUND SHIP.
  - 24. An Irishwoman.
  - 27. ELISABETH FEE.
  - 28. Mr WILLIAM DAVIS Citisen & Merchant of London.
  - 29. RICHARD HOWES.
  - 30. WILLIAM ASTIN.
- August. 1. Capt. THOMAS BROWN, from ye Almshous.
  - ANTHONY HALL.
  - 2. DANIEL NEAL, from ye Almshous.
  - 3. MARTHA NEAL.
  - RICHARD MENDAM, a child.
  - 5. MARGARET BLAND.
  - WILLIAM BUNNEL.
  - 7. MARY CONNET.
  - M^s SARAH FRITH.
  - 9. JOHN TAYLOR.
  - 12. ELISABETH GUY.
  - 14. Mr THOMAS LARKHAM.
  - 16. MARY HORN, Widdow.
  - ANDREW, from ye Almshous.
  - ALICE TOWNSEND.
  - 17. MARY WHITE.
  - WILLIAM LEIGH ye Son of CHARLS & MARTHA LEIGH.
  - 19. JOHN RADFORD.

1678.

August. 19. SARAH COOK.
   EDWARD CHAMBERLAIN.
   20. Mr RICHARD DUTTON.
   BARTHOLOMEW JONES.
   22. ALEXANDER HILGROVE.
   26. THOMAS WILLIAMS.
   MARY HACKWOOD.
   28. LAKE ye Son of Capt. WILLIAM MARSHAL.
   30. ELISABETH ye daughter of JOHN & SUSANNA NEWPORT.
   31. RALPH HENLY.
September. 1. HENRY BANKS.
   MARY SMITH.
   4. KATHARIN CRADDOCK.
   5. LAWRENCE PETERSON.
   7. SUSANNA MOYSE.
   8. SAMUEL JONES.
   A Child of DANIEL & MARGARET SUILLIVANT.
   FRANCES ye daughter of ROBERT & ELISABETH CODRINGTON.
   10. ANN MARSHAL.
   12. JANE y Wife of ROBERT HOLMAN.
   15. ELISABETH ye Wife of JOHN PEERS, Esqr
   19. NICHOLAS BREWER.
   21. THOMAS HOG.
   22. HAGAR a Christian Negro.
   ELISABETH PIERCE.
   25. HANNAH ye daughter of Mr BERNARD SCKENKEN.
   RALPH ye Son of CHRISTOPHER & JANE SMITH.
   26. ROBERT ALDRIDG.
   28. Mr EDWARD BUSHEL Merch^t
   HUGH DAVIS.
   29. NICHOLAS CONEY.
   30. M^s PICKERING.
   JONE PERRY.
October. 1. JONE ye wife of CHRISTOPHER HODGES.
   ELISABETH ye daughter of ROBERT & ELISABETH WEBSTER.

1678.

October. 2. Mr THOMAS ORESBY.
   3. Mr HUGH STONE.
    ROBERT READING.
    ELISABETH WEBSTER.
   9. ROGER ye Son of ROGER COWLEY Esqr & SUSANNA his Wife.
    ANN ye Wife of THOMAS HATTON.
  10. MARY ye Wife of PATRIC GOLANE.
  13. ANN ye daughter of JOHN SMITH.
    MARGARET ye Wife of ROBERT CHANDLER.
  14. JOHN HART.
  15. DEARMAN SUILLIVANT, out of prison.
  16. CHRISTOPHER ye Son of Major JOHN HALLET & MARY his wife.
  17. JOHN LOCKTON.
    JANE ELLIOT.
  19. SAMUEL OKELLY.
  21. MARY ye daughter of WILLIAM RICHARDSON.
  23. JAMES BAYNS.
    JOHN KELLEY from ye Almshous.
  24. ELISABETH BLANCHFLOWER.
    THOMAS MARSHAL.
  31. Mr JOSEPH RUMSEY from ye prison.
    WILLIAM SHIRLEY.

November. 1. SARAH BLACKMAN.
    JOHN ye Son of WILLIAM & DORCAS MORRIS.
   3. SUSANNA ye daughter of HENRY & ANN BUNTING.
   4. JOHN ye Son of JOHN & ELISABETH MURRIL.
   5. ELISABETH HUNT.
   6. GEORG ELLIOT.
   7. ZECHARIAH DUNSTHORP.
  15. KATHARIN ye Wife of DANIEL ONEAL.
  16. MARY ye Wife of ABEL DEAN.
  18. JOHN ye Son of JOHN BAILY & JANE CONNER.
  19. MARY ye Wife of Mr RICHARD TUDOR.

1678.

November. 23. MARY yᵉ Wife of JOHN BRUSH.
    24. Mʳ THOMAS BONNET.
    26. THOMAS GRANT.
        ANNA HENRY yᵉ daughter of ANTHONY HENRY.
    27. WILLIAM yᵉ Son of JOHN & ANN SHREWSBURY.
    30. JAMES JONAS.
December. 2. ELISABETH SMITH.
        ROBERT CLARK.
    3. GEORG POET.
    5. FRANCIS PETERSON.
    6. Mʳ JOSEPH HUSSEY.
    11. HANNAH HARRIS.
        WILLIAM BROUGHTON.
    12. ELISABETH yᵉ daughter of MARY TANNER.
    15. JANE DAVIS.
    16. JOHN WALKER.
    17. MARY yᵉ daughter of WILLIAM BLACKMAN.
        A poor woman from Dʳ DE VILLERMARSK.
    19. PHOEBE yᵉ Wife of Mʳ WILLIAM CAPS.
    24. THOMAS yᵉ Son of THOMAS & JANE PARIS.
    25. ANN yᵉ Wife of Mʳ JOSEPH WARREN.
    26. ABIGAIL yᵉ Wife, and ELISABETH yᵉ daughter of THOMAS COOPER.
    29. NATHANIEL LANE.
        ELISABETH MACKARTEE.
    30. BENJAMIN GODBEHERE.
January. 4. WILLIAM PARSONS.
    7. HENRY FERN.
    8. ROBERT GILBERT.
    10. BENJAMIN yᵉ Son of BENJAMIN & AMEY JONES.
    11. EDWARD MACKLOGHLIN.
        ELISABETH yᵉ Wife of JOHN ADAMS, alias ADAMSON.
    12. ELISABETH yᵉ Wife of CHRISTOPHER BANCROFT.
        JOHN HORTON.
        ELISABETH RUMLEY.

1678.

January. 14. Mrs Barnet ye Wife of Mr William Barnet.
  15. Mr Edward Crisp, Merch^t^
    Charls ye Son of Charls Cavenaugh.
  17. David Mayo.
  30. Samuel Collins.
  31. Cornelius Suillivant.
February. 4. David Miller.
  6. John ye Son of Mr John Ham & Susanna his Wife.
    Bernard Cornelius, a Norman belonging to y^e^ *Endeavor* of N. England, Sam. Smith, Com^r^
  9. Edward Berridg.
  10. Elisabeth ye daughter of Edward & Jone Gislingham.
  12. Margaret ye Wife of Peter Beal.
  13. Rebecca ye daughter of Robert & Grace Griffith.
  14. Ann Patric Servt to Susan Hall.
    Barbara ye daughter of Mary Tailor.
  15. Edward Farthing belonging to y^e^ *Endeavor* of London, James Gilbert Com^r^
  20. Mary ye daughter of Mr John Smith & Philippa his Wife.
    James ye Son of Roger & Sarah Dyer.
  21. Michael Rogers, belonging to his M^ties^ Frigat, y^e^ *Europa*, Capt. Will. Long Com^r^
  26. John Buckly Servt to Mr Brooks.
  27. Jonathan ye Son of Thomas & Sarah Ellarce.*
  28. John Richardson.
March 3. Georg Adson.
  6. Henry Smith.
  9. Jonathan ye Son of Robert & Elisabeth Pain.
  10. William Rose.
    Elisabeth Brown.
    Elisabeth Tester.
  12. Georg Bradley.
  13. Elisabeth ye daughter of Mues Walford.
  21. Mary Letherland.

---

* [This name *may* be read Ellaree.]

1679.

March. 26. WALTER BUSH.
26. 28. Capt. ANDREW RICHES Com^r of y^e *White Fox* of London, & his Son SAMUEL RICHES, who were both killd by ye bursting of a gun.
26. 31. JACOB BASTIONS, Servt to Mr LATIMER RICHARDS of St Georges.
April. 1. JAMES FOWLER.
   GRISSEL ALLEN.
2. ELISABETH WILSON, from ye almshous.
   SARAH ye daughter of CHARLS & MARTHA LEIGH.
5. RICHARD THOROGOOD.
12. JOHN SUTTON.
14. ZEBULON ye Son of Mr JOHN CUNNINGHAM & ANN his Wife.
   ELISABETH ELLIOT, Widdow.
15. THOMAS ye Son of DANIEL & ELISABETH FRISSEL.
17. THOMAS STRANFELLOW.
   ELISABETH WILLIAMS.
18. ELISABETH ye daughter of STEPHEN & MARY WILSON.
20. MARY ye Wife of Mr JOSEPH SMITH, Merch^t
   CORNELIUS MACKELLY.
21. ELISABETH DICK.
   STEPHEN ye Son of JOHN LIZARD.
22. ELISABETH BEACHAM.
   WILLIAM AVERY.
24. HENRY GITLY.
26. MARY UNDERWOOD.
27. THOMAS FERRIMAN.
May. 1. JOSEPH ye Son of GEORG & HANNAH OATS.
2. EDWARD LEEK.
   GEORG SPAR.
3. JOHN BRUNCOCK.
4. ELIAS BLACKWELLER.
6. ANN TROWSDALE.
   THOMAS BOON.

1679.

May 7. Mr ROBERT BLAKE.
    9. MARY ye Wife of DENIS COCKLIN.
   15. HUMPHREY KELLEY.
      JANE ATKINS.
      Mr GREGORY HALLET.
   23. ANN RAYMENT.
   24. TEAG MULLINS.
      ROBERT DANES.
   25. PHILLIS ye Wife of JOHN KINGSTON.
   29. JOHN JONES
   30. JAMES ye Son of Mr WILLIAM BOWEN.
   31. Mr JOHN GILLIARD of y^e *Guianabo* of London, SAM. JONES Com^r

June 1. SAGE ye Wife of JAMES ANDREWS.
      ELISABETH ye Wife of THOMAS LAMBERT.
      RICHARD HENDY of y^e *Coast Frigat*, Capt. VARLOW, Com^r.
    2. SUSAN ye wife of EDWARD WALKER.
      ISAAC HOGDON.
      GEORG POTTER.
    3. PRUDENCE ye wife of Mr GEORG PEARSON.
    4. EDWARD REEVS.
      Mr WILLIAM BRAG.
    5. ARTHUR Servt to JOHN RICHARDSON.
    7. JOYCE ye daughter of EDENDEN.
    8. Capt. HENRY HAWLEY.
    9. ANN ye Wife of HENRY BRADLEY.
   11. HENRY KIRBY, a Seaman.
      WILLIAM WATSON of y^e *Ruth*, THEOPHILUS POMEROY, Com^r
      ISAAC COLE belonging to a Guiney-ship, JEHU HAL Com^r.
   12. JOHN ye Son of ANTHONY & ELISABETH SUILLIVANT.
      ANN ye Wife of THOMAS HENWOOD.
   13. ELISABETH ye Wife of Mr EDWARD PARIS.
   16. JOHN BROWN of y^e *Friendship*, JOHN WILLIAMS Com^r.
   17. THOMAS ATKINS.
   18. ELISABETH TAGGARD.

1679.

- June. 19. RICHARD MAY.
  - 20. NICHOLAS FRANCKLIN.
  - 21. SARAH yᵉ daughter of Mʳ GABRIEL MORGAN & MARY his Wife.
  - 23. WILLIAM MANSFIELD.
  - 24. Mʳ RICHARD PIERCE.
    KATHARIN CARVIS.
    EDWARD yᵉ Son of EDWARD WALKER.
  - 27. ROBERT LANE, from yᵉ almshous.
  - 28. BARNS PASTOR.
    MATTHEW BENTHAM, Servᵗ to L.Col. CODRINGTON.
  - 29. SARAH BLACKWELLER.
  - 30. ANTHONY HAYLEY.
- July. 2. ELISABETH yᵉ daughter of GABRIEL & MARY MORGAN.
  - 3. Capt. EVAN MORGAN.
  - 4. Capt. WILLIAM LONG Comʳ of his Mᵈⁱᵉˢ Ship yᵉ *Europa*, buried in yᵉ Sea.
  - 6. GRACE HARVEY, Widdow.
  - 7. MARY yᵉ Wife of THOMAS STRATTON.
  - 8. JOHN DICK.
    JOHN BUCKLY, from yᵉ almshous.
  - 9. GABRIEL MORGAN.
    DAVID FOGO, from yᵉ almshous.
    Mʳ THOMAS BALDWIN.
  - 11. JANE yᵉ Wife of HENRY KARVIS.
    Mʳ JOHN CUNNINGHAM.
  - 12. Mʳ EDMUND DAWSON.
  - 13. TIMOTHY GARMAN.
  - 14. CASSANDRA yᵉ wife of EDWARD WILLIAMS.
    Mʳ JOHN COTTON.
  - 15. JANE BAGGET.
    ROBERT yᵉ Son of JANE DEMPSTER, Widd.
  - 17. JANE WARD.
  - 18. JOHN ROBERTS, from yᵉ prison.

1679.

July 18. PETER GASCOIGN.
  19. MARY BUCKLY.
   MARTIN STITH.
   PHILLIP BRIAN.
  21. RICHARD VANLANG.
   SARAH ABBEY.
   WILLIAM BUNNEY, from ye almshous.
   ELENOR daughter of MARY BRIAN, Widd.
  22. MARY MORRIS a Christian Negro.
   PHILIPPA ye Wife of Mr JOHN SMITH, Mercht.
  23. Sr THOMAS WARNER, K^t
  24. GEORG SMITH, a Trumpetter to C. ROBINSON.
  25. MARY ye daughter of JOHN WOODLAND.
   Mr JOHN RICHARDSON.
  26. WILLIAM ABRAHAM.
   JOHN ye Son of MARY WOODYARD.
  27. NATHANIEL THOMAS.
August. 4. WILLIAM ANDERSON.
   ANN ye wife of PATRIC CAMPEL.
   SARAH ye daughter of C. JOHN JOHNSON & SARAH his Wife.
  5. EDWARD PARSONS.
  6. FRANCIS ye son of C. FRANCIS BURTON & JUDITH his Wife.
  7. JOHN VINCENT.
  8. ELISABETH ye daughter of Mr RICHARD & HANNAH BUNNY.
   Col. GEORG THORNBURGH.
  9. RALPH MONTREVERS.
   JAMES DODSWORTH.
   JOHN WILLIAMSON.
  15. MARY ye Wife of Mr JOHN COCK.
   THOMAS BANKS.
  17. ELISABETH FREEMAN.
   Mr GULLIVER.
  18. ISAAC ye Son of ANTHONY SANDS.
   DANIEL LAWRENCE.

1679.

August. 18. JANE, from y⁶ almshous.
JAMES, ditto.
19. ELISABETH DICK.
20. TEAG CONNER.
21. ELISABETH JEFFRYS.
MANUS CALLEN.
23. MARY y⁶ Wife of JOHN WORSAM, Esqʳ
26. JOHN BAL.
27. ELISABETH yᵉ daughter of Mʳ WILLIAM BARNS & SARAH his Wife.
28. THOMAS STRAFFORD.
CHARLS HARRISON.
MUNDUSIA yᵉ daughter of JOHN & ELISABETH SMITH.

September. 2. CICILY yᵉ Wife of JOHN MILES.
4. ESTHER yᵉ daughter of FRANCIS & ELISABETH HAL.
5. Mˢ JULIAN NELSON Widd. aged 92 years.
6. Mʳ ROBERT PALMER aged 95 years.
7. JOHN GREENWOOD.
JANE DEMPSTER.
Capt. THOMAS CRUTCHFIELD Comʳ· of yᵉ *Lisbon Merchᵗ* of London.
11. EDWARD HARDING aged 70 & odd years.
DOROTHY SUTTON.
12. JOSEPH yᵉ Son of JOSEPH & MARGARET SALMON.
14. NICHOLAS BARNWEL from Mʳ REYNOLDS'S.
16. DANIEL OREE, from yᵉ almshous.
ESTHER MORGAN.
ELISABETH ERPEY.
MARTIN SWAIN.
17. THOMAS SMITH.
18. MARY y⁶ Wife of JOHN HARE.
19. ALICE yᵉ Wife of THOMAS FOLINSBY.
20. Mʳ HENRY TURPIN aged 87 years.
23. KATHARIN CARYL.

438 PARISH REGISTERS.

1679.

September. 24. Mr EDWARD PRESTON.
   GEORG ye Son of Capt. FRANCIS BURTON & JUDITH his Wife.
25. ALEXANDER MACKRERY from L.Col. JELLY'S.
   ELISABETH RUL.
   RICHARD ye Son of RICHARD & JONE ELLIOT.
26. SUSANNA ye daughter of Mr THOMAS & SUSANNA REYNOLDS.
   WILLIAM LAWLESS, out of prison.
27. JOHN COOPER.
29. JOHN ye Son of Mr THOMAS & JANE FORRESTER.

421.

Año: 1680

BARBADOS

 LIST of the Inhabitants in and about the Towne of St Michaells wth their children hired Seruants, Prentices, bought Seruants and Negroes.

	childrn	hired Seru^{ts} & Prefit	bought Seru^{ts}	Neg^{rs}
ALLAN LYDE & wife............	3			6
HENRY MOSELY & wife	..		..	6
Wm BISHOP & wife......... ...	5		..	5
EDWARD DUFFEILD & wife......	1			2
BENJ^a GRACE jun^r & wife........	2		..	2
ANTHONY MICHELL & wife......	5		..	2
THOMAS GARROTT & wife	2		..	2
SARAH WAKER			0	2
ABRAHAM LANGFORD		..	..	1
GEORGE PEARCE & wife		1	0	2

	children	hired Serv[ts] & Prefit	bought Serv[s]	Neg[rs]
JOHN BARKER		1	0	1
JOHN BORROWS................		2		1
GEORGE TUTHILL..............	..			3
OLLIUER HUTTON & wife	1			4
SAMUELL BRUNTTS & Comp[a] ...	..			4
DANIELL CLANEY & wife	1		..	2
REBECCAH JONES		..	..	3
JOHN ORPEN & wife............	..	3	2	5
JOSEPH SMITH	..	..		4
W[m] BULKLY	..	1		1
ALLEXANDER HARBIN & wife ..	..	..		1
W[m] HARDING & wife	1	1		6
WALTER BENTHALL & wife		..		6
SAMUELL CARPENDER..........	..	..		4
JOHN COSTEEN & wife..........	..	3		8
JOSEPH HARBIN & wife	3	1	..	8
W[m] STICKLAND & wife.........	1		..	3
THOMAS EMPEROR & wife	2		1	10
RICHARD WILLIAMS & wife	3	..	2	3
STEPHEN LANGTON & wife......	..	..	1	4
HENRY DEUILLERMAS & wife ..	2	1	1	2
JAMES SICKLEMORE	..	..		2
JOHN BUSSHELL Senior & wife ..	2	..		7
THOMAS DOXY & wife	1	1		3
JOHN HUTTON & wife	5	..	..	..
THOMAS WATTSON & wife	1	2	2	8
LUCY BUTTLER.................	..	1		3
JOHN WHETTSTON & wife	2			5
HENRY CROFTS & wife	2	..		5
CHRISTOPHER FOWLER	..	1		5
RICH[D] DEARSLEY & wife	..	..		2
THOMAS SMITH & wife	1	5		3
PETER BAKER & wife		..		2

	children	hired Serv^{ts} & Presit^s	bought Serv^{ts}	Slaves
Thomas Clarke & wife	1	..	2	1
J^{no} Oglesby & wife	4	3	1	6
Lettecia Bate	..	1	..	4
Rob^{tt} Draper	..	2	..	5
J^{no} Smith	2	3	1	12
J^{no} Haruey	1	..	..	3
Richd Forstall	..	..	2	..
Joseph Groue	..	1	..	4
J^{no} Mercer	..	..	..	1
Thomas Perce & wife	2	4	5	8
Richd Lennon & wife	..	..	..	4
J^{no} Felton & wife	1	3	5	16
James Poke & wife	6	2	1	4
Francis Cristian & wife	7	3	2	3
Muse Walford & wife	4	..	1	1
Anne Owen	..	..	2	6
Charles Collins & wife	2	1	..	8
Richd Shetman & wife	..	..	..	3
Wm Critchlow & wife	2	1	2	7
George Harper & wife	..	2	..	..
Coll^o Batte	..	1	..	1
Cap^{tt} J^{no} Johnson & wife	4	4	3	20
Olliuer Smitth	..	4	..	..
J^{no} Smartt	..	1	..	2
Thomas Brearly & wife	..	1	1	6
Jeremiah Cooke & Comp^a	..	6	..	5
Elizabeth Bancks	2	..	..	4
Wm Smith & wife	..	..	..	1
J^{no} Pitt	..	..	..	3
Owen Dauis	..	..	..	1
Widd^o Crisp	1	..	..	4
Paul Gwyne & wife	1	..	..	6
Wm Gold & wife	..	..	..	5

PARISH REGISTERS. 441

	children	hired serut[ts] & l'rent[s]	bought seru[ts]	Slaues
HUMRY BROWNE & wife	..	..	..	3
JNº COSSENS	..	..	..	1
GEORGE FLETTCHER & wife	..	4	2	12
CAP[T] THOMAS MORRIS & wife	3	3	..	11
JNº RAYMON	..	1	..	
THOMAS MOUNTAINE & wife	..	..	..	1
JAMES SHARPE & wife	2	..	..	3
THOMAS HOLLARD & wife	3	2	11	18
JNº HIGGINBOTHAM & wife	..	..	2	3
JNº NEWBOTT & wife	..	7	..	1
JNº COCK	..	..	..	1
Wid[do] THORNBRUGH	3	..	1	8
THOMAS SEARLE & wife	1	..	..	6
THO: BLAKE & wife	..	..	..	2
THO: ASHENDINE	..	..	..	2
GEORGE MASON	..	..	..	1
M[rs]: MAGETTESS	..	..	..	4
KATH: TOYER	..	..	..	1
THOMAS LAMBORNE & wife	..	..	..	2
RICH[D] BRISTOW & wife	..	2	..	
W[M] HOLLYDAY & wife	4	..	1	
W[M] BROOKE & wife	3	..	..	5
JNº HALLETT Esq[r] & wife	5	3	2	14
ROGER CORBITT & wife	..	..	..	9
ANTH[O] PRINCE & wife	..	1	..	5
W[M] BICKNALL	..	0	1	2
MARTIN CREAMER	..	..	..	2
JNº CHOLEMLEY	..	..	..	2
W[M] EMBEREE	..	..	2	2
JNº CRISP jun[r] & wife	..	..	..	2
RICH[D] PARKER & wife	1	1	..	4
JNº STUARD & wife	..	1	..	8
RICH[D] TRANTT	..	..	1	4

56

PARISH REGISTERS.

	children	hired serv[ts] & Pren[tis]	boug[t] serv[ts]	Slaus
Hugh Archer & wife.........	..	3		6
George Snouks	..	1		
George Nedham & wife	2	1		6
W[m] Sanders		1		1
Widd[o] Turpin		0		
Rob[tt] Tatt's.................		02		
W[m] Price		..		
W[m] Baynes & wife		0	0	0
James Vickars & wife.........		2	2	1
Thomas Bishop & wife	..	..		2
Roger Dyer & wife	..	0		1
Rich[d] Bunney & wife	1	1		3
Charles Jues [?Ives] & wife....	1	1		2
J[no] Hancock & wife	..	1	..	
Rich[d] Nusom & wife	1	..	1	4
Mary Doue		..	..	1
Rich[d] Attwood & wife		2	..	5
M[rs] Dauis	..			1
Samuell Mead & wife	3	..		9
Widd[o] Laroch	..	..	..	2
W[m] Capps	..	..	1	3
J[no] Puddiford & wife.........	..	1	..	3
Daniell Brewer	..	1		1
Gamaliell Ellis		..		2
Widd[o] Bush		1		..
Stephen Scar & wife.........		1		3
Nathaniell Eldred & wife....		1		2
J[no] Johnson & wife	..	..		1
Rich[d] Poore & wife...........	..	1		1
Roger Anderson & wife	1			3
J[no] Boles				2
Nicholas Molder & wife		..		4
J[no] Hudson & wife...........		2		2

	children	hired seru^{tts} & Prentt^s	bough^t seru^{ts}	Slaues
J^{no} Prince & wife		..	..	1
J^{no} Hopcroftt & wife		0	1	2
Rob^{tt} Landall & wife		..	5	..
Rob^{tt} Gray & wife		3		4
Widd^o Smith		..	..	1
Abell Deane		1	..	1
Thomas Forrestor & wife		1	1	5
Xtopher Akers & wife		3		..
J^{no} Creswell & wife		..	..	2
Andrew Hawkins & wife		..	1	1
Hester Lane			..	1
Henry Jacobs & wife			1	5
Thomas Wrightt & wife			..	3
J^{no} Coocke & wife			..	4
Tho: Read & wife		..	..	1
J^{no} Coppin sen^r & wife		..		5
Thomas Simson & wife		..		1
Francis Bestt & wife		..		2
Ambross Addams		..		1
Wm Cragg	..	..		1
Wm Parris	..	..		2
Rob^{tt} Lanier & wife	..	3		..
Xtopher Frankling & wife	..	..		2
Abraham Fifeild & wife	1	..		1
John Olliuer & wife	..	1		1
Widd^o Baines	4	..		4
Beniamin Rawlings & wife	..	..		2
J^{no} Peirceson	..	..		3
Samuell Sourton	..	4		1
Richd Hallett	..	1		4
Benj^a Mattson & wife	2			2
Edward Sturdiuantt	..			1
Hugh Hall & wife	2			8

56—2

	child[r]	hired seruan[ts] & Prett[s]	bought seru[ts]	Slaues
J[no] Barnes	..		1	2
J[no] Deuenish & wife	2		..	4
J[no] Firebrass & wife	..	..	1	
Rob[tt] Hussey & wife	2	..	..	6
Mathew Hauiland	..	2	..	1
Jacob Legay	..	1	1	3
J[no] Man & wife	5	..	..	6
Rob[tt] Beckles & wife	3	..	1	4
Judith Sparrow	1	..	..	11
Henry Fissher & wife	3	..	..	11
Rob[tt] Rich jun[r] & wife	1	..	..	13
Widd[o] Bragg	3	..	..	2
Samuell Gifford & wife	2	..	1	5
Martin Hayes & wife	1	..	1	
Samuell Stoker & wife	2	..	..	4
Thomas Warner & wife	3	..	1	7
W[m] Cannings & wife	2	..	..	8
Bridgett Collett	2	1		4
Thomas Lowe & wife	..	1		2
Samuell Ballard & wife	1	1		1
Thomas Fercharson & wife	5	2	..	17
Phillip Trauers	..	..	1	10
George Newton	..	..	1	1
J[no] Bayley & wife	2	1		5
Edward Parsons & wife	2	2		12
Widd[o] Barrowman	..	..		2
Gabriell Newman & wife	3	..		4
Mary Chapman	1	..	..	5
Rich[d] Addamson & wife	4	1	..	9
Benj[a] Hassell	..	..	1	2
Rob[tt] Stone & wife	1	..	..	1
Thomas Dod & wife	5	1		2
W[m] Wilson & wife	2	3		11

	children	hired seruantˢ & Prenttˢ	bougtt seruttˢ	Slaues
Joseph Borden & wife	2	1		14
Samuell Parris	..	1	..	1
Rich⁰ Tudar & wife	2	..	3	16
Mathew Deane & wife	2	2	0	2
Jn⁰ Hasell & wife	3	2	..	20
Samuell Shenton & wife	..	2	..	3
Guy & wife	..	1		..
Wᴹ Litton & wife	5	1		1
Henry Lelland & wife	3	..		3
Jn⁰ Legay	2	1		11
Thomas Heslerton & wife	1	..		3
Edmond Jefferres & wife	..	..		6
Widd⁰ Seay	2	..		6
Thomas Pilgrim & wife	..	2	..	..
George Bread & wife	..	..	..	3
Wᴹ Jordan & wife	1	1	1	5
Wᴹ Cope & wife	5	..	..	6
Thomas Eles & wife	1	4	..	4
Thomas Horner & wife	2	..		3
Wᴹ Preswell	..	2		..
Theophilus Barrodall	3	..		2
Downes Daniell	..	..		2
James Taggartt & wife	..	..	..	4
Nathaniell Claire & wife	..	3	1	10
Jn⁰ Hudson & wife	2	1	2	3
Olliuer Gilhampton & wife	3	..	1	3
Thomas Clouan & wife	2	..	..	1
Nicholas Maynard & wife	5	..		2
George Oates & wife	..	1		2
Barnard Man & wife	..	1		2
Jn⁰ Dauis & wife	..	..		2
Jn⁰ Murrell & wife	2	..	..	2
Widd⁰ Bouey	..	..	1	..

	children	hired seruants & Prentt[s]	bougtt serutt[s]	Slaues
W[m] Harding Vintner & wife....		1	1	1
Thomas Tickner & wife	..	..	2	3
Vallentine Copman & wife....	1	..	..	4
W[m] Shipton & wife	1	2	..	5
George Cheyney & wife	1	1	..	2
J[no] Bradham	..	1	..	..
Owen Dayley & wife..........	1	1	1	1
Francis Wood & wife	1	..	..	4
Henry Byrch & wife..........	1	1	..	6
Rob[tt] Hole & wife	1	..	1	8
Mathew Willox & wife	1	..	1	3
J[no] Heaton	..	..	1	1
Rich[d] Wilson & wife	2	1	..	4
W[m] Biddle & wife	2	1	..	3
M[rs] Hoskins	2	..	1	0
Benj[a] Elly & wife	1	..	1	
George Hannah & wife	2	4	2	10
J[no] Hunter & wife............	..	..	1	4
Rich[d] Alford & wife..........	2	3	3	5
Thomas Whiteing & wife......	1	8	3	14
Thomas Bringhurst & wife....	..	5	2	5
J[no] Haywood & wife	1	..	..	3
Henry Freman & wife	2	5	1	3
J[no] Plumly p El: Browne ...	..	..	..	9
Edward Towne & wife	..	..	..	3
Laughline Bayne & wife	..	1	..	0
Thomas Walden & wife	1	..	..	2
Benj[a] Jones & wife	..	..	..	1
W[m] Cliggatt & wife	1	3	1	
Lawrance Reed & wife........	..	..	..	1
Rob[tt] Hewitt & wife	1	3	..	13
Edward Huntt & wife	3	..	..	5
Nathaniell Branker & wife ..	1	..	..	5

	children	hired serv^ts & Pren^ts	bough^t serv^ts	Slaues
NATHANIELL SMITH & wife	2	..	..	1
STEPHEN GASCOYNE Esqr & wife .	..	7	1	0
EDWINE STEED Esqr & wife	2	1	..	7
BENJ^A DWEIGHTT & wife	3	..	..	12
THOMAS REYNOLDSON & wife ..	..	..	3	3
HENRY STEPBING	..	3	..	1
RICH^D FORD & wife	1	..	..	2
HENRY HARUEY & wife		1	..	3
J^NO FREDERICK & wife..........		6	..	
THOMAS PARKER	..	1	3	1
JAMES ELY & wife	3	1	1	13
JONATHAN HUTCHINSON........	..		..	5
URSELAH PEA	..		..	4
RICH^D: HALL & wife	3		..	7
W^M WELDING	1		..	3
THEOPHILUS BOWDEN..........	..		..	1
J^NO LEGARD	..		..	2
J^NO SANDERS & wife............	2	..	..	1
STEPHEN CLAY & wife..........	1	..	..	2
JACOB: MACKERNESS & wife	..	2	..	4
W^M SIDNEY & wife	5	3	..	7
THOMAS BIFFIN & wife	2	..	..	2
RICH^D BARRETT	..	..	..	7
THOMAS ROWSE & wife	..	7	..	3
M^RS TOTHILL	1	..	..	1
SAMUELL SMARTT & wife	1	2		13
SUSANAH BEEKE		..		5
W^M MICHLEBORNE & wife	..	1		2
J^NO FISHER	..	..		1
JACOB: LEGAY sen^r	2	1		3
CHRISTOPHER JACSON & wife....	1	1		5
W^M MACKERNESS	1	3		2
Widd^o HAYWOOD	..	..		2

	children	hired seru^(tts) & Pren^(tts)	bought seru^(tts)	Slaues
Edward Prestton	..	..	..	1
Widd° Baldwine	..	1	..	7
J^(no) Townsend & wife	2	..	..	4
J^(no) Munrow & wife	..	..	..	1
J^(no) Shroesberry & wife	1	..	..	1
J^(no) Mills & wife	..	..	..	7
Isaac Roett..... ,............	..	1	1	5
Charles Lee & wife	..	..	..	1
Benj^a Bird & wife	2	1	..	1
Basell Dunkly & wife	..	1	..	
Martin Dallison & wife	..	2	..	6
Mary Lister	..	..	..	1
Anne Kew	..	..	..	1
Kathrine Whiteing...........	..	..		2
J^(no) Hunter	2	..	..	1
J^(no) Spencer & wife.............	2	3	..	3
Wm Maxwell & wife	1	..	..	1
Doctor Richard Lawford	..	..	..	1
Thomas Parris & wife	2	..	..	1
Edward Rainsford	..	2	..	4
Samuell Dyer	..	1	..	2
Edward Peireson & wife	1	..	..	1
Marke Noble & wife	1	1	..	4
Francis Louell...............	..	1	..	9
John Chason & wife	2	1	..	..
Wm Beale	..	..	..	2
Daniell Jones	..	1	..	5
Peter Swaine & wife..........	3	..	1	4
J^(no) Ladston & wife	..	..	..	3
Ellinor Walter	2	..	..	2
J^(no) Williams & wife	4	..	..	2
J^(no) Lamply & wife	1	..	..	1
Mary Busher	..	..	..	3

	children	hired seruen[ts] & Pren[ts]	bought seru[ts]	Slaues
Mary Wilson			..	1
J[no] Rawlings & wife		..	2	1
James Miller & wife	..	1		1
Edward Fennell & wife	1	..	..	4
Jonathan Taylor & wife	..	..	..	3
W[m] Simmes & wife	1	..	..	8
Rob[tt] Webster & wife	..	..	1	..
Rob[tt] Paine & wife	6	1	1	2
J[no] Paine & wife				1
J[no] Stedham				2
Madam Fits James				2
THE JEWES	Jewes			
Jacob Franco Nunes	4			1
Aron Nauaro	7			11
Aron Barruch	5			5
Paul Deurede	2		..	3
Isaac Perera	2		..	4
Dauid Ralph Demereado	3		..	11
Lewis Dias	6		..	8
Abraham Qay	2		..	2
Abraham Barruch	3		..	3
Dauid Israell	5		..	3
Anthony Rodrigus	3			10
Abraham Sousa	2			2
Leah Medinah	7			
Isack Abof	2	..		1
Abraham Burges Aron	2	..		2
Moses Hamias	2	..		1
M[rs] Leah Decompas	3	..		1
Hester Bar Simon	5	..		1
Daniell Boyna	3	..		11
Abraham Lopes	2	..		1
Abr: Valuerde	2	..		4

	Psons	slaues		Psons	slaues
JUDIEAH TOREZ	2	2	SAMUELL NAUARRO	4	1
MOSES MERCADO	5	2	RACHELL BURGES	6	2
JAELL SERANO	1	5	MORDECAH PALACHE	1	
ELIAH LOPEZ	5	2	REBECAH PACHECO	2	4
ISAAC GOMEZ	3	2	REBECAH BARRUCH	1	1
JOSEPH SENIOR	3	4	JACOB PACHECO	5	4
ISAAC PERERA	6	3	RACHELL LOPEZ	4	1
ISACK MEZA	3	4	JACOB FONCECO VALE	5	4
SOLOMAN CORDOZA	3	2	MORDECAH SARAH	4	1
ABRAHAM OBEDIENTE	2	2	SAMUELL DECHAUIS	2	4
JUDITH RISSON	4	2	DAUID SWARIS	5	2
DAUID NAMIAS	9	5	JUDITH NAUARO	2	1
MOSES ARROBAS	4	2	HESTER NOY	2	
GABRIELL ANTUNES	2	4	JUDIH ISRAELL	2	
JACOB PREETT	1	1	MOSES DESAUIDO	5	3
SARAH ATKINS	1	..	ISACC NOY	6	2
ABRAHAM COSTANIO	2	6			

Total of Inhabit.......... 404.

Mem^d that y^e Town of St Michael only has returnd an Acco^{t.} of Children

Total of Inhabitants .. $\begin{Bmatrix} \text{Men......404} \\ \text{Children ..402} \end{Bmatrix}$ 806.

Total of White servants 412

Total of Negroes .... 1325.

[BARBADOES.]

LIST of Owners and possessors of land Hired Seruants & Apprentices, Bought Seruants & Negroes in yᵉ Parish of Sᵗ. Michaells.*

A	acres land	hired Seruᵗˢ	bought Seruᵗˢ	Neg ⁿ
Thomas Ashendine	5	..		3
Bartho Aldsworth	46	..		16
Anthony Anthony	19	1		15
Cornelious Austrian	6	..		6
Allin Thomas................	7	3		10
Allexander Antor	7	..		2
Jacob. Allen	..	1		3
B	Ac'			
Theo: Barradall	4	..	..	1
Borden Joseph	9	..	..	..
Bonett Edwᴰ Plantᴬ	88	2	1	94
Francis Bond Esqʳ............	160	3	5	93
Collº Wᵐ Bate	125	1	1	60
Francis Burton..............	130	—	—	60
Thomas Batson	35	2	3	20
Jnº Battyne junʳ	32	1	..	21
Jnº Boucher	3	2	..	1
George Birkehead	8	1	..	10
Hugh Brandon	25	1	—	6
Jnº Bird	6			2
Jnº Barron	14		..	6
Humphry Brogdon	10	..	..	14
Allice Baines................	30	1	2	16
Jnº Barnes	15	1	3	11

* [Totals are given in the original at the end of every page of MS., but are not carried forward; as it is impossible to keep page for page with the MS., we have omitted them altogether, with the exception of the sum-totals at end.]

	acres land	hired serv:ts	boug:t Ser:ts	Neg:ro
W:m Barron	19	1	..	15
W:m Barnett	15	..	1	11
J:no Brett	4	..	..	5
Joseph Beedle	8	..	3	4
W:m Busshey	10	1	..	14
J:no Bignall sen:r	7	..	4	11
J:no Bignall jun:r	10	1	2	14
M:rs Burnell	6	..	..	2
W:m Bragg	10	..	..	2
Allexander Barraman	4	..	..	8
Jerreard Boucher	..	..	..	3
Phillip Brewster	5	..	..	3
Cornelious Bryan	14	1	1	9
Daniell Boyna	10	1	..	14

C	ac'	hired serv:ts	boug:tt Ser:ts	Slav.
Capps. William	12	1	..	5
J:no Crisp sen:r	56	1	2	7
Roger Cowley Esq:r	88	1	3	40
W:m Cannings	7	..	..	5
M:rs Coather	15	1	..	8
Tho: Carnock P~~owis~~*	8	1	..	2
J:no Chace	60	1	2	24
Patick Carney	5	..	..	1
Kathrin Cleaner †	20	1	..	4
W:m Cliggatt	13	1	1	6
Chrictopher Coale	5	..	..	1
James Cissell	22	1	..	16
J:no Cleaner†	10	..	..	—
Tho: Clark ~~dead~~*	20	..	..	—
Nicho. Chandler	5	..	..	—
Henry Cleauer	20	1	..	3

* [Thus erased in the original.]
† [So in the original: but see Cleauer [Cleaver] at the bottom of the page.]

	ac.'	hired seru.ᵗˢ	boug.ᵗᵗ Ser.ᵗˢ	Slau.ˢ
Tho: Coale	39	..	..	4
Jno Coddrington Esqʳ	300	1	5	137
Tho. Child	7	1	..	13
Benjᵃ Caime	13	2	..	8
Wᵐ Cockman	14	3	—	11
George Clarke	20	..	..	6
Symon Cooper	80	3	2	26
Allex: Coachman his Estate	8	..		..
Henry Clark	8			..
Cordiu Paulus	..			7
Jno Cattlin	5			..
Boham Carter	5			..

D.	land	hired Seru.ᵗˢ	bog.ᵗᵗ Ser.ᵗˢ	Slaues
Benjᵃ Dwight	25	1	..	13
Dauis Wᵐ	101	2	..	35
Dunidge Wᵐ	15	1	..	4
Thomas Drayton	12	1	1	7
James Daneff	5		..	4
Jno Dick	5	..	..	2
Giles Deboyce	16	1	2	7
Dennis Dowell	5		..	..
Roger Dunn	7			2

E	acres land	boug.ᵗᵗ serutt.ˢ	hired seru.ᵗˢ	Negros
Wᵐ Embree	10	..	..	1
Jno Elliott	35	1	..	6
James Ard	7	..	1	1
Mʳˢ Ellacott	27	1	2	6
Lawrance England juʳ	10			3
Seaborne Egginton	2			1

	acres land	hired serv⁽ᵗˢ⁾	bough⁽ᵗ⁾ serv⁽ᵗˢ⁾	Negroes
F.				
Rich⁽ᴰ⁾ Forstall	294	4	6	129
George Fletcher	10	..	..	..
J⁽ɴᴼ⁾ Farmer	179	3	5	93
Henry Feake	8	1	..	3
Rich⁽ᴰ⁾ Fifeild	12	..	1	8
J⁽ɴᴼ⁾ Fowler	8	1	..	1
Philip Fonseire	25	1	3	19
Roger Fauell				
Rob⁽ᵀᵀ⁾ Feauer	10	..	..	3
Joane Fuller	30	1	1	16
Francis Frostt	..		..	7
G.				
Benjamin Grace	10	1	2	10
Rich⁽ᴰ⁾ Gayton	26	1	1	26
Ellizab: Gritton	50	1	2	26
Ellz: Goodman	10	1	..	8
J⁽ɴᴼ⁾ Griggory	204	1	4	85
Peter Goding	7	..	..	4
	land Ac'.	hired serv⁽ᵗˢ⁾	boug⁽ᵗ⁾ Serv⁽ᵗˢ⁾	Neg⁽ʳᵒˢ⁾
H.				
Harris J⁽ɴᴼ⁾	20	1	..	6
Hallett J⁽ɴᴼ⁾ Esq⁽ʳ⁾	220	4	5	84
Hutchinson J⁽ɴᴼ⁾	5	..	..	5
Hawksworth J⁽ɴᴼ⁾	63	1	..	18
Samiell Hanson	101	..	..	..
Ralph Hassell	10	1	..	10
Rich⁽ᴰ⁾ Howell & Guy Esq⁽ʳˢ⁾	605	5	20	405
Symon Huntt dead	40	1		24
Francis Harding	10			..

	land Ac'.	hired seru^tts	boug^tt Seru^tts	Neg^rs:
Daniell Hurlow	17	1	1	5
Christopher Hooper	25	1	..	10
Francis Hall	26	1		30
Edward Huntt	5	..	..	..
J^no Hawksworth*............	63	1	1	20
Daniell Harwood............	10	..	..	2
J^no Handy	56	1	2	49
Edward Harding	3	..		3
Samuell Hyatt	30	..		7
Francis Hardwick	10	..		..
J^no Ham.....................	20	..		..
Widd^o Hamblin	4	..		1
Georg Harper	20	1	..	10
Wm Hecthrop	14	..	..	12
Wm Hearst	10	..	..	9
J^no Hill	10	..	1	5
J^no Hare	..			3
J^no Higginbotham............	5			..
Ralph Hollinsworth	10			5
Samuell Hathway	10			5

I	ac'	hired seru^tts	boug, Seru^tts	Negroes
Jacson Xtoph:................	11	1	2	28
Thomas Jelly	200	3	10	70
J^no Jefferres	5	2	—	4
Allex Jennison	3	..		..
J^no Johnson...................	6	..		..
Wm Jacobs	..	..		3
K.				
Humry Kentt................	52	1	1	17

* [This name will also be found six lines from the bottom in p. 454; the number of servants, however, is different.]

	ac'	hired serv.ts	bough.t Serv.ts	Negroes
L				
Leer Thomas	234	2	18	160
Roger Louell................	13	..	..	5
Xtopher Lyne	53	..	..	..
Phillip Lancaster	50	1	2	25
J.no Ledra	27	..	..	7
W.m Litton	4	..	..	3
Rich.d Layton	50	1	2	27
M.rs Lucomb	9	..	..	6
Nicholas Langworthy	12	..	..	11
Georger Lillington	32	..	..	..
M.rs Louell	7	1	..	27
Thomas Links...............	6	..	..	12
Thomas Lucomb	9	..	..	5
M				
Morris Thomas	144	3	..	100
Euan Morgan................	140	2	3	72
Gabriell Martin	10	..	..	5
W.m. Marchall	180	1	2	52
Rich.d Morris	35	1	1	12
J.no Macklaire	6	..	..	6
W.m Murrell	11	..	..	8
M.rs Mullinax	7	..	..	3
Rich.d Mullinax	9	..	..	5
Anthony Michell............	5	1	..	4
Bryan Murphe	9	3	..	14
J.no Murrow..................	3	..	..	3
J.no Murrell	..	..	..	2
N.				
Neale Tho:	50	2	1	16

	ac'			
O				
Samell Osborne	40	0	1	33
Thomas Odiarne	101	1	..	17
Francis Oakley	6	..	..	..
J^{no} Odell	5	..	..	2
P				
Nicholas Prideaux	230	2	6	76
Richd Pearce	15	..		80
Thomas Pilgrim	20	1		34
Edward Parris	35	1		12
J^{no} Piggott	5	..		1
Mrs Panton	3	..		3
George Parris	32	1		23
Adrian Paily	5	..		1
Wid^{do} Pirkins	16	..		6
J^{no} Perriman	7	..		..
Job Perridge	7	..		4
Samuell Perry	4	..		.7
Henry Price	5	..		..
J^{no} Plumley	15	1		6
J^{no} Pollard	5	..		..
Richd Pollard	3	..		..
R				
Edward Rundall	11	1	..	16
Anne Rowe	22	..	..	3
Richd Robinson	12	0	..	3
Wm Robinson	186	2	3	76
Thomas Reynolds	28	..	..	12
Isacc Roett	5	..	..	..

	land ac'	hired Seru[ts]	bougt Seru[ts]	Negroes
S				
Barnard Shenkingh	10	..	..	..
Jno Strode	50	1	2	40
Mrs Stanly	10	..	..	4
Benja Scott	10	..	..	..
Simmons Phill.	39	..	..	18
Mrs Spenswick	30	1	..	22
Simmons Phillip*	39	..	..	18
Steede Edwyne Esqr	12	2	..	30
Capt Jno Sutton	129	1	3	105
Alice Smith	12	..	..	6
Jno Springham	22	1	..	28
Joseph Salmon	10	1	..	12
Allex: Sinklaire	10	1	..	7
Richd Sweeting	19	1	..	8
T				
Turpin Henry Senr	10	..	..	3
Tudar Richard	8	..	..	..
Allex Taggartt	4	..	..	2
Francis Turton	25	..	..	3
Xtopher Terry	12	..	..	3
Widdo Twine	10	..	..	6
George Tyrwhitt	49	1	2	33
Roger Thomas	5	3	..	4
Herculous Tyrwill	5	..	..	4
Henry Turpin junr	7	..	..	5
Dauid Thomas	4	..	..	4
Phill. Trowell	9	..	..	..

PARISH REGISTERS.

W	ac'			
WILLIS J^{no}	5	1	..	5
WARREN JOSEPH	6	1	..	14
FRANCIS WOOD	10	..	..	10
Wm WELDING	10	..	..	..
Wm WITHINGTON	20	..	..	9
MARY WATERS	15	1	..	9
J^{no} WILLOUGHBY	5	..	..	..
GEORGE WALTON	30	..	..	6
GEORGE WILLOUGHBY	26	..	1	8
SAMUELL WARNER	10	..	..	8
J^{no} WILLIAMS	..	..	..	2
DAUID WELCH	5	..	..	..
NATH: WHITE	13	1	..	13
BRIDGET FERRELL (*sic*)	5	..	..	..
Y				
JOHN YOUNG	40	1	..	13
	*			

Tot. of Inhabitants............ 225.
Total of Acres............... 7063.
Total of Serv^{ts}............... 303.
Total of Negro's .... 3746.

---

* [There are 227 names entered, but 2 have been entered twice, viz. HAWKSWORTH and SIMMONS.]

[BARBADOES.]

Masters & mistreses names yt are Owners of Land in the Parish of St Georges in ye Island of Barbados taken by the command of his Excellency Sr Jonathan Atkins Kt ye 23th Day of December: 1679	Number of Acres	Number of White Seruants	Number of Negroes
Robert Dauers Esqr	305	8	200
Mr Robert Dauers Junior	47	..	..
Mr James Robinson	6	2	1
Mr John Robinson	12	..	4
Mr William Dauis	10	1	10
Mr John Koker	..	..	5
Mr Thomas Browne	..	..	3
Mrs Sarah Horswood	..		4
Mrs Margaret Roe..............	40	..	6
M's Ellinor Bowdler	..	..	2
Mr Job: Lullman	6	..	2
Edward Pye Esqr	400	..	190
Mr Thomas Prothers	55	..	15
Mr William Catline............	..	..	5
Mr Henry Euans	106	..	42
Mrs Francis Holdip	19	..	9
Mr John Holdip	..	..	7
Mr Brian Blackman	10	1	10
Mr Fran: Smith Jujo'	6	..	18
Mr Miles Toppin...............	30	..	38
Mr Henry Burrell	15	..	3
Mr Michaell Weyly	10	..	10
Mr Fran: Bell..................	12	..	8
Mr John Jemot	8	..	5
Mr Henry Eastwick	50	1	37
Mr John Goldingham	118	..	76
Mr Richard Eastwick	40	..	20

Masters & mistreses names yt are owners of Land in the Parish of St Georges in ye Island of Barbados taken by the command of his Excellency Sr Jonathan Atkins K, y, 23th Day of December: 1679	Number of Acres	Number of White Seruants	Number of Negroes
Mr MARMADUKE NICHOLES	30	..	13
Mr FRAN: BOND	105	1	60
Mr JOHN GIBBONS	7	..	3
Mr EDWARD CLEYPOLE	325	12	86
Mr RICHARD SUTTON	106	5	60
Mr GEORGE BRIGGS	140	1	64
Mr JOHN BATTINE Senjor	172	1	81
Mr SAMUELL WEBB	..	..	1
Mr THOMAS BLACKMAN	..	1	1
The Lady ANN WILLOUGHBY	317	..	160
Mr SAMUELL COWARD	20	..	4
Mrs GRACE SILUESTER	515	10	220
Mr THO: WILBRAHAM	20	..	6
Mr HENRY HARDING	95	..	54
Collo XTOPHER LINE & Sonn	272	..	..
Mr WALTER CHAMELL	33	..	27
Mrs MARTHA ALT	36	1	22
Mr JOHN WILKINS	40	..	8
Mr JOSEPH MILES	..	2	6
Mr JOSEPH ROBINSON	5	1	3
Major PAULE LYTE	235	8	120
capt JOHN COUSSINS	70	1	50
Mr JOHN COUSSINS Senjor	60	..	50
Mr WILLIAM SNIPE	..	..	4
Mr LATYMORE RICHARDS	12	..	8
Mr SAMUELL SEDGWICK	12	..	5
Mr JOHN SEDGWICK	10	..	5
Mr JOHN LAHANE	10		4
Mr PHILLIP FUSHEIR	7		3
Mr WILLIAM WEAUER	100		30
Mrs MARY RIDGWAY	39		5

Masters & M^rs: names that are owners of Land in ye Parish of St Georges in The Island of Barbados Taken by the Command of His Excellency Sr Jonathan Atkins K^t ye 23th December —1679—	Number of Acres	Number: of White Seru^ts	Number of Negroes
Mrs ELIZABETH BARNES	57	..	40
Mrs ELIZABETH WOLUERSTONE	20	..	6
Mr JOHN PRICE	10	..	1
Mr JOSEPH RIDGWAY	40	..	6
Mr EDWARD ROBERT'S	10	..	7
Mr WILLIAM BRADSHAW	10	..	8
Mr ROBERT CUSTIS	10	..	7
Mr RICHARD LINTOTT	144	2	60
Mr WILLIAM SAPSTER	46	..	14
Mr JOHN MARSHALL	..	..	2
Mr HENRY GORGES	125	..	58
Mr BENJA MIDDLETON	379	..	130
Mr JOHN WILTSHEIR	140	..	43
Mr BASILL DIXWELL	37	..	19
Mr WILLIAM GREENE	100	..	42
Mr ROBERT HOOPER	219	2	117
Mr RICHARD SALTER	217	4	120
Mr SAMUELL HANSON	57	6	105
Mr WILLIAM HARMER	32	1	12
Mr SAMUELL WARNER	4	..	16
Mr JOHN BATTINE Juj^or	190	5	80
Mr JOHN TULL	10	..	8
Mr DAUID MORGAN	20	..	19
Mr THOMAS GUNSTONE	165	1	42
Mr JOHN RENNEY	15	..	8
Mr WILLIAM HARRIS	29	..	2
Mr GABRILL DEANE	22		14
Mr GEORGE KEYSER	104	1	42
Mr JOHN MORECOTT	55	..	27
Mr BARNES Widdoe	15	..	13
Mr RICHARD BRITLAND	25	..	19

Masters & mistreses Names yt are owners of Land in ye Parish of St Georges in ye Island of Barbados taken by the command of his Excellency S, Jonathan Atkins Kt ye 23th December —1679—	Number of Acres	Number of White Servts	Number of Negroes
Mr GEORGE WILLSON	16	2	7
Mr JAMES BUTLER	..	1	3
Mr THOMAS LEARE	127	1	75
Sr PETER LEARE	336	8	123
Mr THOMAS BATTSON	110	4	75
Mr SAMUELL PALMER	70	..	35
Mr CHARLES BUTTALL	48	1	44
Mr GEORGE GREENE his Plantā	258	..	52
Collonell HEN: DRAX	705	7	327
WILLIAM BULKELY Esqr & his sonn	380	2	174
SAMUELL HUSBANTS Esqr	420	3	220
Mr THO: WILTSHEIR Deceased	180	3	93
Mr JAMES BUTT & MARY MIDDLETON	42		2
Mr SAM: SMITH	26		6
Mr JOHN WHEELER	20		..
Mr ROBERT RICH	40		..
Mr JONATHAN ANDREWES	37		..
Mr PEIRSE POOR	9		..
Mrs. APPLEWHITE Widdoe	169		..
Mrs BOOTH Widdoe	10		..
Mr JOHN RENNEY Jujor	7		..
Mr JOHN ROBINS	7		..
Mr JOHN ELLIOTT	10		..
Sr THOMAS BENDISH	72		..
Mr JOHN EVANS	10		..
Mr DARBY MACKONE	7		..
Mr WILLIAM CLARKE	6		..
Mr MICHAELL POORE	6		..
Mr ANTHO: LORD	6		..

Master & mistreses Names y^t are owners of Land in y^e Parish of St Georges in y^e Island of Barbados taken by the command of his Excellency Sr Jonathan Atkins K^t y_e 23th December —1679—	Number of Acres	Number of White Seru^ts	Number of Negroes
Mr ROBERT DAWSON	15	..	..
Mr BITLER & COLETON	15	..	..
Sūme Totall	9569	111	4316

Baptized in The aboue S^d pish p the Register Booke from y^e 25 march 78: to y^e 29: 7^ber 1679 } 36

Buried in S^d Parish in y^t time.................... 66

p J^no COUSSINS & PAULE LYTE, Church Wardens

(In-dorso

    Acco^t of Inhabitants   122
    Land &c in the parish
    of St George.

        Rec^d 3^d June 1680.

BARBADOS.   BAPTISMES.

CHILDREN BAPTIZED in the parish of St Georges from march the 25th. 1678. till September ye 29th 1679

d
MILES ye Sonne of MILES TUPPIN: ....baptized......Aprill—01—78
JOHN ye Sonne of JOHN PITTS ....baptized......Aprill—04—
JOHN ye Sonne of LAWLAND CLAREE ..baptized......Aprill—12—
JDETH ye daughter of JOHN ROBBISON..baptized ......May—30—
ANNE ye Daughter of MICHAEL PORE;.. baptiz'd ......July—06—
MARY, & ELIZABETH ye daughters of THOMAS WHITE ..July—18—
SAMUEL, ye Sonnne [sic] of JAMES DOWNING.. baptiz'd ..July—21—
SARAH ye daughter of MARMADUKE NICOLLS.. baptiz'd ..July—26—
GEORGE ye Sonne of JOHN SEDGEWICKE ....baptized ..July—30—
ELIZABETH ye daughter of WILLIAM GREENE, baptized August—07—
ANNE ye daughter of MATTHEW JENNINS ....baptized august—25—
PAUL ye Sonne of PAUL LYTE ....baptized august—31—
HENRY ye Sonne of DANIEL GUNNE ....baptized ..7ber.—14—
JOHN ye Sonne of EDWARD MORGAN ....baptized...7ber.—22—
MARGARET ye daughter of GEORGE KEYZAR...........8ber—03—
SAMUEL ye Son of BONAVENTURE JELLFES baptized....8ber—13—
JOHN ye Sonne of JOHN WHITING baptized ....8ber—25—
THOMAS ye Sonne of JOHN DOLLSTAN baptized........8ber—31—
HESTER ye daughter of ALEXANDER CROOKSHANK ....9ber—03—
JOHN y^e Sonne of WILLIAM ALLEN baptized ....9ber—24—
HENRY y^e Sonne of JOHN GOULDINGHAM .... xber—04—
ELIZABETH y^e Daughter of ANNE REES widdow ......xber—06—
JOHN y^e Sonne of ROBERT PART baptized ....xber—09—
JOHN y^e Sonne of JOHN BRADFORD baptized........January—26—$\frac{78}{9}$
JOHN y^e Sonne of JOHN JEMMOT baptized ....february—19—
ELIZABETH y^e daughter of CHARLES SAWYERS ....march—06

SARAH y^e daughter of EDWARD GIBBS baptized ....march—21—
GEORGE y^e Sonne of JOHN PITTS baptized ....Aprill. 23–1679
BENJAMIN y^e Sonne of Widdow WILTSHEIR ....Aprill—25—
NATHANAEL y^e Sonne of HENRY HARDING baptiz'd......June—10—
WILLIAM ye Sonne of JONATHAN ANDREWES baptiz'd ...June—15—
ELIZABETH the daughter of JOHN HANDY baptized.........July—20—
MARMADUKE ye Sonne of MARMADUKE NICOLLS............July—22—
RICHARD ye Sonne of JOHN TULLS baptized ....7ber—04—
JOHN ye Sonne of JOHN IPSLEY baptized ....7ber.—07—
WILLIAM ye Sonne of MILES TAPPIN; baptiz'd ....7ber—15—

Coppied out of ye register-   p. me. DANIEL DYKE Cleric
  booke for ye parish of St Georges—
  in ye Island of Barbados. December ye 8th 1679.

BARBADOS.

BURIALLS in ye parish of St Georges from ye 25th. of March: 1678. untill ye 29th September. 1679.

                                                        BURIALLS

JOHN ye Sonne of LAWLAND CLAREE ....buried   Aprill-14-1678
WILLIAM PLOWMAN ....buried ......May—12—
THOMAS, ye Sonne of BARBARY STEELE ......buried ......May—31—
SARAH ye Wife of WILLIAM DAVIS ....buried ......June—13—
JOHN BOOTH ....buried ......June—14—
JOHN ye Sonne of THOMAS NEALE...............buried ......July—07—
ANNE ye daughter of MICHAEL PORE .... buried ......July—07—
SARAH ye daughter of MARMADUKE NICOLLS ....august—01—
RICHARD LACON's daughter ....buried ...august—05—
NICHOLAS WILLSON ....buried ...august—26—

		Burialls
William ye Sonne of John Palmer	buried	7ber—07—
Thomas Wiltsheir Junior	buried	7ber—19—
Joyce Williams	buried	7ber—20—
Amy ye Wife of William Brettland	buried	7ber—28—
Amy ye Wife of Thomas Brookman	buried	8ber—07—
Elizabeth ye daughter of William Greene	buried	8ber—09—
Robert Quarree*	buried	8ber—14—
Richard Harris	buried	8ber—25—
John Whiting	buried	8ber—28—
James ye Sonne of John Holman	buried	8ber—29—
William ye Sonne of William Matthewes	buried	8ber—30—
Elizabeth Jones		9ber—02—
Nathan Morris		9ber—11—
Robert Hoskins	buried	9ber—20—
Charles ye Sonne of Charles Chevny	buried	xber—17—
Anne ye Wife of James Gad	buried	xber—28—
Thomas Wiltsheir Senior	buried	xber—31—
Bridget ye daughter of Edward Morris	buried	January—04—$\frac{1678}{9}$
Peter Littlewood	buried	January—30—
Richard Posslet	buried	January—30—
Bridget ye wife of William Sapster	buried	February—01—
Rose ye daughter of Robert Graves	buried	Febr—02—
Matthew Macklond	buried	Febr—09—
John Crage	buried	Febr—12—
Daniel Morton	buried	Febr—28—
Sarah ye wife of John Weaver	buried	march—02—
Richard Foot	buried	march—19—
Moses Naseby	buried	March—27-1679
Samuell Brookes	buried	Aprill—03-1679
John Teene	buried	Aprill—04—
Mary Graves	buried	Aprill—16—
Peirce Pore	buried	Aprill—17—
George Nice	buried	May—02—

* [The first letter in the MS. is blotted, but I do not think there can be much doubt as to the name.]

	Burialls
PETER MORE ....buried......	May—04-1679
THOMAS COLTON................buried......	May—05—
MARY ye Daughter of SAMUEL BOYS.........	May—06—
ALEXANDER BUCKLE................buried......	May—07—
CHARLES ANDREWES................buried......	May—22—
JOHN HOLLOWELL................buried......	June—05—
BENJAMIN WOLVERSTON ....buried......	June—11—
TEAGE ONAN ....buried......	June—14—
HENRY JONES................buried......	June—24—
FRANCES ye Wife of OLIVER COTTOM ......buried......	July—01—
ABIGAIL ye daughter of EDWARD CLAYPOLE........	July—16—
JANE ye daughter of WILLIAM AVERY	July—25—
MARGARET ye Wife of JOHN PRICE	July—28—
GEORGE ye Sonne of BARBARY STEELE ......buried......	July—31—
JOHN ye Sonne of RICHARD HARLOW.......buried...	august—10—
MARY ye daughter of THOMAS READ ......buried...	august—11—
MARTHA ye wife of ANGUIS BANES ......buried...	august—12—
WILLIAM DAVIS ....buried...	august—25—
LAWRENCE ye Sonne of THOMAS WILTSHEIR Junior, deceasd ....buried......	7ber. 03—
BENJAMIN ye Sonne of THOMAS WILTSHEIR junior deceasd ....buried......	7ber—06—
WILLIAM CRAFTS ....buried......	7ber—07.—
SAMUEL ye Sonne of BONAVENTURE JELLFES buried......	7ber—23—
MARY ye Daughter of ROBERT PART ......buried......	7ber—23—

(66)

Coppied out of ye register- December ye 8th
booke for ye parish of St Georges. 1679.
in ye Island of Barbados. pr. me DANIEL DYKE Cleric.

[endorsed]   BARBADOS
　　　　　　Accot of Christnings . 36.
　　　　　　Burials........... 66.
　　　　　　in the Parish of
　　　　　　St. George.
　　　　　　　Recd 3d June. 1680.

List of the Masters & Mistresses names wth what Lands & Seruants & negrees they haue, & Asoe what Christenings & Burialls hath been in the Parish of S^t. Andrews.

Masters & Mistriṣ names	Acres of Land	Seruants	Negroes:	Christnings	Burialls:
Leu^t BASSILL GIBBES	130	2: men	045	one MARY	1: man
JOHN FOORD Esqr:	280	4: men	120	one ELIZ^a: BURGES	4: men
Cap^tn JOHN GIBBES	200	1: man	093	....	2: Children
THOMAS LEAKE Esqr	150	......	060		
Mr RICHARD EDWARDS	30	......	031	one SARAH	1: SARAH
Cap^tn ABBLL* ALLEYNE	316	1: man	115	....	1: man
Cap^tn SAMUELL WOODWORD	120	......	046		
Mr JOHN HOULDER	57	......	041	....	3: men
The Widdow HUTCHINS	10	......	003		
Mr JOHN SWANN	42	......	014		
Mr SAMUELL AUSTEN	6	......	002		
JOHN BODEN Esqr	250	12:men	143	....	1: man
Mr RICHARD MORRIS	115	1:man	035		
Mr EDWARD JORDAN	28	......	010	....	2:
THOMAS RICHARDS	12	......	008	....	1:
Doctor EDWARD LAMMY	14	......	005		
Mrs MARTHA HAMERLY	86	......	019	....	2:
Mr GEORGE HURST	110	1: man	040		
JOHN SAVERY	53				
Mr WILLIAM HAWKSWORTH	18	......	006		
Cap^tn TYMOTHY THORNHILL	170	1: man	150	....	3: men
Mrs ANNE JOHNSTON	105	......	041	....	3: men
Lt CHARLES SANDIFORD	15	......	004	one RICHARD	
Lt WILLIAM HALL	40	......	009	one ANNE	
Cap^tn ARCHIBALD JOHNSTON	60	3: men	036	two Sonns	1: boy
Mr Wm DOTTEN	109	3: men	60		

* [? ABELL.]

Masters & mistris names	Acres of Land	Seruants:	Negroes:	Christnings	Burialls:
Lt JOHN SANDIFORD	75	1: man	033		
Doctor JOHN HAYWARD	30	......	006	....	1: Boy
JOHN SOMERHAIES Esqr	140	2: men	051	one ANNE	1: Girle
JOHN MERRICK Esqr	266	6: men	167		
Mr ALLEXANDER BARTLETT ..	12	......	006		
Mr JOHN JEPHSON	10	......	003		
WILLIAM ROACH	4	......	001	....	1: Boy
Mr JOHN BURGES	40	......	016		
Mr DAVID SMITH	6	......			
Mr STEPHEN SMITH..........	50	......	008		
Mrs MARY COBHAM	87	2:	26	....	2:
Mr ROBERT HAYTE	18	......	005		
Doctor STEPHEN GIBBES......	28	......	014		
Mr HUGH WILLIAMS	10	......	005		
Mr THOMAS BROOKES	12	......	021		
Mr Wm RAWLINGS............	9	......	004		
The Widdow ELLICOTT	86	......	010		
Mr JOHN TAYTE	16	......	005		
Mr HUGH DUNN	10				
Mr JOHN BELFORD	8	......	002	....	1:
DENNIS MURFEY	14	......	..	I	
Mr THOMAS CADLE	9	......	..	1:	1:
JOHN BOOTHMAN	5	......	001		
DANIELL DONAVAN..........	4	......	000	....	1:
CALEB ROUSE*			003		
Mr JOHN SWAN..............			14		
Mr HENRY COLLETT			02		
JOHN THOMAS			003		
ANDREW FALLIN			001		
DANIELL SHANIS			001		
JAMES STOLLARD			001		
WILLIAM ROCH*			001		

* [A pen has been drawn through these names in the Orig. MS.]

PARISH REGISTERS. 471

Masters & mistris names	Acres of Land	Seruants:	Negroes:	Christnings	Burialls:
GEORGE DENT			006		
JAMES WEBB			001		
Mr ROBERT ENGLISH			004		
PHILIP CHARLES			001		
JOHN SMITH			002		
TEAGUE Boy			001		
Mr JOHN SLYE	26	......	005		
Mr THOMAS COPPIN	12	......	009		
Capt ABELL GAY	100	......	028		
The Widdow GAY	100	......	019		
Lt JOHN MILLS	260	......	90	....	3:
Mr HENRY JEENES	68	......	12	....	2:
Mr ANDREW FOLLYN	26	......	01	one ANDREW	1:
Mr DANIELL SHAHANISSE	10	......		....	2:
Mr GEORGE BUSTIAN	10	......	001		
Mr JOHN WELCH	19	......	001		
Mr ROBERT HIUE	10	......		two Sonns	
Mr ROBERT HEWITT	10	......	005	two Sonns	
Mr HENRY KELSOLL	105	......	030	one Daughter	1:
Mrs HELLEN CANTEY	20	......	007		
Mr BARTHOLOMEW REESE	152	......	051	....	1:
Mr THOMAS BERESFORD	180	2	028	1:	
Lt BENNETT REESE	60	......	006		
Mr NATHANIELL SNOW	180	......	048		
Mr CALEB ROUSE	76	......	003		
Mr EDWARD PAINE	5	.....		1:	
Lt HUMPHERY WATERMAN ..	186	......	092		
Mr ROBERT RICHARDS	60	3:	25		
Mr WILLIAM DAVIES	82	1:	22		
Mr JOHN WAYTE	93	......	050		
Mr PHILLIP ROSSE	12	......	004	....	1:
Mr RICHARD WILLIS	5	......	001		
DANILL DYNEGELL	5	......			

masters & mistris names	Acres of Land	Seruants	Negroes	Christnings	Burialls
RALPH FRETTWELL Esqr		1:			
Mr JOHN LOCKE		......	006		
Mr THOMAS RUSSELL	25	......	005		
Mr ANDREW BLACK	20	......	014		
Mr DAVID MICHELL	10				
JOHN NOBB			003		
W^M CAMPION...................			005		
JAMES BINNEY			003		
W^M HENDERSON			001		
W^M PURSS			002		
THOMAS JOHNSTON			008		
SYMON RUD			001		
RICHARD WILLIS			001		
DANIELL DOUGLE			001		
DERMOTT MAHONT			002		
DENNIS MACKHALA...........			002		
JOHN DANIELL................			003		
THOMAS LAYTON			003		
HENRY LAYTON & JANE WEBB......			005		
Total............. 109	5597	47	2248	18	44

Lands in dispute between the Lady YEAMANS Madam FARMER Madam SPARKS Amo^{ts} } 719

Lands in this parish & the owners lives in other parishes Amounts to .... } 1260

Totall 7576

MATTHEW GREY Minister
JOHN FOORD
BASILL GIBBES.. Churchward

(endorsed) BARBADOS.
Acc^t of Inhabitants .. 109
Christnings .... 18.
Burials 44
Land &c in St Andrew's parish.
Rec^d 3^d June. 1680.

Año: 1680 (?)

True and Perfect List of all yᵉ Names of yᵉ Inhabitants in yᵉ Parrish of Christ Church. with an Exact accompt of all yᵉ Land, white Seruants; and Neg'ˢ within yᵉ Said parrish Taken This 22ᵗʰ Decemb' 1679

A

	acres Land	wᵗᵗ Seruants	Negʳˢ
ADAM......JOHN............	..192	3	64
ARNETT....DAUID..........	..50	1	20
ANDREWS..ROGER..........	..10	......	18
ADAMS......CONRADT.......	..10	......	21
ALCORN....JOHN............	5	2	5
ANDERSON..ADAM...........	5	......	......
ASHBURNER.WILLIAM........	..13	......	6
AUSTINE....THOMAS..........	5	......	......
ALSOPP....RICHARD........	5	......	1
ADDICE....EDWARD..........	..20	......	11
ADDIS JOHN ORPHANT........	3	......	......
ANDERSON..WILLIAM........	2	......	......
AUSTINE....JOHN............	..30	......	16
ALSOPP....EDWARD........	..10	......	2
ASHURST....JOHN..........	..33	......	11
ASHURST....BENIAMIN........	......	......	7
ANDREWS..THOMAS........	5	......	......
ARTHUR....MICHAELL......	......	3	......
ARNETT....PATRICK........	3	1	3
ARCH......JOHN..........	....7½	......	......
ANDERSON..THOMAS........	....2½	......	......
	411	10	..185

B.	acres Land	wth Seruants	Neg's
BISHOPP......JOAN..........	..202	2	65
BUCKWORTH..RICHARD......	..188	5	65
BONNETT....THOMAS dec'd....	..138	......	......
BOND........FRANCIS........	..60	......	......
BROWNE......STEPHEN......	..85	1	16
BARRY........JOHN..........	..14	......	12
BLANCHARD..WILLIAM......	..15	......	4
BULL........CHRISTOPH^R....	..18	......	3
BOXFIELD....THOMAS........	5	......	......
BAKER........ESIAS..........	5	......	1
BRIGSTOCK....RICHARD......	....7½	......	......
BARNES......OLLIVER........	1	......	......
BURTON......AGNES Widdow..	..55	......	17
BURBON......JOHN and Comp^{lt}.	....8¼	......	2
BOURNE......JOHN..........	..12	......	1
BOURN........JOHN Junio'....	7	1	11
BENTLY......MARTYN Esqu'..	..245	5	..154
BROOKS......JOHN..........	..30	......	8
BLAKE........NICHOLAS......	9	......	7
BAYLY........ROBERT........	7	......	2
BOURNE......SAMUELL......	5	......	2
BUENNO......BENIAMIN......	......	......	1
BOULINE (?)..HENRY........	4	1	......
BRIGGS......WILLIAM......	..12½	......	7
BURK........TOBIAS........	4	......	2
BARRY........ALCE..........	..10	......	4
BATEMAN....JOHN..........	7	......	......
BAYLY........CHARLES......	..32	......	3
BRADLY......RALPH........	5	......	......
BRADLY......ROBERT........	2	......	1
BANBRIGG....ROBERT........	..33½	......	9
BUTTLER....WILLIAM......	..10	......	1
BOYNER......JOHN..........	....3¼	......	......

	acres Land	wtt Seruants	Negrˢ
BURK .... JAMES	....8½	......	......
BUDDING .... RICHARD........	... 10	......	 8
BAYLY........ RICHARD	5	......	 6
BAXTER ...... EDWARD........	8	......	......
BEARD........ RICHᴰ dec̄d	4	......	......
	1256¼	.. 14	412

C	acres Land	wtt Seruants	Negrˢ
CLARK ...... MARGARETT	.. 167	 5	78
COOPER ...... THOMAS	.. 21	......	17
CLEMENT .... WILLIAM........	.. 14	 3	 7
CLARK ...... FRANCIS	.. 12	......	 6
CONOWAY .... CORNELIUS......	 3	......	 1
COUGHLAN.... TEAGUE	7	......	 4
CHAFFIN...... DANIELL		 1	 2
CONNER ...... BRYEN	6	......	......
COCKTON .... DANIELL........	7	......	 2
CLARK ...... EDWARD	 1	......	......
COPPINGER.... JOHN	8	......	......
CARNER [?CARVER] MICHAELL ..	6	......	 1
CRICHLOW .... ELIZABETH		......	 5
CHRICHLOW .. JAMES	9	......	 6
CLARK ...... ROGER..........	.. 20	......	11
CLARK ...... CHRISTOPH'	.. 60	......	31
CASON ...... THOMAS	8	......	 5
CRICHLOW .... HENRY	.. 15	......	 4
CLANCEY .... CORNELIUS......	.. 10	......	 3
CUDDEN ...... JOHN	8	......	 3
COLLYER .... TOBIAS		......	 2
COMELL ...... DUGWELL	.. 10	......	 3
CLARK .... WILLIAM and Complt	7	......	......
CONNEY ...... EDMOND........	....1⅓	......	......

	acres Land	wth Seruants	Neg^s
CLOUGHAN....ELIZABETH......	2	......	......
CREEDE ......JOHN	.. 26	......	 2
COLLEY ......THOMAS	.. 10	......	 4
CORTEENE ....ELLINOR........	6	......	......
CHIZELL......DANIELL........	....2½	......	......
CAUAN ......JOHN	2	......	 1
CHAPPELL ....JONAH Decd	....2½	......	 1
COOKE......MARGRETT Widdow	5	......	 3
CHASE........STEPHEN	9	......	 6
CONNEYLAND . PATT: and Comp^{lt}	.. 12½	......	 2
COPPINE ......JOHN	5	......	......
CAREW ......RICHARD	.. 38	......	 6
CHURCHER ....THOMAS........	5	......	......
CLARK........THOMAS	.. 15	......	......
CODD ....JAMES..........	.. 13	......	......
CAMMELL ....GILBERT........	4	......	......
	558	.. 9	216

	acres Land	wth Seruants	Neg^s
D			
DORN ....JOHN	.. 56	 2	31
DORN ....FRANCIS	.. 37	......	......
DOWELL......RICHARD	3	......	 1
DAWSON......MILLES	5	......	 1
DAUIS........EDWARD	1	......	......
DANIELL ....NICHOLAS	.. 10	......	 8
DRURY ......RICHARD	.. 61	......	25
DENNIS ......JOHN	....2½	......	......
DOLLAR ......JOHN	......	......	 2
DUKE ....HENRY	.. 23	......	 4
DUMESNILL .. CAREW..........	.. 70	......	37
DAUIS........MARGARETT	.. 10	......	 2

	acres Land	w^{tt} Seruants	Neg'^{s}
DENHAM......JOHN	......	......	1
DEMSTER ....JOHN	6	......	......
DILLON ......GARRETT	20	......	9
DURANT......NATTHAN	8	......	9
DENNIS ......JOHN	5	......	......
DOWLING ....WILLIAM........	3	......	......
DANIEL ......JOHN	5	......	......
DANBY ......JOHN	2	......	......
DURANT......THOMAS	6	......	4
	333	2	134

E	acres Land	w^{tt} Seruants	Neg'^{s}
EYTON ......WILLIAM........	...98	3	70
EDNEY ......PETER	...52	......	......
ELLIOTT......JOAN	...10	......	2
EUANS ......JOHN	3	2	4
ENES ....PHILLIPP	4	......	3
EARL ....THOMAS	...12	......	......
ELLIOTT......RICHARD........	......	1	20
	179	6	..99

F	Acres Land	w^{tt} Seruants	Neg'^{s}
FRERE........TOBIAS Esqu'....	395	5	..150
FRERE........JOHN Esqu'	180	......	..80
FRERE........WILLIAM	120	......	..40
FITZGERALD..MORRIS	..15	......	9
FA'WELL [*i.e.* FAREWELL]..JAMES	..18	......	2
FORESTALL....RICHARD	..10	......	......
FAWNE ......JOHN	5	......	......
FRERE........WILLIAM	1	......	...
FARROW ......ROBERT	1	......	......

	acres Land	w't Seruants	Neg's
Foy..........Hugh............	3	......	......
Frame ......William........	.. 10	......	......
Ford ....Thomas	.. 15	......	9
Foster ......John	.. 25	......	10
Field........Anthony	.. 11	......	5
Feyfield ....Richard........	.. 23	......	......
Fell ....Thomas	5	......	......
	842	5	305

G.	acres Land	w't Seruants	Neg's
Gunning ....John	..267	......	47
Gray ....Richard decd ..	..150	5	55
Greenidge ..Richard........	.. 40	......	9
Gray ....Robert	.. 18	......	4
Greenidge ..Jean	9	......	4
Gaslee ......John	.. 20	......	16
Gorman ......Matthew	.. 10	......	1
Gilham ......John	4	......	......
Garuey ......James..........	5	......	3
Goodman ....Richard	8	......	9
Griggs........John	.. 10	......	......
Gilbert ......Natthan^ll.	5	......	2
Gary ....Edward	8	......	1
Gregory......Ormond	5	......	4
Griffin ......Edward	.. 30	......	3
Gilles ......Edward........	.. 10	......	6
Gorden ......Peter..........	8	......	......
Gilles........Edward Junio'..	5	......	1
Grigson ......Robert	.. 10	......	......
George ......Thomas........	......	......	7
Gibbs ....John	......	......	10
	622	5	182

H

	acres Land.	w[t] Seruants	Neg[s]
HARDING ....HENRY Decd	220	 1	90
HARGRAUES ..ALLIS	126	 1	56
HASELWOOD ..THOMAS	170	 2	78
HOOPER ......JONATHAN	.. 50	......	17
HAWEN [or HAUSEN] SAMUELL..	.. 50	......	......
HOOPER ......CRISPINE	..100	......	......
HARLSTONE ..EDWARD	.. 30	 1	11
HORNIOLD ....WILLIAM	.. 12	......	 3
HAGTHORP....WILLIAM	9	......	......
HYDE ....HENRY	5	......	 3
HANMERRY ..NICHOLAS	6	......	......
HUTTON......OLLIUER	.. 36	......	......
HARRIS ......ZACHARIAH	......	......	 1
HOLMES......JOHN deēd	.. 15	......	 8
HUMPHRYES ..EDWARD	.. 25	......	14
HUMPHRYES ..EDWARD	2	......	......
HOLMES......JAMES	9	......	 3
HOLDER......NICHOLAS	.. 33	......	18
HERRINGMAN WILLIAM	.. 14	......	 4
HART........EDWARD	.. 32	......	......
HALLAM ....W[m] Decd........	.. 20	......	10
HALEY ......THOMAS	.. 12	......	......
HARRIS ......ANTHONY	.. 10	......	 6
HARMAN ....WILLIAM........	.. 10	......	 2
HENDERSON ..FRANCIS	5	......	......
HUGHINIS ....PATTRICK	9	......	 7
HOGMAN ....ELIZABETH	.. 10	......	......
HATTON ......CHARLES	.. 28½	......	15
HAYWOOD ....JOHN	.. 15	......	 6
HOLMES ......HENRY	.. 12	......	 4
HACKETT ....WILLIAM	7	......	......
HART........WALTER	.. 80	......	28
HAYES........THOMAS	.. 37	......	16

	acres Land	w^{tt} Seruants	Neg's
HARBERT ....EDWARD	.. 13	......	 6
HACKETT ....ANN & Comp^{lt} ..	.. 21	......	......
HAUGHTAINE . RICHARD........	.. 30	......	......
HANBURY ....NICHOLAS	5	......	......
HOOPER......DANIELL	......	......	 9
HOUGH ......WILLIAM	......	......	 4
	1268	.. 10	419

I	acres Land	w^{tt} Seruants	Neg's
IRELAND......THOMAS	.. 18	......	 6
ILAM ....RICHARD	.. 10	......	......
JONES........ANTHONY	3	 1	 2
JELPH'S ......JOHN	5	......	......
JEAMES ......MARGARETT	.. 10	......	 2
JONES........ROBERT	......	......	 1
JEAMES ......MARGARETT	......	......	 5
	.. 46	.. 1	.. 16

K.	acres Land	w^{tt} Seruants	Neg's
KINSLAND .. NATTHAN^{LL} Esqu'..	340	 5	170
KIRTON........PHILLIPP dec̃d....	360	 9	130
KIPPS........JEAN............	.. 10	......	 3
KELLY ......DAUID	.. 13	......	 3
KEZAR ......TEAGUE	3	......	......
KEY ....WILLIAM........	.. 16	......	 1
KNIGHTS ....JOHN	.. 20	......	 6
KNOWLES ....ANDREW........	1	......	......
KENDALL ....WILLIAM decd ..	5	......	......
KING ....RICHARD........	.. 12	......	 2
	779	.. 14	315

L	acres Land	w^{tt} Seruants	Neg's
LEWIS .... EDMOND........	214	 8	72
LEIGH .... SARAH	172	......	52
LEWIS .... DAUID..........	 10	......	 1
LUCAS .... RICHARD	 15	 1	10
LAMBERT...... ARTHUR	 4	......	 2
LINCK .... THOMAS	 9	......	......
LEWIS .... JOHN	 15	......	 6
LEE .... JAMES..........	19	......	 4
LETTIS........ THOMAS........	42	......	24
LACON .... THOMAS........	 9	......	 1
LELAND ...... CHRISTOPH'	30	......	 9
LOCKSMITH.... THOMAS........	....3½	......	......
LOWRE........ JOHN	 7	......	 6
LOUELL........ CONSTANCE....	.. 17½	......	 6
LONGSTAFF .... ELIZABETH	 9	......	......
	576	 9	193

M	acres Land	w_{tt} Seruants	Neg's.
MAXWELL ..... THOMAS	24	 2	30
MATTSON ..... MATTHIAS	11	 2	12
MOORE .... ROBERT	 5	......	 2
MURFORD .... RICHARD	12	......	 3
MERRICKS .... JOHN dec̄d......	 5	......	......
MASON........ THOMAS........	 7	......	...3
MOORE........ ALCE	 2	......	......
MITCHELL .... THOMAS........	 1	......	......
MACC GRAUGH..DANIELL	 2	......	 2
MOODY........ DAUID	13	......	 2
MORRIS........ WILLIAM	15	......	 2
MATTSON...... SMITHELL	20	......	 3
MACC DANIELL..ALLEXAND'	13	......	 1
MUNROW ...... ANDREW	 5	......	 3
MORRIS .... HUGH..........	 5	......	 1

	acres Land	wᵗᵗ Seruants	Negʳˢ
MARSAN ...... EDWARD	10	......	 6
MARKLAND .... HENRY	44	......	20
MACC GRAUGH .. JOHN	 5	......	 2
MORRIS ...... EDMOND........	10	......	......
MACC BREECLY BRYEN	19	......	 8
MONK .... HENRY	 2	......	 2
MOHOLLAND .. JAMES..........	10	......	 2
MAY .... JOHN	....4½	......	......
MUNROW ...... ALLEXAND'.....	13	......	......
MILLINGTON .. JOHN	......	......	 2
	257½	.. 4	106

	N	acres Land	wᵗᵗ Seruants	Negʳˢ
NEWTON ...... SAMUELL Esqu'..		.. 581	15	.. 260
NEMIAS ...... DAUID a Jew		20	......	12
NOBLE........ MARK		 5	......	......
NORRON ...... KATHERINE		10	......	 7
NUSUM ...... ARTHUR		48	......	 7
NUSUM ...... ARTHUR Junio' ..		13	 1	12
NEWMAN ...... MARGARETT		28	......	 9
NIXON .... MARY		 5	......	......
NURSE........ ROBERT		 5	......	 2
		715	16	.. 309

	O	acres Land	wᵗᵗ Seruants	Negʳˢ
OKER .... GEORGE		69	......	22
OWTRAM ...... DOROTHY		.. 116	......	28
OISTINE ...... JAMES		67	 1	17
OUERTON .... ROBERT		 5	......	......
OISTINE ..... NICHOLAS		 4	......	 1

PARISH REGISTERS. 483

	acres Land	wtt Seruants	Neg's
OLLIUER......MARGARETT	4	......	......
OUTRAM......ROBERT	10	......	......
	275	1	68

P.	Acres Land	wtt Seruants	Neg's
PEARS........JOHN Esqu'......	910	8	..180
PERRIMAN....RICHARD	37	1	20
PINCHBACK....THOMAS........	38	......	11
PILE..........THEOPHILUS	45	1	12
PILE..........SARAH	20	......	3
PERRY........JOHN	15	......	......
PEAD........JOHN	....4½	......	7
POCKETT......WILLIAM	3	......	......
PAYNE........ELIZABETH......	4	......	......
PERROTT......RALPH	70	......	15
PECOCK ......ROBERT	7	2	7
POYER........THOMAS	13	......	3
PARSONS......WILLIAM deēd ..	4	......	......
PITTMAN.....ARTHUR........	15	......	5
PITTS........HUGH..........	8	......	2
PEAK ....CHRISTOPH'....	4	......	2
PRICE ....MATTHEW	5	......	2
PRICE ....HENRY	35	......	15
PRICE ....WILLIAM	1	......	......
PERRY........EDWARD........	5	......	......
POTTER ......ROBERT	4	......	......
PORTER ......ROBERT	5	......	7
PIKE ....OLLIŭ deēd......	....2½	......	......
POORE........PETER	3	......	......
PUMFRETT...ANN............	5	......	......
PHELOMY....JOHN	10	......	......
PHILLIPPS WILLIAM 5 acrs 2 Neg's			
	1273	..12	291

61—2

	acres Land	wth Seruants	Neg's
Q			
QUIGGEN......JOHN..........	..12	......	6
	acres Land	wth Seruants	Neg's
R			
RICHBELL ....ROBERT........	..315	8	140
RISLEY........CRESSENT......	..148	1	84
RUSHBROOK ..HENRY.........	..50	1	13
RODMAN......SARAH..........	..75	......	2
RODMAN......JOHN...........	7	......	3
RODMAN......JOHN Junio'.....	..47	......	13
RICHARDS ....JOHN...........	..10	......	7
RICHARDSON ..MARY...........	..33	......	10
RYCRAFT......SARAH.........	..45	......	12
RICHARDSON..DAUID..........	....4½	......	2
REYNOLD ....JEAN Widdow ..	......	......	8
ROBINSON ....THOMAS........	..10	......	8
ROBINSON ....ROBERT........	..12½	......	6
ROGERS ......JOHN..........	..12½	......	3
RAWLINES ....JOHN...........	..15	......	8
ROSE........ELIZABETH......	8	......	3
RICHARDSON ..GEORGE........	..10	......	7
ROBINSON ....MANUSS (?)......	..17	......	6
ROSSE........JOHN..........	1	......	......
ROBINSON ....WILLIAM........	......	......	3
RAINSFORD ...JOHN..........	3	......	1
RENNY......TEAGUE.........	5	......	......
RENNY.......TEAGUE Jun'....	..10	......	1
RYCORD......SAMUELL......	2	......	1
RUCK........JOHN..........	..44	......	16
REDMAN......RICHARD......	..10	......	......
ROBINSON ....EDWARD........	7	......	......
RENTFREE ....ROBERT........	..10	......	......
RYMORE......ALLEXAND'......	1	......	......

S

	acres Land	wth Seruants	Neg's
SCAWELL [or SEAWELL] } RICH^D Esqu'	550	 8	.. 206
SEARL .... JOHN Esqu'	365	 11	.. 184
SILUESTER .... Madam	180	 1	 40
SCOTT .... BENIAMIN	.. 108	 2	 41
SHURLAND .... JOHN	.. 30	 00	 12
STANFORD .... ROBERT	.. 27	......	 9
SMITH .... ELIZABETH	 5	......	 6
STEPHENS .... JOHN	 5	......	......
SHELTON ..... SAMUELL	.... 1½	 2	 3
STRODE ...... HENRY	.. 30	......	 32
STRAWNE ..... HENRY	 5	......	 2
SHERON ...... GEORGE	.. 10	......	 6
SIMPSON ...... JAMES	.... 1½	......	 1
SPEGHT ...... WILLIAM	.. 22	......	 21
SISTERS ...... ELIZABETH	.. 36	......	 19
SNERLING .... ROBERT	......	......	 1
SADLER ...... THOMAS	.. 21	......	......
SLANY ...... ANTHONY	......	......	 2
STONE........ JOHN	.. 20	......	 1
SKAROS ..... GEORGE	 5	......	 1
SPAROWHAWK .. JAMES	 5	......	 4
STRODE ...... MARGRETT......	......	 1	 4
SPENCER...... JOHN	.. 23	......	 7
SAUNDERSON .. JOHN	 4	.... .	 1
SLAUGHTER .. THOMAS	 3	......	 2
STUDDY ...... THOMAS	 8	......	 3
SHORTE ...... OWEN	 6	......	......
SCRUTTON [or STRUTTON] .. JOHN	 5	......	 1
SAWYER ...... MARGARETT	.. 10	......	 4
SNIPE .... JOHN	......	......	 2
SHORE........ RICHARD	.. 10	......	......

	acres Land.	w^{tt} Seruants	Neg's
SAUNDERSON..ROBERT	.. 10	......	......
SUTTON ......HENRY	5	......	......
	1511	25	615

	acres Land.	w^{tt} Seruants.	Neg's.
T			
THORNBURGH...GEORGE	.. 40	......	10
TROWELL ....PHILLIPP	.. 34	......	21
TYLER........ROBERT	.. 21	......	 4
TAYLOR ......JOHN	.. 12	......	 6
THOMPSON ....JOHN	8	......	 4
THOROWGOOD..THOMAS	1	 1	 1
TERRILL......SAMUELL	....3¾	......	 2
TUBBS........EDWARD	....7½	......	......
TILNEY ......THOMAS	.. 10	......	 1
THOMAS......THOMPSON	8	......	 1
THISTLETHWAITE..PETER	8	......	 1
TICHBOURN....WINNEFRED	.. 17	......	 6
TYSOE ....WILLIAM	1	......	 1
	171¼	 1	.. 58

	acres Land	w^{tt} Seruants	Neg's
V			
VINTON [or VNITON]..THOMAS	.. 17	......	 9
VFFORD......··JOHN	5	......	......
	.. 22	......	 9

	acres Land	w^{tt} Seruants	Neg's
W			
WATTKINES ..DAUID	.. 20	......	 6
WYNN........RICHARD	.. 60	......	 8
WALTERS ....CHRISTOPH'	..112	......	28
WATTKINES ..ROBERT	5	......	......

	acres Land	wᵗʰ Seruants	Negʳˢ
WRIGHT ...... WILLIAM	2	......	 3
WALROND .... THOMAS	.. 340	 18	.. 170
WASLEY ...... JOHN	1	......	......
WATTKINES .. THOMAS	.. 10	......	 5
WEBSTER .... JOHN	5	......	 1
WISE .... CHRISTOPH'	.. 19	......	 7
WILLIAMS .... RICHARD	..406	 2	.. 200
WRIGHT ...... JOHN	.. 40	 4	 7
WARNER...... STEPHEN	.. 18	......	11
WATT .... DAUID..........	.. 10	......	 10
WILSON ...... ANTHONY	6	......	......
WHITE........ PATRICK	.. 13	......	 6
WILSON ...... EDWARD........	6	......	 4
WILSON ...... CHARLES	.. 20	......	 6
WILSON ...... CHARLES Junio'..	5	......	 4
WALTER ...... RICHARD	....2½	......	......
WHITE........ MILICENT	....2½	......	......
WARD .... WILLIAM	.. 14	......	 3
WILSON ...... WILLIAM	9	......	 2
WELLS........ JOHN	5	......	......
WILSON ...... MARGARETT	5	......	......
WARD .... RICHARD	2	......	......
WADDINE .... THOMAS	2	......	......
WYATT ...... CHRISTOPH'	.. 10	......	 3
WHITEHEAD .. THO: dec̄d	.. 25	......	 6
WALTON ...... RICHARD	.. 11	......	 2
	1112	.. 24	492

Total of Inhabitants } 410

The Sum Totall of Euery Lott Conteined in ye w^thin
List Alphabettically Drawne and Cast upp att ye Foote

acres Land	w^tt Seru^tts	Negros
12978¾	..178	4723

JN^o KENNEY
RICH ELLIOTT } Church Wardens
JN^o ADAMS

BARBADOS

AN Extract from ye Register of Christ Church of ye Christnings within ye Said Parish from March ye 25: 78. to ye 29th: of 7b^r: 79

Anno Dom. 1678
Aprill.

JANE ye Daughter of THOMAS and JANE WITHERING was bap^t y^e: 2^d
GRISSEL ye Daughter of TIMOTHY and MARY HUDLEY was bap^t y^e: 26th

June
MARGRET ye Daughter of WILLIAM and MARY WALTON was bap^t y^e: 27th

July
THOMAS ye Sonn of CORNELIUS and MARGRET STAPONS bap^t y^e: 2^d
THOMAS ye Sonn of NICOLAS and MARIE CLARE............ bap^t y^e: 3^d

August
MARY ye Daughter of HUMPHREY and ELIZABETH BALL bap^t y^e: 1st
MARY ye Daughter of WILLIAM and MABELL HOWARD bap^t y^e: 18th
JOAN ye Daughter of BENJ^A and KATHERINE FINCH bap^t y^e: 25th
RICHARD ye Sonn of THOMAS and ELIZABETH HASELWOOD bap^t y^e: 26th

1678

JOHN ye Sonn of THOMAS and ELIZABETH SERLE .... bap^t y^e: 30th
MARY y^e [sic] of JOHN and MABELL GITTINGS of ye Age of
  Eighteen years and Seaven moneths was bap^t in ye P'sence } y^e: 31th
  of EDWARD WASSON and ANNE PACKSON Wittnesses ......

September

NICOLAS ye Sonn of HUGH and MARY MORRICE   was bap^t y^e: 8th
MARY ye Daughter of DOWGALL and MARY CAMPBELL   bap^t y^e: 8th
FRANCIS ye Sonn of JOHN and ANN HANSON   was bap^t y^e: 19th
ROBERT ye Sonn of ROBERT and MARY STANFORD   was bap^t y^e: 24th
JOHN ye Sonn of JOHN and ABIGAILL COLLINS   was bap^t y^e: 29th

October

CHRISTOPHER ye Son of JOHN and ANNE SNIPE   was bap^t ye 13th
WILLIAM ye Son of JOHN and MARGERY HINCH   was bap^t y^e: 20th
LANCELOTT ye Son of LANCELOT and MARY THOMPSON   bap^t ye 20th
JANE ye Daughter of W^m and ELIANOR DAVIES   was bap^t ye 24th
MACHELL ye Daughter of EDWARD and MACHELL ALSOPE bap^t ye 31th

November

RICHARD ye Sonn of RICHARD and MARY BRIDGESTOCK   bap^t ye 10th
ISABELL ye Daughter of ROBERT and KATHERINE CHURCH bap^t ye 17th
MARTHA ye Daughter of JAMES and HANNA ANDERSON   bap^t ye 24th
W^m ye Son of OBAH a Christian Negroe Woman   was bap^t ye 24th
SUSANNA a Negroe Woman of JOHN OSBOURN'S   was bap^t ye 24th
  whose vndertakers were HERBERT GRIFFITH, ANN KELLY, and
  ELIZ: WATKINS
W^m ye Son of ye Said SUSANNA, whose vndertakers were RALPH
  BRETTON, and EDWARD PRICE, and MARY SMITH was baptized ye 24th
MARTHA a Moletto Daughter of ye s^d JOⁿ OSBURN and SUSANNA
                                                             bap^t ye 24th
THEOPHILUS ye Son of RICHARD and ELIZABETH LUCAS was
                                                             baptized ye 26th
ALEXANDER ye Sonn of THOMAS and ANN IRELAND was bap^t ye 28th

1678

MARGRET ye Daughter of ROBERT and ELIZABETH BRADLY
 was bap^t y^e: 28th
MARY ye Daughter of ROBERT and ELIZABETH JONES was bap^t ye 28th

December

SARAH ye Daughter of GEORGE and ELVY HARE was...... bap^t y^e 1st
GRACE y^e Daughter of OLIVER and GRACE PIKE was ...... bap^t y^e: 10th
ANNE y^e Daughter of JOHN and SUSANNA WEBSTER was bap^t y^e 17th
RICHARD y^e Sonn of ZACHARIE and ELIZABETH HARRIS was
 bap^t y^e 26th
MARY y^e Daughter of W^M and MARY PHILLIPS was bap^t y^e 30th

January 167$\frac{8}{9}$

JOB y^e Son of WALTER and DOROTHY HART of about.
 22. years of Age his Chosen wittnesses WALTER HART } bap^t y^e 2^d
 and THOMAS HAYES ....
CHARITY y^e Daughter of WALTER and DOROTHY HART
 of about 19 years of Age whose Wittnesses were
 WALTER HART THOMAS HAYES and ELIZABETH } bap^t y^e 2^d
 JEWSON and JANE HAYES............................
ELIZABETH of ye age of 8 years, and KATHERINE of y^e
 Age of Seaven years and AMARINZIA of ye Age of 5
 years, and BENJ^A of ye Age of 7 moneths, all children } bap^t: ye 3^d
 of BERNARD and ELIZABETH SCHENCKINGH were bap^t
ELIZABETH ye Daughter of NATHANIEL and ANN
 RIDGEWAY of ye Age: 11: years .... was bap^t ye 4th
JOHN ye Sonn of ROBERT and ANNE SNELLIN ...... was bap^t ye 7th
ELIZABETH ye Daughter of WILLIAM and ANNE MERCER
 was bap^t ye 19th
PHILOCLEON ye Daughter of RICHARD and JANE GREENIDGE
 was bap^t ye 21th
CHRISTOPHER ye Sonn [of] CHRISTOPHER and ANN BULL was bap^t ye 22th
ARTHUR ye Son of ARTHUR and SUSANNA NUSUM was bap^t ye 22th

February.

1674

MARY of ye Age of 5 years and 6 moneths, and HENRY⎫
the Age of 4 months, Daughter and Son of JAMES and ⎬ bap^t ye 13th
MARY SIMSON ....were⎭
JOHN ye Son of DANIELL and MIRIAM MAGRAUHAN was bap^t ye 18th
KATHERINE ye Daughter of RICHARD and ELIZABETH
              CAREW was bap^t ye 28th
ANTHONY ye Sonn of GEORGE and MARY RICHARDSON was bap^t ye 28th

March

ANNA ye Daughter of PETER and MARY JARRET was bap^t ye 7th
ANNE ye Daughter of RICHARD and ANNE PERRYMAN bap^t ye 11th
SAMUELL ye Sonn of JAMES and ELIZABETH MADDER was bap^t ye 12th
J^{no} the Sonn of JOHN and MARY BYNO ....was bap^t ye 13th
LUCY of ye Age of 2 years and Six moneths, and ANTHONY⎫
ten dayes old, Daughter and Son of ANTHONY and MABELL ⎬ ye 13th
HARRIS ....were bap^t⎭
CONRAD ye Son of CONRAD and ELIZABETH ADAMS...was bap^t ye 23th
ROBERT ye Son of ROBERT and REBECCA HANSON ...was bap^t ye 23th
ELIZABETH ye Daughter of W^m and MARIE SPEIGHTS was bap^t ye 23th

Aprill

JAMES ye Son of HENRY and SUSANNA CHRUCTHLOE was bap^t ye 4th
ELIZABETH ye Daughter of PEREGRINE and ISABELL GUARD
                was bap^t ye 6th
ELENOR ye Daughter of ALEXANDER and ELENOR OSBOURN
                was bap^t ye 19th
J^{no} ye Sonn of JOHN and LOWRIE SPENLOVE........... was bap^t ye 26th
JAMES ye Sonn of PATRICK and JANE OHAIN (or OHANI) was bap^t ye 26th
KATHERINE ye Daughter of ISAAC and SUSANNA RAGG was bap^t ye 26th

May

MARY ye Daughter of J^{no} and HESTER ADAMS ...... was bap ye 3^d

1679

WILLIAM yᵉ Son of WILLIAM and ANN BRIDGESTOCK was bapᵗ yᵉ 11ᵗʰ
JOHN the Son of JAMES and MARY HOLMES............ was bapᵗ yᵉ 15ᵗʰ
WILLIAM yᵉ Son of MARGARET COOK Widdow......... was bapᵗ yᵉ 14ᵗʰ

June

ELIZABETH yᵉ Daughter of SMITHY and MARTHA MATSON
                                              was bapᵗ yᵉ 14ᵗʰ
JAMES the Sonn of JOHN and MARY JELPII .... was bapᵗ yᵉ 29ᵗʰ

July

JAMES yᵉ Son of JAMES and ANGELETTA OISTINS ... was bapᵗ yᵉ 2ᵈ
SUSANNA yᵉ Daughter of JOHN and ELIZABETH GASELEE was bapᵗ yᵉ 3ᵈ
EDWARD yᵉ Son of STEPHEN and MARGRET CHASE   was bapᵗ yᵉ 8ᵗʰ
GEORGE yᵉ Son of GEORGE and ANN GILES was bapᵗ .... yᵉ 8ᵗʰ
NICOLAS yᵉ Son of NICOLAS BIDLECOMB by a Negroe Woman
                                              was bapᵗ yᵉ 9ᵗʰ
ANNE yᵉ Daughter of Jⁿᵒ and ANNE CREED   .... was bapᵗ yᵉ 13ᵗʰ

August

JOHN yᵉ Son of JOHN and ANNE DANIELL .... was bapᵗ yᵉ 7ᵗʰ
MARY yᵉ Daughter of ROGER and MARY CLARKE ... was bapᵗ yᵉ 7ᵗʰ
JOHN yᵉ Son of JOHN and ELIZABETH SMITH was .... bapᵗ yᵉ 28ᵗʰ
DANIELL yᵉ Son of DARBY and ELIZABETH MALLONEE was bapᵗ yᵉ 17ᵗʰ
THOMAS yᵉ Son of OWEN and JOAN MALLONEE ...... was bapᵗ yᵉ 31ᵗʰ

September

WILLIAM of yᵉ Age of ten moneths Son of WILLIAM and FRANCES
                                              SMITH bapᵗ yᵉ 3ᵈ
WILLIAM yᵉ Son of Wᴹ and ELIZABETH WOODFINE   was bapᵗ yᵉ 7ᵗʰ
SAMUEL of yᵉ Age of 7 months Son of DAVID and JANE ARNET.
                                              was bapᵗ yᵉ 9ᵗʰ
KATHERINE yᵉ Daughter of TEAGE and KATHERINE KEYZAR
                                              was bapᵗ yᵉ 9ᵗʰ

1679
ANNE ye Daughter of JOHN and KATHARINE ROGERS was bapt ye 15th
Wm ye Son of WILLIAM and JOAN COLE .... was bapt ye *th
WALTER ye Son of RICHARD and CHARITY HICKMAN was bapt ye 25th
DAVERS ye Son of RICHARD and ELIZABETH SEAWELL was bapt ye 26th

October

THOMAS ye Son of THOMAS and ELIZABETH HUGHS. was bapt ye 13th
JOHN ye son of JOHN and SUSANNA MERICK .... was bapt ye 16th
JOHN ye Sonn of JOHN and MARY BUNNYON .... was bapt ye 16th
ELIZABETH ye Daughter of JAMES and REBECCA CRUTCHLOE
                                              was bapt ye 17

Total 93†

JNo KENNEY ⎫
RICH: ELLIOTT ⎬ Church Wardens
JNo: ADAMS ⎭

BARBADOS

N Extract from ye Register of Christ Church of ye Burialls wthin ye Said Parish from March ye 25th 1678. to September ye 29th 1679

Anno Dom 1678
May

JOHN ye Son of JOHN MARKLAND .... buried ye 31th

June

ANNANIAS MAN Senio' .... buried ye 4th
MARY ye Wife of Wm HALLUM .... buried ye 17th
JANE BRYAN... buried ye 20th
WILLIAM HARGROVE .... buried

---

* Date doubtful, owing to the orig. MS. being split.
† [It should be 98.]

July

1678
FRANCIS yᵉ Wife of JOHN STONE	buried yᵉ 12ᵗʰ
WILLIAM LEIGH	buried yᵉ 19ᵗʰ
JANE yᵉ Wife of JOHN COPPIN	buried yᵉ 29ᵗʰ

August

JOHN ARCH	buried yᵉ 5ᵗʰ
JANE the Daughter of THOMAS and ELIZABETH HASELWOOD	būr yᵉ 26ᵗʰ
CHARLES the Son of THOMAS and ANNE IRELAND	buried yᵉ 30ᵗʰ

Septemb'

MAJ' RICHARD GRAY	buried yᵉ 10ᵗʰ
HESTER the Wife of Jnᵒ PEERSE Esq'	buried yᵉ 15ᵗʰ

October

JOSHUAH CHAPPELL	buried yᵉ 5ᵗʰ
THOMAS CRAWFORD	buried yᵉ 21ᵗʰ
KATHERINE the Wife of Wᴹ HORNIOLDE	buried yᵉ 28ᵗʰ

November

SIMON REYNOLDS	buried yᵉ 2ᵈ
CHARLES yᵉ Son of JOHN and ELIZABETH BURTON	buried yᵉ 28ᵗʰ
GEORGE STRODE was buried	yᵉ 29ᵗʰ

Decemb'

ARTHUR yᵉ Son of ARTHUR and SUSANNA NUSUM	buried yᵉ 28ᵗʰ

January 167$\frac{8}{9}$

MARGARET OLIVER	buried yᵉ 29ᵗʰ
JANE yᵉ Wife of Jnᵒ THOMPSON	buried yᵉ 31ᵗʰ
MABEEL the Wife of ZACHARIAH HARRIS	buried yᵉ 31ᵗʰ

167 2/7

February

STEPHEN SMITH	buried y^e 8th
JOHN BUSSIE	buried y^e 9th
JOHN BURTON Junio'	buried y^e 10th
EDWARD ADDISON Junio'	buried y^e 10th
J^{no} BURTON Senio'	buried ye 13th
JOHN and his Wife JANE LITTLE	buried ye 13th
CHRISTIAN a Negroe Servant of MAJ' KINGSLANDS	buried ye 13th
JOHN HOLMES	buried ye 15th
WILLIAM KENDALL	buried ye 18th
DELIVERANCE ADDISON	buried ye 18th
CHRISTOPHER CLANCY	buried ye 18th
JANE the Wife of EDWARD MARSON	buried ye 26th

March

Wm COOK	buried ye 2^d
Sr ROBERT HACKET	buried ye 3^d

Aprill

HENRY HARDING	buried ye 21th
OLIVER PIKE	buried ye 22th
REBECCA POTTER	buried ye 23th
SARAH ye Daughter of ALEXANDER and MARY BLOWDEN	buried ye 26th

May

SUSANNA ye Wife of HENRY HOLMES	buried ye 17th

June

DAVID ROBINSON	buried ye 10th
MATHEW GORMON	buried ye 23th
JAMES ye Son of JOHN JELPH	buried ye 24th
THOMAS CHESTER	buried ye 30th

1679

July

PETER ALSOPE..	buried ye 1st
JOHN BASHFORD	buried ye 3^d
WILLIAM SILCOMB	buried ye 5th
EDWARD the Sonn of STEPHEN and MARGRET CHASE...	buried ye 9th
ANTHONY RICHARDSON...................................	buried ye 13th
HENRY HOLMES	buried ye 22th
RICHARD BEDFORD...	buried ye 23th
MARTHA CAULDWALL......................................	buried ye 28th

August

MICHAELL CLARK	buried ye 5th
DOROTHY CALLAHAN.....................................	buried ye 10th
MACHELL ye Daughter of EDWARD ALSOPE	buried ye 19th

September

SAMUELL ye Son of Capt DAVID, and JANE ARNET	buried ye 13th

      J^No KENNEY
      RICH: ELLIOTT } Church Wardens.
      J^No: ADAMS

BARBADOS

AN account of all the Persons who have been baptized within the Parish of St James since the 25th of March 1678 to the 29th of September 1679

1678 May— 23—ELIZABETH ye Daughter of THOMAS SERTAIN
       August 11—ELIZABETH ye Daughter of DAVID POOR
       Aug— 17—MARY ye Daughter of FRANCIS WALTHO
       Aug— 25—ANNE ye Daughter of JAMES WALWYN Esq'

     Septemb 1—JOAN ye Daughter of WILLIAM HABBERD

1678 Sept— 5—Elizabeth ye Daughter of WILLIAM THOMAS
Sept— 8 ELIZABETH ye Daughter of ALEXANDER CUTHBERT
—MARY the Daughter of RICHARD MIDDLETON
October—10—JOHN the Son of JOHN HILL
Octob—15—WILLIAM ye Son of JOHN LEECH
Oct— 15—GEORGE ye Son of JOHN LEECH
Oct— 15—SUSANNA ye Daughter of JOHN LEECH
Oct— 15—WILLIAM ye Son of WILLIAM FOSTER
Oct— 20—JOHN ye Son of JOHN MIRCH

November—17—RALPH ye Son of THOMAS KEMP
Nov—17—MARY ye Daughter of THOMAS KEMP
Nov—24—ANNE ye Daughter of RICHARD CHOM

December 8 HENRY ye Son of Mr WILLIAM CHESTER
February 23 DORCAS ye Daughter of HENRY WRIGHT

1679 August 24 PIERCE ye Son of HENRY WATTY
Aug— 27 ANDREW ye Son of Lt Col^l ANDREW AFFLECK
September 5 JOHN the Son of Mr JOHN HOOKER
Sept— 25 THOMAS ye Son of JOHN DANIEL Esq'.

       Concordat cū Registro
       C. LEGARD
        vicarius ibid

Baptized in the Parish
of St James since y^e
25th of march 1678 } 23
to ye 29 of Septemb 1679

BARBADOS

AN acc^t of all the Persons that have been buried within the Parish of St James since the 25 of March 1678 to the 29 of September 1679

1678 March 28—MATTHEW ye son of MATTHEW PEDDER

Burialls

1678 Aprill— 8—RALPH y^e son of Mr JOHN HOOKER
Apr — 13—HENRY YATES
April— 29—JOHN HUDSON—who was casually drownd

May — 6—ELEANOR PAYN
May — 7—ELIAS WILLIAMS
May — 8—MARY y^e Daughter of JOHN SLAUGHTER
May — 23—ROBERT BELL
May — 31—JOHN THOMAS

June — 1—NICOLAS LAWRENCE of S_t Thomas's Parish
June — 27—MARY SLATE,—Servt to Capt JOSIAS COX

July — 1—MATTHEW WHETTY
July — 3—MARY DRISKELL
July — 10—JOHN OSDELL

September—4—DAVID CALLAHONE
Sept 16—JOHN SPARKE Esq'
Sept — 18—JOAN y^e Wife of RALPH CARR

October—9—MARY y^e Daughter of RICHARD MIDDLETON
Octob —14—Cap_t ROBERT ARUNDELL
Octob —16—WILLIAM LINCKLATE, serv^t to Judge REID
Octob 30—JOHN DOWNS

Novemb 1—ALEXANDER ROBINSON
Novem— 4—JOHN NICOLLS
Nov— 14—ELIZABETH COOK.

December 1—MICHAEL y^e Son of JAMES GOFFE
Decemb 22—JOHN SEATON
February 12—WILLIAM JONES

Burialls.

1679 May— 8—FRANCES ye Wife of JOHN GOEING
June— 7—MARY ye Wife of MORGAN MURPHY
June— 13—EDWARD WEBB.
June— 29—JOHN DUDLEY
July— 4 ALICE ye Wife of THOMAS WALTER
July 14—JAMES INNIS
July— 22—TOBIAS PAYNE
July 27—JOHN ye son of Mr JOHN BATT
July 29—OWEN COLLOHONE

August 6 ANTHONY STEERMAN
Agu—— 7 JOHN ARMITAGE of the Parish of St Peters who was casually drowned
August—19 FRANCIS BEARNE
Sept 6 JOHN ye Son of Mr JOHN HOOKER
Sept 7 JAMES ye Son of ALEXANDER MURREY
Sept 8—CORNELIUS ye Son of DEARMAN DRISKELL
Sept 11 JAMES PURSLEY
Sept 22 ELIZABETH ye Wife of WILLIAM SPENCE

Buried in ye Parish of St James from ye 25 of March 1678 to ye 29 of September 1679 } 44

Concordat cū Registro
C LEGARD vicarius
ibid

[indorsed] BARBADOS

Accot of Christnings 23.
Burials............ 44
in St James Parish.
Recd 3d June 1680.

63—2

ANN: Acco:t of the: land As Itt: Stondeth: In yͤ church Books: With the Number of Servants And Negros With the Names: of the Owners thereof In the psh: of Sᵗ James: As: Was taken by the Church Wardens of the Said Parrish the 20ᵈ December 1679

A	Seruᵗˢ,,	land,,	Neg'ˢ,,
AFLICK: ANDREW; Leuᵗ Colᵒ	 2	96	70
ANDREWS: EUEN	......	20	 7
ANDREWS: Wᵐ	 2	......	 2
ALLING JACOB Very pore	......	 4	......
B.			
BAYLYE: RICHARD: Colᵒ	......	.. 228	......
BOND: FRANCIS: Esqʳ	 2	.. 120	67
BURHALL: GEORGE	......	10	11
BANBRIG: ROBERT: Docto'	......	......	 4
BURROWES JOHN	......	10	 2
BATT: JOHN Senj'	 1	40	17
BALAM: CHARLES Capᵗ	......	78	22
BURGIS THOMAZING m'ˢ	......	20	 7
BURTON FRANCIS: Capᵗ	......	15	......
BISSEX WILLIAM m'	 1	 9	 4
BYRNE: DINNIS	 1	10	11
BLAKE: JOHN	......	24	......
BELCHEM: JOHN Very pore	......	 3	......
BIGGNELL Wᵐ Very pore	......	 3	......
BALL: JOHN—Decᵈ his Widdow is pore	......	 3	 1
C			
CHESTER WILLIAM: mʳ	 1	120	45
COX: JOSIAS: Capᵗ	 9	247	122

	Serv^{ts}	land	Neg^s
CHAMBERLAINE: FRANCIS: Capt	......	20	16
COLLINGS: JAMES	 2	121	 10
CHACE JOHN	......	27	 8
CHRISTOPHER WILLIAM	......	16	 8
COURTYERE GEORGE	......	23	 8
CAMERRAME JOHN	......	45	......
CHAPEMAN RICHARD	 1	......	 5
CHALLENER ROB^T	......	 2	 1
CRESSWELL JOHN	......	 9	......
CUTA MATHEW: DAY: THOMAS: MILLER: JN^o: pore..................	......	 6	......
CLEMENTS ROBERT pore	......	 5	......

D.

DANIELL JOHN: Esqr	......	.. 160	55
DYMOCKE: WILLIAM: Capt	 3	57	60
DYER: WILLIAM Dec^d his Estates	 6	.. 317	.. 120
DOLLATHY: ELIZABETH	......	40	16
DALBEY: JOANE.....................	 1	 8	 6
DOWNES HENRY	......	18	 3
DUCE: GYLES	......	10	 7
DAMERALL THOMAS pore	......	 3	 1
DUNEING HENRY pore	......	 4	......

E

EUENS: RICHARD Esqr..............	 7	171	78
ELDING: EDWARD: Capt	 3	176	70
ELMES: JOHN:......................	......	 5	 3

F.

FEAKE: HENRY	 8	.. 245	.. 120
FITTE: ROBERT:	......	30	14

	Serv[ts]	Land	Negrs
FOSTER: ROBERT: Docto'	......	7	5
FLINT: GEORGE	......	10	1
FUTER THOMAS	......	32	......
FEAK RICHARD for: NATH[ll]: WILLIAMSON	......	7	......
FUREY CHARLES pore	......	4	......
FREEMAN WILLIAM pore	......	3	......

G

	Serv[ts]	Land	Negrs
GIBBES: PHILLIP	7	..174	60
GIBBES: JOSEPH:	......	25	......
GIBBSON JOHN	......	7	......
GIBBSON: MATHEW	......	10	......
GRAVE: WILLIAM	......	6	2
GILLHAM EMANUELL	......	4	......
GARRET: EMOND	......	4	2
GRONEARE JOHN pore	......	5	......
GARNER: MARY pore	......	5	......
GARNER: MILLER & Comp[a] pore	......	4	......

H

	Serv[ts]	Land	Negrs
HELMES THOMAS Maj'	4	..134	52
HELMES: THOMAS: Cap[t]	3	60	50
HOOKER JOHN	......	......	7
HABING THOMAS	......	6	7
HIGGINSON MARG[t]	......	10	4
HALL: JOHN	......	14	1
HEWES JOHN	......	6	4
HOLDER: MELITIAH	3	100	32
HOLDER: JOHN: Jun'	......	98	......
HOPEKINGS SAMUELL	......	4	3
HILL JOHN	......	......	2

	Serv^{ts}	Land	Negros
HOUSFEILD JOHN pore	......	 5	......
HARRISON: ABRAHAM	......	 4	......

I
	Serv^{ts}	Land	Negros
JEFFORDS: ELIZ^A	......	20	 6
JOHN JOHNSON	......	13	 1

K
	Serv^{ts}	Land	Negros
KNIGHTS BENJ^A: Esqr	 3	.. 300	.. 150
KELLEY: ROB^T:	 3	62	37
KING ROB^T	......	 5	 3
KNATCHBULL JOHN	......	 4	 3
KENN MATHEW Docto'	 2	15	 9
KELLEY JOHN			
KNIGHTINGALL NATHANIELL pore	—— 0	 4	......
KANTY: DARBY pore	......	 3	......

L.
	Serv^{ts}	Land	Negros
LITTLETON: EDWARD: Esqr	 3	.. 205	.. 120
LANE ANTHONY Capt	......	20	 4
LOWTHER: LUKE	......	12	 6
LEACH: JOHN	......	16	 5
LOUE MARY	......	......	 3
LAWRANCE HENRY	......	10	 6
LEWIS: HUGH: Capt	......	40	15
LEGAYE JACOB Senj'	......	21	......
LUKE: ELIAS:	......	20	 3
LANGHAM THOMAS	......	 5	.....
LEAGER: Widdow pore	......	 7	......

M
	Serv^{ts}	Land	Negros
MELLOWS: ELISHA: Capt	 1	47	24

	Seruants"	Land"	Negros"
MUNDY: ELIZA	2	75	35
MULLENEX WILLIAM		17	10
MERRELL THOMAS: Capt		35	19
MELL: WILLIAM		20	
MARTING: JOHN		10	1
MADDOX THOMAS pore		5	
MIDDLETON: RICHARD			4
MACCONY DINNIS		3	
MASSLING WILLIAM		8	3
MUNNS: THOMAS: Ensigne		2	2
MORRAINE JOHN		5	
MORGAINE ROBT: pore		5	
MACCONY: DINNIS pore		2	
MACKGERRY WILLIAM pore		1	
MACKWARD: FELLEN pore		2	

N.

NELSON THOMAS		4	1
NORRIS SAMUELL Capt			3

O

ODAM WILLIAM		7	1
ODGNE: EDMOND		15	6

P

PAIGE SARAH		30	2
PARKER RICHARD		7	
PEREING SABASTING		24	13
PARE EDWARD	1		3
PEARCE: BENONY			
PAINE TOBIAS		26	3
PETTER SAMUELL		14	8

	Seruants	Land	Negros
Q			
QUALE HUGH..................	......	5	......
QUERKE RICHARD...............			
: R :			
REID JOHN Esqr	2	..198	85
RICHARDS THOMAS	2	20	10
RAMSEY ROAS m^{ls}	1	30	29
RUSSELL PHILLIP	...2	13	5
RIUERS WILLIAM	......	......	1
ROASS THOMAS: Docto'.........	......	20	9
REID: ADAME pore	......	6	......
RAUEN: XTOPHER pore..........	......	5	......
RICHARDSON: NICHOLAS pore	......	5	......
REEUES THOMAS pore	......	4	......
ROBINSON: JOHN pore	......	......	1
S			
STANFAST JOHN: Col^{lo}	.10	0351	..238
SPARKS: JOYE: Madam	12	..133	..150
SCOTT: WALTER: Capt	2	..107	52
STEWARD: AMEY	......	10	1
SMITHWICKE W^m	......	10	1
STURMAN MARY	1	20	7
STOUT JOHN Leu^t	......	10	5
SMITH MARG^T	......	12	......
SUMERS THOMAS	......	7	2
SAMPSON JOHN: Capt	......	25	......
STROUDE JOHN m^{ls}	......	5	......
SCOTT: JOHN	......	10	1
STRETCH: JOHN	......	......	1
STAYSMORE FRANCIS	......	......	1

	Seruants,	Land,	Negros,
SAGE RICHARD Liueing On: Cott^o BAYLYS land	....	....	 3
SPENCER: MARG^T Very pore	,......	 6	 2
SHEPEHERD JOHN pore.............	....	 5	....
SHAWE DANIELL pore:	....	 6	....
SHOUELL ELIAS pore:	....	 5	....
STEEUENS JOHN pore	....	 3	....
T			
THORNEHILL TIMOTHY: Cott^o........	 7	.. 268	.. 150
THORPE JAMES Capt	....	96	27
TEMPROE JOHN	....	12	 2
TAYLOR WALTOR	....	13	10
THOMPSON: XTOPHER Docto'	....	 9	 3
TOUEY RICHARD	....	15	 7
THORNEHILL TIMOTHY Capt	....	10	....
TUCKER ANN pore	....	 2	....
THOMAS: JOHN pore	....	 4	....
TINDALL RICHARD pore	....	 3	....
V.			
VEREING ALCE:.....................	....	25	11
VEREING JOSHUA	....	10	11
W			
WALWYNE JAMES: Esqr	 7	.. 305	.. 160
WALTORS RICHARD	 3	.. 206	.. 140
WARDLE: CHRISTOPHER	....	15	 1
WALE JOHN	....	.. 159	80
WILLIAMS THOMAS	....	 7	15
WILLIAMS WILLIAM................	....	 5	 2
WHATSON RICHARD pore...........	....	 5	....

	Seruants	Land	Negros
WALLEY HENRY pore	......	 2	......
WRIGHT HENRY pore	......	 2	......
WILLEY: RAWLEY pore	......	 3	......
YEAMONS ELIZ^A^	 2	 50	18
Tot. of Inhabitants is 183	.. 113	6742	2895

JOH:N: STANFAST -
JAS. WALUYN - } Church Wardens

CHILDREN Baptized in y^e^: Parrish of St Johns from ye 25th day of March 1678 to the 29th day of Sep^t^: 1679 According to the parrish Register

1678

March	31	JOHN, Sonne of JOHN JONES
May—	12	ELIZABETH, Daughter of THOMAS POOLER
	26	RICHARD, Sonne of RICHARD POOLER
June—	20	ANN Daughter of JOHN SUMMERS
	21	ELIZABETH Daughter of ROCKINGHAM BASON
	25	SAMUELL, Sonne of JEFFERY BATTALA
October—	3	JOHN, Sonne of Capt: JOHN LESLIE
	20	JOANE, Daughter of HUGH HALL
November—	3	WILLIAM, Sonne of JOHN MILLWARD
,, ,,		THEADOCIA, Daughter of LAWRANCE REESE
,, ,,		DOROTHY, Daughter of RICHARD MOORE
	24	WILLIAM, Sonne of THOMAS GARDNER
,, ,,		JOHN, Sonne of ARON JACOBSONE
	26	SARAH, Daughter of Mr JOHN VAUGHAN
,, ,,		KATHARINE, Daughter of JOHN PEIRCE
,, ,,		THOMAS, Sonne of THOMAS ROOME

1678	December	9	ELIZABETH, Daughter of Docter JAMES KEITH
		27	ANTHONY, Sonne of WILLIAM SHOREY
1679			
	Aprell—	13	THOMAS & ELIZ^A^: } Sonne & Daughter of JOHN DENT
	„ „		SARAH, Daughter of HENRY POLLARD
	„ „		HENRY, Sonne of THOMAS QUINTYNE
	August—	9	JOHN, Sonne of JAMES PEMBERTON
		24	MARY, Daughter of BENJAMEN CORBETT
	„ „		MARY, Daughter of Capt: THO: BALDWYN
		28	WILLIAM & CHARLES— } Sonns of Mr JAMES PEMBERTON
	September—4		LEOLIN, Sonn of LEOLIN LLOYD

28: persons Baptized

BEN: CRYER: Clerk.

INDEX.

AAUSTINE, Thomas, 317*
Abbe, Thomas, 217
Abbey, Sarah, 436
Abbitt, Elizabeth, 179
Abbott, John, 49
———, Marie, 49
———, Richard, 51, 120
Abbs, Edward, 124
Abby, Jo., 35
Abdy, Mathew, 98
Abo-Cromby, Mr., 310
Abof, Isack, 449
Abraham, Agnus, 348
———, William, 436
Abrock, Jo., 111
Absolon, Geo., 132
Abudient, Abraham, 349
Ackland, George, 187, 250
———, Mary, 187, 250
———(or Aukland), Robert, 267
———, Tho., 313
Acklin, Daniell, 414
———, Jo., 50
Adam, John, 473
Adams, see also Addams
———, Andrew, 102
———, Conrad (or Conradt), 473, 491
———, Dorothie, 107
———, Edward, 327, 329
———, alias Adamson, Elisabeth, 431
———, Elizabeth, 491
———, George, 348
———, Hester, 491
———, John, 51, 316*, 327, 329, 342, 488, 491, 493, 496
———, alias Adamson, John, 431
———, Mary, 284, 491
———, Mary Cheame, 284
———, Mr., 178
———, Rachell, 109

Adams, Raph, 185
———, Richard, 91, 119, 284
———, Suzan, 91
———, Thomas, 115, 158, 347
———, William, 76, 126, 308
Adamson, see also Addamson
———, Elisabeth Adams, alias, 431
———, George, 347
———, John Adams, alias, 431
———, Richard, 331
Adaudly, Margaret, 428
Addams, see also Adams
———, Ambross, 443
———, Ann, 174, 223
———, Robert, 239
Addamson, see also Adamson
———, Richard, 444
Adderford, Lawrence, 128
Addice, Edward, 473
Addis, John Orphant, 473
Addison, Deliverance, 495
———, Edward, Junr., 495
———, Mathew, 128
———, Thomas, 184
Aden, Luke, 187
Adson, Georg, 432
Adward's, Robert, 192
Ady, John, 365
Aflick (or Affleck), Andrew, 497, 500
Aires, see also Ayres
———, Samuell, 294
Akers, Christopher, 443
Alambridge (Allambridge, or Alimbridge), John, 327, 329
Albans, see St. Albans
Albemarle, Christopher, Duke of, 162, 164*, 165
———, George, Duke of, 161
Albercht, Hennigo, 347
Albert, Ann, 348

Albon, Alice, 131
Alborn, Edward, 171
Alburie, William, 133
Alcocke, Frauncis, 300
Alcorn (or Alchorne), John, 338, 473
Aldburgh, John, 278
Aldcock, Annis, 98
Alder. Richard, 174
Allerley, Richard, 122
Alderman, Grace, 105
Aldersey, Samuel, 158
Alderson, Thomas, 349
Alderton, Wm., 114
Aldin, Edward, 133
———, George, 121
Aldon, Richard, 240
Aldred, Robert, 84
Aldridg (or Aldridge), Robert, 236, 429
Aldsworth, Bartho., 451
Aldwell, Katherin, 138
Aldworth, Edward, 86
———, Eliz., 133
Alemby, William, 343, see Allamby
Aleworth, Edward, 86
Alexander, Sir William, 158, 159
———, William, 335
Alford, Nico., 135
———, Richard, 232, 446
Alimbridge, see Alambridge
Alington, Giles, 273
Alis, Protherock, 37
Alkynn, Sampson, 137
Allamby, William, 338, see Alemby
Allambridge, see Alambridge
Allcott, Elizabeth, 113
Allen, see also Allin, and Allyn
———, 178
———, Abell, 343
———, Anne, 90

INDEX.

Allen, Elisabeth, 423
———, Grissel, 433
———, Jacob, 423, 451, *see* Alling
———, John, 90, 465
——— (or Allens), John, 327
———, Jone, 425
———, Priscilla, 423
———, Regnald, 298
———, Richard, 328, 336, 340
———, Samuel, 165*
———, Thomas, 326, 327, 329, 330, 398
———, William, 183, 217, 307, 465
Allens (or Allen), John, 327
———, Richard, 327
Allerton, George, 80
Alley, Hugh, 97
Alleyne, Abbll [Abell], 469
Alliday, Jo., 52
Allin, *see also* Allen, and Allyn
———, Edward, 133
———, Eliazer, 348
———, George, 284
———, Gregorie, 120
———, James, 122
———, Joan, 123
———, John, 38, 125, 331
———, Richard, 122, 333
———, Thomas, 64, 84, 125, 138, 451
———, William, 40
Alling, Jacob, 500, *see* Allen
Allington, William, Lord, 162
Allinson, Andrew, 194
———, Wm., 114
Allis, Richard, 150
Allison, Thomas, 348
Allumby (or Alumby), Thomas, 355, 391
Allyn, *see also* Allen, and Allin
———, George, 284
———, Katherin, 284
———, Mathew, 284
———, William, 284
Almond, Awdry, 93
———, Wm., 93
Almie (or Almy), Annis, 93
———, Chri., 93
Alnutt, Mr., 230
———, Mrs., 179
———, Thomas, 179, 225
Alport, Sara, 113
Alsop (Alsope, or Alsopp)
———, Edward, 473, 489, 496
———, Jo., 79
———, Joseph, 58
———, Katherine, 349
———, Machell, 489, 496

Alsop, Peter, 496
———, Richard, 473
———, Robert, 129
———, Tho., 78
Alston (or Alstone), John, 327, 328
Alt, Martha, 461
Althrop, Richard, 184
Alumby, *see* Allumby
Alxarson, Anne, 289
———, Marey, 289
Ambrose, 242
———, Isack, 113
Ames, Joane, 294
———, John, 294
———, Ruth, 294
———, William, 294
Analin (or Avalin), Abram, 189, *see* Avelin, &c.
Anderson, Adam, 473
———, Hanna, 489
———, James, 41, 489
———, Jo., 35, 74
———, Margret, 348
———, Martha, 489
———, Richard, 85, 102, 117
———, Robert, 70
———, Roger, 442
———, Thomas, 37, 473
———, William, 75, 436, 473
Andrew, 428
———, Anthony, 194
Andrews, Andrewes, Anndrews, Androwe, Androwes
———, Anto., 113
———, Charles, 468
———, Elizabeth, 60
———, Euen, 500
———, James, 434
———, Jane, 60
———, Joachim (or Joakin), 221, 271
———, Jocomb, 174
———, John, 316*, 317*
———, Jonathan, 463, 466
———, Owen, 70
———, Roger, 473
———, Sage, 434
———, Samuell, 60
———, Thomas, 473
———, William, 120, 137, 188, 277, 280, 281, 289, 466, 500
Andros, Sir Edmund (or Edmond), 164*, 165, 165*, 168
———, William, 264
Angelo (Negroes), 174, 224
Anley, Nathan, 102
Anmer, Henry, 36
Ann (a maid) 173

Anndrews, *see* Andrews
Anthony (or Anthonie)
———, Anthony, 451
———, John, 258
———, (Negro), 172, 182, 185
Antonio (Negro), 241
Antony (Antoney, or Antonye)
———, Arthur, 269
———, Henry, 142
———, (Negro), 244
———, Walter, 81
Antor, Allexander, 451
Antrobuss, Joan, 45
Antunes, Gabriell, 450
Apleby, *see* Appleby
Apleton, *see* Appleton
Aplewhite (or Applewhite)
———, Henry, 352, 400
———, Mrs., 463
Appleby (or Apleby), William, 83, 192, 196
Appleton (or Apleton), Richard, 185, 244
Ap Roberts, John, 190
Ap Thomas, Thomas, 122
Ap Williams, Rice, 179
Arch, John, 473, 494
Archbold, Tho., 129
Archdin, Tho., 138
Archer, Hugh, 442
———, Jo., 116
———, Joseph, 193
Ard, James, 453
Ardinton, Edmond, 116
Are, Sarah, 349
Argall, Sir Samuell, 218, 270
Aris, John, 80, 347
Armestronge, *see* Armstrong
Armitage (or Armetage)
———, Henry, 347
———, John, 499
———, Thomas, 140
Armsby, Jo., 120
Armstrong (or Armestronge)
———, 243
———, Ann, 348
———, Henry, 102
———, Jocky, 194
———, Katherin, 82
Army, John, 184, 242
Arndell, John, 261
———, Peeter, 262
Arnet (or Arnett)
———, David, 473, 492, 496
———, Jane, 492, 496
———, Patrick, 473
———, Samuel, 492, 496
Arnold, Ann, 98
———, Benedict, 163
———, James, 111

INDEX. 511

Arnold, Jesper, 98
———, Robert, 120
———, Tho., 39, 79
Aron, Abraham Burges, 449
Arp, Jo., 103
Arras, Nicholas, 180
Arres, Samuell, 289
Arrobas, Moses, 450
Arthur, 434
———, John, 303
———, Katherine, 348
———, Mathew, 153
———, Michaell, 473
Arundel (or Arrundell)
———, Elizabeth, 184, 222
———, John, 184
———, Margreat (or Margrett), 184, 215
———, Petter, 184, 274
———, Richard, 173, 222
———, Robert, 498
———, William, 94
Ascam, Abigaile, 225, *see* Longman
———, Peeter, 225
Ascomb (or Ascombe)
———, Abigall, 175
———, Goodman, 191
———, John, 188
———, Mary, 175
Aser, *see* Asser
Ash, Christo., 194
———, Edward, 38
———, Richard, 141
Ashbey, Abraham, 89
———, Alce, 89
———, Hanna, 89
———, Jeremy, 89
———, Mary, 89
———, Sarra, 89
Ashborn, Francis, 85
Ashburner, William, 473
Ashcrofte, Jo., 137
Ashendine, Tho., 441, 451
Ashford, Ambrose, 326, 331
Ashley, Ann, 175, 226
———, Anthony, Lord, 161, 162
———, Mary, 37
———, Mr., 110
———, Sam., 37
Ashmole, Elie, 160*
Ashmore, Anthony, 141
Ashon, George, 102
Ashton, Alice, 123
———, Henry, 160
Ashurst, Beniamin, 473
———, John, 74, 473
Askew, Tho., 109
———, William, 171, 207

Askume, John, 264
Askyn, Robert, 95
Asser, (or Aser) Godheard, 306 308
Assueros, Walter, 373, 399
Ast, Richard, 37
Astin, William, 428
Aston, Brian, 139
———, Edward, 141, 186
———, James, 86
———, Robert, 240
———, Wm., 52
Astwood, Jo., 46
Atherson, Jo., 63
Atherton, Wm., 349
Atkins (or Attkins), *see* Atkyns
———, Abigall, 240
———, Jane, 434
———, Jeremy (Jeremiah, &c.), 332, 339, 340
———, John, 182, 241
———, Sir Jonathan, 162*, 460, 461, 462, 463, 464
———, Mr., 191
———, Richard, 176, 191, 240
———, Robert, 74
———, Sarah, 450
———, Thomas, 133, 434
Atkinson (or Attkinson)
———, Ann, 183
———, Charles, 182
———, Edward, 117
———, Frances, 193
———, Geo., 136
———, James, 122
———, Jo., 36, 37, 68
———, Love, 68
———, Martin, 116
———, Miles, 109
———, Richard, 103
———, Robert, 51, 193
———, Samuell, 310
———, Tho., 109
Atkyns, Henry, 40, *see* Atkins
Atterhorn, George, 136
Attkins, *see* Atkins
Attkinson, *see* Atkinson
Atwell, Wm., 143
Atwood, Phillipp, 49, 59
Attwood, Richard, 442
Aualin, *see* Avalin, Avelin, &c.
Aubony, Thomas, 407
Auborn, Edward, 216
Aukland (or Ackland), Robert, 267
Aust, Henry, 348
Austen, Samuell, 469
Austin, Ann, 427
———, Edward, 83
———, John, 118, 364, 427

Austin, Richard, 298
———, Thomas, 316*, 324, 344
Austine, John, 473
———, Robert, 174
———, Thomas, 473
Austrian, Cornelious, 451
Avalin, *see* Avelin
Avelin, Avalin, Aualin, or Analin
———, Abram (or Abraham), 189, 253
———, Arthur, 253
Averie (or Avery)
———, George, 121
———, Jacob, 121
———, Jane, 468
———, John, 96, 136
———, Marie, 113
———, Mary, 349
———, Thomas, 70
———, William, 433, 468
Avoake, John, 340
Awbrey, Alice, 67
———, Lewes, 81
———, Peter, 67
Awde, Samuell, 95
Awdry, Humfrey, 126
Awdley, Wm., 140
Awman, John, 422
———, Margaret, 422
Axstell, Tho., 121
Axton, Jacob, 308
Aymie, Wm., 84
Aymies, Jo., 112
Aynis, Jo., 104
Ayres, Anna, 66
———, Benjamin, 66
———, Christian, 66
———, Dorothy, 66
———, Eliz., 126
———, John, 379
———, Marie, 66
———, Rabecca, 66
———, Sara, 66
———, Symon, 66
———, Tho., 66
———, *see* Aires

BABB, 123
———, Mr., 144
———, Tho., 110, 130
Babbington, *see* Babington
Babell, Hugh, 394, 403
Baber, Francis, 283
——— John, 168
Babington, Babbington
———, Jo., 119
———, Randall, 316*
———, Thomas, 356

INDEX.

Backford, Clement, 141
Backley, Jo., 59
Bacon, Daniell, 129
——, Edward, 71
——, George, 55, *see* Mason
——, John, 55
——, Samuell, 55
——, Susan, 55
Badcocke, Wm., 154
Baddam, Jo., 125
Badeley, John, 230
Badland, John, 153
Badston, John, 176
Bagbie, Jo., 118
Bagford, Henry, 193
Bagg, John, 334, 337
——, Roger, 363, 371, 372, 380, 381, 388, 396, 406
Baggelay, Baggley, *see* Bagley
Bagget, Jane, 435
Baglen, Thomas, 228
Bagley, Baggley, Baggelay
——, Jo., 37
——, Judith, 133
——, Phillip, 104
——, Tho., 135
Bagin, Henry, 51
Bagnall, John, 350
Bagwell, Francis, 351
——, Henry, 170, 208, 268
——, Pr., 318*, 320, 323
——, Robert, 208
——, Thomas, 170, 229
Bailife, George, 234
Baily, John, 430
——, Mary, 271
——, Temperance, 269
——, William, 269
——, *see* Bailey, Baley, Baly, &c.
Baines, Allice, 451
——, Robert, 193
——, Widow, 443
——, *see* Banes, Baynes
Bainham, John, 270, 272, *see* Baynam
Baker, Alexander, 69
——, Christian, 69
——, Daniell, 40
——, Dorothie, 96
——, Elizabeth, 69, 96, 113, 289
——, Ellis, 101
——, Esias, 474
——, Francis, 45
——, Handgate, 111
——, James, 333, 338, 341
——, John, 67, 111, 118, 194, 262, 289, 294, 316, 316*, 318, 318*, 320, 324, 343

Baker Margerie, 111
——, Marie, 95
——, Mary, 67
——, Morice, 192
——, Peter, 439
——, Richard, 238
——, Robert, 39
——, Samvell, 78
——, Smith, 63
——, Thomas, 105, 289
——, William, 171, 176, 216, 232, 240
Bakewell, Francis, 113
——, Theodorus, 111
Bal, John, 437
——, Thomas, 427
——, *see* Ball
Balam, Charles, 500
Baldin, Jo., 106
——, Wm., 106, 117
Baldry, Robert, 120
Baldwin, Baldwine, Baldwinn, Baldwyn, Baldwyne, Baldwynn
——, Hugh, 177, 220
——, John, 114, 115, 180, 234
——, Mary, 508
——, Nicholas, 215
——, Susan, 220
——, Thomas, 173, 186, 435, 508
——, Widow, 448
——, William, 79, 185, 187, *see* Bauldwin
Bales, Tho., 114
Baley, Baly, *see* Baily, &c.
——, Ann, 216
——, Lewis, 179
——, Mary, 205
——, Nicholas, 170, 216
——, Temperance, 210
——, Thomas, 205
——, William, 205, 268
Ball, Elizabeth, 488
——, Geo., 81, 304
——, Goodwife, 188
——, Humphrey, 488
——, James, 351
——, John, 500
——, Joseph, 351, 363, 384, 405, 415
——, Mary, 488
——, Richard, 113, 234
——, Robart, 265
——, Robertt, 188
——, *see* Bal
Ballance, Jo., 117
Ballard, Elizabeth, 107
——, Hester, 107

Ballard, Jo., 107
——, Samuell, 444
——, Wm., 107
Balls, Robert, 195
Balme, Jo., 115
Balrick, Thomas, 351
Baly, *see* Baley, Baily, &c.
Bambury, Thomas, 316*
Bamford, John, 36, 172, 217
Banbridge, Christo., 116
——, Henry, 114
Banbrig (or Banbrigg), Robert, 474, 500
Bancks, Banckes, *see* Bank's
Bancroft, Christopher, 431
——, Elisabeth, 431
Banes, Anguis, 468
——, Martha, 107, 468
——, *see* Baines, Baynes
Bangton (or Baugton), Isacke, 173
Banister, Henry, 103
——, Richard, 355
Bank's, Bancks, Banckes
——, Edward, 75, 194
——, Elizabeth, 125, 440
——, Francis, 182, 241
——, George, 255
——, Henry, 104, 429
——, James, 85, 125
——, Joseph, 350
——, Thomas, 125, 177, 436
——, William, 43, 51
Bankus, Christopher, 223
Banner, Ri., 313*
Banshott, Tho., 299
Banton, Ivie, 213
Banum, Elzabeth, 249
——, John, 249
——, *see* Baynam
Baram, Anthony, 241
——, Elizabeth, 241
——, *see* Barham
Barbe, Adrian, 199
Barber, Ann, 186, 195
——, Francis, 79
——, Geo., 102
——, Henry, 186
——, Susan, 179
——, Tho., 42
——, Wm., 81, 129
Barcrofte, Jane, 150
——, John, 150
Barcott, Symon, 86
Bard, Tho., 113
Bardin, Nichas., 296
Barefoote, Tho., 103
Barham, Anthony, 272, *see* Baram
Barke, Francis, 192

INDEX.

Barker, Alice, 136
———, Francis, 121
———, Henry, 95, 176
———, John, 138, 354, 439
———, Lawrence, 112
———, Mary, 82
———, Robert, 357, 386, 413
———, Steephen, 239
———, William, 95
Barkly, Barkley
———, Edward, 184, 236, 267
———, Jane, 236
Barloe, Jo., 82
———, Wm., 120
Barlow, Henry, 180
Barnaby, Barnabe, Barnabie
———, John, 188, 247
Barnard, Humphry, 350
———, Richard, 40
———, William, 184, 241, 333, 338, 340
Barnardo, Mrs., 180
Barne, Robert, 134
Barnes, Barns
———, Barnabie, 103
———, Edward, 51, 182
———, Elizabeth (or Elisabeth), 423, 437, 462
———, Giles, 70
———, Henrie, 102
———, James, 122
———, Jonathan, 129
———, John, 86, 444, 451
———, Nicholas, 351
———, Olliver, 474
———, Richard, 111
———, Sarah, 423, 437
———, Tho., 127
———, Widow, 462
———, William, 71, 119, 133, 166*, 167, 296, 423, 437
Barnet, Barnett
———, John, 142, 189, 226
———, Mrs., 432
———, Thomas, 172, 222
———, William, 215, 432, 452
Barnewel, Nicholas, 437
Barnewell, Robert, 356
Barnie, Ann, 95
———, Debora, 121
Barnit, Francis, 139
Baron, William, 342, see Barron
Barradall (or Barrodall), Theophilus, 445, 451
Barrasman, Alexander, 452
Barran, Margerie, 71
Barrat, Annis, 75
Basret, Barrett
———, Frances, 185, 236
———, John, 70

Barret, Richard, 447
———, Tho., 66
———, Walter, 256
———, William, 172
Barrey, see Barry
Barrith, Wm., 133
Barrodall, see Barradall
Barron, John, 451
———, Robert, 129
———, Wm., 452, see Baron
Barrow, Rebecca, 356
———, Thomas, 193
Barrowe, Jo., 79
Barrowman, Widow, 444
Bar Simon, Hester, 449
Barruch, Abraham, 449
———, Aron, 449
———, Rebecah, 450
Barry, Barrey
———, Alce, 474
———, Clement, 154
———, James, 296
———, John, 474
———, William, 183, 260
Bartcherd, Tho., 117
Bartlett, Allexander, 470
———, John, 334, 336, 340
———, Richard, 182
———, Robert, 150
Barton, Christopher, 355
———, Isack, 68
———, James, 350
Barwell, John, 350
Barwick, Lawrence, 125
Bascomb, Georg, 303
Basden, William, 303
Basford, William, 82
Basher, Jo., 41
Bashford, John, 496
Baskervile, Robert, 137
Bason, Elizabeth, 507
———, John, 340
———, Rockingham, 507
Basse, Mrs., 171
———, Nathaniell, 184, 241, 272
———, Samwell, 184
———, William, 171
Bassett, John, 63, 297
———, Olliver, 75
———, Tho., 42
———, Wm., 93
Bassit, Thomas, 86
Bastions, Jacob, 433
Batcheller, John, 134
Bate, Alice, 68
———, James, 68
———, John, 241
———, Lettecia, 440
———, Lyddia, 68
———, Margaret, 68

Bate, Marie, 68
———, Nicholas, 120
———, Wm., 120, 451
Bateman, Elizabeth, 113
———, John, 474
———, Mathew, 119
———, Robert, 103
Bates, Ann, 48
———, Ben., 48
———, Clement, 48
———, James, 48
———, John, 217
———, Joseph, 48
———, Rachell, 48
———, Richard, 119, 350
———, Wm., 86
Bath, John, Earl of, 160*, 165
Bathe, John, 63
Bathoe, Wm., 128
Bathurst, Joseph, 165*
Batley, Edward, 424
———, Jeffry, 424
———, Priscilla, 424
Batson (or Battson), Thomas, 451, 463
Batt, Anne, 299
———, Christopher, 299
———, Dorothie, 299
———, Ellin, 220
———, John, Senr., 500
———, —, 182, 499
———, Michaell, 176, 220
———, Robert, 319
Battala, Jeffery, 507
———, Samuell, 507
Batte, Coll*., 440
Batten, Robert, 298
Battersby, George, 350, 357
Battine, Battyne, Battyn
———, Doctor, 338
———, John, Senr., 461
———, —, Junr., 451, 462
Battison, Julian, 355
Battrick, Wm., 59
Battyn, &c., see Battine
Baugh, Thomas, 170, 202
Baugton (or Bangton), Isacke, 173
Bauldwin, William, 247, see Baldwin
Bawde, Randall, 208
Bawden, John, 343
Bawdrye, Mary, 192
Baxter, Edward, 475
———, Robert, 109
Bay, Jo., 122
Baycock, Tho., 111
Bayley, Baylie, Bayly, Baylye
———, Ann, 170
———, Charles, 474

Bayley, George, 180
———, Henry, 117
———, John, 86, 103, 191, 444
———, Margaret, 121
———, Robert, 130, 474
———, Roger, 304
———, Richard, 82, 300, 475, 500
———, Wm., 128
Baylife, Temperance, 171
Baylys, Col., 506
Baynam, Elizabeth, 186, *see* Bainham, Banum
Baynan, John, 185
Bayne, Laughline, 446
Baynes, Wm., 442, *see* Baines
Bayns, James, 430
Beacham, Elisabeth, 433
Beacon, Hugh, 105
Bead, John, 41
———, William, 84
Beads, Mathew, 139
Beadslie, Beadsley, Beardsley
———, John, 45
———, Joseph, 45
———, Marie, 45
———, Wm., 45
Beal, Margaret, 432
———, Peter, 432
———, Rebecca, 323
Beale, Sara, 88
———, Wm., 448
Beamond, John, 60
———, Wm., 60
Beanam, John, 193
Beane, Christopher, 170, 215
———, Steeven, 101
———, Tho., 114
———, William, 189, 250
Beard, John, 354
———, Richard, 475
Beards, Elizabeth, 66
Beardsley, *see* Beadslie, &c.
Beare, Richard, 128
———, Walter, 221
Bearne, Francis, 499
Beaton, Nathaniel, 319
———, Wm., 75
Beauford, Richard, 118
Béava, George, 198
Beck, Henry, 108
Beckett, Stephen, 278
Beckkitt, William, 52
Beckles, Elisabeth, 424
———, Robert, 424, 444
———, Susanna, 424
Beckwith, Robert, 103
Beddell, Jo., 79
Bedding, Rabecca, 71
Beddle, Wm., 50

Bedford (or Beeford), Ann, 129
———, Nathaniell, 70
———, Richard, 496
———, William, 179, 232
Bedlam, Tho., 71
Bedwell, John, 304
Bee, Jo., 86
Beeby, Jo., 83
Beeckman, Geerrard, 166*
Beeding, Wm., 359, 369, 395
Beedle, Joseph, 452
Beeford (or Bedford), Ann, 129
Beeke, Susanah, 447
Beere, Henry, 82
Beeresto, Geo., 131
———, Wm., 131
Beeston, Sir William, 167*, 168
———, William, 166*
Bectell, Jo., 115
Beetes, John, 279
Belchamber, Thomas, 165*
Belchem, John, 500
Belcher, Edward, 98
———, Jeremy, 59
Belford, John, 470
Belfour, James, 355
Belk, Tho., 122
Bell, Fran., 460
———, James, 71
———, John, 122, 124
———, Robert, 498
———, Tho., 81, 84
———, William, 307
Bellamy (or Bellemie), Edward, 316*, 317, 343
Bellis, Edward, 129
Bellomont, Richard, Earl of, 167*, 168
Bellowes, Jo., 49
Belson, Thomas, 263
Belt, Humfrey, 96
———, Isack, 129
Belton, Jo., 63
Beman, John, 193
Benbricke, John, 194
Bendige, Edward, 195
Bendish, Sir Thomas, 463
Benes, Richard, 142
Benfield, Brasil, 422
———, Edward, 422
———, Rebeccah, 422
Benford, Jo., 118
Benge, William, 235
Beniamin, Jo., 150
———, Richard, 150
Benet, Benett, *see* Bennett, &c.
Benn, Wm., 128
Bennerman, Wm., 136
Bennett, Bennet, Benet, Benett
———, Bartholomew, 70

Bennett, Benjamin, 167*
———, Charles, 316
———, Edward, 241
———, Jane, 72
———, Joane, 259
———, John, 80, 118, 182, 316*
———, Katherine, 209
———, Margery, 230
———, Mary, 242
———, Mathew, 104
———, Mr., 243
———, Robert, 178, 191, 248
———, Samuel, 107, 183, 259
———, Thomas, 95, 230, 242, 326, 330
———, William, 196, 209, 327
Benning, Elizabeth, 71
Benson, Henry, 143, 170, 207
———, John, 128
———, Mary, 355
———, William, 40
Benstedd, Jo., 73
Benthall, Walter, 439
Bentham, Matthew, 435
Bentley, Bently, Bentlie
———, Abram, 119
———, Alice, 131
———, Jo., 109, 132
———, Martin, 356, 474
———, Mary, 107
———, William, 131, 251, 273
Benton, Robert, 115
Beomont, Gamaliell, 76
———, Tho., 126
Beresford, Berresford, Berrisford
———, Henrie, 140
———, Thomas, 323, 471
Beriston, Theoder, 171
———, Theophilus, 222, 267
Berkeley, John, Lord, 162
———, Sir William, 159*, 162*
Berkynn, Tho., 51
Berman, Margrett, 170
Bernard, John, 278, 279, 280, 282, 283, 307
———, Mary, 279, 283
———, Musachiell, 283
———, Nathaniell, 128, 283
———, Phebe, 280
———, Samuell, 282
———, William, 96
Bernardo, ———, 180, Sheppard
———, Mr., 235
Berne, Olough, 119
Berresford, *see* Beresford
Berridg, Edward, 432

Berrisford, see Beresford
Berrow, Christopher, 549, 352, 383
Berry, John, 272
——, Richard, 84
——, William, 104
Besford, Jo., 74
Beson, Tho., 112
Bessy, Anto., 107
Best, Christopher, 174
——, Richard, 140
——, Thomas, 124, 186, 327, 330
Bestt, Francis, 443
Bethell, James, 122
Bett, Wm., 84, 136
Betton, Samuell, 192
Betts, Leonard, 103, 145
Bew, Robert, 174, 180, 224
Bewlie, Grace, 59
Bevenister, Eliam, 354
Bever, Isack, 137
——, Jo., 83
Bibbie (or Bibby), William, 188, 265
Bick, Francis, 101
—— Richard, 102
Bickham (or Brickham), Richard, 334, 336, 340
Bickle, Thomas, 350
Bickley, Richard, 237
Bicknall, William, 441
Bickwell, Agnis, 284
——, John, 284
——, Zachary, 284
Bicroft, Edward, 80
Biddle, Wm., 446
Biddleston, Henrie, 63
Bidlecomb, Nicholas, 492
Biffin, Thomas, 447
Bigg, Rachell, 68
Biggnell, Wm., 500
Biggs, Elizabeth, 83
——, Mrs., 171
——, Phillipp, 83
——, Richard, 170, 171, 205, 268
——, Sarah, 205
——, Thomas, 108, 171, 192
——, William, 171, 319*, 322
—— (or Briggs), William, 319
Bignall, John, Junr., 452
——, ——, Senr., 452
Bilford, James, 350
Bill, Jo, 46
——, Marie, 49
Billiard, John, 186, 266
Billinge, Cornelius, 67
Billinghurst, John, 136
Billingsley, Sir Henry, 155

Billins, Jo., 112, 123
Bills, Robert, 110
Binckes, Bincks, Bink's
——, Ann, 220
——, Charles, 351
——, Goodwife, 180
——, William, 180, 220
Bindloss, John, 163
Bingham, Wm., 63
Bink's, see Binckes
Binney, James, 472
Binsley, William, 261
Bird, Benjamin, 328, 448
——, Henry, 353
——, John, 451
——, Peter, 319, 319*, 320*
——, see Burd
Birkehead, George, 451
Birkenhedd, Francis, 140, see Byrkenhead
Bishop, Bishopp
——, Joan, 474
——, Jo., 105
——, Robert, 325, 352
——, Thomas, 355, 442
——, Valentine, 125
——, William, 438
Bissex, William, 500
Bitler, Mr. 464
Bitton, James, 66
Bixe, David, 298
Black, Andrew, 472
Blackborne, James, 262
Blackett, Tym., 79
Blackgrove, Anto., 39
Blackleech, John, 352
Blackler, Peter, 139
Blacklock, George, 139
Blacklocke, Thomas, 189
Blackly, Tho., 110
Blackman, Brian, 460
——, Humfrey, 122
——, Jeremy, 119
——, Mary, 431
——, Nicholas, 170, 207
——, Sarah, 430
——, Thomas, 461
——, William, 431
Blackston, Eliza., 299
—— (or Blakeston), Nathaniel, 167*, 168
Blackwell, Jeremy, 131
Blackweller, Elias, 433
——, Sarah, 435
Blackwood, Susan, 176, 223
Blades, Anto., 40
——, Edward, 383, 395, 411
——, John, 375
——, Nicholas, 41

Blake, Bartlomew, 229
——, Francis, 125
——, John, 145, 349, 500
——, Nicholas, 376, 406, 474
——, Robert, 434
——, Tho., 441
——, Walter, 171, 238
Blakeston, see Blackston
Blanch, Eliz., 109
Blanchard, William, 474
Blanche, James, 296
Blanchflower, Elisabeth, 430
Blanck's, Thomas, 220
Bland, Jo., 120
——, Luke, 79
——, Margaret, 428
Blaney, Edward, 174, 224, 232
Blason, Ann, 63
Blathwaite, William, 163
Bliss, Owen, 63
Blithe, Tho., 119
Block, Steeven, 101
——, Wm., 126
Bloes, Tho., 86
Blogget, Bloggett
——, Daniell, 61
——, Samvell, 61
——, Suzan, 61
——, Tho., 61
Blomfield, Sarah, 280, 282
——, William, 280, 282
Blore, Francis, 264
——, John, 264
Blorke, William, 145
Blosse, Mary, 278, 279
——, Richard, 278
Blouncker, Henry, 162
Blowden, Alexander, 495
——, Mary, 495
——, Sarah, 495
Blower, Gody, 189
——, John, 189, 266, 274
——, Tho., 132
Bloxam, alias Ingles, Nicholas, 139
Bloxsall, Jo., 69
Blunt, George, 355
Boddy, Robert, 121
Boden, John, 469
Bodilies, Arthur, 124
Bodingham, John, 354
Bodkin, Martin, 353
——, Nicho., 354
Boeman, Richard, 135
Bold, Margaret, 129
Boldsworth, Anto., 64
Boles, John, 442
Bolt, Gabriell, 63
Bolte, Amias, 206
Bolton, Ambross, 352

INDEX.

Bolton, Nathaniell, 70
———, Richard, 267
———, Samuell, 353
———, Tho., 37
Bomer, Emanuell, 36
Bonales, Mr., 262
Bonall, Anthony, 184, 261
———, James, 184
Bond, Elisabeth, 423
———, Francis, 342, 423, 451, 461, 474, 500
———, Giles, 366, 377
———, Samuell, 316, 318, 342
———, Thomas, 352
Bonett, Edward Plantᵉ, 451
Bonfilly (or Bonfolly), John, 129
Bonham, George, 94
Bonn, Jo., 128
Bonner, James, 213
———, John, 139, 390
———, Richard, 145
Bonnett, Thomas, 431, 474
Bonnick, Nathaniell, 132
Booghert, Barnard, 359
Boole, Joseph, 154
Boomer, Thomas, 96
Boon (or Boone)
———, Jo., 52
———, Samuell, 332, 339, 340
———, Thomas, 433
Boot, Francis, 169
Booth, Elizabeth, 186, 255
———, Gregorie, 143
———, Henry, 174, 177, 223
———, John, 127, 178, 466
———, Mary, 186
———, Marie, 123
———, Mrs., 463
———, Reynold, 116, 255
———, Sir William, 326, 328, 331, 332, 335, 341
———, William, 339
Boothman, John, 470
Borden, Eliz., 78
———, Joan, 78
———, John, 78
———, Joseph, 445, 451
———, Mathew, 78
Borebancke, Joseph, 91
Borinthon, Thomas, 154
Borne, Marmaduke, 134
———, Richard, 38
———, Tho., 38
Borowe, Anne, 294
———, John, 294
Borrows, John, 439
Boss, Peter, 418
Bossinger, Tho., 393
Bostock (or Bostocke)

Bostock, Edmond, 106
———, Edward, 89, 105, *see* Boswell
———, Henrie, 140
———, Loughton, 36
———, Thomas, 89, 98, 99, 100
Boswell, Edward, 89, 91, *see* Bostock
———, Jo., 81
———, Samvell, 115
Bottam, John, 179
Bottell, Paul, 81
Bottom, John, 181
Bottomly, Jo., 115
Boucher, John, 451
———, Jerreard, 452
Bouett, *see* Bovett
Bouey, *see* Bovey
Boughei, Jo., 135
Bouldin, Mary, 274
———, Thomas, 274
Bouldinge, Thomas, 255
———, William, 255
Bouline, Henry, 474
Boulle, Bridgett, 289
Boult, Annis, 171
Boulten (or Boulton), Richard, 187, 251, 273
Bourbicth, Edward, 219
Bourk, Bryan, 71
Bourn (or Bourne)
———, John, 474
———, ———, Junr., 474
———, Robert, 268
———, Samuell, 474
Bovett, Edmond (or Edmund), 319, 320, 320*, 322
———, Edward, 320*
———, John, 318*, 319*, 325
———, Thomas, 327, 329
Bovey, Widow, 445
Bowden, Joan, 105
———, Michaell, 153
———, Theophilus, 447
Bowdler, Andrew, 349
———, Ellinor, 460
Bowen, James, 434
———, William, 434
Bowes, John, 38, 112
———, Katherin, 95
Bowhane, Teag., 353
Bowler, William, 119
Bownd, John, 41
Bowton, Jo., 111
Bowyer, Daniell, 124
———, Tho., 119
Box, Ann, 352
———, Beniamine, 195
———, John, 195, 214

Boxfield, Thomas, 474
Boyce, Chri., 137
———, Francis, 151
———, Joseph, 140
———, *see* Boyse, Boys
Boyden, Thomas, 279
Boyle, Naamy, 193
Boylson, Tho., 99
Boyna, Daniell, 449, 452
Boyner, John, 474
Boys, Francis, 425
———, Luke, 169
———, Mary, 468
———, Mrs., 169
———, Samuel, 468
———, *see* Boyce, Boyse
Boyse, Allice, 202
———, Chyna, 208
———, Luke, 202
———, Humphry, 191
———, *see* Boyce, Boys
Braban, Robert, 51
Brabant, Alexander, 133
Braby, Elizabeth, 172
———, Stephen, 172
Brackley, Edward 305
———, Mary, 121
———, *see* Brakley
Braddock, Nathan, 117
Bradford, Henry, 224
———, John, 465
———, Tho., 117
Bradham, John, 446
Bradley, Bradly, Bradlie
———, Ann, 434
———, Dorothie, 105
———, Elizabeth, 490
———, Georg, 432
———, Henry, 434
———, Margret, 490
———, Michaell, 353
———, Ralph, 474
———, Robert, 474, 490
Bradshaw, Richard, 172
———, William, 462
Bradston, John, 184, 226
Bradstreet, Anna, 282
———, Bridgett, 280
———, Humphry, 280, 282
———, John, 282
———, Martha, 282
———, Mary, 282
Bradway, Bradwaye
———, Adria, 204
———, Allexander, 170, 204
———, Sisley, 204
Bragg, John, 341
———, Widow, 444
———, William, 434, 452

INDEX.

Braghton (Braughton, or Broughton), Charls, 319*, 324
Brakley, Jane, 185
——, William, 193
——, see Brackley
Branch, Christopher, 169, 201
——, Mary, 201
——, Thomas, 201
——, see Braunch
Brancker, Branker
——, Edward, 423
——, Mary, 423
——, Nathaniell, 423, 446
Brandby, Eliz*., 354
Brandon, Hugh, 451
——, Marttin, 269
Brane, Thomas, 97
Brangman, Edward, 307
——, Samuell, 303, 307
Branker, see Brancker
Branlin, Ann, 211
——, William, 211
Bransby, Thomas, 181, 230
——, William, 94
Bransbyes, Mr., 231
Brasey, Wm., 61
Brasier, Abraham, 166*
Brass, Alice, 137
Braughton (Braghton, or Broughton), Charls, 319*, 324
Braunch, Jo., 138, see Branch
Bray, John, 340
Bread, Arthur, 356
——, George, 445
——, Thomas, 353, 356
Brearly, Martin, 351
——, Thomas, 440
Breddy, Patrick, 101
Breedon, Thomas, 160*
Brent, Robert, 165
Bressett, John, 340
Brett, James, 75
——, John, 351, 452
Brettland, Amy, 467
——, William, 467
Bretton, Ralph, 489
Brewer, Daniell, 150, 442
——, Elizabeth, 137
——, Nicholas, 429
Brewett, George, 138
——, Kat., 136
Brewood, Thomas, 274
Brewster, Phillip, 452
——, Richard, 271
Brewynn, Tho., 134
Brian, Elenor, 436
——, Mary, 436
——, Phillip, 436

Brian, Robert, 110
——, see Bryan, Mac Brian
Briar, Joseph, 367, see Bryer
Brice (or Price), John, 319
Bricke, Edward, 174
Brickham (or Bickham), Richard, 334, 336, 340
Bridges, Edmond, 107
——, Elisha, 67
——, Henry, 195
——, Thomas, 234
Bridgestock (or Bridgestocke)
——, Ann, 492
——, Mary, 489
——, Richard, 489, see Brigstock
——, William, 492
Bridgwatter, Isbell, 218
——, Richard, 177, 218
Bridle, John, 326, 330
Briers, Robert, 79
Briggham, Tho., 62
Briggins, Leonard, 139
Briggoll, Mark, 102
Briggs, George, 461
——, James, 135
——, Jo., 108
—— (or Biggs), Wm., 319
——, William, 474
Brighton, Tho., 132
Brigstock, Richard, 474, see Bridgestock
Bringhurst, Thomas, 446
Brint, Morgan, 81
Brisco, Ann, 102
Brishitt, Petter, 191
Bristow, Bristowe
——, Eliz., 124
——, John, Junr., 303
——, ——, 305, see Marshall
——, Richard, 441
Britland, Richard, 462
Brittaine, Britten, Brittin, Britton
——, Dennis, 142
——, Jo., 138
——, Robert, 184, 246
——, Tho., 79
Broad, Thomazin, 123
Broadshaw, Richard, 217
Brock, Brocke
——, John, 259
——, Lawrence, 140
——, Richard, 70
——, Robert, 71
——, Thomas, 332, 337, 340
——, William, 173, 205
Brodbanke, Thomas, 195
Broderick, Brodricke
——, Allen, 167*

Broderick, William, 165*, 167
Brodley, Daniell, 53
Brogan, Nico., 141
Brogden, John, 193
Brogdon, Humphry, 451
Brograve, Henry, 353
Bromby, Jo., 64
——, Tho., 64
Brome, John, 352
Bromedg, Sarah, 230
Bromley, Davie, 95
——, Launcelott, 141
Bromwell, Isack, 110
Bronsford, Jonathan, 95
Broockes, William Morgan, alias, 247
Brook, Brooke, Brookes, Brooks
——, Alice, 113
——, Ann, 84
——, Barnabie, 128
——, Bazill, 35
——, Chidley, 166, 167*
——, Cutberd, 195
——, George, 96
——, Gilbert, 93
——, James, 113, 183, 259
——, John, 87, 474
——, Mr., 432
——, Richard, 62, 77, 81, 123, 129
——, Robert, Lord, 159
——, ——, 79
——, Samuel, 467
——, Sibile, 187
——, Thomas, 62, 77, 128, 171, 217, 356, 470
——, Walter, 95
——, William, 81, 93, 96, 140, 187, 273, 441
Brookehaven, Jo., 70
Brooker, Geo., 116
Brookes, see Brook
Brookman, Amy, 467
——, Thomas, 467
Brooks, see Brook
Brooman, Freese, 129
Broome, Roger, 132
Broomer, Joan, 62
——, Marie, 58
Broomish, Edward, 127
Broque, Gillain, 198
——, Louis, 199
——, Robert, 198
Brotherton, Hester, 102
Broughton (Braghton or Braughton), Charls, 318*, 319*, 324
——, Henry, 73
——, Thomas, 96
——, William, 431

INDEX.

Browing, *see* Browning, &c.
Browinge, William, 201
Brown, Browne
———, Christopher, 117, 170, 203
———, Edward, 41, 129
———, El., 446
———, Elisabeth, 432
———, Francis, 354
———, Hugh, 353
———, Humry, 441
———, James, 356, 386, 392, 410
———, John, 61, 63, 68, 87, 91, 111, 122, 135, 140, 150, 171, 173, 181, 214, 311, 327, 328, 331, 335, 339, 372, 434
———, Jonas, 316*, 318, 343
———, Josiah, 166*
———, Liddia, 88
———, Mary, 109
———, Michell, 36
———, Nicholas, 187, 253
———, Phil., 279, 280, 281, 282
———, Rachaell, 349
———, Ralph, 125
———, Rebecca, 252
———, Richard, 83
———, Robert, 132, 141, 187, 252
———, Roger, 304
———, Stephen, 474
———, Suzan, 77
———, Thomas, 42, 74, 122, 191, 194, 428, 460
———, Weston, 185, 257
———, William, 109, 114, 119, 183, 231, 250, 259, 327, 328, 352
Browning, Browninge
———, Ann, 350
———, John, 242
———, Joseph, 126
———, William, 169
Brownley, Richard, 52
Browton, Jo., 127
Bruer, John, 317*, 342
Bruister, Wm., 132
Brumwell, John, 64
Bruncock, John, 433
Brufing, Jo., 80
Brunt, Edward, 39, 128
———, Jo., 127
Bruntts, Samuell, 439
Brush, John, 431
———, Mary, 431
Bruster, Abram, 104
———, Elizabeth, 71
———, Richard, 112

Bruton, Robert, 297
———, William, 39
Bruxston, Tho., 114
Bryan, Cornelious, 452
———, Edward, 186
———, Sir Ernest, 162
———, Henry, 139
———, Jane, 493
———, Jo., 36
———, Joseph, 40
———, *see* Brian, O'Bryan, &c.
Bryant, Barnard, 326, 330
———, Roger, 318*, 320, 324
———, Thomas, 151,
Bryer, John, 316, *see* Briar
Bucher, Frances, 177
Buck, Bucke
———, Benamy, 175, 225
———, Christian, 108
———, Francis, 142
———, Gercyon (or Gercian), 175, 225
———, Isack, 135
———, Mara, 175, 225
———, Peleg., 175, 225
———, Richard, 142, 270
———, Roger, 65
———, Thomas, 125
———, William, 65
Buckam, Richard, 78
Buckingham, George, Marquis of, 156
———, ———, Duke of, 157, 158
Buckland, Chri., 74, *see* Bucland
Buckle, Alexander, 468
———, Henry, 123
———, Lucie, 120
Buckley, Buckly
———, Ben., 63
———, Daniell, 63
———, Humfrey, 119
———, John, 432, 435
———, Mary, 436
———, William, 139, 403, 414
———, *see* Bulkly, &c.
Buckmuster, John, 227
Bucks, Mr., 226
Buckworth, Richard, 474
Bucland, William, 96, *see* Buckland
Budd, Jo., 113
Budding, Richard, 475
Budge, John, 334, 337, 340
Buenno, Beniamin, 474
Bugby, Bugbye
———, Edward, 278, 279
———, Rebecca, 279
———, Sarah, 278

Bugland, Henry, 128
Buglar (or Bugler), Thomas, 316*, 343
Bulfell, Richard, 116
Bulkly, Bulkley, Bulkely
———, Grace, 76
———, Peter, 77
———, Tho., 79
———, William, 354, 356, 367, 372, 373, 379, 397, 439, 463
———, *see* Buckley
Bull, Ann, 490
———, Christopher, 474, 490
———, Edward, 63
———, Henry, 57, 107
———, Isack, 95
———, Joseph, 212
———, Richard, 67
———, Thomas, 86, 130, 190
Bullaker, Andrewe, 297
Bullar, Jo., 138
Bullard, Tho., 124
Bullen, Silvester, 227
Bullington, Nicholas, 176
Bullman, Jo., 73
Bullock, Bullocke
———, Anto., 86
———, Edward, 68
———, Francis, 121
———, Henry, 88
———, Mary, 83
———, Susan, 88
———, Tho., 88
———, William, 179, 240
Bullt, Jan, 198
Bumstedd, Wm., 41
Bun, *see* Bunn
Bunce, Jo., 52
Bundock (or Bundicke), Wm., 44, 46, 49
Bunn, Bun
———, Bridgitt, 220
———, Mrs., 177
———, Thomas, 177, 220
Bunnel, William, 428
Bunny, Bunney
———, Elisabeth, 424, 436
———, Hannah, 424, 436
———, Richard, 424, 436, 442
———, William, 436
Bunnyon, John, 493
———, Mary, 493
Bunting, Ann, 430
———, Henry, 430
———, Richard, 132
———, Sarah, 426
———, Susanna, 430
Burback, Marie, 118
Burbon, John, 474

INDEX. 519

Burch, Burche
———, Capt., 73
———, Daniell, 75
———, William, 35, 304
———, see Byrch
Burchard, Ann, 131
————, Elizabeth, 131
————, Jo., 131
————, Mary, 131
————, Marie, 131
————, Sara, 131
————, Suzan, 131
————, Thomas, 131
Burcher, John, 181
————, Robert, 307
————, William, 181
Burd, John, 35
———, Symon, 59
———, see Bird
Burdin, Geo., 97
Burditt, William, 262
Burges, Burgess, Burgis,
————, 294
————, Anthony, 378, 417
————, Aron Abraham, 449
————, Eliz^a., 460
————, Ellin, 95
————, Humphry, 298
————, James, 49
————, John, 334, 337, 340, 470
————, Rabecca, 142
————, Rachell, 450
————, Thomazing, 500
Burgoss, Abraham, 351
Burhall, George, 500
Burk, Burke
———, James, 475
———, Jeoffery, 356
———, Thomas, 338
———, Tobias, 474
Burket, Henry, 103
Burkitt, Jo., 143
Burlacy, Walter, 154
Burland, John, 180
Burles, John, 107, 108
Burley, Roger, 113
————, Timothy, 194
Burlie, Alexander, 102
Burlingham, Geo., 37
Burne, Dennis, 352, see Byrne
———, Randall, 119
Burnell, Mrs., 452
Burnham, Tho., 140
————, Wm., 128
Burnhouse, William, 195
Burnet, Samvell, 104
Burnett, Jo., 138
Burr, Jeremy, 82
———, Mathew, 114

Burr, Robert, 126
Burrage, Charles, 316, 318, 344
Burrell, Henry, 460
Burren, Mr., 181
Burridge, Robert, 327, 329
————, Thomas, 327, 330
Burrin, Anthony, 179
Burrowes, Burrow, Burrowe, Burrows, Burroughes, Burrocs
————, Anthony, 154, 171, 175, 250
————, Bridgett, 225
————, Ellin, 87
————, Jane, 82
————, John, 136, 175, 225, 270, 500
————, Mihil, 308
————, Mr., 231
————, Mrs., 175
————, William, 59, 134, 333, 337, 340
Burston, John, 330
Burt, Ann, 93
———, Anthony, 259
———, Edward, 93
———, Hugh, 93, 98
———, James, 63
———, John, 314
———, William, 38, 237
———, see Burtt
Burton, Agnes, 474
————, Charles, 494
————, Elizabeth, 494
————, Francis, 423, 425, 436, 438, 451, 500
————, Georg, 141, 425, 438
————, John, Junr., 495
————, ———, Senr., 495
————, ———, 75, 494
————, Judith, 423, 425, 436, 438
————, Richard, 254
————, Tho., 71
————, Wm., 119, 126
Burtt, Jane, 173
———, William, 177
———, see Burt
Burtwezill, Mary, 124
Busbie, Busbee, Busby
————, Abraham, 289
————, Bridgett, 289
————, Edward, 177
————, John, 289
————, Nicho., 289
————, Sarath, 289
————, Thomas, 83
Bush, John, 74, 101, 188, 257, 273
———, Susan, 249
———, Walter, 433

Bush, Widow, 442
Bushel, Bushell
————, Edward, 429
————, George, 324, 343
————, Nicholas, 192
————, Ruth, 98
————, Wm., 351
————, see Busshell
Busher, Mabell, 117
————, Mary, 448
Bushnell, Francis, 49
————, Jo., 49
————, Marie, 49
————, Martha, 49
Busket, James, 42
Bussell, Jo., 74
Busshell, John, Senr., 439
————, see Bushell
Busshey, Wm., 452
Bussie, John, 495
Bustian, George, 471
Buston, John, 332, 337, 338
Butcher, John, 355, 423
————, Mary, 423
————, Richard, 423
Buth, John, 191
Butler, Buttler
————, Edward, 173
————, Elinor, 354
————, Francis, 219
————, Ger., 129
————, Henry, 113
————, James, 463
————, John, 111, 123, 125, 142, 353
————, Lucy, 439
————, Walter, 355
————, William, 474
Butt, James, 463
Buttall, Charles, 463
Butterey, Richard, 193
Butterfeild, John, 189, 232
Butterfield, Nathaniell, 304
Butterick, Wm., 53
Buttler, see Butler
Buttolph, Ann, 73
————, Tho., 73
Button, Thomas, 180
Buttry, Grace, 108
————, Martha, 107
————, Nico., 107
Buwen, Thomas, 195
Bycroft, Grace, 85
Bygraue (Bygrave), Elizabeth, 181, 238
Byham, Nathaniell, 93
Byley, Henerey, 299
———, John, 299
———, Mary, 299
Byno, John, 491

Byno, Mary, 491
Bynstedd, Jo., 119
Byrall, Jo., 128
Byrch, Henry, 446, *see* Burch
Byrkenhead, Mathew, 158, *see* Birkenhedd
Byrne, Dinnis, 500, *see* Burne

CADDY, William, 41
Cades, Thomas, 378, 402
Cadge, Edward, 225
Cadle, Thomas, 470
Cadwold, Anto., 142
Caime, Benja., 453
Calcker, Mr., 175
———, Mrs., 175
Calcott, Edward, 387
Calder, Thomas, 261
Call . . ., Alles, 294
——— . . ., Augsten, 294
Callahan, Dorothy, 496
Callahane, Charles, 367
Callahone, David, 498
Calland, Mathew, 74
Callay, Thomas, 360
Callen, Manus, 437
Calthrop, Charles, 182
Calverlie, Geo., 86
Calvert, Sir George, 157
Came, Francis, 333, 335, 340
Caminge, John, 171
Cammell, Gilbert, 476
Cammerrame, John, 501
Campanell, Mordicay, 358
Campbell, Dowgall, 489
———, Mary, 489
Campel, Ann, 436
———, Patric, 436
Campion, Clement, 136
———, Jean, 198
———, Philippe, 198
———, Robert, 202
———, Wm., 472
Can (or Caus), Mr., 189
Cane, George, 194
———, John de, 137
Cann, Mr., 176
Cannelly, Daniell, 136
Cannings, Wm., 444, 452
Cannion, Wm., 38
Cañon, Elizabeth, 85
———, John, 206
———, Richard, 85
Cant, William, 41
Canter, Capt., 309
Canterbury, George, Archbp. of, 158
———, William, Archbp. of, 160
Cantey, Hellen, 471

Canting, Dennis, 358
Cantlebury, John, 334, 336, 341
Cantwell, John, 193
Capell, William, 104
Caplin, Robert, 103
Caps, Capps
———, Cathrin, 194
———, Phœbe, 431
———, William, 187, 274, 431, 442, 452
Carew, Elizabeth, 491
———, Katherine, 491
———, Richard, 476, 491
———, Thomas, 359
Carkille, William, 151
Carlisle, Charles, Earl of, 162*
———, James, Earl of, 158, 160
Carlowe, Edward, 218
Carlton, Mary, 37
Carman, Henry, 171, 215
Carmichael, Archibald, 163*, 165, 167
Carn (or Corn), Elisabeth, 426
———, Jane, 426
———, John, 426
Carner [?Carver], Michaell, 475
Carney, Patick, 452
Carning, John, 183
Carnock, Tho., 452
Carnoll, Christopher, 36
Carow, Peter, 369, *see* Carrow
Carpender, Samuell, 439
Carpent, William, Junr., 299
Carpenter, Abigael, 299
———, Dixi, 190
———, Elias, 143
———, Henry, 168*
———, Tho., 39
———, Tomazin, 59
———, Wm., 140, 299
Carpentier, Martin de, 198
Carpentry, Jan de, 198
Carr, Andrew, 71
———, Calebb, 77
———, Joan, 498
———, John, 268
———, Ralph, 498
———, Richard, 98
———, Robert, 77
Carraway, Joan, 137
Carre, Henry, 165
Carrell, Henry, 117
Carrington, Thomas, 150
Carrow, George, 332, 336, 340, *see* Carow
Carsley, Henrie, 243
Carter, Cartter
———, Anto., 120
———, Boham, 453

Carter, Christopher, 153, 188
———, Edmond, 194
———, Elinor, 357
———, Erasmus, 180
———, Geo., 128
———, Henry, 86
———, James, 50, 192
———, John, 38, 96, 121, 170, 176, 220, 268, 272
———, Margery, 126
———, Martha, 46
———, Rosamus, 234
———, Thomas, 46, 122
———, William, 228
Carteret, Sir George, 161, 162
Carterett, James, 161
Cartrack, Mildred, 58
———, Sara, 58
Cartwright, John, 174
Cartwrite, Phillipp, 41
———, Wm., 135, 142
Caruear [Carvear], Elizabeth, 291
——— ———, Grace, 291
——— ———, Richard, 291
——— ———, Susanna, 291
Carven, Richard, 177
[?Carver] Carner, Michaell, 475
Carvis, Katharin, 435
Cary, Richard, 115, 357
Caryl, Katharin, 437
Casewell, Caswell, Caswells
———, Lawrence, 319, 319*, 323
———, Mr., 305
———, Richard, 309
Cason, Casson
———, John, 133
——— (or Coson), Nehemiah, 111
———, Thomas, 475
Casse, Wm., 133
Cassedy, John, 41
Casson, *see* Cason
Castell, George, 123
———, Henry, 101
Caswell, *see* Casewell
Catesby, Jane, 84
———, John, 193
Catline, William, 460
Catoir, Ernou, 199
Caton, Richard, 129
Cattlin, John, 453
Catts, Jo., 121
Cauan, *see* Cavan
Cauldwall, Martha, 496
Caunt, Richard, 122
Caus (or Cans), Mr., 189
Causey (or Cawsey), Mrs., 171

INDEX.   521

Causey, Nathaniel, 171, 213, 268
———, Thomas, 181, 212
———, Thomasine, (171), 213
Cavan, John, 476
Cave, John, 81
———, Richard, 37
Cavenaugh, Charls, 423, 432
Caverlie, Charles, 81
Cawcott, George, 267
Cawdle, Wm., 67
Cawfeild, Richard, 360
Cawood, Richard, 71
Cawsey, *see* Causey
Cawt, Bryan, 175
Chace, John, 323, 452, 501
Chadd, Mary, 126
Chaddock, Marie, 67
Chaffin, Daniell, 475
Chalk, Jo., 117
Challener, Robert, 501
Challoner, Sir Thomas, 156
Chaloner, Morris, 192
Chamber, Henry, 317*, *see* Chambers
Chamberlain, Chamberlaine, Chamberlin, Chamberline, Chamberlins, Chamberlyne
———, Edward, 429
———, Frances, 195
———, Francis, 186, 254, 501
———, James, 257
———, John, 317*, 342
———, Marmaduke, 358
———, Mr., 257
———, Rebecca, 186, 254
———, Thomas, 84, 316*
———, Wm., 127
Chambers, Alice, 224
———, Chri., 137
———, Elizabeth, 75
———, Henry, 316, 342, *see* Chamber
———, James, 188, 235
———, Jane, 37
———, John, 145, 215
———, Josua, 129
———, Robert, 130
———, Thomas, 217
Chamblis, Richard, 39
Chambney, Marie, 113
Chamell, Walter, 461
Champ (or Chump), Alice, 75
———, John, 192
Champante, Hen., 300
Champer, Robert, 169
Champin, Pasta, 185
Champion, Pascoe, 244
———, Richard, 37
Chancy, Charles, 198

Chandler, Chandeler, Chaundler
———, Arthur, 177, 219
———, George, 95
———, John, 186, 248
———, Margaret, 430
———, Nicholas, 452
———, Robert, 430
(?———), Thomas, 248
Channce (or Chaunce), Ellin, 136
Chantry, Robert, 180
Chapeman, Richard, 501
Chaplain, Edward, 303
Chaplaine, Isacke, 173, 213
———, John, 173, 213
———, Mary (173), 213
Chaplin, Chapline
———, Clement, 69
———, Edward, 133
———, Isacke, 267, 269
———, Jeremiah, 357
———, Thomas, 361
———, Wm., 83
Chapman, Ann, 212
———, Frances, 175
———, Francis, 232, 270
———, Geo., 52
———, Henry, 115
———, Jo., 140
———, Mary, 444
———, Mathew, 324
———, Nicholas, 169, 233
———, Phillip, 186, 250
———, Ralph, 57
———, Richard, 51, 118
———, Thomas, 121, 171, 212, 274
———, Walter, 111
———, *see* Chappman
Chappell, George, 43
———, John, 82, 112, 333, 338, 340
———, Jonah, 476
———, Joshuah, 494
———, Thomas, 95
Chappman, Luke, 241
Chard (or Charde)
———, Ann, 202
———, Josuah, 170, 202, 267
Charles, 208
———, Dorothie, 102
———, Evan, 361
———, Philip, 471
———, Wm., 112
Charlton, Henrie, 263
Chase, Edward, 492, 496
———, Margret, 492, 496
———, Stephen, 476, 492, 496
Chason, John, 448

Chater, Barnabas, 324
———, Jo., 140
Chaunce (or Channce), Ellin, 136
Chaundler, *see* Chandler
Chauntree (or Chauntrie), Robert, 175, 232
Cheame, Mary, 284, *see* Adams
Cheek (or Cheeke), Phillip, 316, 318, 344
Cheesman, Cheeseman, Chesman
———, Edward, 185
———, John, 185, 274
———, Richard, 323
———, Thomas, 185
———, Wm., 133
Cheney, Elisabeth, 423
———, Georg, 423
———, Mary, 423
———, *see* Cheyney
Cherrall, Vrsula, 109
———, William, 109
Chester, Henry, 497
———, Sampson, 360
———, Thomas, 495
———, William, 323, 342, 497, 500
Chesterman, Adam, 81
Chesting, John, 142
Cheswood, Hugh, 139
Chew, John, 237
———, Sarah, 237
Cheyney, Cheyny, Cheynei
———, Abram, 140
———, Charles, 467
———, George, 446
———, *see* Cheney
Chickin, Joseph, 285
Chilcot (Chilcott, or Chillicott), John, 334, 337, 341
Child, Michaell, 322, 343
———, Tho., 453
Childs, Tho., 82
Chillicott, *see* Chilcot
Chilton, Edward, 167*
Chinnery (or Chinery), Thomas, 375, 400, 405
Chippfield, [*i.e.*, Chipperfield], Edmond, 130
Chipps, Edmond, 95
Chisman, Edward, 252
———, John, 252
Chitting, Richard, 39
Chittingden, Hen., 61
———, Isack, 61
———, Rabecca, 61
———, Tho., 61
Chittwood, Marie, 45
Chizell, Daniell, 476
Cholmeley, John, 441

66

INDEX.

Cholmle, Robert, 221
Chom, Anne, 497
——, Richard, 497
Choupouke (an Indian), 185
Chrichlow, *see* Crichlow
Chrismus, Dictras, 187
——————, Elizabeth, 187
Christian (a Negro), 495
————, Francis, 424, 440
————, Matthew, 424
————, Thomasin, 424
Christo. (Welshman), 195
Christopher, William, 501
Chructhloe, *see* Crutchloe
Chubnell, Jo., 142
Chump (or Champ), Alice, 75
Church, Edward, 74
————, Isabell, 489
————, John, 64.
————, Katherine, 489
————, Martin, 122
————, Robert, 489
————, Wm., 50
Churcher, Thomas, 476
Churchman, John, 150
Chyn, Thomas, 319
Cinduare (or Cindnare), James, 190
Cisely (a maid), 194
Cisse, Mr., 248
Cissel, James, 452
Clackson, John, 186
Claddin, Wm., 113
Claire, Nathaniell, 445
Clancey, Cornelius, 475
Claney, Christopher, 495
————, Daniell, 439
Clanton, Jo., 138
Clare, Marie, 488
————, Mr., 196
————, Nicolas, 488
————, Thomas, 488
Claree, John, 465, 466
————, Lowland, 465, 466
Clark, Clarke
————, Ann, 357, 422, 427
————, Brigett, 175
————, Christopher, 475
————, Daniell, 79
————, Edmond, 82
————, Edward, 35, 171, 475
————, Elisabeth, 87, 422, 427
————, Francis, 101, 475
————, George, 64, 182, 229, 453
————, Gilbert, 134
————, Giles, 317
————, Henry, 453
————, John, 35, 41, 137, 138, 139, 161, 357, 362, 393
————, Lœtitia, 427

Clark, Margaret, 116, 475
————, Mary, 130, 359, 492
————, Michaell, 496
————, Nicholas, 104, 150
————, Porcas, 358
————, Richard, 40, 52
————, Robert, 143, 318*, 319*, 323, 431
————, Roger, 427, 475, 492
————, Sycillie, 49
————, Thomas, 73, 85, 128, 139, 143, 174, 191, 422, 427, 440, 452, 476
————, William, 74, 79, 84, 116, 153, 185, 186, 243, 256, 318*, 319*, 324, 327, 329, 349, 363, 366, 368, 388, 405, 411, 415, 463, 475
————, *see* Clearke, Clerke
Clarkson, Mathew, 166
Clatworthy, Mathew, 114
Clay, Martha, 425
————, Stephen, 358, 382, 385, 394, 402, 447
————, *see* Claye
Claybourne, Wm., 271, 272, 274, *see* Cleiborn
Claye, Ann, 211
————, John, 211
————, *see* Clay
Claypole, Abigail, 468
————, Edward, 468
————, *see* Cleypole
Claypool, John, 357
Claypoole, Norton, 357
Clayton, Obediah, 164
————, Richard, 104
————, *see* Cleyton
Claxon, John, 234
Claxson, Abraham, 86
Cleaner, John, 452
————, Kathrin, 452
Clearke, Fayth, 278
————, John, 281
————, Thurston, 279
————, *see* Clark, Clerke
Cleaver, Henry, 452
Cleiborn, Edward, 120, *see* Claybourne
Clemens, William, 170
Clement, Clements
————, Elizabeth, 174, 223, *see* Hamor
————, Ezechell, 39
————, Jeremy, 174, 223, *see* Hamor
————, Robert, 501
————, Thomas, 138
————, William, 190, 475
Clere, Jo., 42

Cleri, Tho., 280, 281, 282
Clerke, Wm., 47, *see* Clark, Clearke
Cleven, Joan, 130
Clever, Tho., 117
Cleypole, Edward, 461, *see* Claypole
Cleyton, Ralph, 124
————, Sara, 120
————, *see* Clayton
Cliffe, George, 38
Clifford, Marie, 59
————, Olliver, 115
Clift, James, 316*, 317, 343
Clifton, Tho., 114
Cliggatt, Wm., 446, 452
Clinch, Tho., 311
Clinton, Jo., 81, *see* Clynton
Clitden, François, 198
Clitson, Robert, 297
Cloake, Edmond, 188
Clood (or Clode), John, 334, 337, 341
Close (or Closse), Phettiplace, 179, 231, 266
Clouan, *see* Clovan
Clough, Humphry, 192
Cloughan, Elizabeth, 476
Clovan, Thomas, 359, 361, 445
Clowdeslie (or Clowdlslie), Wm., 125
Clowes, Robert, 161*
Cluffe, Jo., 56
Clymer, Jo., 134
Clynton, Richard, 39, *see* Clinton
Coachman, Alexander, 453
————, John, 94
Coale, Chrictopher, 452
————, Thomas, 453
————, William, 185
————, *see* Cole, Coles
Coarten, Myndert, 166*
Coates, James, 409
Coather, Mrs., 452
Cobb, Elizabeth, 246
————, Joseph, 246
————, Nico., 128
Cobbet, Josias, 72
Cobbett, James, 72
Cobcrafte, Geo., 85
Cobham, Mary, 470
————, Nathaniell, 40
Cock, Cocke
————, Allan (or Allen), 351, 352, 359, 400, 411
————, Geo., 100
————, James, 355, 370, 408
————, John, 128, 319*, 351, 436, 441, *see* Cooke

INDEX.

Cock, Joseph, 100
——, Mary, 436
——, Richard, 153, 378, 417
Cockerell, William, 297
Cockey, Tho., 39
Cocklin, Denis, 434
——, Mary, 434
Cockman, Richard, 64
——, Wm., 453
Cockram, Christen, 295
——, James, 316*, 317, 342
——, John, 316*, 318, 343
——, William, 295
Cock's, Wm., 128
Cockton, Daniell, 475
Codd, James, 476
Codrington, Alice, 428
——, Christopher, 166, 167*, 379, 398, 409, 435
——, Elisabeth, 422, 429
——, Frances, 422, 429
——, John, 386, 427, 453
——, Robert, 422, 428, 429
Coe, Jane, 59
Coert, John, 139
Coggin, Sara, 113
Cogley, Daniell, 188
Coke, Adrian, 52
——, Elizabeth, 67
——, Henrie, 142
——, John, 71, 97, 137
——, Marie, 49
——, Miles, 137
——, Richard, 38
——, Robert,.79, 80
——, Tho., 52, 114
——, Wm., 141
Coker, John, 79, 253
Cokes, Edward, 75
Colborn, Edward, 107
Colbron, Wm., 107
Colburne, Robert, 107
Colchester, Joan, 105
Cole, Clement, 59
——, Francis, 245
——, Isaac, 434
——, James, 360
——, Joan, 493
——, Jo., 74
——, Thomas, 359
——, William, 166, 245, 273, 493
——, *see* Coles, Coale
Colebank, Sara, 96
Coleman, John, 139
——, Wm., 113

Colerack, Jane, 126
Coles, Edward, 84
——, Eliza., 118
——, Margaret, 136
——, Thomas, 102
——, *see* Cole, Coales
Colethorpe, Christopher, 247
Coleton, Mr., 464
Colleton, Thomas, 343
Collett, Bridgett, 444
——, Henry, 470
Colley, Thomas, 476
Collie, Robert, 41
Collier, Daniell, 104, *see* Collyer
Collings, James, 501
——, Nicholas, 318
——, *see* Collins
Collingworth, David, 75
Collins, Abigaill, 489
——, Ann, 97
——, Charles, 440
——, David, 193
——, Elizabeth, 105
——, Emanuell, 326, 330
——, Giles, 104
——, Henry, 97
——, John, 97, 161, 206, 319, 319*, 323, 360, 489
——, Josias, 193
——, Margery, 97
——, Mr., 191
——, Nicholas, 343
——, ——, Junr., 316
——, Petter (or Peeter), 182, 241
——, Samuell, 316*, 432
——, Susan, 206
——, Thomas, 182
——, Walter, 81
——, Wm., 79
——, *see* Collings
Collis, Alexander, 360
——, James, 194
Colliton, Sir Peter, 162
Collohon, Charles, 113
Collohone, Owen, 499
Collon, Nicholas, 139
Collopp, Jo., 126
Collowe, Stephen, 244
Colly, Thomas, 181
——, Walter, 137
Collyer, Ambross, 358
——, Tobias, 475
——, *see* Collier
Colman, Abram, 193
——, Barnard, 85
Colthrough, Peter, 359
Coltman, Ann, (170), 204
——, Henry, 170, 204

Colton, Thomas, 468
Colture, Wm., 112
Colwell, Samuell, 358
Combe, William, 334, 341
Comberbatch, Thomas, 290
Combes, Austen, 173
Comell, Dugwell, 475
Comes, John, 235
——, William, 236
Comin, Nicholas, 180, *see* Comon
Commins [*i.e.*, Commins], Edward, 112
Comon, Nicholas, 234, *see* Comin
Compeare, Leonard, 161*
Compton, Frances, 178
——, Jo., 141
Conaway, *see* Conway
Coney, Conney, Conny, Cony
——, Edmond, 475
——, John, 38
——, Nicholas, 429
——, Richard, 163*, 164
Congrave. Winnifredd, 113
Conisby [*i.e.* Connisby], Wm. 143
Conly (or Couly), Patrick, 7
Conne, Jacque, 197
Conner, Bryen, 475
——, Jane, 430
——, Phillipp, 37
——, Teag, 437
Connet, Mary, 428
Connett, John, 318*, 319*, 324, *see* Cunnet
Conney, *see* Coney
Conneyland, Patt, 476
Connier, Tho., 126, *see* Conyer
Conniers, Jo., 39, *see* Conyers
Conny, *see* Coney
Connyer, Patrick, 71, *see* Connier
Conoway, *see* Conway
Conway, Conaway, Conoway
——, Aron (or Aaron), 179, 233
——, Cornelius, 475
——, George, 350, 356, 386, 393, 414
——, Margaret, 75
Cony, *see* Coney
Conyard, Nathaniel, 314
Conyers, Moses, 190, *see* Conniers
Cocke, *see* Cooke, John
Coocke, John, 443
——, Phillip, 257
Cooe, Anna, 279
——, Beniamin, 278

524 INDEX.

Cooe, John, 278
———, Robert, 278, 279
Cook, Elizabeth, 498
———, Sarah, 429
———, William, 492, 495
Cooke, Ann, 187
———, Arthur, 192, 196
———, Christopher, 221
———, Edward, 134, 173
———, Ellin, 206
———, Garret, 115
———, George, 195
———, Jeremiah, 440
——— (or Cocke), John, 36, 98, 104, 113, 175, 226, 319, 319*, 323
———, Margarett, 476
———, Mathew, 316, 318, 343
———, Richard, 109, 120
———, Wm., 103, 187
Cooker, John, 186
Cookins, Danniell, 254
Cooksey, William, 169, 178, 228
Coomb, William, 337
Coombes, John, 135
Coomes, John, 188
———, William, 188
Coop, see Cooper
Cooper, 286
———, Abigail, 431
———, Ann, 124
———, Ant°., 86
———, Beniemen, 293
———, Christopher, 319, 319*, 325
———, Elizabeth, 56, 293, 431
———, Ellin, 67
———, George, 135
———, John, 44, 104, 109, 142, 188, 438
———, Lawrance, 293
———, Martha, 44
———, Mary, 44, 293, 358
———, Peter, 59
———, Rebeca, 293
———, Richard, 35, 102
———, Roger, 57, 58, 61, 69, 72, 76, 77, 78
———, Symon, 453
———, Thomas, 43, 44, 236, 357, 461, 475
———, Walter, 169, 233
———, Wibroe, 44
———, Wm., 69
Coose, Sara, 151
Covell, Cesara, 92
Cop [i.e., Coper], see Cooper
Cope, Richard, 93
———, William, 93, 445

Copeland, Jo., 112
Copeland, Mary, 427
———, Mr., 312
Copley, James, 119
———, Lionel, 165*
Copman, Vallentine, 446
Coppin, Jane, 494
———, John, 443, 494
———, Thomas, 471
Coppine, John, 476
Coppinger, John, 475
Coppyn, Robert, 119
Corbett, Benjamin, 508
———, Mary, 508
———, William, 361
Corbitt, Roger, 441
Cordelion (Cordelon, or Cordylion), Peter (or Petard), 319, 319*, 325
Cordell, Robert, 60
Corder, Thomas, 181
Cordiu, Paulus, 453
Cordoza, Soloman, 450
Cordylion, see Cordelion
Corie, Richard, 127
Cork, Margaret, 492
Corker, Elizabeth, 102
Corn, see Carn
Cornbury, Lord, 168*
Cornelius, Bernard, 432
———, Francis, 358
———, Thomas, 327, 329
Cornew, Barth., 154
Cornie, William, 184
Cornille, Pierre, 198
Cornish, Edward, 359
———, Elisabeth, 423
———, John, 423
———, Stephen, 423
———, Thomas, 188, 262, 353, 354, 360, 364, 366, 383, 392, 402
Cornwell, William, 142
Corrington, Jo., 63
———, Mary, 63
Corser, William, 41
Corteene, Ellinor, 476
Cosker, Henry, 394
Coson (or Cason), Nehemiah, 111
Cossen, Elizabeth, 143
Cossens } see Coussens, &c.
Cosson, Wm., 142
Costanio, Abraham, 450
Costeen, John, 439
Cote, Eliz., 117
Cotes, James, 81, 136
———, Jo., 113
Cotesworth, James, 143
Cotinho, Moses Henriques, 361

Cotter, Garrett, 162*, 163
Cottingham, George, 114
———, Katherine, 360
Cottom, Frances, 468
———, Oliver, 468
Cotton, John, 435
———, Richard, 122
———, Rowland, 95
Coubber, Rebecca, 187
Coughlan, Teague, 475
Coulburne, John, 359
Couly (or Conly), Patrick, 71
Councell (or Counsell), Edward, 332, 335, 341
Countwane (or Countway), John, 191, 192
Couper, Walter, 258
Courser, William, 77
Courtney, James, 151
———, Jo., 104
———, Sybbill, 105
———, Wm., 361
Courtyere, George, 501
Coussens, Coussins, Cossens, Cosson, Cozens
———, John, 441, 461, 464
———, Junr., 461
———, Wm., 142, 327, 329
Covell, Jo., 126
Covells, Capt., 308
Coventrie, Miles, 80
Coventry, Thomas, Lord, 160
Covett, Robert, 103
Coward, Rob., 333, 336, 341
———, Samuell, 461
Cowdell, Thomas, 141
Cowley, Elisabeth, 423
———, Roger, 423, 430, 452
———, Susanna, 423, 430
———, William, 95
Cowly, Bryan, 142
Cowper, Averyn, 37
———, Ro., 54
Cox, Francis, 360
———, John, 303
———, Josias, 498, 500
———, Mrs., 307
———, Phillip, 318*, 319*, 320*
———, Samuel, 167*
Coxe, William, 255
Coxsall, John, 150
Coxshedd, Jo., 105
Coxson, Tho., 81
Cozens (or Coussens), Wm., 327, 329
———, see Coussens
Crabbtree, Edward, 129
Craddock, Craddocke
———, Francis, 159*
———, Isabell, 50

INDEX. 525

Craddock, Katharin, 429
———, Mr., 106
Cradouke, William, 267
Craford, Patrick, 158
Craft, Crafts
———, Mathew, 318, 344
———, ———, Junr., 316*
———, William, 468
Crag, Cragg, Crage
———, John, 357, 424, 467
———, Susanna, 424
———, Wm., 443
Crampe, Thomas, 188
Crane, John, 316
———, Richard, 126
Cranfield, Ann, 37
———, Edward, 37, 164, 167
———, Thomas, 101
Cranich, John, 240
Cranwell, Geo., 125
Crapp, John, 40
Crapplace, Mr., 191
Crashaw, Rawleigh, 183, *see* Crawshaw and Croshaw
Crauen, *see* Craven
Craven, Richard, 272
———, Thomas, 112
———, William, Earl of, 162
Crawford, Thomas, 494
Crawshaw, William, 244, *see* Crashaw and Croshaw
Creamer, Martin, 441
Crean, Paul, 412
Creed, Creede
———, Ann (or Anne), 120, 492
———, John, 476, 492
———, Wm., 347, 366
Crenne, Jan de, 199
Crepy, Abel de, 199
Cressitt, Edward, 85
Creswell, Cresswell
———, John, 443, 501
———, William, 135
Crew, Joseph, 219
———, Josua, 177
———, Marie, 64
———, Randall, 209
———, Robert, 230
Cribb, Jo., 43
———, Richard, 74
Crichlow (or Chrichlow)
———, Elizabeth, 475
———, Henry, 475
———, James, 475
Crillick, James, 357
Cripp's, Zachary, 235
Crisp, Crispe
———, Edward, 432
———, John, Senr., 452

Crisp, John, Junr., 441
———, ———, 421
———, Joseph, 163
———, Margaret, 421
———, Roger, 361
———, Sarah, 421
———, Thomas, 187
———, Widow, 440
———, Zacharia, 180
Crispin, Tho., 63
Cristian, Francis, 440
Cristie, Richard, 127
Critch, Richard, 101
Critchlow, Wm., 440
Crocker, Henery, 221, 237
———, Jone, 237
———, Richard, 181
Croft's, Croftes
———, Ann, 123
———, Henry, 439
———, John, 70, 96
———, Thomas, 380, 396, 400
Cromby, Mr. Abo—, 310
Crome (or Crowe), Wm., 74
Crompe, Bridget, 117
———, Thomas, 227
Crompton, Sir Thomas, 156
Croney, William, 243
Croninburgk, Peter, 141
Crooke, Wm., 84
Crookshank, Alexander, 465
———, Hester, 465
Crosby, Ann, 62
———, Marmaduke, 64
———, Symon, 62
———, Tho., 62
Croshaw, Raughly, 274, *see* Crashaw and Crawshaw
Cross, Crosse
———, Ann, 280
———, Henry, 66
———, James, 84
———, John, 280, 316*, 318, 342
———, Jonas, 333, 335, 341
———, Thomas, 177, 221
———, William, 316*, 342
Crossing, Wm., 358
Crouch, Richard, 177
———, Robert, 121
———, Thomas, 175, 180, 232
Crowder, Hugh, 234
———, James, 209
———, Richard, 51
———, Thomas, 40
Crow, Crowe
———, Adam, 126
———, Benjamin, 326, 328
———, Mitford, 168*
———, (or Crome), Wm., 74

Crowley, Ro., 61
Croy, Jan de, 198
Cruder, Hugh, 180
Crudge, Richard, 268
Crust, Thomas, 225
Crutchfield, Thomas, 437
Crutchloe, Chructhloe
———, Elizabeth, 493
———, Henry, 491
———, James, 491, 493
———, Rebecca, 493
———, Susanna, 491
Cryer, Ben., 508
Cudden, John, 475
Cuffe, Martin, 194
Cugley, Danniell, 264
Culley, Samuell, 181, 239
Cullidge, Geo. 112
Cullimor, James, 41
Culpeper, Alexander, 161*, 163*
———, Thomas, Lord, 161*, 163, 165
Culverwell, John, 316
Cunnet (or Connet), John, 319*
Cunningham, Ann, 433
———, John, 433, 435
———, William, 83
———, Zebulon, 433
Cunstable, Robert, 178
Cuppledike, Henry, 38
Curden, Jo., 82
Curke, Wm., 153
Curle, Tho., 381
Currier, William, 343
Curstis, John, 359
Curtis, Elizabeth, 64
———, Henry, 76
———, James, 136
———, John, 123, 253
———, Thomas, 243, 254
———, William, 126, 150
Curtise, John, 186
———, Thomas, 184
Custis, Robert, 462
Cuta, Mathew, 501
Cuthbert, Alexander, 497
———, Elizabeth, 497
Cutler, Clinton, 80
———, Tho., 51
Cutling, Henry, 125
Cutt, Lawrence, 372, *see* Cutts
Cutting, Cuttinge
———, Jane, 123
———, John, 277, 279
———, Richard, 282
———, William, 281
Cutts, John, 163
———, Roger, 124
———, *see* Cutt

INDEX.

Cvlloe (Culloe), Steven, 185

DABB, Tho., 73
Dabbin, Nicholas, 153
Dabyn, Robert, 283
Dade, John, 268
Daggett, Tho., 114
Dainty, Henry, 297
Dalbey, Joane, 501
Dalbie, William, 169
Dalby, William, 233
Dale, Niccolas, 255
——, Sir Thomas, 270
——, Tho., 71
—— (or Deale), Wm., 319*, *see* Deale
Dales, Francis, 67
Dalleper, Henry, 122
Dallinger, Jo., 63
Dallison, Martin, 448
Dally, Richard, 83
Dalton, Hanna, 65
———, Philemon, 65
———, Samuell, 65
Damand [*i.e.* Dammand], Jane, 58
Damerall, Thomas, 501
Dameron, Bridgett, 195
Damont, Jan, 199
Damport, Lanslott, 175, 180
————, Lawley, 233
Dan, John, 427
Danby, John, 477
Dancy, John, 234
Dandg, Henry, 313*
Dane, Tho., 77
Daneff, James, 453
Danes, Richard, 51
——, Robert, 434
—— (or Daues), Suzan, 108
Dang, Margarett, 361
Dangerfield, Walcup, 363
Daniel, Daniell
————, 190
————, Anne, 492
————, Christopher, 272
————, Daniell, 37
————, Downes, 445
————, Elizabeth, 65
————, Henry, 127, 163
————, John, 362, 472, 477, 492, 497, 501
————, Nicholas, 476
————, Richard, 317*, 319*, 325
————, Robert, 358, 362
————, Thomas, 497
————, Wilbert, 365
Dannell, Edward, 115
Dapwell, Robert, 367

Daries, James, 180
Darkin, Robert, 401
Darno, Penelope, 107
Darrell, John, 294
Dart, Jane, 133
Darvall, Charles, 297
Dauers, *see* Davers
Daues, *see* Daves
Daughton, Richard, 86
————, Wm., 135
Dauis, *see* Davis
Davenport, Jo., 141
Davers, Robert, 63, 460
———, Junr., 460
Daves, Richard, 145
—— (or Danes), Suzan, 108
——, *see* Davis
David, Lewes, 74
Davidson, William, 160*
Davie, Geo., 137
——, Morrice, 136
——, Tho., 140
——, *see* Davy
Davies, Arthur, 187
———, Barnabie, 108
———, Chri., 79
———, Daniell, 51
———, Dorothie, 113
———, Edmond, 51
———, Edward, 37, 111, 133, 193
———, Elianor, 489
———, Elizabeth, 68, 186, 195, 362
———, Ellin, 113
———, Emanuell, 138
———, Gabriell, 80
———, George, 186
———, Humfrey, 38
———, Isbell, 113
———, Jane, 363, 489
———, Joane (or Jone), 174, 187
———, John, 40, 65, 68, 71, 104, 137, 171, 179, 186, 212, 217, 236, 363, 364
———, Joseph, 43
———, Katherine, 237, 364
———, Margaret, 68
———, Marie, 68
———, Nicholas, 43, 186
———, Peter, 364
———, Philip, 115
———, Richard, 104, 187
———, Robert, 94, 111
———, Rowland, 127
———, Samuell, 105, 179, 233, 363
———, Sara, 43
———, Tho., 140, 143, 186

Davies, William, 122, 128, 135, 189, 195, 471, 489
Davis, David, 422
——, Edward, 476
——, Hugh, 422, 429
——, James, 236
——, Jane, 222, 421, 422, 431
——, Joane (or Jone), 237, 421
——, John, 254, 445
——, Margaret, 476
——, Mrs., 442
——, Niccolas, 248
——, Owen, 440
——, Randall, 307
——, Richard, 201, 256
——, Robert, 176
——, Sarah, 466
——, Thomas, 254, 257
——, William, 265, 428, 453, 460, 466, 468
——, *see* Daves
Davison, Alice, 173
Davy, Robert, 365, *see* Davie
Daw, William, 332, 338, 340
Dawe, Geo., 105, 127
Dawes, John, 159*
————, William, 48
Dawlen, Henry, 177
Dawse, Margery, 176
Dawson, Edmund, 435
———, Georg, 217
———, Hugh, 139
———, Milles, 476
———, Richard, 51, 94
———, Robert, 464
———, Tremmitt, 364
———, William, 171, 210
Day, Anthony, 104
——, Dorothy, 105
——, Hanna, 77
——, James, 378, 408, 417
——, John, 133, 169, 238, 308
——, Mary, 280
——, Richard, 79
——, Robert, 46, 280
——, Samuel, 167
——, Thomas, 501
Dayes, Tho., 40
Dayhurst, Thomas, 179
Dayley, Alice, 427
———, Denis, 427
———, Katherine, 427
———, Owen, 446
Daynie, Jo., 124
Deacon, Avis, 109
————, Tho., 111
Deale (or Dale), Wm., 318*, 319*, 322

Dean, Deane
——, Abel, 430, 443
——, Gabrill, 462
——, Mary, 430
——, Mathew, 445
——, Nathaniel, 104
——, Rachell, 56
Dearsley, Richard, 439
Death, Elizabeth, 96
——, Suzan, 96
Deboyce, Giles, 453
De Cane, John, 137
Decborn, John, 40
De Carpentier, Martin, 198
De Carpentry, Jan, 198
Dechauis, Samuell, 450
Decke, William, 297
Decompas, Leah, 449
Dederix, Baltazar, 141
De Forest, Jesse, 199
De La Garde, Alexander, 75
De La Hay, Daniell, 297
—— ——, John, 296
De La Met, Jan, 198
De La Montagne, Mousnier, 197
Delavall, Ralph, 350, 373, 399, 411
De La Ware, Esaw, 184, *see* Delywarr
Delbridge, Mr., 308
De Lecheilles, Jacques, 198
De Le Marlier, Nicolas, 199
De Le Mer, Philippe, 198
De Lielate, Anthoine, 199
Delk, Roger, 237
Dellahay, Jo., 75.
Dellicat, Francis, 115
Delywarr, Isaye, 243, *see* De La Ware
De Maine, Petter, 191
Demereado, David Ralph, 449
Demon, Martin, 231
De Moone, Martine, 179
Dempster, Jane, 435, 437
——, Robert, 435
Demster, John, 477
Denbigh, Henry, Earl of, 159
Dench, Wm., 73
Dency (or Deucy), John, 180, *see* Densy
Dene, Francis, 41
——, Tho., 86
Denham, John, 319, 477
——, William, 182
Denison, Doctor, 144
—— ——, Edward, 213
Denman, Jo., 132
Denmarke, John, 180
Denner, John, 338

Dennis, Daniell, 52
——, John, 116, 476, 477
——, Robert, 85
——, Tho., 75, 332, 336, 340
Denny, Mary, 91
Densy, Jane, 363, *see* Dency
Dent, Elizabeth, 508
——, George, 471
——, John, 52, 508
——, Richard, 64
——, Thomas, 508
Denton, Jacob, 126
——, John, 362
——, Robert, 81
Denum, William, 241
De Pasar, Paul, 198
Dermot, Jo., 111
Derrick, Victor, 36
Desart, Francis, 297
Desauido [*i.e.*, Desavido], Moses, 450
Desendre, Anthoin, 199
Desworth, Edward, 362, 375
De Trou, Jan, 199
Deucy (or Dency), John, 180
Deuenish, *see* Devenish
Deuillermas, *see* Devillermas
Deurede, *see* Devrede
Deusbury, Daniell, 324
Devenish, John, 362, 444
Deverill, George, 172, 222
De Villermask, Dr., 431
Devillermas, Henry, 439
Devocion, Margaret, 98
Devorax, Stephen, 331
Devrede, Paul, 449
Dew, Ann, 109
——, Elizabeth, 109
Dewer, Stephen, 365
De Wever, Lewin, 365
Dexter, Abell, 129
——, Francis, 48
——, Wm., 365
Deyking, Alice, 98
——, John, 98
Diamond (Dyamond, or Dimand), Jasper, 327, 329
——, *see* Dymond
Dias, Lewis, 449
Dible, Francis [Frances], 285
——, Thomas, 285
Dichfeild, Edward, 157
Dick, Elizabeth, 433, 437
——, John, 435, 453
——, *see* Dick's
Dicken, Hugh, 187
Dickenson, Florence, 67
——, Geo., 83
——, Jeremy, 185
——, John, 84, 139

Dickenson, Peeter, 257
——, Wm., 124
Dickerson, Feleaman, 293
Dickins, Wm., 353
Dickinson, Elizabeth, 248
——, Francis, 362
——, Jane, 174
——, Jeremiah, 248
Dickonson, Robert, 303
Dick's, Edward, 118
——, Eliz., 113
——, *see* Dick
Dickson, Petter, 185
——, Stephen, 261
——, *see* Dixon
Dier, Mary, 192
——, William, 192
Digaud, Barthelemy, 199
Digglin, Tho., 137
Dikes, Henry, 115
Dilke, Clement, 175
——, Mrs., 175
Dill, Lawrence, 303
Dillimager, Thomas, 171
Dillon, Garrett, 477
Dimand, *see* Diamond
Dimsdale, John, 236
Dingley, N., 300
Dinse, John, 191
Disbrough, Isack, 46
Disherd, Jo., 52
Disnall, Nathaniell, 94
Ditchfield, Jo., 128
Ditty, Edmond, 352, 353, 366, 369, 375, 376, 381, 383, 388, 389, 390, 400, 405
Dix, Abegell, 290
——, Joane, 290
——, Margaret, 63
——, Presella, 290
——, Samuell, 290
Dixon, Adam, 218
——, Alice, 71
——, Ann, 191
——, Chri., 112
——, Edward, 83
——, Mathew, 111
——, Richard, 125
——, Steven, 183
——, Wm., 85
——, *see* Dickson
Dixson, Adam, 272
——, Rachell, 293
Dixwell, Basill, 462
Dobell, Henry, 138
Docker, John, 179, 236
Dockkie, James, 128
Dod, Dodd, Dod's, Dodd's
——, Geo., 82
——, James, 98

INDEX.

Dod, Jane, 202
——, John, 169, 202, 267, 270, 319, 319*, 323
——, Margaret, 425
——, Mrs., 169
——, Thomas, 425, 444
Dodderidge, Davie, 141
——————, Jarvice, 40
——————, Tho., 117
Dodington, Richard, 165*
Dodson, Edward, 134
——, Elisabeth, 427
——, Georg, 427
Dodsworth, James, 436
Doe, Jo., 81
——, Thomas, 122, 177
Doged, Thomas, 295
Dolbeare (or Dolebeer), Samuell, 318*, 319*, 324
Doldron, Grace, 362
Dole, Peter, 35
Dolebeer, *see* Dolbeare
Doleberry, Andrew, 362
Doleman (or Toleman), Susan (or Susannah), 320*
——————, Thomas, 236
Dolfemb, Richard, 179
Doll, Richard, 37
Dollar, John, 476
Dollathy, Elizabeth, 501
Dollen, Thomas, 320*, 323
Dolling, Thomas, 318*
Dollstan, John, 465
——————, Thomas, 465
Dolphinbe, Richard, 231
Domelawe (or Domelow), Richard, 172, 272
Donavan, Daniell, 470
Done, John, 132
Donn, Clement, 115
——, Henry, 113
——, Jo., 133
——, Tho., 106
——, Wm., 81
Donnard, Marie, 54
Donoldson, Henrie, 79
Donthorne (or Dunthorne), Eliza., 273, *see* Dunthorne Douthorn
Dore, James, 213
Dorie, *see* Dory
Dorifall, Anne, 281
Dorington, Nicholas, 193
Dorn, Francis, 476
——, John, 476
Dorrell, Tho., 85
——————, William, 219
Dorset, Edward, Earl of, 159
Dory (or Dorie), Gregory, 182, 260

Dotten, Wm., 469
Doue, *see* Dove
Doughty, Doughtie
——, Ann, 172, 216
——, Thomas, 172, 181, 216, 238
——, *see* Dowtie
Douglas, Douglass
——, Captain, 114
——, Hugh, 137
——, William, 188
——, *see* Dowglas, Duglas
Douse, Bridgett, 365
——, Thomas, 267
——, *see* Dowse
Douston, John, 181
Douthorn, Elizabeth, 188
——————, Samwell, 188
——————, Thomas, 188
——————, *see* Donthorne, &c.
Dove, Mary, 442
Dowe, Henrey, 292
——, Joane, 292
Dowell, Dennis, 363, 453
——, Richard, 476
Dowglas, William, 269, *see* Douglas, and Duglas
Dowling, William, 477
Downe, John, 326, 331
——, Robert, 135
Downeman, Elizabeth, 185, 244
——————— (or Downman), John, 185, 244, 274
——————, Mary, 257
Downes, Daniell, 445
——, Eustice, 212
——, George, 134
——, Henry, 501
——, Richard, 79, 177, 240
——, Walter, 101
——, William, 138, 194
——, *see* Downs
Downing, Francis, 208
——————, James, 465
——————, John, 365
——————, Samuel, 465
Downman, *see* Downeman
Downs, John, 498, *see* Downes
Dowse, Mr., 262
——, Mrs., 183
——, Thomas, 183
——, *see* Douse
Dowsell, Anto., 67
Dowtie, Henery, 220, *see* Doughty
Doxey, Thomas, 405, 439
Doyer, Isack, 342
Doyley, Edward, 160*
Drake, Diana, 75
——, Isack, 134

Drake, Jo., 128
Dran, Maren, 364
Drap, *see* Draper
Draper, Bartholmew, 71
——, Cleare, 279
——, Henry, 185, 245
——, Joseph, 63
——, Robert, 249, 440
——, Tho., 104
Drax, Henry, 363, 384, 463
Drayton, Thomas, 363, 453
Dreadd, John, 40
Drebble, James, 161
Drew, Drewe
——, Edward, 189, 263
——, Tho., 41
——, Will., 332, 337, 340
——, *see* Drue
Drewrie, Geo., 92
——, Robert, 113
——, *see* Drury
Drinker, Edward, 98
——, Elizabeth, 98
——, Jo., 98
——, Phillip, 98
Driskell, Cornelius, 499
——, Dearman, 499
——, Mary, 498
Driver, James, 74
——, Robert, 92
Drudg, Andrewe, 296
Drue, Edward, 103, *see* Drew
Drury, Richard, 476, *see* Drewrie
Dry, William, 188
Duboyes, John, 364
Duce, Gyles, 501
——, Robert, 74
Dudley, Andrew, 171, 209
——, John, 499
——, Joseph, 163*, 168*
Dudman, Henry, 104
Duffeild, Edward, 350, 354, 356, 361, 372, 379, 382, 391, 393, 399, 402, 409, 438
Duffill, John, 213
Duffy, John, 173
Dufour, Theodore, 198
Dugdell, Henry, 122
Duglas, William, 256, *see* Douglas and Dowglas
Duhurst, Henry, 105
Duke, Henry, 476
——, Jo., 56
Dukes, Wm., 362
Dukkarth, Jo., 52
Dulinare, George, 96
Dum' [*i.e.*, Dummer], *see* Dummer
Dumesnill, Carew, 476

INDEX.   529

Dummer, Alce, 299
———, Dorathie, 299
———, Jane, 299
———, Joane, 299
———, Richard, 299
———, Steephen, 299
———, Tho., 299
Dumpont, John, 191
Dun, *see* Dunn
Dunbarr, Wm., 128
Duncomb, Jo., 110
Dundas, Wm., 364
Dune, Thomas, 172
Duneing, Henry, 501
Dungan, Thomas, 164*
Dunham, Robert, 125
Dunidge, Wm., 453
Dunkly, Basell, 448
Dunn, Dun
———, Hugh, 470
———, Jo., 37
———, Petter, 193
———, Roger, 453
———, Thomas, 222
———, Wm., 153
Dunnell, Henry, 36
Dunnohoe, Cornelius, 364
———, Jeffory, 364
———, Teag, 363
Dunstarr, Robert, 142
Dunsthorp, Zechariah, 430
Dunthorne (or Donthorne), Elizabeth, 255, 273
———, Thomas, 255
Dunton, Andrew, 37
Du Pon, Michel, 198
Dupper, Edward, 195
Durant, Natthan, 477
———, Thomas, 477
Durdal, Heugh, 299
Duston, John, 154
Dutton, David, 238
———, Richard, 429
Dweight (or Dwight), Benjamin, 447, 453
Dyamond, *see* Diamond
Dye, Henry, 63
Dyer, Ananiah, 127
———, Isack, 316*, 317
———, James, 432
———, Jo., 42
———, Roger, 432, 442
———, Samuell, 448
———, Sarah, 432
———, William, 501
Dyke, Daniel, 466, 468
———, Richard, 319
Dykes, Mr., 308
Dymett [*i.e.*, Dymmett], Thomas, 96

Dymocke, William, 501
Dymond, Robert, 40, *see* Diamond
Dynegell, Danill, 471
Dynley, Richard, 71
Dyos, Geo., 137

EACH, Samuell, 269
Eakins, Wm., 67
Earl, Earle
———, John, 366
———, Robert, 316, 318, 343
———, Thomas, 477
Easemond (Easman, or Eastmond), John, 318*, 319*, 323
East, Easte
———, Richard, 187, 257
———, William, 103, 133
Eastchurch, William, 366
Easte, *see* East
Eastmond, *see* Easemond
Easton, Rob., 332, 336, 340
Eastwick, Henry, 460
———, Richard, 460
Easy, Ben., 84
Eaton, Abigall, 58
———, George, 81
———, John, 40
———, Mabell, 120
———, Mary, 58
———, Tho., 58
Ebdon, George, 318*
Ebes, Thomas, 257
Ebsworth, Anne, 243
———, Agnes, 184
———, Anthony, 184, 243
Eccallowe, Peter, 249
Eden, Alles, 291, *see* Edens, and Eeden
Edenburrow, Tho., 37
Edenden, 434
———, Joyce, 434
Edens, Jo., 140, *see* Eden
Ederife, Ester, 224
Edgar, Richard, 334, 336, 339
Edge, Robert, 130
Edger, William, 190
Edlow, Mathew, 169, 201
Edlyn, Henry, 162
Edmond, Edmondes, Edmond's, Edmund's
———, Jo., 36, 190
———, Michaell, 296
———, Richard, 39, 193
———, Robert, 189, 235
———, Titus, 46
Ednall, Edward, 112
Edney, Peter, 477
Edward, 188
———, ———, 190

Edward (a Negro), 178, 229
Edwards, Anthony, 266
———, Arthur, 191
———, David, 416
———, Edmond, 117
———, John, 180, 234, 326, 329, 340, 366
———, Richard, 154, 255, 469
———, Robert, 130, 141, 144
[?———], Sarah, 469
———, Thomas, 94
———, William, 117, 192
Edwardson, Jo., 84
Edwin, James, 112
Edwynn, Edward, 133
———, Tho., 111
Edye, Rawleigh, 153
Eeden, Jo., 84, *see* Eden
Eeke, Geo., 81
Eeles, Edward, 80
———, Henry, 116
———, John, 96
———, *see* Eles
Eelie, Robert, 115, *see* Ely
Eester, Thomasin, 256
Egerton, Wm., 135
Egginton, Seaborne, 453
Eggleston, Richard, 102, 104
Ekkersoe, Tho., 128
Elbridg, William, 194
Elding, Edward, 501
Eldred, Nathaniell, 442
Eldridg, Giles, 424
———, Mary, 424
Eles, Thomas, 445, *see* Eeles
Elinor, ———, 175
Elison, *see* Ellison
Elizabeth, ———, 203
——— (a Maid), 195
Ella, Marmaduke, 117
Ellacott, Mrs., 453, *see* Ellicott
Ellarce (or Ellaree), Jonathan, 432
———, ———, Sarah, 432
———, ———, Thomas, 432
Ellatt, John, 231
Ellerton, James, 41
Ellesmere, Thomas, Lord, 155, 156
Elley, Benj^a., 446
Ellgate, Margrett, 47
Ellicott, Vines, 366
———, Widow, 470
———, *see* Ellacott
Ellinsworth, Wm., 367
Elliot, Elliott
———, Elizabeth, 46, 433

67

Elliot, Georg, 430
——, Henry, 367
——, Jane, 430
——, Joan, 438, 477
——, John, 137, 179, 453, 463
——, Lyddia, 46
——, Marie, 46
——, Phillip, 46
——, Richard, 438, 477, 488, 493, 496
——, Sara, 46
——, Thomas, 161
Ellis, David, 173, 176, 220
——, Elizabeth, 92
——, Gamaliell, 442
——, Margrett, 220
——, Mary, 422
——, Richard, 36
——, Robert, 137, 422
——, William, 422
Ellison, Ellin, 230
——, George, 231
—— (Elison), John, 181, 230
——, William, 250
Elliston, George, 366
——, William, 132
Ellitt, Walter, 135
Ellmer, Edward, 150
Ellotts, Henry, 142
Ellvyn (or Elvyn)
——, Mark, 38
——, Wm., 81
Ellwood, Ralph, 131, *see* Elwood
Elmes, Richard, 134
——, Rodolphus, 56
Elson, Elizabeth, 64
——, Wm., 365
Elsword, Hener., 181
Elvyn, *see* Ellvyn
Elwood, Henery, 237, *see* Ellwood
Ely, Ann, 259
——, Elizabeth, 259
——, James, 447
——, Walter, 183, 259
——, *see* Eelie
Emarson, *see* Emerson
Embree (or Emberee), William, 441, 453
Embrie, Henry, 96
Emerson, Emarson, Emerson [*i.e.*, Emmerson]
——, Allice, 239
——, Ann, 239
——, Ellis, 239
——, Jo., 98
——, Mr., 239
[?——], Robert, 239
——, Thomas, 239
——, William, 171, 212

Emery, John, 366
Emmerton, Ann, 105
Emperor, Thomas, 439
Enderbee, Oliver, 365
Endick, Daniell, 117
Enes, Phillipp, 477
England, Allen, 318°, 319°, 324
——, John, 316°, 423
——, Lawrence, 423
——, ————, Junr., 453
——, Mary, 423
English, John, 218
——, Richard, 171, 210
——, Robert, 471
——, Thomas, 426
Enims (Euines, or Euims), John, 192, 193
Ennis Wm., 119
Ennys, Margaret, 424
——, Timothy, 424
Eason, William, 94
Epes, Margrett, 262
——, William, 262
Epps, Elizabeth, 100
——, Mrs., 188
——, Petter, 188
——, William, 188
Eritage, Roger, 141
Erle, Bryan, 39
——, Edward, 126
Erpey, Elisabeth, 424, 437
Estplynn, Michell, 71
Estwicke, Thomas, 342
Etherington, John, 39
Euans, *see* Evans
Euens, *see* Ewens
Euers, *see* Ewers
Euims (Euines, or Enims), John, 192, 193
Eumes, John, 501
Evan, Evan ap, 111
Evand's, Clement, 249
——, Richard, 242
——, Thomas, 244
——, William, 261
Evans, Andrew, 70
——, Clement, 188
——, Christo., 191
——, Cornelius, 304
——, David, 50
——, Edward, 140, 366
——, George, 185
——, Griffinn, 143
——, Henry, 460
——, Hugh, 139
——, John, 52, 84, 124, 185, 189, 463, 477
——, Lawrance, 171, 213
——, Leonard, 37
——, Lewis, 134, 366

Evans, Marke, 185
——, Nico., 52
——, Richard, 134, 184
——, Samuell, 357, 393, 402
——, Thomas, 52, 143, 185
——, William, 95, 114, 185, 366
Evars, Robert, 236
Evens, John, 235
Evenson, John, 298
——, Tho., 298
Evere, Ester, 174
Everedge, Sara, 118
Everett, Aron, 104
Everie, Tho., 41
Ewens, Richard, 501
——, William, 270
Ewer, Elizabeth, 88
——, Sara, 88
——, Tho., 88
Ewers, Robert, 270
Ewin's (Euines, &c.), John, 192
Ewis, John, 192
Ewynn, Tho., 86
Exson, Jo., 116
Eyres, Nicholas, 234
Eyton, William, 477

FABERR, Joseph, 72
Fabin, Elizabeth, 76
Facy (or Facey), John, 317°, 319°, 322
Faierbrother, Nathaniell, 82, *see* Farebrother
Fairbore, Stafford, 167°
Fairechild, Joane, 258
Fairfax, William, 271
Fairefax, Nicho., 375, *see* Fearfax
Faldoe, Barthol., 49
Falkland, Anthony, Lord, 165
Fall, Charles, 63
Fallin, Andrew, 470, *see* Follyn
Fallowes, Edward, 214
Fance (or Fauce), Robert, 80
Fane, Richard, 75
Fanning, Andrew, 367
Fanshaw, Richard, 117
Farbracke, Roger, 187
Farbrase, Roger, 245
Farebank, James, 140
Farebern, Lawrence, 95
Farebrother, Suzanna, 106, *see* Faierbrother
Farepoynt, James, 95
Farest, Robert, 102
Farewell, James, 477
Farley, Farly
——, Ann, 230
——, Jane, 230

INDEX.

Farley, Thomas, 181, 230
Farman, Alice, 108
——, Mary, 108
——, Ralph, 108
——, Tho., 108
Farmer, Charles, 188
——, Elizabeth, 75
——, James, 303
——, John, 135, 329, 334, 336, 337, 340, 454
——, Madam, 472
——, Thomas, 52, 170, 204
Farmor, Henry, 174
Farnarcque, Thomas, 198
Farnell, Robert, 169
[Farquaharson], Fercharson, Thomas, 444
Farr, Edward, 134
Farraby, Tho., 114
Farrands, Robert, 53
Farrar, John, 194
——, Robert, 101
——, William, 171, 268
Farrell, Edmond, 122
——, Hugh, 370
——, Roger, 370
——, Simon, 138
Farren, John, 153
Farrer, James, 369
Farring, Miles, 74
Farrington, Edmond, 44
——, Edward, 44
——, Eliza., 44
——, John, 44
——, Mathew, 44
——, Sarra, 44
Farron, Samuell, 75
Farror, Edmond, 370
Farrow, Robert, 477
Farthing, Edward, 432
Fassitt, James, 142
Fatrice, Nicholas, 192
Fauce (or Fance), Robert, 80
Faucey, Thomas, 324
Fauell, see Favell
Faulkner, Thomas, 184, 250
Faux, John, 40
Favell, Christopher, 370
——, Roger, 454
Favor, Jo., 36
Fa'well, see Farewell
Fawn (Foane, or Fowne), Robert, 318*, 320*, 324
Fawne, John, 477
Fayrie, Oliver, 114
Feaghery, Thomas, 368
Feak, Richard, 502
Feake, Henry, 454, 501
Fear, Francis, 370
Fearfax, Tho., 51, see Fairfax

Fearne, Henry, 194
——, Paul, 118
Feat's, Robert, 116
Featlie, Tymothie, 94
Feaver, Robert, 454, see Fever
Fedam, George, 178
Fee, Elizabeth, 428
Feeld, Henrie, 134, see Feld
Feeldes, Henrie, 247
Feeldhouse, Jo., 36
Feelding, Jo., 129
Feild, James, 246
——, William, 233
——, see Field
Feld, Tho., 67
Fell, Henry, 192
——, Lidia, 369
——, Thomas, 478
Feld, Jo., 124, see Feekd
Felkynn, John, 140
Felloe (or Fellow), William, 45, 425
Felton, John, 440
Felver, Joan, 67
Fenn, Alderman, 50
——, Richard, 50, 179
Fennell, Edward, 449
——, Robert, 188, 264
Fenner, Rabecca, 131
Fennick, Eliz., 106
Fenton, Agnis, 329
——, James, 194
——, Mr., 257
Fercharson [Farquaharson], Thomas, 444
Fergusson, Elisabeth, 423
——, Thomas, 423
Fern, Henry, 431
Fernall, Robert, 233
Ferneley (or Fernley), Thomas, 166, 190
Ferrar, William, 209
Ferrell, Bridget, 459
Ferriman, Thomas, 433
——, William, 426
Fetherston, John, 190
Fever, William, 284, see Feaver
Feversham, Earl of, 165
Feyfield, Richard, 478
Field, Anthony, 478
——, Henry, 139
——, Richard, 123
——, see Feild
Fifield, Abraham, 443
——, Henry, 165, 166
——, Richard, 454
Figiss, Arthur, 125, 126
Filborne, Robert, 141
Filenst, Thomas, 172
Filks, John, 427

Fillingham, Francies, 293
Filmer, John, 178
Finch, Benjamin, 488
——, Frances, 211
——, Joan, 488
——, Sir John, 162
——, Katherine, 488
——, see Fynch
Fine, Richard, 240
Finn, Teage, 368, see Fynn
Firebrass, John, 444
Firmin, John, 281
Fish, Christopher, 70
Fisher, Edward, 36, 51, 177, 219
——, Gabriell, 122
—— (or Fissher), Henry, 171, 444
——, Jane, 194
——, John, 176, 188, 326, 329, 447
——, Katherine, 210
——, Robert, 36, 132, 210
——, Samuell, 192
——, Sarah, 219
——, Sisly, 210
——, Thomas, 191
——, Wm., 138
Fister, Constance, 125
Fitch, Abigall, 101
——, Enecha, 236
——, James, 101
——, Jo., 107, 108
——, Samuell, 390
——, Tho., 236
Fits, Fitt, Fitte, Fitts
——, Alice, 179
——, Ann, 227
——, Robert, 178, 127, 227, 501
——, Thomas, 179
——, see Fitz
Fits James, Madam, 449, see Fitz James
Fitzgerald, Morris, 477
Fitzgerard, Elenor, 424
——, James, 424
——, John, 424
Fitz James, Edward, 367, see Fits James
Fitz Jarrell [? Fitzgerald], John, 368
Fitziefferys, Mr., 191
Fitz Nichols, Mary, 368
Fitzrandolph, Phillip, 367
Flaming, Peter, 74
Flane, Charles, 79
Flatter, Nico., 141
——, Wm., 143
Fleetwood, Alexander, 134
Flege, Thomas, 291

67—2

INDEX

Flemg [? Fleming], Edmond, 369
Flemïng, [*i.e.*, Flemming], Abram, 65
———, Richard, 79
Fletcher, Benjamin, 165*, 166*, 167
———, Edward, 38, 192
——— (or Flettcher), George, 441, 454
———, Henry, 87
———, John, 115, 352
———, Lodowick, 118
———, Miles, 95
———, Noah, 427
———, William, 425
Flewellin (or Flewilling), Peter, 323, 328
Flexney, Thomas, 105
Flexny, Robert, 349, 356, 373, 391
Flint, George, 502
——— (or Flynt), Thomas, 183, 259
Flinton, Elizabeth, 187
———, Farrar, 251
———, Joane, 187, 251
———, Pharaoh, 273
Flit, Marie, 198
Flitcroft, Nicolas, 63
Floid, Nathaniell, 232, *see* Floyd
Flower, John, 132
———, Thomas, 138, 179, 247
Floyd, Thomas, 170, *see* Floid
Fludd, David, 104
———, Elizabeth, 96
———, Jane, 96
———, John, 211
———, Joseph, 96
———, Margett, 211
———, Obediah, 96
———, Tho., 75
———, William, 211
Flude, Bartholmew, 38
Flynt, *see* Flint
Foane (Fowne, or Fawn), Robert, 318*, 320*, 324
Fogg (or Fogo), David, 348, 352, 363, 384, 395, 400, 405, 415, 418, 435
Fokar, Jo., 65
Folinsby, Alice, 437
———, Thomas, 437
Follett (or Follitt), John, 319, 319*, 323, 357
Folly, Nico., 127
Follyn, Andrew, 471, *see* Fallin
Fonceco Vale, Jacob, 450
Fonseire, Philip, 454

Fontleroy, James, 369
Foockes, William, 243, *see* Fookes
Foode, Wm., 327
Fookes, Henry, 39, *see* Foockes
Foord, John, 469, 472, *see* Ford
Foot, John, 319, 319*, 323
———, Richard, 467
Forbush, James, 367
Forcey (or Forcy), Thomas, 318*, 319*
Ford, Adrian, 103
———, Barbara, 62
———, Charles, 105
———, Francis, 369
———, George, 128, 152
———, Jn., 285
———, Mary, 85
———, Richard, 447
———, Rose, 425
———, Thomas, 478
———, Tristram, 143
———, *see* Foord
Foreman, Samuell, 190
Forest, Jesse de, 199
Forestall, Richard, 477
Forgiue [*i.e.*, Forgive], Samuell, 154
Forrester, Agnes, 426
———, Jane, 426, 438
———, John, 438
———, Thomas, 426, 438
Forrestor, Thomas, 443
Forstall, Richard, 342, 440, 454
Forster, Josias, 87
———, Thomas, 304
Forten, Jo., 131
Fortescue, Sir Nicholas, 157
———, Symon, 268
Forth, George, 120
———, John, 186, 254
Foskew, Thomas, 181
Fossitt, Fossett
———, Ann, 123, 172
———, Robert, 101
———, Thomas, 172
———, Wardin, 84
Foster, Christopher, 92
———, Elizabeth, 324
———, Francis, 92, 124
———, Hester, 325, 329, 368
———, Hopestill, 68
———, James, 95
———, John, 93, 173, 182, 478
———, Nathaniell, 93
———, Patience, 68
———, Rabecca, 93
———, Richard, 122
———, Robert, 502
———, Sylus, 84

Foster, Tho., 85
———, William, 390, 497
Fouch, Tho., 126
Fouche, Hugh, 127
Fouks, William, 186
Foulfoot, Tho., 42
Foulke, Thomas, 192
———, William, 254
Fouller, Frances, 174
———, William, 183
Fountaine, Edward, 97
———, John, 36
Fourdrin, François, 198
Fousher, Phillip, 329
Fowle, Ann, 59
Fowler, Christopher, 439
———, Francis, 232
———, Geo., 114
———, James, 327, 329, 433
———, John, 41, 271, 454
———, Joshua, 369
———, Margrett, 259
———, Widow, 183
———, William, 259
Fowne (Foane, or Fawn), Robert, 318*, 320*, 324
Fox, George, 124
———, Hugh, 95
———, John, 39, 93, 103, 308
———, Nicholas, 104
———, Phillis, 368
———, Richard, 93
———, Stephen, 368
———, Wm., 115
Foxcrofte, Tho., 113
Foxen, John, 179, 236
Foxsley, Jane, 123
Foy, Hugh, 478
Frame, William, 478
Framerie, Martin, 198
Francis, 209
——— (a Negro), 182
———, William, 296
Francisco, Mathias, 254
Francke, Daniell, 190
Francklin, Nicholas, 435
Franklin, Jonathan, 74
——— (Francklyn, Franklyn, or Francklyon), Thomas, 318*, 319*, 323, 367
Frankling, Christopher, 443
Fransum, Joseph, 368
Fraser, Malcum, 320*
Frazill, John, 71   [210
Freame (or Freme), John, 171,
Frebourne, *see* Freebourne
Frederick, John, 447
Free, John, 40
Freebourne, Freebourn, Frebourne, Fribourne

INDEX. 533

Freebourne, Mary, 278, 279
———, Sarah, 278
———, William, 278, 279
Freeman, Alice, 98
———, Anthony, 130
———, Bennet, 103
———, Bridges, 182
———, Edmond, 93, 98
———, Edward, 98
———, Elizabeth, 98, 134, 436
——— (or Freman), Henry, 446
———, John, 92, 98
———, Joseph, 358, 367, 384, 404
———, Marie, 92
———, Raph, 209
———, Sycillie, 92
———, Thomas, 93, 139
———, William, 138, 502
Freme, see Freame
Freman, see Freeman
French, Elizabeth, 99, 100
———, Francis, 99
———, John, 50, 99, 152
———, Judeth, 283
———, Marie, 99
———, Roger, 326
———, Samuell, 369
———, Wm., 100
Frere, John, 477
———, Tobias, 329, 477, see Frier
———, William, 477
Fresey, Ambrose, 191
Frethram, Richard, 193
Frethy, Tho., 153
Fretwell (or Frettwell), Ralph, 329, 472
Frey, John, 298
Fribourne, see Freebourne
Friccar, Jo., 111
Frie, Geo., 128, see Fry
Frier, George, 218
———, Tobias, 79, see Frere
———, Vrsula, 218
———, see Fryer
Frisbie, Richard, 260
Frisby, Elizabeth, 123
Frisle, Frissel, Frissell
———, Daniel, 423, 433
———, Elizabeth, 423, 433
———, Margery, 194
———, Thomas, 423, 433
Frister, Robert, 123
Frith, Robert, 111
———, Samuell, 369
———, Sarah, 428
———, Tho., 118
Frogmorton, John, 176

Frost, Frostt
———, Francis, 454
———, Reignold, 153
———, Tho., 134
Fry, Frye
———, Henry, 191
———, John, 187, 190
———, Richard, 145
———, see Frie
Fryer, George, 117, see Frier
Fryme, Richard, 38
Fulcock, Henry, 133
Fulder, Kat., 113
Fulford, Jo., 82
Fulham, Thomas, 195
Fuller, Alice, 105
———, Joane, 454
———, Jo., 73
———, Marie, 48
———, Wm., 73
Fulshaw, Samuell, 193
Fulwood, John, 181
Fullwood, George, 141
Furbank, Bartholm, 127
Furbredd, Margerie, 37
Furey, Charles, 502
Furlow, Mr., 191
Furse (alias Voss, Fusse, or Fuss), Morris, 333, 338, 340
Fusheir, Phillip, 461
Fusse, see Furse
Futer, Thomas, 502
Fyers, Jone, 367
Fynch, Jo., 125, see Finch
Fynn, John, 136, see Finn

GAD, Anne, 467
———, James, 467
Gadling, Henry, 121
Gadsby, Tho., 126
Gage, Joseph, 318*
Gaich, Joseph, 319*, 323
Gaile, Elias, 175, 226
Gale, John, 172, 334, 337, 340, see Gall, Joseph
———, Richard, 70
Galhampton (Galhamton, Gilhampton, or Gilhamton), Thomas, 332, 335, 340, see Gilhampton
Gall, Andrew, 349, 361, 370, 379, 409
———, Joseph, 334, see Gale, John
Galler, Wm., 135
Galley, Tho., 135
Gallop, Ann, 337
Galloway, Charles, 75
Gamlin, Robert, 149

Gammage, Gamage, Gamadge, or Gamidge
———, Stephen, 327, 330
———, Thomas, 333, 336, 341
Gane, Richard, 40, see Gayne
Ganey, Henry, 187, see Gany
Gannock, Robert, 120
Ganter (or Gunter), Lester, 131
Gantois, P., 198
Gany, Anna, 187, 256
———, Henrie, 251
———, William, 187, 256, 273
———, see Ganey
Gard, Margeret, 123, see Guard
Garde, Alexander de la, 75
Gardener, Wm., 85
Gardiner, Edward, 170
———, Thomas, 507
Gardner, Ann, 75
———, Charles, 317, 342, 344
———, Edward, 107
———, George, 370
———, John, 371, 374
———, Lyon, 118
———, Mary, 118
———, Peter, 68
———, Thomas, 123
———, William, 507
Garland, Hugh, 36
———, Jo., 112
Garman, Timothy, 435
Garner, Mary, 502
———, Miller, 502
Garnett, Elizabeth, 187, 255
———, Judith, 279
———, Susan, 187, 255
———, Thomas, 187, 255
Garney, James, 478
Garr, Symon, 137
Garrard, Edward, 71
Garret, Garrett
———, Emond, 502
———, Francis, 83
———, Owen, 71
———, Steeven, 50
———, Richard West—, 135
———, Tho., 81
———, William, 217
Garrott, Thomas, 438
Gary, Edward, 478
Gascoign, Peter, 436
Gascoyne, Savill, 116
———, Stephen, 447
———, see Gaskoyne
Gaselee, or Gaslee
———, Elizabeth, 492
———, John, 478, 492
———, Susanna, 492
Gasko, Thomas, 172

INDEX.

Gaskoyne, Thomas, 264, *see* Gascoyne, &c.
Gaspar, Pierre, 198
Gass, Edward, 51
Gastrell, Ebedmelech, 169
Gater, Joan, 111
——, Jo., 111, 112
Gates, Elizabeth, 232
——, Sir Thomas, 155
——, Thomas, 179, 232, 270
Gather, John, 173
Gaton, Tho., 40
Gatter, John, 240
Gaughton, Nico., 86
Gault, William, 294
Gaumon, Natha., 184
Gauntlett (or Gawntlett), William, 183, 195
Gaurd, La, 184
Gavett, John, 194
Gavyn, Richard, 127
Gawntlett, *see* Gauntlett
Gawyn, *see* MacGawyn
Gay, Abell, 471
——, James, 171
—— (or Guy), John, 326, 328
——, Widow, 471
Gayer, Francis, 112
Gayne, William, 187, 253, *see* Gane
Gayton, Richard, 454
Geales, William, 194
Gean, Pontus Le, 199
Gedney, Hanah, 294
——, John, 290, 294
——, Ledia, 294
——, Sarah, 294
Gee, John, 102, 229
——, Samuel, 320, 328, 341
Geere, Dennis, 87
——, Elizabeth, 87
——, Sara, 87
Geerie, Jo., 117
Geies, Wm., 135
Genney, Richard, 124
Gentler, Vallentyn, 191
George, 188
——, Henry, 112
——, Thomas, 478
Gerden, Bridget, 64
Gerish, Benjamin, 371
Gew, Henry, 126
Ghiselin, Claude, 199
Gibbes, *see* Gibbs
Gibbins, Oliff, 125
Gibbons, Henry, 332, 338, 340
——, James, 60
——, John, 461
——, Mathew, 140

Gibbs, Gibbes
——, Bassill, 469, 472
——, Edward, 86, 371, 466
——, Francis, 223
——, Jane, 126, 144
——, John, 105, 131, 171, 213, 260, 316, 318, 323, 343, 469, 478
——, Joseph, 502
——, Lieut., 309
[?——], Mary, 469
——, Nicholas, 342
——, Phillip, 502
——, Richard, 371
——, Sarah, 466
——, Stephen, 349, 476
——, Thomas, 323
Gibbson, Gibson
——, Ann, 62
——, Francis, 174
——, John, 122, 502
——, Mathew, 502
——, Nico., 112
——, Richard, 141
——, Walter, 52
——, William, 40, 139
——, Yeoman, 118
Giddins, Geo., 45, 46
——, Jane, 45
Gidion, Rowland, 373
Gifford, Edward, 122
——, Francis, 272
——, Samuell, 444
Giggon, Jesper, 64
Gilbert, ——, 195
——, Henry, 122
——, James, 347, 358, 362, 394, 399, 432
——, Nathaniell, 478
——, Robert, 80, 431
——, Roger, 122
——, Thomas, 141, 365, 383, 386, 398
——, William, 297
Gilby, Robert, 39
Gilder, Henrie, 64
Gildingwater, Tho., 74
Giles, Ann, 492
——, George, 492
——, Jonathan, 177, 222
——, Margrett, 184
——, William, 322
——, *see* Gyles
Gilgate, Jo., 82
Gilhampton, Olliver, 445
——, *see* Galhampton
Gilham, Gillham, *see* Gillam
Gill, Alexander, 174, 240
——, John, 104, 319°, 323
——, ——, Junr., 319

Gill, Mark, 120
——, Richard, 115
——, Thomas, 129
Gillam, Gilham, Gillham
——, Ann, 97
——, Ben., 97
——, Emanuell, 502
——, Jo., 124, 478
——, Tho., 124
——, Wm., 137
Gille, Jan., 199
Gilles, Edward, 478
——, ——, Junr., 478
Gillett, Richard, 194
Gilliard, Anto., 85
——, John, 434
Gilson, Thomas, 74
Gislingham, Edward, 432
——, Elisabeth, 432
——, Jone, 432
Gitly, Henry, 433
Gittes, Henry, 371
Gittings, John, 489
——, Mabell, 489
——, Mary, 489
Gladdin, Tho., 356
Glade, Joseph, 38
Gladwell, Aymes, 66
Glaister, Richard, 37
Glasbrooke, Wm., 118
Glassenden, John, 133
Gleadston, Nicholas, 193
Glenester, Robert, 123
Glifford, Hanna, 109 [? Clifford]
Gloster, Jo., 122
——, Mathew, 170, 206
Glouer [*i.e.*, Glover]
Glover, Alexander, 128
——, Henry, 178, 280
——, John Jarvice, *alias*, 181
——, Richard, 111
Glower, Charles, 150
Glynn, Bryan, 101
Goad, John, 112, 142
——, Tho., 100
——, Wm., 141
Goadby, Jo., 46
Goald, John, 319
Goard, Richard, 72, 76
Godbehere, Benjamin, 431
Godbitt, Tho., 79
Godby, Joane, 253
——, Thomas, 187, 253, 273
Goddard, John, 166
Goddin, Edward, 85
——, George, 71
——, Jo., 135
——, *see* Goding

Godding, Gooden or Goden, Abraham, 319, 320*, 325, *see* Goding
Godffree, Gilbert, 372
Godfrey, Andrew, 422
———, Jo., 101
———, Sarah, 422
Godfrie, Henrie, 140
Godfry, Mary, 371
Goding, Peter, 454, *see* Godding, &c.
Godsall (or Godsal), John, 316*, 317, 343
Godwin, Reinould, 258, *see* Goodwyn
———, Robert, 261
Goeing, Frances, 499
———, John, 499
Goff, William, 136
Goffe, Eliza, 107
———, James, 498
———, Marie, 87
———, Michael, 498
Gogin, William, 372
Golane, Mary, 430
———, Patric, 430
Gold, Edward, 54
———, Eliz., 123
———, Jarvice, 48
———, William, 440
Goldenham, Jonas, 133
Golder, Wm., 124
Golding, George, 168
———, John, 70
———, Percivall, 371
———, *see* Goulding
Goldham, Alice, 67
Goldingham, James, 41
———, John, 324, 460
———, *see* Gouldingham
Goldsmith, Arthure, 234
———, Farford, 63
———, *see* Gouldsmith
Goldwell, Ann, 113
Golthorp, Ralph, 103
Gomez, Isaac, 450
Gonn, Ann, 107
———, Jasper, 107
Good, Thomas, 299
Goodale, Abraham, 282
———, Isaacke, 282
———, Mary, 282
———, Robert, 282
Goodall, Katherin, 280
———, Robert, 280
Goodbarne, John, 119
Goodby, Jone, 187
Goodchild, Richard, 195
———, Chrismus, 195

Gooddens, Adam, 291
Gooden, *see* Godding
Goodenuff, Sam., 69
Goodfaith, Joseph, 304
Goodhew, Jane, 108
Goodhue, Nico., 108
Goodin, Anne, 293
Gooding, Joseph, 371
Goodladd, Richard, 80
Goodman, Ellz., 454
———, Richard, 478
———, Robert, 183, 260
———, Tho., 37
———, Tymothie, 75
Goodridge, Jo., 125
Goodson, John, 101, 125
Goodwene, John, 145
Goodwinn, Mary, 134
Goodwyn, Goodwynn
———, Jane, 134
———, Marie, 67
———, Reinold, 183, *see* Godwin
———, Tho., 81
———, William, 150
Gookines, Daniell, 243
Goold (or Gould), Enock, 316*, 317, 343
———, Thomas, 316, 342
———, *see* Gould
Goose, William, 293
Gorden, Edmond, 59
———, George, 372
———, Peter, 478
Gorges, Sir Ferdinand, 159*
———, Henry, 462
———, Richard, Lord, 162
Gorham, John, 94
———, Thomas, 94
Gorhie, Donough, 129
Gorman (or Gormon), Matthew, 478, 495
Gorton, John, 372
———, Richard, 372
———, Steven, 122
Gosling, Tho., 81
Goslinn, Jo., 81
Gosnel, Elisabeth, 422
———, John, 422
Gosselin, Wm., 142
Gosselyng, George, 161*
———, James, 161*
Gother, Henry, 372
Gough (or Gowgh), Mathew, 121, 137
Gould (or Goold), Enock, 316*, 317, 343
———, Grace, 90
———, John, 90
———, Petter, 191

Gould, Thomas, 318
———, William, 316*
———, *see* Goold
Gouldfinch, Nicholas, 226
Goulding, Thomas, 239, *see* Golding
Gouldinge, Jane, 152
———, Sara, 249
Gouldingham, Henry, 465
———, John, 465
———, *see* Goldingham
Gouldocke, Sara, 185
Gouldsmith, Arthur, 179
———, Nicholas, 175
———, *see* Goldsmith
Gouldson, Gouldston
———, Anne, 281
———, Henery, 281, 282
———, Mary, 282
Gouldwell, Henry, 186
Gourdeman, Jean, 198
Gourney, William, 151
Governeur, Abraham, 166*
Gowde, Henry, 140
Gowen, Tho., 119
Gowgh, *see* Gough
Grace, Benjamin, 454
———, ———, Junr., 438
———, Geo., 121
Grafton (or Graston), James, 37
———, John, 364, 385, 397
Grame (or Grand), James, 37
Grane (or Graves), George, 175
Granger, Niccolas, 262
———, Robert, 39
———, Thomas, 129
———, *see* Graunger
Grant, Thomas, 431, *see* Graunt
Grasson, Wm., 123
Graston (or Grafton), James, 37
Graue, Graues, *see* Grave, Graves
Graunger, Nicholas, 188, *see* Granger
Graunt, John, 121
———, Zeth, 150
———, *see* Grant
Grave, Elnor, 225, *see* Snow
———, George, 225
———, Joan, 130
———, John, 225
———, Mary, 130
———, William, 286
Graves (or Grane), George, 175
———, Mary, 467
———, Richard, 92
———, Robert, 217, 467
———, Rose, 467

536 INDEX.

Graves, Thomas, 188, 263
Gray, Edward, 51
———, Francis, 79
———, George, 339
———, John, 342
———, Mathew, 342
———, Richard, 137, 478, 494
———, Robert, 372, 443, 478
———, *see* Grey
Graye, Jone, 176, 228
———, Margrett, 228
———, Thomas, 176, 228
———, William, 176, 228, 502
Grazbury, John, 307.
Grazebury, James, 311
Greefeson, William, 139
Green, Jacob, 348, 369, 380, 383, 389, 406, 411, 416
———, Richard, 317*, 319*, 324
———, *see* Greene
Greene, Abigall, 150
———, Aderton, 192
———, Alexander, 125
———, Ambrose, 140
———, Daniell, 36
———, Darcas, 278
———, Edward, 125
———, Elizabeth, 465, 467
———, Ellin, 62
———, George, 36, 463
———, Jacob, 150
———, John, 70, 74, 81, 150, 176, 182, 194, 279
———, Joseph, 150
———, Nicholas, 71
———, Percivall, 62
———, Perseverance, 150
———, Richard, 86, 179, 236
———, Robert, 102, 170
———, Roger, 138
———, Saloman (or Solloman), 189, 264
———, Sara, 113
———, Sisley, 174
———, Suzan, 71
———, Thomas 38, 45, 46, 83, 103, 142
———, William, 71, 126, 127, 141, 254, 462, 465, 467
Greenelefe, Wm., 128, *see* Greenleafe
Greenewood, John, 39
———————, Robert, 141
———————, *see* Greenwood
Greenhill, Nicholas, 230
Greenidge, Jane, 490
———————, Jean, 478
———————, Philocleon, 490
———————, Richard, 478, 490
Greenleafe, Ann, 204

Greenleafe, Robert, 204
———————, Susan, 204
———————, Thomas, 204
———————, *see* Greenelefe
Greenly, Jo., 51
———, Steeven, 52
Greenoway, Ursula, 57
Groenslatt, Thomas, 373
Greenway, Robert, 357, 408
———————, Wm., 317*, 319*, 320*
Greenwich, Jo., 74
Greenwood, John, 37, 437
———————, Tho., 51
———————, *see* Greenewood
Greevett, Ellin, 227
———, John, 227
———, *see* Grevett
Gregorie, Alexander, 138
———, Ben, 115
———, Tho., 121
———, *see* Griggory
Gregory, Ormond, 478
———, Richard, 171, 222
———, Thomas, 327, 331
———, *see* Griggory
Greigs, John, 352
Grenier, Antoine, 198
Grensild, Barbrey, 294
———, Marey, 294
———, Samuell, 294
Gressam, Edward, 128
———, Jo., 127
Grestninh, Jacobus, 370
Gretrick, Thomas, 297
Grevett, John, 178, *see* Greevett
Grey, Matthew, 472
———, Ralph, 167*, 168
———, Thomas, 162
———, Ursula, 425
———, *see* Gray, Graye
Gribell, Thomas, 145
Griddick, Jo., 135
Griffige, Joan, 123
Griffin, Griffine, Griffinn
———, Ann, 113, 133
———, Dennis, 372
———, Edward, 417, 478
———, George, 154
———, Gualter, 428
———, Henry, 427
———, John, 136, 226, 267
———, Marie, 68
———, Mathew, 192
———, Rice (or Rise), 185, 243
———, Richard, 190, 195
———, Thomas, 133, 194
———, Wm., 115

Griffin, *see* Griphin and Gruffin
Griffith, Ambrose, 183
———, Edward, 138
———, Grace, 432
———, Herbert, 489
———, Jo., 120
———, Josua, 97
———, Rebecca, 432
———, Robert, 432
———, Wm., 119
———, *see* Gyffith.
Griffiths, Richard, 41
Griff's, *see* Griffith, Griffiths
Griggory, John, 454, *see* Gregory, Gregorie
Grigg's, Grigg
———, Alyce (or Alce), 44, 370
———, Elisa, 44
———, Geo., 44
———, James, 44
———, John, 478
———, Mary, 44
———, Robert, 370
———, Tho., 44, 119
———, Wm., 44
Griggson, Grigson
———, Richard, 80
———, Robert, 478
———, Wm., 38
Grimes, Ann, 173
———, Gilbert, 73
———, George, 190
———, (or Grines), George, 267
Grimscroft, Jo., 36
Grimston, Anthony, 102
———————, Justice, 43
Grind, Richard, 135
Grindall, Edward, 135, 180
Grinder, Thomas, 172
Grindon, Edward, 270
Grindry, John, 187
———, Jone, 187
———, Mary, 187
Grines (or Grimes), George, 267
Griphin, Raph, 178, *see* Griffin, &c.
Gritton, Ellizabeth, 454
Croncare, John, 502
Groue, Groues, *see* Grove, Groves
Ground, Robert, 39
Grove, Benjamin, 353, 377
———, Joseph, 440
———, Richard, 231
———, Wm., 129
———, *see* Groves
Grover, Samuel, 132

INDEX.

Groves, Benjamin, 401
———, Elizabeth, 87
———, Jo., 87
———, *see* Grove
Growce, Samuell, 118
Grubb, John, 271
———, Thomas, 228
———, William, 70
Grubthorn, Edward, 133
Grudge, Humfrey, 84
Gruffin, John, 192, *see* Griffin, &c.
Gualmay, Thomas, 64
Guard, Elizabeth, 491
———, Isabell, 491
———, Peregrine, 491
———, William, 347, 358, 362, 379, 387, 392, 403, 412, 413
———, *see* Gard
Gudderidge, Ann, 102
———, Tho., 113
Guine (Gunie, or Gume), Griffine, 177
——— (———), Thomas, 191, 192, 193
Guise, Christopher, 164*
Gullifer, Tho., 71
Gulliver, Mr., 436
Gulstons, Chad., 195, *see* Gunston
Gume (Guine or Gunie), Griffine, 177
Guffly [*i.e.*, Gummy], Richard, 95
Gun, Daniel, 424
———, Sarah, 424
———, Thomas, 424
———, *see* Gunne
Gundrie, John, 251
———, Marie, 251
Gunie (Guine, or Gume) Griffine, 177
——— (or Guine), Thomas, 191, 192, 193
Gunne, Daniel, 465
———, Henry, 465
———, *see* Gun
Gunnery, John, 274
Gunning, John, 478
Gunston, Chad., 189, *see* Gulstons
Gunstone, Thomas, 462
Gunter (or Ganter), Lester, 131
———, Wm., 142
Guppy, Justinean (or Juztipher, 332, 335, 341
———, Wm., 318*, 319*, 320*
Gurge, William, 151
Gurr, George, 180, 236
Gurrish, Jeffery, 117

Gutsall, Walter, 92
Guy, 445, 454
———, Alice, 75
———, Elisabeth, 428
———, James, 205
——— (or Gay), John, 326, 328
———, Richard, 120
———, Robert, 171, 228
———, Whitney, 195
———, William, 35
Gwyne, Paul, 440
Gyffith, Ambrose, 255
———, Joyse, 255
———, *see* Griffith
Gyles, Wm., 318*, 319*, *see* Giles

HABBARD, Joan, 496
———————, William, 496
Habbittell, Geo., 123
Habing, Thomas, 502
Habroll, James, 24
Hach, Thomas, 171
Hacker, Ferdinando, 375
———, James, 296
———, John, 233
Hacket, Hackett
———, Ann, 480
———, Sir Robert, 494
———, Robert, 376
———, William, 479
Hackwell, Hackewell
———, , 88, 89, 90
———, H., 87
———, Jo., 66
———, Richard, 73, 100
———, Robert, 91, 92, 96, 97
Hackwood, Mary, 429
Hadbie, Tho., 81
Hadborne, Anna, 91
———, Anne, 91
———, Geo., 91
———, Rebecca, 91
Hadnet, Humfrey, 101
Haeward, Thomas, 149, *see* Haieward, Haiward, Hayward
Haffell, *see* Hasfell
Hagar (a Negro), 429
Haggar, Robert, 109
Haggat, Othniell, 338
Hagthorp, William, 479
Haiden, Tho., 128, *see* Heydon, Heiden
Haies, Ant*., 121
———, James, 137
———, John, 41
———, Robert, 72
———, William, 50

Haies, *see* Hayes
Haieward, John, 70
———, Samuell, 56
———, Sith, 110
———, Richard, 121
———, *see* Haeward, Hayward, Haiward
Haieword, James, 43
Haile, Sarah, 132
———, Thomas, 173
Haine (or Hanie), John, 184, *see* Hayne
Haines (or Hames), Thomas, 128
———, ————, William, 180
———, *see* Haynes
Haiward, Robert, 111, *see* Haeward, &c.
Hakes, Thomas, 191
Hakesby, Isabell, 113
Hal, Elisabeth, 437
—, Esther, 437
—, Francis, 437
—, Jehu, 434
—, *see* Hall
Halam, Robert, 169, *see* Hallam, Hallum
Haldin, Richard, 133
Hale, Barnabie, 379
—, Jo., 119
—, Thomas, 206
Haler, Henrie, 112
Hales, Jo., 112
Haley, Dennis, 376
———, Thomas, 479
———, *see* Hayley, Haly, Heylei
Halford, Tho., 43
Halfyard, Aymies, 135
Halingworth, *see* Hallingworth
Hall, Agnis, 283
———, Anne, 421
[?—], ———, 469
———, Anthony, 428
———, Christopher, 176, 227
———, Dorothy, 283
———, Elizabeth, 283, 421
———, Esther, 421
———, Francis, 421, 455
———, George, 173, 222
———, Giles, 377
———, Grissell, 283
———, Hugh, 186, 252, 443, 507
———, James, 115
———, Jeffery, 185
———, Joane, 283, 507
———, John, 114, 141, 178, 227, 421, 426, 502
———, Joseph, 283
———, Richard, 447

INDEX

Hall, Robert, 414
———, Samuell, 76
———, Susan, 173, 222, 227, 432
———, Susanna, 421
———, Temperance, 283
———, Thomas, 79, 80, 87, 111, 137, 188, 194, 235, 304
———, Tristram, 283
———, William, 112, 236, 332, 338, 341, 469
———, *see* Hal
Hallam, Wm., 479, *see* Halam, Hallum
Hallers, Julian, 219
Hallett, Hallet
———, Andrewe, 286
———, Christopher, 422, 430
———, Gregory, 434
———, John, 328, 337, 366, 422, 430, 441, 454
———, Joseph, 326
———, Mary, 422, 430
———, Richard, 443
———, Thomas, 327, 329
Halliack, John, 92
Halliers, Idye, 210
Hallingworth, Halingworth
————————, Edward, 74
————————, Eliz., 108
————————, Richard, 108
————————, Suzan, 108
————————, *see* Hollingworth
Halloway, Abraham, 63
————, Darby, 424
————, Lanthil, 424
————, Mary, 424
Hallowell, Huyn, 81
Hallum, Mary, 493
———, Wm., 493
———, *see* Halam, Hallum
Halock, Edward, 94
Halsey, Jo., 76
———, Richard, 112
Haly, Ellin, 116, *see* Haley, Hayley, &c.
Ham, John, 432, 455
———, Joseph, 245
———, Susanna, 432
Haman (or Hamun), John, 191, 192
———, Joseph, 185
———, Mathew, 179
———, *see* Hayman
Hamar, *see* Hamor
Hamblen, Mathew, 67
Hamblin, Widow, 455
Hamdy (or Hamey), Richard, 110
Hamer, *see* Hamor
Hafferly, *see* Hammerly

Hames, Clement, 136
———, Richard, 143, *see* Hamis
———, Tho., 41
——— (or Haines), Tho., 128
——— (————), William, 180
Hamey (or Hamdy), Richard, 110
Hamias, Moses, 449
Hamilton, Adam, 374
————, James, Marquis of, 160
Hamis, Richard, 141, *see* Hames
Hamlin, Giles, 360
Hammerly, Martha, 469
Hamock, Allin, 120
Hamon, Mathew, 235
Hamond (or Hammond)
————, Christopher, 121
————, Daniell, 86
————, Elizabeth, 67, 279
————, John, 41, 279
————, Sarah, 279
Hamor, Hamar, Hamer, Hamors
————, Elizabeth, 223
————, Mrs., 174
————, Raphe, 174, 223, 236, 271, 272
Hampton, Joane, 253, 261
————, John, 84, 183
————, Mrs. 184
————, William, 253, 261
Hamun (or Haman), John, 191, 192, *see* Hayman
Hanbury, Daniell, 48
————, Nicholas, 480
Hancock, Alexander, 378
————, John, 137, 442
————, Tho., 121
Hand, Tho., 124
———, Winnifred, 64
Handcleare, Beniamine, 184, 243
Handley, Robert, 112
Hands, Richard, 41
Handy, Elizabeth, 466
———, John, 455, 466
———, Samuell, 111
Hanes (or Haues), Luke, 120
Haney, John, 261
Hanford, Eglin, 56
————, Eliz., 56
————, Margaret, 56
Hanger, Phillip, 377
———, Sarah, 303
Hanie, Elizabeth, 262
——— (or Haine), John, 184
Haning, Wm., 142

Hankworth (or Haukworth), Nathaniell, 243
Hanmer, George, 86
———, Tho., 128
Hanmerry, Nicholas, 479
Hannah, Andrew, 379
———, George, 164, 167, 446
———, James, 167
Hannay, George, 163°, 343
Hannis, Richard, 141
Hanson, Ann, 489
———, Francis, 489
———, John, 489
———, Rebecca, 491
———, Robert, 491
———, Samuell, 454, 462
Hanway, George, 165°
Harbert, Edward, 480
———, Jo., 91
———, Wm., 102
Harbin, Allexander, 439
———, Joseph, 439
Harbynn, Peter, 127
Harcombe (or Hercombe), John, 319, 319°, 323
Hardcastell, Mathew, 252
Hardeman (or Hardiman), John, 326, 330
Harding, Christopher, 190, 269
———, Edward, 437, 455
———, Eliz., 73
———, Francis, 421, 454
———, Henry, 461, 466, 479, 495
———, Hugh, 307
———, John, 350, 374, 394, 404
———, Katharine, 421
———, Margery, 71
———, Mary, 421
———, Nathanael, 466
———, Sara, 133
———, Thomas, 182
———, Wm., 133, 439, 446
Hardiss, Joan, 102
Hardisse, William, 102
Hardon, John, 121
Hardwick, Francis, 455
Hardy, Joseph, 357, 358, 374, 394, 404
———, Robert, 73
Hare, Bryan, 124
———, Elvy, 490
———, George, 490
———, John, 437, 455
———, Mary, 437
———, Sarah, 490
———, Suzan, 125
Harecourt, Robert, 156
Harefinch, Wm., 104

Hargrave, Richard, 35
Hargraves, Allis, 479
Hargrove, William, 493
Harison, *see* Harrison
Harker, John, 378
Harkwood, Jo., 133
Harlakenden, Eliza, 100
———, Mable, 100
———, Roger, 100
Harlow, Harlowe
———, Anthony, 178
———, John, 82, 187, 250, 468
———, Richard, 468
Harlstone, Edward, 479
Harman, Captain, 47
———, Charles, 264
———, Ellis, 115
———, Francis, 109
———, Jo., 109
———, Richard, 37
———, Sara, 109
———, Tho., 43, 51
———, William, 462, 479
Harper, George, 343, 440, 455
Harries, Maryes, 152
Harrington, Elias, 111
Harris, Adria, 203
———, Alice, 113, 186
———, Anthony, 479, 491
———, Dorithe, 170
———, Edward, 377
———, Elinor (or Ellnor), 184, 243
———, Elizabeth, 490
———, Geo., 64
———, Hannah, 431
———, Henry, 297
———, John, 42, 82, 103, 170, 252, 268, 333, 338, 341, 359, 454
———, Lieut., 180
———, Lucy, 491
———, Mabell, 491, 494
———, Richard, 87, 128, 467, 490
———, Robert, 36, 116, 142
———, Thomas, 170, 203
———, Walter, 149
———, William, 39, 70, 114, 135, 186, 193, 462
———, Zachariah, 479, 490, 494
Harrison, Abraham, 502
———, Ann, 186
———, Charls, 437
———, George, 269
———, Hugh, 104
———, John, 39, 102
———, Raphe, 195

Harrison, Richard, 96
——— (Harison, or Harrison), Robert, 138, 323, 331
———, William, 106
Harrowigg, Marie, 67
Harrwell, Tho., 143
Harrwood, *see* Harwood
Hart, Harte, Hartt
———, Captain, 176
———, Charity, 490
———, Chri., 85
———, Dorothy, 490
———, Edward, 479
———, Isacke, 291
———, Job, 490
———, John, 94, 108, 149, 430
———, Josias, 191
———, Mary, 108, 152
———, Robert, 85
———, Tho., 91, 128, 137
———, Walter, 479, 490
———, Wm., 102
Hartey, John, 316
Hartforde, Margrett, 47
Hartlie, Christopher, 140
Hartley, Jeremy, 71
———, William, 174, 180, 233
Haruey, *see* Harvey
Harvey, Harvye, Harvy, Harvie
———, Alexander, 122
———, Ann, 45
———, Grace, 435
———, Griffith, 373
———, Henry, 447
———, Sir John, 160
———, John, 158, 440
———, Nicholas, 37
———, Richard, 45, 83
———, Samuell, 195
———, Thomas, 232, 416
———, William, 334, 338, 341
Harwood, Harrwood
———, Ann, 423
———, Augustin, 105
———, Daniell, 455
———, Grace, 241
———, John, 423
———, Margarett, 151
———, Mary, 423
———, Paule, 187, 253
———, Ralph, 40
———, Richard, 329, 337
———, Robert, 122
———, Thomas, 120, 178, 241
———, William, 181, 238
Hasfell, Marie, 55
———, Martha, 55
———, Rachell, 55
———, Richard, 55

Hasfell, Ruth, 55
———, Sara, 55
Hasell, John, 445
———, Peter, 378
———, William, 374
———, *see* Hassell, Hazel
Haselwood, Elizabeth, 488, 494
———, Jane, 494
———, Richard, 488
———, Thomas, 479, 488, 494
Haslewood, Walter, 237
Hasley, John, 181, 238
Hassard, Edward, 67, *see* Hazard
Hassell, Benjamin, 444
———, Ralph, 454
———, Wm., 122
———, *see* Hasell, Hazel
Hastings, Edward, 69
———, Susan, 280
———, Thomas, 280
Hatch, Rebecca, 187
———, Thomas, 222
Hatchet, Tho., 102
Hatfeild, Hatfield, Hattfild
———, Joseph, 183, 260
———, William, 172, 210
Hathorn, Jo., 103
Hathorne, Tho., 47
Hathoway, Jo., 108
Hathway, Samuell, 455
———, Suzan, 96
Hatrell, George, 135
Hatterton, Jo., 80
Hattfild, *see* Hatfeild
Hatton, Ann, 430
———, Charles, 479
———, John, 248
———, Olive, 248
———, Robert, 373
———, Thomas, 430
———, Wm., 129
Hanby, Richard, 39
Haues (or Hanes), Luke, 120
Haughtaine, Richard, 480
Haughton (or Houghton), Epaphroditus, 165*, 166
———, Gerrard, 298, *see* Hawton
Hauiland, *see* Haviland
Haukins, *see* Hawkins
Haukom, *see* Hawlkom, &c.
Haukseworth, Tho., 43, *see* Hawksworth
Haukworth (or Hankworth), Nathaniell, 243, *see* Hawksworth
Haulkom, *see* Hawlkom
Haulton, William, 279

68—2

INDEX.

Hausen (or Hawen), Samuell, 479
Havercamp, Francis, 126
Haviland, Mathew, 329, 444
———, Miles, 374
Haward, Henry, 278.
———, Hugh, 218
———, Susan, 218
———, see Hayward
Haway, Thomas, 172
Hawen (or Hausen), Samuell, 479
Hawes, Ann, 131
———, Anna, 131
———, Obediah, 131
———, Reginoll, 37
———, Richard, 131
Hawker, Timothy, 334, 338, 341
Hawkes, Ellin, 117
———, Mary, 117
———, Wm., 124
Hawkins, Abraham, 424
———, Andrew, 443
———, Clement, 74
———, Geo., 83
———, James, 125
———, Job, 56
———, Mary, 424
———, Richard, 59
———, Thomas, 180, 234, 424
———, William, 151
———, see Hawkynns
Hawksworth, John, 454, 455, 459
———, William, 469
———, see Haukworth
Hawkynns, Marie, 58
———, Robert, 58
———, see Hawkins
Hawley, Geo., 120
———, Henry, 126, 160, 426, 434
———, Jane, 426
Hawlkom (Haulkom, Haulkon, Haukom, or Holcombe), Andrew, 319, 319*, 323
Hawton, Gerard, 374, see Haughton
Haxley, Robert, 64
Hay, Daniell de La, 297
———, John De La, 296
———, Peter, 160
Hayem, Abraham, 373
Hayes, Jane, 490
———, Martin, 402, 444
———, Thomas, 479, 490
———, see Haies
Hayley, Anthony, 435, see Haly, Haley, Heylei

Hayman, Nathan, 400, 404, 414
———, William, 39
Hayman, see Haman
Hayne, Haynes
———, John, 318*, 319*, 324
———, Michell, 119
———, William, 318*, 319*, 322, 333, 337, 340
———, see Haine, Haines
Hayse, Thomas, 331
Hayte, Robert, 470
Hayward, John, 470
———, William, 70
———, see Haward, Haeward, &c.
Haywood, John, 331, 446, 479
———, Widow, 447
———, see Heywood
[?Hazard], Henry, 188
———, Joane, 188
———, John, 188, 248
———, see Hassard
Hazell, Toby, 64, see Hasell, Hassell
Healy, Wm., 375, see Hely
Hearst, Wm., 455
Heath, Elizabeth, 130
———, Isack, 130
———, Martha, 130
———, Robert, 135
———, Thomas, 121
———, William, 150
Heathfeild (or Heatchfeild), John, 318*, 319*, 323
Heaton, John, 446
Hebbs, Thomas, 175
Hebden, Tho., 37
Heck, Katherin Van, 101
———, Olliver Van, 101
———, Peter Van, 101
Hecthrop (or Hectrop), Wm., 347, 455
Hedges, Francis, 87
———, Robert, 174, 240
Hedley, Hedly
———, Edward, 86
———, Michell, 124
———, Tho., 86
Hedsall, Thomas, 54
Heed, Robert, 84
Heelis, Geo., 134
Heford, Nathan, 45
———, Roger, 242
Heiden, Henry, 111, see Haiden, Heydon
Helawe, Wm., 81
Helcott, Thomas, 177, 265
Helin (Hellin, Helline, or Helyn), John, 176, 181, 313*

Hellier, see Hellyer
Hellin, &c., see Helin
Hellue, Robert, 193
Hellyer (Hellier or Hillier), Robert, 327, 329
——— (———), Thomas, 327, 329
Helmes, John, 376
———, Thomas, 502
Hely, John, 171, 210
———, Mathew, 81
———, see Healy
Helyn, see Helin
Heming [i.e., Hemming], Jo., 122
Henderson, Francis, 479
———, Wm., 472
Hendly, Daniell, 374
———, Eliz*., 374
Hendry, Jo., 123
Hendy, Richard, 434
Henley, Edward, 324
Henly, Ralph, 429
Henman, Jo., 134
Henry, 184, 188
———, Anna, 431
———, Anthony, 431
———, Wm., 86
Henson, Phillipp, 52
Henton, Elias, 236
Henwood, Ann, 434
———, Thomas, 434
Hepworth, Joseph, 41
Herbert, Elisabeth, 424
———, Charles, 162*
———, Henry, 378
———, William, 424
Hercombe (or Harcombe), John, 319, 319*, 323
Hereford, Peter, 184
Hernden, Tho., 134
Hero, Oble, 261
Heron, John, 105, 140
Herrick, Isaac, 373
Herring, Jo., 75
Herringman, William, 479
Herrott, Edward, 137
Hersey, Richard, 95
Heslerton, Thomas, 445
Heth, Jo., 132
Hetherington, Katherine, 374
Hethersall, Thomas, 188, 272
Hethersell (or Hethersall), John, 330, 338, 343
Hewbrayne, John, 154
Hewes, John, 502
———, Thomas, 254
———, see Hughes, Hughs, Hues

INDEX. 541

Hewitt, Robert, 446, 471, *see* Huett
Heydon, J., 303, *see* Haiden, Heiden
Heylei, Richard, 43, *see* Haley, Hayley
Heywood, John, 374, *see* Haywood
Hibbins, James, 63
Hibbott's, Katherin, 96
Hichcocke, Kilibett, 173
———, Thomas, 177, 189
———, William, 181
———, *see* Hitchcock
Hickcombottom, Jo., 36, *see* Higginbotham
Hickey, Wm., 104
Hickles, Jane, 143
Hickman, Charity, 493
———, Richard, 493
———, Walter, 493
Hickmore, Mr., 174
Hicmott, James, 224
Hide, James, 81
———, Richard, 125
———, *see* Hyde
Higges, Miles, 306
Higginbotham, John, 441, 455, *see* Hickcombottam
Higgins, Elizabeth, 185
———, John, 39, 206
Higginson, Ann, 124
———, Humfrey, 124
———, Margaret, 502
Higgison, Henry, 375
Higley, John, 374
Hilgrove, Alexander, 429
Hilk, John, 378
Hilman, *see* Hillman
Hill, Edward, 186, 257, 273
———, Elizabeth, 152, 186, 252
———, Frances, 187
———, Francis, 260
———, George, 94, 426
———, Hanna, 186
———, Henry, 85, 295
———, Jane, 207
———, Joan, 134
———, John, 37, 39, 74, 80, 122, 126, 138, 186, 249, 377, 455, 497, 502
——— (or Gill), John, 319*
———, Katherin, 64
———, Marmaduke, 207
———, Robert, 106
———, Thomas, 187
———, William, 107, 149, 152, 186
———, *see* Hills
Hilliard, Charles, 35

Hilliard, Gregory, 195
———, John, 81, 140, 195
———, Wm., 77
Hillier, *see* Hellyer
Hillman, Ellner, 98
——— (or Hilman), James, 333, 337, 340
Hills, Ismale, 188
———, Rose, 123
———, *see* Hill
Hilton, Alice, 71
———, Hugh, 128, 170, 203
———, Tho., 307
Hinch, John, 489
———, Margery, 489
———, William, 489
Hinde, Margaret, 105
———, William, 104
———, *see* Hynd
Hindsley, Wm., 123
Hine, Robert, 471
Hingle, James, 112
Hinkynn, Wm., 141
Hinshawe, Wm., 125
Hinson, Jo., 128
Hinton, Ellias, 179
———, John, 175
———, *see* Hynton
Hippsley, Jo., 135
Hitchcock, Hitchcocke
———, Captain, 195
———, John, 319*, 324
———, Mathew, 59
———, Tho., 104
———, Wm., 79
———, *see* Hichcock, Hitckock
Hitchcott, John, 318* [? Hitchcock]
Hitchy, John, 228
Hitckock, Alice, 237
———, Thomas, 237
———, *see* Hitchcock, Hitchcock, &c.
Hiter, George, 40
Hoare, Edward, 319*
———, Richard, 318*, 319*, 324
——— (or Hoar), Thomas, 326, 330
———, *see* Hore
Hobbs, Hobs, Hobes
———, Elizabeth, 378
———, Humility, 426
———, Oliver, 318*, 319*, 324
———, Robert, 140
———, Roger, 326, 331
———, Tho., 69, 113
Hobcraft, Elinor, 421

Hobcraft, John, 421
———, Lovel, 421
Hobes, *see* Hobbs
Hobin, Tho., 139
Hoble, John, 286
Hoblyn (or Holbin), Christopher, 316*, 317, 342
Hobs, *see* Hobbs
Hobson, Edward, 104, 169, 201
———, John, 121
———, Nicholas, 41
———, Thomas, 169, 268
Hocksley, John, 152
Hoddins, Jo., 81
Hodges, Christopher, 429
———, Elizabeth, 177, 220
———, Jo., 36, 54, 104, 193
———, Jone, 429
———, Mr., 50
———, Roger, 86
———, Tho., 81
Hodgskines, Hodgkins, Hodskyns, Hodskynns
———, Antonio, 124
———, Edward, 120
———, Henrie, 135
———, Jesper, 125
———, Margrett, 264
———, Nicholas, 264
———, Temperance, 264
Hodgson, William, 39
Hodson, Tho., 137
Hoeman, Elizabeth, 118
———, Wm., 89
———, Winifrid, 89
Hog, Thomas, 429, *see* Hogg
Hogdon, Isaac, 434
Hogg, Jo., 129, 142, *see* Hog
Hoggin, Dennis, 111
Hogman, Elizabeth, 479
Holbin (or Hoblyn), Christopher, 316*, 317, 342
Holbrooke, Anne, 285
———, Elizabeth, 285
———, Jane, 285
———, John, 285
———, Thomas, 285
Holburd, Walter, 64
Holcombe, *see* Hawlkom, &c.
Holder, John, 336
———, Junr., 502
———, Meletiah, 502
———, Nicholas, 479
———, Wm., 336
———, *see* Houlder
Holdip, Frances, 423, 460
———, Hilliard, 362, 375, 423
———, John, 423, 460

INDEX.

Holdred, Wm., 53
Holdsworth, Arther, 378
———, Gilbert, 71
———, Jo., 109
Hole, Robert, 446
Holeman, Roger, 379
———, Thomas, 324
Hollam, Robert, 202
Holland, Abram, 139
———, Ann, 123
———, Gabriell, 169, 228
———, Henry, Earl of, 159, 160
———, John, 38
———, Martha, 105
———, Rebecca, 228
———, Robert, 38
———, Thomas, 96
———, Wm., 110
Hollard, Angell, 285
———, Katheryn, 285
———, Thomas, 373, 441
Holliday, Mary, 375, see Hollyday
Hollidge, Roger, 102
Hollingworth, Wm., 108, see Hallingworth
Hollin, John, 427
Hollinbrigg, Edward, 120
Hollinby, Richard, 52
Hollinsworth, Ralph, 455]
Hollis, Edith, 171
———, Nico., 51
Holloway, Edmond, 70
———, Eedie, 113
———, Elizabeth, 123
———, Hannah, 304
———, Jo., 72
———, Richard, 373
Hollowell, John, 468
Holly, Eliza., 93
Hollyday, Wm., 441, see Holliday
Holman, James, 467
———, Jane, 429
———, John, 467
———, Robert, 429
Holmar, Edward, 150
Holme, Robert, 38
Holmes, Alice, 180
———, Captain, 175
———, Henry, 41, 479, 495, 496
———, James, 479, 492
———, John, 51, 479, 492, 494
———, Mary, 492
———, Mathew, 111
———, Richard, 40
———, Samuell, 83

Holmes, Susanna, 495
———, Thomas, 297
Holsey, Richard, 376
Holt, Humfrey, 132
———, Joseph, 379
———, Randall, 221
———, Rowland, 375
———, Wm., 85
Holton, Bartholmew, 95
Home, John, 265
Homer, Roger, 353, 360, 361, 369, 382, 385, 408, 412, 417
Homes, Margaret, 123
———, Thomas, 290
Honniborn, Robert, 102
Hoode, Ralph, 242
Hooe, Ryce, 96
Hook, Wm., 376
Hooke, Beniamin, 105
Hooker, John, 497, 498, 499, 502
———, Ralph, 498
———, Thomas, 173
Hookham, Olliver, 74
Hooks, John, 192
Hooper, Crispine, 479
———, Christopher, 455
———, Daniell, 377, 480
———, John, 319
———, Jonathan, 479
———, Robert, 462
———, Wm., 86, 107
Hopcroft, John, 416, 443
Hopekings, Samuell, 502, see Hopkins
Hopes, Henry, 119
Hopkicke, William, 194
Hopkins, Annis, 117
———, Barthelmew, 183
———, Richard, 121
———, see Hopekings
Hopkinson, Michell, 36
Hoppine, Mary, 152
Hopson, Thomas, 233
Hopwood, Jo., 63
Hordesnell, Henry, 164*
Hore, Richard, 37, see Hoare
Horn, Mary, 428
Horne, Gustavus Adolphus, 377
———, Henry, 179
———, Jo., 103
———, Richard, 141
Horner, James, 125
———, Thomas, 193, 445
Horniold, Horniolde
———, Katherine, 494
———, William, 479, 494
Hornn, Richard, 179
Hornwood, Jo., 121

Horribynn, Richard, 80
Horrock's, Tho., 126
Horsham, Dorcas, 68
———, Edward, 67
———, Elizabeth, 67
Horswood, Sarah, 460
Horton, John, 431
———, Robert, 427
Horwood, James, 42
Hosier, ———, 192, 196
Hoskins, Hoskyns
———, Bartholmew, 121, 274
———, Sir John, 167
———, Katharin, 428
———, Mrs., 446
———, Nicholas, 189
———, Robert, 467
Hosmer, Hossmer
———, Ann, 54
———, James, 54
———, Marie, 54
Hoten, Margery, 378
Hough, William, 377, 480
Houghton, Chri., 83
———— (or Haughton), Epaphroditus, 166, 165*
———, John, 89
———, Wm., 65
Houlder, John, 469, see Holder
Houlding, Just, 279
———, Richard, 279
Housfeild, John, 502
How, Eliz*., 376
———, John, 189, 330
———, Tho., 379
———, see Howe
Howard, Francis, Lord, 163*, 164, 165*
———, John, 258, 360, 372, 417
———, Mabell, 488
———, Mary, 488
———, Sir Philip, 163*
———, William, 119, 488
Howe, Edward, 131, 143
———, Elizabeth, 131
———, Ephraim, 131
———, Isack, 131
———, Jeremie, 131
———, Rice, 206
———, Sara, 131
———, Wm., 131
———, see How
Howell, Andrew, 175, 226
———, Arthur, 35
[?———], Guy, 454
———, James, 190
———, John, 177
———, Richard, 454

Howell, Sarah, 375
———, Tho., 125
Howes, Marie, 67
———, Richard, 428
Howgate, Jo., 120
Howlett, Randall, 174
———, William, 191
Hownesfield, John, 140
Howse, Jo., 74
Howseman, Richard, 73
———, Wm., 51
Howson, Ellin, 42
———, Peter, 42
Huatt (or Hutt), Nathanill, 271
Hubbard, George, 132, 303
———, James, 80
———, John, 68, 106, 303
———, Judith, 106
———, Marie, 130
———, Mary, 107, 108
———, Martha, 107
———, Nathaniel, 107
———, Richard, 81, 107
———, Samuell, 86
———, Tho., 41, 58
———, Wm., 58, 68, 106
Hubbart (or Hubbert), Edward, 394
———, George, 308
———, John, 312
Hubberstead, Edward, 217
Hubbert (or Hubbart), Edward, 350, 394
Huchens, John, 145, see Hutchins
Huchinson, John, 300, see Hutchinson
Hucker, Walter, 316*
Huckle, Wm., 73
Hudlice, John, 296
Hudley, Grissel, 488
———, Mary, 488
———, Timothy, 488
Hudson, Chri., 109
———, Edward, 174, 180, 266
———, Eliz., 62
———, Francis, 127
———, Hanna, 62
———, John, 62, 442, 445, 498
———, Marie, 62
———, Ralph, 62, 84
———, Richard, 122
———, Robert, 173, 213
———, Suzan, 38
———, Thomas, 139, 357, 387, 399
———, Wm., 37, 102
Hues, Hugh, 181, see Hewes, Hughs, &c.

Huett, Ambrose, 51, see Hewett
Huff, Francis, 252
Hugens, see Hutchins
Huges, Thomas, 186
Huggins, Nico., 137
Hughens, see Hutchins
Hughes, Charles, 137
———, Edward, 109
———, Griffith, 125
———, John, 40, 80
———, Lewes, 74
———, Owen, 84
———, Richard, 35, 104, 143
———, William, 105
———, see Hewes, Hues, Hughs
Hughinis, Pattrick, 479
Hughs, Andrew, 377
———, Ann, 238
———, Elizabeth, 493
———, Hugh, 238
———, John, 425
———, Richard, 428
———, Thomas, 493
———, see Hewes, Hues, Hughes
Hughson, Elizabeth, 113
Huies, Edward, 192
Hulett, Wm., 137
Hull, Jefferey, 236
———, Katherin, 130
Hulls, Andrew, 130
Humfrey, Jo., 112, 140
Humfrie, Aymie, 116
Humphryes, Edward, 479
Hunckes, Henry, 160
Huncote, Wm., 113
Hundley, Godfrey, 115
Hunking, Marke, 352, 380
Hunt, Abraham, 319, 319*, 324
———, Dennis, 376
———, Edward, 103
———, Elisabeth, 430
———, Job, 316*, 318, 343
———, John, 124, 377
———, Leonard, 81
———, Luke, 379
———, Ralph, 115
———, Wm., 137, 138
———, see Huntt
Hunter, Christian, 108
———, Eliz., 108
———, Francis, 85
———, John, 190, 446, 448
———, Thomas, 108, 257
———, Wm., 108
Huntley, Margaret, 37
Huntt, Edward, 446, 455

Huntt, Symon, 454
———, see Hunt
Hurles, Eliza., 375
Hurlestone (or Hurlestons), John, 270, 273, see Hurlstone
Hurlie, Darby, 81
Hurlock, C. John, 427
———, Tho., 111
Hurlow, Daniell, 455
Hurlstone, Edward, 344, see Hurlestone
Hurst, George, 469
———, Tobias, 256
———, Wm., 376
Hurt, John, 304, 306
———, Richard, 86
———, Robert, 140
———, Toby, 186
Husband, Mary, 105
Husbants, Samuell, 463
Husse, Hussey, Hussy, Hussye
———, Joseph, 431
———, Lawrence, 333, 338, 340
———, Mr., 194
———, Robert, 218, 444
Huste, Robert, 286
Huswith, David, 85
Hutchins, Anthony, 139
——— (or Hugens), John, 303, 327, 329, 331
——— (or Hughens), Mathew, 326, 331
———, Nevill, 40
———, Robert, 273
———, Widow, 469
——— (or Hutchings), William, 334, 335, 341
———, see Huchens
Hutchinson, Clement, 70
———, Jo., 37, 124, 454
———, Jonathan, 447
———, Michell, 127
———, Robert, 177
———, William, 185, 244
———, see Huchinson
Hutley, Richard, 180
Hutt (or Huatt), Nathanill, 271
———, Robert, 79
Hutton, Elizabeth, 186
———, Francis, 116
———, John, 109, 186, 439
———, Olliver, 439, 479
———, Wm., 36
Hyatt, Samuell, 455
Hyde, Edward, 168*
———, Henry, 479
———, Robert, 317, 320, 328, 341

544 INDEX.

Hyde, *see* Hide
Hye, John, 136
Hyet, Tho., 36
Hynd, Jo., 52, *see* Hinde
Hynton, Wm., 83, 84, *see* Hinton
Hywood, Tho., 51

IBOTSON, Ibottson, Ibbison
———, Ann, 186
———, Elizabeth, 186, 254
———, Persivall, 186, 254, 272
Ilam, Richard, 480
Iles, Henry, 39
Illett, Jonadab, 188
Inchiquin, William, Earl of, 166
Ingleby (Inglebee, or Inglebe), John, 349, 361, 406, 415
———, Nicholas, 381
Ingles, *see* Bloxam
Inglish, Mary, 75, *see* English
Ingram, Edward, 108
Inman, John, 250
Innis, James, 499
Ipsley, John, 466
Ireland, Alexander, 489
———, Ann (or Anne), 489, 494
———, Charles, 494
———, Marie, 65
———, Martha, 65
———, Samuell, 65
———, Thomas, 133, 480, 489, 494
Ireson, Edward, 93
———, Elizabeth, 93
Irish, George, 381
———, Henrie, 36
———, Tho., 63, 142
Ironmonger, Thomas, 212
Isaacke, Rebecca, 281
Isabell (Negress), 244
Isgraue [*i.e.*, Isgrave], John, 175
Isham, Robert, 120
Ison, Edward, 103
Israell, David, 449
———, Judith, 450
Issabella (Negress), 185
[?Ives] Jues, Charles, 442
——— (or Joes), Wm., 131
Iveson, Richard, 75, 134
———, Tho., 51

JACCSON, George, 379
———, James, 381
———, Wm., 379
———, *see* Jacson

Jacckson, *see* Jackson
Jack, John, 135
Jackman, John, 325
———, Saloman, 217
Jackson, Ann, 116, 239
———, Barnard, 173, 209
———, Charles, 71
———, Elizabeth, 37
———, Ephraim, 175
———, Henry, 58, 79
———, James, 51
———, Jer., 367
———, John, 75, 76, 100, 108, 175, 181, 183, 187, 225, 229, 239, 257
———, Launcelot, 96
———, Margaret, 108
———, Mary, 427
———, Nico., 112
———, Richard, 39
———, Samuell, 117, 136
———, Tho., 137
———, Walter, 217
———, Widow, 181
———, William, 41, 104, 140, 192, 196
———, *see* Jaccson, Jacson
Jacob, Henry, 104
———, John, 380
Jacobs, Henry, 443
———, Wm., 445
Jacobsone, Aron, 507
———, John, 507
Jacson, Christopher, 447, 455
———, Jeremiah, 413
———, *see* Jaccson, Jackson
Jago, Walter, 41
Jakes, Dorothy, 116
———, Jo., 111
Jakins, James, 191
James, ———, 437
———, Lewes, 125
———, Richard, 125, 126, 382
———, Robert, 127
———, Roger, 136
———, Thomas, 36, 134, 427
———, Ursula, 126
———, William, 79, 126, 150, 381
——— (a Frenchman), 182
——— (an Irishman), 194
———, called the Piper, 188
Jane, ———, 437
Janes, Jane, 424
———, John, 424
———, Thomas, 424
Jarman, Precilla, 77
Jarmin, Symon, 379
Jarratt (or Jerratt), Samuell, 268

Jarret, Anna, 491
———, Mary, 491
———, Peter, 491
——— (or Jerratt), William, 269
Jarvice, Francis, 115
———, *alias* Glover, John, 181
Jay, Sir Thomas, 43
———, Thomas, 137
Jeames, Margarett, 480
Jeenes, Henry, 471
Jefferie, Jefferies, Jeffereys, Jefferres, Jefferyes, Jeffery, Jefferys, Jeffreyes, Jeffreys, Jeffrys, Jeofferies
———, Andrew, 35
———, Edward, 132
———, Edmond, 445
———, Elisabeth, 77, 437
———, Goodwife, 229
———, Herbert, 162°
———, Job, 112
———, John, 191, 192, 455
———, Marie, 77
———, Mary, 77
———, Nathaniell, 175, 225
———, Peter, 348, 415
———, Rice, 367, 403
———, Robert, 77
———, Stephen, 316°
———, Tho., 77, 112
Jefferson, John, 183, 226, 271
Jeffords, Eliz., 503
Jellfes, Bonaventure, 465, 468
———, Samuel, 465, 468
———, *see* Jelph's
Jelly, L.-Col., 438
———, Mary, 421
———, Richard, 421
———, Thomas, 421, 455
Jelph, James, 492, 495
———, John, 480, 492, 495
———, Mary, 492
———, *see* Jellfes
Jelson, Joell, 381
Jemmot (or Jemot), John, 460, 465
Jenings, *see* Jennings
Jenkin, Joane, 260
———, Oliver, 260
———, *see* Jinkines, Jenkins, Jenkynns
Jenkins, Edmond, 122
———, Elizabeth, 131
———, Jane, 382
———, John, 182
———, Jone, 186
———, Owen, 381
———, Mary, 186
———, Morgan, 139

INDEX. 545

Jenkins, see Jenkin, Jinkines, Jenkynns
Jenkinson, Fra., 109
———, Oliver, 186
———, Robert, 101
Jenkynn, Jo., 107 } see
Jenkynns, Tho., 39 } Jenkin,
Jenkyns, Walter, 137 } &c.
Jennicom, Tho., 87
Jennings, Henry, 87
———, Jane, 129
———, John, 141, 402
———, Michaell, 382
———, Mathew, 192
———, Nicholas, 279
———, Phillipp, 51
———, Richard, 133
———, Sara, 133
———, William, 382
———, see Jennins, Jennyngs
Jennins, Anne, 465
———, Matthew, 465
———, Richard, 303
———, see Jennings, Jennyngs
Jennions, Tho., 122
Jennison, Allex, 455
———, Henry, 425
Jennor, Jenor, Jenour, Jenoux
———, Anthony, 370, 379, 382, 398, 409
———, Edward, 38
———, Thomas, 368, 404
Jennoway, Suzan, 127
Jennyngs (or Jenyngs), Richard, 307, 310
Jephson, John, 470
Jermayne, Thomas, 152
Jernew, Eliz., 120
———, Joan, 120
———, Nicholas, 120
Jerratt, see Jarratt, Jarret
Jesop, Walter, 283
Jesope, , 283
Jesopp, Tho., 36
Jeune, Gregoire le, 198
Jewell, Christopher, 317*, 319*, 323
———, Tho., 53
———, Walter, 96
Jewson, Elizabeth, 490
Jinkines, Allexander, 252
———, Joane, 252
———, Oliver, 252
———, see Jenkin, Jenkins, &c.
Jipson, Sarah, 380
Jiro (a Negro), 179
Jnoson, see Johnson
Jo., see John
Joane [? Medcalfe], 258
Joanes, Richard, 286

Joanes, Thomas, 295
———, see Jones, &c.
Jobe, Joan, 96
Joes (or Ives), Wm., 131
John, , 188, 189, 191
———, (Irishman), 194
———, Morgan, 382
———, (Negro), 86, 172
Johnes, David, 38
———, Hugh, 74
———, Jo., 49
———, Oliver, 135
———, Sara, 150
———, see Jones, Joanes, &c.
Johns, Phillipp, 111
Johnson, Abram, 38
———, Alice, 127, 424
———, Ann, 228
———, Archibald, 342
———, Bridget, 424
———, Edmond, 107
———, Edward, 41, 126, 183, 258
———, Eliza., 108, 127
———, George, 102
———, Hamond, 304
———, Henrie, 13;
———, James, 136
———, John, 40, 60, 79, 108, 112, 113, 115, 133, 138, 178, 228, 271, 319, 327, 329, 330, 365, 379, 380, 387, 399, 436, 440, 442, 455, 503
———, Joseph, 181, 231
———, Major, 338
———, Margaret, 116, 231
———, Mary, 127
———, Sir Nathaniel, 164*
———, Nathaniell, 380, 382
———, Peter, 94
———, Richard, 94, 171, 210
———, Robert, 52, 127
———, Sarah, 436
———, Suzan, 42, 108
———, Thomas, 96, 102, 108, 119, 130, 424
———, Widow, 183 [376
———, William, 116, 153, 348,
Johnston, Anne, 469
———, Archibald, 469
———, Thomas, 472
Joliffe, John, 319
Jolly, Mary, 126
Jonas, James, 431
Jones, Alice, 107
———, Amey, 431
———, Anthony, 171, 222, 480
———, Bartholomew, 429
———, Benjamin, 431, 446
———, Chadwallader, 230

Jones, Charles, 88, 163, 164
———, Daniell, 448
———, Davie, 138
———, David, 86, 214
———, Edith, 75
———, Edmond, 126
———, Edward, 38, 140, 168, 236
———, Elizabeth, 106, 129, 218, 381, 467, 490
———, Ellin, 36, 92
———, Evan, 80
———, Giles, 272
———, George, 194
———, Grace, 105
———, Griffin, 84
———, Hector, 383
———, Henry, 233, 468
———, Hester, 92
———, Isack, 92
———, John, 59, 64, 98, 103, 106, 112, 121, 124, 140, 192, 380, 426, 434, 507
———, Joseph, 342
———, Katherin, 118
———, Lewes, 135
———, Margrett, 219
———, Marie, 71
———, Mary, 93, 311, 490
———, Maudlin, 110
———, Morgan, 74
———, Morrice, 140
———, Morris, 84
———, Peter, 140, 217
———, Phillip, 101, 194
———, Rabecca, 106
———, Rebeccah, 439
———, Richard, 38, 83, 116, 185, 190, 380
———, Robert, 64, 135, 380, 480, 490
———, Roger, 425
———, Ruth, 106
———, Samuell, 381, 429, 434
———, Sara, 92, 106
———, Symon, 101
———, Tedder, 129
———, Theoder, 187
———, Theophilus, 106
———, Thomas, 40, 86, 92, 169, 177, 182, 219, 220
———, Walter, 73
———, William, 84, 137, 157, 178, 191, 195, 217, 311, 382, 498
———, see Joanes, Johnes, Joones
Joones, Elizabeth, 255
———, Sara, 255
———, Theodore, 246
———, see Jones, Joanes, &c.

69

INDEX.

Jope, Wm., 118
Jordan, Edward, 469, *see* Jourden
———, James, 382
———, Margery, 171
———, Margrett, 210
———, Mary, 171, 210
———, Samuell, 269
———, Sisley, 171, 209
———, Thomas, 177
———, Wm., 380, 445
Jorden, Joane, 91
———, Peter, 169, 201
———, Thomas, 219
Jornall, John, 185, 246
Jostlin, Dorothy, 55
———, Eliza, 55
———, Mary, 55
———, Nathaniell, 55
———, Rebecca, 55
———, Tho., 55
Jourden, Edward, 342, *see* Jordan
Joy, Edmund, 426
———, William, 182
Joyce, Henery, 145
———, William, 261
Joyner, Jo., 52
———, Tho., 132
Judd, Harbert, 103
Jues (or Ives), Charles, 442
Juiman, John, 187
Julian, Robert, 227
———, Sara, 185, 247
———, William, 185, 247, 273
Jumrey, *see* Pomre, &c.
Justin (or Justine) Humphry, (&c.) 316*, 317, 342

KALLAHANE, Charles, 355, 356, 359, 361, 373, 378, 379, 382, 386, 391, 409, 416, 417
Kamplinn, *see* Kemplin
Kanniday, Ann, 422
———, Mary, 422
———, Thomas, 422
Kanty, Darby, 503
Karsewell, William, 123
Karvis, Jane, 435
———, Henry, 435
Kay, *see* Mac Kay
Keal, Keale, Keel, Keele, Kerle
———, George, 333, 335, 341
———, John, 335, 339, 340
Kean, Alice, 178, 228
Keatch (or Keech), Richard, 326, 330
Kedby, Tho., 138

Keech, *see* Keatch
Keel, *see* Keal
Keele, Edward, 46, *see* Keal
Keie, Sarah, 214
———, Thomas, 214
———, *see* Key
Keith, Elizabeth, 508
———, Henry, 383
———, James, 508
———, *see* Keth
Kelly, Ann, 489
———, Brian, 122
———, David, 480
———, Robert, 343, 503
Kelley, Humphrey, 434
———, John, 430, 503
Kellum, Richard, 115
Kelsoll, Henry, 471
Kelum, Robert, 117
Kemball, Elizabeth, 281, 282
———, Henery, 280, 282
———, John, 282
———, Martha, 282
———, Mary, 282
———, Richard, 280, 282
———, Susan, 280, 282
———, Thomas, 282
———, Ursula, 280
Kember, Robert, 240
Kemp, Anthony, 218
———, Edward, 73
———, Humfrey, 133
———, Isack, 112
———, Margrett, 218
———, Mary, 497
———, Ralph, 497
———, Thomas, 497
———, William, 177, 185, 218, 247
Kemplin (Kemplyn, Kamplinn, or Scamplyn), John, 319, 319*, 325
Kendall, Henry, 129
———, James, 165, 166, 326, 328
———, William, 480, 495
Kendridd, William, 109
Keninston, Thomas, 195
Keniston, Allen, 218
——— (or Kniston), Thomas, 221
Kenn, Mathew, 503
Kenneday, Jo., 117
———, Symon, 36
Kennedy, Ellinor, 383
———, John, 383
Kennell, Samuell, 183, 258
Kenney, John, 488, 493, 496
Kennyon, Geo., 85
———, Jo., 85

Kent, Edward, 316, 318, 343
———, Humfry (&c.), 215, 268
———, Joane, 215
———, Jo., 129
———, Nico., 79
———, Peter, 317*, 319*, 324
Kentt, Humry, 455
Kerbie, Jo., 130 } *see* Kirbie,
Kerby, Humfrey, 75 } Kirby
Kerfitt, Thomas, 227
Kerill, John, 193
Kerle, *see* Keal
Kersey, Thomas, 303
Kersley, Henry, 184
———, Robert, 36
Kerton, William, 191
Keth, George, 248
———, John, 248
——— (or Keyth), Mr., 188, 229, 273
———, Susan, 229
———, *see* Keith
Kett, Robert, 38
Kettell, Peter, 73
Kevynn, Robert, 101
Kew, Anne, 448
———, Nicholas, 383
Key, John, 41, 141
———, William, 480
Keyne, Ann, 107
———, Ben., 107
———, Robert, 107
Keyser, *see* Keyzar
Keysie, Lawrence, 143
Keyth, *see* Keith, Keth
Keyzar, Kezar, Keyser
———, George, 462, 465
———, Katherine, 492
———, Margaret, 465
———, Teague, 480, 492
Kibe, Jo., 81
Kid (or Kidd), Roger, 176, 221
Kiddall, Sara, 177
Kidson, Marmaduke, 101
Kiffin, David, 122
Kilborne, Dunston, 40
———, Elizabeth, 280
———, Francis [Frances], 66
———, Jo., 66
———, Lyddia, 66
———, Margaret, 66
———, Marie, 66
———, Thomas, 66, 280
Kilby, Henry, 125
Kildale, Edward, 219
Kildridge, William, 186
Kilhammy, Patric, 426
Kilin, John, 293
Killinghall, Margaret, 132

INDEX.

Killson, Thomas, 249
Kimp, Michell, 73
Kinderslie, Marie, 71
King, Allin, 116
———, Edward, 119, 129
———, Henery, 238
———, John, 143, 324
———, Mary, 424
———, Richard, 71, 316, 317*, 343, 480
———, Robert, 503
———, Suzan, 94
———, Thomas, 93, 128, 141, 279, 282, 424
———, William, 51, 98, 137, 383, 404
Kinge, Dorothy, 285
———, Hanna, 285
———, Katheryn, 285
———, Percy, 61
———, Mary, 285
———, William, 285
Kinghman, *see* Kingman, John
Kingman, Anne, 285
————, Edward, 284
————, Henry, 284
————, Joane, 284
————, (or Kinghman), John, 285
————, Thomas, 285
Kingsland, Major, 495
————, Robert, 347, 393
Kingsley, William, 234
Kingsmeale, Mr., 178
————, Mrs., 178
Kingsmell, Jane, 229
————, Mr., 230
————, Nathaniell, 229
————, Richard, 229, 230, 271
————, Susan, 229
Kingsmill, James, 111
Kingston, James, 140
————, John, 434
————, Phillis, 434
Kinham, Alice, 285
Kinnoul, William, Earl of, 161*
Kinsland, Nathaniell, 480
Kinston, Thomas, 176
Kinton, John, 190
Kipps, Jean, 480
Kirbie, Richard, 112 } *see* Kerbie
Kirby, Henry, 434 } Kerby
Kirk, Chri., 124
———, Judith, 62
Kirton, Phillipp, 480
Kitchin, John, 117, 284
————, Robert, 352
Kithly, Phillip, 235

Knatchbull, John, 503
Knell, Phillip, 348, 416
Knibb, Tho., 121
Knight, Beniamin, 189, 262
———, Dorothie, 107
———, Christopher, 316*
———, Edmond, 38
———, John, 195, 299, 316*
———, Mordecay, 236
———, Richard, 191, 192, 193
———, Robert, 298
———, Sara, 107
———, Thomas, 80
———, Wm., 64, 82
Knights, Benjamin, 503
———, John, 480
Knightingall, Nathaniell, 503
Knipe, Samuel, 128
Kniston (or Keniston), Thomas, 221
Knore, Noll, 92
———, Sara, 92
———, Thomas, 92
Knott, Abraham, 364, 369, 377, 380, 396
———, James, 188, 264
———, John, 354
———, Joseph, 360, 364, 366, 372, 390, 397, 408, 412
———, Wm., 353, 407, 412
Knowles, Andrew, 480
———, Henry, 62
———, Isarell, 195
———, John, 139
———, Tho., 64
Koker, John, 460
Koorbe, Roger, 79
Kullaway, John, 174
Kyrtland, Nath., 44
———, Phillip, 44
Kyte, John, 383

LACIE, Robert, 81
Lacon, Launcelott, 141
———, Mary, 193
———, Richard, 466
———, Thomas, 481
Lacton, Henery, 223
Lacy, Wm., 85
Ladson, John, 385
Ladston, John, 448
La Garde, Alexander De, 75
La Guard, 184
Lahane, John, 461
La Hay, Daniell De, 297
—— ———, John De, 296
Laine (or Lame), Nethaniel, 194
Lake, Jacob, 52

Lake, Jo., 86, 139
———, Mr., 181
———, Wm., 75, 111
Lakeland, Sibbell, 102
Lamb, Jo., 129
———, Robert, 96
Lambard, Richard, 83
Lambart, Wm., 59
Lamberd, Tho., 52
Lambert, Arthur, 481
———, Elisabeth, 434
———, Charles, 139
———, Henry, 198
———, Robert, 331
———, Sammuell, 257
———, Thomas, 434
Lambertt, William, 190
Lambeth, Marie, 75
Lamborne, Thomas, 441
Lame (or Laine), Nethaniel, 194
Lammas, Edward, 59
Lammy, Edward, 469
Lampeugh, Edward, 38
Lampley, James, 127
Lamply, John, 448
Laffiyn [*i.e.*, Lammyn], Wm., 51
Lancaster, Gowen, 101
————, Phillip, 456
Land, George, 285
———, Sarah, 285
Landall, Robert, 443
Landman, John, 172
Landsdale (or Lansdale), Margaret, 421, 422
————————, Stephen, 421, 422
————————, William, 421, 422
Landsdell, William, 274
Lane, Alice, 68, 253
———, Anthony, 503
———, Henery, 211
———, Hester, 443
———, Jo., 68
———, Nathaniel, 431
———, Oziell, 68
———, Rabecca, 102
———, Ralph, 324
———, Richard, 67
———, Robert, 435
———, Samuel, 68
———, Thomas, 183, 253
Laners (or Lavers), Joane, 152
Lang, *see* Land
Langbridge (or Laughbridge), Francis, 327, 329
Langden, Peter, 184
Lange, Jo., 81

69—2

548   INDEX.

Langford, Abraham, 438
———, Harry, 385
———, Marcie, 95
Langham, Thomas, 503
Langley, Mr., 196
———, Sara, 174
———, Wm., 64, 384
Langman, Mary, 225
———, Peeter, 225, 229
Langram, Rowland, 127
Langridge, Robert, 39
Langstedd, Edward, 120
Langton, Stephen, 439
———, Thomas, 384
Langworth, Francis, 83
Langworthy, Nicholas, 456
Laniere, Clement, 422
———, Rebecca, 422
——— (or Lanier), Robert, 422, 443
Lankfeild, , 183
———, John, 182
Lansdale, *see* Landsdale
Lapworth, Michaell, 233
———, Robert, 201
Larbee, Jacob, 218
Larkham, Thomas, 428
Larkynn, Richard, 135
———, Tho., 86
Larmount, James, 183
Laroch, Widow, 442
Lasey, John, 190
———, Susan, 227
———, William, 227
Lathom, Robert, 240
Lathrop, John, 217
Lattner, Francis, 104
Lauckfild, Alice, 258
———, John, 258
Lauericke, *see* Lavericke
Lauers, *see* Lavers
Laughbridge (or Langbridge), Francis, 327, 329
Launder, Tho., 97, *see* Lawnder
Lavericke, John, 282
Lavers (or Laners), Joane, 152
Lavor, Wm., 79
Lawes, [F]rancis, 280
———, Liddea, 290
———, Marey, 290
Lawford, Richard, 448
Lawless, William, 438
Lawnder, Jo., 143, *see* Launder
Lawrance, Henry, 503
———, Sir Thomas, 165*
———, *see* Lawrence
Lawrell, William, 177
Lawrence, Ann, 424
Lawrence, Barbara, 424

Lawrence, Blackwell, 139
———, Daniel, 424, 436
———, Dorothy, 67
———, Elizabeth, 67
———, John, 45, 75
———, Marie, 45
———, Nicolas, 498
———, Richard, 38, 79
———, Samuel, 327, 329
———, Sir Thomas (165*), 167*, 168
———, Thomas, 168
———, William, 45, 138
———, *see* Lawrance
Lawson, Alce, (174), 232
———, Christopher, 174, 232
———, Thomas, 192
Lawsone, Samuell, 145
Lawters, John, 94
Laycock, Robert, 71
Layden, John, 267
———, Katherin, 207
Laydon, Alice, 185, 245
———, Anne, 185, 244
———, John, 185, 244
———, Katherin, 185, 245
———, Margerett, 245
———, Virginia, 185, 245
———, Wm., 70
Layfield, Ann, 124
Layton, Edward, 40
———, Henry, 472
———, Richard, 456
———, Thomas, 472
Lea, John, 277
———, Phillip, 303
———, Robert, 55, 57, 60, 61, 64
———, Thomas, 217
———, Wm., 49
———, *see* Lee
Leach, John, 503, *see* Leech
———, Margaret, 49, 59
Leachman, James, 135
Leager, Widow, 503
Leak, Augustine, 239
———, Winifred, 239
Leake, Alexander, 94
———, Anne, 91
——— (or Leaker), John, 332, 336, 340
———, Richard, 111
———, Robert, 128
———, Thomas, 70, 469
Leaker, *see* Leake, John
Leane (or Leave), Tego, 153
Leare, Sir Peter, 463
———, Thomas, 463
Leas, George, 141
Leaue, *see* Leave

Leauer, *see* Leaver
Leave (or Leane), Tego,
Leaver, Robert, 195
Leaves, Ellin, 131
Leay, Andrew, 69
———, Jo., 69
Leca, Jan., 198
Lecester, Jo., 93, *see* Leister
Lester
Lecheilles, Jacques de, 198
Lecraift, Thomas, 303
Ledra, John, 456
Lee, Anthony, 112
———, Charles, 448
———, Christopher, 224
———, Daniell, 82
———, George, 64, 114
———, Henry, 51, 113, 384, 386
———, James, 143, 481
———, John, 36, 102, 115, 143, 145, 351, 371
———, Marie, 113, 114
———, Richard, 74, 81, 385
———, Robert, 75
———, Tho., 40
———, Walter, 134
———, William, 86, 111, 318, 344, *see* Ley
———, *see* Lea
Leech, George, 497
———, Millicent, 67
———, John, 497
———, Richard, 51
———, Susanna, 497
———, William, 497
———, *see* Leach
Leed, Tho., 118
Leeds, Joane, 292
———, Richard, 292
Leek, Edward, 433
Leer, Thomas, 136, 456
Lees, Christopher, 218
Leet, Mr., 178
———, William, 163
Legard, C., 497, 498
———, John, 447
Legardo, Elias, 261
Legay (or Lagaye), Jacob, Senr., 447, 503
———, Jacob, 444
———, John, 445
Le Gean, Pontus, 199
Legg, Christopher, 114, 119
———, John, 164*
———, Samuell, 359, 384, 389, 401, 407
Leigh, Charls, 424, 428, 433
———, Martha, 424, 428, 433
———, Sarah, 424, 433, 481

Leigh, William, 428, 494
Leinster, Mainhardt, Duke of, 166*
Leisler, Jacob, 166*
Leister, Thomas, 174, 221, see Lecester, Lester
Le Jeune, Gregoire, 198
Lelam, Alice, 425
———, Henry, 425
———, Mary, 425
Leland, Christopher, 481
Lelland, Henry, 445
Lemi [i.e., Lemm], Mathew, 79
Leman, Katherine, 218
Le Marlier, Nicolas De, 199
Lemon (or Lennon), Wm., 120
Lendall, Robert, 122
Lene, Edward, 120
Lennon, Richard, 440
——— (or Lemon), Wm., 120
Lennox, James, Duke of, 159*
———, Ledowick, Duke of, 156
Leonard, Tho., 112
Le Rou, Jan, 198
Leroux, Jacob, 364, 385
Le Roy, Hugh, 123
———, Jerome, 199
Lerrigo, Marie, 123
Leslie, John, 507
Lester, John, 108
———, see Pester, Lecester, Leister
Letherland, Mary, 432
Lett, Tho., 63
Letteny, Tho., 40, see Lettyne
Lettis, Thomas, 481
Lettyne, Tho., 60, see Letteny
Leusier, Michel, 199
Levant, Isabella, 428
Leverett, John, 163
Levett (or Livett), George, 172, 255
Levins, John, 149
Levitt, Alice, 124
Le Voh, Phillip, 427
Levynns, Ann, 120
Levyns, Wm., 41
Lewes, Edward, 119
———, Eliz., 108
———, John, 35, 126
———, Richard, 127
———, Robert, 79, 103, 108
———, Roger, 207
———, William, 120, 150
———, see Lewis
Lewgar, John, 385
———, William, 328

Lewis, David, 481
———, Edmond, 280, 281, 481
———, Hugh, 503
———, John, 281, 481
———, Mary, 280
———, Roger, 172
———, Thomas, 281
———, see Lewes
Ley, Thomas, 173
———, William, 161, 316, see Lee
Lickburrowe, James, 36
Liddicott, John, 153
Lieford, Ann, 77
Lielate, Anthoine de, 199
Lightbound, Richard, 140
Lightfoote, John, 174, 223
Lilburne, Richard, 386, 393
Lillie, Edward, 125
Lillington, George, 329, 343, 456
Lilliot, Martha, 134
Limrick, Launcelott, 104
Lince, Robert, 220
Linch, Thomas, 159*, see Lynch
Linck, Thomas, 481
Lincklate, William, 498
Lincoln, Elizabeth, 102
———, John, Bishop of, 157
———, see Linkon
Lincolne, Cap., 195
Lincorne, Samuell, 290
Lindsey, Robert, 179
Line, see Lyne
Ling (or Linge), John, 41, 172
Linge, Henry, 172
Linicker, John, 218
Linkon, Ann, 171, see Lincoln
Links, Thomas, 456
Linsey, Daniell, 290
Linton, Thomas,' 324, see Lynton
Lintott, Richard, 330, 462
Lipps, John, 216
Lister, Mary, 448
———, Thomas, 104
Liswel, Hanna, 422
———, John, 422
———, Mary, 422
Little, Jane, 495
———, John, 495
Littlefeild, Annis, 299
Littleton, Edward, 503
Littlewood, Peter, 467
Litton, John, 194
———, Wm., 445, 456
Liversidge, Richard, 112
Livett, see Levett
Lizard, John, 433

Lizard, Stephen, 433
Lloyd, David, 129
———, John, 344, 385
———, Judith, 136
———, Katherin, 71
———, Leolin, 508
———, Maudlin, 117
———, Nowell, 124
———, Richard, 102, 166
———, Tho., 79
———, Walter, 130
———, see Loyd
Lock, Ann, 383
———, Richard, 50
———, Wm., 43, 141
Locke, John, 195, 472
———, Robert, 186, 254
Lockbeare (or Lockebeare), Elias, 316*, 317*
Lockley, Richard, 111
Locksmith, Thomas, 481
Lockton, John, 430
Lockwood, Nicholas, 348, 358, 362, 363, 368, 370, 371, 380, 387
Lodge, Wm., 52
Loe, Jo., 132
———, Peter, 116
Loftis, John, 41
Lone (or Love), Tho., 71
Long, Elizabeth, 64
———, Henry, 40
———, Jane, 235
———, John, 52, 193, 327, 330, 380, 388
———, Katherin, 102
———, Nic*·, 108
———, Will., 432, 435
Longe, Alice, 242
———, Anne, 90
———, Elias (or Ellias), 170, 285
———, Eliza, 89, 90
———, Ellyn, 60
———, John, 90
———, Joshua, 90
———, Mary, 90
———, Michell, 90
———, Nicholas, 181
———, Rebecca, 90
———, Richard, 184, 242
———, Robert, 89, 90, 242
———, Sarra, 90
———, William, 184, 243
———, Zachery, 90
Longman, Petter, 189
Lonnin, James, 43
Longsha, Henry, 74
Longson, William, 385
Longstaff, Elizabeth, 481

INDEX.

Longwith, William, 71
Looker, Joan, 127
Loomes, Edward, 68
Lopes, Lopez
———, Abraham, 384, 449
———, Eliah, 450
———, Rachell, 450
———, Telles Abraham, 386
Lord, Ann, 72
———, Antho., 463
———, Aymie, 72
———, Dorothy, 72
———, John, 72
———, Robert, 72
———, Thomas, 72
———, William, 72
Lort, Sampson, 133
Lostell, Peter, 64
Lottis, Rowland, 180
Loue, *see* Love
Louell, *see* Lovell
Loueridge, *see* Loveridge
Love, Mary, 503
———, Richard, 81
——— (or Lone), Tho., 71
——— Valentine, 64
Loveley, Lovely
———, Ann, 52
———, Mary, 52
Lovell, Anne, 285
———, Constance, 481
———, Elizabeth, 74, 285
———, Ellyn, 285
———, Francis, 448
———, James, 285
———, John, 285
———, Mrs., 456
———, Phillipp, 74
———, Robert, 285
———, Roger, 456
———, Zacheus, 285
Lovely, *see* Loveley
Loveridge, Bernard (&c.), 316, 318, 344
——————, John, 326, 329
——————, William, 326
Lovett, Gurtred, 129
———, Mary, 126
———, Robert, 112
Lowder, James, 82
Lowe, Dorothie, 132
———, Thomas, 444
Lowis, Originall, 81
Lowman, Barnard (&c.), 318*
Lownd, John, 122
Lowre, John, 481
Lowther, Christopher, 384
———, Luke, 503
———, Wm., 122
Lowynn, Tho., 128

Loxmore, Thomasin, 187
Loyd, Edward, 182
———, John, 184
———, Math., 175
———, Morice, 179
———, Nath., 180
———, Silvester, 342
———, *see* Lloyd
Lucas, Elizabeth, 489
———, Charles, 339
———, Richard, 112, 481, 489
———, Theophilus, 489
Luccom, Henry Van, 143
Luch (or Lush), Arthur, 327, 330
Lucie, Mary, 127
Luck, Robert, 35
———, Wm., 116
Lucock, Margaret, 52
Lucomb, Mrs., 456
———, Thomas, 456
Lucott, William, 195
Ludcole, Joan, 124
Luddington, Christiom, 49
Ludken, Elizabeth, 290
———, William, 290
Luke, Elias, 503
Lullett, John, 191
Lullman, Job, 460
Lumbard (or Lumberd), Robert, 326
Lumus [*i.e.*, Lummus], Edward, 59
Lunthorne, Robert, 176
Lupo, Albiano, 185, 245, 273
———, Elizabeth, 185, 245, 273
———, Phillip, 185, 248
———, Temperance, 245
———, William, 194
Lupton, Davie, 136
———, Jo., 115
———, Mary, 141
Lupworth, Micheall, 179
Lurting, Thomas, 41
Lusam, William, 233
Lush (or Luch), Arthur, 327, 330
———, Henry, 286
Luther (or Lutter), Edward, 326, 330
Lutterell, Walter, 75
Lyddale, John, 308
Lyde, Allan, 438
———, Edward, 340
———, Robert, 359
———, Sylvester, 316, 317*
Lydiatt, Timothy, 384
Lyllant, Richard Nash, *alias*, 319
Lynch, Alice, 383

Lynch, Morgan, 386
———, Nicholas, 383
———, Richard, 386
———, Sir Thomas, 164
———, *see* Linch
Lynlie, Wm., 67
Lynley, Robert, 41
Lyne (or Line), Christopher, 386, 456, 461
———, Mary, 100
———, Phelix, 73
Lynn, Robert, 385
Lynt, Robert, 129
Lynton, Nico., 142, *see* Linton
Lyon, Elizabeth, 173
———, John, 41
———, Wm., 130
Lyte, Paul, 461, 464, 465
Lyttcot, Leonard, 384
Lyvermore, John, 279

MABIN, Edward, 182
Mac Brian, Dennis, 74
Macc Breecly, Bryen, 482
Macc Cartie, Charles, 79
——— ———, Owen, 79
——— ———, *see* Mackartee
Macc Daniell, Allexander, 481
——— ———, Patrick, 390
Maccenree, John, 390
Macc Graugh, Daniell, 481
——— ———, John, 482
Macclahen, Owen, 390
Maccmash, Charles, 388
Mac Conry, John, 75
Maccony, Dinnis, 504
Maccowdin, Wm., 52
Mace, Alce, 47
———, John, 96
Mc Gawyn, Brian, 101
Machem, Jo., 104
Mackartee, Elisabeth, 431, *see* Macc Cartie
Mc Kay, Malashus, 83
Mackelly, Cornelius, 433
Mackenny, Cornelius, 424
———, John, 424
———, Susanna, 424
Mackerness, Jacob, 447
———, John, 447
Mackgerry, William, 504
Mackhala, Dennis, 472
Macklaire, John, 456
Mackloghlin, Edward, 431
Macklond, Matthew, 467
Muckone, Darby, 463
Mackrery, Alexander, 438
Mackward, Fellen, 504
Macock (or Macocke), Sara (or Sarah), 174, 223

INDEX. 551

Macquin, Archibald, 423
———, Frances, 423
———, Nicholas, 423
Macy (or Masey), George, 327, 331
Madder, Elizabeth, 491
———, James, 491
———, Samuell, 491
——— (or Mader), 319*, 325
Madders, John, 327, 330
Maddeson, Maddison
———, Isacke, 172, 209, 268
———, John, 320*
———, Mary, 172, 207
Maddockes, Jane, 47
Maddocks, Margaret, 37
Maddox, Alexander, 138
———, Jo., 43
———, Jone, 387
———, Thomas, 194, 504
Maden, Patrick, 391
Mader, Wm., 325
Madford (or Wadford), William, 326, 330
Madin, Henry, 112
Mageridge, Maggeridge, see Mogeridge
Magettes, Mrs., 441
Magitt, Henry, 114
Magner (or Magnor), Charles, 215, 268
Magrauhan, Daniell, 491
———, John, 491
———, Miriam, 491
Magridge, see Mogeridge
Magwaine, Owen, 389
Mahane, John, 389
Mahewe, see Mayhew
Mahone, James, 390, see Mahony
Mahont, Dermott, 472
Mahony, Daniell, 388
Maicockes, Samuell, 269
Maies, Cornelius, 122, see Mayes
Maijor, Robert, 297, see Maior, and Major
Main, Andrew, 425
———, Mary, 425
Maine, Petter De, 191
Maior, Edward, 36
———, Thomas de la, 228
———, see Maijor
Major, Peter, 405
———, Wm., 388
Makynn, James, 135
Maldman, John, 182
Mallion, Jo., 71
Mallocke, Malachi, 318*

Mallonee, Daniell, 492
———, Darby, 492
———, Elizabeth, 492
———, Joan, 492
———, Owen, 492
———, Thomas, 492
Maltman (or Multman), Tho., 127
Man, see Mann
Manby, John, 192, 196
Mandeville, Henry, Viscount, 157
Manerick, Nathaniell, 391
Manifold, John, 108
———, Wm., 120
Maning, see Manning
Mann, Manne, Man
———, Ann, 75
———, Annanias, Senr., 493
———, Barnard, 445
———, Edward, 279, 280, 281, 282
———, John, 139, 160*, 444
———, Percivall, 193
———, Tho., 84
———, Wm., 84
Mannell (or Manuell), Robert, 171
Mannen, Andrew, 387
Mannering, Joseph, 149
Manning, Manning's, Maning
———, Anne, 292
———, Edmond, 92
———, Francis, 140
———, John, 120, 192, 326, 330
———, Peter, 124
———, Tho., 115
Mannington, Roger, 129
Mansell, Robert, 390
Mansfield, Davy (or David), 180, 234
———, Jo., 59, 133
———, Richard, 52
———, William, 435
Manton, William, 138
Manuell (or Mannell), Robert, 171, 210
Manzer, James, 73
Mapes, John, 279
Marburie, Gilbert, 249
March, Collice, 239
———, Samuell, 181, 239
Marchall, Wm., 456, see Marshall
Marchant, Emanuell, 316, 343
———, Silus, 338
———, William, 316, 324, 338

Marfutt, Tho., 39
Margaret, 426
Margrett (Negress), 182
Markcom, Robert, 104
———, Thomazin, 113
Markes, Mark's
———, John, 327
———, Richard, 117
———, Walgrave, 226
Markland, Henry, 482
———, John, 493
Marlett, Thomas, 169
Marlier, Nicolas De la, 199
Marloe, Thomas, 220
Maroh, Mary, 390
———, Sarah, 390
———, Thomas, 390
Marritt, Wm., 141
Marriott, Robert, 392
Marrow, Cornelius, 389
———, Daniel, 310
———, Katherine, 389
———, Wm., 41
Marsan, see Marson
Marsden, Francis, 137
Marsh, Edward, 318*, 320*, 323
——— (or Mursh), Francis, 115
———, John, 80, 115
———, Wm., 80
Marshall, Marshal
———, Ann, 228, 429
———, Charle, 194
———, Edward, 183, 260
———, Francis, 43, 75
———, Henrie, 111
———, Jane, 75
———, Jarvis, 386
———, John, 80, 113, 130, 462
———, John Bristowe, 304, 305(?), see Bristowe
———, Lake, 422, 429
———, Mathew, 35
———, Richard, 74
———, Robert, 176, 228
———, Thomas, 107, 327, 330, 430
———, Walter, 115
———, William, 92, 329, 422, 429
Marson (or Marsan), Edward, 482, 495
———, Jane, 495
Marteaw, Nicholas, 184
Martha (a Mulatto), 489
Martin, Marting, Marttin, Martyn
———, Antoine, 198

Martin, Christopher, 350, 375, 384
———, Edward, 96
———, Francis, 143
———, Gabriell, 456
———, Giles, 219
———, Jeanne, 198
———, Joane, 286
———, John, 67, 122, 123, 154, 258, 269, 504
———, Marie, 54
———, Nicholas, 176
———, Petter, 191
———, Richard, 58, 365
———, Robert, 237, 286
———, Saloman, 107
———, Simon, 154
———, Thomas, 70, 91, 154, 161*
———, Wm., 75
Martue, Niccolas, 249
Marvynn, Marvyn, Marvinn
———, Elizabeth, 65
———, Hanna, 65
———, Marie, 65
———, Marthaw, 65
———, Mathew, 65
———, Sara, 65
Marwood, John, 120, 316*
Mary, ———, 182, 186
——— (a Negress), 241
Mascrie, Robert, 121
Masey (or Macy), George, 327, 331
Masie, Alexander, 114
Mason, Alice, 251
———, Ann (or Anne), 99, 117
———, Beniamin, 74
———, Captain, 150
———, Elizabeth, 195
———, Frances, 188
———, Francis, 251, 268
———, George, 55, 441, see Bacon
———, Hester, 279
———, Hugh, 279
———, John, 70, 94, 142
———, Mary, 188
———, Ralph, 99
———, Richard, 99, 129
———, Samuell, 99
———, Susan, 99
———, Sylam, 389
———, Thomas, 115, 193, 481
———, Walter, 185
———, William, 36, 102
——— (or Masonn), Wyatt, 247
Massingburd, Wm., 109

Massling, William, 504
Masters, Jo., 138
———, Michell, 124
———, Wm., 42
Maston, John, 291
Mastus, Joseph, 387
———, Martha, 387
Mathelin, Richard, 304
Matheman, John, 173, 222
Mather, George, 389
———, Jo., 52
Mathew, Mathews, Mathewes, Matthews, Matthewes
———, Edward, 421, 427
———, George, 154, 390
———, Hannah, 421
———, Jo., 132
———, Robert, 179, 233
———, Roger, 138
———, Rowland, 74
———, Samuell, 118, 179, 233, 234, 270, 272
———, Thomas, 335, 338, 340
———, William, 75, 138, 317*, 467
Maton, Philippe, 199
———, Richard, 101
Matson, Mattson
———, Benjamin, 387, 425
———, Elizabeth, 425, 492
———, Margaret, 425
———, Marthe, 492
———, Mathew, 390
———, Matthias, 481
———, Smithell, 481
———, Smithy, 492
Matthews, Matthewes, see Mathew
Mattison, Alexander, 391
Mattson, see Matson
Maudsley, Henry, 123
Maul, Thomas, 387
Maulder, Febe, 107
Mawfrey, Edward, 82
Max, Robert, 112
Maxwell, Marie, 136
———, Thomas, 481
———, Wm., 448
May (or Maye), Cornelius, 186, 247, 272, see Maies
———, Elizabeth, 186
———, Henry, 186
———, James, 320, 320*, 322, 325
———, John, 88, 107, 320*, 482
———, Mathew, 75
———, Richard, 435
———, Willyam, 152
Maybank, Edward, 241
Maye, see May.

Mayes, Robert, 111, see Maies
Mayhew (or Mahewe), Thomas, 160, 159*, 295
Maymor, Griffin, 137
Maynard, Elizabeth, 116, 422
———, James, 316, 318, 343, 386
———, Mary, 422
———, Nicholas, 323, 422, 445
———, Thomas, 125
Mayo, David, 432
———, Samuell, 87
Mayor, John, 190
Mayro, James, 173
Mead, John, 319
———, Samuell, 442
———, William, 333, 335, 341
Meade, Thomas, 316*, 318, 343
Mecham, Wm., 52
Medcalfe, George, 183, 258
[? ———] Joane, 258
———, Sara, 258
———, see Metcalfe
Medcalfe [Medcalfe], 183
Meddowes, Henry, 102
Medgley, see Medley
Medinah, Leah, 449
Medley (or Medgley), John, 140, 141
———, Robert, 103
Medwell, Tho., 41
Meggeridge, see Mogeridge
Mekins, Edward, 134
Mell, William, 504
Mellison, Wm., 140
Melloly, James, 391
Mellowes, John, 364, 366, 406
Mellows, Elisha, 503
Melony, Timothy, 387
Melton, Henry, 129
Mendam, Arthur, 422, 427
———, Richard, 422, 427, 428
———, Sarah, 422, 427
Mentis (or Meutis), Thomas, 175
Mer, Philippe de le, 198
Mercado, Moses, 450
Mercer, Anne, 490
———, Dorcas, 113
———, Elizabeth, 490
———, John, 440
———, Luce, 90, 107
———, William, 490
Merchant, Emanuel, 317
Mere, Elizabeth, 92
———, John, 92
———, Robert, 92

INDEX. 553

Mere, Samuell, 92
Meredith, Philip, 119, *see* Merideth, &c.
Merick, John, 493
———, Susanna, 493
———, *see* Merrick
Meriday (Meridie or Meridien), John, 191, 192, 193.
Merideth, Julian, 120, *see* Meredith, Merredith
Merie, Jo., 115, *see* Merry
Merrell, Thomas, 504
Merres, Thomas, 259
Merrick (or Merricks), John, 470, 481, *see* Merick
Merridith, Walter, 111, *see* Merideth, &c.
Merrifield, Edward, 50
Merriman, Geo., 75
———, Sara, 125
Merriton, Marie, 136
Merry, John, 154, *see* Merie
Met, Jan De La, 198
Metcalf, Metcalfe
———, Chri., 82
———, Elizabeth, 289
———, James, 35
———, Joane, 289
———, Marey, 289
———, Martha 289
———, Michill, 289
———, Oswell, 134
———, Rebeca, 289
———, Sarrah, 289
———, Thomas, 64, 289
———, *see* Medcalfe
Meutis (or Mentis), Thomas, 175
Meverill, Sampson, 86
Meyer (Mire or Myre), Henry, 333, 338, 340
Meza, Isack, 450
Micell, *see* Michill
Michaell, Ann, 173
———, John, 209
Michell, Anthony, 438, 456
———, David, 472
———, Francis, 187
———, John, 388
———, Richard, 368, 388
———, *see* Mitchell
Michill (or Micell), George, 332, 335, 340
Michleborne, Wm., 447
Middleton, Midleton
———, Anthony, 182
———, Arthur, 391
———, Benjamin, 342, 428, 462
———, Edward, 132, 304

Middleton, Henrie, 257
———, Jo., 111
———, Marie, 113
———, Mary, 463, 497, 498
———, Richard, 497, 498, 504
———, Thomas, 333, 337, 340
Midland, Geo., 103
Mighill, Ann, 213
Milborn, William, 303
Milburne, Jacob, 166*
Mildmay, Sir Henry, 91
Mileman, John, 257
Miles, Antonio, 137
———, Cicily, 437
———, John, 437
———, Joseph, 461
———, Lewes, 117
Miller, Benjamin, 87
———, David, 432
———, James, 80, 449
———, John, 133, 316*, 317*, 342, 501
———, Joseph, 130
———, Katherine, 426
———, Phillipp, 142
———, Richard, 96
———, William, 126, 192, 425
Millet, Tho., 57
Millett, Frances, 192
———, Marie, 57
Millington, John, 482
———, Rowland, 80
Mills, Edward, 115
———, John, 304, 448, 471
———, Joseph, 125
———, Robert, 40
———, Thomazin, 116
Millward, Milward
———, Henry, 268
———, John, 507
———, Marie, 68
———, Tho., 81
———, William, 507
Milner, John, 307
———, Michell, 107
———, Robert, 170, 208
———, Samuell, 94
Milnhouse, John, 219
Milton, Richard, 212
Milward, *see* Millward
Mimes, Thomas, 172
Ming, David, 309
Minifie (or Minify), George, 175, 226
———, John, 326
Mintrene, Mintren
———, Edward, 250
———, Richard, Senr., 187

Mintrene, Richard, Junr., 187
———, ———, 250
Mirch, John, 497
Mire (Meyer or Myre), Henry, 333, 338, 340
Mitchell, Edward, 113
———, Francis, 245
———, (or Mitchill), John, 133, 137, 245, 327, 331, 334, 338, 341
———, Maudlin, 245
———, Rob., 333, 336, 340
———, Thomas, 481
———, William, 124
———, *see* Michell
Mixer, Isaacke, 280, 282
———, Sarah, 280
Modyford, Sir James, 162
Mogeridge, (Mageridge, Maggeridge, Magridge, Meggeridge, or Mogridge), John, 316, 317*, 318, 319*, 324, 342
Moholland, James, 482
Moier, Hugh, 150
Moises, *see* Moyses
Molder, Nicholas, 442
Molesworth, Sir Hender, 165
Moleton, *see* Moulton
Molin, Jo., 116
Mollins, *see* Mullins
Molton, Thomas, 135, 232
Moncaster, Richard, 142
Mofiing's, *see* Mohnings
Monk, Henry, 482
———, Peter, 38
Monmouth, Duke of, 321
Monning's, Mofiing's
———, Anna, 92
———, Mary, 92
———, Michelaliell, 92
Monnvs, Joseph, 84
Montagne, Mousnier de La, 197
Montecue, Peeter, 233
Montgomery, Edmond, 75
———, James, 75
———, Phillip, Earl of, 158
———, Thomas, 164*
Montrevers, Ralph, 436
Moody, David, 481
———, Symon, 119
Moone, John, 219
———, Martine de, 179
Moor, George, 399
Moore, Alce, 481
———, Dorothy, 507
———, Henry, 303
———, John, 308

70

INDEX.

Moore, Joseph, 310
———, Leonard, 202
———, Richard, 507
———, Robert, 481
———, Thomas, 316*
———, Wm., 310
———, see More
Moper, Nathanieli, 184
Morcock, Elizabeth, 219
———, Revolt, 219
———, Thomas, 219
———, see Morecock
Mordin, Tho., 86
More, Alexander, 41
———, Elizabeth, 260
———, Geo., 120
———, Henry, 85, 136
———, Isack, 65
———, James, 257
———, John, 38, 39, 43, 62, 113, 183, 260
———, Leonard, 169
———, Mrs., 183
———, Peter, 468
———, Richard, 93
———, Robert, 37, 183, 259
———, Sara, 173
———, Suzan, 71
———, Tho., 75, 102, 103, 111, 132, 137
———, Wm., 115, 190
———, see Moore
Morecock, Morecocke
———, Bennet, 78
———, Marie, 78
———, Nic°., 78
———, Reignold, 177
———, Thomas, 124, 391
———, see Morcock
Morecott, John, 462
Moredecah, Sarah, 450
Moreland, Thomas, 262
Moreton, Sir William 162
———, see Morton
Morewood, Mr., 180
———, Richard, 173
Morfin, Jo., 115
Morfy, James, 109
Morgan, Morgaine, Morgon
———, Andrew, 96
———, David, 462
———, Edmond, 243
———, Edmund, 425
———, Edward, 184, 389, 465
———, Elisabeth, 425, 435
———, Esther, 425, 437
———, Evan, 435, 456
———, Gabriel, 435
———, Geo., 86
———, John, 111, 382, 388, 465

Morgan, Mary, 435
———, Pierce, 141
———, Richard, 94
———, Rob., 504
———, Robert, 94, 195
———, Sarah, 435
———, Sibill, 257
———, Thomas, 192, 266, 388
———, Walter, 35
———, William, 141
———, alias Broockes, William, 247
Morison, Richard, 160, see Morrison
Morley, Henry, 84
———, Richard, 161*
———, Wm., 127
Morlin, Phillipp, 139
Morraine, John, 504
Morrell, Margaret, 424 [424
———, Nicholas, 376, 389,
Morrey, Geo., 132, see Mory
Morrice, Hugh, 489
———, John, Senr., 304
———, Mary, 489
———, Nicolas, 489
———, Richard, 138
Morris, Bridgett, 467
———, Davie, 87, 95
———, Dorcas, 430
———, Dorothy, 423
———, Edmond, 482
———, Edward, 132, 151, 467
———, Hugh, 481
———, Humfrey, 63
———, Isaac, 46, 387
———, John, 129, 185, 244, 430
———, Katharin, 427
———, Mary, 244, 436
———, Nathan, 467
———, Richard, 82, 192, 456, 469
———, Sarah, 423
———, Samuell, 176, 240
———, Thomas, 344, 423, 441, 456
———, Thomasin, 423 [481
———, William, 387, 430,
Morrish, Jo., 128
Morrison, Elizabeth, 46
———, Robert, 125
———, Wm., 47
———, see Morison
Morse, Elizabeth, 64
———, John, 316*
———, Joseph, 65
———, Samuell, 64
Mortagh, Dennis, 52
Morten, see Morton

Mortimer, Tho., 115
Morton, Morten
———, Daniel, 467
———, (or Moreton), Edward, 326, 329
———, Henry, 75
———, Jo., 128
———, Mathew, 120
———, Nic°., 122
———, Rowland, 81
———, William, 186, 249
Mory, Jo., 93, see Morrey
Mosdell, Jo., 132
Moseley, Geo., 112
Mosely, Henry, 438
———, Jo., 37
———, Richard, 389
Mosley, Joseph, 185, 243
Moss, Jo., 84
———, Richard, 123
Mosse, Joseph, 280
Moston, Henry, 120
Mothropp, Tho., 125
Mott, Adam, 99, 300
———, Elizabeth, 99
———, Jo., 99
———, Jonathan, 99
———, Mary, 99
———, Sara, 99
Moulston, Thomas, 174
Moulton, Anne, 291
———, Bridgett, 291
———, Henry, 291
———, (or Moleton), Humphry, 327, 331
———, Jane, 291
———, John, 291
———, Marey, 291
———, Merrean, 291
———, Ruth, 291
———, William, 291
Mounday, Mary, 185
———, Robert, 185
———, see Munday
Mountack, Andrew, 391
Mountain, Mountaine
———, John, 50, 391
———, (late Stow), Mary, 308
———, Thomas, 441
Mountfort, Edward, 84
Mountney, Alexander, 186, 257, 273
———, Lenord, 257
Mountstephen, Samuell, 316*
Mountsteven, John, 163*, 164
Mowser, Jo., 83
Moyle, Dorothy, 123
Moyse, Susanna, 429
Moyser, James, 35

INDEX. 555

Moyses, Mathew, 50
———— (or Moises), Theoder, 169, 202
Much, Roger, 190, *see* Mutch
Mudge, William, 176
Mulleneux, Edmond, 122
————, Jo., 134
Mullenex, William, 504
Mulfinax, Mrs., 456
————, Richard, 456
Mullins, Mullens, Mollins
————, George, 332, 337, 340
————, Robert, 318*, 319*, 322
————, Teag, 434
Multman (or Maltman), Tho., 127
Mumford, Richard, 229
Munday, Robart, 244
————, William, 35
————, *see* Mounday
Mundy, Eliz*a*., 504
Munjoy, George, 397
Munnes, William, 262, *see* Munns
Munning's, Abigail, 282
—————, Elizabeth, 280, 282
—————, George, 280, 282
Munns, Thomas, 504, *see* Munnes
Munrow, Allexander, 482
————, Andrew, 481
————, John, 448
Munson, Susan, 281
————, Thomazin, 94
Murfey, Dennis, 470 ⎫ *see*
Murfie, Tho., 36 ⎭ Murphy
Murfitt, Nathan., 142
Murford, Richard, 481
Murphe, Bryan, 456
Murphy, Daniell, 388
————, Mary, 499
————, Morgan, 499
————, William, 354, 361, 382, 383, 393, 409, 412, 413, 418
————, *see* Murfey, &c.
Murral, David, 421
————, Elisabeth, 421
————, John, 421
————, *see* Murril
Murrell, John, 445, 456
————, Wm., 456
Murrey, Alexander, 499
————, James, 499
Murril, Murrill
————, Elisabeth, 430
————, Isack, 150
————, John, 430
————, *see* Murral

Murrin, Elizabeth, 134
Murrow, John, 456
Mursh (or Marsh), Francis, 115
Musgrave, Sir Christopher, 344
————, Jo., 125
————, Symon, 344
Musick, John, 135
Muskett, Simon, 43
————, Wm., 391
Mussell, Jo., 54
————, Robert, 75
Mutch, Margery, 226
————, William, 226
————, *see* Much
Mynnikyn, Christian, 39
Mynter, Jo., 104
Myre (Mire, or Meyer), Henry, 333, 338, 340

NACTON, Teague, 74
Naile, *see* Nayle
Nailer, Elizabeth, 309, *see* Naylor, &c.
Namias, David, 450
Nancarro, Ellin, 153
Nancy, Robert, 60
Naseby, Moses, 467
Nasfeild, Henrie, 252
Nash, Ann, 96
————, Edmond, 75
————, Richard, 319*, 323
————, Thomas, 377
————, Wm., 120
————, *alias* Lyllant, Richard, 319
Nasy, Daniell, 392
Nathaniell, 243
Natt, Richard, 109
Navaro, Aron, 449
————, Judith, 450
Navarro, Samuell, 450
Naxston, Moules, 118
Nayle (or Naile), William, 179, 231
Nayler, Edward, 128 ⎫
————, Jo., 128 ⎬ *see*
Naylor, Thomas, 190 ⎭ Nailer
Neagle, Martin, 392
Neal, Daniel, 428
————, Martha, 428
Neale, John, 466
————, Jonathan, 101
————, Thomas, 165*c*, 166*b*, 456, 466
————, *see* Neele
Neares, Thomas, 183
Neave, Margrett, 293
Nedham, George, 442

Nedsom (or Neesom), Jo., 74
Needes, John, 316*
Needham, Tho., 121
——————, William, 168
Needler, John, 392
Needome, John, 180
Neele, Marie, 124, *see* Neal, &c.
Neesam, Wm., 125
Neesom (or Nedsom), Jo., 74
Neimart (Neinneart, Nevmart, or Newmart), Petter, 266, 267
Nelme, Richard, 81
Nelson, George, 173, 219
————, Joseph, 79
————, Julian, 437
————, Thomas, 504
Nemias, David, 482
Nepho, Jerome, 317*, 319, 320, 321, 322, 325
Nesse, Wm., 101
Netbie, Anto., 80
Nettellford, Geo., 119
Nettleton, James, 140
Nevell, Nicholas, 141
Nevill, John, 392
Nevitt, Roger, 125
Nevmart, *see* Neimart
Newberry, Joseph, 341
Newbolt, Richard, 143
Newbott, John, 441
Newby, Henry, 84
Newcom, Francis, 48
—————, Jo., 48
—————, Marie, 64
—————, Rachell, 48
Newcome, William, 187
Newdon, John, 154
Newell, Abraham, 278, 279
————, Fayth, 278
————, Francis [Frances], 279
————, Grace, 277
————, Isacke, 278
————, John, 278
Newham, Christopher, 374
Newman, Abraham, 362, 413
—————, Elizabeth, 88
—————, Gabriell, 444
—————, John, 123, 297
—————, Margarett, 482
—————, Mountford, 111
—————, Robert, 188, 253
—————, Thomas, 79
—————, William, 184, 242, 311
Newmart, *see* Neimart
Newport, Elisabeth, 422, 429
—————, John, 422, 429
—————, Susanna, 422, 429

INDEX.

Newton, Abigall, 392
———, George, 444
———, John, 141
———, Samuell, 382, 402, 482
Nice, George, 467
Nichcott, Huch, 195
Nicholas, ———, 195
Nicholes, *see* Nicolls
Nichollas, William, 170
Nicholls, Elizabeth, 59
———, Jer., 135
———, John, 305
———, Thomas, 193
———, William, 211
———, *see* Nicolls
Nicholson, Francis, 166*, 167*, 168
———, Tho., 129
———, Garret, 136
———, Ralph, 37
Nickerson, Anne, 290
———, Elizabeth, 290
———, Nicho., 290
———, Robartt, 290
———, William, 290
Nicklin, Jo., 133
Nicks, John, 40
Nicolas, 492
Nicolls, John, 498
——— (or Nicholes), Marmaduke, 461, 465, 466
———, Sarah, 465, 466
———, *see* Nicholls
Nisbett, Robert, 41
Nisom, Jo., 40
Nixon, Mary, 482
Nobb, John, 472
Noble, Ann, 67
———, Geo., 128
———, Marke, 448, 482
Noden, Hugh, 163*
Nokes, Henrie, 128
———, Jo., 41
Nonn (or Noun), Goodwife, 194
Nordin, Nathaniell, 140
Norman, Geo., 85
———, Jo., 85, 115
———, Matthew, 304
Normansell, Edward, 192
Norris, Jo., 85
———, Samuell, 504
Norron, Katherine, 482
North, John, 59, 111, 115
———, Nathanael, 310
———, Thomas, 182
Northampton, Henry, Earl of, 155, 156
Northin, Jo., 79
Norton, Geo., 73

Norton, William, 144, 149
Norwood's, Richard, 304
Nott, Tho., 51
Noun (or Nonn), Goodwife, 194
Nowell, George, 333, 337, 340
———, John, 240
———, Peternell, 133
Nowes (or Nowis), Percivall (or Percivall), 316, 318, 342
Noy, Hester, 450
———, Isaac, 450
Nubold, Joan, 37
Nuce, George, 183
Nunes, Jacob Franco, 449
Nuftick, *see* Nunnick
Nunn, Richard, 66
———, Tho., 129
Nunnick, Addam, 129
———, Elizabeth, 37
Nurse, Robert, 482
Nusom, Richard, 442
Nusum, Arthur, 482, 490, 494
———, ———, Junr., 482, 490
———, Susanna, 490, 494
Nutbrowne, Francis, 107
Nuttall, Robert, 114
———, Thomas, 392

OAGE, Ann, 203
———, Edward, 203
———, Thomas, 170, 203, 268
Oakley, Francis, 457
Oats (or Oates), George, 424, 433, 445
———, Joseph, 424, 433
———, Hannah, 424, 433
Obah (a Negress), 489
Obediente, Abraham, 450
O'Bryan, Dermond, 75
Odam, William, 504
Odell, John, 457
Odgne, Edmond, 504
Odiarne, Thomas, 457
Offient, John, 81
Offword, John, 40
Ogden, Randall, 42
Ogell, Gregorie, 52
———, Jo., 35
Ogilby, Ogilsby, Oglesby
———, Elisabeth, 424, 427
———, Frances, 424, 427
———, John, 424, 427, 440
Ogle, John, 393
Ohain, Ohani
———, James, 491
———, Jane, 491
———, Patrick, 491

Oistine, Oistines
———, Angeletta, 492
———, James, 482, 492
———, Nicholas, 482
Okelly, Samuell, 430
Oker, George, 482
Okley, Robert, 172, 217
Old, Susan, 205
Older, Richard, 51
Oldham, John, 78
———, Tho., 78
Oldrick, Robert, 112
Oldridge, Abell, 393
Oliues, *see* Olives
Oliver, Olliver
———, Edward, 176
———, John, 149, 295, 443
———, Marey, 295
———, Margaret, 483, 494
———, Marie, 113
———, Robert, 154
———, Thomas, 149, 295
Olives, John, 172
Olmstedd, James, 150
Olney, Epenetus, 45
———, Marie, 45
———, Tho., 45
O, Mullin, Jo., 112
Onan, Teage, 468
Oneal, Ann, 393
———, Daniel, 430
———, Katharin, 430
Onge, Mary, 279
Onion, Elizabeth, 227
———, George, 227
Onyon, Robert, 94
Oram, Jo., 70
Orchard, Richard, 109
———, Thomas, 359
Oree, Daniel, 437
Oresby, Thomas, 430
Orpen, John, 439
Orris, George, 76
Osborn, Osborne, Osbourn, Osburne
———, Alexander, 491
———, Elenor, 491
———, Jenkin, 172, 208
———, John, 178, 228, 489
———, Mary, 228
———, Moses, 316*
———, Ralph, 182, 261
———, Richard, 40
———, Robert, 393
———, Samell, 457
———, Thomas, 169, 177, 201, 219
———, Walter, 318*
Osdell, John, 498
Osmotherly, Wm., 119

INDEX. 557

Ossebrooke, Tho., 141
Otland, Ant°., 112
Ottawell (or Ottowell), Thomas, 180, 232.
Ottway, Thomas, 175
Ouerton, *see* Overton
Ouills [*i.e.*, Wills], William, 189
Outmore, Robert, 128
Outram, Robert, 483, *see* Owtram
Overbury, Henry, 428
Overton, Robert, 482
Owdell, Isack, 94
Owdie, John, 65
Owen, Anne, 440
———, David, 135
———, Elizabeth, 68
———, Evan, 312
———, John, 41
———, Lazarus, 313
———, Tho., 121
———, Wm., 40
———, *see* Owin
Oweth, Hutinne, 152
Owin, Beniamin, 179, 258, *see* Owen
Owly (or Owlye), John, 267
Ownstedd, Arnold, 142
Owtram, Dorothy, 482, *see* Outram.
Ox (or Oxe), Robert, 365, 410
Oxenbridge, Jo., 87
Oxford; Michaell, 297

PACE, Richard, 270
Pacheco, Jacob, 450
———, Rebecah, 450
Pack, Stephen, 137
———, Wm., 104
Packe, Richard, 187, 253
Packer, Thomas, 170
Packson, Anne, 489
Page, Elizabeth, 58
———, Frances, 291
———, John, 87, 398
———, Katherin, 58
———, Lucea, 291
———, Margrett, 291
———, Mary, 87
———, Mathew, 71
———, Robert, 115, 291
———, Sara, 87
———, Susanna, 291
———, Tho., 58, 142
———, Wm., 101
———, *see* Paige
Paget, William, Lord, 157
Pagitt, Anthony, 217
———, Tho., 111

Paige, Sarah, 504, *see* Page
Paily, Adrian, 457
Pain, Elisabeth, 424, 432
———, Jonathan, 432
———, Robert, 424, 432
———, Susanna, 424
———, *see* Payn
Paine, Dorothey, 293
———, Edward, 471
———, Elizabeth, 293
———, John, 179, 293, 449
———, Marey, 293
———, Robert, 154, 449
———, Sarah, 293
———, (or Payne), Silvanus, 360, 364
———, Tobias, 504
———, Thomas, 293
———, *see* Payne
Painter, Elin, 176
Palache, Mordecah, 450
Pall, Thomas, 227
Palliday, Jo., 79
Pallister, James, 40
Palmer, Ann, 136
———, Anthony, 338
———, Ellis, 133
———, Francis, 227
———, Geo., 86, 133
———, Joane, 210
———, John, 81, 114, 137, 165*, 281, 342, 344, 467
———, Mrs., 171
———, Nicholas, 326, 330
———, Prisilla, 210
———, Rabecca, 124
———, Richard, 107, 133
———, Robert, 437
———, Samuell, 463
———, Thomas, 67, 140, 171, 210
——— (or Pallmer), William, 104, 127, 467
Palmerley, Jo., 58
Pancrust, Anns, 87
Panke, Richard, 142
Panton, Mrs., 457
Paple, Jo., 81
Paramour, *see* Parramore
Pardy, Joseph, 39
Pare, Edward, 504
Paris, Parris
———, Ann, 423
———, Edward, 434, 457
———, Elisabeth, 434
———, George, 457
———, Jane, 431
———, Owen, 394, 398
———, Samuell, 445
———, Thomas, 425, 431, 448

Paris, William, 423, 443
Parish (or Parrish), Thomas, 65, 187, 188, 252
Park, Jo. de, 41
Parke, Thomas, 189
Parker, Charles, 135
———, Daniell, 318*, 319*, 322
———, Geo., 77
———, John, 398
———, Mary, 137
———, Nathanuel, 300
———, Nicholas, 104
———, Ralph, 350, 358, 373, 374, 383, 398, 399
———, Richard, 318*, 319*, 323, 441, 504
———, Robert, 83
———, Samuel, 134
———, Thomas, 59, 119, 202, 447
———, Walter, 109
———, William, 82, 188, 249, 334, 337, 340
Parkhurst, Ant°., 138
Parkins, Andrew, 118
———, Gressam, 126
———, Thomas, 194
Parkinson, Dorithie, 194
———, James, 74
Parler, Symon, 73
Parlin, John, 140
Parmeton, Rabecca, 113
Parnell, Edward, 86
———, John, 331
———, Walter, 179
———, William, 179, 258
Parr, Elisabeth, 422
———, Georg, 422
———, Jo., 127
———, Petronilia, 422
Parramore, John, 264
——— (or Paramour), Robert, 181, 218
Parratt (or Parrett), John, 186, 243
Parreck, John, 377
Parrett, *see* Parratt
Parrie, Edward, 132, *see* Parry
Parris, *see* Paris
Parrish, *see* Parish
Parry, John, 115
———, Morris, 84, 128
———, Wm., 115
———, *see* Parrie
Parryer (or Purryer), Wm., 44
Parsons, Daniell, 342
———, Edward, 167, 436, 444
———, (or Parsones), Francis, 395

INDEX.

Parsons, Henry, 96
———, John, 102, 188, 235, 316
———, Phillipp, 96
———, Samuell, 237
———, Tho., 36, 331
———, (or Passens), Thomas, 326
———, William, 431, 483
Part, John, 465
———, Mary, 468
———, Robert, 465, 468
Parter, Thomas, 186
Partin, Partlin, Partten
———, Avis, 206
———, Margrett, 170, 206
———, Rebecca, 206
———, Robert, 170, 206, 267, 268
Partridge, Jo., 113
———, William, 167
Pasar, Paul De, 198
Pascall, Henry, 349
Pascoll, James, 249
Passeman, John, 208
Passens (or Parsons), Thomas, 326
Passmore, Jane, 227
——— (or Pasmore), Thomas, 175, 227
Pastor, Barns, 435
Patient, Arthur, 104
———, Nathaniell, 102
Patric, Ann, 432
Patrick, Tho., 136
Patten, James, 316*
Patteson, Edward, 43
Pattison, James, 122
———, John, 193
Pattman, Jo., 52
Paty, Eliza, 393
Paul, Joseph, 327, 331
———, Richard, 327, 331
———, Robart, 334, 335, 340
———, Samuell, 351
———, Wm., 86
Paulett (or Pawlett), Thomas, 170, 207
Paulson, Wm., 79
Paulus, Cordin, 453
Pawlett, *see* Paulett
Payn, Eleanor, 498, *see* Pain
Payne, Anna, 65
———, Daniell, 65
———, Edward, 59, 62, 76
———, Elizabeth, 113, 483
———, Jo., 65, 82, 93
———, Robert, 135
——— (or Paine), Silvanus, 364
———, Suzan, 66
———, Tho., 101

Payne, Tobias, 499
———, William, 65, 92
———, *see* Paine
Payson, Giles, 46
Payton, Henry, 195
———, Peter, 120
———, Robert, 36
Pea, Urselah, 447
Peach, Arthur, 79
———, Jonathan, 423
———, Sarah, 423
Peacock, Charles, 109
———, Samuel, 427
———, Tho., 125, 139
———, Wm., 46
———, *see* Pecock
Pead, John, 210, 483, *see* Peede
———, Thomas, 394
Peak, Christopher, 483
Penke, Marie, 49
———, Robert, 172, 222
———, *see* Peke
Peale, Larence, 246
Pearce, Pearse, Peerce, Peerse, Peirce, Peirse
———, Anth., 153
———, Benony, 504
———, Edmond (or Edward), 89
———, George, 438
———, Hester, 494
———, John, 393, 494, 507
———, Katherine, 507
———, Mr., 89, 90
———, Mrs., 229
———, Nicholas, 233
———, Richard, 343, 457
——— (or Pearc), Robert, 316, 318, 319, 319*, 324, 342
———, Thomas, 323
———, Wm., 271
———, *see* Pierce
Pearcey, *see* Peircy
Pearns, Mr., 191
Pears, John, 483
Pearse, *see* Pearce
Pearshouse, Chester, 396
Pearson, Georg., 434
———, John, 393, 428
———, Prudence, 434
———, Peirson, Pierceson
Peas, Wm., 127
Pease, Elisabeth, 422, 427
———, John, 278, 279
———, Robert, 278, 279
———, Ursula, 422, 427
Peat, Jo., 46
Peboddy, Francis, 45
Pechey, Lambert, 396

Peck, Francis, 73
———, Tho., 39
Pecock, Robert, 483, *see* Peacock
Pedder, Matthew, 497
Pedler, Francis, 154
———, Robert, 154
Pedro, John, 258
Peede, John, 171, *see* Pead
Peele, Lawrence, 185
Peerce, *see* Pearce
Peers, Elizabeth, 429
———, John, 429
Peerse, *see* Pearce
Peeter, , 242, 257, *see* Peter
Peeters, Mary, 205
Pegden, Mr., 191
Peirce, *see* Pearce
Peirceson, John, 443, *see* Pearson, Peirson
Peircy (or Pearcey), Richard, 316*, 317
Peirsby, Richard, 183
Peirse, *see* Pearce
Peirsey, Abraham, 217, 224
———, Elizabeth, 224
———, Mary, 224
Peirson, Cutbert, 182
——— (or Peireson), Edward, 392, 397, 448
———, *see* Pearson, Peirceson
Peke, Dennis, 71, *see* Peake
Pell, Marie, 49
———, Richard, 52
———, Tho, 49
Pellam, Penelopy, 60
———, Jo., 59
Pelsant, Sampson, 194
———, Wolston, 194
Pelteare, Abraham, 248
Pelton, George, 231
Pemberton, Charles, 508
———, James, 508
———, John, 508
———, William, 508
Pembroke, William, Earl of, 156, 158
Pemmell, Thomas, 396
Pen, *see* Penn
Pendleton, Mary, 397
———, Wm., 85
Pendred, Robert, 52
Penford, Tho., 138
Penington, John, 153, *see* Pennington
Peniston, Richard, 303
———, Samuell, 394
Penn, Francis, 80
———, Robert, 233

INDEX.

Penn (or Pen), William, 117, 163
Pennaird, Robert, 144
———, Tho., 144
Penne, *see* Penny
Penniman, Jane, 395
Pennington, Wm., 132, *see* Penington
Penrice, John, 186
Penrise, Robart, 254
Penson, Tho., 75
Penny (or Penne), George, 51, 320, 322
——— (———, or Pinney), John, 320*, 322, 325, 327, 330, *see* Pinney
Pepp [*i.e.*, Pepper]
Pepper, Fra., 121
———, Mary, 278, 279
———, Richard, 278, 279
Peppet (or Peppett), Gilbert (or Gibert), 172, 272
Perce, Jone, 174
———, Phebe, 66
———, Richard, 38
———, Thomas, 440
———, Wm., 115, 174
———, *see* Perse
Percy, Annis, 52
———, Robert, 35
———, *see* Persey
Pereing, Sebasting, 504
Perera, Isaac, 449, 450
Perk, Elizabeth, 105
———, Isabell, 105
———, Margery, 105
———, Richard, 105
Perkin, Elisabeth, 421
———, John, 421
———, Richard, 421
———, *see* Perkynn, Pirkins
Perkins, Martin, 119
———, Robert, 122
———, William, 149
———, *see* Perkyns
Perkinson, Elizabeth, 169
Perk's, Ann, 79
Perkynn, Martin, 40
———, Thomas, 71
———, *see* Perkin
Perkyns, James, 36, *see* Perkins
Perley, Allin, 45
Perpoynt, Henry, 79
Perrie, *see* Perry
Perridge, Job, 457, *see* Perwidg
Perriman, John, 457, *see* Perryman
Perrin, Henry, 399
———, Margarett, 394

Perrin, *see* Perryn.
Perrot, Samuel, 422
———, Sarah, 422
Perrott, Ralph, 483
Perry, Ben., 37
———, Dorothy, 37.
———, Edward, 483
———, George, 271
———, Hugh, 143
——— (or Perrie), John, 167, 483
———, Jone, 429
———, Marie, 64
———, Mrs., 175
———, Samuell, 457
———, Tho., 37, 126
———, William, 266
Perryman, Anne, 491
——— (or Perriman), Richard, 483, 491
———, *see* Perriman
Perryn, John, 123, *see* Perrin
Pers, Barbre, 290
———, Elizabeth, 290
———, John, 290
———, Judith, 290
Perse, Nicholas, 169
———, Richard, 178
———, *see* Perce
Persey, Abra., 269, *see* Percy
Persivall, Andrew, 398
Persons, Richard, 283
Perwidg (or Perwidge), Job, 394, *see* Perridge
Pester (Pestor, or Lester), Thomas, 318*, 319*, 323
Peter (a Negro), 182
———, Isack, 38
———, John, 120
———, *see* Peeter
Peterson, Francis, 431
———, John, 266
———, Lawrence, 429
Petite, Bastian, 135
Petley, Richard, 102
Petter, 184
———, Samuell, 504
Petters (a Maid), 171
Petting, Nic*., 114
Pew, Elizabeth, 83
———, Jo., 114
———, Richard, 83
Pewsie, Geo., 110
Phelomy, John, 483
Phelpes, William, 316
Phildust, Thomas, 222
Philkynn, Robert, 52
Phillip, Phillipes, Phillipp, Phillips, Phillipps
———, 188

Phillip, Eliazer, 396
———, Elizabeth, 96, 242
———, Elmer, 170
———, Henry, 182
———, James, 102
———, John, 38, 40, 74, 116, 195
———, Mary, 490
———, Phillip, 44
———, Richard, 83, 126
———, Thomas, 111, 127, 173, 180, 185, 236, 242
———, William, 74, 143, 318, 343, 483, 490
Philmott, John, 236
Philpe, Richard, 75
Philpott, John, 41
———, Phillipp, 40
Phinloe, 229
Phinnei, Richard, 135
Phippin, Judith, 43
——— (Phippen, or Shippin), William, 334, 337, 341
Phipps, Thomas, 141
———, Sir William, 164*, 165*
Phlinton, Pharow, 186
Picke, Andrew, 153
Pickering, John, 129
———, Mr., 429
Pickett, Adam, 353
Pickford, Robert, 397
Picto, Frend, 71
Piddington, Christopher, 82
Piddock, Wm., 395
Pidgion, Robert, 192, *see* Pigeon
Pierce, Danyell, 281
———, Elisabeth, 230, 422, 429
———, John, 139
———, Jone, 224
———, Richard, 230, 435
———, Steven, 118
———, Thomas, 70, 422
———, William, 224, 240
———, *see* Pearce
Pigeon, Jo., 122, *see* Pidgion
Piggott, John, 457
———, Walter, 138
———, Wm., 79
Pike, Grace, 490
———, John, 139
———, Oliver, 483, 490, 495
Pile, Sarah, 483
———, Theophilus, 483
———, Wm., 394
Pilgrim, Thomas, 445, 457
Pilkinton, Margrett, 235
———, William, 235

INDEX

Pillard, Benjamin, 111
Pilson, Edward, 397
Pim, Thomas, 410
Pinchback, Thomas, 483
Pinder, Joanna, 59
———, Katherin, 59
———, see Pynder
Pine, Richard, 318*, 319*, 323
Pinffe, Henry, 182
Pinke, Henery, 241
———, John, 395
Pinkley, John, 128
Pinney, Azarias, 318*, 320, see Penny
Pinsen, William, 184
Pinson, Samuel, 318*, 319*, 323
Piper, James, called the, 188
———, Wm., 393
Pippin, Mathew, 67
Pirkins, Widow, 457, see Perkins, &c.
Piscer, Elizabeth, 123
———, Robert, 123
Pitcher, Tho., 79
Pitney, Pitnei, Pittnei
———, Margaret, 56
———, Samuell, 56
———, Sara, 56
Pitt, John, 440
———, Richard, 36
———, Thomas, 342
———, Wm., 140
———, see Pitts
Pittman, Arthur, 483
———, Christo., 193
———, Henry, 319, 320*, 325
——— (or Puttman), Wm., 319, 320*, 325
Pittnei, see Pitney
Pitts, Francis, 184
———, George, 466
———, Hugh, 483
———, John, 327, 329, 465, 466
———, Thomas, 135, 316*, 317
———, William, 316, 317*, 343
———, see Pitt
Pitway, Mary, 121
———, Robert, 121
Pix, Richard, 389
Place, John, 39, 308
———, Peter, 131
Plant, Mathew, 113
———, William, 236
Platt, John, 396
———, Lawrence, 84
Play, Wm., 365, 387, 404, 414
Plomer, Wm., 141

Plowman, Mathew, 165
———, William, 466
Pluffer [i.e., Plummer], John, 394
Plumley, George, 326, 330
——— (or Plumly), John, 446, 457
Plunckett, Geo., 52
Plunket, Edward, 74
Plunkett, Rowland, 74
———, Tho., 74
Pockett, William, 483
Podd, Samuel, 59
Poet, Georg., 431
Poke, James, 440
———, Rice, 136
Polegreen, John, 395
Pollard, Abraham, 334, 338, 340
———, Henry, 508
———, John, 457
———, Joseph, 397
———, Richard, 457
———, Sarah, 508
———, Tho., 153
Pollen, John, 145
Pollentin, John, 182
———, Margrett, 182
———, Rachell, 182
Pollington, Charles, 71
———, John, 272
Pomell, Elizabeth, 173
Pomeroy (Pomre, Pumrey, Pumroy, or Jumrey), Daniel, 332, 338, 340
——— (or Pomrey), James, 326, 329
———, Theophilus, 434
Pomfrett, Thomas, 316*, see Pumfrett
Pon, Michel Du, 198
Pond, Rebecca, 299
Ponnt (Pound, or Pount), Tho., 72, see Pownd
Pofites [? Pountes], John, 174
Poole, Edward, 284
———, Daniell, 235
——— (or Pool), Jeremiah, 316, 317, 343
———, John, 340
———, Robert, 86, 224
———, Simon, 334, 335, 340
——— (or Pool), Sylvester, 316*, 318, 343
———, Tho., 116, 272
Pooler, Elizabeth, 507
———, Richard, 507
———, Thomas, 507
Pooley, Grivell, 172, 215
Pooly, Jo., 112

Poor, Poore, Pore
———, Abram, 83
———, Alce, 300
———, Anne, 465, 466
———, Danyell, 300
———, David, 496
———, Elizabeth, 496
———, Innocent, 195
———, Mary, 397
———, Michaell, 463, 465, 466
———, Miles, 397
———, Peirce, 463, 467
———, Peter, 483
———, Richard, 442
———, Samuel, 300
Pope, Anto., 143
———, Charles, 395
———, Elizabeth, 187, 256
———, George, 178
———, Humphery, 333, 337, 340
———, Jo., 124
———, Thomas, 193
Popeley (or Popely), Richard, 182, 256
Popkin, Thomas, 178, 229
Popleton, William, 212
Popple, Magnus, 398
Pore, see Poor
Porte, Nicholas, 145
Porter, Abraham, 175, 225
———, Edmond, 137
———, Edward, 135
———, Henry, 102
———, James, 348, 363, 368, 388, 389, 400, 406
———, Jane, 423
———, John, 71, 286
———, Luke, 316, 318, 342
———, Martha, 129
———, Mathew, (&c.), 326, 330
———, Peeter, (&c.), 188, 244, 262
———, Richard, 286
———, Robert, 40, 423, 483
———, alias Thomas, Peter, 423
Portman, Christopher, 398
Poslett (or Posslet), Richard, 395, 467
———, Thomas, 94
Postell, Wm., 105
Pott, Elizabeth, 174, 223
———, John, 174, 221, 223
———, Wm., 73
———, see Potts
Potter, Ann, 260
———, Francis [Frances], 97
———, Georg., 434

Potter, Henry, 183, 260
——, Jo., 104
——, Joseph, 98
——, Rebecca, 495
——, Robert, 483
——, Vyncent, 76
——, William, 66, 97
Pottle, Christopher, 396
Potts, Anto., 104, *see* Pott
Poulter, Tho., 129
Pound (Pount, or Ponnt), 72, *see* Pownd
?Pountes (Poñtes), John, 174
Povey, Richard, 159*
Powel, Caleb, 421, 426
——, Elizabeth, 421, 426
——, Mary, 421, 426
Powell, Arthur, 397
——, Daniell, 151
——, Cathren, 184
——, Elizabeth, 114
——, Gody, 189
——, Jacob, 316*
——, James, 84
——, John, 184, 246, 273
——, Kathren, 246, *see* Powell, Cathren
——, Mary, 71
——, Micell (or Michaell), 334, 336, 340
——, Richard, 74
——, Robert, 304
——, Samuel, 111
——, Thomas, 82, 181, 189, 236, 263
——, Wm., 73, 86
—— (or Powle), Wm., 270
Powis, Tho., Carnocke, 452
Powle, Nathaniell, 269
—— (or Powell), Wm., 270
Pownd, Jo., 103, *see* Pound
Pownder, Garret, 36
Poyer, Thomas, 483
Poyett, Luce, 293
Pran, Georg., 181
Prater, Thomas, 246
Pratt, Isabell, 178, 229
——, Isack, 52
——, Richard, 139, 269
——, Thomas, 96
Praul, John, 402
Preett, Jacob, 450
Preist, Henry, 316*, 317*, 343
——, Lawrence, 316*
——, Thomas, 316, 318, 343
——, *see* Priest
Pressey, Henry, 297
Preston, Daniell, 70
—— (or Prestton), Edward, 43, 438, 448

Preston, Eliz., 131
——, George, 138
——, Jo., 131
——, Joseph, 127
——, Lawrence, 85
——, Marie, 131
——, Mathew, 135
——, Richard, 51, 122
——, Roger, 53, 171, 210
——, Sara, 131
——, Wm., 131
Preswell, Wm., 445
Prew, John, 318*, 320*, 323
Price, Ann, 203
——, Edward, 175, 193, 489
——, Henry, 457, 483
——, Hugh, 170, 204
——, John, 125, 170, 203, 204, 266, 319, 360, 378, 392, 396, 397, 462, 468, *see* Brice
——, Judith, 204
——, Margaret, 468
——, Mary, 203
——, Mathew, 125, 483
——, Peter, 104
——, Rebecca, 92
——, Richard, 67
——, Tho., 128
——, Walter, 214
——, William, 142, 169, 202, 442, 483
——, *see* Prise, Pryse
Prichard, Henry, 186
——, John, 70
——, Joseph, 136
——, Margaret, 82
——, Maximillian, 142
——, Thomas, 95, 177, 192
——, Wm., 39, 136
——, *see* Pritchard
Prichett, Margery, 187
——, Miles, 187, *see* Prickett
Prickett, Miles, 245, 273, *see* Prichett
——, Thomas, 194
Priday, Samuel, 75
Prideaux, Nicholas, 330, 343, 424, 457
——, Rebecca, 424 [&c.
Prier, Jo., 130, *see* Pryer, Prior
Priest, Walter, 173, *see* Preist
Primatt, Humphry, 395
Prince, Anth°., 441
——, John, 443
Prior (or Pryor), John, 327, 330, *see* Prier, Pryer, Pryor
Prise, Edward, 226
——, Thomas, 190
——, *see* Price, Pryce

Pritchard, Thomas, 221, *see* Prichard
Procter, Ant°., 112
——, John, 59, 266
——, Marie, 59
——, Martha, 59
——, Wm., 128
Proctor, Allis, 231
——, John, 179, 231
——, Mrs., 179
Prophett, Jacob, 191
Prosser, Thomas, 40
Prouse (or Prowse), George, 181, 231
Prothers, Thomas, 324, 460
Prout, Edward, 421
——, Katherine, 421
——, Thomas, 421
——, Timothy, 353, 377, 381, 396, 401
Prowd, Ralph, 73
Prowse, *see* Prouse
Pryce, Howell, 141
——, Launcelot, 37
——, Thomazin, 37
——, *see* Price, Prise
Pryer, Daniell, 130
——, Peter, 105
——, *see* Prier, Prior, Pryor
Pryme, Edmond, 103
Pryñi [*i.e.*, Prymm], Jane, 116
Prynn, Michell, 125
Pryor (or Prior), John, 327, 330, *see* Prier, Pryer
Puddiford, John, 442
Pugett, Christopher, 172
Puggett, Cesar, 238
Pullin, Edward, 41
Pumfrett, Ann, 483, *see* Pomfrett
Pumrey, &c., *see* Pomeroy
Purefoy, Samuell, 154
Purefray (Purfrey, or Purfry), Thomas, 180, 247
Purnell, Richard, 41
——, Thomas, 125
Purryer, Alyce, 44
——, Kathren, 45
——, Mary, 45
——, Sarra, 45
—— (or Parryer), Wm., 44, 45
Pursell, Tho., 136
Pursley, James, 499
Purss, Wm., 472
Purstynn, Henry, 39
Puttex, William, 40
Puttman, *see* Pittman
Pye, Edward, 460
——, Georg., 426

Pynch, Tho., 115
Pynder, Anna, 59
———, Francis, 59
———, Jo., 59
———, Margaret, 133
———, Marie, 59
———, Mary, 59
———, Sir Paul, 159
———, Tymothie, 133
———, see Pinder
Pyndon, Alice, 118
Pynkston, John, 135

QAY, Abraham, 449
Quaile, Ann, 192
Quale, Hugh, 505
Quant, Henry, 333, 336, 340
Quarree, Robert, 467
Quarrier, James, 94
Querk, John, 398
Querke, Richard, 505
———, William, 188, 251
Quesnee, Pierre, 199
Quicke, Elizabeth, 152
——— (or Quick), Thomas, 317*, 319*, 324
Quiggen, John, 484
Quillin, Teague, 127
Quintin, Roger, 113
Quinton, Henry, 36
Quintyne, Henry, 337, 390, 508
———, Richard, 398
———, Thomas, 508
Quithor, Geo., 125
Quyle, Jo., 125
Quyñie (or Q'ny), Wm., 104, 122

RABEY, Kathren, 292
Raddish, Jo., 79
Radford, Cornelius, 316, 318, 343
———, Henrie, 134
———, John, 428
———, Richard, 356, 361, see Ratford
Raffe, Robert, 191
Ragg, Isaac, 378, 491
———, Katherine, 491
———, Susanna, 491
Railey (Rawley, or Ralye), Andrew, 175, 184, 228, see Rayley
Rainolds, Richard, 41, see Reynolds
Rainsecrofte, Jo., 140
Rainsford, Edward, 93, 401, 448
———, John, 484

Rainy, James, 347, 348, 366, 384, 404, 405
———, Luke, 400
Ralye, see Railey, Rayley
Ram, George, 98
———, Tho., 84
Ramsey, Jo., 119
———, Roas, 505
———, Robert, 132, 425
Ramshaw, William, 181, 237
Rand, Isaac, 386, 391, 392, 418
Randall (or Rendell), Bartholomew, 333, 338, 340
———, Henry, 316
———, Wm., 69
Randolph, Edward, 163, 163*, 165
Ranke (or Rauke), Richard, 190
Ranse, Wm, 41
Ranton, see Raynton
Rapen, William, 73
Rapier, Richard, 182
Rapson, Andrew, 327, 330
Rasbottom, Tho., 38
Rastell, Henry, 83
Ratcliffe, Ratlife, Ratliffe
———, Ann, 208
———, Elkinton, 174, 236
———, Isack, 208
———, Roger, 170, 208
Ratford, Francis, 115
——— (Rattford, or Radford), Richard, 356, 361, 365, 370, 398, 410, 412, 413
Ratlife, see Ratcliffe
Rauen, see Raven
Raughton, Ezekiah, 202
———, Margrett, 202
———, see Rawton
Rauke (or Ranke), Richard, 190
Raven, Christopher, 505
Ravenett, William, 174
Ravenscroft, Benjamin, 400
Ravish, James, 112
Rawlin, Rawlines, Rawlings, Rawlins
———, Beniamin, 443
———, Henry, 139
———, Jane, 66
———, John, Senr., 303
———, John, 80, 449, 484
———, Wm., 470
Rawse, Richard, 170
Rawson, Chrͬ., 193
Rawton, Esaias, 169, see Raughton
Ray, Abram, 68

Ray, Jo., 125
Rayley, Jonas, 170, see Railey, &c.
Rayment, Ann, 434
Raymie, see Rayne
Raymon, John, 441
Raymond, Arthur, 122
Raymont, William, 240
Raynard, Elizabeth, 113
Raynberd, Niccholas, 262
Rayne (Raynes, Raynne, or Rayinne), Francis, 87, 162
———, Sarah, 111, see Raynne
Rayner, Raynor
———, Edward, 281
———, Elizabeth, 280, 281
———, Joane, 226
———, Joseph, 281
———, Lidia, 281
———, Sarah, 281
———, Thurston, 280, 281
———, Wassell, 175, 226
———, William, 427
Raynes, Raynne, see Rayne
Raynor, see Rayner
Raynton, Elizabeth, 105
——— (or Ranton), Sir Nicholas, 47, 60
Read, Anthony, 182
———, George, 106
———, Hanna, 284
———, James, 40
——— (or Reid), Justice (or Judge), 106, 498
———, Lusan, 284
———, Mabell, 106
———, Marmaduke, 81
———, Mary, 468
——— (or Reid), Osmond (or Symon), 334, 337, 340
———, Ralph, 106
——— (or Reede), Stephen (or Steeven), 95, 187, 253
———, Susan, 284
——— (or Reade), Thomas, 241, 267, 443, 468
———, William, 67, 106, 113, 284
———, see Reed, Reid
Reading, Robert, 430, see Reding, Redding
Reason, Barbaric, 75
———, James, 86
———, John, 326
———, Ralph, 50
———, Thomas, 330
Rebbell, Wm., 111
Reddam, John, 94
Reddhedd, John, 40, see Redhead

INDEX.

Reddin, Katherine, 402
Redding, Henry, 36
———, James, 35
———, Jeremy, 37
———, *see* Reading, Reding
Reddish, John, 178, 230
———, Wm., 127
Reddman, Jo., 121
———, Thomas, 70
———, Wm., 102
———, *see* Redman
Redes, Roger, 179
Redford (or Reeford), John, 132
Redhead, Christopher, 177, 232, *see* Reddhedd
Reding, John, 191, *see* Reading, Redding
Redman, Richard, 484, *see* Reddman
Reed, Elizabeth, 152
———, Lawrence, 446
———, *see* Read, Reid
Reefe, Mary, 190
Reeford (or Redford), John, 132
Reene (or Reeve), Nathanall, 170
Rees, Anne, 465
———, Elizabeth, 465
———, Thomas, 176
Reese, Bartholomew, 471
———, Bennett, 471
———, Lawrance, 507
———, Theadosia, 507
Reeue, Reeues, *see* Reeves
Reeves, Reeve, Reevs
———, Edward, 434
———, John, 42, 319, 319*, 323
——— (or Reene), Nathanall, 170
———, Thomas, 81, 145, 299, 505
———, Wm., 72
Reid, Adame, 505
———, John, 505
———, *see* Read, Reed
Reignolds, Reinolds, *see* Reynolds
Reld, Gabriell, 131
Remington, Remnington
———, Alice, 96
———, Elizabeth, 96
———, Phillipp, 95
Remnant, James, 400
———, Jone, 400
Ren, Clare, 219
Renalles, Paule, 234
Rendell (or Randall), Bartholomew, 333

Rennam, Ezechell, 128
Renney, John, 462
———, ———, Junr., 463
Renny, Teague, 484
———, ———, Junr., 484
Rensby (or Reusby), Henry, 153
Rentfree, Robert, 484
Resburie, Jo., 79
Reusby (or Rensby), Henry, 153
Revell, James, 136
Reynolds, Reignolds, Reinolds
———, 192
———, Christopher, 83, 182, 241
———, Hugh, 368, 380
———, James, 427
———, Jean, 484
———, John, 50, 82
———, Mr., 174, 437
———, Nico., 120
———, Paule, 180
———, Richard, 67
———, Robert, 192
———, Sarah, 280
———, Simon, 494
———, Susanna, 438
———, Thomas, 81, 123, 128, 438, 457
———, *see* Rainolds
Reynoldson, Thomas, 447
Riall, Alice, 113, *see* Ryale
Ricard, Peter, 126
Rice, James, 402
———, John, 402
———, *see* Ryce
Rich, Robert, 401, 402, 444, 463
Richard, 221, 251
———, James, 396, 401
———, Jo., 74 [484
Richards, John, 86, 125, 162*,
———, Katherin, 83
———, Latimer (or Latymore), 433, 461
———, Nathaniell, 150
———, Richard, 231
———, Robert, 40, 316*, 318, 342, 471
———, Thomas, 40, 85, 469, 505
———, Wm., 195
Richardson, Anthony, 491, 496
———, Daniell, 339
———, David, 484
———, Elisabeth, 426
———, George, 62, 484, 491
———, Henrie, 137

Richardson, John, 104, 113, 342, 344, 432, 434, 436
———, Leonard, 125
———, Luke, 115
———, Manley, 129
———, Margaret, 426
———, Mary, 430, 484, 491
———, Nicholas, 505
———, Richard, 142, 426
———, Robert, 50, 128
———, Symon, 95
———, Tho., 103
———, William, 134, 179, 240, 430
Richbell, John, 401
———, Richard, 400
———, Robert, 401, 484
Riches, Andrew, 433
———, Samuel, 433
Richier, Isaac, 166
Rickard, Margaret, 113
———, Samuel, 358, 362
Ricord, Charles, 396, 400
Ricrofte, James, 35
Riddall, Sara, 174
Riddell, William, 104
Riddlesden, Marie, 59
Ridgdell, William, 36
Ridge, Jo., 115
———, Tho., 115
Ridges, Richard, 111
Ridgeway, Ann, 490
———, Elizabeth, 490
———, Nathaniel, 490
———, *see* Ridgway
Ridgley, Tho., 36
Ridglie, Geo., 74
Ridgway, Joseph, 462
———, Mary, 461
Ridley, Daniell, 362
———, Elizabeth, 133
———, George, 399
———, Richard, 48
———, Robert, 133
Rigglie, Robert, 111
Righton, William, Senr., 304
Riley, Elizabeth, 102
———, Garrett, 35
———, Miles, 35
———, Tho., 133
Rilsden, Charles, 116
Rimwell, Adam, 260
Ripen, *see* Ripping
Riply, Richard, 371
Rippin, Allin, 121
———, Nicholas, 94
Ripping (or Ripen), Christopher, 177, 219
———, Ellis, 208

71—2

INDEX.

Risby, Thomas, 183
Rishford, Geo., 50
Rising, James, 132
Riskymer [Riskymmer], Nicholas, 69
Risley, Cressent, 484
Risson, Judith, 450
Rivers, John, 314
———, William, 505
Roach, William, 470
Roads, George, 183 ⎫ see
Roades, Margreat, 179 ⎬ Rodes
Roane, Bancks, 399
Roas, Ramsey, 505
Roass, Thomas, 505
Robard's, James, 52
Robb, Elizabeth, 143
———, Ellin, 143
Robbison, Jdeth, 465
———, John, 465
Robensone, Ellen, 292
Robert, 100, 192, 239, see Robertt
Roberts, Blanch, 87
———, Edward, 38, 116, 425, 462
———, James, 178
———, John, 112, 312, 435
———, John, ap., 190
———, Joseph, 150
———, Robert, 75
———, Thomas, 64, 190
———, Wm., 399.
———, see Robertts
Robertson, Nic*., 93
Robertt ———, 292, see Robert
Robertts, Christopher, 194
———, William, 194
———, see Roberts
Robesonn, James, 220
Robins, Edward, 127
———, John, 164*, 316, 463
———, Tho., 83
Robinson, Allexander, 399, 498
———, Ann, 425
———, C., 436
———, Christopher, 166*, 167
———, David, 52, 495
———, Edward, 38, 484
———, Elizabeth, 93
———, Henrie, 114
———, Isack, 130
———, James, 143, 460
———, Jeremy, 296
———, John, 52, 85, 94, 95, 140, 187, 251, 426, 460, 505
———, Joseph, 461
———, Joyce, 121

Robinson, Kat., 94
———, Leonard, 142, 425
———, Manuss, 484
———, Mathew, 95
———, Mary, 94, 124
———, Richard, 182, 457
———, Sir Robert, 164*
———, Robert, 43, 484
———, Sara, 93
———, Thomas, 71, 111, 141, 484
———, William, 80, 193, 425, 457, 484
Robinsonn, Mathewe, 244
Robisonn, Richard, 249
Robson, Thomas, 163, 163*
Robotham, William, 402
Roch, William, 470
Rockly, Raph, 194
Rocks, Michell, 41
Rodes, Tho., 135, see Roads
Rodeway, see Rodway
Rodgers, George, 180
——— (or Rogers), John, 333, 335, 338
———, see Rogers
Rodman, John, 484
———, ———, Junr., 484
———, Sarah, 484
Rodrigus, Anthony, 449
Rods, John, 39
Rodway (or Rodeway), Stephen, 333, 337, 340
Roe (or Row), Christopher, 316*, 317*, 343
———, Edward, 103
———, Margaret, 460
———, Robert, 52
———, Tho., 75
———, see Row, Rowe
Roed's, Roger, 225
Roett, Isaac, 448, 457
Rofe, Barbary, 131
———, Wm., 143
Roffin, Wm., 112
Rogers, Anne, 493
———, Bryan, 257
———, David, 427
———, Edward, 262
———, Ellener, 102
———, Georg., 232
———, Henry, 37
———, James, 66
———, John, 63, 125, 143, 484, 493
——— (Rodgers, or Roggers), John, 316, 318, 333, 335, 338, 340, 343
———, Katherine, 493
———, Mary, 129, 423

Rogers, Mathew, 70
———, Michael, 432
———, Mr., 423
———, Nathaniel, 119
———, Raph, 193
———, Richard, 111
———, Roger, 423
———, Sym., 107
———, Tho., 124, 125
———, Wm., 94
Rogerson, Ellin, 102
———, Theoder, 124
Roker, Arthur, 71
Rolfe, Elizabeth, 174, 223
———, James, 209
———, John, 270, 271
———, Robert, 135
Rolinson, John, 37
Rolles, Jo., 80
Rollright, Margaret, 67
Rolls, Benedict, 119
Romney, Tho., 82
———, Sir William, 155
Romsey, James, 38
Rooby, Martin, 153
Rookeman, Rookman
———, John, 93
———, Elizabeth, 93
Rookines (or Rookins), William, 183, 260
Roome, Thomas, 507
Root, John, 238
Roote, Mary, 97
———, Nicholas, 177
———, Ralph, 92
Ropear, Alles, 292
———, Elizabeth, 292
———, John, 292
Roper, Clement, 217
———, Hanna, 51
———, Margaret, 423
———, Thomas, 191
———, William, 423
Rosdell, Tho., 84
Rosden, Wm., 132
Rose, Christopher, 399
———, Daniell, 102, 278
———, Dareas, 278
———, Elizabeth, 278, 484
———, John, 176, 278, 316, 316*, 317, 317*
———, Margery, 279
———, Mary, 278
———, Rebecca, 207
———, Robert, 278, 279
———, Samuell, 278
———, Sarah, 278
———, Susanna, 426
———, Thomas, 240
———, William, 342, 344, 432

INDEX. 565

Roseter, Thomas, 154
Rosman, James, 152
Ross, William, 399
Rosse, Henry, 133
———, John, 484
———, Phillip, 471
———, Rebecca, 171
———, Thomas, 161, 267
Rosser, Humphrey, 427
Roswell, Mr., 183
Roth, Richard, 400
Rottrie, Sophia, 109
Rou, Jan le, 198
Rouse, Caleb, 470, 471, *see* Rowse
Rousell, George, 317, *see* Rowsell
Rovenson, John, 156
Row (or Roe), Christopher, 316*, 317*, 343
———, Lawrence, 400
———, Nich., 184
———, Peter, 326, 329
———, *see* Roe
Rowe, Anne, 457
———, Mary, 262
———, Nicholas, 262
———, *see* Roe
Rowes, John, 183
Rowinge (or Rownige), Henry, 172, 217
Rowland, Jo., 132
———, Richard, 82
Rowles, Henrie, 135
Rowlidge, Jo., 117
Rowlson, Francis, 110
———, Thomas, 236
Rowlston, Sionell [? Lionell], 254
Rownige (or Rowinge), Henry, 172, 217
Rowse, Thomas, 447, *see* Rouse
Rowsell, George, 316*, *see* Rousell
Rowsewell, Thomas, 316
Rowsley, Elizabeth, 191
———, William, 191
Rowton, Ann, 62
———, Edmond, 62
———, Richard, 62
Roy, Hugh Le, 123
———, Jerome, Le, 199
Royall, Joseph, 169, 202
———, Sibill, 229
Roydon, Wm., 399
Royston, Thomas, 118
Ruce, Roger, 240, *see* Reuse
Ruck, John, 484
Rud, Symon, 472

Rudge, Jo., 140
———, Thomas, 401
Rudle, Robert, 402
Rudston, Eliz., 118
Ruese, Roger, 174, *see* Ruce
Ruggells, Barbarie, 46
———, Jo., 46
Rul, Elisabeth, 438
Rule, Thomas, 401
———, Wm., 136
Rumball, Tho., 132
Rumell, Adam, 182
Rumley, Elisabeth, 431
Rumsey, Joseph, 430
Rundall, Edward, 457
Rusco, Marie, 57
———, Rabecca, 57
———, Samuel, 57
———, Sara, 57
———, Wm., 57
Rush, Clinion, 219
———, William, 81
Rushbrook, Henry, 484
Rushmore, George, 182
Russell, Edward, 401, 426
———, Francis, 132, 167
———, George, 54, 342
———, James, 160*
———, John, 36, 103, 119, 180, 224
———, Katherin, 71
———, Phillip, 505
———, Randolph, 162*
———, Thomas, 472
Rutten, Elizabeth, 180
Rutter, Daniell, 316, 317, 342
———, Tho., 74
Ryale, Joseph, 218, *see* Riall
Ryce, Ann, 117, *see* Rice
Rycord, Samuell, 484
Rycraft, Sara, 484
Ryder, Symon, 399
Rydie, James, 115
Ryle, Tho., 117
Rymes, Henry, 39
Rymore, Allexander, 484

SABYN, Geo., 142
——— (or Sabin), Robert, 96, 186, 250
Sacker, John, 261
Sad, Abraham, 296
Sadd, Richard, 95
Saddock, Tho., 137
Sadler, Hugh, 70
———, Rowland, 116
———, Thomas, 342, 344, 485
Saford (or Safford), Christopher, 171, 211
Sage, Jan, 198

Sage, Richard, 506
Saie, Wm., 125, *see* Say
Saiewell, Arthur, 83
———, Francis, 70
———, James, 93
———, Robert, 93
———, Suzan, 94
Sailes, Richard, 404 [162
St. Albans, Henry, Earl of,
? St. Parlin, Thomas, 141
Saires, Geo., 86, *see* Sares
Sakell, Samuell, 135
Saker, Jo., 116
———, Marie, 116
———, Tho., 115
Salford, John, 186, 250, 273
———, Mary, 186, 250
———, Robert, 186, 250, 273
———, Sara, 190
Salisbury, Robert, Earl of, 156
Sall, Edward, 70
Salmon, Joseph, 437, 458
———, Margaret, 437
———, Peter, 135
———, Wm., 81
Salsbury, William, 192
Salt, Samuell, 404
Salter, Edward, 103
———, Elizabeth, 174, 223
———, George, 409
———, James, 326, 329
———, John, 185
———, Nicholas, 317*, 319*, 324
———, Rich., 407
———, Richard, 342, 462
———, Robert, 118
Saltonstall, Merriall, 59
———, Richard, 59
Salvadge, Ensign, 274
———, Robert, 183
Sam, Gregory, 153
———, John, 318*, 319*
Sames, Elizabeth, 102
Samond, Wm., 72
Sampson, John, 330, 338, 505
Samuell, 290
Sams, John, 323
Sandby, Tho., 38
Sanderick, *see* Standerwick
Sanders, Alexander, 173, 238
———, Benj^a., 404
———, David, 181
———, George, 181
———, Henery, 217
———, John, 154, 194, 351, 411, 447
———, Richard, 177, 219
———, William, 330, 342, 442
———, *see* Saunders, Sawnders
Sanderwick, *see* Standerwick

566   INDEX.

Sandford, John, 408
Sandiford, Charles, 469
———, Henry, 404
———, John, 470
[———?], Richard, 469
Sandley, Robert, 82
Sandome, Richard, 406
Sandrs, *see* Sanders, Saunders
Sands, Sand's
———, Anthony, 436
———, David, 233
———, George, 174, 234
———, Isaac, 436
———, William, 179, 236
Sandwich, Edward, Earl of, 162
Sandy, Robert, 318*, 319*, 324
Sandys, George, 270
Sanford, Roger, 142
Sankey, Hamblet, 135
———, Robert, 60
Sankster, Eliz., 118
Sansom, Richard, 78
Santen, Lucas, 165
Sape, Marey, 295
Sapster, Bridget, 467
———, William, 462, 467
Saracole, Jo., 69
Sarah, Mordecah, 450
Sares, Wm., 86, *see* Saires
Satchill, Wm., 119
Sauewell, Daniell, 195
Saundby, Michell, 118
Saunders, Edward, 122
———, John, 117, 387
———, Judith, 48
———, Lea, 48
———, Marie, 48
———, Martin, 47, 48
———, Mary, 37
———, Rachell, 47
———, Thomas, 102, 122
———, William, 121, 316, 318, 327
———, *see* Sanders, Sawnders
Saunderson, Jo., 135, 485
———, Robert, 486
———, Tho., 112
Savadge, Robert, 259
———, Thomas, 189, 256
Savage, Ann, 263
———, Edward, 39, 51
———, Thomas, 45, 263
Savery, John, 469
Savory, Wm., 119
Sawcott, Jo., 52   [217
Sawell, Thomas, 120, 172
Sawier, Thomas, 225

Sawier, William, 175, 232
———, *see* Sawyer
Sawkynn, Wm., 106
Sawnders, Edward, 126
———, Jo., 128
———, *see* Sanders, Saunders
Sawter, Roger, 64
Sawyer, Margarett, 485
———, Thomas, 182
———, William, 180
———, *see* Sawier
Sawyers, Charles, 465
———, Elizabeth, 465
Say, Geo., 63, *see* Saie [159
Say & Sele, William, Lord,
Sayer, William, 35   [319
Scamplyn (or Kemplyn), John,
Scar, Stephen, 442
Scarburgh, Edward, 162
Scarfield, William, 120
Scarsbrick, Wm., 50
Scawell (or Seawell), Richard, 485
Schenckingh, Amarinzia, 490
———, Benjn., 490
——— (or Shenkingh, Sckenken), Bernard, 429, 458, 490
———, Elizabeth, 490
——— (———), Hannah, 429
———, Katherine, 490
Scot, Jane, 421
———, Mary, 421
———, *see* Scott, Skott
Scotchmore, Robert, 124, 221, 239, *see* Scottesmore
Scott, Abigail, 282
———, Apphia, 263
———, Benjamin, 404, 458, 485
———, Elizabeth, 67, 282
———, Goodwife, 188
———, Henry, 176, 221
———, James, 120
———, Jane, 84
———, John, 64, 105, 143, 505
———, Martha, 280
———, Percis, 263
———, Richard, 325
———, Thomas, 282, 407
———, Walter, 188, 263, 331, 336, 505
———, Wm., 125
———, *see* Scot, Skott
Scottesmore, Robert, 176, *see* Scotchmore
Scotts, Mr., 313*
Scriven, Robert, 120
Scrubs, George, 342

Scrutton (or Strutton), John, 485
Scurrier, William, 316*, 317
Sea, Mary, 38
Seabright, Richard, 141
Sealy, Henry, 408, 412, *see* Seely
Seaman, George, 337
———, Rob., 333, 340
———, Thomas, 408
Seamer (Seaman, or Seymer), John, 332, 337, 340
Searl, John, 485
Searle, Brigett, 194
———, Francis, 104
———, Richard, 409
———, Thomas, 441
———, *see* Serle
Sears (or Sease), Robert, 332, 337, 340
Seaton, John, 119, 498
Seaward, John, 188, *see* Seward
Seawell, Davers, 493
———, Elizabeth, 493
———, Richard, 493
——— (or Scawell), Richard, 485
Seay, Widow, 445
Seden, Nic*., 51, *see* Seeden
Sedgewicke, George, 465
Sedgwick, John, 131, 461, 465
———, Marie, 83
———, Ralph, 405
———, Samuell, 461
Seeden, Annis, 105, *see* Seden
Seely, Wm., 74, *see* Sealy
Seemes, Richard, 116
Seere, Wm., 41
Seirson, Cutbert, 260
Sell, Edward, 86
———, Jo., 133
Selleck, John, 405
Selley, John, 243
Sellin, Ann, 68
———, Joan, 68
Sellock, John, 384
Selman, George, 41
Selwyn, William, 168*
Senior, Jacob, 409
———, Joseph, 450
Sennodd, Robert, 71
Sennott, Wm., 63
Sension, Nico., 58
Sentence, Henry, 51
Serano, Jaell, 450
Sere, John, 236
Serfatty, Joshua, 407
Sergeant, Tho., 47
Seriff, William, 40

INDEX.   567

Serjeant, Richard, 224, 402
Serle, Elizabeth, 489
———, John, 489
———, Thomas, 489
———, see Searle
Sertain, Elizabeth, 496
———, Thomas, 496
Session, Geo., 36
Sessions, Jo., 52
Severne, Jo., 124
Sewar, Robert, 84, see Sewer
Seward, John, 249
———, William, 39
———, see Seaward
Sewer, John, 404, see Sewar
Sexton, Richard, 108
———, Thomas, 192
Sexston, Peter, 102
———, Robert, 136
Seymer, John, 340, see Seamer
Seymor, Florentio, 310
Seywell, Thomas, 255
Sfrane, Almons, 405
Shakerly, William, 427
Shaftesbury, Anthony, Earl of, 161*
Shafto, Wm., 363, 371, 388, 413
Shahanisse, Daniell, 471, see Shanis
Shahany, John, 324
Shale, Robert, 326
Shanis, Daniell, 470, see Shahanisse
Sharks, George, 191
Sharp, Boaz, 303
———, Elizabeth, 205
———, Isack, 205
———, Judith, 191
———, Mrs., 170
———, Richard, 101
———, Robert, 93, 114
———, Samuell, 172, 205
———, Tho., 119, 132
———, William, 119, 170, 205
Sharpe, Aser, 360, 372, 381, 385, 390, 391, 398, 403
———, Elizabeth, 215
———, Henry, 308
———, James, 441
———, Mary, 410
———, Samuell, 215, 268
Sharpes, William, 267
Sharples, Edward, 173
———, Tho., 84
Shaw, Annis, 224
———, Thomas, 303, 304, 355, 398, 418
Shawe, Abram, 142
———, Anne, 110

Shawe, Daniell, 506
———, John, 80, 94, 95
———, Sara, 95
———, Wm., 115
Sheaperd, see Sheppard
Sheere, Strenght, 244, see Shere
Sheering, Jo., 63
Sheffield, Thomas, 266
Sheicrofte (or Shercrofte), Wm., 141
Shetlam, Thomas, 374
Shelley, John, 174, 184, 232
———, Robert, 150
Shelton, Samuell, 485
Shenkingh, see Schenckingh
Shenton, Grace, 422
———, Jane, 422
———, Samuell, 422, 445
Sheppard, Sheaperd, Shepeheard, Shepheard, Shepherd, Sheppeard
———, Humfrey, 286
———, John, 99, 506
———, Justice, 43
———, Lieutenant, 184
———, Margaret, 99
———, Ould, 180, see Bernardo
———, Ralph, 97
———, Robert, 175, 180, 232, 235
———, Samuell, 100
———, Sara, 97
———, Thankes, 97
———, Tho., 99
Sheppey (or Sheppy), Thomas, 170, 204
Sherborn, Henrie, 150
Sherborne, James, 85
Shercrofte (or Sheicrofte), Wm., 141
Shere, Stephen, 185, see Sheere
Sheres, Francis, 63
Sherewood, see Sherwood
Sherhack, Benedicter, 64
Sherin, Robert, 280
Sherland, John, 406
Sherley (or Shurley), Daniell, 169, 201
———, Lidia, 213
———, Susan, 213
Sherly, Tho., 84
———, see Shirley
Sherlock, Edward, sen., 303
———, Jo., 134
Sherlocke, Elizabeth, 111
Sherman, John, 280
———, Tho., 41

Sheron, George, 485
Sherrick, Jo., 114
Sherringham, Phillipp, 119
Sherwin, John, 410
Sherwood, Alice, 279
———, Anna, 278
——— (or Sherewood), Peaceable, 176, 236
——— (——————),
   Peeter, 243, 254
———, Rebecca, 278
———, Rose, 278
———, Samuell, 403
———, Suzan, 85
———, Thomas, 278, 279
Shettleworth, John, 38
Shetman, Richard, 440
Sheword (or Shewoud), Thomas, 184, 243
Shilborn, Wm., 118
Shingle, Richard, 296
Shinglewood, Robert, 80
Ship, Edmund, 428
———, Jefferie, 140
Shipley, Jo., 115
Shipman, Wm., 82
Shippin (or Phippin), William, 334
Shipton, Wm., 446
Shirley, William, 430, Sherley, &c.
Shoare, James, 355
Shore, Ellin, 118
———, Mathew, 141
———, Richard, 485
Shorey, Anthony, 508
———, William, 508
Short, Martha, 408
———, Samuell, 86
———, Walter, 406
Shorte, Joane, 152
———, Owen, 485
Shorter, Jo., 84
———, Marie, 114
Shotten (or Shotton), Nicholas, 181, 230
Shovell, Elias, 506
Shrawley, Margrett, 191
Shreife, Richard, 190
Shrewsbury, Ann, 431
——— (or Shroesbury), John, 431, 448
———, William, 431
Shule, John, 180
Shurke, George, 178
Shurland, John, 485
Shurley, see Sherley
Sibery, Thomas, 182
Sibsey, John, 185
Sicklemore, James, 439

Siddy, Henry, 409
Sides, Thomas, 178, 229
Sidney, John, 410
———, Wm., 447
Siggins, Tho., 129
Silby, Robert, 112, *see* Sylbie
Silcomb, William, 496
Silsby, Mathew, 124
Silvester, Abram, 37
———, Grace, 461
———, Madam, 485
Simes, Beniamin, 184, 242
——— (Sims or Sunes), Henry, 318°, 319°, 323
———, Sarra, 100
———, *see* Symes
Simes [*i.e.*, Simmes], Symon, 104, *see* Symes
Simmes, Symon, 104
———, Wm., 449
Simmons, Phillip, 458, 459
———, Richard, 343
Simnell, John, 257
Simon, Hester Bar, 449, *see* Symon
Simons (or Symonds), Richard, 316°, 318, *see* Symons
Simpkins, Nathaniel, 128, *see* Symkynn
Simpson, Edward, 133
———, James, 485
———, Jo., 132
———, Thomas, 104, 136, 181
———, Mr., 133
Sims, *see* Simes
Simson, Henry, 491
———, James, 491
———, Mary, 491
———, Thomas, 443
Sindry, John, 410
Singer, Tho., 36
Singleton, Jo., 83
Singnell, William, 139
Sinklaire, Allexander, 458
Sipsey, John, 274
Sismore, Martha, 172
———, William, 172
Sister, Gerrart, 297
Sisters, Elizabeth, 485
Sizemore, William, 269
Skahane, Teige, 406
Skaros, George, 485
Skarvill, Robert, 38
Skene, Alexander, 167°
Skerry, Elizabeth, 291
———, Henry, 291
Skinner, John, 179, 231
———, Nicholas, 182
———, *see* Skynner
Skofield, Richard, 59

Skooler, Anthony, 74
Skorie, Jehn, 36
Skorier, Phillip, 128
Skose, Richard, 151
Skott, Elizabeth, 280
———, Thomas, 280
———, *see* Scott
Skudder, Jo., 88
Skyddell, Tho., 142
Skynggle, Ann, 75
Skynner, Richard, 135
———, Sam., 142
———, *see* Skinner
Slade, John, 316, 318
Slany, Anthony, 485
Slate, John, 342
Slater, Anne, 246
———, Henry, 166
———, John, 246
———, Mary, 498
Slatier, Martin, 239
Slaughter, John, 498
———, Mary, 498
———, Thomas, 485
———, William, 402
Slavelie, Richard, 153
Slawcome, Davey, 145
Sleight, James, 183, 252
Sleman, Tho., 154
Slie, Jeremie, 112
———, Richard, 67
—, *see* Slye
Slograve, William, 338
Sluce, Lawrence, 418
Slye, John, 471, *see* Slie
Smal, Ann, 428
Smale, Hugo, 194
Smalepage (or Smalpage), Lawrence, 177, 220
Smalewood, *see* Smalwood
Small, Wm., 113
Smalle, Walter, 297
Smallie, John, 149
Smallman, Edward, 51
Smalpage, *see* Smalepage
Smalwood (or Smalewood), Randall, 176, 225
Smart, John, 323, 410
———, Richard, 140
———, Samuell, 337
———, Wm., 85
Smartt, John, 440
———, Samuell, 447
Smith, Alexander, 40, 304
———, Alice, 56, 458
———, Ann, 424, 426, 430
———, Anne, 290, 421
———, Antonio, 141
———, Arthur, 186
———, Charles, 120

Smith, Christopher, 253, 429
———, Daniell, 38, 41
———, David, 470
———, Dorothy, 68
———, Edward, 117, 179, 231, 403
———, Elisabeth (or Elizabeth), 123, 280, 282, 292, 424, 431, 437, 485, 492
———, Frances, 492
———, Francis, 63, 67, 231, 317°, 319°, 324
———, Junr., 460
———, George, 80, 82, 125, 436
———, Hanna, 49, 59
———, Henry, 115, 292, 421, 424, 426, 432
———, Hester, 403
———, Humfrey, 87
———, Isaac, 406
———, James, 74, 141
———, Jane, 429
———, Joan, 71, 223
———, John, 56, 57, 70, 74, 82, 109, 111, 117, 135, 139, 140, 177, 178, 179, 220, 229, 231, 258, 292, 334, 337, 409, 410, 422, 424, 427, 430, 432, 436, 437, 440, 471, 492
———, Jonas, 83
———, Joseph, 433, 439
———, Judith, 422, 427
———, Katherin, 123
———, Leonard, 67
———, Lewes, 122
———, Margaret, 118, 405, 505
———, Margerie, 123
———, Marie, 49, 59
———, Mary, 68, 282, 422, 427, 429, 432, 433, 489
———, Mrs., 174, 191
———, Mundusia, 424, 437
———, Nathaniel, 447
———, Nicholas, 180, 234
———, Olliver, 440
———, Osborne, 183
———, Osmond, 223
———, Osten, 175
———, Peter, 101
———, Phillip, 282, 402
———, Philippa, 422, 432, 436
———, Ralph, 429
———, Richard, 48, 111, 134, 139, 177, 219, 239
———, Robert, 172, 185, 243
———, Roger, 174, 223, 232, 271

INDEX.

Smith, Samuell, 280, 282, 305, 432, 463
——, Sithe, 292
——, Stephen, 470, 495
——, Susanna, 231
——, Thomas, 37, 39, 40, 53, 86, 115, 120, 137, 174, 177, 194, 220, 224, 407, 421, 426, 437, 439
——, Thurlo, 408
——, Walter, 126
——, Widow, 443
——, William, 35, 67, 74, 138, 184, 189, 190, 243, 246, 263, 326, 329, 332, 334, 404, 406, 440, 492
——, ——, Junr., 335, 336
——, see Smyth
Smitheman, Jo., 51
Smithick, Henry, 119
Smithson, Robert, 37
Smithwicke, Wm., 505
Smyth, Arthur, 252
——, John, 341
——, Sir Thomas, 156
——, Wm., 341
Snacknell, Richard, 405
Snales, Margaret, 123
Snape, John, 135
Snapp, Thomas, 188
Snathe, Richard, 64
Snellin, Anne, 490
——, John, 490
——, Robert, 490
Snerling, Robert, 485
Snipe, Christopher, 489
——, Elizabeth, 489
——, John, 485, 489
——, William, 461
Snoden, Luke, 114
Snouks, George, 442
Snow, Snowe
——, George, 316*, 317*, 343
——, Henry, 110
——, Nathaniell, 471
——, Rebecca, 175, 225, see Grave, Elnor
——, Richard, 141
——, Sara, 175, 225, see Grave
——, Wm., 59
——, see Swnow
Snowood, John, 246
Soanes, Mary, 126
[Somerhaies?], Anne, 470
——, John, 470
Somers, Cornwall, 164
——, Sir George, 155
——, James, 95
——, see Summers
Somersall, John, Senr., 303

Somersall, Thomas, 191
Somerton, John, 103
Sommer, Elisa, 91
——, Henry, 91
Sone, George, 408
Sothey (or Soothey), Ann, 176, 226
—— (————), Elizabeth, 191, 226
——, Henry, 191
——, Mary, 191
——, Mr., 191
——, Mrs. 176
——, Thomas, 191
Sotterfoyth, Jo., 36
Sourton, Samuell, 443
Sousa, Abraham, 449
Southampton, Earl of 313*
————, Henry, Earl of, 156
Southern, John, 175, 225, 273, see Sowthern
Southernes, Mr., 308
Southward, Henry, 143
Southwood, Marie, 110
Southworth, Francis, 405, 418
Sowth, Francis, 38
——, Martin, 128
Sowthern, Jane, 111, see Southern
Spalden, Edmond, 187
Spalding, Edward, 176
Spar, Georg, 433
Sparke, Sparkes, Sparks
——, Edward, 58
——, George, 180
——, James, 112
——, John, 195, 234, 498
——, Joye, 505
——, Madam, 472
——, Samuell, 407
——, Thomas, 265, 307
S. Parplin [?St. Parlin], Thomas, 141
Sparowhawk, James, 485
Sparrow, Judith, 444
Sparshott, Edward, 173, 208
Speckman, Henrie, 41
Speed, Richard, 52
Speere, Eliz., 82
Speering, John, 326, 329
Speights, Elizabeth, 491
——, Marie, 491
——— (or Speghts), William, 485, 491
Spence, Elizabeth, 499
——, James, 327, 331
——, John, 327
——, Mrs., 191
——, Sara, 178, 249

Spence, William, 178, 191, 271, 499
Spenceley, John, 141
Spencer, Allice, 228
——, Sir Edward, 106
——, Francis, 35
——, James, 142
——, John, 142, 448, 485
——, Kathren, 173
——, Margaret, 506
——, Nicholas, 163, 163*
——, Peter, 141
——, Robert, 84, 163
——, Thomas, 182
——, William, 82, 117, 228, 229
Spendergrass, Tho., 51
Spendley, Mary, 75
Spenlove, John, 491
——, Lowrie, 491
Spenswick, Mrs., 458
Spicer, Ann, 71
——, Edward, 122, 129
——, Gregory, 233
——, Henry, 129
——, Richard, 36
——, Samuell, 405
——, Wm., 112
Spight, Fra., 84
Spilman, Hanna, 252
—— (or Spillman), Thomas, 175, 186, 188, 226, 252, 273
Spillmans, Captain, 269
Spittle, Robert, 409
Sprad, Elinor, 179
Spraging, Radulph, 95
Spratt, Mary, 108
——, Tho., 112
Sprawe, Oliff, 102
Sprawson, William, 114
Spreate, Jo., 101
Spring, Elinor, 280
——, Henry, 281
——, John, 280, 281
——, Mary, 281
——, William, 281
Springall, Jo., 36
Springham, Hannah, 422
————, John, 338, 422, 458
————, Sarah, 422
Sprite, Robert, 74
Spurling, Richard, 172
Spurr, Robert, 51
Spurway (Spurwey, or Spurnay), Robert, 326, 329
Spyer, Jo., 63
Spynk, Robert, 82
Sqire, John, 303
Squier, Phillipp, 38

INDEX.

Srayne, Richard, 132
Staber, Peter, 178
Stacie, Elizabeth, 105
Stacy, W., 403
Stafferton, Mr., 176
Stafford, Jane, 71
———, Mr., 309
———, William, 249, 251
Stagg, Wm., 48, 53, 56, 57, 60, 61, 68
Stalvers, Henry, 306
———, Mrs., 305
Stamford, John, 257
Stamp (or Stump), Tho., 79
Stanbridg, Nathanel, 194
Stanbridge, William, 95
Standerick (Standericke, Standerwicke, Sanderick, or Sanderwike), Nathaniell, 319, 320*, 323
Standich, Dorothy, 96
Standish, James, 221
Standon, Mary, 421
———, William, 421
Standy, Robert, 78
Stanfast, John, 505, 507
Stanford, Jo., 73
———, Mary, 489
———, Richard, 115
———, Robert, 485, 489
Stanley, Christopher, 72
———, Francis, 138
———, Hugh, 126
———, Morris, 261
———, Robert, 408
———, Roger, 221
———, Suzanna, 72
———, William, 135
Stanly, Mrs., 458
Stann, Jo., 129
Stannadge, Thomas, 407
Stannion, Ant°., 48
Stansley, Tho., 56
Stanson, John, 191
Stantley, Jo., 98
Stanton, Daniell, 367
———, Pearce, 406
———, Tho., 36
Staple, see Staples
Staplehill, Allexander, 151
Staples (or Staple), Leonard, 73, 316, 318, 342
———, Richard, 271
Stapleton, Pierce, 81
———, Walter 405
———, William, 161*, 162*
Stapons, Cornelius, 488
———, Margaret, 488
———, Thomas, 488
Stares, Thomas, 42

Starkey, Elizabeth, 175
Starkie, Peter, 125
Starling, Wm., 114
Staueling, see Staveling
Staughton, Edward, 87
Staunton, Jo., 126
Staveling, Mathew, 193
Staysmore, Francis, 505
Stebing, Eliz., 278
———, John, 278
———, Rowland, 278, 279
———, Sarah, 278, 279
———, Thomas, 278
Steddall, William, 79
Stede (Steed, or Steede), Edwyn, 162, 321, 325, 331, 335, 339, 344, 424, 447, 458
———, John, 166
———, see Steed
Stedham, John, 449
Stedman, Elizabeth, 68
———, Isack, 68
———, Nathaniell, 68
———, Susanna, 426
Steed, Calia, 424
———, see Stede
Steel, Mary, 403, 404
Steele, Barbary, 466, 468
———, George, 468
———, Thomas, 466
Steephens, see Stephens
Steere, Richard, 136
———, Robert, 111
Steerer, Eliz., 107
Steerman, Anthony, 499
Steevens, Alice, 98
———, Edward, 139
———, Henry, 99
———, John, 40, 129, 506
———, Mathew, 86
———, Tho., 73, 101
———, Wm., 83, 126, 128
———, see Stevens, Stephens
Steevenson, Christopher, 127
———, Richard, 120
Stepbing, Henry, 447
Stephen, ———, 192
Stephens, Steephens, &c.
———, (or Stevens), Elias, 326, 329
———, John, 239, 485
———, Nathaniell, 405
———, Philip (?Philippa), 151
———, (or Stevens), Richard, 175, 193, 226, 333, 336, 339
———, Sylvester, 406
———, see Steevens, Stevens

Stepney, Thomas, 256
Sterry, Geo., 140
Steven, 196
Stevens (or Stephens), Elias, 326, 329
———, Hector, 426
———, (or Stevans), John, 181, 296
———, Judeth, 151
———, (or Stephens), Richard, 333, 336, 339
———, Robert, 43
———, Thomas, 426
———, see Steevens, Stephens
Steward, Amey, 505
———, John, 424
———, Margaret, 424
———, William, 139
———, see Sheard
Stewart, John, 329
Stibbs, Jo., 120
Stickland, Margaret, 422
———, William, 379, 422, 439
Stiffchynn, Wm., 128
Stiles, Francis, 42
———, Henry, 43
———, Joan, 43
———, Jo., 43
———, Rachel, 43
———, Tho., 42
Stilgo, Anto., 111
Stint, Henry, 140
Stirrup, James, 306
Stith, Martin, 436
Stoak's, Stoakes, see Stokes
Stocbridge, Ann, 94, see Stockbridge, Stuckbridge
Stock, Robert, 85
Stockbridge, Jo., 93, see Stocbridge, Stuckbridge
Stockdell, Edward, 186
Stocker, William, 177, 237
Stockley, John, 403
———, Mary, 403
Stockton, Jonas, 187, 256
———, Timothy, 187, 256
———, Tho., 132
Stockwell, Gabriell, 85
Stoe, Wm., 80, see Stow
Stoiks, Goodman, 178
Stoker, Samuell, 444
———, Wm., 132
Stokes, Stoak's, Stoakes
———, Ann, 227
———, David, 304
———, George, 39
———, Grace, 130
———, John, 227
———, Jonathan, 305, 306
———, Luke, 52

INDEX. 571

Stokes, Michaell, 403
——, Tho., 132
——, Wm., 335, 336, 338, 339
Stollard, James, 470
Ston, Henry, 119
——, Jo., 54
——, Moyes, 175, *see* Stones
——, Richard, 193
—— (Stor, or Stow), Samuel, 63
Stone, Ann, 66
——, Elizabeth, 238
——, Francis [*i.e.*, Frances], 494
——, ——, 66
——, Hugh, 430
——, Joan, 66
——, John, 66, 180, 181, 234, 237, 408, 485, 494
——, Marie, 66
——, Maximillian, 238
——, Richard, 75
——, Robert, 444
——, Sisly, 237
——, Symon, 66
Stones, Moyses, 244, *see* Ston
Stonhouse, Wm., 84
Stonword, Hen., 86
Stoodly (or Stoodley), John, 333, 336, 340
Stope, Chri., 122
Stor, Samuel, 63
——, *see* Ston, &c.
Storey, William, 290
Stott, Fra., 51
Stotter, Jo., 143
Stout, John, 505
Stow (or Stowe), John, 303, 309
——, Mary, 308, *see* Mountain
—— (Ston or Stor), Samuel, 63
——, Thomas, 303, 309
——, *see* Stoe
Stowes, Mr., 312, 313
Strachey, William, 171, 238
Strafford, Thomas, 437
Stramige (?), *see* Straunge
Stranfellow, Thomas, 433
Strange, Ben., 86
——, William, 104, 222
——, *see* Straunge
Stratford, Robert, 38
Strattergood, John, 41
Stratton, Mary, 435
——, Thomas, 435
Straughan, Wm., 83, *see* Strawne
Straunge (or Stramige ?) William, 172

Strause, Elias, 407
Strawne, Henry, 485, *see* Straughan
Streaton, Elizabeth, 66
Street, Alice, 59
Streme, Jo., 131
——, Thomas, 131
Stretch, John, 505
Stretcher, Andrew, 122
Streter, Thomas, 143
Stringer, Mr., 309
——, Samuel, 120
Strong, Charles, 327, 330
Strode, George, 494
——, Henry, 485
——, John, 162, 163, 458
——, Margarett, 485
Stroude, Mrs. John, 505
Strowde, John, 93, 115
Strutt, James, 352, 359, 371, 395, 400, 406
Strutton (or Scrutton), John, 485
Stuard, John, 441, *see* Steward
Stubber, Jo., 113
Stucbridge, Charles, 93, *see* Stocbridge, Stockbridge
Studdy, Thomas, 485
Studman, Isack, 53
Stump (or Stamp), Tho., 79
Sturdevant, Roger, 37
Sturdivantt, Edward, 443
Sturdy, Jo., 80
Sturgis, Wm., 64
Sturman, Mary, 505
Sturton, Jo., 140
Suckliff, Michell, 136
Sudburrowe, Peter, 79
Sudgerner, Rowland, 109
Suffolk, Thomas, Earl of, 156
Suillivant, Anthony, 424, 434
——, Cornelius, 432
——, Daniel, 426, 429
——, Dearman, 430
——, Elisabeth, 424, 434
——, John, 424, 434
——, Margaret, 428, 429
Sulley, Thomas, 178
Sully, Maudlyn, 247
——, Thomas, 247
Sumerfild (Summerfild), Nicholas, 262
Suffles (Summes), John, 140
Sumfill (Summfill), John, 188
Summers, Ann, 507
—— (or Sumers), John, 338, 343, 507
——, Thomas, 505
——, *see* Somers
Sunes, *see* Simes, Henry

Surgisson, Wm., 36
Susan, ——, 245
Susanna (negress), 489
Sussames, Alexander, 194
Sutton, Dorothy, 437
——, Ellin, 116
——, George, 38
——, Henry, 377, 486
——, John, 84, 323, 343, 407, 423, 433, 458
——, Katharin, 423
——, Mary, 423
——, Nicholas, 173, 215
——, Richard, 163, 461
——, Robert, 121
——, William, 179
Swain, Martin, 437
Swaine, Peter, 376, 415, 448
——, *see* Swayne
Swales, Geo., 81
Swan (or Swann), John, 120, 425, 469, 470
Swanley, Jo., 112
——, Robert, 410
Swarbeck, John, 220
Swarris, David, 450
Swayne, Ann, 117
——, Elizabeth, 49, 59
——, Francis, 54
——, Tho., 116
——, Wm., 54, 69
——, *see* Swaine
Sweet (or Sweete), Robert, 185, 249
Sweeting, Jo., 51
——, Richard, 409, 458
——, Samuell, 316*
Sweetland, James, 386
——, William, 349, 373, 402, 403
Swift, Mr., 180
Swifte, Abram, 114
——, Jane, 126
——, Jo., 114
——, Thomas, 234
——, Wm., 115
Swinhow, Thomas, 220, 268
Swinny, Thomas, 409
Swnow, Thomas, 177, *see* Snow
Swynden, Wm., 76
Syard, Jo., 103
Sydlie, Tho., 59
Syer, Tho., 113
Sylbie, Tobie, 138, *see* Silby
Symes, Alexander, 138
——, Margrett, 243
Symes (Symmes), Beniamin, 126
—— (——), John, 38

72—2

INDEX.

Symes, *see* Simes, &c.
Symon, Oliver, 114
———, Stephen, 153
——— (an Italian), 194
———, *see* Simon
Symondes, Tho., 36
Symonds, Dorothy, 141
———, Francis, 41
———, James, 137
———, Jo., 52, 114
———, Richard, 112, 154
———, Samuell, 104
———, Wm., 122
———, *see* Simons
Symons, John, 194
——— (or Simons), Richard, 269, 316*, 318
———, Samuell, 403
———, *see* Simons
Symper, Robert, 142
Sympkynn, Ralph, 122, *see* Simpkins
Sympson, Daniell, 101
———, Geo., 83
———, John, 52
———, *see* Simpson

TABOR, Anne, 283
———, Jane, 283
———, Sarah, 283
———, Timothy, 283
Tadd, Alexander, 81
Taggard, Elisabeth, 434
Taggartt, Alexander, 458
———, James, 445
Tailor, Barbara, 432
———, Mary, 432
———, *see* Tayler, Taylor
Talbott, Geo., 80
———, Jo., 83
———, Thomas, 95
———, Wm., 120
Tallcott, John, 150
Tanner, Daniell, 185, 247
———, Elisabeth, 431
———, Josias, 228
———, Mary, 431
Tapper, Thomas, 128, 412
Tappin (Toppin, or Tuppin), Miles, 460, 465, 466
———, William, 466
Tarborer, Richard, 180
Taselie, Eliz., 87
Tatam (or Tattam), Nathaniel, 170, 209
Tate, James, 70
———, Tho., 121
———, *see* Tayte
Tathill, William, 173
Tatnum, Henry, 40

Tatt's, Robert, 442
Taverner, Henry, 126
Tawyer, Hugh, 71
Tayler, Dyonis, 59
———, George, 124, 131, 141
———, James, 85
———, Jasper, 194
———, John, 40, 112, 118
———, Nicholas, 119
———, Richard, 86, 136
———, Steeven, 138
———, Thomas, 75
———, Wm., 86, 140
Taylor, Ann, 87
———, Anto., 71
———, Chri., 79
———, Dorothy, 203
———, Elizabeth, 77
———, Fortune, 174
———, John, 94, 122, 253, 428, 486
———, Jonathan, 449
———, Kat., 58
———, Mary, 203
———, Mrs., 181
———, Rebecca, 253
———, Richard, 170, 203, 267, 268
———, Robert, 103, 193
———, Thomas, 36, 273
———, Waltor, 506
———, William, 71, 94, 396
———, Zachary, 84
———, *see* Tailor
Tayte, John, 470, *see* Tate
Teage, John, 412
Teague (boy), 471
Teape (or Teap), Robert, 332, 338, 341
———, Walter, 319
Tedder, Tho., 52
Teed, John, 294
Teene, John, 467
Teirrer, John, 135
Temple, Edward, 173, 190, 205
———, Sir Richard, 161*
———, Thomas, 161
Temproe, John, 506
Tems (or Tenis), George, 81
Terrett, Ralph, 40
Terrill, James, 143
———, Samuell, 486
———, Tho., 80
Terry, Anto., 84
———, Bassell, 63
———, Christopher, 411, 458
———, Giles, 85
———, Jo., 98
———, Richard, 107
———, Robert, 107

Terry, Thomas, 84, 107
Terwight, Geo., 330
Tester, Elisabeth, 432
Tetloe, Nic^o., 82
Thatcher, Francis, 423
———, Jo., 120
———, Mary, 423
———, Samuel, 423
———, Sylvester, 104
Thayer, Nathaniel, 412
Theody, Mark, 38
Thimbleby, Nicholas, 192
Thistlethwaite, Peter, 486
Thomas, 182, 188, 194, 195, 243, 248, 427
———, Abraham, 317*, 320, 324
———, Charls, 321, 322, 325, 342, 344
———, Christopher, 79, 124
———, David, 133, 458
———, Davie, 80, 141
———, Elizabeth, 497
———, Gabriell, 138
———, George, 411
———, Henry, 153
———, John, 51, 80, 116, 130, 152, 179, 233, 470, 498, 506
———, Nathaniell, 172, 217, 436
———, Richard, 80, 83
———, Robert, 95
———, Roger, 80, 458
———, Thomas, 115, 122, 149
———, Thompson, 486
———, William, 95, 112, 132, 293, 497
——— (an Indian), 188, 255
Thomkins, John, 104
Thomlins, Ben., 62
———, Edward, 62
Thomlinson, Joseph, 141, *see* Tomlinson
Thompson, Ann, 222
———, Christopher, 506
———, Jane, 494
———, John, 486, 494
———, Lancelott, 489
———, Mary, 489
———, Roger, 222
(?)———, Thomas, 486
———, William, 195
———, *see* Tompson
Thomson, Chri., 134
———, Edward, 81, 103
———, Georg, 185
———, Jo., 52, 76, 81, 84, 134, 135
———, Morris, 273
———, Paule, 185

INDEX. 573

Thomson, Robert, 128
———, Tho., 86, 98, 128
———, William, 124, 142, 185, 244
———, *see* Tomson
Thornbrugh, Widow, 441
Thornburgh, George, 436, 486
Thorncome, Wm., 114
Thorne, Arthur, 133
———, Henry, 173, 213
———, Peter, 56
———, Thomas, 122
Thornebury, Thomas, 253
Thornegood (or Thorngood), Thomas, 176, 182
Thornehill (or Thornhill), Timothy, 164, 469, 506
Thornton, Joanna, 59
———, Nicholas, 303
———, Robert, 68, 162*
———, Walter, 59
———, Wm., 411
Thorogood (or Thorougood), Adam, 187, 253
———, Richard, 433
Thoroughgood, Edw., 286
———, *see* Thurrowgood, &c.
Thorowden, Allice, 218
Thorowgood, Edward, 159
———, Thomas, 226, 486
———, *see* Thurrowgood, &c.
Thorp, Elizabeth, 67
———, John, 47
———, William, 67
Thorpe, James, 329, 506
———, John, 412
Thrasher, Robert, 261
Thredder, Niccolas, 249
Threlcatt, Anto., 74
Threnorden, Edward, 216
———, Elizabeth, 216
Thresher, Robert, 183
Throgmorton, John, 189, 208
Througood, *see* Thorogood
Thurrogood, Jo., 142
———, Mary, 96
Thurrowgood, Wm., 118
———, *see* Thorowgood, &c.
Thursby, James, 192
Thurston, John, 293
———, Margrett, 293
———, Thomas, 293
Thwait's, Alexander, 49
Thwing, Ben., 62
———, John, 357
Tibbalds, Tho., 131
Tibott, *see* Tybbott

Tichbourn, Winnefred, 486
Tickin (or Tinkin), Peter, 318*
Ticknall, Henrie, 130
Tickner, Thomas, 446
Tiffin, Tho., 142
Tiffing, Jo., 125
Tighton, W., 121
Tiler, Elizabeth, 259
———, William, 259
———, *see* Tyler
Till, John, 136
Tilly, Wm., 88, *see* Tylly
Tilney, Thomas, 486
Timothy, John, 316*, 317, 343
Tindall, Richard, 506
———, Thomas, 191, 267
———, Widow, 176
Tine, Elisabeth, 424
———, John, 424
———, Margaret, 424
Tingley, Palmer, 53
Tinico, Jacob, 411
Tinkin, *see* Tickin
Tippin, John, 411
Tippsley, Francis, 138
Tissall, Robert, 143
Titcomb, Samuell, 329
Titloe, Josua, 111
[Titus], Edmond, 46
———, Jo., 46
———, Hanna, 46
———, Robert, 46 [340
Tiverton, William, 333, 336,
Todd, Robert, 259
Toleman (or Doleman), Susannah, 320*
Toller, Marie, 66
Tollie, Tho., 84
Tollo, Demeuerez Lewis, 412
Tomkins, Elizabeth, 131
———, Kat., 131
———, Marie, 131
———, Ralph, 131
———, Samuel, 131
Tomlinson, Mathew, 80, *see* Thomlinson
Tompson, Ann, 172
———, Nicholas, 180, 234
———, Roger, 172
———, *see* Thompson, &c.
Tomson, George, 244
———, Hather, 256
———, Mr., 257
———, Paule, 244
———, William, 255
———, *see* Thomson
Tooke, James, 178, 220, *see* Tuke
Tooles, Morgan, 411
Toolie, Tho., 85
Tooly, Nathan, 127

Toothaker, Margaret, 130
———, Roger, 130
Topleife, Wm., 140
Topliss, Wm., 79
Toppan, Abraham, 293
———, Elizabeth, 293
———, Petter, 293
———, Susanna, 293
Toppin, *see* Tappin
Topsall, Humfrey, 36
Torez, Judieah, 450
Tothill, Mrs., 447
Totle, William, 206
Totman, Jo., 150
Totnell, Jo., 67
Toulban, Robert, 138
Touey, *see* Tovey
Tounsend, *see* Townesend, &c.
Tovey, Richard, 506
Towers, Edward, 116
Towne, Edmund, 291
———, Edward, 446
———, John, 39
Townesend (or Townsend), Thomas, 327, 329
Townsend, Alice, 428
———, Francis, 121
———, John, 448
———, (or Townshend), Richard, 120, 134, 174, 223, 363, 411
———, Tho., 37
Townson, James, 51
———, Tho., 36
Towse, John, 37
Toyer, Kath., 441
Trachern, John, 173
Tracy, Thomas, 266
Trallopp, Tymothy, 122
Tramorden, Edward, 172
Trane, Jo., 63
Trantt, Richard, 441
Trarice, Nic*., 43, 45, 47, 55
Trash (or Trask), Suzan, 95
Tratt, Robert, 70
Travel, Samuel, 164
Travers, Phillip, 444
Travis, Richard, 410
Tredwell, Mary, 110
———, Thomas, 110
Tree, John, 227
———, Richard, 227, 272
Tregagell, Richard, 132
Trehearne, John, 214
Tremills, Wm., 412
Tremineere, Edward, 153
Trendall, Richard, 67
Treneighan, Robert, 153
Trent, Jo., 79
Trentum, Tho., 108

INDEX

Trese, Samuel, 84
Trethewy (or Trethewey), John, 161, 162
Trevas, Geo., 118
Trewin, Jane, 153
Trigg, Thomas, 41
Triggs, Thomas, 192
Trim, Trim̃, [i.e., Trimmer], Valentine, 370, 373, 414
Trippatt, Jo., 86
Trodd, Richard, 296
Troope, Samuel, 129
Trott, Perient, 307, 309
Trou, Jan de, 199
Trowell, Phillipp, 458, 486
Trowsdale, Ann, 433
Trubbs, George, 316, 317*
True, Ant⁰., 82
——, John, 103
Trueman, Richard, 42
Trumball, Thomas, 94
Trump (or Trumpe), Humphery, 334, 337, 340
Truren, John, 327
Trusdal, William, 425
Trusedell, Phines, 142
Trussell, John, 170, 207
Trye, John, 221
Tubbs, Edward, 486
Tubley, Grace, 123
Tuck, Warram, 112
Tucke, William, 296
Tucker, Ann, 506
——, Charles, 163
——, Elizabeth, 244
——, Francis, 305, 306
——, Geo., 122
——, Henry, Senr., 303
——, ——, 305, 327, 330
——, John, 163*, 164*
——, Margaret, 98
——, Mary, 185, 244
——, St. George, 303
——, Thomas, 119
——, William, 184, 244, 273, 274, 327, 330
Tudar, Richard, 445, 458
Tudor, Mary, 430
——, Richard, 430
Tuke, Chri., 85, see Tooke
Tull, John, 461
Tullie, Jo., 126
Tulls, John, 466
——, Richard, 466
Tuppin, see Tappin
Turdall, John, 412
Turgis, Symon, 170, 208
Turk, Geo., 133
Turner, Elizabeth, 46, 123
——, Henry, 173, 177, 214, 219

Turner, Joan, 123
——, John, 83, 411
——, Jonathan, 303
——, Joseph, 193
——, Marmaduke, 63
——, Martha, 424
——, Martin, 180, 234
——, Mary, 424
——, Mathew, 51
——, Robert, 85, 93, 170, 210
——, Sara, 37
——, Symon, 170
——, Thomas, 79, 80, 112, 144, 205, 297
Turnor, George, 255
——, Roger, 192
Turpin, Henry, Junr., 458
——, ——, Senr., 458
——, ——, 437
——, John, 70
——, Widow, 442
Turton, Francis, 458
Tustin, Jo., 133
Tuthill, George, 439
Tuttell, Abigall, 45
——, Ann, 48, 49
——, Anna, 48
——, Elizabeth, 49, 83
——, Isbell, 48
——, Joan, 45
——, Jo., 45, 48, 49
——, Rebecca, 48
——, Richard, 48
——, Sara, 45
——, Symon, 45
——, Tho., 49
——, William, 49
Twine, Widow, 458
Tyack, William, 164*
Tybbott, Tybbot, Tibott
——, Elizabeth, 108
——, Henry, 108
——, Jeremy, 108
——, Remembrance, 108
——, Samuell, 108
Tyers, John, 188
Tyler, Elizabeth, 181
——, Jo., 121
——, Robert, 486
——, Thomas, 70
——, William, 181
——, see Tiler
Tylly, Nathaniell, 73, see Tilly
Tynkler, Sara, 94
Tynman, Robert, 102
Tyos, John, 235
Tyres, Samuell, 83
Tyrwhitt, George, 458
Tyrwill, Herculous, 458

Tyse, Wm., 137
Tysoe, Wm., 486
Tyzacke, John, 166*

UBANK, William, 135
Ufford, John, 486
Underwood, Andrew, 111
——, John, 35, 96
——, Marable, 291
——, Martha, 281
——, Martin, 281
——, Mary, 433
——, Peter, 50
——, Robert, 104
Union (Vnion or Vinon), George, 181
Uniton (or Vinton), Thomas, 486
Unyon, Tho., 143
Upgate, Richard, 121
Upham, Elizabeth, 286
——, John, 286
——, ——, Junr., 286
——, Nathaniell, 286
——, Sarah, 286
Uppcott, Richard, 94
Upson, Steeven, 66
Upton, John, 172, 217
Uree, John, 369
Urquhart, Allexander, 413
Usfitt, Thomas, 150
Usher, Ann, 206
——, Beniamine (or Beny), 192, 193
——, John, 38
——, William, 39
Usherwood, Thomas, 142
Ushur, James, 267
Utie (or Uty), Ann, (181), 237
—— (——), 181, 237, 270
Vaghan, see Vaughan
Vale, Jacob Fouceco, 450
Vallin's, Joan, 113
Valuerde, Abr., 449
Vanderspike, John, 407
Van Heck, Katherin, 101
—— ——, Olliver, 101
—— ——, Peter, 101
Vanlang, Richard, 436
Van Luccom, Henry, 143
Vardell, Robert, 132
Varier, William, 342
Varloe, Phillip, 364, 376
Varlow, Capt., 434
Varnam, Francis, 425
Vass, Ezekiah, 396
——, Robert, 121
Vassall, Ann, 93, 94
——, Fra., 94
——, Judith, 94
——, Margaret, 93

Vassall, Mary, 93
———, Wm., 93
Vater, *see* Vawter
Vaughan, Davie, 119
——— (or Vaghan), John, 118, 135, 260, 305, 507
———, Ralph, 47
———, Rowland, 109
———, Sarah, 507
Vause, Richard, 205
Vaux, John, 413
Vawter (or Vater), Robert, 318*, 319*, 320*
Veazey, Nathanael, 313
Veiyard, William, 316
Venn, Edward, 318*, 319*, 320*
———, Tho., 81
Vennable, Ralph, 86
Vennell, John, 296
Venner, Thomas, 319, 319*, 320*
Ventimer, Geo., 73
Verdin, Richard, 125
Vereing, Alice, 506
———, Joshua, 506
Vergo, Daniell, 173
———, John, 179
Verin, John, 234
———, Nathaniell, 413
Vernie, John, 176
Vernnillie, John, 166*
Vernon, James, 165*
———, Peter, 413
Verryard, William, 318
Verulam, Francis, Lord, 157
Vicars, John, 193
———, Severn, 304
Viccars, Jo., 109
———, Zeverin, 85
Vickars, James, 442
Victor, Michell, 119
Viero, Daniell, 209
Vildy, Edward, 332, 336, 341
Villermarsk, Dr. De, 431
Vincencio, Mr., 180, 235
Vincene, Joane, 202
———, William, 202
Vincent, John, 318*, 319*, 324, 436
———, Mrs., 169
———, William, 169, 267
———, *see* Vyncent
Viner, Anthony, 412
Vinicott (or Vincott), Joseph, 333, 338, 340
Vinon (or Union), George, 181
Vinson, Tho., 115
Vinter, Richard, 324 [486
Vinton (or Uniton), Thomas,
Viper, Tho., 80
Virbritt, 261

Virgo, John, 240
———, Susan, 240
Visher, Ann, 116
Vizard, Joan, 126
Voh, Phillip le, 427
Voss, John, 102
———, Morris Furse, *alias*, 340, *see* Fuss, &c.
Vynall, Jo., 117
Vyncent, Edward, 86
———, Ezia, 133
———, Marthew, 133
———, *see* Vincent
Vynn, Jo., 52
Vyons, Francis, 122

WACKEFEILD, Anne, 300
———, William, 300
Wadd, Anne, 291
Waddine, Thomas, 487
Waddington, Hanna, 123
Wade, Dinah, 286
———, Edward, 103
———, Elizabeth, 286
———, Geo., 82, 115
———, Hannah, 426
———, John, 136, 426
———, Jonathan, 150
———, Nic*., 63
———, Richard, 286
———, Robert, 50
———, Wm., 153
Wadford (or Madford), Wm., 326
Wadham, Richard, 334, 338, 340
———, Roger, 328, 331
———, Tho., 370
Wadsworth, William, 150, 243, 254
Waggitt, Edward, 109
———, Tho., 85
Waine, Amyte, 250
———, Ann, 187
———, John, 187, 250
Wainwright, James, 418
———, John, Senr,, 303
———, *see* Waynewrite
Wakefield, Thomas, 95
Waker, Sarah, 438
Wakers, Jo., 118
Walden, Humphrey, 181, 239
———, Samuell, 84
———, Thomas, 446
Wale, John, 340, 506, *see* Wall
Walford, Elisabeth, 432
———, Muse, 343, 432, 440
Walker, Edward, 101, 434, 435
———, Grace, 75
———, James, 61, 81
———, John, 192, 193, 196, 431

Walker, Joseph, 70
———, Margaret, 129
———, Mathew, 81
———, Richard, 60, 191
———, Roger, 184, 243
———, Sarra, 61
———, Susan, 434
———, Thomas, 134, 426
———, Walter, 124
———, William, 40, 60, 169, 294
Walkin, Robert, 190
Wall, Joan, 92
———, John, 332, 336, *see* Wale
———, Samuel, 417
———, Thaobald, 128
———, Walter, 128
Waller, Andrew, 298
———, Charles, 174, 223
———, Edmond, 162
———, Jo., 103, 140
———, Peter, 102
Walley, Henry, 507, *see* Whaley
Wallinger, Charles, 96
Wallington, Joseph, 70
———, William, 101
Wallis, George, 92
———, Ralph, 92
———, Tho., 64, 120
Walrond, Thomas, 487
Walston, Jane, 132
Walter, Alice, 499
———, Ellinor, 448
———, Richard, 487
———, Robert, 162*
———, Thomas, 499
———, William, 39
Walters, Ann, 343
———, Christopher, 486
———, John, 332, 337, 340
———, Richard, 322
———, William, 40, 41, 140, 233, 334, 338, 341
Waltho, Francis, 496
———, Mary, 496
Walton, George, 459
———, John, 186, 257
———, Margaret, 488
———, Mary, 488
———, Richard, 41, 487
———, William, 39, 488
Waltors, Richard, 506
Waltum, Robert, 121
Walwyn, Anne, 496
——— (or Walwyne), James, 496, 506, 507
Wamsley, John, 193
Wandall, Ann, 102
Wafierton [Wannerton], William, 229

576 INDEX.

Ward, Eliza, 55
———, Elizabeth, 123
———, Henry, 314
———, James, 79
———, Jane, 435
———, John, 182, 260
———, Richard, 121, 487
———, Robert, 80
———, Thomas, 181, 239, 314
———, William, 174, 180, 233, 487
Wardd, Richard, 115
Warden, Thomas, 262
Wardle, Christopher, 506
Ware, Esaw de La, 184
Warner, Ann, 427
———, Ciprian, 104
———, John, 65, 427
———, Nathaniell, 418
———, Ralph, 426
———, Samuell, 338, 459, 462
———, Stephen, 487
———, Sir Thomas, 436
———, Thomas, 84, 105, 158, 427, 444
———, Wm., 121
Warr, William, 140
Warren, Anne, 431
———, Edward, 81
———, Elizabeth, 75
———, George, 333, 336, 340
———, Henry, 84
——— (or Warrin), John, 79, 85, 112, 135, 333, 337, 340
———, Joseph, 431, 459
———, Nicholas, 326
———, Richard, 297
———, Thomas, 351, 363, 375, 384, 395
Warrington, Robert, 82
Warrwell, Joseph, 125
Wartumbee, Richard, 139
Warwick, Robert, Earl of, 159
———, Earl of, 309
Wasey, Joseph, 374
Washborn, Washborne, Washburn, Wasborne
———, John, 57, 189, 257, 263, 426
———, Joseph, 36
———, Margerie, 57
———, Phillipp, 57
Wasley, John, 487
Wassell, Jo., 93
Wasson, Edward, 489
Waterman, Ann, 123
———, Humphery, 471
———, John, 324
———, Katherin, 85
———, Mr., 309
———, Nicholas, 154

Waterman, Tho., 40
Waters, Watters
———, Edward, 187, 253, 272
———, Grace, 187, 253
———, Jo., 101
———, Margarett, 253
———, Mary, 459
———, William, 187, 253
Wathin, Tho., 137
Watkines, Watkins, Watkyns, Wattkines, Wattkins
———, Arthur, 52
———, Daniell, 189, 231
———, David, 354, 486
———, Eliz., 489
———, Henry, 189
———, Peregree (or Peregrin, &c.), 189, 265
———, Phillip, 416
———, Rice, 181, 232
———, Richard, 138
———, Robert, 486
———, Thomas, 487
Watkinson, John, 39
Watler, Robert 127
Watlington, Francis, 351, 354, 368, 375, 388, 408
———, Mary, 417
Watson, Wattson
———, Abram, 50, 121
———, Alice, 124
———, Christopher, 80
———, Francis, 87
———, James, 172, 207
———, John, 36, 82, 150, 169, 201, 256
———, Margaret, 102
———, Nic°., 74, 122
———, Thomas, 50, 172, 439
———, William, 103, 434
———, see Whatson
Watt, David, 487
Watters, see Waters
Wattkines ⎫ see Watkines
Wattkins ⎭
Wattlin, Richard, 279
Watton, John, 119, 128, 191
Watts, Watt's
———, James, 74
———, Jeremy, 104
———, Jo., 51, 73, 141
———, Josias, 116
———, Medusala, 41
———, Nico., 81
———, Richard, 115
———, Thomas, 171, 238
———, Wm., 139
Wattson, see Watson
Watty, Henry, 497
———, Pierce, 497

Wautre, George, 198
Waycome, William, 190
Waymoth, James, 134
Waynewrite, Richard, 83, see Wainwright
Wayte, John, 471
Wazell, Thomas, 71
Wazen, Jo., 121
Weare, John, 296
Weasell (or Wesell), Niccolas, 182, 261
Weaver, Edmond, 46
———, James, 46
———, John, 467
———, Margrett, 46
———, Samuell, 181, 238, 319, 320°, 322
———, Sarah, 467
——— (or Weavor), Thomas, 167°, 417
———, William, 329, 461
———, see Wever
Webb, Anthony, 153
———, Edward, 136, 499
———, Goodman, 176
———, James, 316, 317, 343, 471
———, Jane, 472
———, Katherin, 67
———, Richard, 114
———, Samuell, 461
———, Stephen, 177, 232
———, Thomas, 63, 104, 118, 143
Webbs, Mr., 308
Webber (or Wheeler), Nathaniel, 326, 329
Weblin (or Webling), Wassell, 182, 241
Webster, Anne, 490
———, Edward, 415
———, Elisabeth, 429, 430
———, Francis, 103
———, Henry, 414
———, Joan, 237
———, John, 487, 490
———, Ralph, 141
———, Richard, 135
———, Robert, 429, 449
———, Roger, 181, 237
———, Susanna, 490
Weeden, Edward, 59
Weekeham, Gyles, 296
Weekes, Anna, 130
———, Jo., 116, 130
———, Marie, 130
———, Thomas, 139
Weeks, Symon, 152
Welby, William, 168
Welch, David, 459
———, Edmond, 416
———, John, 303, 362, 471

Welch, *see* Welsh
Welchman, John, 183
———, Lewis, 183
Welder, William, 169
Welding, William, 447, 459
Weldon, William, 201
Wellyn, Richard, 41
Wellman, Christian, 133
———, Tho., 40
Wells, Ann, 49, 59
———, Henrie, 38
———, John, 487
———, Mathew, 129
———, Richard, 113, 120
———, Robert, 127
———, Tho., 59
———, William, 86
Welsh, Jacob, 54
———, John, 143, 304
———, *see* Welch
Weltden, Anthony, 413
Wendever, Robert, 80
Wentworth, Hugh, 87
Wesell, *see* Weasell
West, Anthony, 176, 235
———, Francis, 157, 158, 172, 257, 268
———, ——— [Frances], 179
———, ———, Mrs., 257
———, Henry, 194
———, Jane, 424
———, John, 82, 92, 178, 179, 227, 424
———, Nathaniell, 133, 190, 257
———, Richard, 115
———, Thomas, 87, 178, 229, 424
———, Twiford, 130
West—Garrett, Richard, 135
Westbury, Thomas, 417
Westerlink, Martin, 138
Westgarth, Jo., 51
Westlake, Philip, 120
Westlie, Wm., 117
Weston, Edmond, 76
———, Francis, 266
———, Hugh, 116
———, Jesper, 36
———, Jo., 51, 74, 125, 143
———, Josias, 140
———, Sicillia, 116
———, Thomas, 209
———, William, 37, 51, 173, 208
Westwood, Westwoode
———, Bridgett, 279
———, Mathew, 52
———, William, 277, 279
Wethered, John, 298
Wetherell, Sackford, 258
Wetherfield, Leonard, 36
Wethersby, Wethersbie

Wethersby, ———, 257
———, Bartholmew, 185, 251
———, Dorythie, 251
Wethersly, Albiano, 185
Wever, Richard, 103, *see* Weaver
Weyer, Archibald, 40
Weyly, Michaell, 460
Whaley, Roger, 164*, *see* Walley
Whaplett, Tho., 120
Wharton, Phillipp, 86
Whatson, Richard, 506, *see* Watson
Wheat, Josua, 57
Wheatlie, Richard, 102
———, Wm., 85
Wheatly, Christopher, 84
Wheeler, Sir Charles, 161*
———, Charles, 162
———, Edward, 79
———, Henry, 183, 259
———, John, 111, 416, 463
———, (or Webber), Nathaniel, 326
———, Richard, 127
———, Wm., 132, 415
Wheler, Christopher, 417
Whetenhall, Charles, 303
Whetston, Christian, 67
———, (Whetstone or Whettston), John, 116, 149, 321, 322, 325, 331, 335, 339, 344, 439
Whetty, Matthew, 498
Whicker (or Whitker), Benjamin, 318*, 320, 324
———, John, 318, 320, 325
Whitby, Richard, 181
White, Andrew, 136
———, Ann, 125
———, Anthony, 279
———, Charles, 115, 320
———, Cornelius, 303
———, Edward, 90, 118, 235
———, Ellin (or Elen), 102, 422
———, Elizabeth, 465
———, Francis, 68
———, Gamaliel, 117
———, George, 39, 74
———, John, 39, 42, 51, 75, 95, 150, 330
———, (Witte, or Wittes), John, 326, 327, 331
———, Isack, 136
———, Jacob, 136
———, Jeremy, 233
———, Katharine, 87
———, Mark, 104

White, Martha, 90
———, Mary, 90, 428, 465
———, Michell, 38
———, Milicent, 487
———, Nath., 459
———, Patient, 136
———, Patrick, 487
———, Richard, 7/, 422
———, Thomas, 126, 422, 465
———, William, 38, 65, 84, 102, 103, 115, 257
———, *see* Wite
Whitefoot, Amos, 414
Whitehead, Joseph, 418
———, Tho., 487
Whitehedd, John, 40
Whiteing, Kathrine, 448
———, Thomas, 446
———, Wm., 416
———, *see* Whiting
Whiteliff, George, 414
Whiteman, Robert, 88
Whitfeild, Mathew, 415
———, Roger, 355, 382
———, (or Whitfild), Gilbertt, 184, 243
Whitfield, John, 119
Whitehand, George, 238
Whithedd, James, 116
———, John, 71
———, Nico., 141
———, Tho., 128
Whithorn, Gabriel, 320*
Whithorse, Lawrence,
Whitimor, Sir William,
Whittimor, Whitmore
Whiting, John, 465, 467
———, Richard, 427
Whitinge, James, 248
———, *see* Whiteing
Whitker, *see* Whicker
Whitley, Michell, 120
Whitlock, Wm., 52
Whitman, Sara, 131
———, Zacharia, 131
Whitmarck, Whitmarcke, Whitmarke, Whytemark
———, Alce, 284
———, Jane, 284
———, John, 284
———, Ouseph (or Onseph), 284
———, Richard, 284
Whitmore, Alce, 151
———, (or Whitmor), Sir George, 47, 100
———, Robert, 175, 233
———, *see* Whitimor, Whittimor
Whitney, Ellin, 58

INDEX.

Whitney, Jo., 58
———, Jonathan, 58
———, Nathaniell, 58
———, Richard, 58
———, Samuel, 308
———, Tho., 58
Whitt, Edmond, 180
——, Jerime, 180
——, Robert, 194
——, William, 173
Whittaker, Geo., 112
Whittakers, Elizabeth, 183
———, Isacke, 182
———, Mary, 182
Whittee, Mary, 414
Whitteredd, Whittredd
———, Elizabeth, 56
———, Tho., 56
———, Wm., 56
Whittington, Stephen, 152
Whittimor, Elizabeth, 46
———, Lawrence, 46
———, *see* Whitimor, Whitmore
Whitton, Awdry, 76
———, Jeremy, 78
———, Thomas, 78
———, *see* Witton
Whitreed, *see* Whiteredd
Whitwham, Jo., 119
Whurter, Vyncent, 116
Whytemark *see* Whitmarck
Wickham, Benj^a., 415
———, Eliz^a., 417
———, Joseph, 332, 335, 341
———, Tho., 417
Wicks, Jo., 115
———, Matthew, 308
Wiett, Wm., 154, *see* Wyatt
Wiffe, Richard, 257
Wigg, John, 37
Wigge, Edward, 241
Wiggin (or Wiggins), Tho., 114, 125
Wiggmore, Elias, 125
Wilbraham, Tho., 461
Wilby, George, 59
Wilcockes, Mihell, 246
Wilcocks, John, 188
———, Maudlin, 188
———, Micheall, 188
———, Nic^o., 81
———, *see* Willcockes
Wilcockson, Margaret, 45
———, Wm., 45
———, *see* Willcockson
Wild, Alice, 56
——, Jo., 56
—— (or Wile), Robert, 104
—— (or Wilde), William, 56, 418

Wild, *see* Wylde
Wile, *see* Wild
Wiley, Jone, 426, *see* Wylie
Wilkenson, *see* Wilkinson
Wilkines, Briggett, 265
———, John, 264, 265
Wilkins, Goodwife, 189
———, Humfrey, 111
———, John, 189, 415, 461
———, *see* Wilkyns
Wilkinson, Daniell, 414
———, Edward, 70
———, Hen., 72
———, Jane, 84
———, Jo., 36, 84, 122
———, Mathew, 140
———, Parnel, 310
———, Tho., 111
Wilks, John, 40
——, Nathaniell, 414
Wilkyns, Roger, 127, *see* Wilkins
Willard, Jo., 127
Willcockes, Elizabeth, 246
———, John, 263
———, *see* Wilcocks
Willcockson, Jo., 45, *see* Wilcockson
Willer, Thomas, 193
Willerton, Elizabeth, 95
Willet, Tobie, 150
Willett, Ann, 121
Willey, Rawley, 507
William, ——, 188
—— (Negroes), 172, 244, 489
Williames, Alles, 292
———, Ann, 98
———, Anne, 290
———, Elizabeth, 292
———, Roland, 261
———, William, 292
Williams, Ann, 422
———, Anto., 82
———, Arthur, 418
———, Cassandra, 435
———, Christopher, 324
———, David, 169, 236
———, Davie, 70, 137
———, Edward, 226, 435
———, Elias, 498
———, Elizabeth, 180, 433
———, Ellis, 140
———, Henry, 171, 211
———, Hugh, 174, 329, 338, 470
———, Humfrey, 116
———, John, 41, 70, 132, 139, 141, 349, 351, 385, 397, 412, 427, 434, 448, 459
———, Joyce, 467

Williams, Katharin, 422
———, Lewes, 73
———, Matthew, 386, 413
———, Maurice, 52
———, Michell, 124
———, Mrs., 189
———, Owen, 41, 74, 138
———, Pierce, 217
———, Rice ap, 179
———, Richard, 116, 117, 154, 329, 351, 439, 487
———, Robert, 84, 114, 179, 192
———, Roger, 86, 137, 233
———, Rowland, 165*, 183
———, Simon (or Symon), 415, 422
———, Susan, 211
———, Teage, 154
———, Thomas, 81, 102, 113, 166*, 171, 210, 326, 330, 369, 385, 390, 392, 396, 401, 407, 413, 416, 418, 429, 506
———, William, 112, 127, 138, 189, 329, 506
——— (or Wills), William, 326, 327, 329
Williamson, Ann, 130
———, John, 96, 436
———, Marie, 107
———, Michell, 46 [501
———, Nathaniel, 86,
———, Wm., 107
Willis, Ann, 222
——, Elizabeth, 96, 423
——, Henry, 413
——, John, 50, 319, 319*, 320*, 423, 459
——, Mary, 120
——, Richard, 471, 472
——, Thomas, 83, 423
——, Wm., 74
Willkisson, Beniamone, 145
———, Larence, 145
Willmott (or Willmatt), Edward, 327, 328
——— (———), Hugh, 327, 330
Wilms, *see* Williams
Wrlmson, *see* Williamson
Willoughby, Lady Ann, 461
———, Ann, 423
———, Dorcas, 423
———, Francis, Lord, 160*, 161
———, George, 459
———, John, 162*, 459
———, Nicholas, 423
———, Oliver, 417

INDEX.

Willoughby, William, Lord, 161*
——, ——, 162
Willoughbye (Willowbey, Willoby, or Willowsaby), Thomas, 185, 248, 274
Willox, Mathew, 446
Wills, John, 152, 413
——, Roger, 52
—— (or Williams), William, 326, 327, 329
?——, see Ouills
Willson, Henry, 173
——, Nicholas, 466
——, Wm., 416
——, see Wilson
Wilmose, John, 177
Wilse, Francis, 415
Wilson, Anthony, 487
——, Charles, 487
——, ——, Junr., 487
——, Clement, 193
——, Edward, 79, 487
——, Elisabeth, 433
——, George, 463
——, Henry, 127, 188, 215, 262
——, Jacob, 86
——, James, 296
——, John, 102, 109, 172, 327, 329, 427
——, Katherin, 105, 117
——, Margarett, 487
——, Mary, 433, 449
——, Nathan, 124
——, Reginald, 163*, 166
——, Richard, 94, 105, 446
——, Robert, 105
——, Stephen, 433
——, Thomas, 69, 223
——, William, 444, 487
——, see Willson
Wilton, Francis, 202
Wiltsheir, Benjamin, 466, 468
——, John, 462
——, Lawrence, 468
——, Thomas, 463
——, ——, Junr., 467, 468
——, ——, Senr., 467
——, Widow, 466
Winch, Sir Humphry, 162
Winche, Mary, 278
——, see Wynch
Winckoll, Elizabeth, 54
——, Jo., 54
Windebank, Secretary, 114
Windmile (or Wynwill), Christo., 182, 260
Windor, Ann, 181

Windor, Edward, 193
Windsor, Thomas, Lord, 160*
Wing, Hugh, 240
Winge, Judith, 279
——, Robert, 279
Wingfield, Harbottle, 162*
Wingate, Roger, 159*, see Wyngate
Wingatt, John, 415
Winke, Debora, 71
Winne, Griffin, 219, see Wynn
Winscomb, Joane, 213
Winslow (or Winsloe), Edward, 348, 376, 381, 385
——, Josias, 163
——, Simon, 163
——, Thomas, 193
——, see Wynsloe
Winter, Ambross, 332, 336, 340
——, Robert, 190
——, Thomas, 272
——, see Wynter
Wintersall, Thomas, 194
Winthropp, or Wynthropp
——, Deane, 100
——, Elizabeth, 100
——, John, 100
Wise, Abraham, 357
——, Christopher, 487
——, John, 36, 37, 102
Wiseman, Katherin, 84
Witchfield, John, 150
Wite, Daniell, 133, see White
With (or Withie), Mary, 130
——, Symon, 195
With'e [i.e., Withere], Richard,
Withering, Jane, 488 [185
——, Thomas, 488
Withers, Susanna, 426
Withie (or With), Marie, 130
——, Robert, 130
——, Suzan, 130
——, see Withy
Withington, Tho., 368, 405
——, Wm., 459
Withy, Jesper, 36, see Withie
Witte (Wittes, or White), John, 326, 327, 331
Witton, Jo., 103, see Whitton
Witts, Goodman, 191
Wm, see Williams
Wodall, Francis, 104
——, Jo., 101
——, Patrick, 102
Wolfe, Emanuell, 416
Wolfinden, Jeremiah, 416
Wolhouston, Marie, 48
Wolley, Richard, 79
Wollman, Richard, 120
Wolrich, John, 177

Wolrich, Mrs., 177
——, Richard, 303
Wolton, James, 143
Wolverstone, Benjamin, 468
——, Elizabeth, 462
Wood, Abraham, 179, 233
——, Alexander, 363, 364
——, Andrew, 426
——, Ann, 240
——, Anne, 100
——, Constunt, 87
——, Elizabeth, 66, 130
——, Francis, 446, 459
——, Henry, 112, 180
——, James, 416
——, John, 35, 80, 82, 130, 190, 283
——, Leonard, 105
——, Nathaniell, 66
——, Percivall, 179, 240
——, Patrick, 138
——, Richard, 95
——, Symon, 75
——, Thomas, 39, 140, 176, 240, 303
——, William, 130
——, see Wood's
Woodall, Henry, 182
Woodbridge, Elizabeth, 124
——, Jo., 112
Woodcock, Josua, 132
——, Thomas, 407, 417
Wookcocke (or Woodcoke), William, 316*, 317, 344
Woodcooke, John, 286
Woolcott, Francis, 85
Woodfine, Elizabeth, 492
——, Wm., 492
Woodford, Thomas, 149
Woodgrene, Jo., 82
Woodland, John, 436
——, Mary, 436
——, Peter, 296
Woodlase, Ann, 203
Woolley, Ann, 170
Woodliffe, Jo., 269
Woodman, Henry, 116
——, Richard, 98
Wood's, Robert, 190, see Wood
Woodson, Frances, 182
——, John, 172, 216
——, Sarah, 172, 216
Woodstock, Robert, 81
Woodward, Christopher, 193, 206
——, George, 47, 54, 281
——, Henry, 181, 182, 237, 242
——, Jane, 237
——, John, 281

INDEX.

Woodward, Mary, 173
———, Richard, 280, 281
———, Rose, 280
Woodword, Samuell, 469
Woodyard, John, 436
———, Mary, 436
Wooley, John, 184
Woolridge, William, 334, 339, 341
Worden, Isaac, 66
———, Jane, 43
Worlidge, Henry, 104
———, William, 185, 254
Wormley, Ralph, 167
Worrall, Wm., 128
Worsam, John, 437
———, Mary, 437
Worthall, Thomas, 251
Worton, Nathanell, 266
Wragg, Beniamin, 96
Wrast, Marie, 45
Wray, Ralph, 80
Wrench, Wm., 140
Wrenn, Tho., 123
Wright, Alice, 126
———, Dorcas, 497
———, Henry, 497, 507
———, Horten, 229
———, Jeffery, 87
———, Joane, 261
———, John, 109, 194, 256, 487
———, Lubas, 132
———, Mary, 414
———, Mr., 196
———, Ralph, 306
———, Richard, 123, 414
———, Robert, 183, 261, 414
———, Thomas, 443
———, William, 487
———, see Write
Wrighton, Mr., 309
Write, Arthur, 73
——, Jo., 74, 122
——, Nathaniell, 64
——, Wm., 112
——, see Wright
Writters, John, 268
Wulfris, Tho., 300
Wy, Parry, 75
Wyatt, Christopher, 487
———, Sir Francis, 157, 160, 173, 221, 273
———, Hant, 173
———, Margaret, Lady, 173

Wyatt, Ralph, 162*
———, see Wiett
Wydhouse, Jo., 52
Wygon, Edward, 104
Wylde, Geo , 77, see Wild
Wylie, John, 76, see Wiley
Wynch, Jeffery, 120, see Winch
Wynchester, Jo.. 48
Wyncott, Ann, 83
———, Dorothie, 83
Wynd, Arthur, 40
——, James, 80
——, Mary, 136
Wyndell, Jo., 66
Wynes, Tho., 116
Wyngate, Charles, 84, see Wingate
Wynkles, Jo , 52
Wynn, Christopher, 121, see Winne
——, Jo., 125
——, Richard, 486
Wynnstonly, Hugh, 71
Wynsloe, Edmond, 149, see Winslow
Wynter, John, 140, see Winter
Wynthropp, see Winthropp
Wynwill (or Windwile), Christopher, 182, 260
Wyon, Robert, 111
Wythins, Jo., 137

YARD, Wm., 84
Yardley, see Yeardley
Yarwood, Thomas, 418
Yateman, William, 135
Yates, Edward, 238
——, Charls, 421
——, Henry, 498
——, Joice, 421
—— (or Yat's), John, 41, 86, 95
——, Kat., 37
——, Margaret, 421
——, Mr., 183
——, Robert, 119
——, Thomas, 418
——, Wm., 93
Yatman, Henry, 74
Yeamans, Eliz*., 507
———, Lady, 472
Yeardley, Yardley, Yeardly, Yeartley
————, Argall, 173, 222
————, Elizabeth, 173, 222

Yeardley, Frances, 173, 222
————, Sir George, 157, 173, 222, 238, 274
————, Temperance, Lady, 173, 222
Yeats, Leonard, 172
Yemanson, James, 174
Yeomans. Arthur, 41
Yonge, Joane, 245
———, Richard, 245
[?——], Susan, 245
———, see Young, &c.
Yonges, Anne, 294
———, Joan, 294
———, John, 145, 294
———, Josueph, 294
———, Marey, 294
———, Rachel, 294
———, Tho., 294
———, see Young, &c.
Yore, Elizabeth, 102
York, James, Duke of, 160*, 161, 161*, 162. 164
——, James, 94
——, John, 140
——, Kat., 116
Yott, Tho., 135
Young, Andrew, 127
———, Francis, 125, 342
———, Harford, 70
———, John, 41, 459
———, Joseph, 109
———, Marmaduke. 84
———, Mathew, 418
———, Nathaniell, 137
———, Richard. 95
———, Samuell, 79, 342, 344
———, William, 74
———, see Yonge, Yonges, &c.
Younge, ———, 173
———, Jone, 176
———, Richard, 176
———, Thomas, 159
Younglove, Margaret, 130
———, Samuel, 130

ZOROBABELL, 190
Zouch, Edward, Lord, 156

………es, Debra. 290
…………es, Elizabeth. 290
…………es, John. 290
…………es, Samuell, 290

THE END.

BILLING, PRINTER, GUILDFORD, SURREY.

www.ingramcontent.com/pod-product-compliance
Lightning Source LLC
Chambersburg PA
CBHW071216290426
44108CB00013B/1196